# Handbook of Youth and Young Adulthood

The parameters within which young people live their lives now have changed radically. Changes in education and the labour market have led to an increased complexity of the youth phase and to an overall protraction in dependency and transitions.

Written by leading academics from several countries, this handbook introduces up-to-date perspectives on a wide range of issues that affect and shape youth and young adulthood. It provides an authoritative and multi-disciplinary overview of a field of study that offers a unique insight on social change in advanced societies and is aimed at academics, students, researchers and policy-makers.

*Handbook of Youth and Young Adulthood* introduces some of the key theoretical perspectives used within youth studies and sets out future research agendas. Each of the ten parts covers an important area of research – from education and the labour market to youth cultures, health and crime – while discussing change and continuity in the lives of young people. This work introduces readers to some of the most important work in the field while highlighting the underlying perspectives that have been used to understand the complexity of modern youth and young adulthood.

**Andy Furlong** is Professor of Social Inclusion and Education in the Faculty of Education at the University of Glasgow and editor of the *Journal of Youth Studies*.

# Handbook of Youth and Young Adulthood

## New perspectives and agendas

Edited by
Andy Furlong

Routledge
Taylor & Francis Group

LONDON AND NEW YORK

First published 2009
by Routledge
2 Park Square, Milton Park, Abingdon, Oxon OX14 4RN

Simultaneously published in the USA and Canada
by Routledge
270 Madison Avenue, New York, NY 10016

*Routledge is an imprint of the Taylor & Francis Group, an informa business*

Typeset in Bembo by
Taylor & Francis Books
Printed and bound in Great Britain by
TJ International Ltd, Padstow, Cornwall

*British Library Cataloguing in Publication Data*
A catalogue record for this book is available from the British Library

*Library of Congress Cataloging in Publication Data*
Handbook of youth and young adulthood : new perspectives and agendas /
   edited by Andy Furlong.
      p. cm.
   1. Youth–Social conditions. 2. Young adults–Social conditions. I. Furlong, Andy.
   HQ796.H2559 2009
305.235–dc22                                        2008035735

ISBN 978-0-415-44540-5 (hbk)
ISBN 978-0-203-88196-5 (ebk)

**To Gerda with love**

# Contents

*List of illustrations*                                                                          xii
*List of contributors*                                                                           xiii

## Part I: Reconceptualizing youth and young adulthood                                           1

1  Youth transitions in an age of uncertainty                                                    3
   *Walter R. Heinz*

2  Socio–economic reproduction                                                                   14
   *Ken Roberts*

3  Youth and generation: in the midst of an adult world                                          22
   *John Goodwin and Henrietta O'Connor*

4  Models of navigation and life management                                                      31
   *Manuela du Bois-Reymond*

5  The emergence of 'emerging adulthood': the new life stage between
   adolescence and young adulthood                                                               39
   *Jennifer Lynn Tanner and Jeffrey Jensen Arnett*

## Part II: Divisions                                                                            47

6  Social class, youth and young adulthood in the context of a shifting global
   economy                                                                                       49
   *Lois Weis*

7  New masculinities and femininities: gender divisions in the new economy                       58
   *Linda McDowell*

8   Young people, 'race' and ethnicity                                      66
    Colin Webster

9   Young people and social capital                                         74
    Cherylynn Bassani

10  Disability, exclusion and transition to adulthood                       81
    Sheila Riddell

11  Young refugees                                                          89
    Elizabeth Heger Boyle

**Part III: Education**                                                     95

12  Educating for late modernity                                           97
    Johanna Wyn

13  Explaining cross-national differences in education-to-work transitions  105
    David Raffe

14  Young people's subjective orientations to education                    114
    Andy Biggart

15  Mass higher education                                                  121
    Andy Furlong and Fred Cartmel

16  Vocationalism                                                          127
    David B. Bills

17  Keeping kids on track to a successful adulthood: the role of VET in improving
    high school outcomes                                                   135
    James R. Stone III

**Part IV: Employment and unemployment**                                   145

18  Changing experiences of work                                          149
    Jeylan T. Mortimer

19  Youth unemployment and marginalization                                157
    Illse Julkunen

20  Precarious work: risk, choice and poverty traps                       167
    Robert MacDonald

21  NEETs, freeters and flexibility: reflecting precarious situations in the new
    labour market                                                          176
    Akio Inui

22  The stratification of youth employment in contemporary China                182
    *Jieyu Liu*

23  What makes a young entrepreneur?                                              188
    *David G. Blanchflower and Andrew Oswald*

**Part V: Dependency and family relations**                                      201

24  Leaving the parental home in young adulthood                                 203
    *Clara H. Mulder*

25  Young, free and single? The rise of independent living                       211
    *Sue Heath*

26  Intergenerational support during the transition to adulthood                 217
    *Teresa Toguchi Swartz and Kirsten Bengtson O'Brien*

27  Early childbearing in the new era of delayed adulthood                       226
    *Frank Furstenberg Jr*

28  Homeless youth and the transition to adulthood                               232
    *Bill McCarthy, Monica Williams and John Hagan*

**Part VI: Youth, culture and lifestyles**                                       241

29  Leisure activities, place and identity                                       243
    *Joan Abbott-Chapman and Margaret Robertson*

30  Young adults and the night-time economy                                      249
    *Robert G. Hollands*

31  Young people and consumption                                                 255
    *Amy L. Best*

32  Spectacular soundtracks: youth and music                                     263
    *Andy Bennett*

33  Young people, drugs and alcohol consumption                                  269
    *Shane Blackman*

34  Spectacular youth? Young people's fashion and style                          276
    *Paul Hodkinson*

35  The experience of youth in the digital age                                   283
    *Philippa Collin and Jane Burns*

## Part VII: Civic engagement and disengagement                                          291

36  Young people's civic engagement and political development                             293
    *Constance Flanagan*

37  Young people, politics and citizenship                                               301
    *Anita Harris*

38  Youth and trade unionism                                                             307
    *Jan Carle*

39  'Riots' or 'urban disorders'? The case for re-politicizing urban disorders           313
    *Sadiya Akram*

40  Young people and armed conflict                                                      321
    *Colette Daiute*

## Part VIII: Physical and mental health                                                 329

41  Health in youth: changing times and changing influences                             331
    *Patrick West*

42  HIV and AIDS, STIs and sexual health among young people                             344
    *Frederick Mugisha*

43  Progress, culture and young people's wellbeing                                       353
    *Richard Eckersley*

44  Health-related behaviours in context                                                361
    *Patrick West*

## Part IX: Identities, values and beliefs                                               373

45  Youth-identity studies: history, controversies and future directions                375
    *James E. Côté*

46  Values and related beliefs                                                           384
    *Monica Kirkpatrick Johnson and Maria Monserud*

47  The influence of aspirations on educational and occupational outcomes                392
    *Nathan Jones and Barbara Schneider*

48  Generation Y, flexible capitalism and new work ethics                                399
    *Peter Kelly*

49  Understanding the sexual lives of young people                                       406
    *Janet Holland*

50  Religiosity in the lives of youth                                     413
    *Lisa D. Pearce and Melinda Lundquist Denton*

**Part X: Crime and deviance**                                           421

51  Juvenile delinquency and desistance                                  423
    *Shelly Schaefer and Christopher Uggen*

52  Young people and anti–social behaviour                               430
    *Alan France*

53  Youth in a world of gangs                                            436
    *John M. Hagedorn*

54  Young people, crime and justice                                      444
    *Rob White*

55  Youth and punishment                                                 452
    *Angela Harvey and Aaron Kupchik*

    *Indexes*                                                            459

# Illustrations

## Figures

10.1  Destinations of moderate learning difficulties (MLD) school and other
      school leavers in Glasgow, 2002                                         84
42.1  Framework of service provision and accountability relationship         350

## Tables

8.1   Socio-economic and demographic characteristics of selected ethnic groups   70
10.1  Adults with a disability or long-term illness by sex and age, 2001–02       82
10.2  Categories of disability used by HESA and percentages of undergraduates
      in each category in 1994/95 and 2002/03                                     86
23.1  Self-employment rates among workers only, 2001–06                          190
23.2  Probability of being self-employed in the UK, Canada and the USA,
      2001–07 (dprobits)                                                         192
23.3  Probability of being self-employed and choosing self-employment,
      2002–04                                                                    194
23.4  Probability of being self-employed and life satisfaction, Europe, 1973–2006   196
23.5  Satisfaction with work in Europe, 2001                                     197
33.1  Proportion of 16–24 year-olds in England and Wales reporting to
      having used drugs in the last year (%)                                     271
42.1  Direction of change in the probability of females marrying, having
      premarital sex, and having sex by age 18                                   345
42.2  Percentage of young women currently using condoms in successive
      demographic and health surveys                                             346
45.1  Fundamental assumptions in Identity Studies regarding epistemology and
      social order, by individual/social focus                                   377
45.2  Culture, youth, and identity: structure of transitions to adulthood and
      parameters of social identity formation by socio-historical period         379

# Contributors

**Joan Abbott-Chapman**, University of Tasmania, Australia

**Sadiya Akram**, University of Birmingham, UK

**Jeffrey Jensen Arnett**, Clark University, USA

**Cherylynn Bassani**, University of British Columbia, Canada

**Andy Bennett**, Griffith University, Australia

**Amy L. Best**, George Mason University, USA

**Andy Biggart**, Queen's University, Belfast, UK

**David B. Bills**, University of Iowa, USA

**Shane Blackman**, Canterbury Christ Church University, UK

**David G. Blanchflower**, Dartmouth College, USA

**Elizabeth Heger Boyle**, University of Minnesota, USA

**Jane Burns**, University of Melbourne, Australia and Inspire Foundation

**Jan Carle**, University of Gothenburg, Sweden

**Fred Cartmel**, University of Glasgow, UK

**Philippa Collin**, University of Sydney, Australia and Inspire Foundation

**James E. Côté**, University of Western Ontario, Canada

**Colette Daiute**, City University of New York, USA

**Melinda Lundquist Denton**, University of North Carolina, USA

**Manuela du Bois-Reymond**, Leiden University, The Netherlands

**Richard Eckersley**, Australian National University, Australia

**Constance Flanagan**, Pennsylvania State University, USA

**Alan France**, University of Loughborough, UK

**Andy Furlong**, University of Glasgow, UK

**Frank Furstenberg Jr**, University of Pennsylvania, USA

**John Goodwin**, University of Leicester, UK

**John Hagan**, Northwestern University, USA

**John M. Hagedorn**, University of Illinois-Chicago, USA

**Anita Harris**, University of Queensland, Australia

**Angela Harvey**, The Ohio State University, Newark, USA

**Sue Heath**, University of Southampton, UK

**Walter R. Heinz**, University of Bremen, Germany

**Paul Hodkinson**, University of Surrey, UK

**Janet Holland**, London South Bank University, UK

**Robert G. Hollands**, University of Newcastle-upon-Tyne, UK

**Akio Inui**, Tokyo Metropolitan University, Japan

**Nathan Jones**, Michigan State University, USA

**Illse Julkunen**, Helsinki University, Finland

**Peter Kelly**, Monash University, Australia

**Monica Kirkpatrick Johnson**, Washington State University, USA

**Aaron Kupchik**, University of Delaware, USA

**Jieyu Liu**, University of Leeds, UK

**Robert MacDonald**, University of Teesside, UK

**Bill McCarthy**, University of California, USA

**Linda McDowell**, University of Oxford, UK

**Maria Monserud**, Washington State University, USA

**Jeylan T. Mortimer**, University of Minnesota, USA

**Frederick Mugisha**, Economic Policy Research Centre, Uganda

**Clara H. Mulder**, University of Amsterdam, The Netherlands

**Kirsten Bengtson O'Brien**, University of Minnesota, USA

**Henrietta O'Connor**, University of Leicester, UK

**Andrew Oswald**, Dartmouth College, USA

**Lisa D. Pearce**, University of North Carolina, USA

**David Raffe**, University of Edinburgh, UK

**Sheila Riddell**, University of Edinburgh, UK

**Ken Roberts**, University of Liverpool, UK

**Margaret Robertson**, Latrobe University, Australia

**Shelly Schaefer**, University of Minnesota, USA

**Barbara Schneider**, Michigan State University, USA

**James R. Stone III**, National Research Center for Career and Technical Education, University of Louisville, USA

**Teresa Toguchi Swartz**, University of Minnesota, USA

**Jennifer Lynn Tanner**, Rutgers, The State University of New Jersey, USA

**Christopher Uggen**, University of Minnesota, USA

**Colin Webster**, Leeds Metropolitan University, UK

**Lois Weis**, State University of New York and University of Buffalo, USA

**Patrick West**, Social and Public Health Sciences Unit, Medical Research Council, University of Glasgow, UK

**Rob White**, University of Tasmania, Australia

**Monica Williams**, University of California, USA

**Johanna Wyn**, University of Melbourne, Australia

# Part I

# Reconceptualizing youth and young adulthood

*Andy Furlong*

## Changing contexts, changing lives

Young people's lives have changed quite significantly in the past few decades with key contexts such as education, labour market experiences and patterns of dependency having been transformed. Young people spend a greater proportion of their lives in education, increasingly entering higher education, and enter forms of employment that are very different to those experienced by their parents. Transitions take longer to accomplish, they are less likely to involve a linear movement from education to work and independent living with 'backtracking' and mixing of statuses that were once distinct becoming ever more common.

These changes have encouraged researchers to attempt theoretical reconceptualizations of transitions and of the life course, with some of these approaches having gained widespread acceptance. Compared to perspectives developed in the 1970s and 1980s, for example, contemporary researchers tend to regard individual agency as being more significant, while structural perspectives have become less prominent. There are certainly disagreements over the extent to which individuals are able to exercise choices and shape their biographies, but most new models make some room for reflexivity, even when they are underpinned by an acceptance that individuals are differentially empowered to make choices.

While researchers have been somewhat eager to highlight changes and apply new theoretical perspectives to the experiences of young people, fewer commentators have balanced an appreciation of change with a recognition of continuity. In many respects, the lives of young people today have things in common with earlier generations: inequalities such as class and gender exert a powerful influence over their lives and many do continue to experience smooth and highly structured transitions. For social scientists, the study of young people's lives provides a unique opportunity to study processes of change, to understand the way in which inequalities are reproduced between generations and to reflect on the ways in which structure and agency combine to shape lives.

Part I is primarily concerned with ideas used to conceptualize youth, young adulthood and processes of transition. Chapters 1–5 provide an overview of change, outline the ways in which social scientists have understood the lives of young people and contextualize

1

the processes of social reproduction that underpin transitions. Authors differ strongly over the extent to which they emphasize change or to which they highlight continuity between generations and different perspectives are explored throughout these chapters.

In Chapter 1, Heinz sets the scene by looking at youth transitions in the context of life course theory, arguing that the borders between different phases of the life course have become increasingly fuzzy and less dependent on chronological sequence with combinations of statuses having become common. Young people are forced to manage multiple transitions, cope with unexpected sequences of events at the same time as constructing biographies that help make sense of these discontinuities. While highlighting the importance of reflexivity in the shaping of modern transitions, Heinz is concerned to demonstrate the way in which class contexts, opportunities and institutions frame processes of navigation and restrict choices.

For Roberts, in Chapter 2, the focus on processes of social reproduction is of crucial importance and he explores changes in the ways in which researchers have tried to understand how young people from different social positions have come to occupy particular class locations. To make sense of processes of mobility, it is necessary to understand the transitions which underpin the reproduction of socio-economic inequalities. Thus changes in the contexts of education and employment have led to an individualization of experiences, yet links between class of origin and class of destination remain strong. Inequalities are being reproduced in different ways, but outcomes remain relatively stable.

These themes of continuity in the experiences of young people of different generations come across powerfully in Chapter 3 by Goodwin and O'Connor. Drawing on data collected by a team led by Norbert Elias in the 1960s, Goodwin and O'Connor argue that the 1960s generation experienced complex, individualized, transitions rather than the smooth and linear transitions assumed by some contemporary researchers. Indeed, they argue that generations should not be regarded as distinct but as strongly interrelated figurations which involve processes of cross-generational learning.

While Goodwin and O'Connor stress generational continuity, in Chapter 4, du Bois-Reymond is concerned to show that in western societies the life course has become more diverse and less uniform and the future has become less predictable. Navigation and life management have increased in significance, with education representing a central resource through which transitions are shaped. The centrality of processes of navigation mean that class, gender and ethnicity are no longer 'predetermining' forces and that opportunities have become more open. At the same time, du Bois-Reymond appreciates the continued relevance of class and acknowledges the existence of barriers that constrain individual agency.

In discussing the protracted nature of transitions, many researchers have begun to appreciate the inadequacy of the term 'youth' for understanding processes that may shape the lives of individuals well into their twenties and even beyond. In this context, terms such as young adulthood have been used to come to terms with a phase of the life course in which individuals may be dependent in one context, but independent in others. A phase in which they are well beyond adolescence and responsible for many aspects of their lives, but not yet regarded as fully autonomous adults. In Chapter 5, Tanner and Arnett refer to this stage as 'emerging adulthood', regarding it as having a psychological as well as a social base and arguing that it has become a critical phase in human development involving the potential for far-reaching personality change.

Taken together, the chapters that make up Part I of this book introduce the reader to some of the new and emergent ways of thinking about youth and young adulthood. They highlight changes in the ways in which social scientists think about this phase in the life course and discuss patterns of change and continuity in the lives of young people.

# Youth transitions in an age of uncertainty

*Walter R. Heinz*

## Introduction

In this chapter, youth transitions will be discussed in the framework of life course theory and with a focus on the consequences of the restructuring of work for the timing of adulthood in a comparative perspective. For youth research, the concepts 'transitions' and 'pathways' are of special importance because they refer to the timing and duration of the passage to adulthood and stimulate investigations on how life chances, institutional regulations and individual decisions are related.

The social age markers, which used to define the timing of transitions, have lost their normative force in the course of the last decades of the twentieth century, though they are still used by young adults, institutions and parents as a means of orientation. Today, individual biographical timetables do not follow socially expected and culturally transmitted age-norms. The borders between all phases of the life course have become fuzzy, the timing and duration of transitions between childhood, adolescence, youth, adulthood, and old age are less age-dependent and demand a series of individual decisions.

Some youth researchers, representing developmental or cultural positions, see the structural changes of the life course as a sign of more autonomy, but a more down-to-earth explanation would take into account the labour markets and social policies of post-industrial service societies which have restructured youth transitions and created the new life phase of young adulthood. Standard employment has been replaced by flexible work and precarious careers, a development which makes it difficult to individually coordinate the multiple transitions which mark the route to adulthood and require special programmes for preventing the social exclusion of disadvantaged youths.

I shall argue that the instabilities of the life course stem from the tension between uncertain life chances and the culture of individualism which expects that people actively shape their biographies. At the level of cultural expectations, there is a double-edged message: perform your transitions and pathway choices according to market opportunities and institutional rules and do this according to your individual, self-determined timing.

In the following, first, the concepts of transition and pathways will be outlined, then the changing social contexts of youth transitions are sketched out, followed by a discussion of how young people navigate pathways and use their experiences for self-socialization and shaping their biographies, finally, research issues concerning the relationship between life course policy and transitions are outlined.

## Transitions and social pathways

The notion of transition should be regarded as a heuristic concept, rather than as a descriptive one with a specific focus on youth. It is part of the life course approach which connects social time and space with individual biographies and the sequence of life events of cohorts.

There are many transitions that people must navigate from cradle to grave, and it is a misconception to equate the concept of transition with the life phase of youth (e.g. Wyn and Woodman 2007). Based on my involvement in comparative transition research over 30 years, I regard youth transitions neither as linear nor as emergent. On the contrary, they are contingent and linked to complex interactions between individual decisions, opportunity structures, and social pathways with more or less institutionalized guidelines and regulations.

In this perspective, youth is not a self-contained phase, but rather a component of the life course which is impossible to clearly distinguish from adolescence and adulthood, except in terms of legal definitions of the maturity age.

The concept of transitions neither implies psychosocial or developmental assumptions or normative expectations regarding the correct timing and sequencing of becoming adult, it rather gains relevance in the life course framework which rests on the following five assumptions (e.g. Heinz and Marshall 2003; Mortimer and Shanahan 2003):

- Each life phase affects the entire life course: life-span development.
- Individuals actively construct their biography: human agency.
- The life course is embedded in historical events: time and place.
- Social circumstances and events influence transitions: timing of decisions.
- Social relationships and networks contribute to the shaping of biographies: linked lives.

According to this theoretical perspective, transitions in post-industrial service societies are time-dependent passages of individuals between life spheres. Core transitions to adulthood concern the matching of education and employment which is the backbone for implementing one's aspirations and to coordinate participation in the spheres of family life, consumption and citizenship.

Social change has restructured all life phases, therefore each new generation of young people, as well as adults and the elderly, have to find a balance in life by managing, defending, claiming its place in society through shaping their biographies in the course of transitions. Therefore, the study of the concept of transitions is crucial, especially in relation to the following:

- differences within and between cohorts or generations in regard to the timing, duration and outcomes of status changes across the life course (based on longitudinal cohort surveys);
- differences and similarities within and between societies in regard to the bearing of institutional arrangements (education, employment, welfare) on the shape and

duration of status changes over the life course (based on cross-national surveys and policy analysis);

■ the balance of individual agency, opportunity structures, and institutional regulations in the shaping of biographies (based on case studies of biographies in different contexts).

Transition studies in a life course framework attempt to integrate individual and structural perspectives in a longitudinal design and ask how social pathways are restructured, for whom and what consequences they have for young persons' life chances (e.g. Bynner and Chisholm 1998). Methodologically speaking, such research should be conducted as a dialogue between variable-based surveys and biographical case studies.

In order to focus my argument, the concept of pathway must be clarified. According to Raffe (2003), pathways can be analysed from three perspectives: (1) how they structure transitions; (2) how they are interrelated; and (3) how they are navigated by young people. The first perspective concerns the institutional fabric, the second, the issue of social inequality or permeability of pathways, and the third, the young person's choices and actions in and between pathways. Though it is evident that education-to-work transitions are interdependent with changes in family, household and lifestyle, I will concentrate on pathways between training and employment because this transition determines the pathway options for other life spheres and it also reduces analytical complexity.

## Youth and social change

Youth is constructed and modified as a social category according to social expectations regarding age brackets for participation in education, work, marriage, parenthood, consumption, and social welfare. Regular and non-standard transitions are products of living circumstances and individual decisions regarding pathways. Social origin, education, and opportunity structures are determinants of the extent to which young people have the material, social and individual resources for constructing a self-determined and subjectively meaningful transition to work, therefore, the links between pathways and navigations are a crucial theme for transition research.

The transitional arrangements for moving towards adulthood differ between societies according to their respective cultural traditions, education, employment, and welfare systems. In the second half of the twentieth century, these systems contributed to the formation of an institutionalized (male) life course pattern, consisting of education, work, and retirement, mirroring the life phases of youth, adulthood and old age. This pattern was based on age-graded, standard transitions between these life spheres. Hence, J. S. Coleman noted more than 30 years ago that the student role keeps the young from adult responsibilities and productive activities: 'they are held in a dependent status and they do not learn independence' (1974: 10).

But 'the times they are changing' (Bob Dylan): in post-industrial service society the young generations are expected to self-direct their decisions regarding education, training and employment in order to become flexible participants in volatile labour markets. They must identify the most promising pathways to adult independence and navigate multiple transitions with uncertain outcomes. In the first decade of the twenty-first century, the age-bound notion of youth must be re-assessed in the light of the transformation of socio-cultural and economic contexts and regarded as an extended period of semi-adulthood. Female and male life courses do not follow a step-wise progression to adulthood in an age sequence, rather, they combine education and work, work, and family formation. The discontinuity of biographies becomes obvious at transitions between life phases, where age-related criteria, rules and rites concerning the timing and procedures of status changes only survive in some institutional contexts, e.g. graduation and marriage ceremonies. Young mothers (and some fathers), for example, must reconcile education, child rearing and employment and try to come to terms with biographical discontinuities which result from non-standard employment.

The dimension of historical time and place must be considered in order to understand the restructuring of the youth phase. The coordinates of this period of life vary according to the economy and the educational and social policies of the state: the life course and its component 'youth' are path-dependent social structures. Modern societies differ in their institutional arrangements concerning life transitions: education and training provisions, labour market regulations, exclusion mechanisms, social assistance rules, and to the extent to which there is an explicit youth policy. Consequently, the focus of youth issues differs between societies.

For example, in Britain in the 1980s, the decline of the labour market for school leavers and the effects of training programmes were the dominant themes of youth research and policy studies, whereas in the 1970s youth (sub)cultures and alternative life styles were the main themes. Keeping young people in school and channelling them into post-secondary education became research and policy issues in the 1990s, as a response to the skill needs of the knowledge society.

Today, discontinuities between education and work are experienced by a rising number of school leavers, skilled young workers and college graduates, alike. Young men and women are confronted with a variety of pathway options, albeit with uncertain destinations in regard to employment, partnerships, and life styles options. In the past decade, a number of comparative surveys recorded the effects of different transition regimes on the biographies of young people. Most studies, however, are cross-sectional and tend to confirm well-known social structural effects on education, training, and labour market entrance. Initial employment outcomes shape work careers and family formation and reinforce the persistent social inequalities of origin and gender. Since education and training regimes also differ in the permeability of pathways in the vocational and academic segments, drop-outs and low achievers may only have access to schemes which do not improve their transition outcomes. European cross-sectional data (Müller and Gangl 2003) show that young people who graduate from vocational education and training (VET) pathways leave with portable skills and enter relatively stable employment faster compared to the ones who look for work after a school-based preparation. And a recent 14-country study by Blossfeld et al. (2005), based on longitudinal panel surveys, shows widespread uncertainty among young people in respect to the timing and type of employment, partnership and family formation. This uncertainty occurs in the context of increasing social inequality of life chances, especially in regard to living conditions, skills, and social capital.

It is crucial for my argument to note that the impact of uncertainty on the timing of life events and biographical decisions is 'institutionally filtered' by the respective welfare regimes, educational provisions, employment conditions and industrial relations, and family structures as well as by social provisions for coordinating young parents' careers.

## Navigating social pathways

Navigation is a concept which translates the abstract term of agency into the transition terminology. It denotes the series of individual decisions and activities in regard to social pathways that lead from one life phase to another and connect their participation in various life spheres (Evans and Furlong 1997). Young people want to, and many are required to, become their own scouts of opportunities and to come to terms with temporary engagements in many life spheres. Today, becoming adult requires the coordination of multiple transitions and the construction of biographical continuity in view of discontinuities, reversals, and detours. Despite their uncertain future, many young adults attempt to adapt their aspirations and decisions by actively shaping their life course with an eye on the future. Through this process they can accumulate resources that help them shape biographies and make individual decisions in the context of fragmented pathways and changing opportunity structures. There is an obvious contradiction between the early stress on preparing for independent decision-making and the extended period of actually reaching full adulthood.

Recently, the notion of 'emerging adulthood' (Arnett and Tanner 2006) has gained some prominence in youth research. The years from 18–25 are defined as a distinct period of the life course between adolescence and adulthood in industrial societies, a period which is supposed to characterize the entire population in this age group, regardless of country, social class, gender and ethnicity. This is a daring assumption in the light of comparative research about the impact of globalization and social structural changes on individual options for shaping their life course (see Shavit and Müller 1998; Heinz 1999; Bynner 2001; Blossfeld et al. 2005; see also the recent debate between Bynner 2005 and Arnett 2006).

Longitudinal survey and case studies in the UK and Germany have shown that uncertainty is linked to a condition of 'structured individualization' (Evans and Heinz 1994; Roberts 1997). Transitions have become more individualized, but still occur in the context of social inequality, which is evident in unequal access to promising pathways. As Bynner (2005) convincingly argues not just for the UK, social class modifies the form and content of 'emergent adulthood' because it opens or restricts access to pathways which support young people to act according to the criteria for being adult.

In addition to social inequality, there is also the question of cross-national validity of the metaphor 'emerging adulthood'. For example, British young people aspire and experience adult responsibility earlier than their continental counterparts, compared to German youth, they enter the labour market at least two years earlier (Evans and Heinz 1994). These differences are caused by institutional structures, whereas the German transition system for the non-college-bound youth provides a well-established VET framework for portable skills, in Britain, staying in school longer and a later job start are favoured.

The cross-national validity of 'emergent adulthood' can be checked in regard to the institutional provisions for the transition to adulthood. For example, in contrast to the UK, the USA, and Canada, for the young cohorts in Germany the school-to-training-to-employment transition is structured by the institutions of a welfare-and-training state. Up to two-thirds of school leavers engage in vocational and technical education and training because it still promises to provide knowledge, skills and credentials necessary for entering the occupationally structured German labour market. Their actions and perceptions reflect less their efforts to match work with their identity than with their skill profile and job search experiences. In the light of the impact of institutions and opportunity structures on youth transitions, 'emergent adulthood' should be regarded as a hypothesis about the self-definition of college students and graduates in societies that provide social pathways to adulthood which are characterized by a low degree of institutionalization and demand a high degree of individual risk-taking and exploration of life chances. It is likely that emerging adults' decision-making about work is primarily identity-based for those who are navigating self-selected pathways with definite destinations, (e.g. medical, law or business school or high quality vocational training with Volkswagen or Siemens). For the less privileged, there tends to be a step-wise correction or retrospective construction of an occupational identity, as qualitative longitudinal studies suggest (Heinz *et al.* 1998; Devadason 2007).

Thus, it cannot be taken for granted that all young people in their twenties experience this period as 'having the most control over the significant events in their lives' as Arnett and Tanner (2006: 24) assume. On the contrary, many struggle to gain control over conditions and outcomes of their choices in order to emerge as adults and to shape their life course. In Germany, the major reason for delayed transitions is the widening gap between demand and supply of training places, especially in manufacturing and construction occupations. Less qualified school-leavers are referred to intermediate education pathways in order to upgrade their skill level (the number of young people using such provisions has doubled since the early 1990s). Being channelled into such routes is still related to social origin: youth from advantaged families only took three months to find a training place, compared to a year for those from disadvantaged homes (BIBB 2007). In the UK, those who leave education at the earliest possible age face social exclusion in a labour market which demands technical and social skills. They form the bulk of up to 20 per cent of young people who are neither in education, employment or training (NEET).

There are a variety of structural influences on the social differentiation of youth which make pars-pro-toto notions like 'emerging adulthood' or generalized portraits like 'new social generation' questionable if youth studies are presenting a realistic account of the interaction between life chances and transition biographies.

## Youth transitions as self-socialization

A biography is not just a subjective narrative about one's life history but a time- and space-related reflection of past events, the timing of transitions, and future plans. The evolving biography reflects personal agency and is the temporary sum total of the young person's aspirations and assessments of past successes and failures and interpersonal recognition and rejection in the social arenas where autonomy and self-responsibility are expected.

In regard of the loose coupling of social pathways and biographies, I proposed a model of self-socialization (Heinz 2002) which integrates personal agency (self-reflexive action, navigation, and learning loops) with opportunity contexts in training and employment.

Recent research (Heinz 1999; Shanahan 2000; Bynner 2001; Lehmann 2007; Stauber *et al.* 2007) shows that there are different schedules of identity formation which are influenced by social class, institutional provisions of educational improvement and social assistance, and employment opportunities. Qualitative transition studies show clearly that youth identities develop and change as a biographical process of self-reflection and learning in the context of pathways that are embedded in different economic conditions and institutional contexts. Young people (and their parents) tend to experience these contexts as complex when they look for training places, or after completion of VET or college graduation, for a suitable job or career. This situation requires that young persons develop their own navigation competence in order to manage labour market entry and related partnership and family transitions. In respect to work demands and employment conditions, they must find arrangements with contingent, provisional options and settle with short-term commitments without the promise of continuity (Heinz 2003). For example, young people who start to work straight after leaving school have much more restricted opportunities to explore their interests and a higher risk of unemployment compared to those who enter and finish a college or a university course.

For an adequate explanation of the variations in the biographical timings that young women and men develop during their passages into the labour market, we must analyse their orientations and actions towards different occupational and relationship commitments and their variable responses to discontinuous careers. This sheds light on the ways in which young adults construct their living arrangements and apply their vocational and social skills so as to shape their biographies in the process of multiple transitions. For a majority of young men and women, this is less a process of exploration (i.e. experimenting with different roles) than of coming to terms with turning points and unintended consequences of their biographical decisions and actions.

New insights about the impact of unstable and short-term contexts of opportunity on a young person's transitions to work are possible when we take into account that their interpretations of skill demands and career options depend to a large extent on their biographical action orientations. According to the model of self-socialization (Heinz 2002), these orientations result from experiences, with opportunities and outcomes of self-initiated as well as enforced decisions in regard to choice of occupation, employer, continuing education, return to education, or job change. The process of self-socialization differs from socialization in family, school and training in regard to the involvement of the learner who actively pursues the acquisition of skills and knowledge and responds to the outcomes of their pathway choices. Making sense of the consequences of one's decisions and performances in education, training and employment transitions is the matter of self-socialization by which persons develop their own guidelines in respect to the criteria of adulthood in the context of work and its relation to private life (Heinz 2002).

## Transitions and biographical agency

The biographical dimension of transitions is the empirical centre-piece of self-socialization because it illuminates the variability of young people's arrangements with training, work and career opportunities and highlights obstacles. Recently, there has been progress in delineating empirically grounded typologies of biographical agency which explain how young women and men approach and manage their status passage into the employment system (cf. Shanahan 2000; Stauber et al. 2007).

The typology of 'Biographical Action Orientations' (BAO) delineates several ways of constructing a personally meaningful passage in view of the balance of success and disappointment in school, VET and job search in the context of uncertain occupational opportunities and institutionalized cultural codes of individual flexibility. In a longitudinal study (Heinz et al. 1998; Heinz 1999; Kühn and Witzel 2000), 2,000 young skilled workers in six major German trades completed questionnaires and participated in semi-structured interviews. These data highlighted young adults' interpretations of factors that shaped their occupational transitions over a period of eight years, from the beginning of their training until the first five years in the labour market.

In this study, BAO refers to the individual guidelines for decisions, activities and commitments concerning work and private life. The concept has three characteristics: first, the personal guidelines are responsive to changing opportunities; second, they are patterns of orientations and actions that are basic to the self-management of transition; and third, they are valid across specific transition events. Hence, modes of biographical agency in the world of work illuminate the various reasons developed by young adults, to shape their occupational life and to come to terms with the outcomes of their decisions.

Six types or modes of biographical agency could be distinguished:

- *Company identification*: The firm is regarded as a kind of home; work satisfaction depends on the social relationships at the workplace and on job. The biographical guideline is – work as a means of maintaining social ties and receiving a decent wage.
- *Wage worker habitus*: Routine work conditions are preferred, effort depends on rewards. Biographical guideline – work is merely a means of material reproduction through a fair wage.
- *Career involvement*: Work is assessed in regard to a limited range of career options that the firm offers. Biographical guideline – promotion, climbing up the company's ladder of advancement.
- *Optimizing opportunities*: Work conditions are expected to combine variable challenges with a wide scope for initiative. Biographical guideline – work is a means of accomplishing occupational goals in exchange for career options.
- *The mode 'personal growth and autonomy'*: This relates to an image of work as a field of exploration in the service of self-realization. Biographical guideline – work is a means of expressing and developing one's personality.
- *Self-employment habitus*: Work is seen as a way of gaining autonomy in respect to both the conditions and results of occupational activities. Biographical guideline – work is a means of setting up one's own business.

In a comparative, retrospective, life history study of British and Swedish young adults (Devadason 2007), young people created coherent transitions as a subjectively meaningful linkage of self-projects, experiences, and social contexts, orientations were found which have some similarity to the BAOs. Five types or modes of biographical shaping were distinguished: climbing the career ladder; personal development; avoiding monotony and boredom; not getting ahead; and disappointed expectations.

To explain variations in young adults' action orientations, their transition history was reconstructed. The ones who developed the guidelines of company identification and wage worker habitus had a difficult passage from school to VET, applying often for an apprenticeship that at the end was their second or third choice. This experience led to a stepwise 'cooling-out' of occupational aspirations. Young workers with the biographical guidelines of career involvement and optimizing opportunities were better at school and had a more successful passage into an apprenticeship of their choice. The small number of young workers who developed the biographical modes of autonomy and self-employment had a good school record and a history of actively exploring options in order to match their talents and skills with occupational opportunities. Only the few young adults, who also had the option of an academic pathway, managed to develop a self-determined, though distant relationship to the world of work; an adaptive strategy which shows some resemblance to emergent adulthood

These findings suggest that there is indeed a 'loose coupling' between occupational conditions, career opportunities and the biographical arrangements that young persons develop in their transition to adulthood. Training pathways and occupational contexts are used in different ways as a resource for shaping, applying and revising biographical orientations and actions.

## Conclusion: life course policy and transitions

In this chapter I wanted to show that assumptions about the causal effects of social structures on transition outcomes are masking the personal shaping of biographies. Individual aspirations and pathway decisions are a crucial mediating force which explains the loose coupling of social structure and individual lives. What may appear as the deliberate postponement of career and marriage commitments in fact reflects a realistic assessment of labour market uncertainties Biographical research documents that young adults' transitional experiences in the contexts of training and employment are used as building blocks for self-reflections which lead to a range of actions, from playing it safe to partial corrections and even revisions of past decisions in regard to education, employment and continuing training. This indicates that the majority of young adults do not react to employment conditions as one homogeneous social generation or as emergent adults, rather, they respond with a specific mode of biographical agency by applying their respective guidelines to construct life course continuity. These guidelines mirror individuals' social pathways and correspond to the respective occupational cultures and work contexts.

The analysis of personal meanings attached to transitional events and their consequences for self-socialization, however, must be complemented by investigating the institutional provisions which accompany young people on their road to adulthood: are these arrangements only focused on the life phase of youth or are they a component of a coherent life course policy (Leisering 2003) which connects the life phases from childhood to old age? By establishing pathways, the state expects that young people actively decide between different transition routes and also makes them accountable for the long-term consequences of their pathway choices.

Societies' life course policies prepare young adults in different ways to navigate pathways and follow their life plans. The transformation of the temporal sequence of becoming an adult has extended the stage of the life-span in which adulthood is socially and subjectively achieved. When looking at young peoples' modes of biographical agency, it is evident that they reflect their transition and employment contexts, which in turn are structured by life course policies that offer different possibilities for taking the initiative and accomplishing continuity. Through processes of self-socialization during the passage from school to work, young adults develop specific guidelines for their adult life which in different ways respond to the norm of flexibility. Autonomy and the optimization of opportunities represent individual efforts of self-direction by using certified skills in innovative ways. However, the other modes of biographical agency are less well coordinated with the demands of lifelong learning and employability.

11

For further research it is important to find out, first, how different life course policies help stabilize transition biographies and provide launch pads into a self-directed adulthood. In neo-liberal societies, like the UK and the USA, early economic independence* is expected and the social monitoring of pathways is less institutionalized, thus life course policies stress the notion of individual responsibility to accomplish the transitions to adulthood. In these countries young people begin work early and jobs are often low paid and insecure. In social welfare and training societies, such as Germany, Denmark and the Netherlands, standardized vocational and academic pathways, which allocate young people to social positions after an institutionalized process of qualification, are promoted. Here transitional outcomes depend to a large extent on the active matching of skills and credentials with employment opportunities and, in cases of risk, monitoring by state agencies.

Second, research concerning the five dimensions of the life course must be expanded: we know more about the impact of time and space, institutions, and personal agency on the timing of transitions than about the ways in which linked lives, the relationships between young adults and parents, peers, or partners, contribute to the course and outcome of transitions. Thus, there is an empirical question concerning the balance of public investment and institutional guidance, on the one hand, and private transition support, on the other.

Though there are no easy answers, it is likely that an active education and social policy, which covers the whole life course, can guarantee that young adulthood is not experienced as a period of continued economic dependence on the family and social assistance, but as one of biographical options. This means that employability cannot be the main criterion of adulthood but the competence to connect the participation in all life spheres in a self-directed way. Such a policy is best suited to promoting the anticipation of the potential effects of transition risks on the entire life course.

Life course theory contributes to the explanation of the complex configuration of pathways and transition biographies because it specifies the linkages of time and space (life course policy) with the timing and outcomes of multiple youth transitions. In order to better understand this complexity, a combination of comparative longitudinal research and case studies, which link institutional with individual level analysis, are called for.

## References

Arnett, J. J. (2006) 'Emerging adults in Europe: a response to Bynner', *Journal of Youth Studies*, 9: 111–23.

Arnett, J. J. and Tanner, J. L. (eds) (2006) *Emerging Adults in America*, Washington, DC: APA.

BIBB (Bundesinstitut für Berufsbildung) (2007) *BIBB-Report 2/07*, Bonn: BIBB.

Blossfeld, H.-P. *et al.* (eds) (2005) *Globalization, Uncertainty, and Youth in Society*, London: Routledge.

Bynner, J. (2001) 'British youth transitions in comparative perspective', *Journal of Youth Studies*, 4: 5–23.

—— (2005) 'Rethinking the youth phase of the life course: the case for emerging adulthood?', *Journal of Youth Studies*, 8: 367–84.

Bynner, J. and Chisholm, L. (1998) 'Comparative youth transition research: methods, meanings, and research relations', *European Sociological Review*, 14: 131–50.

Coleman, J. S. (1974) *Youth and the Transition to Adulthood*, Chicago: University of Chicago Press.

Devadason, R. (2007) 'Constructing coherence? Young adult's pursuit of meaning through multiple transitions between work, education and unemployment', *Journal of Youth Studies*, 10: 203–21.

Evans, K. and Furlong, A. (1997) 'Metaphors of youth transitions: niches, pathways, trajectories, and navigations', in J. Bynner, L. Chisholm, and A. Furlong (eds) *Youth, Citizenship, and Social Change in a European Context*, Aldershot: Ashgate, pp. 17–41.

Evans, K. and Heinz, W. R. (eds) (1994) *Becoming Adults in England and Germany*, London: Anglo-German Foundation.

Heinz, W. R. (1999) 'Job-entry patterns in a life course perspective', in W. R. Heinz (ed.) *From Education to Work: Cross-National Perspectives*, New York: Cambridge University Press, pp. 214–31.

—— (2002) 'Self-socialization and post-traditional society', in R. A. Settersten and T. J. Owens (eds) *Advances in Life Course Research: New Frontiers in Socialization*, New York: Elsevier, pp. 41–64.

—— (2003) 'From work trajectories to negotiated careers: the contingent work life course', in J. T. Mortimer and M. J. Shanahan (eds) *Handbook of the Life Course*, New York: Kluwer/Plenum, pp. 185–204.

Heinz, W. R., Kelle, U., Witzel, A. and Zinn, J. (1998) 'Vocational training and career development in Germany: results from a longitudinal study', *International Journal for Behavioral Development*, 22: 77–101.

Heinz, W. R. and Marshall, V. W. (2003) *Social Dynamics of the Lifecourse*, Piscataway, NJ: Aldine Transaction.

Kühn, T. and Witzel, A. (2000) 'Orientierungs- und Handlungsmuster beim Übergang in das Erwerbsleben', in W. R. Heinz (ed.) *Übergänge: Individualisierung, Flexibilisierung und Institutionalisierung des Lebenslaufs*, Weinheim and München: Juventa.

Lehmann, W. (2007) *Choosing to Labour? School-to-Work Transitions and Social Class*, Montreal: McGill-Queen's University Press.

Leisering, L. (2003) 'Government and the life course', in J. T. Mortimer and M. Shanahan (eds) *Handbook of the Life Course*, New York: Kluwer/Plenum, pp. 205–25.

Mortimer, J. T. and Shanahan, M. J. (eds) (2003) *Handbook of the Life Course*, New York: Kluwer/Plenum.

Müller, W. and Gangl, M. (eds) (2003) *Transitions from Education to Work in Europe*, Oxford: Oxford University Press.

Raffe, D. (2003) 'Pathways linking education and work: a review of concepts, research, and policy debates', *Journal of Youth Studies*, 6: 3–19.

Roberts, K. (1997) 'Structure and agency: the new youth research agenda', in J. Bynner, L. Chisholm and A. Furlong (eds) *Youth, Citizenship and Social Change in a European Context*, Aldershot: Ashgate, pp. 56–65.

Shanahan, M. J. (2000) 'Pathways to adulthood in changing societies', *Annual Review of Sociology*, 26: 667–92.

Shavit, Y. and Müller, W. (eds) (1998) *From School to Work: A Comparative Study of Educational Qualifications and Occupational Destinations*, Oxford: Clarendon Press.

Stauber, B., Pohl, A. and Walther, A. (eds) (2007) *Subjektorientierte Übergangsforschung*, Weinheim and München: Juventa.

Wyn, J. and Woodman, D. (2007) 'Generation, youth and social change in Australia', *Journal of Youth Studies*, 9: 495–514.

# 2

# Socio-economic reproduction

*Ken Roberts*

## Introduction

Reproduction theories were introduced to youth studies in the 1970s by Marxist sociologists who were challenging (explicitly or implicitly) functionalist accounts of social role allocation and socialization. Previously these processes had been regarded as achieving the best possible compromises between the capabilities of individuals and the needs of society, save for a tendency for individuals to stick close to their social class origins which, it was assumed, would be corrected by meritocratic educational reforms. Reproduction theorists have continued to insist that the tendency to 'stick' is not an aberration but the norm to which it is exceptions (where social mobility occurs) that require a special explanation.

There are two dimensions to socio-cultural reproduction. The first concerns the tendency for children to inherit their parents' class positions. This helps to explain the second set of reproduction processes whereby social forms and relationships endure while ageing actors retire and are replaced by upcoming cohorts. Reproduction theorists insist that the maintenance of class relationships must be regarded as perpetually hazardous given that one class of people is not just relatively disadvantaged but is actually exploited and has an objective interest in the breakdown of reproduction and the ensuing revolutionary transformation.

## Mechanisms of reproduction

### Education: correspondences

The first reproduction theorists noted 'correspondences' between the organization of education and the organization of work in capitalist economies. They noted how, beneath the banner of 'equal opportunity', children from different social class backgrounds tended to receive different kinds of schooling that prepared them for their future roles in the class structure. In their influential book, *Schooling in Capitalist America* (1976),

Bowles and Gintis noted how school children became accustomed to attending regularly and punctually, performing daylong routine tasks, and accepting the authority of teachers (corresponding to their future workplace bosses). They noted how lower achieving (generally working-class) children learnt to recognize their limited capabilities, and realized that they were best suited to and destined for future positions among the led rather than among the leaders. Simultaneously, children learnt basic skills (such as literacy and numeracy) that would be required in their future adult roles as workers.

This type of 'mechanistic' reproduction theory came under instant attack (see Collins 1971). It was dubbed 'Marxist functionalism', and criticized along with the 'technical functionalism' that it was intended to replace for exaggerating the correspondences to which it drew attention. Critics noted that most knowledge imparted at school bore no obvious relationship to knowledge required in the wider society. Furthermore, far from aligning pupils' ambitions with their future employment, it was noted that America's schools produced cohorts of excessively ambitious school-leavers.

## Education: resistance

It proved far easier to map correspondence theories onto European school systems which divided secondary age pupils into academic and non-academic tracks, often taught in entirely different schools, rather than the comprehensive American high schools in which all pupils were encouraged to compete for the highest possible adult positions.

In his widely acclaimed book, *Learning to Labour* (1977), Paul Willis studied the responses of a small group of working-class male pupils (known as 'the lads') to their experiences in the lower streams of a secondary modern school (to which 11 year-olds who failed to gain grammar school places were allocated at that time), in a town in England's heavily industrialized Midlands. 'Mechanistic' reproduction theories had portrayed working-class pupils as accepting working-class futures because they had no alternative but to be realistic. However, in Willis's account, 'the lads' were far from docile and played active roles in enthusiastically embracing working-class futures. 'The lads' were bringing into school knowledge and values acquired from their working-class homes. They realized that most school knowledge was useless, and knew they did not need the qualifications that would confer access to 'sissy', effeminate, office jobs because the lads intended to become 'real men' doing 'real work', earning good money in the local factories. Thus their school-lives became essays in 'resistance'. They would disrupt classroom learning whenever possible. Through their attitudes, dress and daily demeanour, they displayed contempt for teachers. They were in fact 'learning to labour'; learning the techniques of resistance and the virtues of solidarity that would stand them in good stead when facing the demands of management in their future shop-floor jobs. This resistance perspective was subsequently applied to young people on the vocational courses and training schemes that were introduced in the context of rising levels of youth unemployment in Britain in the 1970s and 1980s (see Riseborough 1993).

## Youth cultures: more resistance (through rituals)

One of British sociology's most distinctive (and well-known) contributions to international youth research has been the interpretation of working-class youth cultures offered by investigators based at or associated with Birmingham University's Centre for Contemporary Studies (CCCS) in the 1970s. They alleged that post-war youth cultures (specifically

Teddy boys, rockers, mods and skinheads) embodied distinctively working-class values. They argued that working-class members of these youth sub-cultures (which were 'subs' of class cultures) were reworking values that they had acquired from their families, and through their youth cultures were addressing class-specific problems encountered in growing up in post-war Britain. Rather than mindless yobos, seduced by commercial purveyors of pop music and fashions, the young people were credited with using these cultural products to express their own meanings – typically pride in who they were, and defiance towards all authority figures. The young people were credited with creating 'styles' which were clearly effective judged by their ability to provoke moral panics throughout the wider society. This youth cultural resistance was acknowledged by all concerned to be 'ritualistic' (see Hall and Jefferson 1976). The young people knew (as did their sociological investigators) that after their weekend fun, they would return to their working-class homes and jobs. Even so, as a mechanism of socio-cultural reproduction, and a process of socialization into class struggle, participation in youth cultures could be highly effective.

The Teddy boys, mods and rockers of the 1950s and 1960s have their present-day equivalents, namely the 'chavs' or 'charvers', with Burberry the latest 'theft' of upper-class attire, and bling, trainers and tracksuits paraded with pride in an age-old working class spirit of defiance.

## Social and cultural capital

While British sociologists were noting ways in which working-class youth resisted efforts to incorporate them into middle-class society, French sociologists, most notably Pierre Bourdieu, were noting how the French middle classes deployed their social and cultural capital to advantage their own children and exclude others from similar life chances (see Bourdieu and Passeron 1977).

Bourdieu adopted an economic concept – capital – and applied it to social and cultural resources, indicating how these resources could also be accumulated and invested in the expectation of a dividend. Social capital comprises trusted social relationships. Unlike Robert Putnam (2000), an American political scientist who treats social capital as an asset of entire communities (where social capital is high, so are educational attainments, people are healthier and crime rates are lower), Bourdieu's social capital is the property of particular classes of people who use it to separate insiders from the excluded. Cultural capital comprises non-material assets: knowledge (which may be certified in education), and tastes (in music, art, etc.). All classes of people possess social and cultural capital. For example, they can all use 'connections' to assist in job search. All classes of people feel most comfortable, at ease, with others who possess similar tastes. However, Bourdieu explains how different classes' social and cultural capitals are not of equal value. Some types of capital yield far better rates of return when converted into economic capital via occupational attainments. Bourdieu contends that when actors enter any 'field', which may be education or the labour market, those with similar cultural capital will tend to act in similar ways and recognize each other as people like themselves.

Another of Bourdieu's contentions is that middle-class culture is the dominant culture in all education. Children who enter school already equipped with this cultural capital, signalled by valuing the right kinds of knowledge and expressing 'correct' tastes, are liable to be identified instantly as educable and destined for success. Working-class pupils find that their own culture is disparaged. Thus class advantages and disadvantages are transmitted down the generations in what appears to be an impartial meritocratic process, thereby not just reproducing but simultaneously legitimating social inequalities.

The British and the French explanations of socio-cultural reproduction (as described above) are best treated as complementary rather than as alternatives. Working-class youth learn to prefer and actively seek out working-class futures for themselves. Meanwhile the middle classes use their own social and cultural capital to impede any aspiring lower-class youth.

## Challenges

### *Can reproduction theories cope with change?*

Throughout their history, reproduction theories have faced challenges. Reproduction theories may create an impression that class cultures and relationships are transmitted intact and unchanging from generation to generation. Yet we know that major changes in class structures and relationships have occurred throughout the histories of modern societies. Neither the present-day middle class nor the present-day working class is a replica of its mid-twentieth-century counterpart. In practice, reproduction theories have no problem in addressing changes because these are facilitated by the changeover in personnel that occurs from generation to generation. Upcoming working, and middle, class young adults help to create new working and middle classes.

The British middle class, defined here in terms of its members' employment in man-agement and professional occupations, more than doubled in size during the second half of the twentieth century. This change in the shape of the class structure induced upward mobility from the working class, and the upwardly mobile appear to have been largely responsible for changing the character of middle-class culture from highbrow to omni-vore (see van Eijck 1999). Existing, older members of the middle class have not needed to change their tastes or lifestyle habits. The 'new blood', often rising from below, has imported what were formerly working-class tastes and accomplished a cultural transformation of the middle class.

The working class has also changed. Most traditional working-class masculine jobs in coal mines, steel mills and other heavy industries have been lost, sometimes to new technology, sometimes to lower wage cost countries. New working-class jobs have been created, but these are generally low-skill and low-paid jobs in service sectors – retailing, bars, restaurants, sports and leisure centres, security firms and suchlike. How have working-class young males, destined for working-class employment, coped with this change? A great deal of evidence suggests that such working-class males have not changed: they still see themselves as equipped for masculine jobs which require strength and manual skills, in which they will earn the wages to be effective 'breadwinners' for their families (McDowell 2003). If they are unable (as many are) to enact these identities in employment and in the domestic sphere, they can turn to leisure with 'the lads' who convince each other that the bravado that they display on nights out is 'real life' (see Blackshaw 2003).

According to Beverly Skeggs (1997), young working-class women have responded to the changes rather differently. The young women in Skeggs' research (who were attending a further education college to prepare for careers in care occupations) were sensitive to the denigration (from politicians and the media) endured by the working class since the 1970s. Rather than the 'salt of the earth' whose hard work and skills were to be

17

admired, the working class was being portrayed as lacking relevant skills and qualifications, willing to depend on social housing and sometimes on state welfare, and even lacking proper parenting skills as evidenced by the low achieving school children and teenage delinquents who they reared. The response of Skeggs' young women was to seek respectability. Being working class was experienced as a stigma. The young women wanted to avoid being regarded as 'common', and they sought to consolidate their respectability through the marriage market. Needless to say, these young working-class women's aspirations to respectability were liable to be thwarted by a shortage of eligible males. Hence the postponement of marriage, withdrawal by women from marriages deemed unsatisfactory, sub-replacement fertility and the rising incidence of single parenthood.

We can note here that both masculine and feminine responses to the changing conditions of working-class life set those concerned at risk of becoming members of, and then reproducing, an underclass or excluded groups.

## Youth's new condition

This new condition has arisen as part of a set of inter-related trends since the 1970s: de-industrialization, economic and occupational restructuring, higher levels of unemployment, and, as part of these changes, a shortage of entry jobs for statutory age school-leavers (16 year-olds in Britain). More young people have been continuing in post-compulsory education, adding to their qualifications, joining training schemes, and most likely gaining work experience in part-time and temporary jobs. The outcomes include a prolongation of school-to-work transitions and the individualization of youth biographies. There are now few places where young people in specific neighbourhoods all attend the local school, after which high proportions progress into jobs in a dominant local industry – the coal mine, the steel mill or the shipyard. These collective biographies have splintered. A result is that young people are less likely to be aware of what they share in common with others in any social category. They are more likely to be sensitive to their individuality, and these circumstances oblige them to be reflexive – to repeatedly take stock of their opportunities as well as their own abilities and inclinations and, on this basis, take charge of their own career development.

Classlessness is another alleged feature of youth's new condition. Nowadays in Britain, young people from all social class backgrounds receive a common schooling up to age 16. Thereafter they intermingle in post-compulsory education. Higher education has expanded. Graduates can no longer rely on being offered traditional graduate jobs. Few young people can be certain as to what their adult occupations will be. Individuals from all social class backgrounds also intermingle in the youth scenes associated with music, alcohol and sports. They form crowds on the basis of common tastes, which do not map in any obvious way onto any other social divisions.

Reproduction theories may appear to have been more suited to an era when young people were divided into different career groups while still in compulsory education, after which they exited into corresponding kinds of employment in which they could expect to remain for life. However, reproduction theorists have a convincing answer to their alleged obsolescence. They can point to the fact that links between social class origins and destinations remain as tight as ever. These links may be less visible, and young people and other lay actors may be less aware of these links than in the past, but sociologists who assume that these links have weakened commit what Furlong and Cartmel (2007) describe as an 'epistemological fallacy'.

## Social mobility

This is the Achilles' heel of reproduction theories. The problem is not that the theories may appear (this is only a superficial impression) to suggest that everyone should remain in the classes into which they are born. As we saw earlier, reproduction theories can accommodate mobility in so far as this is forced by changes in the shape of the class structure. Where reproduction theories falter is in trying to explain the precise volume of mobility and exactly who becomes mobile. Savage and Egerton (1997) propose that the changing shape of the class structure explains the volume of mobility, while individuals' abilities and educational attainments determine exactly who is mobile, but their own evidence shows that the volume of mobility is in excess of what is structurally required.

Moreover, as soon as individual level variables are admitted to explain exactly who becomes mobile, investigators who do not start from the premises of reproduction theories can claim that individual factors explain not only who becomes mobile but also exactly how much mobility occurs. For example, Saunders (1997) rejects the hypothesis which contends that individuals' life chances depend primarily on social advantages and disadvantages (SAD), and claims that individual ability (measured by IQ tests) is by far the best single predictor of outcomes, followed by individual motivation. On the basis of this evidence, Saunders (1995) argues that Britain is a more meritocratic society than reproduction theories suggest, and that the tendency for individuals to stick close to their levels of origin is actually due to the distribution of merit. Indeed, Saunders shows that the volume of social mobility in Britain is more or less exactly what one would expect from the relationship between parental social class and children's measured abilities.

Rational action theories offer an alternative socio-cultural explanation of inter-generational mobility and immobility to the accounts favoured by orthodox reproduction theorists (see Goldthorpe 1996). The latter stress the contrasts between different classes' cultures and values, whereas rational action theorists stress the similarities. They argue that most families in all social classes subscribe to achievement values in so far as they want their children to succeed and get ahead. The difference is said to be that lower-class families are satisfied with more modest levels of success than middle-class families. According to rational action theorists, this is because the 'investments' that are necessary to pursue upward mobility are greater relative to a lower-class family's resources than for a better-resourced higher-class family. This is most easily illustrated in financial terms – the costs of supporting a child through higher education – but the position is the same in respect of socio-emotional investments. Long-range upward mobility from the working class risks a family 'losing' a child. The outcome is said to be that working-class families will invest only when the risks of failure are low, for example, to support an exceptionally able child through university. Middle-class families, in contrast, will invest whatever is necessary for all their children – private schooling, private coaching, securing a place at a good secondary school, then at a good university (see Devine 2004). This view of the ambitions of working-class families accords with the findings of youth researchers who have found that 'resisters' are a minority among working-class youth, and that 'ordinary' or 'normal' working class young people are ambitious, albeit moderately so compared with middle-class peers (see Jenkins 1983; Brown 1987).

Moreover, the 'gradational' view of the relevant social class cultural differences in rational action theory fits the evidence on class differences in educational attainments, and on chances of reaching a middle-class destination, more closely than the 'relational'/oppositional

19

view of class cultures in orthodox reproduction theories. The latter postulate a 'clear break' between middle- and working-class cultures. Rational action theories appear to have the better explanation of why there are differences in life chances between children from the upper and lower middle classes, and from the skilled and unskilled working classes, and why the 'step' from the working class to the middle class is just one step (and not a particularly large step) among many.

## Conclusion

Reproduction is a major process, if not *the* main process, that youth researchers are required to investigate. This is because youth itself is a process, a transitional life stage, during which individuals' lives change constantly. The core task of youth research is to identify patterns in these changes, and thereby discover how children from different backgrounds reach different adult destinations. Youth researchers need to investigate everything that happens during the life stage – young people's consumption practices, their experiences with the welfare and justice systems, their political activities, their housing, their inter-personal relationships, their family and domestic contexts as well as their experiences in education and labour markets. We need to distinguish events and experiences that have long-term implications for adult outcomes from those which are relatively inconsequential. We know that childhood origins (specifically family backgrounds and education) are excellent predictors of adult outcomes, and the strength of these childhood predictors has not diminished despite all the changes in education, in youth labour markets, the extension of the life stage, and the individualization of biographies since the mid-twentieth century.

We need to know more and, first of all, this will involve recognizing that studying processes of reproduction requires equal attention to mobility and immobility, and to changes as well as continuities in class structures and relationships. An explanation of 'one side of the coin' necessarily contains an explanation of the other. Second, up to now, there has been rather too much assertion and too little testing hypotheses about reproduction processes. We need to compare systematically the merits of gradational (as in rational action theories) and relational/oppositional views of class divisions. We also need to set alongside each other the contributions of socio-cultural and bio-psychological factors in reproduction processes. The prize will be a convincingly and coherent explanation of the stability of the links between childhood origins and adult destinations throughout the late twentieth-century prolongation of youth transitions, individualization of biographies, the spread of uncertainty about outcomes among individuals passing through the youth life stage, and all the manifestations (of which there are many) of classlessness among young people.

## References

Blackshaw, T. (2003) *Leisure Life: Myth, Masculinity and Modernity*, London: Routledge.
Bourdieu. P. and Passeron, J-D. (1977) *Reproduction in Education, Society and Culture,* London: Sage.
Bowles, S. and Gintis, H. (1976) *Schooling in Capitalist America*, London: Routledge.
Brown, P. (1987) *Schooling Ordinary Kids: Inequality, Unemployment and the New Vocationalism,* London: Tavistock.

SOCIO-ECONOMIC REPRODUCTION

Collins, R. (1971) 'Functional and conflict theories of educational stratification', *American Sociological Review*, 36: 1002–11.

Devine, F. (2004) *Class Practices: How Parents Help Their Children Get Good Jobs,* Cambridge: Cambridge University Press.

Furlong, A. and Cartmel, F. (2007) *Young People and Social Change*, Maidenhead: Open University Press.

Goldthorpe, J. H. (1996) 'Class analysis and the re-orientation of class theory: the case of persisting differentials in educational attainment', *British Journal of Sociology*, 47: 481–505.

Hall, S. and Jefferson, T. (eds) (1976) *Resistance Through Rituals*, London: Hutchinson.

Jenkins, R. (1983) *Lads, Citizens and Ordinary Kids*, London: Routledge.

McDowell, L. (2003) *Redundant Masculinities? Employment Change and White Working Class Youth,* Oxford: Blackwell.

Putnam, R. D. (2000) *Bowling Alone: The Collapse and Revival of American Community,* New York: Simon & Schuster.

Riseborough, G. (1993) 'GBH – The Gobbo Barmy Army: one day in the life of the YTS boys', in I. Bates and G. Riseborough (eds) *Youth and Inequality*, Buckingham: Open University Press.

Saunders, P. (1995) 'Might Britain be a meritocracy?' *Sociology*, 29: 23–41.

—— (1997) 'Social mobility in Britain: an empirical evaluation of two competing explanations', *Sociology*, 31: 261–88.

Savage, M. and Egerton, M. (1997) 'Social mobility, individual ability and the inheritance of class inequality', *Sociology,* 31: 645–72.

Skeggs, B. (1997) *Formations of Class and Gender: Becoming Respectable,* London: Sage.

van Eijck, K. (1999) 'Socialisation, education and lifestyle: how social mobility increases the cultural heterogeneity of status groups', *Poetics,* 26: 309–38.

Willis, P. (1977) *Learning to Labour,* Farnborough: Saxon House.

# 3

# Youth and generation

## In the midst of an adult world

*John Goodwin and Henrietta O'Connor*

## Introduction

The relationship of young people to the generations that surround them, either younger or older, has been of interest to sociologists, psychologists and policy-makers for some time, with the categories of childhood, youth and adolescence, adulthood and old/third-age all becoming both important conceptual tools and widely used units of analysis. However, despite a wealth of literature from the past fifty or so years, the concept and meaning of youth and generation remain complex – at the same time youth is an age that is both ambiguous and ill defined but is also a time of life that is perceived to be the most difficult for individuals with the problem of making the transition from education to work, the problem of 'growing up' and the problem of youth culture with its associated moral panics (see Brake 1985; Clay 2003). It becomes easier then to adopt Mannheim's view of generation as 'a common location in the social and historical process' (Mannheim 1952: 291) and group young people into homogenous generations labelled 'delinquents', 'Baby Boomers', 'Generation X', 'Generation Y', and so on. Yet how we *understand* these groupings, and their relationship to older generations, remains heavily contested and largely dependent upon the perspective adopted in the literature – be it functionalist, structuralist, lifecourse, cohort, transitional or interpretavist (see Pilcher 1995).

As MacDonald *et al.* (2001) have argued, historically the study of youth developed with research focused on one of two distinct strands. Early studies of youth, dating from the 1960s, were interested in what can be termed as youth culture and the associated moral panics around this life stage. Later studies, which emerged in the 1970s, were more interested in youth transitions from school to work and understanding how young people made the transition into work and on to adulthood. However, as Macdonald *et al.* (ibid.: 4.9) argue, 'there is more to becoming an adult than simply making a transition from school to work'. As such, the complexity of youth transitions is now becoming more widely understood as the focus has shifted from looking merely at issues of youth culture and/or the move from school to work to encompass other significant elements such as the transition out of the family home to independent living. Alongside the broadening of the debate around transition it is increasingly argued that not only

22

have transitions to work become more complex, but other transitions at this life stage, based on traditional signifiers of adulthood such as independent living, marriage and secure work/career have become more protracted than past transitions.

One of the most important recent contributions to these debates has come from Wyn and Woodman (2006) and their argument that the concept of generation is far a more powerful analytical tool than 'youth in transition'. Wyn and Woodman (ibid.: 498) argue that 'youth as transition' is too psychosocial, too developmental, too deterministic, that it underestimates the importance of young people's own subjectivities and that it leads to youth being viewed as a 'linear process or position on the lifecourse' between childhood and adulthood.

> If we understand that the adulthood that was available to the Baby Boomer generation was a historical artefact, a product of a particular combination of economic realties, social policies and industrial settlements that have long since ceased to exist, it becomes possible to see what is missing from the conceptualisation of youth simply as transition.
>
> (ibid.: 498)

They support this assertion with an exploration of the experiences and attitudes of young people born in the early 1970s. From this analysis, they develop the concept of new adulthood which

> signals the emergence of significant new priorities and subjectivities that are anchored in the political and material conditions of young people's lives. It is suggested that these subjectivities are not simply transitional (or age effects), and implies that a generational shift has occurred.
>
> (ibid.: 500)

While Wyn and Woodman's analysis is clearly important in that it re-states the case for the concept of generation, it is limited by only using youth (or generations of youth) as a metaphor of social change. Their analysis does not fully explore the interconnections or interactions between one generation and another, for example, do young people in Wyn and Woodman's analysis not interact with their parents and teachers? Who do they interact with when they enter work for the first time, is it exclusively their own peer group and generation or is it, as is more likely, are they interacting with individuals from different generational groups? They also fall foul of what Furlong and Cartmel (1997) refer to as 'the epistemological fallacy of late modernity' – that somehow everything is separate from and different to the past. Rather than seeing social life as a snapshot in the way that Wyn and Woodman's analysis implies, there is a need to see it as a continuum and understand that both the past and present are interrelated. This in turn means that behaviours of today emerge out of, but are not separate from, those of the past. In highlighting the distinctiveness of generations Wyn and Woodman's analysis often underplays the similarities between generations. For example, they draw a clear distinction between the Baby Boomers in their twenties during the mid-1970s to the post-1970 generation who would be in their twenties in 2001. Yet in our own analysis of historical youth transitions data, we have highlighted the common experiences between youth from 1960s and young workers now (see Goodwin and O'Connor 2005). Our analysis suggests that young people in the 1960s experienced very similar individualized, non-linear and complex transitions to contemporary generations of youth. This is despite the huge economic and social transformation, between the early 1960s and the present, to which Wyn and Woodman (2006) refer.

In this chapter, we seek to examine intergenerational relationships in Norbert Elias's 'Adjustment of Young Workers to Work Situations and Adult Roles' project from the 1960s. In particular, we aim to answer four broad questions. First, what can we learn from Eliasian sociology about the relationship between young and older people? We want to use Eliasian theory to support our analysis and underscore what Furlong and Cartmel (1997) view as the epistemological fallacy of late modernity that is apparent in some writings on age and generation. Second, to what extent did young people then mix with members of other generations, especially older workers? Third, to what extent were those interactions positive and beneficial for the young workers in helping them develop and make the transition to adulthood? Finally, to what extent is Elias' work useful for understanding current debates on youth and generation?

## Using Eliasian sociology to explore youth and generation

As suggested above, one of the main limitations with much of the writing on youth and generation is the tendency to highlight the apparent 'distinctiveness' of young people from older generations around, focusing on what is unique about them and what is different between them and older generations rather than considering the interconnections between the two. However, we feel that the work of Norbert Elias allows us to understand youth and generation slightly differently, he allows us to view generations not as 'static objects' or separate groups of relationships, but as figurations or sets of inter-relationships through which young people learn the acceptable adult behaviours from the adults around them (Goodwin 2007). Of particular importance here is Elias's critique of the *homo clausus* or 'closed personality' perspective that has come to dominate sociology. For Elias,

> The conception of the individual as *homo clausus*, a little world in himself who ultimately exists quite independently of the great world outside ... every other human being is seen as a *homo clausus*; his core, his being, his true self likewise as being divided within him by an invisible wall from everything outside, including every other human being.

> (Elias 2000: 472)

Such a conception leads sociologists to continually view the individual as something existing outside of society and society as existing beyond individuals (ibid.: 472). The central thrust of Elias's work, as Mennell (1993) argues, is underpinned not by *homo clausus* but by *homo aperti* – a sociological analysis that emphasizes the interdependence of people and traces 'changes in personality structure hand in hand with changes in the structure of human relations in societies as parts of an overall process' (ibid.: 193). Embracing the notion of *homo aperti* and a sociological analysis that emphasizes the interdependence of people has important implications for how youth and generation are perceived in sociological analysis. Elias articulates this view further, and more fully in his writings (see Elias 2000; 2001) and argues that 'I' is an outcome of interactions and relationships with others. In Elias's analysis:

[T]here can be no 'I' without 'he', 'she', 'we', 'you' or 'they'. It is plainly misleading to use such concepts as 'I' or ego independently of their position with
the web of relationships to which the rest of the pronouns refer. Taken together,
the personal pronouns are in fact an elementary form of expression of the fact
that every person is fundamentally related to other people, and that every human
individual is fundamentally a social being.

(Elias 2001: 124)

In this sense, 'I' is not a singular but is instead a plurality with 'I' and 'we' being inextricably linked. As such, youth cannot solely be about an 'individual' or a generation of
individuals that are 'unique'. Instead, generations are historically and spatially located and
analysis of generations provides insight into changing group identities, behavioural standards,
changing relationships, interactions, configurations, and power balances.

It is the web of social relations in which individuals live during their most impres-
sionable phase, that is childhood and youth, which imprints itself upon their unfolding
personality in the form of the relationship between their controlling agencies, super-
ego and ego and their libidinal impulses. The resulting balance ... determines how an
individual person steers him or herself in his or her social relations with others ...
However, there is no end to the intertwining ... it never ceases entirely to be
affected by his or her changing relations with others throughout his or her life.

(Elias, 2000: 377)

This process of constant change Elias conceptualized as the inter-relationship between
*sociogenesis* (the processes of development and transformation in social relations) and *psychogenesis* (the processes of development and transformation in the psychology, personality or habitus that accompany such social changes) (van Krieken 1998). Elias argues that
habitus is not inherent or innate but 'habituated' and becomes a constituent part of the
individual by learning through social experience and develops as part of a continuous
process beginning at birth and continuing through childhood and youth (ibid.: 59).
Given the interrelationship between sociogenesis *and* psychogenesis, Elias argued that the
socialization of children cannot take place behind closed doors and the learning of adult
behaviours is only possible due to the presence of others.

Elias's specific writings on youth are located in two places: first, in the archived notes
and memorandum that accompanied the archived material associated with the Adjustment of
Young Workers to Work Situations and Adult Roles' project, and, second, his paper 'The
Civilising of Parents' (Elias 1980). From these writings, it is clear that Elias thinks there
are two, parallel, long-term processes occurring. First, that in order for young people to
acquire appropriate adult behaviours, interaction with adults both at home and at work is
essential. Second, however, compared to more primitive societies, contemporary societies
are marked by a growing separation between adults, children and young people. In the
context of this later process Elias identified eight particular problems for young people:

- the prolonged separation of young people from adults;
- the indirect knowledge of the adult world;
- the lack of communication between adults and children;
- the social life of children in the midst of an adult world with limited communication
  between the two;

25

- the role of fantasy elements in the social and personal life of the young vis-à-vis the reality of adult life;
- the social role of young people is ill-defined and ambiguous;
- striving for independence through earning money constitutes a new social dependence (on work rather than parents);
- the prolonging of social childhood beyond biological maturity:

He states:

> Human social life in the form of urban-industrial nation-states encloses each individual person in a complex network of longer, more differentiated chains of inter-dependence. In order to claim to be an adult … in order to fulfil an adult's functions … it is necessary to have a very high degree of foresight, restraint of momentary impulses, for the sake of long-term goals and gratifications … it requires a high degree of self-regulating restraint of drives and affects.
>
> (Elias 1980: 201–2)

The more complex a society the more complex this process of transition to adulthood or the learning of adult norms becomes. Elias suggested that this is radically different from the children growing up in 'simpler' societies of previous periods in which children and young people had more direct contact with adults. To illustrate this, Elias suggests that in Eskimo society there is a direct developmental line between children's play behaviour (playing with bows and arrows or learning to treat skins) and adult behaviour such as hunting, tent making and survival (ibid.: 202). The young person's behaviour corresponds to a high degree with adult reality whereas in complex industrial societies it does not. As such, in a simpler society, he argues the individual civilizing transformation is temporally shorter and less deep-rooted (ibid.: 202). Yet despite these problems and the apparent increasing separation of young people from the older generation, the interaction between adults and young people is essential if the young people are to make a successful transition to adulthood – or, in Eliasian terms, to acquire appropriate behavioural standards of the time. The process of separation may make the learning of these adult behaviours more complex but the interaction must still take place.

We would now like to explore some of the above themes using data from Elias's 'Adjustment of Young Workers to Work Situations and Adult Roles', undertaken in Leicester between 1962 and 1964. To explore these themes, data were collected via interviews with a sample of young people drawn from the Youth Employment Office index of all Leicester school leavers from the summer and Christmas of 1960 and the summer and Christmas of 1962 – 882 interviews were completed, of which 851 of the original interview schedules were rediscovered by the authors (see Goodwin and O'Connor 2005; 2006; 2007).

## Youth and generation at work in 1960s Leicester

One of Elias's central concerns focused on understanding more about the way that younger people interacted with older people, in particular, to probe the notion that interaction with adults is essential to the acquisition of appropriate adult behaviour. Most respondents, when asked about their relationships with older people, reported that they had good relationships with older workers and many commented that they interacted better with the older staff than with people of the same age:

> All right – Tack (45) who's just come – he's nice. I seem to get on better with the older ones because the young ones try to be 'lairy' and that – I'd sooner have older ones.
>
> I don't have much contact with young people of my own age at work, and I prefer it that way, if you get a lot of young lads together, they are going to lark about and not get on with the job. I get on with the boys at the boys' club. As far as working with them, I resent it. Even girls as old as 19 seem immature about their job, secretaries or trainee secretaries are alright but I don't bother with the others.
>
> Very well. I find that whenever I go I always get on with older folk best. Probably with working with them a lot. I get on alright with younger people but not as well as older folk. [Why?] As I say, probably because I've had to work with older people.

Many were very clear that it was 'right' to respect older and more experienced workers. These young workers explained that as long as they respected the older workers, by displaying appropriate adult behaviours themselves, then their workplace relationships were good. This is significant given Elias's argument that young people only learn appropriate adult behaviour through interaction with older people. Indeed, the quotes that follow provide support for Elias's contention that the learning of adult behaviours is only possible due to the presence of others:

> I get on alright with them [older workers], I don't go shooting my mouth off, that's what they don't like, people shooting their mouths off, there is a lad who has just started who shoots his mouth off and nobody likes him. Everything they've got, he's got something better.
>
> Generally, very well, but they have their own way of doing things, and you have to be very tactful not to upset them.
>
> I'm not cheeky with them, I just respect that they're older.
>
> Very well. I get on with them all the time. They don't treat me as the youngster and push any old job on me, they treat me as they treat the other men.
>
> Quite well. You know I used to do as I was told. Sometimes I was a bit cheeky and I used to get a back hander, like – off the chaps especially. I used to get on pretty well with everybody.

Furthermore, some respondents commented that they were not comfortable when adults acted in a way the young person felt was inappropriate: 'Some of them are alright, but others act stupid, throwing things about and so on.'

For those who commented on positive relationships with other young people, the emphasis was on shared understandings, stressing the similarities within and among their own generation or the 'collective exposure to the same historical set of cultural … experiences' (Brannen, 2003: 1.2):

> [With] my own age? It's just like being at school with some of them – you talk about records and things like that.
>
> Alright, better than with the old [Why?] we have more in common – records and so on.

Others, however, demonstrated that they felt little separation from older workers, regardless of their differing generations, by talking about their shared activities. The quotes below suggest that, for some young workers, appropriate behaviour in the adult world was easily learnt:

> Very well, the older blokes are very nice. I have a game of darts with them at dinner time.
>
> They're great. Play football with about 20 of the chaps at dinner on the back of the playing field. We have a fab old time.

In terms of learning work-based skills, the young workers seemed to have clear idea of the separation that existed between themselves and the older, more experienced workers. Here, the concept of learning appropriate adult behaviour, in this case, work-specific skills, was understood by the younger generation in a very explicit way. They had no doubt that the older workers were 'superior' not only in age but also in experience:

> Well, they're all right. They were willing to show you a trade, specially the chaps who were ready for retiring. They were more willing than a younger person.
>
> All right ... They're more grown up and obviously talk about more grown-up things.
>
> Very well, in general. For a start, they regard you as incompetent until they get to know your capabilities.
>
> Usually very well, some look down on you a bit, thinking you don't know the job very well, but usually get all the co-operation you need.
>
> Very well – you know if you get in a bit of a muddle, they'll always give you a hand. The managers come down on to the warehouse floor to give you a hand with anything as long as they aren't too busy.
>
> I get on all right – they try to be a bit, telling you this and telling you that. They try to appear too fatherly at times, about work and things in general but that's all.

It is clear then that among this group of young workers there was evidence of young people learning adult norms through the presence and behaviour of the adults around them, in this case, at work. The majority of young people recognized a clear separation between themselves and the older workers (or adults) on starting work and this was evident in their deference towards older workers and their understanding of their place at work as the most junior employees. However, over time these individuals began to acquire and adopt appropriate forms of social and professional behaviour and this was increasingly recognized and respected by their older colleagues. Recognition for the changes in behaviour at work is important because, as Blatterer explains:

> Adult recognition through commitment and responsibility, productivity and performance ... implies that being adult is not something we can simply claim for ourselves. Individuals' adult status ultimately relies on the extent to which the things they do and say, and the attitudes and beliefs they hold and express, match the social norms or criteria and expectations of what constitutes adult behaviour and attitudes in society.

(2007: 9.2)

## Conclusion

In this chapter we have suggested that the concept of generation is important but that generations should not be seen as separate groupings but, instead it should be used to denote interrelated groupings. The young workers in the data we have used here were clearly working with colleagues who had been born any time between 1900 and the 1930s – so without doubt were of a different generation to the young workers themselves and therefore an ideal context in which to examine the interrelationships between adults and young people. The data reveal very clearly, that in the context of the workplace, the young workers and older workers interacted and that the young workers themselves thought that this was an essential part of growing up and becoming more adult in their behaviour. The question then remains, for those who critique the transitional approach to generation, how do young people learn appropriate adult behaviours if they only interact within their own generational group? Indeed, using Elias, we can see that young people cannot learn appropriate adult behaviour from within their own generation group alone.

The broadening out of the debates around transition and the recognition of the complexity of this life stage provides support for Elias's argument that as societies become more complex then so too does the transition from youth to adulthood and the learning of adult norms. However, appropriate adult behaviour still has to be learnt by young people and this can only happen through interaction with older generations. Maintaining a view that generations are independent of each other is fallacious as it de-emphasizes the interaction and underestimates the contact that young people have with older people in society.

## References

Blatterer, H. (2007) 'Adulthood: the contemporary redefinition of a social category', *Sociological Research Online*, 12, http://www.socresonline.org.uk/12/4/3.html

Brake, M. (1985) *Comparative Youth Culture*, London: Routledge.

Brannen, J. (2003) 'Towards a typology of intergenerational relations: continuities and change in families', *Sociological Research Online*, 8, http://www.socresonline.org.uk/8/2/brannen.html

Clay, A. (2003) 'Keepin' it real black youth, hip-hop culture, and black identity', *American Behavioral Scientist*, 46: 1346–58.

Elias, N. (1961) 'Application for a grant for special research to DSIR', unpublished, University of Leicester (Teresa Keil Collection).

—— (1980) 'The civilising of parents', in J. Goudsblom and S. Mennell (eds) (1998) *The Norbert Elias Reader*, London: Blackwell.

—— (2000) *The Civilising Process*, London: Blackwell.

—— (2001) *The Society of Individuals*, New York: Continuum Publishing.

Furlong, A. and Cartmel, F. (1997) *Young People and Social Change: Individualization and Risk in Late Modernity,* Buckingham: Open University Press.

Goodwin, J. (2007) 'The transition to work and adulthood: becoming adults via communities of practice', in J. Hughes, N. Jewson and L. Unwin (eds) *Communities of Practice: Critical Perspectives*, London: Routledge.

Goodwin, J. and O'Connor, H. (2005) 'Exploring complex transitions: looking back at the "Golden Age" of youth transitions', *Sociology*, 39: 201–20.

—— (2006) 'Norbert Elias and the lost young worker project', *Journal of Youth Studies*, 9: 159–73.

—— (2007) 'Researching forty years of learning for work: the experiences of one cohort of workers', *Journal of Vocational Education and Training*, 59: 349–67.

MacDonald, R., Mason, P., Shildrick, T., Webster, C., Johnston, L. and Ridley, L. (2001) 'Snakes and ladders: in defence of studies of youth transition', *Sociological Research Online,* 5, http://www.socresonline.org.uk/5/4/macdonald.html

Mannheim, K. (1952) 'The problem of generation', in T. Kesckkemeti (ed.) *Essays on the Sociology of Knowledge*, London: Routledge.

Mennell, S. (1993) *Norbert Elias: An Introduction*, London: Blackwell.

Pilcher, J. (1995) *Age and Generation in Modern Britain*, Oxford: Oxford University Press.

Van Krieken, R. (1998) *Norbert Elias*, London: Routledge.

Wyn, J. and Woodman, D. (2006) 'Generation, youth and social change in Australia', *Journal of Youth Studies*, 9: 495–514.

# 4

# Models of navigation and life management

*Manuela du Bois-Reymond*

## Introduction

Navigation is a nautical term. Nautical charts must lead the ship and its crew safely through the endlessness of unknown oceans and bring them safely back to their home harbour. Why is it that this metaphor is used so frequently by youth sociologists to characterize the lives of young people who live in contemporary societies? Obviously their status and life circumstances are not clear but need active and informed navigators to do the intricate navigation work. The antagonistically intertwined concepts of *structure* and *agency* can teach us how to investigate that work and their workers.

What makes the navigation work difficult and the outcome uncertain is the growing tension between intended actions and unintended risks and outcomes. That tension is caught in the much discussed concept of 'risk society', originally introduced by the German sociologist Ulrich Beck (Beck 1992). Living in contemporary risk societies intensifies feelings of contingency, feelings of never being sure if personal decisions will take me where I want to arrive.

The motor which transforms traditional societies into risk societies is the speed with which new technologies are developed, applied, spread and further developed. That development disquieted and fascinated philosophers and social scientists like Max Weber, Georg Simmel and Emile Durkheim at the turn of the nineteenth into the twentieth century and many scholars again after the Second World War and up to the present. Interestingly (and disquietingly?) the fear of abusively used technology and knowledge has ceased these days. The 'knowledge society' seems to have sunny rather than dark connotations for most people (or not?). The term signifies that the acquisition of knowledge is worthwhile and even necessary to cope with modern life.

Rapid structural changes are not restricted to certain societies and continents but are spread over the globe, although at an uneven pace and with different outcomes. One of the many results of these developments is increased mobility of people within their own society and between countries and continents, resulting, among many other effects, in growing heterogeneity of national populations. Western-type societies willingly or unwillingly become host societies for people emigrating to find employment in the richer continents of Europe and North America. Youth in a given society is no longer identical to autochthonous young people and can therefore not only be analysed within the traditional categories of social class and gender, but must now be conceived as an ethnically and culturally mixed group.

Incalculable risks, growing knowledge and diverse ethnic-cultural composition of the population are three influential conditions which steer the navigation work of young people today – or fail to do so. Youth sociologists have developed over the past three or so decades useful concepts to describe and analyse that navigation work – and its failures. Those concepts we now discuss in the remainder of this chapter.

## Navigation work

In what follows we have to distinguish between youth-sociological *discourses* and *empirical evidence*. We will show that the two do not always match: discourses may exaggerate societal developments and their impact on the lives of young people. There may also be blank spots in discourses overlooking developments which are influential for the lives of young people.

### De- and re-standardization of the life course

It is not easy these days to define who is young, and why. Age, once a strong marker, is no longer a trustworthy indicator. The traditional life course stages of childhood, youth and adulthood have lost their former clear meanings and have become blurred. Children behave in many respects like young autonomous persons, certainly concerning their consumptive behaviour. While childhood ends earlier, the youth phase is prolonged; it begins earlier and might stretch well into the third life decade – adulthood arrested. The main reason for the prolongation lies with education. In comparison to earlier generations, it takes contemporary youth much longer to pass through school and further education. This expresses the need of knowledge societies for ever more and better qualified workforces.

These processes not only prolong the youth phase, it is even open for discussion – and is indeed discussed quite controversially by youth researchers – if it makes sense at all to perceive the life course in distinct phases which follow each other in neat sequence. Empirical evidence rather points to 'yo-yo biographies' of young people who switch between life stages and phases; a young mother who goes back to study; a young man who is 30 and still lives with his parents; a married couple, both of whom go back to a youth-cultural lifestyle after separation. In other words, young people can feel young *and* adult, they can reverse life stages – from employee back to student, or they can – and do – question the notion of adulthood altogether (du Bois-Reymond and Chisholm 2006; Walther *et al.* 2006).

If education is the driving force behind this prolongation of youth, it matters what and how much education one receives. Youth researchers continually point to the gulf between slow and fast trackers (Bynner and Parsons 2002), a distinction which still corresponds closely to middle- and lower-class affiliations as well as to certain ethnic minority groups, while gender has lost its discriminatory rigor: females have caught up with males in terms of educational acquisition in all western-style countries (and many others as well).

That leaves us with the question about the relationship between prolongation and destandardization: is it that the longer educational trajectories become, the more destandardized the life course becomes? Or is it that we have to think in terms of *different forms* of destandardization? As so often with causes and effects of modernization, it is both: looked at from a generational perspective, *all* late modern life courses show less uniformity and more diversity, and education does play a major role in prolongation. But if we compare the life courses of well and badly educated persons, of white and black persons, of females and males, we find very different forms of destandardization and the main difference would have to be sought in the *degree of autonomy* a person is granted by societal institutions and the extent to which they are able to make their own decisions and live according to them.

Finally, there is the question of *re*standardization, in other words, are there new standards developing to which late modern life courses have to comply? We have partly answered this question already by pointing to the greedy need of knowledge societies for highly qualified people. Fast trackers with insufficient education run much higher risks in the labour market than they did in earlier times when more blue-collar work was available; gaining as much education as possible has become a new standard. Also restandardization takes place in that the majority of young Europeans cohabitate before they get married.

In other life spheres, restandardization is less evident: whom you choose as an intimate partner you decide wholly yourself, not your parents, not the church and not your sex. And getting married at all is also an individual choice. Really? Again: that is both true and untrue. It is true in that in late modern societies the range of choices for the individual has hugely increased in comparison to former times, certainly in the private and consumption sphere. It is questionable, though, if we think, for instance, about the retraditionalization in gender relations after the birth of the first child, reinforcing a more traditional share of care and work between young parents.

Evaluating the work of scholars in the field, we come to the conclusion that much attention has been given to structural and biographical processes of de- and restandardization. There is also a sound body of research on the effects of such processes on different groups of young people. Valuable work has been done on demographic statistics and time studies which show, for example, destandardization of marriage norms from the 1970s onwards but at the same time restandardization when ever more people are adhering to similar behaviour, like delaying the birth of the first child.

## Learning in the life course

The 'navigation discourse' in youth sociology concentrates strongly on the transition from school to work. As already indicated, for many young people there is not much navigation room, certainly not when they are fast trackers. Also in most European (and other) countries, educational systems seem resistant to fundamental reforms and force their student populations to follow calibrated paths. In formal education, pupils can only navigate within fixed curricula.

Since the Lisbon Summit of 2000, when the European Commission launched educational and labour market policies designed to make Europe 'the most competitive continent in the world', pressure has mounted to produce more educated young Europeans (see EC 2001). The regularly conducted PISA studies (Programme for International Student Assessment) of the OECD contribute to the spirit of competition by making public the strengths and weaknesses of national educational systems. Lifelong learning inside and outside school is in vogue and has resulted in a growing literature (Nicole 2006).

The increasing importance of the production of knowledge in late modern societies has revitalized discussions about human capital. Youth sociology in particular has picked up and deepened the notion of social and cultural capital as originally developed by scholars like Bourdieu, Coleman and Putnam. For our topic – models of navigation and life management of young people in late modern societies – these notions have positive and a negative connotation for navigation spaces. Here *positive* connotations refer to personal traits and coping strategies of actors which can enhance their life chances, not only by using the cultural and social capital of their family and social surroundings, but also by producing new sorts of capital, and here a valuable resource is the motivation to learn and acquire new insights in all kinds of settings (see Csikszentmihayi 1997).

Motivation to learn and accumulate knowledge has become a potent steering wheel for navigating the ship of life through good and bad weather. And, as social class, gender and ethnic-cultural backgrounds lose their predetermining force for the destiny of individuals, the possibilities to make use of options widen. Successful learning leads to more learning and more chances and can thereby make up for lacking social and cultural capital. Young learners become lifelong learners (by the way, the notion of lifelong learning corresponds with the previously discussed blurring of distinct life phases).

The *negative* connotation which is implied in the notion of social and cultural capital refers to structural barriers and constraints which are difficult or impossible to overcome through the agency of young persons. As early as the 1970s, Bourdieu and many other scholars demonstrated the indestructible nexus between social class and educational success or failure; much of their writing is still relevant (see, more recently, Bourdieu 1993). This nexus might not be as close-knit as it was but it has certainly not dissolved. It is therefore all the more important to think about measures to encourage young disadvantaged persons to develop learning motivation and use the opportunities in educational systems productively.

And this is precisely what the new ideology of neo-liberalism proposes: you yourself are the captain on the ship, you have your luck in your own hands, don't blame your parents, teachers, politicians, do it yourself!

Transferring responsibilities to the individual and thereby unburdening the state from welfare costs is a political strategy by which risks are put on the shoulders of the individual, denying that there are some essential risks that cannot be avoided by individual effort: you might have done your very best at school but still cannot get a good job – or even a job at all; you discover that 'lifelong learning' is not a waterproof solution to labour market problems; you might hear every day that you live in a democratic society but you still experience discrimination because you have the wrong colour of skin; you might be a very successful learner, but if you happen to be female and want to become a mother, you should be modest in your occupational ambitions (see Raffo and Reeves 2000).

As a matter of fact, much of the work by youth sociologists is spent untangling the threads of the nexus between social class, ethnic background and gender, on the one hand, and educational and labour market chances, on the other, making suggestions about how to design promising policies and interventions to reduce the discrepancies between the demands of knowledge societies, personal needs and existing societal barriers (Bradley and Van Hoof 2005; Bekerman 2006; du Bois-Reymond and López Blasco 2003).

An interesting and recently discussed concept in this context is given with the idea of *network learning*. The clue to networks is their non-hierarchical character which stimulates the exchange of experiences as well as mental and real products between all kinds of learners and age groups, not only peers. Networking is greatly facilitated through information communication technologies which may lead to creating new resources which are relatively independent of social and cultural capital, and also of formal educational credits (Diepstraten *et al.* 2006).

## Open life courses

Human life develops in time and space. In that very general sense, the life courses of contemporary people, and young people in particular, are no different from earlier generations. But youth sociologists discuss the question in a more restricted meaning. When they assume that the future is open, they refer to the decades after the Second World War when life courses were strongly determined by gender and class and corresponding behaviours and were thereafter transformed into more individualized biographies with more options to choose from. At the same time, more options increase real and felt contingencies: you never know what will be the result of a certain choice and you feel therefore constantly uncertain if you have made the 'right' choice at the right time (Furlong and Cartmel 2003).

This dilemma is harder for young people than older persons who have already made more choices and have incorporated the results of them in their lives. Further decisions are more limited and better calculable because of the implied path dependency while younger people have not yet accomplished much of their life paths. Their future is still less determined, certainly in contemporary societies with less binding standards and background givens.

Young people react to that situation essentially with two coping strategies. One is to overcome growing uncertainty about future developments, especially concerning the labour market, by drawing up plans. The other is to refrain from making long-term plans and rather stick to short-term planning, or even no deliberate planning at all. *Both* these strategies are sensible in the face of late modern circumstances and risks. A young person may begin her or his life as a student at school with certain occupational wishes and definite plans about how to arrive at that goal. On the way s/he might come across interesting alternatives and switch educational or vocational trajectory. That might not lead to the desired result and demand further switches: – yo-yo biographies in the making. Eventually that person might find that long-term planning is useless and may stick to the ad hoc strategy of making decisions by the day. Many young people whom you ask: 'What do you think your life will be like in five (ten) years from now?' would say one of two things: either, 'By then I will probably have a job in such and such a field and will have a family', or 'How can I know?'

Youth research shows that young people are by and large optimistic about their future, even when they are aware of its 'openness'. They assume that things will work out alright one way or the other. But this general optimistic attitude is not independent of socio-economic developments and geo-political regions. The more prosperous the labour market, the more optimistic (young) people are about the future in general and their own in particular. And vice versa, as, for example, the last Shell Study of German young people demonstrated: with less bright economic prospects in 2006 as compared to four years earlier and correspondingly less optimistic attitudes (cf. Jugend 2006). That study is particularly interesting in that Germany consists of a prosperous western and a less prosperous eastern part. Young East Germans with less bright labour market prospects are more pessimistic about their future than their contemporaries some kilometres further west; they are simply *forced* to plan short term because their original plans for training in a certain field are all too often frustrated and redirected outside their own will. Under such unfavourable circumstances, choices are plainly brought back to zero and the notion of an open future is painted black.

That also happens to the NEETs; young people not in education, training or employment, whom we find in all European countries, albeit in different proportions and targeted in different youth populations. The recent UNICEF Report (2007) gives figures for 15–19 year-olds in a range from under 5 per cent (Norway) to over 10 per cent (France) (and 25 per cent for Israel).

Also sex and gender play a role in choice space. For example, young Italian females are more restricted in their future choices than young Dutch women because of traditional social and family values. Italian women might make short-term plans because they have no other choice while their Dutch contemporaries may do that also, but for different reasons; they may have so many alternatives that they experience 'choice dilemmas' (see various contributions in Leccardi and Ruspini 2006).

So when youth sociologists talk and write about late modern life and open life courses of young people, one must be attentive to two trends, one delineating generality and the other specificity. It is quite safe to state that, in comparison with former generations, the future has become generally less predictable in personal life courses: a young man starting studying philosophy might end up as an employee in an advertisement firm; a young female Moroccan might become an independent self-employed fashion designer. Such unforeseen switches in life courses were less common in the past than they are today.

Another new development is that young people are aware of the contingencies of their lives, be that a pessimistic awareness, as with the NEETs (Yates and Payne 2006), or a more optimistic awareness ('it will be okay').

Specification of general trends has to be taken carefully into account. One fruitful research strategy is by making regional or national comparisons which point to cultural, ethnic, gender and economic factors, types of welfare state regime and many other influences co-determining the future prospects of young people.

## A new life model?

Taking together the three topics discussed in this chapter – de- and restandardization, learning, and open future – do they indicate a new life model to which contemporary youth populations adhere? At first sight the answer seems banal, it is again yes *and* no. Yes, obviously, young people today do conduct their lives according to quite different behavioural standards and with different resources (and lacking different resources!) than their parents – let alone grandparents. Not only do most of them (not all!) have more educational choices and stay young longer, it also takes longer for (almost all) young people to become economically independent, resulting in a delay in family building, and not only do they have innumerable more choices in the field of consumption, they also live in a time which is characterized by the breathtaking acceleration of developments unknown in former times (Rosa 2005). Destandardization and the development of new standards leading to – possibly short-lived – restandardization will be caught in the unforeseeable turmoil of such acceleration and make constant adaptation a necessity. Navigation work will therefore become ever more complex for young people and preparation for such work through broad educational strategies is already of essential importance (Heinz and Krüger 2001). Not all young people will be up to that task.

But there is also an extent to which life models can be regarded as unchanged: despite rapid changes, many young people stick to family traditions, realize normal biographical life plans and adhere to the 'old' values of religion and moral obligations.

The real challenge in conceiving that what is 'old' and what is 'new' does not lie in either/or; it lies in fact in theorizing the *relationship* between the two, and how that relationship affects which groups of young (and old) people in what ways. And not only that: one must realize that the 'old' is never the same old as it was but changes content and form under the pressure of general change. A normal biographical life course, developing according to the 'old' rules: finishing education, getting a job, getting married and beginning a family, is not the same today as it was for former generations, simply because it takes place in another time which allows options *even* if they are not used.

For youth researchers, the task is to bring the trends of continuity and discontinuity together in their work if they are interested in how social change influences the life courses of contemporary young people.

# References

Beck, U. (1992) *Risk Society: Towards a New Modernity*, London: Sage.

Bekerman, Z. (ed.) (2006) *Learning in Places: The Informal Education Reader,* New York: Peter Lang.

Bourdieu, P. (1993) *La Misère du Monde*, Paris: Editions du Seuil.

Bradley, H. and Van Hoof, J. (eds) (2005) *Young People in Europe: Labour Markets and Citizenship*, Bristol: Policy Press.

Bynner, J. and Parsons, S. (2002) 'Social exclusion and the training from school to work: the case of young people not in education, employment or training (NEET)', *Journal of Educational Behaviour,* 60: 289–309.

Csikszentmihayi, M. (1997) *Finding Flow: The Psychology of Engagement with Everyday Life,* New York: Basic Books.

Diepstraten, I., du Bois-Reymond, M. and Vinken, H. (2006) 'Trendsetting biographies: concepts of navigating through late-modern life and learning', *Journal of Youth Studies*, 9: 175–93.

du Bois-Reymond, M. and Chisholm, L. (2006) *The Modernization of Youth Transitions in Europe,* San Francisco: Jossey-Bass.

du Bois-Reymond, M. and López Blasco, A. (2003) 'Yo-yo transitions and misleading trajectories: towards integrated transition policies for young adults in Europe', in A. Blasco, W. McNeish and A. Walther (eds) *Young European People and Contradictions of Inclusion,* Bristol: Policy Press.

European Commission (EC) (2001) *A New Impetus for European Youth*. Online. Available: www.europa. eu.int/comm/youth/whitepaper/index_en.html (accessed June 2007).

Furlong, A. and Cartmel, F. (2003) 'Explaining transitions through individualized rationality', in L. Roulleau-Berger (ed.) *Youth and Work in the Post Industrial City of North America and Europe,* Leiden: Brill.

Heinz, W. and Krüger, H. (2001) 'The life course: innovations and challenges for social research', *Current Sociology*, 49: 29–45.

Jugend 2006 (2006) *15. Shell Jugend Studie*, Frankfurt am Main: Fischer Verlag.

Leccardi, C. and Ruspini, E. (eds) (2006) *A New Youth? Young People, Generations and Family Life,* Aldershot: Ashgate.

Nicole, K. (2006) *Flexibility and Lifelong Learning: Policy, Discourse and Politics*, London: Routledge.

Raffo, C. and Reeves, M. (2000) 'Youth transitions and social exclusion: developments in social capital theory', *Journal for Youth Studies*, 3: 147–66.

Rosa, H. (2005) *Beschleunigung. Die Veränderungen der Zeitstrukturen in der Moderne* [Acceleration: Changes in Time Structures in Modernity], Frankfurt am Main: Suhrkamp.

UNICEF (2007) *Child Poverty in Perspective: An Overview of Child Well-being in Rich Countries,* Florence: UNICEF Innocenti Research Centre.

Walther, A., du Bois-Reymond, M. and Biggart, A. (2006) *Participation in Transition: Motivation of Young Adults in Europe for Learning and Working,* Frankfurt am Main: Peter Lang.

Yates, S. and Payne, M. (2006) 'Not so NEET? A critique of the use of "NEET", in setting targets for interventions with young people', *Journal of Youth Studies*, 9: 329–44.

# 5

# The emergence of 'emerging adulthood'

## The new life stage between adolescence and young adulthood

*Jennifer Lynn Tanner and Jeffrey Jensen Arnett*

## Introduction

Theoretical and empirical understanding of development during the first stage of adulthood has undergone contemporary revision. Arnett (2000; 2004; 2006) introduced the theory of *emerging adulthood* to describe an extended period of development between adolescence and young adulthood, typically extending from ages 18–25. Central to the theory is the tenet that emerging adulthood is a distinct period of development, different from the stage of adolescence that precedes it and the young adult period that follows. The theory of emerging adulthood stresses the psychological and subjective experiences of individuals aged 18–25, characterizing the age period as one of identity explorations, feeling 'in-between', instability, self-focus, and possibilities. The distinctive features of the 18–25 age period call for an apposite term conferring the distinctiveness of the stage. Correspondingly, terms that include the years 18–25 as a non-distinct stage of development – *late adolescence, post-adolescence, youth, young adulthood, the transition to adulthood* – are inadequate descriptors of this unique stage of development (Arnett 2000; 2004).

## Historical basis of emerging adulthood

Emerging adulthood is historically embedded and culturally constructed (Arnett 1998; 2006). Three primary factors gave rise to emerging adulthood: (1) the change from an industrial to an information-based economy and the corresponding increase in the need for post-secondary education; accordingly, transitions to careers, marriages, and parenthood took place later than ever before; (2) dramatic increases in the educational and occupational opportunities available to women, so that more of them sought to obtain post-secondary education and develop their careers rather than becoming married and having children in their early twenties; and (3) greater tolerance of premarital sex, allowing young people in many societies to begin an active sexual life long before contemplating marriage.

In most OECD countries, prior to the 1950s few people obtained post-secondary education, and most young men became employed by the end of their teens, if not sooner. For example, in 1950, only 25 percent of Americans obtained any higher education, and nearly all of them were young men. Most young women, as well as many young men, remained in their parents' household until they married in their late teens or very early twenties. The median marriage age in the United States as recently as 1960 was just 20.3 for women and 22.8 for men (Arnett 2000). The entry to parenthood came about a year later, on average. Thus most young people went directly from adolescence to a settled young adulthood by their early twenties.

Over the past half-century, the changes related to the age period from the late teens through the twenties have been dramatic. Participation in post-secondary education has risen steeply, especially among young women. Now over 60 percent of young Americans enter higher education the year after graduating from high school, and 57 percent of American undergraduates are women (Arnett 2004). The median age of first marriage has risen steeply as well, to its current record-high of 26.0 among women and 27.5 among men, with a corresponding rise in the median age of entering parenthood. Median marriage ages are even later in European countries (Arnett 2006). Furthermore, changes in attitudes toward premarital sex have taken place in Western societies, and the majority of young people in these societies have sexual intercourse for the first time in their late teens, a decade or more before they enter marriage.

## Recentering: a development task of emerging adulthood

Arnett's work provides a portrait of emerging adulthood as a distinct life stage. Tanner's work (2006) complements Arnett's perspective, arguing that distinct population features are reflected in individual pathways of development from adolescence, into emerging adulthood, and beyond to young adulthood. From this developmental perspective, Tanner argues that emerging adulthood is not only a distinct, but also a critical juncture in human life development. Findings from life span research point to emerging adulthood as a critical era in human development when marker life events are most likely to occur (Grob *et al.* 2001). Events experienced in the late teens and twenties are integrated into individuals' identities and memories more so than those events occurring during younger and older life stages

According to Tanner (2006), from a life span developmental perspective, *recentering* is the primary psychosocial task of emerging adulthood. The concept of recentering assumes the interdependence of development, and considers the individual-in-context with the unit of analysis that is changing over time. Specifically, recentering is achieved in three stages. In stage 1, the adolescent transitions into emerging adulthood proper. During this stage, individuals' relationships and roles which formerly identified them as dependent, as the recipient of guidance, support and resources, undergo a shift in dynamic toward relationships in which power is shared, mutual, and responsibility for care and support gain in reciprocity. In stage 2, the individual engages in the developmental experiences of emerging adulthood proper. During this stage, commitments to roles and relationship are temporary and transitory in nature. Individuals explore a series of commitments to inform themselves of the available opportunities in love and work. Following exploration, and transitory associations with others, careers, and contexts, the emerging adult enters stage 3, making commitments to enduring roles and responsibilities of adulthood (e.g., careers, marriages and partnerships, commitments to the parental role).

Studies that use longitudinal, developmental methods (e.g., growth modeling, trajectory modeling) provide empirical support for the proposition that recentering is the fundamental process underlying development during emerging adulthood. Such studies demonstrate that emerging adults renegotiate relationships with parents by relinquishing residential and financial support and moving toward commitments to others, such as life partners and children. For example, Cohen *et al.* (2003) found increases from age 17 to 27 in financial, romantic, residential independence and family-formation. Evidence for emerging adulthood proper is revealed in findings showing a lack of linearity, but rather both progression and also regression in pathways toward adult roles and responsibilities in emerging adulthood. Furthermore, transitions to residential, financial, relationship independence and family formation were interdependent (Sneed *et al.* 2007).

The concept of recentering extends itself beyond the theoretical into the applied realm of developmental science which seeks to understand how to maintain and optimize healthy human development and adaptation. Implicit to the concept of recentering is the assumption that progress in recentering should predict proximal and distal adaptation and optimal development (Tanner 2006). Emerging adults scaffold recentering by selecting and identifying, as well as prioritizing personal life goals. Life goals change as individuals move from adolescence, through emerging adulthood. Salient tasks of emerging adulthood include friendship, academic, and conduct goals, giving way to occupational and romantic goals as emerging adults move into young adulthood. In a Finnish study, over the course of ten years, university students first interviewed when they were 18–28 year-olds disengaged from goals related to education, friends, and traveling, and engaged in goals related to work, family, and health (Salmela-Aro *et al.* 2007).

## Other psychological characteristics of emerging adulthood

In addition to recentering and the five features of emerging adulthood emphasized by Arnett (2004), other cognitive, emotional, and behavioral features distinguish 18–25 year-olds from younger and older individuals. Emerging adult thinking, feeling, and acting reveal underlying physiological and neurological development unique to the age period. The brain's center for reasoning and problem-solving fully develops during the emerging adult age period, accomplished by a pruning of gray matter following adolescence into the twenties and an increase in white matter across this same period through the mid-thirties (Giedd *et al.* 1999). The plasticity of the emerging adult brain, then, indicates that maturation remains sensitive to environmental conditions and experiences during these years and that opportunity to enhance adaptational capacities and to reduce risk of trauma and stress is salient to understanding the role of emerging adulthood in life span human development.

Cognitive capacities, strategies, and organization shift during emerging adulthood. The attainment of wisdom-related knowledge and judgment occurs primarily during emerging adulthood, from ages 15–25 (Baltes and Staudinger 2000). Across multiple measures of aptitude, numerical ability, verbal aptitude, clerical perception, finger dexterity, and general intelligence, maximum levels are achieved in emerging adulthood. Some studies indicate that, after age 25, there is a point of divergence for cognitive performance where crystallized intelligence stabilizes (i.e., intelligence as cultural knowledge), but fluid intelligence begins to decline (i.e., intelligence as basic information processing; Baltes *et al.* 1999).

Emerging adults are different from older adults with regard to their processing of socio-emotional information. This is explained partially as a function of increasing neural stability from young to older adulthood. Emerging adults' responses to emotional stimuli are more sensitive compared to older adults; specifically, selectivity of and reactivity to negative-stimuli are heightened. In cognitive studies, this is demonstrated in differences in activation of the medial prefrontal cortex (MPFC, the brain region that has been implicated in planning complex cognitive behaviors, personality expression and moderating correct social behavior) which reveals that responses to fear stimuli decrease after emerging adulthood and reactions to happiness-stimuli increase. Evidence that emerging adulthood is a period associated with greater sensitivity to fear and negative stimuli is interpreted as a function of brain maturation; with age comes greater control over emotional reactions which gives older adults a greater opportunity to reframe emotional reactions with cognitive interpretations that are more positive (Williams *et al.* 2006).

Personality change from adolescence through emerging adulthood reflects increases in global maturity. Over this period, people's personalities tend to make gains in forcefulness and decisiveness; become more goal-directed in work-related efforts; show increases in self-control, reflecting tendencies to become more reflective, deliberate and planful; and decrease in negative emotionality, including aggressiveness and alienation (Donnellan *et al.* 2007). In regard to the Big Five dimensions of personality, emerging adulthood can be characterized by increases in social vitality (i.e., sociability, positive affect, gregariousness and energy level) during the college years followed by decreases in the 22–30 year-old age period; decreases in social dominance (i.e., dominance, independence, and self-confidence in social contexts) that begin in the adolescent years and continue through young adulthood; and small increases in emotional stability that, again, begin in the teens and continue through the thirties.

Emerging adulthood is an age period during which there is stronger potential for personality change compared to earlier and later decades (Roberts *et al.* 2006). Change in personality is considered an outcome related to emerging adults' experiences establishing careers and committing to interpersonal relationships and family roles: 'as all dominant cultures support if not promote these activities, they may be the catalysts for the widespread pattern of personality trait development found in adulthood and across cultures' (Roberts *et al.*, 2006: 18). Following emerging adulthood proper, stability of personality increases as a function of planful competence, planning for and making commitments to work and family.

Emerging adults are relatively healthy in some respects. During emerging adulthood, fitness peaks, self-reported health is high, and rates of disease and disability are low (Park *et al.* 2006). However, risky behaviors among some emerging adults put them at risk for unintended, sub-optimal health outcomes. Substance use and sexual risk-taking peak in emerging adulthood, including rates of STIs, unintended pregnancy and abortion.

Like physical health, mental health in emerging adulthood is complex and diverse. Psychiatric disorder peaks in prevalence in emerging adulthood (Tanner *et al.* 2007). However, overall, emerging adults are hopeful and optimistic about their futures (Arnett 2004) and non-clinical measures demonstrate increases in well-being and decreases in depressive symptoms from 18 to 25 (Schulenberg and Zarrett 2006). Incomplete brain maturation in emerging adulthood suggests the age period may be a 'sensitive period' or window of opportunity for changing pathways of early, compromised mental health to more salutary trajectories of mental health following intervention or absence of trauma during emerging adulthood.

## Cultural themes and variations in emerging adulthood

Emerging adulthood is different from certain other life stages, such as infancy or late adulthood, in that it is historically recent and culturally-based, so that it exists in some cultures and not others, and takes different forms in different cultures. Nevertheless, the historical changes underlying the rise of emerging adulthood have taken place world-wide, across many economically developed countries, and are taking place now in many developing countries. Despite between-country variation in educational systems and school-to-work policies, increasing rates of post-secondary education are evident across countries. Correspondingly, age at first marriage has increased worldwide, as well as age-at-first birth. Similar changes have take place across countries in the roles and opportu-nities available to women, and young women now exceed young men in educational attainment in every region of the world. The acceptability of premarital sex varies widely among cultures, but the prevalence of premarital sex has grown worldwide.

The study of cultural themes and variations in emerging adulthood is just beginning, but already some important findings have been presented, in regions including Europe, Latin America, and Asia. With respect to Europe, Douglass and colleagues have exam-ined relationships between prolonged education and delayed fertility in European countries and concluded that 'Europeans seem to [be] postponing childbearing due to the activities of emerging adulthood' (Douglass 2007: 4) which include 'exploration, consumption of experience, and freedom from responsibilities associated with careers, marriage, and parenthood' (ibid.: 13). Important variations also exist within Europe. In southern European countries such as Italy and Spain emerging adults tend to remain at home with their families-of-origin, whereas in northern Europe they are more likely to leave home in their late teens or very early twenties.

With respect to Latin America, emerging adulthood has been observed to exist, but in most countries it is mainly a privilege enjoyed by the middle class rather than a normative stage of development (Galambos and Martinez 2007). The more economically developed a country is, the more widespread emerging adulthood tends to be. For example, in Argentina, one of the most economically developed Latin American countries, a longitudinal study demon-strated that emerging adults' experiences are similar to those identified in US samples: diverse employment situations, multiple intimate relationships, and postponement of marriage and parenthood consistent with continuing education after graduating from high school (Facio *et al.* 2007). However, in contrast to the American pattern, the majority of emerging adults in Argentina who are not married or cohabitating live with their parents or other relatives.

In Asia, a study of young Japanese women concluded that many of them experience a prolonged emerging adulthood into their thirties, as they resist pressure to enter tradi-tional roles of wife and mother now that they have a wide range of career possibilities (Rosenberger 2007). In China, emerging adult college students have been found to resemble American college students in many ways (Nelson and Chen 2007), but about 800 million of China's 1.2 billion people are rural villagers who are unlikely to experience anything resembling emerging adulthood.

## Social class variations in emerging adulthood

In addition to between-culture heterogeneity, the question of whether emerging adult-hood is a normative stage of development within societies has been raised. Specifically, there is some question of whether there is a bifurcation of the age period within countries, with emerging adulthood experienced mainly by the middle class and less by the working class. For example, Bynner (2005) emphasizes the structural determinants of adult transitions, including economic and political forces that shape and constrain opportunities of individuals during the first years of adulthood, and contends that the stage of emerging adulthood is experienced mainly by the middle class. Côté (2000) advanced the term *arrested adulthood* to reflect the influence of market forces in delaying adulthood, resulting in great disadvantage, hazard, and vulnerability to individuals who are distanced from the resources available via labor market participation.

While Arnett emphasizes the role of society in structuring and shaping emerging adulthood, and recognizes the key importance of educational attainment in structuring work and income paths in emerging adulthood and beyond, he contends that structural and socialization forces are limited in their determination of emerging adulthood (Arnett 2006). For example, in the United States, few differences exist between middle-class and working-class emerging adults in their conceptions of adulthood or their optimism about their personal possibilities in love and work (Arnett 2004). Further empirical comparisons between middle-class and working-class emerging adults should help to clarify this issue.

## Future research directions

The theory of emerging adulthood identifies a distinct stage of life span of human development tied to Westernization and post-industrialization trends. This framework promotes understanding of the distinct, contemporary experiences of individuals in their late teens and twenties. It follows from this conceptualization of the age period that emerging adulthood is predicted as a normative stage of human development in cultures that experience specific trends, including: increasing proportions of emerging adults, in particular, women, completing higher levels of education in their early twenties; delaying transitions to marriage and parenthood; and, weakening of ties between sex, marital unions, and family formation.

These specifications of the theory of emerging adulthood make the theory testable and lead to testable predictions. Specifically, the theory predicts that as developing countries industrialize and urbanize, the proportion of people who experience emerging adulthood should grow, i.e., the proportion who obtain post-secondary education will increase, ages of entering marriage and parenthood will rise, young women will be more likely to enter the workplace rather than become wives and mothers in their early twenties, and premarital sex will become more prevalent.

Accumulated findings suggest that future studies should also explore within-culture heterogeneity in emerging adult experiences. A particularly interesting frontier is the extent to which socio-economic factors including structural inequalities dictated by race, class, ethnicity, and rural vs. urban geography influence the likelihood that emerging adulthood is a normal, expected stage of human development.

## References

Arnett, J. J. (1998) 'Learning to stand alone: the contemporary American transition to adulthood in cultural and historical context', *Human Development*, 41: 295–315.

—— (2000) 'Emerging adulthood: a theory of development from the late teens through the twenties', *American Psychologist*, 55: 469–80.

—— (2004) *Emerging Adulthood: The Winding Road from the Late Teens through the Twenties,* New York: Oxford University Press.

—— (2006) 'Emerging adulthood in Europe: a response to Bynner', *Journal of Youth Studies*, 9: 111–23.

Baltes, P. B. and Staudinger, U. M. (2000) 'Wisdom: a metaheuristic (pragmatic) to orchestrate mind and virtue toward excellence', *American Psychologist*, 55: 122–36.

Baltes, P. B., Staudinger, U. M. and Lindenberger, U. (1999) 'Lifespan psychology: theory and application to intellectual functioning', in M. R. Rosenzweig and L. W. Porter (eds) *Annual Review of Psychology*, vol. 50, Palo Alto, CA: Annual Reviews, pp. 471–507.

Bynner, J. (2005) 'Rethinking the youth phase of the life-course: the case for emerging adulthood?' *Journal of Youth Studies*, 8: 367–84.

Cohen, P., Kasen, S., Chen, H., Hartmark, C. and Gordon, K. (2003) 'Variations in patterns of developmental transitions in the emerging adulthood period', *Developmental Psychology*, 39: 657–69.

Côté, J. (2000) *Arrested Adulthood: The Changing Nature of Maturity and Identity*, New York: New York University Press.

Donnellan, M. B., Conger, R. D. and Burzette, R. G. (2007) 'Personality development from late adolescence through young adulthood: differential stability, normative maturity, and evidence for the maturity-stability hypothesis', *Journal of Personality*, 75: 237–64.

Douglass, C. B. (2007) 'From duty to desire: emerging adulthood in Europe and its consequences', *Child Development Perspectives*, 1: 101–8.

Facio, A., Resett, S., Micocci, F. and Mistrorigo, C. (2007) 'Emerging adulthood in Argentina: an age of diversity and possibilities', *Child Development Perspectives*, 1: 115–18.

Galambos, N. L. and Martinez, M. L. (2007) 'Poised for emerging adulthood in Latin America: a pleasure for the privileged', *Child Development Perspectives*, 1: 109–14.

Giedd, J. N., Blumenthal, J., Jeffries, N. O., Castellanos, F. X., Liu, H., Zijdenbos, A., *et al.* (1999) 'Brain development during childhood and adolescence: a longitudinal MRI study', *Nature Neuroscience*, 2: 861–3.

Grob, A., Krings, F. and Bangerter, A. (2001) 'Life markers in biographical narratives of people from three cohorts: a life span perspective in historical context', *Human Development*, 44: 171–90.

Nelson, L. J. and Chen, X. (2007) 'Emerging adulthood in China: the role of social and cultural factors', *Child Development Perspectives*, 1: 86–91.

Park, M. J., Mulye, T. P., Adams, S. H., Brindis, C. and Irwin, C. E., Jr. (2006) 'The health status of young adults in the U.S.', *Journal of Adolescent Health*, 39: 305–17.

Roberts, B. W., Walton, K. E. and Viechtbauer, W. (2006) 'Patterns of mean-level change in personality traits across the life course: a meta-analysis of longitudinal studies', *Psychological Bulletin*, 132: 1–25.

Rosenberger, N. (2007) 'Rethinking emerging adulthood in Japan: perspectives from long-term single women', *Child Development Perspectives*, 1: 92–5.

Salmela-Aro, K., Aunola, K. and Nurmi, J-E. (2007) 'Personal goals during emerging adulthood: a 10-year follow up', *Journal of Adolescent Research*, 22: 690–715.

Schulenberg, J. E. and Zarrett, N. (2006) 'Mental health during emerging adulthood: continuity and discontinuity in courses, causes, and functions', in J. J. Arnett and J. L. Tanner (eds) *Emerging Adults in America: Coming of Age in the 21st Century*, Washington, DC: American Psychiatric Association.

Sneed, J. R., Hamagami, F., McArdle, J. J., Cohen, P. and Chen, H. (2007) 'The dynamic interdependence of developmental domains across emerging adulthood', *Journal of Youth and Adolescence*, 36: 351–62.

Tanner, J. L. (2006) 'Recentering in emerging adulthood: a critical turning point in life span human development', in J. J. Arnett and J. L. Tanner (eds) *Emerging Adults in America: Coming of Age in the 21st Century*, Washington, DC: American Psychiatric Association.

Tanner, J. L., Reinherz, H. Z., Beardslee, W. R., Fitzmaurice, G. M., Leis, J. A. and Berger, S. R. (2007) 'Change in prevalence of psychiatric disorders from ages 21 to 30 in a community sample', *Journal of Nervous and Mental Disease*, 195: 298–306.

Williams, L. M., Brown, K. J., Palmer, D., Liddell, B. J., Kemp, A. H., Olivieri, G. *et al.* (2006) 'The mellow years? Neural basis of improving emotional stability over age', *The Journal of Neuroscience*, 26: 6422–30.

# Part II
## Divisions

*Andy Furlong*

## Social divisions and inequalities

The analysis of social divisions among young people and the reproduction of inequalities across generations has long been a central focus in youth studies. Yet to an extent, the focus on the stratification of experiences has become somewhat unfashionable: contemporary researchers are often more concerned with youth cultures and the construction of identities in contexts that can appear to lack the sorts of structure that shaped young lives in a Fordist era. While youth can be considered as a significant crossroad in reproduction of class-based advantage, it also provides an important focus for the study of inequalities related to gender, 'race', ethnicity and disability and an opportunity to understand more about the ways in which such divisions are themselves underpinned by class. In Part II, we focus on social divisions in youth in an attempt to highlight the significance of persistent inequalities.

Noting the tendency for US researchers to neglect the study of social class, in Chapter 6, Weis opens the part by highlighting the relationship between social class and the intensification of inequalities in the new global economy. To Weis, class is regarded as a 'fundamental organizer' of the experiences of young people on both objective and subjective levels. Despite changes in the ways in which young people experience education, she stresses the ongoing importance of youthful resistance in the reproduction of social class.

Weis argues strongly that inequalities linked to class, gender and 'race' should be regarded as nested forms of stratification; an approach that finds resonance in Chapter 7 by McDowell. McDowell argues that the connections between class and gender have changed significantly, with women of all classes having gained most from recent economic changes. Indeed, while many working-class women are drawn into the low paid and casualized sectors of the labour market, working-class males frequently regard new service positions as incompatible with their masculinity or are seen as unsuitable by employers. Among the middle classes, females are deriving benefits from their educational experiences and discovering that gender is not holding them back in the same way as it did for previous generations.

In Chapter 8, Webster's discussion of 'race' and ethnicity is also framed by the over-lapping impact of social class with him arguing that many of the disadvantages faced by minority groups are more strongly linked to class than to 'race' or ethnicity. Ethnicity is regarded as dynamic and Webster suggests that traditional ethnic and racial categories are unable to fully capture the diversity of experiences in the new economic order. Indeed, he argues that the vulnerabilities traditionally associated with minority experiences are more accurately understood as being part of the new, deteriorating, working-class conditions in neo-liberal economies.

An increasingly popular way to try and understand the mechanisms of reproduction in youth has involved a focus on the transmission of social capital. While used widely, Bassani, in Chapter 9, argues that the theory of social capital is under-developed, although poten-tially very useful. Identifying five dimensions of social capital theory that underpin many youth-focused approaches, she attempts to find common ground and shows ways in which the theory can be developed in youth studies.

While vulnerable to social exclusion, disabled young people and young refugees are both under-researched groups. With reference to the disabled, Riddell argues in Chapter 10 that the increased protraction and complexity of transitions may have had a detri-mental effect on a group who already faced a range of difficulties. Recognizing the heterogeneity of disability as a social category, Riddell shows how those who enjoy educational success and enter higher education tend to have specific forms of impairment and are drawn from more advantaged social groups, while those from less advantaged families are particularly prone to negative transitional experiences and outcomes. With respect to young refugees, in Chapter 11, Boyle focuses both on the refugee experience as well as on the process of re-settlement in a new country. Aside from coping with the trauma of change and making adjustments to a new culture, Boyle recognizes that refu-gees face a wide range of other disadvantages; perhaps having lost parents or family members, having to cope with a high level of household responsibilities and often having delayed key educational involvement. Related to these experiences, young refugees often suffer from mental health problems.

Together the chapters in this part encourage us to rethink the ways in which young people's experiences are stratified and the extent to which inequalities tend to be inter-linked. They remind us that while significant changes have taken place that affect the lives of young people, strong continuities exist in the ways in which inequalities are reproduced across generations.

# 6

# Social class, youth and young adulthood in the context of a shifting global economy

*Lois Weis*

## Introduction

This chapter frames an agenda for the critical study of social class and schooling inside the restructured global economy. Here I call for an examination of the deeply woven connections between 'official knowledge' and its global distribution, parental capital and the uneven demands of schools, and the nested nature of class, race and gender in identity formation and class production. Reviewing existing research while simultaneously calling for substantial extension of said research, I suggest that we must extend and explore these connections if we are to unravel the relationship between social class and deepening inequalities in the new global economy.

Noteworthy ethnographic work has been conducted which both elicits class culture and identity and describes and theorizes this identity in relation to schools. Such discussion, however, has been tempered in the USA in particular, if not altogether ignored, since the 1980s, as scholarship targeted more specifically to issues of race and/or gender as well as broader issues of representation has taken hold. Such scholarship, while critically important, has often delved into issues of race, gender and/or representations irrespective of a distinct social class referent, much as earlier scholarship on social class ignored gender and race – a point which critical race theorists (McCarthy 1990), theorists of 'whiteness production' (Fine *et al.* 2004), and feminist theorists across race and ethnicity have commented upon at length (Crenshaw 1989). With the clear turn in the global economy, one accompanied by deep intensification of social inequalities (Reich 2001; Piketty and Saez 2003), the need for serious class-based analyses could not be more pressing.

Bearing in mind the above point, this chapter outlines elements of an agenda for the critical study of social class and schooling. In so doing, I assume that social class, while perhaps a 'phantasmatic' category, organizes the social, cultural and material world in exceptionally powerful ways. The books we read or if we read at all; our travel destinations and mode of travel; the clothes we wear; the foods we eat; whether we have orthodontically straightened teeth; where (and if) our children go to school, with whom, and under what staff expectations and treatment; the 'look' and 'feel' of home-and school-based interventions if our children 'fail'; where we feel most comfortable and with whom; sports/games our children play and where they play them; the extent and type of extracurricular activities our children engage in; where we live and the nature of our housing; and, specifically in the USA, whether we have health insurance and if so, what kind and with what coverage, are all profoundly classed experiences, rooted not only in material realities but in culturally based expectations, whether recognized or not. With deep respect for many of my more poststructurally inclined scholar-friends, then, I analytically embrace categories of social identity while recognizing the ways in which such identities are both 'fiction' and 'real'. Indeed, recognition of the structuring effects of class has never been more pressing, given shifts in the global economy.

This is not to deny the fully and partially independent effects of race in relation to class, a point which is particularly salient in the United States, yet increasingly important in the UK, France, Germany, and Canada, where large immigrant populations of color have significantly altered the social and economic landscape. Rather it is to suggest that class is a *fundamental organizer* of social experience, both 'objective' and 'subjective', an organizer that has been eclipsed over the past 20 years by other forms of interrogation and analyses. As McCarthy (1990) reminds us, however, the experiences and sub-jectivities of racially subordinated groups cannot be read entirely from class. Toward the end of this chapter I take up the ways in which class must be understood and theorized as 'nested' in race and gender rather than as an independent node.

## Shifts in the global economy

> All Americans used to be in roughly the same economic boat. Most rose or fell together as the corporations in which they were employed, the industries comprising such corporations, and the national economy as a whole became more productive – or languished. But national borders no longer define our economic fates. We are now in different boats, one sinking rapidly, one sinking more slowly, the third rising steadily.
>
> (Reich, 1991: 208)

As Reich describes it, the boat holding routine production workers in the US is sinking most rapidly, as the old corporate core is being replaced by

> global webs, which earn their largest profits from clever problem-solving – identifying and brokering. As the costs of transporting things and of communicating informa-tion about them continue to drop, profit margins on high-volume, standardized production are thinning because there are few barriers to entry. Modern factories and state-of-the-art machinery can be installed almost anywhere on the globe.
>
> (ibid.: 209)

Under such conditions, business is not hamstrung by local labor power at all, setting in motion an entirely different set of class dynamics than existed previously. If any given enterprise, no matter how temporary, does not obtain labor at an acceptably low cost, it seeks labor elsewhere as a wide variety of tasks can now be outsourced and/or off-shored, and/or owners simply relocate the business. Nationally based and/or owned US, German, French and British business is tagged to work that can now be done almost anywhere, given high-speed fiber optics, new and quicker modes of transportation, and the internet, serving fundamentally to re-align class in nations throughout the world. By way of example, the old working class, as tied to an industrial economy under which plants are expensive to build, maintain, and move, is not a collective player in this new economy at all, rendering the sons and daughters of the former industrial proletariat exceedingly vulnerable – perched at the competitive edge of new global economic arrangements

The worldwide shift in the economy affects not only first and second wave industrialized nations such as the United States, Japan, Britain, Canada, Australia, Germany, and France. Realignment in the global economy has profound implications for nations such as Singapore, China, Thailand, India, and Mexico, among others, that are now sites of either finance and/or product assembly processes, spurring widespread change inside such nations as well as between and among nations across the globe.

The increasingly interconnected world of commerce and capital, which inevitably sets in motion the production of rearranged class structure in varying nations, coupled with the eclipse of studies of schooling and social class over the past 25 years, demands attention. While such an agenda can arguably take a variety of shapes and forms, I outline, in this chapter, three key areas for research that are related to schooling and class production: (1) official knowledge and its distribution; (2) the 'effects' of parental capital; and (3) production of social and cultural identities. Building on fruitful work already done in these three critical areas, my intent is to pry open discussion as to future research possibilities in shifting context. Although desirous of working toward an agenda for the critical study of schooling and class production in contexts other than first wave industrialized nations, my examples in this particular chapter are drawn largely from the USA and the UK.

## Official knowledge and its distribution

Spurred by calls in England in the 1970s for a 'new sociology of education', scholars addressed questions related to what constitutes 'official' knowledge and the ways in which such knowledge is differentially distributed through schools. As Whitty (1985) makes clear, and as Dimitiradis, McCarthy and I argue elsewhere (Weis *et al.* 2006), mainstream sociologists often assume that the most important question is that of 'access' to a range of educational institutions – what blocks it or what might encourage it. While not an unimportant set of questions, the assumption is that additional schooling will ameliorate the seeming handicaps of a working-class and/or poor upbringing. In sharp distinction, scholars began to focus on the nature of knowledge itself and the ways in which 'legitimate' knowledge works for some and not others. Young (1971), for example, discusses the ways in which particular kinds of knowledge are validated in the academy – knowledge that is 'pure', 'general', and 'academic'. In contrast, knowledge that is 'applied', 'specific' and 'vocational' is marginalized. Although this distinction is arbitrary rather than 'natural', it powerfully serves to keep particular elite groups in control of the official school curriculum (Weis *et al.* 2006).

Apple (1993) offers powerful strategies for understanding the ways in which curricular knowledge is part of a 'selective tradition' that serves ideologically to buttress and naturalize structurally based social and economic inequalities. While Apple's nuanced investigation offers a great deal to our understanding of schooling and social class, a careful look at the 'selective tradition' – what it is, who it works for, how it is forged – inside new global circumstances is needed. Most of the work on the 'official curriculum' was done in the 1970s and 1980s in first wave industrialized nations, with relatively little attention being paid to this subject since, as other forms of investigation, such as those linked to the production of lived culture and identity eclipsed our study of knowledge. Given massive changes in the global economy and accompanying class reconfiguration in countries all over the world, a broad agenda for the study of schooling and class pro- duction must include a focus on issues related to knowledge production and legitimation, particularly the ways in which certain groups are creating class through the instantiation of a newly forged (or alternatively, re-affirmed) selective tradition, one that works to the benefit of some and not others.

Additionally we must track the ways in which knowledge is differentially distributed across groups. Anyon (1981a; 1981b) offers a compelling set of essays related to the ways in which knowledge is differentially distributed across student social class background. Working class students, for example, are offered knowledge as rote memorization and a series of structured tasks, while knowledge distributed to students in executive elite public schools is far more challenging. Students in these latter schools are socialized into an academic culture of excellence while working-class students are socialized into a culture of rote memorization.

While the work of these earlier scholars is noteworthy, it is time both to update such work in the USA and Britain where the majority of such work was originally produced, while simultaneously re-visiting this set of questions in a wide range of social, economic, and national contexts. Here we must ask ourselves not only 'what knowledge is of most worth' in varying national contexts, but *which* students in nations differentially positioned (both in the sense of being positioned and positioning themselves) in the emerging global map are accessing/exposed to what kind of knowledge? This topic swirls through potential quantitative and qualitative studies of tracking in schools, whether in terms of the American track structure associated with ostensibly comprehensive schools, or alter- native forms of tracking such as those associated with varying tests – in institutions in a wide range of national contexts, as well as the ways in which knowledge is codified for varying groups of students. Given that sorting practices common in earlier decades – such as vocational versus college-bound in the United States, for example – are increasingly less relevant given both alterations in the economy and sustained demands from groups formerly locked out of college knowledge (that knowledge linked to college/university access and attendance), it is critically important to update and expand this area of study by focusing carefully on who gets what kind of knowledge, in what context, toward what end, and under what conditions. This involves careful ethnographic work as to the distribution of school knowledge across subject matter and community, as well as quan- titative work revolving around who attends what kind of school and with what con- sequences; the nature of the track structure where relevant; and proportion of students offered high-status knowledge such as Advanced Placement or International Baccalaure- ate courses, including a clear focus on who takes them. While such work has been done over the years, we have remarkably little scholarship that tracks and theorizes social class in relation to schooling under new economic conditions. This is as much the case for first and second wave industrialized nations such as the USA and Japan as it is for recently positioned players in the global economy such as China. In sum, then, we need to take seriously the emerging stratification map as related to 'official' knowledge and its distribution globally.

## Valued parental capital

Large-scale studies attest to the importance of family background in children's academic achievement, academic attainment, occupational status and income We know relatively little, however, with respect to what it is about the family and the family's relationship to the school that produces outcomes of interest.

Engaging in extensive ethnographic work, Lareau (1987) argues that middle-class parents, in contrast to working-class parents, have the cultural capital necessary to actualize positive ties with schools in that they have more information about schooling as well as the social capital to connect with other parents. More recently (Lareau 2003), she turns her attention to class habitus, specifically the ethnographically informed cultural logic of child rearing, arguing that middle-class parents across race (African American and White in the United States) engage in a process of 'concerted cultivation' which results in a 'robust sense of entitlement' among middle-class youth (ibid.: 2), a sense of entitlement that 'plays an especially important role in institutional settings, where middle-class children learn to question adults and address them as relative equals' (ibid.: 2). Working-class and poor children, in contrast, are raised under strictures more closely approximating the 'accomplishment of natural growth' (ibid.: 30). While working class and poor parents may similarly love their children, 'the cultural logic of child rearing at home is out of synch with the standards of institutions' (p. 3), wherein schools, for example, value child-rearing practices associated with concerted cultivation, suggestive of the fact that middle-class children, simply by virtue of parenting practices, will always have an edge in school.

Questions related to habitus and the ways in which class habitus intersects with race/ethnicity in varying national context offer fertile ground for future research. Key here are questions linked to the kind of capital students acquire within their family of origin and the extent to which such capital is actualized and/or valued in varying types of institutions – whether affirmed, dismissed, depended upon for day-to–day operation and/or punished – a set of issues which goes beyond Bernstein's (1990) and Heath's (1983) work on linguistic codes/use in Britain and the USA respectively.

While Lareau offers important work on White and African-American students of varying class background in the United States, extensive work remains, as new forms of parental capital and the meaning of such capital as linked to the production of class (structure and position) are being produced everywhere, and in specific ethnic/racial/gender relation, dependent upon national context. It is arguably the case, for example, that as the economy shifts in directions outlined earlier, schools in first and second wave industrialized nations will demand more of a certain kind of 'preparatory and sustained engagement' from parents (in other words, before children come to school and throughout their schooling career) as they (both parents and schools) position their children to enter and move into a restructured and, for them, tightened economy. In other words, as the 'top' closes down in nations such as the USA, the UK, and Germany, positioning for the 'top' will increasingly demand full-time attention from parents who possess valued social and cultural capital. While obviously calling for empirical work, my larger point is that the micro-moves of differentially positioned parents in varying national context (differentially positioned within nation and between nation in relation to the global economy) constitute an important arena for future research.

Additionally we must factor in the movement of peoples in increasingly globalized contexts, wherein immigrant parents often bring new and intensified demands and attention to American, British and Canadian school systems (Li 2005). This movement means that we must track class structuration while taking into account the movement both of formerly privileged and not so privileged world citizens as they forge class in new national contexts. Globalizing culture and capital means that attention must be paid to the ways in which differentially positioned parents (whether through birth, elected and/ or forced immigration/migration, refugee status, etc.) in varying national contexts both raise children *and* interact with schools, as well as to the construction of valued parental capital among school personnel themselves in differently located institutions. It is the intersection of forged and/or received parental capital coupled with the changing demands of educational institutions in a global context that demands our attention.

## Active production of identities

Rather than mirror passive accounts of socialization, Willis's (1977) ethnographic work on the 'lads' – a group of working-class boys in the industrial Midlands in England – breaks important theoretical ground by focusing our attention on cultural production, wherein the 'lads' actively differentiate themselves from the 'ear 'oles' (so named because they simply sit and listen) and school meanings in general, categorizing both as effeminate and unrelated to the 'real' masculine world of work, thereby reproducing at their own cultural level key elements of social structure. As Willis states:

> In the desire for workers of a certain type, the reach of the production process must pass through the semi-autonomous cultural level which is determined by production only partially and in its own specific terms. In a more general sense it cannot be assumed that cultural forms are determined in some way as an automatic reflection of macro determinations such as class location, region and educational backgrounds ... We need to understand how structures become sources of meaning and determinants on behaviour in the cultural milieu at its own level.
>
> (ibid.: 171)

Taking up the challenge afforded by Willis, we have excellent studies of cultural and identity production processes which span issues of social class, race/ethnicity, gender and schooling. Most such studies, however, have been done in the industrialized West, and we must broaden research to include studies of cultural production in varying national contexts. In addition, while acting back on school meanings appears to constitute a key element of identity work among specific groups of disenfranchised youth across national context, scholars have yet to address, in a sustained fashion, the consequences of such resistance over time, and in relation to new economic circumstances. While Willis suggests, for example, that working-class students' resistance is tied to class-linked labor market possibilities while simultaneously limiting the intensification of demands for production on the shop floor, what we do not know is where such resistance 'sits' as youth grow older, particularly in shifting economic times. Although this genre of study – and specifically the body of work known as 'resistance theory' – offers a great deal with respect to what we know about students and schools, serving ultimately to invert understandings as to the absolute power of educational institutions and their ability to 'name' others, it is less than clear that such focus on resistance productively informs understanding of class. It is critically important then, to call into question the ways in which youth resistance is linked to the production of class, given new and contested social and economic arrangements.

Here I use my own work as an example. Using data collected at two points in time – one point as part of a full-year ethnographic investigation in a White working-class high school in 1985–86 (Weis 1990), and the second, re-interviews with 31 of the original 41 White cohort students in 2000–2001 – *Class Reunion* (Weis 2004) offers an exploration, both empirically and longitudinally of the re-making of the American White working class in the latter quarter of the twentieth century – a time of tremendous upheaval in the global economy with particular implications for this class fraction. Using ethnographic longitudinality to draw out the full analytic power of issues related to social class, race, gender and schooling, I argue that the re-making of the White working class can only be understood in relation to gendered constructions within itself, the construction of relevant 'others' as uncovered ethnographically – in this case African Americans and Yemenites ('Arabians') – as well as deep shifts in large social formations, most particularly the global economy. This twist in method (the longitudinal turn) enables us to focus on the consequences of youth resistant behavior in school rather than simply valorize such behavior as typifies point in time ethnographies. By way of example, those students who would be classified as 'resistors' when they were third-year secondary school students in 1985–86, were nothing more than relatively poor by the time I met them again in their early thirties. Rather than growing up to be part of any kind of romantic collective that capitalizes upon and engages oppositional behavior within the walls of the factory, thereby limiting the power of capital as it intrudes into working-class productivity/life as well as offering dignity for those at the bottom of the class structure, secondary school male resistors in my study are now by and large just low-paid, bouncing between the homes of their mother and current girlfriend, having no steady job to speak of. In times of more robust economic opportunities for the industrial proletariat, such resistors would have perhaps signed on to a factory assembly line and merged with a collective aimed both at preserving dignity and simultaneously drawing boundaries around appropriate worker exploitation. Given male wage earning capacity under the industrial economy, they would, in all likelihood, have begun and sustained a family of their own, cashing in on both the capital-labor accord and the secret guarantees of earning the family wage: sacrifice, reward, and dignity. Now in their early thirties, such high school 'resistors' are marginally employed and bereft of collective, except that which is aimed at the consumption of alcohol, drugs, car races, dirt bikes and the like. The shift in the global economy, then, means that our entire notion of resistance – what it is and where it deposits as youth grow up – must be challenged.

Also key here are the ways in which such a turn toward ethnographic longitudinality (or ethnographic re-visits) allows us to understand the embeddedness of gender construction and form over time and as related to social structure. Gendered forms, meanings and roles are struggled over *within* and *across* particular social class formations. Such struggle is inextricably linked to class formation itself, wherein we cannot understand what has happened to social class in the USA unless we understand what has happened to both women and men in the White working class, for example, and the ways in which they both live and perform gender. Here gender does not sit as a separate node, and the production of social class cannot be understood without clear understanding of the production of gender and the ways in which such production and gender-based challenge, both from outside and inside itself, have changed over time and in relation to new global circumstances; circumstances which may be globally produced but are lived out locally.

I would make the same point about race. Specifically I mean that an understanding of the current position of the White working-class fraction in the United States is fundamentally dependent upon an understanding of whiteness and the ways in which whiteness both invokes privilege and invites 'othering', a set of processes that are brought into sharp relief when we look at the ways in which youth, whether resistant or not, grow into adulthood (Weis 2004). Class, race and gender must, then, be understood as *nested* rather than single nodes of difference, wherein we cannot understand class production, either as lived out forms and/or consequences, without understanding race and gender. Each node embodies and simultaneously embeds another. While race is significant in the USA in relation to class formation, race may or may not be significant in other national contexts, contexts in which ethnicity, for example, and/or religion (often linked) may be key points of class fracture. The extent to which race/ethnicity and gender play in class processes constitutes ground for important empirical work, necessitating cross-sectional and longitudinal design in varying geographic locations.

## Conclusion

Our context is shifting, demanding both increased attention to the production of class and new ways of understanding such production in nations across the world. Gamoran (2001; 2007) argues that inequality in educational outcomes as related to social class background 'will persist largely unabated throughout the 21st century despite much rhetoric and a few policies directed against it' (2001: 135). As I argue in this chapter, this is likely to be even more the case given massive shifts in the global economy which spur widespread inequalities both within nations and between nations across the globe.

It is therefore imperative that the research community focuses specifically on the ways in which parents and children of varying social class backgrounds and across race/ethnicity experience and interact with educational institutions from pre-kindergarden through postgraduate school, moving carefully to understand the ways in which such produced outcomes work in nations positioned differently in relation to globalizing culture and capital. Updating and extending earlier work on knowledge and its distribution; parental capital and its effects; and the production of culture and identities will enable us to make great strides toward understanding the relationship between schooling and class structure in the twenty-first century.

## References

Anyon, J. (1981a) 'Social class and school knowledge', *Curriculum Inquiry*, 11: 3–42.
—— (1981b) 'Elementary schooling and the distinctions of social class', *Interchange*, 12: 118–32.
Apple, M. (1993) *Official Knowledge*, New York: Routledge.
Bernstein, B. (1990) *The Structuring of Pedagogic Discourse*, New York: Routledge.
Crenshaw, K. (1989) *Demarginalizing the Intersection of Race and Sex*, Chicago: University of Chicago Legal Forum.
Fine, M., Weis, L., Pruitt, L. and Burns, A. (2004) *Off White*, New York: Routledge.
Gamoran, A. (2001) 'American schooling and educational inequality', *Sociology of Education, Special Issue, Current of Thought: Sociology of Education at the Dawn of the 21st Century,* 74: 135–53.

—— (2007) 'Persisting social class inequality in U.S. education', in L. Weis, *The Way Class Works*, New York: Routledge.

Heath, S. (1983) *Ways with Words*, Cambridge: Cambridge University Press.

Lareau, A. (1987) 'Social class differences in family-school relationships', *Sociology of Education*, 60: 73–85.

—— (2003) *Unequal Childhoods*, Los Angeles, CA: University of California Press.

Li, G. (2005) *Culturally Contested Pedagogy*, Albany, NY: State University of New York Press.

McCarthy, C. (1990) *Race and Curriculum*, Philadelphia, PA: Falmer Press.

Piketty, T. and Saez, E. (2003) 'Income inequality in the U.S., 1913–98', *Quarterly Journal of Economics*, 118: 1–39.

Reich, R. (1991) *The Work of Nations*, New York: Alfred A. Knopf.

—— (2001) *The Future of Success*, New York: Alfred A. Knopf.

Weis, L. (1990) *Working Class Without Work: High School Students in a De-industrializing Economy*, New York: Routledge.

—— (2004) *Class Reunion: The Remaking of the American White Working Class*, New York: Routledge.

Weis, L., McCarthy, C. and Dimitriadis, G. (2006) *Ideology, Curriculum and the New Sociology of Education*, New York: Routledge.

Whitty, G. (1985) *Sociology and School Knowledge*, London: Methuen.

Willis, P. (1977) *Learning to Labour*, Farnborough: Saxon House.

Young, M. F. D. (ed.) (1971) *Knowledge and Control*, London: Macmillan.

# 7

# New masculinities and femininities

## Gender divisions in the new economy

*Linda McDowell*

## Introduction

In this chapter, I bring together several debates to answer a question about whether there are new patterns of class-based disadvantage and privilege for young people making the transition between education and waged employment in the first decade of the new millennium. My aim is to counter-pose economic debates about the rise of a new polarized service economy in the UK with sociological and educational debates about the risk society, individualism, social mobility, portfolio careers and the loosening of the traditional structural constraints of class and gender. These arguments find an echo in contemporary popular and policy debates about lads and ladettes, yobs, chavs, 'bling' and a form of class condescension that seem to position working-class young people's behaviour as the cause rather the consequence of their disadvantage. The implications of these latter arguments are that policies focusing on young people themselves, modifying their attitudes and behaviour, are sufficient to challenge their disadvantage, leading to the neglect of structural features of economic change.

I focus on the bottom end of the class structure in most detail and on the recent debates about the position of young people who are unable to gain access to secure employment that provides sufficient income for independent living. Many working-class young people, particularly young men, have been disadvantaged by contemporary changes in the labour market in the UK in ways that challenge their sense of self-identity as masculine. Many of these issues are addressed in more detail in the later section on the labour market.

## The new informal economy: feminized service employment

One of the most significant changes in the post-war British economy, with implications for the ways in which men and women construct themselves as gendered social beings, has been a remarkable shift in the nature of waged work. In 1955, almost two-thirds of the labour force – which at that time was dominated by men – worked in the manufacturing sector – made goods for the expanding industrial economy of the time, both at home and for export. For boys in particular, post-war economic expansion and the emphasis on manual labour meant that even young men with few educational credentials and skills were able to secure employment that gave them access to a reasonable wage. Although youth were paid a lower wage than adults (and there was a significant gender gap in wages), their employment facilitated the expansion from the late 1950s onwards of a consumer goods industry and the rise of the 'teenager'. From the late 1950s youth cultures – Teddy boys, mods and rockers, Goths – succeeded one another, distinguishable by clothes, style and iconic consumer durables. While this development – that of youth cultures – is still a marked feature of the ways in which young people distinguish themselves from adults, and while youth purchasing power has continued to expand, 50 years later, the structure of the labour market had been transformed. Manufacturing employment, paying relatively decent wages, is no longer accessible to unskilled working-class youths – boys in the main.

The economy of the new millennium is numerically dominated by service sector employment in which the product typically is not physical goods but forms of service. Britain is now a high-tech knowledge-based informational economy in which education and skills are the main entry requirement to employment: at least to high status and well-remunerated occupations. University education, which in the 1950s was restricted to a tiny middle-class majority, has expanded enormously. In the UK, 38 per cent of the age group between 18–21 now enter university and many students move into well-paid middle-class jobs in the expanding professions and high tech industries. Perhaps the most significant change has been the rise in the number of women with degrees who then enter the labour market on a more permanent basis than women in earlier generations. The old pattern in which women worked for a decade or less and then left waged work when they had children has disappeared as many women take shorter and shorter breaks before returning to employment, although often on a part-time basis. Thus, women's identity has changed in contemporary western economies. 'No longer defined in terms of husbands, fathers of boyfriends, women and in particular younger women have been set free to compete with each other, sometimes mercilessly' (McRobbie 2004: 100). One of the arenas of competition is the labour market. If working-class boys have lost out, it seems as if girls, especially middle-class girls, have been the beneficiaries of economic and social change.

What the shift away from manufacturing employment initially accomplished, however, was a rise in social mobility as young people from a wider class spectrum gained access to education and white-collar work. Throughout the 1960s and 1970s, both many boys and rising numbers of girls entered forms of work that brought them social status and a new middle-class pattern of living. In more recent decades, however, social mobility rates, especially for boys, have stagnated and new class patterns of inequality have become evident (Aldridge 2004). Children from working-class families find access to well-paid work is impossible without significant educational capital. At the same time, patterns of promotion 'on the job' seem to have been stymied by falling rates of occupational mobility in the workplace. The opportunity to move up through the hierarchical structures of a firm or organization has also largely vanished. Indeed, without a first degree, and it seems increasingly a higher level degree, the entry to well-paid employment is now almost impossible.

## Class and income polarization

This pattern of class-based inequality is exacerbated by a structural feature of service-dominated economies. As many scholars have documented, the growth of service employment is associated with an increasingly bifurcated labour market (e.g. Castells 2000). Despite the rhetoric about the knowledge-based information economy, in the UK at least as many low status and poorly paid jobs have been created in the past two decades. This is leading to a new class structure with a hollowed out middle and growing income polarization. Among the fastest growing jobs recently are retail assistants, catering workers, and elder care workers: more than a quarter of all 18–21 year-olds currently work in retail. Many of the jobs at the bottom end of the economy open to those with few educational qualifications are precarious, casualized and insecure, and above all low paid. They demand, however, a particular type of embodied social capital to produce the necessary deferential service performance (McDowell 2003). It has been argued that many of these types of work are 'feminized' in that they draw on the stereotypical attributes of femininity including docility, empathy with the needs of others, and an ability to produce a courteous 'smiling' performance in exchanges with customers and clients. Hochschild (1983) argued that these types of work demand the 'management of emotions' often under stressful conditions. Many working-class young men find it difficult to produce the required workplace performance, seeing deference and courtesy, bending to the will of both superiors and customers, as a challenge to their sense of themselves as masculine. Versions of a street-based, swaggering working-class masculinity – labelled 'protest masculinity' (Connell 2000) – is seldom seen as a positive attribute for employment by putative employers and often, if employment is gained, leads to conflict in the workplace. For many prospective employers, the stroppy, macho, often awkward young men whom they interview when filling vacancies are less appealing prospects than either young women from the same class position or the growing number of older women returning to work as their children go to school, often to make up for the declining incomes of their husband and partners who are also affected by declining opportunities for men. Katherine Newman (1999), for example, and Philippe Bourgois (1995), have shown how working-class young men in New York City, typically disqualify themselves from the only sorts of jobs available – as fast food workers, office messengers, etc. – by unacceptable attitudes and behaviour.

In his study of young minority men in a New York City neighbourhood disadvantaged by the almost complete disappearance of blue-collar jobs, Bourgois (1995) found that the tough, aggressive, sexualized street credibility valorized by young men in that locality disqualified them from most vacancies available in the city. These youths 'find themselves propelled headlong into an explosive confrontation between their sense of cultural dignity versus the humiliating interpersonal subordination of service work' (ibid.: 14). Their social and cultural capital is inappropriate in white-collar workplaces:

> They do not know how to look at their fellow service workers – let alone their supervisors – without intimidating them. They cannot walk down the hallway to the water fountain without unconsciously swaying their shoulders aggressively as if patrolling their home turf.
>
> (ibid.: 142–3)

In the UK (McDowell 2003), I also found that the educational and cultural capital of many young male school-leavers disqualified them from most of the vacancies on offer, whether by their own choice or because prospective employees refused them. Many young men to whom I talked had clear views about the types of work they were prepared to consider, regarding most routine, casualized service sector work as 'women's work' and so beneath their dignity. Even if they were prepared to consider employment in the shops, clubs and fast food outlets that were the main source of work for unqualified school leavers, they often disqualified themselves as potential employees by their appearance (piercings and tattoos as well as inappropriate clothes) and their attitudes during the recruitment process. Employers read the surface signals of bodily demeanour, dress and language as indicators of the underlying qualities they are seeking, or more typically as characteristics they wanted to avoid. If these young men did find work, often their sexualized, aggressive embodied interactions, especially with women co-workers and superiors, soon disqualified them.

A number of terms have been employed to differentiate the two ends of service employment. Castells (2000), for example, has termed 'top-end' high status occupations where skills are highly developed and specific to particular types of work whereas the low status jobs are 'generic' – open to almost anyone who has labour power to sell. Brush (1999) has captured these differences in the concept of 'high-tech' and 'high touch' work. The latter term is particularly appropriate in my view as many of these generic jobs involve close and personal contact with the bodies of the consumers – in gyms, hair salons, nursing homes, massage parlours, etc. Wolkowitz (2006) has dubbed these jobs 'body work'. Women typically are assumed to be more appropriate 'body workers' – more at ease with the messy, leaky boundaries of the human body and the demands it makes for comfort and solace. The combination of Hochschild's (1983) notion of managed emotions – often referred to as 'emotional labour' which similarly involves succour, comfort and deference – and Wolkowitz's idea of 'body work', provides a powerful way of describing the feminization of bottom end work. Typically masculine skills of rationality, a stiff upper lip and embodied strength have relatively little purchase in the world of servicing bodies and young working-class men are the least appropriate of all possible labourers in this new embodied economy.

Young working-class people without educational capital – and men in particular – are now restricted to low-paid work at the bottom end of the labour market, in jobs with few prospects and characterized by instability and high rates of labour turnover, as well as poor terms and conditions. These features are reflected in a new concern in the UK and the USA with stagnation of social mobility for young people. For perhaps the first time in a century or more, young people have fewer prospects than their parents – especially boys in comparison with their fathers. According to recent research (Blanden *et al.* 2005), rates of social mobility are not only declining in the UK but are lower than in other advanced industrial countries such as Canada, Germany Sweden, Norway, Denmark and Finland. Finnegan's (1999) book *Cold New World* provides a fascinating ethnographic view into the world of young men and women in the USA with stalled opportunities and no prospects for mobility, exploring the complex connections between race, class and gender in different regions of the USA with different industrial histories and patterns of economic change. In the UK, the problems of these young people who are trapped, often without work, are such that the ex-Labour Minister Frank Field (2005) suggested that they represent 'the first non-violent loss of a generation'.

In the next section, I consider the ways in which youth – especially troublesome, rebellious and workless youth – are currently constructed in the media, in other forms of popular discourse and by policy-makers.

61

## The discursive construction of class and youth inequalities

While the discussion of the size of the lost generation is in neutral terms, it is typically accompanied by popular and policy discourses that are part of what the social commentator Mount (2004) has termed 'class condescension'. In the past five years or so there has been a remarkably consistent trend to refer to working-class youth, especially young men as 'yobs'. This term, used by Blair, Prescott and Straw in the early 2000s when respectively the PM, Deputy PM and the Home Secretary, as well as the media, has replaced the previous and less vituperative term 'lad' previously the most common way of referring to working-class boys (although the rise of an associated discourse about 'ladettes' to refer to outrageous female behaviour including sexual promiscuity and binge drinking is more pejorative). The term 'yob' is more pernicious and is part of the general process of labelling of the working class as backward, unmodern, and racist Haylett (2001). Skeggs (2004) argues that class increasingly is constructed through a process of inscription, given meaning through systems of cultural attribution which consist not only of economic but also moral exchanges. She documents the growth of discourses that portray the working class in ways that emphasize moral laxity, fecklessness, their propensity to violence and their inability to defer gratification compared to the attributes of morality, discipline and restraint that distinguish the middle classes (or rather used to, as conspicuous consumption, pleasure and self-gratification also now part of middle-class identity, in an economy that relies on consumption) (Bauman 1998).

Class-specific traits are marked on the body through exercise, patterns of movement, weight, posture and clothing: captured in the term 'habitus' (Bourdieu 1984). For working-class youth, these embodied attributes tell against them in applications for deferential 'high touch' work. Young men's macho attitudes, their appearance in caps, body jewellery, often tattooed, relatively inarticulate, with low social skills and an inadequate understanding of appropriate behaviour in shops and offices, are relatively worthless in economic terms. In Britain, the stark associations between looks, threats and youth were made clear in the debate about 'hoodies' – a term that refers to hooded sweatshirts and the working-class youths who wear them. In 2005, hooded youth were banned from a major out-of-town shopping mall. The discursive construction of the working class as morally worthless or as excessive – the social construction of the chav,[1] for example, or the idea of bling (conspicuous but tasteless display of ostentatious jewellery, etc.) to identify a style and a lifestyle – is evidence of the class condescension noted by Mount.

The discursive construction of a new femininity is perhaps more complicated, although the idealized version of deferential and empathetic femininity valued in high touch jobs is contradicted by a version of a raunchy, aggressive femininity captured by the term 'ladette'. This is a media version of sexually confident young women, like young men enjoying themselves in the public world of leisure, less concerned with either economic success or conventional female aspirations for romance than with living for the moment. Against this flashy but optimistic version of a new millennium femininity is the rise of various more pathological versions of femininity – young women anxious about their embodiment as female and subject to, in growing numbers, a number of conditions including bulimia and anorexia, self-harm, and less dangerous but debilitating forms of low self-esteem. Feminist scholars have examined the ways in which regulatory norms operate through the education system, in the media and in other forms of representation to construct these pathological versions of femininity.

McRobbie (2004), in an interesting analysis of the genre of self-improvement TV programmes, brought together a class and gender analysis to explore the forms of symbolic violence that produce young working-class women as inadequate in the new knowledge-based economy and society. She examined the 'reality' television shows in Britain that depend on the humiliation and temporary 'makeover' of typically young working-class volunteers who are given a glimpse of a middle-class world to which they may aspire but are, in general, excluded from in the competitive and individualized neo-liberal economy. She argues that these TV programmes both reflect the arguments about individualization (that I discuss further in the next section) and flexibility, the insistence on mobile performance and the transformative potential of continuous personal reinvention but that, significantly, they also solidify class differentials by revealing the significance of class 'hatred and animosity refracted at a bodily or corporeal level' (ibid.: 100). The distinctive 'bodily failings and unappealing characteristics including voice, manners, facial expressions etc' (ibid.: 100) of working-class women exclude them from the meritocratic and individualized new society and as McRobbie notes 'class makes a decisive re-appearance through the vectors of a transformed individualism' (ibid.: 100).

New class and gender divisions, then, are emerging based on 'the denigration of low class or poor and disadvantaged women by means of symbolic violence' (ibid.: 101). In the USA, talk shows that portend to resolve problems faced by working people but in fact encourage them to humiliate themselves play a similar role in the construction and affirmation of class condescension. These forms of humiliation reflect, or extend, older divisions between women constructed on the basis of class-specific notions of moral worth that divide middle- from working-class women and also differentiate between rough and respectable working-class women. Skeggs (1997), for example, in her ethnographic study of working-class young women in the North of England, documented the ways in which the discourse of respectability, that distinguishes the decent from the rough working class, affected the behaviour of young women in the 1990s.

While the rise of the ladette has valorized a version of non-respectability, for many (most?) young women, class-specific versions of decency still regulate their behaviour. For the middle classes in general and policy-makers in particular, these versions of class condescension provide a space to despise the working class as well as to see their own success as deserved. Thus, they are increasingly able to refuse responsibility for others less fortunate than themselves, so reinforcing the growing individualization of British society. In the final debate linking economic change, youth and inequality, I explore arguments about the growing individualization of society.

## The risk society, portfolio careers and the detraditionalization of class and gender

One of the most influential commentators on recent social changes in industrial societies is Ulrich Beck, a German sociologist. He has argued that western societies have become risk societies (Beck 1992) in which the traditional mechanisms of class solidarity and social movements to ensure security have been destabilized both by greater risks – of famine, disease, war, nuclear threat – and by a shift in economic and social policy towards a neo-liberal version of individualization or individual responsibility. Thus, Beck argues, the traditional constraints of the former industrial society are weakened. Those who are successful in the new economy are able to build portfolio careers, to construct and sell their individual experiences in the knowledge-based economy in which performance, style, confidence are as important a part of working life as more traditional skills. Categorical inequalities (Tilly 1998) – the structural constraints of class and gender – are de-emphasized as notions of individual rights and responsibilities become more important. If these arguments are applied specifically to young people's life transitions, the greater variation and complexity of transitions – into the labour market, for example – are adduced as evidence for Beck's theoretical argument. However, as the discussion above shows, class and gender still matter in the labour market. Indeed, Beck himself suggested that as 'gender is part of an older modernity ... women find it difficult to remove themselves from these social traditions and become individualised subjects' (Beck 2002: 151). I believe instead that gender and class connections remain important but have changed significantly: it is young women – the middle-class women who are entering careers on a lifetime basis and so becoming 'more like men' and working-class women, who may be in relatively low-paid work but who are holding down jobs on a more permanent basis than either their male peers at present or their mothers when generations are compared – who seem to have gained the most from economic restructuring and social change. What seems to be occurring is a reconfiguration of class and gender (McDowell 2006) in the new millennium in which, for middle-class youth, gender perhaps has less salience as a social division than it did for earlier generations, although on childbirth many of the old inequalities may recur. Among the working class, youth remains a period of their lives in which class and gender inequalities continue to structure life chances and opportunities. Young working-class women may have greater social freedom than their mothers, and perhaps better labour market opportunities, but they remain segregated in low-paid feminized parts of the labour market and constrained by hegemonic versions of femininity. Thus, class and gender still matter, although the connections between these divisions have changed.

## Note

1 Chav is a derogatory term used in the middle of the first decade of the new millennium to refer to the despised characteristics of working-class youth. It might be derived from a Romany term 'chavi' or 'chavari' which means child. There is a website www.chavscum.co.uk where examples of the derisive and condescending attitudes may be explored.

## References

Aldridge, S. (2004) *Life Chances and Social Mobility: An Overview of the Evidence*, Prime Minister's Strategy Unit, London: The Cabinet Office.

Bauman, Z. (1998) *Work, Consumerism and the New Poor*, Buckingham: Open University Press

Beck, U. (1992) *Risk Society: Towards a New Modernity*, London: Sage.

—— (2002) 'Zombie categories: interview with Ulrich Beck', in U. Beck and E. Beck-Gernsheim, *Individualisation: Institutionalised Individualism and its Social and Political Consequences*, London: Sage.

Blanden, J., Gregg, P. and Machin, S. (2005) *Intergenerational Mobility in Europe and North America*, London: Centre for Economic Performance, London School of Economics.

Bourdieu, P. (1984) *Distinction: The Social Judgement of Taste*, London: Routledge.

Bourgois, P. (1995) *In Search of Respect: Selling Crack in el Barrio*, Cambridge: Cambridge University Press.

Brush, L. (1999) 'Gender, work, who cares?! Production, reproduction, deindustrialisation and business as usual', in M. M. Ferree, J. Lorber and B. Hess, (eds.) *Revisioning Gender*, London: Sage.

Castells, M. (2000) 'Materials for an exploratory theory of the network society', *British Journal of Sociology*, 51: 5–24.

Connell, R. W. (2000) *The Men and the Boys*, Cambridge: Polity.

Field, F. (2005) *The Lost Generation*, Radio 4 programme, 25 August.

Finnegan, W. (1999) *Cold New World: Growing up in a Harder Country*, London: Picador.

Haylett, C. (2001) 'Illegitimate subjects? Abject whites, neoliberal modernisation and middle class multiculturalism', *Environment and Planning D: Society and Space*, 19: 351–79.

Hochschild, A. (1983) *The Managed Heart: The Commercialisation of Human Feeling*, Berkeley, CA: University of California Press.

McDowell, L. (2003) *Redundant Masculinities? White Working Class Youth and Employment Change*, Oxford: Blackwell.

—— (2006) 'Reconfigurations of class and gender relations', *Antipode*, 38: 825–50.

McRobbie, A. (2004) 'Notes on "what not to wear" and post-feminist symbolic violence', in L. Adkins and B. Skeggs (eds) *Feminism after Bourdieu*, Oxford: Blackwell.

Mount, F. (2004) *Mind the Gap: The New Class Divide in Britain*, London: Short Books.

Newman, K. (1999) *No Shame in My Games: The Working Poor in the Inner City*, New York, Vintage Books and Russell Sage Foundation.

Skeggs, B. (1997) *Formations of Class and Gender*, London: Routledge.

—— (2004) *Class, Self, Culture*, London: Routledge.

Tilly, C. (1998) *Durable Inequality*, Berkeley, CA: University of California Press

Wolkowitz, C. (2006) *Bodies at Work*, London: Sage.

# 8

# Young people, 'race' and ethnicity

*Colin Webster*

> [S]ystematic comparative analysis is essential: it is necessary to demonstrate that 'black' people collectively are treated in a certain manner or experience a particular disadvantage, and that the same treatment and disadvantage are not experienced by any other group.
>
> (Miles and Brown 2003: 80)

## The problematic of race and ethnicity

Before going on to briefly review substantive aspects of black and minority ethnic young people's transitions, this chapter first considers some of the theoretical and conceptual problems that have important implications for how we might understand minority transitions. Racial or ethnic categories cannot be abstracted from their social context or the cross-cutting influences that constitute 'race' and ethnicity at any given point in time. In other words, it cannot be presumed from the outset that race or ethnicity will be the overriding or main factors determining black and minority experiences. Other spatial, demographic, social class and gender factors may be as important or override the significance of race and ethnicity according to social situation and context. It may seem churlish to appear to cast doubt on the distinctiveness or primacy of racial exclusion and ethnic identity in the lives of some young people given plentiful evidence of discrimination across different dimensions of youth transitions. Suffice to say there is little doubt that within Britain and America the disproportionate presence of young African-Caribbean and African-American men in the youth and criminal justice system is both striking and even greater than in the past. Black young people in particular suffer disproportionately in respect of school failure, exclusion from school, being in the care system and joblessness (House of Commons Home Affairs Select Committee 2007; Walker *et al.* 2007). These disadvantages, however, are suffered by other groups too and as MacLeod's (1995) study of working-class white and black boys in the USA shows, class rather than race may be the overriding factor in determining transition outcomes.

Young people's experiences are often shared across similar class groups despite different ethnic identity, while there is considerable class and other forms of polarization both within and between heterogeneous racial and ethnic groups. Therefore intergenerational experiences by young people in their transitions to adulthood are influenced by class as well as ethnic relations. As Furlong and Cartmel (2007: 8) suggest, 'The analysis of the impact of "race" on the life experiences of young people is complex because many of the disadvantages faced by members of ethnic minorities are a consequence of their position within the class structure, rather than being a feature of racial exclusion.' A further complication is that racial and ethnic group identity is subjectively experienced differently and perhaps less strongly than in the past among some individuals and groups while strengthening in others, for example, among some young British Muslims (Lewis 2007). Change in how racial and ethnic identity may be felt does not of course alter the continued efficacy of objective racial and ethnic stratification as an aspect of the reproduction of social divisions and social exclusion for some groups.

Some brief illustrations of these difficulties can be mentioned here so as to begin to think afresh about the problematic of young people, race and ethnicity. Young black men are typically said to be disproportionately involved in offending inferred from their presence in the criminal justice system and that this involvement has deleterious effects on transitions within this group. The couplet *Black youth* has long been employed in racist discourse to signify *criminality* so that terms like 'crime' and 'riot' become racially loaded (Keith 1993: 234). Yet in Britain self-report studies suggest that whites disproportionately offend compared to other ethnic groups and obviously commit the vast bulk of crimes. After all, 85 per cent of offences involving children and young people were committed by those who classify their ethnicity as white, and 92 per cent of black young people and children are not subject to disposals in the youth justice system (House of Commons Home Affairs Committee 2007).[1] Similarly, white working-class boys living in disadvantaged areas are the lowest performing group of pupils in schools after the small population of Traveller children (Curtis 2008). And of course, school failure is a strong predictor of 'failed' transitions, delinquency, crime and anti-social behaviour.

A further set of problems emerge when it is acknowledged that customary ethnic and racial categories in a myriad of western societal contexts hardly capture the increasingly complex ethnic and demographic make-up of societies experiencing recent large-scale immigration. In the case of Britain, customary categories such as 'Black', Asian', 'White', 'Other', and more recently, 'Mixed', hardly do justice to either the diversity within these categories or the influx of new migrants and their children. Similarly, customary descriptions of a white majority and ethnic minorities in some urban areas seem increasingly outmoded in new complexions of inter- and intra-ethnic group relations in western societies. Of course it may still be the case that the particular status of black and minority young people, as the children of earlier or recent migrants, continues to carry particular resonance in terms of intergenerational and area experiences of advantage and disadvantage.

A third and final set of conceptual problems insinuate themselves into discussion of young people, race and ethnicity. As implied above, ethnicity, like class and gender, is relational, productive and active in social relationships rather than a mere fixed or passive descriptor or category. Understanding ethnicity requires consideration of 'white' ethnicity too as whiteness conjures up other ethnicities while at the same time is often rendered invisible, 'normal', 'neutral'. Ethnicity – white and minority – is an identity and a lifestyle, and a set of perspectives on social relationships, marked by varying degrees of self awareness. Acquired in the course of collective and individual history, ethnicity is about becoming, being and staying a particular identity and its distinctiveness is realized in specific social and spatial locations. Certain locations are sought out, others are avoided, becoming one thing and not being something else. The relational and interdependent aspects of race and ethnicity arise from it defining others as also belonging to a different race or ethnicity and thus implicitly or explicitly defining itself as belonging to a race or ethnicity. Changes in the situation, power or status of each group influence the position of the other. In these ways ethnicity is dynamic and changing, accruing advantage and disadvantage in ways that favour some groups while marginalizing others (Webster 2008).

## Immigration and the marginalization thesis

According to some writers (Tonry 1997; Patterson 1997; 1998; Smith 2005), the children and grandchildren of some migrant groups in western societies tend to experience difficulties adapting and assimilating to their adopted or host countries compared to their parents. According to this argument – what we might call the immigration and marginalization thesis – patterns appear in which first-generation immigrants are typically more conformist and law-abiding than the general population, whereas subsequent generations – at least for a while – suffer assimilation problems that produce behaviours strongly associated with typical 'risk factors' in transitions from childhood to young adulthood. These include being raised in a lone parent family, poor parental supervision, truancy and school failure, peer influence, living in a poor area, dependent drug use, joblessness, and later, not forming a stable family. Studies tend to emphasize individual risk factors as proximate causes of anti-social behaviour, delinquency and crime rather than structural background factors such as the effects of poverty on family disruption, school processes and labour market conditions. In Britain, the most recent group to which these risks are said to disproportionately apply are mixed race young people.

The argument as to why this should be the case is in part because subsequent generations – usually natives by birth themselves, relatively new arrivals, or in the case of African Americans relatively recent internal migrants from southern to northern or rural to urban areas – accrue higher expectations of being accepted and culturally assimilating than their parents but that these are thwarted by racial discrimination and hostility, lack of opportunity and deprivation. This in turn leads to disaffection, alienation and among some groups to school failure, delinquency and crime because unfulfilled cultural expectations of American and British life lead to experiences of rejection and then rebellion against white authority. This does not, however, happen to the children of all immigrant groups because of cultural differences that may encourage or inhibit disaffected responses to thwarted aspirations and different national policies that may help or hinder assimilation. For example, economic migrants from many Asian cultures in the USA and the UK bring advantageous cultural, social and economic capital and this is eventually reflected in subsequent generation's educational and occupational mobility and success. Whereas this intergenerational inheritance 'protects' some immigrant groups and their children from 'risk factors', other groups are less fortunate (Mason 2003). This argument is extended to include American, European, Australian and Canadian minorities to show that only some, not all, disadvantaged minority groups are disproportionately exposed to risky transitions.

A particular focus has been the plight of African-American and British African-Caribbean young people. Legacies of slavery and post-slavery societies among these groups are said to have led to the prevention of family formation among African-Americans and rapid changes and dissolution in the African-Caribbean family after migration. African-American and British African-Caribbean groups, in contrast to other similarly discriminated against and disadvantaged groups, have failed to benefit from the role of family and community networks in conserving cultural capital and economic self-sufficiency. These groups are said to hold conceptions of masculinity and unstable relations between men and women which contribute to a high prevalence of lone parent families within these groups, and low proportions of young adults who live with a partner. The failure to form stable families, illegitimacy and family breakdown are said to be important causes of poverty and destabilized transitions rather than that poverty and economic insecurity themselves may cause or make family instability and destabilized transitions likely. In other words, the key explanation for consistent patterns of disrupted and destabilized transitions over the generations is found in the parallel intergenerational lack of stable family structures of the two groups.

There are several criticisms that can be made of the immigration and marginalization thesis and these are rehearsed directly and indirectly in the remainder of this chapter. In essence, the sorts of endogenous explanations offered thus far (that the causes of marginalized transitions are to be found within the legacies and cultures of ethnic groups themselves) are rejected when intergenerational black and minority experiences of transition are placed in their social, political and economic context. Disrupted transitions have been less to do with cultural legacies and much more to do with epochal social and economic change within advanced liberal societies upon which minority intergenerational experiences were contingent.

## Risk and ethnicity

Limiting the discussion here to Britain, although not dissimilar processes and outcomes have occurred in other western societies in the past three decades, (Furlong and Cartmel 2007; Glynn 2006), young people generally have experienced growing 'risks'. Furlong and Cartmel (2007: 8–9) argue that 'growing up in the risk society' has meant growing up in different circumstances to those experienced by previous generations among all groups because of the ways in which social changes over the last three decades have heightened risks and individualized young people's experiences. Transitions have become more uncertain, precarious and extended although particularly among the most vulnerable groups such as minority ethnic and working class groups. As Furlong and Cartmel argue:

> In the modern world young people face new risks and opportunities. The traditional links between the family, school and work seem to have weakened as young people embark on journeys into adulthood which involve a wide variety of routes, many of which appear to have uncertain outcomes.
>
> (2007: 9)

Nowhere has this been truer than in the cumulative, intergenerational, crises faced by black and Asian young people as they attempt to adopt new identities and adapt to economic and social change from the 1970s to the present. Changes in schooling and youth training, in eligibility and entitlement to welfare benefits, in youth labour markets and drug markets, and changes to their neighbourhoods, have marginalized and polarized their experiences. Minority ethnic and white working-class young people's marginalized transitions to adulthood often take place in inner city neighbourhoods and peripheral estates characterized by de-industrialization, destabilization, deprivation and high levels of crime and violence.

If the 1970s were the years of crisis, the 1980s brought the 'solutions' to this crisis – a series of cumulatively repressive measures against working-class young people in general and black young people in particular. Although the new generation of black young people inherited their parents' experience of racial exclusion and isolation, they faced very different conditions and problems. As black youth unemployment began to rise, it was their experience of school that marked the new generation. ESN ('educationally sub-normal') Special Schools contained disproportionate numbers of black children as a result of teachers' prejudice and low expectations of black children's abilities and performance, black young people constituted over a third of detention centre and borstal populations and the numbers of 14–16 year-old males – white and black – sent to custody more than doubled between 1971 and 1981 (Webster 2007). The 1990s followed a similar pattern but took a different turn as collusion between the police and media constructed British 'Asian' ethnicity in the language of criminality, alleging the widespread involvement of Asian young men in street rebellion, gang violence, crime and drugs (Webster 1997). Finally, minority ethnic young people are disproportionately found among those not engaged in education, employment or training (NEET), and from those who have lived in the care system (Britton *et al.* 2002).

Concluding this section, minority young people's cumulative intergenerational experiences of transitions can be summarized as exposing them to particular sorts of risks perhaps not experienced by other groups, as Table 8.1 shows. It is important to note that Table 8.1 does not control for social class which if factored in would no doubt present a somewhat different picture of exposure to risk based on class as much as race. Nevertheless, the disproportionate proximity to risk factors that may destabilize transitions among minorities compared to whites is clear. These risks are greater where a higher proportion of the group is young, where young men and women lack educational qualifications and/or are unemployed and live in deprived and high crime urban areas. And

**Table 8.1** Socio-economic and demographic characteristics of selected ethnic groups

| | % Living in Inner London | % Aged 10–15 | % of males aged 16–24 unemployed | % aged 16–20 with no educational qualifications | % of dependent children living in single parent households |
|---|---|---|---|---|---|
| White British | 5.3 | 19.6 | 7.2 | 16 | 22.1 |
| Mixed White and Black Caribbean | 15.1 | 57.5 | 14.5 | 24.6 | 54.5 |
| Black Caribbean | 33.7 | 20.4 | 15.8 | 16.3 | 59.1 |
| Black African | 47.7 | 30.2 | 6.9 | 12.6 | 44.3 |
| Indian | 8.2 | 22.9 | 5.2 | 10.6 | 10.9 |
| Pakistani | 6.1 | 35.0 | 10.1 | 22.6 | 16.3 |
| Bangladeshi | 45.7 | 38.4 | 9.2 | 21.6 | 15.1 |

Source: UK Census (2001), Fitzgerald (2008).

the more of these factors are present, the more they may reinforce each other (Fitzgerald 2008). These are also the factors that bring the risk of young people coming to the attention of the police.

Although increased precariousness of youth transitions and disengagement from education, employment and training disproportionately affects some minority ethnic young people, for other minority groups, this has not been the case. Growing class, educational and economic polarization between and within different minority ethnic groups complicates processes of social exclusion and disadvantage in respect of these groups. There has been both consolidation and enhancement of initial parental advantages and disadvantages by second and third generation minority young people and there is evidence of both upward and downward inter-generational and intra-generational educational and occupational mobility (Mason 2003). This is clearest in respect of cultural capital where the subsequent relative educational performance of different minority young people has simply reflected the cultural capital that the first generation of parents brought with them. So, for example, for most ethnic minority groups, the second and third generation have made significant educational progress, especially some groups and women, Caribbean, Pakistani and Bangladeshi boys have made least progress. When social class background is taken into account, Caribbean boys in particular, continue to do less well than their white counterparts although not the poorest white boys (Curtis 2008). In addition, Pakistani and Bangladeshi young people are geographically concentrated and segregated in de-industrialized urban areas, disproportionately suffer joblessness and belong to the poorest ethnic groups in British society (Mason 2003). Here, vital class processes interpenetrate with ethnicity to produce enduring structures of disadvantage, but they do not necessarily override the influence of ethnic inequality

## Conclusion: peculiarities of minority young people's transitions?

Returning to the earlier discussion about the theoretical and conceptual issues that accompany discussions of race and ethnicity, we might ask, are then minority transitions significantly different or disadvantaged compared to white and other groups of similar class background and/or neighbourhood? Second, are the claims found in the immigration and marginalization thesis valid in that problematic intergenerational transitions derive thwarted cultural assimilation and cultural legacies of advantage and disadvantage? Combining these questions we might then ask are cumulative intergenerational experiences of marginalization and social exclusion significantly different for some disadvantaged minorities compared to working-class white young people by virtue of the formers' peculiar status as second and third generation children of migrants?

Initial migrants through chain migration tended to concentrate and settle in particular and poor urban areas because of the availability of cheap housing, safety in numbers from racist hostility and violence, the security brought by close social networks, proximity to employment opportunities and discrimination in the housing and labour markets. Far from being motivated by 'self-segregation', as some claim, this geographical concentration offered clear advantages while building in disadvantage from the beginning. The places and occupations that some minority groups found themselves in were most vulnerable to economic restructuring and deindustrialization and this set in train a process of growing spatial inequality that adversely effected neighbourhoods with significant minority settlement (Butler and Watt 2007). The above claims of a crisis in the black family have to be placed alongside a crisis of white working-class families experiencing similar destabilizing effects as neighbourhoods declined and work disappeared. Poor transitions are far from being the preserve of some minority communities and the same sorts of disadvantage have influenced white working-class transitions in the rationing of good schooling, decent work, fair policing and of bridging social capital enabling opportunities beyond those of class- and ethnically-based ghettoes, whether of white estates or inner city areas.

Explanations of the marginalized transitions of some minority young people that rest on notions of thwarted expectations of cultural and racial assimilation found in the experiences of second and third generation young people ignore the actual intergenerational experiences of growing risk among urban working-class young people generally over the past three decades. The intergenerational experiences of minority groups are best understood not in terms of exclusive racial or ethnic phenomenon but rather, as a function of their increased vulnerability, visibility and worsening of social conditions shared among working-class young people – white and minority – in the context of neo-liberal economic and social restructuring.

## Note

1 Presumably, if comparisons of ethnic disadvantage or offending and victimization by current ethnic categories controlled for social class, area of residence or other proxies for SES – something that most surveys omit or is only implicit – then differences between 'whites' and others would disappear or whites show similar or higher rates of disadvantage, offending and/or victimization when similar age and SES were compared.

## References

Britton, L., Chatrik, B., Coles, B., Craig, G., Hylton, C. and Mumtaz, S. (2002) *Missing Connexions: The Career Dynamics and Welfare Needs of Black and Minority Ethnic Young People at the Margins*, Bristol: The Policy Press.

Butler, T. and Watt, P. (2007) *Understanding Social Inequality*, London: Sage.

Curtis, P. (2008) '85% of poorer white boys fall short in GCSEs', *Guardian*, 1 February.

Fitzgerald, M. (2008) '"Race", ethnicity and crime', in C. Hale, K. Hayward, A. Wahidin and E. Wincup (eds) *Criminology*, Oxford: Oxford University Press.

Furlong, A. and Cartmel, F. (2007) *Young People and Social Change*, 2nd edn, Maidenhead: Open University Press.

Glynn, A. (2006) *Capitalism Unleashed: Finance, Globalization, and Welfare*, Oxford: Oxford University Press.

House of Commons Home Affairs Committee (2007) *Young Black People and the Criminal Justice System*, vol. 1, London: The Stationery Office.

Keith, M. (1993) *Race, Riots and Policing: Lore and Disorder in a Multi-racist Society*, London: UCL Press.

Lewis, P. (2007) *Young, British and Muslim*, London: Continuum.

MacLeod, J. (1995) *Ain't No Making it*, Boulder, CO: Westview Press.

Mason, D. (ed.) (2003) *Explaining Ethnic Differences: Changing Patterns of Disadvantage in Britain*, Bristol: The Policy Press.

Miles, R. and Brown, M. (2003) *Racism*, 2nd edn, London: Routledge.

Patterson, O. (1997) *The Ordeal of Integration: Progress and Resentment in America's 'Racial' Crisis*, Washington, DC: Civitas/Counterpoint.

—— (1998) *Rituals of Blood: Consequences of Slavery in Two American Centuries*, New York: Basic Civitas.

Smith, D. J. (2005) 'Ethnic differences in intergenerational crime patterns', in M. Tonry (ed.) *Crime and Justice: A Review of Research*, vol. 32, Chicago: University of Chicago Press.

Tonry, M. (ed.) (1997) *Ethnicity, Crime and Immigration: Comparative and Cross-national Perspectives*, Chicago: University of Chicago Press.

Walker, S., Spohn, C. and DeLone, M. (2007) *The Color of Justice: Race, Ethnicity and Crime in America*, 4th edn, Belmont, CA: Wadsworth.

Webster, C. (1997) 'The construction of British "Asian" criminality', *International Journal of the Sociology of Law*, 25: 65–86.

—— (2007) *Understanding Race and Crime*, Maidenhead: Open University Press.

—— (2008) 'Marginalized white ethnicity, race and crime', *Theoretical Criminology*, 12: 293–312.

# 9

# Young people and social capital

*Cherylynn Bassani*

## Introduction

Social capital is a product of relationships that influences well-being. In youth studies, the concept has a relatively long history, though it has not always been called social capital. The *theory* of social capital, however, has developed only over the past few decades and is still under construction. Although many scholars use social capital in their research, either to explain disparities in well-being or as a contextualization measure, work is needed to improve the theory's external validity.

## Historical development

The *concept* of social capital (the product of relationships) has been discussed and theorized for as long as people have been interested in youths' well-being. The theory of social capital has a shorter history and is typically linked to three main scholars – Coleman, Bourdieu, and Putnam – though countless others have worked to develop the theory across the disciplines (i.e., Morrow 1999; Lin 2001; Ream 2003; 2005; Bassani 2007). In youth studies, social capital theory has developed largely out of Coleman's work.

Social capital was made prominent by American youth education scholar James Coleman in his research on high-school completion, though before Coleman, geographer Lydia Hanifan (1916) discussed social capital in her study of education in rural communities. Coleman (1987, 1988) began to delineate what exactly social capital was and how it was formed in families and schools. After his works were published, an increasing number of youth scholars incorporated social capital into their research. At the same time, French theorist Pierre Bourdieu (1986) integrated social capital into his theory of cultural reproduction. Bourdieu did not focus on youth *per se*, but rather on the way that power is intergenerationally transferred within the educational system. Interestingly, Coleman and Bourdieu worked at the same university for a couple of years, though they were not known to have conducted research on or theorize about social capital together. In the early to mid 1990s, the prominence of social capital was waning in youth studies, but by the late 1990s, political scientist Robert Putnam, although not a youth studies scholar, played a predominant role in making social capital a familiar concept in the public, government, and academic domains. It was US President Bill Clinton's recognition of Putnam's (1999) work (*Bowling Alone*) that made social capital known outside of academic circles. With his wife Hilary's social-policy interests in children's well-being and her book *It Takes a Village* (Clinton 1996) (which incidentally discusses the importance of social capital – though not called such – on the development of youth), it is no surprise that Clinton favoured Putnam's work. As a result, many more researchers began to incorporate social capital into their work, though only a few have worked to develop *social capital theory*. Some, including Coleman, Portes, Morrow, Harpham, and Bassani, among others, focus on children and youths, though other researchers, such as Lin and Putnam, focus on adult–centred aspects of the theory.

## Social capital theory

Coleman began to formulate a theory of social capital in the 1980s. Until very recently, however, there has been limited development of social capital theory (SCT) in youth studies because scholars tend to adopt Coleman's (limited) conceptualization. In fact, the social capital literature is fragmented in that there is no one recognized 'social capital theory'. Some scholars incorporate social capital into their research and do not use social capital theory; others use segments of the theory; while still others have tried to develop the theory. This is a major limitation in the field because researchers in the first two groups comprise the majority and tend to work with Coleman's original ideas; (social capital has a positive influence on well-being and develops in groups and; the importance of bridging – when one or more individuals belong to two or more overlapping groups – in developing social capital) despite theoretical developments. As I have out-lined elsewhere, there are at least five major dimensions of social capital theory upon which youth studies authors (in all three of the aforementioned groups) tend to agree (Bassani 2007).

The first dimension asserts that social capital is but one form of capital from which youths draw. Financial (financial resources of the individual or group), human (education and skills of the individual or group), cultural (cultural knowledge, abilities and experi-ences or the individual or group), and physical (material goods available to the individual or group) capitals are all necessary for understanding youths' well-being, though social capital is recognized as being critically important. Although all five of these capitals are intertwined, social capital is uniquely crucial because it bridges the capital of one group (e.g., the family) with that of another group (e.g., the school). In this sense, social capital has an important, direct influence on well-being, but also an equally important indirect influence. This point will be expanded on later.

Second, authors tend to agree that there is a theoretical and empirical link between social capital and well-being. When SCT was first developed, Coleman (1988) main-tained that it had only a positive influence. Countless empirical studies support this claim, yet some studies also have found that measures of social capital do not play a uniform role in understanding youths' well-being (see Ferguson 2006, for a systematic review and commentary). That is to say, social capital is not consistently statistically significant across studies. This appears to be a measurement validity issue rather than theoretical error. Over the past decade, a growing body of research empirically shows the negative (or perhaps curvilinear) influence that social capital can have on youth well-being, contra-dicting Coleman's original assumption. Such findings tend to come out of the race, ethnicity, and immigrant literatures (Portes and Landolt 1996; Ream 2003; 2005). When youths belong to marginalized groups (i.e., ethnic visible minorities), internal family and community ties tend to be excessively strong; some groups can become fully 'closed', thereby limiting the bridging that can occur with other – outside – groups. As Ream (2003) discussed, such ties tend to choke out or severely limit the ties that youths would otherwise have with other groups (such as other community groups or groups in 'dominant' society). This body of research focuses on Latin and Hispanic American youths, though I suspect that any group that is separated (by self or external forces) from the 'dominant' culture might experience the same negative (or curvilinear) effect of social capital.

Scholars also concur that social resources are transformed into social capital (Coleman 1987; Portes 1998; Lin 2001). As I have discussed elsewhere (Bassani 2007), it is essential to recognize this relationship, though many researchers fail to do so. By delineating the mobilization of social resources into social capital, the last two dimensions of SCT are clarified: that is, the formation of social capital and the mezzo-mezzo bridging of social capital that creates more social capital.

The formation of social capital occurs through a complex interplay between what Coleman referred to as structural and functional resources. *Structural resources* represent the people that are in the group, whereas *functional resources* represent the interaction of group members (including the strength and positive/negative aspects of interaction). When structural and functional *resource efficiencies* are present, structural and functional *resource deficiencies* are absent or limited. The terms 'deficiency' and 'efficiency' do not have standard definitions, but rather represent 'healthy' or 'unhealthy' relationships, as defined by a particular researcher. Ultimately, a healthy relationship is one that produces a heal-thy level of social capital (it does not produce a tightly 'closed' group). What is regarded as a 'healthy' relationship necessarily varies across time, place, and culture.

Youth scholars agree that social capital forms in groups. Research tends to focus on the family and/or school group(s), though social capital also can be formed in non-family groups – such as in various community groups, the workplace, among peers, and in cyber space. For youths, 'the family' acts as the primary (influencing) group, while 'the school' tends to be the main secondary group. As youths pass from childhood into ado-lescence and young adulthood, the primary group changes. During this transformation, the peer group becomes more prominent, perhaps usurping the school group as the main secondary group. Although the family may still be the primary group, its influence erodes. The degree of competition (and thus erosion) between primary and secondary groups varies by culture (whether it be ethnic, national, or otherwise), and thus the theoretical framework needs to be adjusted depending on the age group and culture of youths. Researchers typically do not discuss this, though it is essential for understanding the transformation of a youth's social resources into social capital. In addition, when examining functional social resources, shared values and closure need to be examined. Again, the youth's culture needs to be examined to validly model closure and functional social resource efficiencies. An increase in shared values leads to an increase in group closure, which in turn develops functional social resource efficiencies. Many race, ethni-city, and immigrant youth scholars are taking these considerations into account; however, most researchers use a fixed (Colemanian) SCT.

Finally, youth scholars who use SCT agree on the importance of mezzo-mezzo interactions in the creation of social capital and thus youths' well-being. Bridging links two or more groups and is made possible when the same youth belongs to two or more groups. Following Coleman, family–school bridging is most commonly discussed and tested, though bridging occurs between all groups that youths (or other group members, such as adults) belong to. When groups are bridged, individuals bring resources from one group to another, and if mobilized, these resources will become capital that members of the second group can (potentially) utilize. Not only social resources, but all forms of resources are bridged. Recall, however, that it is social capital that transforms other resources into capital (e.g. human resources into human capital). In sum, the bridging of groups not only influences an individual youth, but also other group members because group dynamics are altered when group membership changes or when members bring in new (or adjusted) resources. This last dimension is perhaps the least examined of the five outlined dimensions, though researchers have increasingly looked at the interrelations between youths and the groups to which they belong (see Bankston and Caldas 1998).

## Main critiques

There are numerous critiques of SCT; some of them are well recognized, while others have yet to be widely acknowledged. A fundamental issue in the literature is the lack of a distinction between the 'concept of social capital' and the 'theory of social capital'. This problem has led to a number of related critiques. Because the concept of social capital is key for understanding youth well-being, many researchers integrate it into their own respective paradigms. This has strengthened our understanding of youth well-being, but it also has created a fractured conceptualization and operationalization of social capital. This fractured conceptualization is attributable to differences in the unit of analysis across disciplines and studies and a non-systematic placing of social capital within theory (peripheral, central, or limited theory). In addition, as a work in progress, there is no definitive understanding of SCT because most youth academics lean on Coleman's original work, while others have tried to develop the theory beyond Coleman. Still others, although it is evident that they are using SCT, do not delineate the fundamental tenets of the theory, and in some cases there is no clear theory or framework.

This disunity is also attributable to the widespread use of secondary datasets that were not created to measure social capital. This, of course, is a general issue across all disciplines, regardless of the research question or theoretical framework. The cross-disciplinary use of social capital, combined with our heavy reliance on secondary data (which leads to measurement error), has led some to critique social capital as becoming a catch-all concept that represents both cause and effect.

A major strength of youth studies is its cross-disciplinary nature. But again, this strength has caused fragmentation in how social capital is viewed (and therefore how it is measured). At a rudimentary level, researchers agree that social capital develops in a group, but they have different views regarding who *holds* social capital: the group or the individual. This disparity tends to be discipline-based and may be caused by differences in the various units of analysis that are prevalent in particular disciplines. Sociology and health sciences, for example, tend to focus on individual youths as the unit of analysis, whereas geography and political science tend to focus on communities. More recently, the focus throughout the social sciences has moved toward embedding youths within the groups to which they belong, thus meshing the dichotomy. This change is likely tied to the development of SCT, as more scholars try to bridge conceptual gaps. More research is needed that considers the interplay among individuals and groups.

As I have reiterated throughout the chapter, a key issue in the literature is that many researchers use (or at least frame their studies around) a stagnant theory, as Coleman (and to a lesser extent Bourdieu) originally developed it. Although it is important to pay tribute to these theorists' work, many of their theoretical points are outdated. For example, Coleman did not consider gender or ethnicity, and his explanation and empirical testing of group dynamics were limited, while Bourdieu's reference to social capital was only one component in his theory of cultural reproduction. Many scholars continue to rely on these early conceptualizations even though they have developed and progressed over time. This reliance is fostered not only by researchers, but also by the gatekeepers of academic knowledge – the editors and reviewers who insist on leaning on theorists (Coleman or Bourdieu) who are seen as the 'canon' in youth studies. That being said, some have tried to create consistency in the literature and thus encourage a reliance on Coleman and/or Bourdieu. Although many researchers value theoretical consistency and the canon, SCT will continue to stagnate if such resistance continues to be met.

A consequence of this over-reliance on the canon theorists is the criticism that SCT does not consider power differences (specifically gender and ethnicity) and time. These critiques are only partially valid because they overlook the large and growing literature that focuses specifically on ethnicity and social capital. Portes and colleagues, and many others have actively published in the area of social capital and ethnicity and immigration, however, critiques tend not to account for changes that have been made in the theory. It would seem that disunity also exists in SCT's critiques. Issues associated with gender and time (i.e., that social capital at one point in time influences social capital at an other point and the fact that group dynamics alter social capital within the group) are still heavily under-theorized (Thorlindsson *et al.* 2007).

Another main critique of SCT is that although it was originally developed in a general youth studies context (Coleman 1987; 1988), it has been essentially adult-centred (i.e., it focuses on adults in the family structure or on student–teacher relations and ratios). Recently scholars have begun to empirically examine youths in youth-centred groups (Bankston and Caldas 1988; Caldas and Bankston 1998; 2001). This research tends to focus on the family and school groups and measures social capital in the context of class/student body constitution (i.e., ethnic composition, family structure composition). When examining group composition, researchers have been focusing their measurement on structural social resource efficiencies, and from this, inferring functional social resource efficiencies, though they do not always use this terminology *per se*. This is a direction that needs to be incorporated and assessed in future studies.

On a related note, the literature tends to focus on social capital in the family and school. These are but two groups to which youths belong; more research is needed on the influence of the workplace, peer networks, and especially internet-based networks. Research on internet networks has been conducted (Wellman *et al.* 2001; Vinken and Ester 2002), though scholars need to increase their awareness of the influence that this quickly emerging and competing secondary group has on youths to stay attuned with youths' changing lives and culture.

Finally, SCT currently regards youths as a homogenous age group. It is important to recognize that each developmental phase is unique, and SCT needs to account for the secondary groups that the youths belong to, in addition to the rivalries that may occur between these groups and the primary group.

## Future developments

Both logically and empirically, social capital is an important concept to understand, measure, and model in youth studies. As this chapter has suggested, several areas need to be explored and expanded.

Foremost, a modernized theory of social capital needs to be pursued. The literature suggests that a canon of SCT has developed, which has led to an over-reliance on Coleman's work. Canons help fields form standardized concepts, but they also stifle theoretical development. As a discipline, youth studies needs to advance both theoretically and empirically by incorporating current developments. Additionally, SCT is heavily rooted in the work of US theorists; the discipline now needs to draw on researchers throughout the world to enhance the theory's validity. A more extensive dialogue among scholars is needed to achieve this.

All dimensions of the theory need to be tested. Currently, researchers tend to focus on testing whether social capital has an influence on youths' well-being (particularly in a US context). Increasingly, researchers have examined the influence of the macro–macro link. This needs to be a primary focus in future studies because knowledge about the influence of secondary groups, apart from the family and school, is limited. The influence of community groups that youths belong to has been understudied (both theoretically and empirically), especially cyber communities, which are becoming increasingly important to youths (as well as everyone else). Additionally, researchers need to take account of the overlapping cultures that youths belong to (such as national, regional, religious, and 'youth' cultures). Membership in and the importance of secondary groups are apt to differ by location; therefore, researchers need to theorize about and then examine these groups based on the country and region they are studying.

Researchers also need to examine the direct and indirect effects of social capital, looking at how social capital works to mobilize other (non-social) resources into capital. Also, scholars need to examine the transformation (mobilization) of social resources into social capital. Such work is imperative in illustrating the foundational importance of social capital.

Social capital is a key determinant of youths' well-being. Researchers increasingly have used the concept and, to a lesser extent, the theory over the past three decades. There are still many holes in the theory that need to be addressed. Consequently, there is a burgeoning need to examine the theory's limitations, both intra- and internationally. Currently, international and national groups are focusing their attention on the development of social capital in communities in order to improve youths' well-being. It is encouraging to see the growth of this theoretical–empirical–policy link, though a stronger theory needs to be developed in order to best guide policy and programmes.

## References

Bankston, C. and Caldas, S. (1998) 'Family structure, schoolmates and racial inequalities in school achievement', *Journal of Marriage and the Family*, 60: 715–23.

Bassani, C. (2007) 'Five dimensions of social capital theory as they pertain to youth', *Journal of Youth Studies*, 10: 17–34.

Bourdieu, P. (1986) 'The forms of capital', in J. Richardson (ed.) *Handbook of Theory and Research for the Sociology of Education*, New York: Greenwood Press.

Caldas, S. and Bankston, C. (1998) 'The inequality of separation: racial composition of schools and academic achievement', *Educational Administration Quarterly*, 34: 533–57.

—— (2001) 'Effect of school population socioeconomic status on individual academic achievement', *The Journal of Educational Research*, 90: 269–77.

Clinton, H. R. (1996) *It Takes a Village: And Other Lessons Children Teach Us*, New York: Touchstone.

Coleman, J. (1987) 'Families and schools', *Educational Researcher*, 16: 32–8.

—— (1988) 'The creation and destruction of social capital', *Journal of Law, Ethics and Public Policy*, 3: 375–404.

Ferguson, K. (2006) 'Social capital and children's wellbeing: a critical synthesis of the international social capital literature', *International Social Welfare*, 15: 2–18.

Hanifan, L. (1916) 'The rural school community center', *Annals of the American Academy of Political and Social Science*, 67: 130–8.

Lin, N. (2001) *Social Capital: A Theory of Social Structure and Action*, Cambridge: Cambridge University Press.

Morrow, V. (1999) 'Conceptualizing social capital in relation to the well-being of children and young people: a critical review', *Sociological Review*, 47: 774–65.

Portes, A. (1998) 'Social capital: its origins and applications in modern sociology', *Annual Review of Sociology*, 24: 1–24.

Portes, A. and Landolt, P. (1996) 'The downside of social capital', *The American Prospect*, 26: 18–21.

Putnam, R. (1999) 'Bowling alone: America's declining social capital', *Journal of Democracy*, 6: 65–78.

Ream, R. (2003) 'Counterfeit social capital and Mexican-American underachievement', *Educational Evaluations and Policy Analysis*, 25: 237–62.

—— (2005) 'Toward understanding how social capital mediates the impact of student mobility on Mexican-American achievement', *Social Forces*, 84: 201–24.

Thorlindsson, T., Bjarnason, T. and Sigfusdottir, I. (2007) 'Individual and community processes of social closure: a study of adolescent academic achievement and alcohol use', *Acta Sociologica*, 50: 161–78.

Vinken, H. and Ester, P. (2002) 'The culture of engagement: the promise of the internet', paper presented at the 2002 International Sociological Association World Congress, Brisbane, Australia.

Wellman, B., Haase, A., Witte, J. and Hampton, K. (2001) *Does the Internet Increase, Decrease, or Supplement Social Capital? Social Networks, Participation and Community Commitment*, Research Bulletin #6, Centre for Urban and Community Studies, University of Toronto.

# 10

# Disability, exclusion and transition to adulthood

*Sheila Riddell*

## Introduction

Disabled young people represent a significant proportion of those who find themselves excluded at an early age, and are likely to experience social marginalization throughout their lives. It has therefore become a policy priority to identify who they are, the nature of the exclusion they experience, in particular at various transition points, and what action is needed to support inclusion. As with many social policy issues, much depends on how 'the problem' is constructed and, in particular, the understandings of disability, exclusion and transition which are employed. In this chapter, current thinking in relation to these central concepts is explored and placed in a wider historical context. Evidence is drawn from recent research to illustrate the complex nature of the social categories employed and the diversity of experiences of young disabled people.

## Emerging understandings of disability

In the welfare states of developed countries, disability has often been defined in terms of administrative categories devised by social security or social services in order to determine access to benefits and services. For example, Stone (1984) noted that disability originated as an administrative category out of a collection of separate conditions understood to be legitimate reasons for not working. Major surveys conducted within the UK have sought to determine how many people are disabled by asking whether the individual has a long-term illness or disability which has an impact on their normal daily activities or ability to work. Surveys conducted in Scotland suggest that about 20 per cent of the adult population defines themselves as disabled, a relatively high proportion of the population compared with the rest of the UK. Statistics from a range of sources show an increasing incidence of disability with age. The Scottish Household Survey 2001, for example, showed that 40 per cent of people aged 65 or over reported a disability or long-term illness, in contrast to 5 per cent of people aged 16–24. Table 10.1 illustrates this increased incidence with age.

**Table 10.1** Adults with a disability or long-term illness by sex and age, 2001–02

|  | No disability or illness (%) | Disability (%) | Long-term illness (%) | Both disability and long-term illness (%) |
|---|---|---|---|---|
| Men | 82 | 7 | 7 | 4 |
| Women | 81 | 7 | 8 | 4 |
| 16–24 | 96 | 2 | 2 | 0 |
| 25–34 | 94 | 2 | 3 | 1 |
| 35–44 | 91 | 4 | 4 | 2 |
| 45–59 | 81 | 6 | 8 | 4 |
| 60–74 | 68 | 11 | 14 | 7 |
| 75+ | 55 | 19 | 18 | 9 |
| Total | 81 | 7 | 8 | 4 |

Source: Scottish Executive (2003).

The surveys referred to above adopt a categorical approach, assuming a dichotomy between disabled and non-disabled people. The Disability Discrimination Act 1995 also operates on the assumption that a distinction may be drawn between disabled and non-disabled people. Under the terms of the Act, a person is disabled if they have a physical or mental impairment which has a significant and long-term adverse effect on their ability to perform normal day-to-day activities.

This categorical view of disability has been challenged by the social model of disability, which drew a distinction between disability and impairment and emphasized the social relational nature of disability (see, for example, Oliver 1990). Within the social model, disability is seen as independent of impairment in that it is a product of the social context in which impairment is experienced. Recently, post-modern and post-structuralist writers have taken these arguments further, critiquing the taken-for-granted distinction between disabled and non-disabled people. Writers such as Corker and Shakespeare (2002), for example, have argued that disability should be seen as the ultimate post-modern category, since it is likely to be experienced differently depending on age, impairment, gender, ethnicity and environment. There is, therefore, an unresolved tension between those who work on the assumption that the categories of disabled and non-disabled are meaningful, having their basis in material reality, and those who see these categories as social constructs.

## Social exclusion and inclusion

Since the election of a Labour administration in the UK in 1997, reducing social exclusion and promoting inclusion have been major government preoccupations, in line with many other European governments. Young disabled people have been identified as a group particularly vulnerable to social exclusion, although this term does not have a fixed meaning. Levitas (1998) identified three particular political discourses associated with the concept of social exclusion and inclusion. The first discourse identifies poverty as the principal reason for social exclusion, and identifies economic redistribution as the most appropriate remedy. The second discourse deploys cultural rather than material explanations of social exclusion, suggesting that, regardless of their economic position, an individual or group may be socially excluded if they lack political and social recognition and respect. The remedy within this discourse is to change social attitudes, so that minority groups are no longer rejected by the wider society. The third discourse envisages lack of labour market attachment as the principal cause of social exclusion, and suggests that a greater degree of social inclusion will be achieved by encouraging or requiring individuals to participate in paid work. These discourses of social exclusion and inclusion are not mutually exclusive, but weave in and out of the welfare policies of developed countries. Within each discourse, it is evident that education, lifelong learning and access to employment are envisaged as playing a major role in promoting inclusion. For those at risk of social exclusion, particularly young disabled people, ensuring future economic independence is vital, but has often been an overlooked aspect of their education (Riddell *et al.* 2001).

## Emerging understandings of transition

As with disability and social inclusion, the meaning of transition to adulthood has shifted over time. Earlier work on youth transitions tended to be based on the assumption that the young person was leaving the malleable condition of youth in order to attain the relatively stable status and identity of adulthood. The life course was viewed as a series of stages which were linear, cumulative and non-reversible, with youth as the stage between childhood and adulthood, with an individual finally achieving a stable subjectivity and social being. In recent years this underlying image has been challenged by arguments about late modernity or post modernity, in which the idea of the stable subjective self is questioned (e.g. Lash and Urry 1993). The labour force of the post-modern economy is imagined as flexible, working on demand across different tasks with varying patterns of work, part-time work and unemployment, training and retraining, as production demands.

The post-modern view of transition coincided with, and was in part informed by, the global economic restructuring of the late 1970s which was driven by the massive increase in oil prices and, in many developed economies, made traditional industries such as mining and manufacturing suddenly appear to be uneconomic. One of the consequences of this economic restructuring was the loss of many male-dominated manual jobs and the virtual collapse (Bynner and Roberts 1991) of the traditional youth labour. Up to that point, young people could leave school at the minimum leaving age and undertake five-year apprenticeships leading into relatively stable trades or, as exemplified by Willis's 'lads', a series of unskilled jobs (Bynner and Roberts 1991; Willis 1977). In 1975, 60 per cent of 16 year-olds were in full-time employment but eight years later only 18 per cent were (Riddell 1998: 190) This has, in large part, been replaced by an 'extended transition' in which young people are increasingly engaged in a period of 'training' for up to ten years after the compulsory school-leaving age. For some 50 per cent of any cohort, this extended transition takes place in and through higher education while, for much of the other 50 per cent, this takes place through the ever extending net of vocational qualifications, part training, part extended job interview. This extended transition has been formalized in law so that parents are duty-bound to provide support for any child up to the age of 25 years who is undertaking education or training.

While much of the public debate about the restructuring of contemporary industrial societies has focused on the transformation of the state and the economy, there is a parallel discourse about the transformation of self. Individuals, it is argued, must choose between different possible identities, thus negotiating a broad variety of global and personal risks. Such risks are not randomly distributed, but are likely to adhere to class patterns with the poor attracting 'an unfortunate abundance of risks' whereas the wealthy 'can purchase safety, freedom from risk' (Beck 1992: 35). For young disabled people, risks are likely to be associated not only with social class, but with other aspects of identity, in particular, impairment. In the following sections, the post-school experiences and outcomes of two distinctive groups of young disabled people are presented, with the aim of underlining the contrasts between them which are related not only to their impairment, but also to their social class position.

## Post-school destinations and experiences of young people with learning difficulties

In Scotland, about 1 per cent of children are educated in special schools or units outside mainstream education. Whereas rural areas have always educated the majority of disabled children in mainstream settings, urban areas developed separate special schools from the 1950s onwards, and these still cater for a proportion of the school population who are particularly likely to come from socially disadvantaged backgrounds. Figure 10.1 contrasts the post-school destinations of Glasgow school leavers from special schools for children with moderate learning difficulties, compared with mainstream school leavers. It is worth

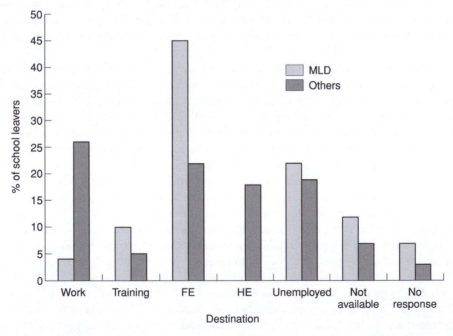

**Figure 10.1** Destinations of moderate learning difficulties (MLD) school and other school leavers in Glasgow, 2002.

Source: Careers Scotland.

noting that in the US, the term 'learning disabilities' is used instead of 'learning difficulties' to denote children with cognitive impairments which are of a global rather than specific nature.

These figures underline the way in which a special school education leads to a special post-school trajectory, leading the young person away from the labour market. About 45 per cent of special school leavers undertake courses in Further Education (FE) compared with 22 per cent of mainstream school leavers. While this might appear to be a positive outcome for the former, in fact the vast majority are in segregated classes providing life skills, whereas mainstream school leavers participate in vocationally orientated programmes designed to lead to employment. A much lower proportion of special school leavers move into employment (4 per cent compared with 26 per cent of the mainstream school population). And whereas 18 per cent of mainstream school leavers enter higher education – a figure which is significantly lower than the rest of Scotland – no special school leaver undertakes higher education. A higher proportion of special school leavers are counted as not available or fail to respond to requests for information.

A study carried out as part of the ESRC's Learning Society Programme (Riddell *et al.* 2001) underlined the problematic nature of post-school transitions for young people with learning difficulties. Education and training opportunities led away from the labour market and often involved ongoing cycles of retraining. Young people were forced to stay in the parental home or else lived in supported accommodation or hostels, reinforcing the status of perpetual child. Very few succeeded in developing independent autonomous friendships and relationships, and they had access to a very restricted form of social capital (ibid.). Even those from relatively privileged social class backgrounds failed to develop autonomous lives, suggesting that disability overrode social class in the distribution of risk. However, it is evident that disabled young people are far from being a homogeneous group, and, as discussed below, young disabled people who manage to access higher education demonstrate that disability does not automatically lead to restricted employment and social opportunities.

## Disabled young people in higher education

As noted above, disabled young people in higher education merit particular attention because their educational outcomes and life chances are markedly better than those of disabled young people who do not progress into higher education. Analysis of HESA data (Riddell *et al.* 2005) shows that disabled young people in higher education reflect the relative social advantage of the majority of higher education students, in particular those in the elite institutions.

However, in relation to the nature of their impairment, they are clearly very different from most young disabled people, with a growing proportion identifying themselves as having dyslexia (specific learning difficulties) and a very small proportion having physical or sensory impairments, mental health difficulties or personal support needs (see Table 10.2). Students with global learning difficulties are entirely absent.

Studies of the experiences of disabled undergraduates (ibid.) show that they experience difficulties in the transition to and experience of university, suffering from restricted social networks, limited physical access and academic pressure due to inaccessible learning materials. They tend to be concentrated in particular disciplinary areas, for example, dyslexic students are particularly likely to study art and design subjects. They are also less likely to obtain

**Table 10.2** Categories of disability used by HESA and percentages of undergraduates in each category in 1994/95 and 2002/03

| Type of disability | 1994/95 (%) | 2002/03 (%) |
| --- | --- | --- |
| Dyslexia | 15 | 49 |
| Blind/partially sighted | 4 | 3 |
| Deaf/hard of hearing | 6 | 4 |
| Wheelchair/mobility difficulties | 6 | 3 |
| Personal care support | 0.1 | 0.1 |
| Mental health difficulties | 2 | 3 |
| An unseen disability | 53 | 23 |
| Multiple disabilities | 5 | 4 |
| Other disability | 10 | 11 |

Source: Higher Education Statistics Agency (HESA).

the highest degree awards. Their chances of obtaining employment post-graduation are somewhat worse than those of non-disabled graduates, although the gap has been narrowing over recent years. For disabled students, it appears that disability still has a negative effect on higher education experiences and post-graduate outcomes, but their overall life chances are vastly better than those of young people with moderate learning difficulties attending special schools. This may be attributable both to their privileged social class position, but also to the particular nature of their impairment. Those with significant cognitive difficulties, it would appear, are particularly likely to experience social stigma and rejection, and the process of transition into adulthood underlines and intensifies their social marginalization.

## Policy responses to the needs of disabled young people

Policy responses to the needs of disabled young people underline their relatively disadvantaged state compared to non-disabled young people, but also the unequal distribution of risk within the group. As noted above, disabled students in higher education are, in general, a socially advantaged group and have a relatively high level of resource expended on them. The Disabled Students' Allowance was established in 1990 and provides funds for individual students to purchase the support they need, reflecting the additional costs of living and studying which they incur. While the funds available are inadequate to meet the needs of those with very significant impairments, such as those requiring 24-hour care, for the majority of students with less significant impairment, including those with dyslexia, the financial support is important both symbolically and practically. Disabled students' support services now exist in all higher education institutions in Scotland, and these provide assessment services and emotional support, as well as pressurizing academic staff to adapt their teaching and assessment practices. Since 2000, institutions have received premium funding from the Funding Councils in relation to the proportion of disabled students they educate who are in receipt of the Disabled Students' Allowance. This incentivizes the recruitment of disabled students, and also encourages a more rigorous approach to assessment of need. The success of these policies is evidenced by the growing proportion of disabled students in higher education in the UK and their relative success in the labour market. While the dangers of social exclusion have not been removed, they have been greatly ameliorated for this group.

By way of contrast, policy and provision for disabled young people who do not progress into higher education have arguably been less effective. The majority of young people in this group have cognitive learning difficulties and/or social, emotional and behavioural difficulties, and many have grown up in poverty or have been looked after by the local authority. Since the 1980s, FE colleges have run special programmes for young people with learning difficulties, but funds have been paid directly to the colleges by the Scottish Government and places have been capped so that demand far exceeds the resources available. This contrasts with the situation with regard to disabled students in higher education, where the young person is given the money to purchase their own support, and while there is a limit on the cash paid to any individual, funds for the Disabled Students' Allowance are not capped. As we have already noted, FE programmes for disabled young people tend to reinforce segregation rather than inclusion (Riddell et al. 2001) and lead on to further training programmes rather than employment.

There has been increasing concern about the position of young people who are not in education, training and employment (known as the NEET group), who in Scotland represent about 14 per cent of school leavers. Young disabled people are over-represented in this group, and, following the recommendations of the Beattie Committee on transitional support for young people with additional support needs (Scottish Executive 1999), a range of initiatives was set up to promote inclusion particularly in terms of accessing the labour market. The importance of employment was also reinforced by the Scottish Executive's review of services for people with learning disabilities (Scottish Executive 2000). Both committees recommended that key workers should be allocated to individuals to help them navigate the period of transition, and that the Careers Service and Local Enterprise Companies should play a much more active role. However, to date, there appears to have been little progress and the Scottish Executive conceded that it has been unsuccessful in its social justice goal of improving the post-school outcomes of disadvantaged young people (Scottish Executive 2004).

## Conclusion

The argument of this chapter has been that full social inclusion, associated with a successful transition to adulthood, has proved an elusive goal for many young disabled people, and that the situation for some groups may have worsened as transitions have become more protracted and complex, and the distribution of economic and social risks have become more polarized and linked to educational attainment. Nonetheless, as noted at the start of this chapter, disabled young people are not a homogeneous group and risks are unequally distributed among them. Young disabled people who enter higher education tend to be from socially advantaged backgrounds and have vastly better outcomes and life chances than others. The policy measures designed to promote their social and institutional inclusion are relatively generously resourced, are not cash-limited and have been largely successful. By way of contrast, young disabled people who do not make it into higher education tend to have different 'types' of impairment (generally learning difficulties and/or social, emotional and behavioural difficulties). They come from socially disadvantaged backgrounds and attract little respect and social recognition. The policy measures designed to promote their chances of social inclusion appear to have been largely ineffective, since there has been little reduction in the number of young people counted as NEET and their post-school outcomes have not noticeably improved. This suggests that there is a need to review the policy measures necessary to reduce disadvantage and disability in the first place, particularly the growing disparity between the richest and the poorest in developed countries.

## References

Beck, U. (1992) *Risk Society: Towards a New Modernity*, London: Sage.

Bynner, J. and Roberts, K. (eds) (1991) *Youth and Work: Transition to Employment in England and Germany*, London: Anglo-German Foundation.

Corker, M. and Shakespeare, T. (2002) *Disability/Postmodernity: Embodying Disability Theory*, London: Continuum.

Lash, S. and Urry, J. (1993) *Economies of Signs and Space*, London: Sage

Levitas, R. (1998) *The Inclusive Society: Social Exclusion and New Labour*, Basingstoke: Macmillan.

Oliver, M. (1990) *The Politics of Disablement*, Basingstoke: Macmillan.

Riddell, S. (1998) 'The dynamics of transition to adulthood', in C. Robinson and K. Stalker (eds) *Growing up with Disability*, London: Jessica Kingsley.

Riddell, S., Baron, S. and Wilson, A. (2001) *The Learning Society and People with Learning Difficulties*, Bristol: Policy Press.

Riddell, S., Tinklin, T. and Wilson, A. (2005) *Disabled Students in Higher Education*, London: Routledge.

Scottish Executive (1999) *Implementing Inclusiveness: Realising Potential: The Beattie Committee Report*, Edinburgh: Scottish Executive.

—— (2000) *The Same as You? A Review of Services for People with Learning Disabilities*, Edinburgh: Scottish Executive.

—— (2004) *Social Justice: A Scotland Where Everyone Matters: Indicators of Progress 2003*, Edinburgh: Scottish Executive.

Stone, D. (1984) *The Disabled State*, Basingstoke: Macmillan.

Willis, P. (1977) *Learning to Labour*, Farnborough: Saxon House.

# 11

# Young refugees

## *Elizabeth Heger Boyle*

## Introduction

Literature on youthful refugees addresses two distinct issues. First, scholars ask whether and how the refugee experience affects young people (sometimes, but not always, in comparison to other age groups). These scholars tend to focus on the trauma of the refugee experience. The work has tremendous potential for innovation because it represents the first foray into a new empirical realm. On the other hand, perhaps for the same reason, the literature in this area also tends to be under-theorized.

The second issue concerning youthful refugees is their post-refugee resettlement experience in a new country. This emphasis is part of the growing attention to youthful migrants and the children of migrants generally. Scholars have come to appreciate that 'acculturation' is a multi-generational process, and this makes the study of young people particularly important. Post-refugee resettlement research is better theorized than the effect of the refugee experience because it evolved as a way to test extensions of, and challenges to, older migration theories.

In this chapter, after discussing the history of refugees, I will elaborate on the work being conducted in each of these lines of inquiry, with a particular focus on Somali refugees and occasional references to other groups. The chapter concludes with a discussion of likely future trends in research on refugee youth.

## The history of international refugee law

Refugees are not simply people who have fled their homes. Rather, 'refugee' is a technical legal term that was created by an international treaty in 1951. It refers to people living outside their countries of origin who have a well-founded fear that they will be persecuted because of their race, religion, nationality, political affiliation, or some other group status. Only individuals who fit within this definition qualify for assistance from the international community when they resettle in new locations.

In practical terms, what this means is that many destitute people driven from their homes are not eligible for protection as refugees. For example, only people who have moved across an international border can claim refugee status. Although the trauma of displacement might be felt just as keenly by someone who is forced to move 200 miles within one country as by someone who moves 20 miles from one country to another, only the latter is a refugee. Furthermore, if a person was displaced by a tsunami, an earthquake, or out of fear of dying of starvation, she is not a refugee. Only individuals who face persecution meet the definition. In fact, although an estimated 32.9 million people were uprooted at the end of 2006, only 9.9 million of those individuals qualified as refugees (UNHCR 2007).

In addition, the formal requirements for refugee status are more likely to be met by adult men than children (or women). Traditionally, courts defined 'persecution' as something done by states. Because adult men are more likely than children to be engaged in the public sphere, they are also more likely to be oppressed in this traditional sense. Children may face grave dangers during conflicts, but these dangers may be diffuse and not directly associated with their 'membership' in some group. Danger itself is not enough to grant them formal refugee status. Likewise, although children are particularly susceptible to extreme poverty in a refugee situation because they may be separated from their adult caretakers, poverty is also an insufficient basis for granting refugee status. The system was set up with adult men in mind; this tends to work to the disadvantage of other groups.

The history of refugee law is also important because it illustrates changing ideas about children in international law. The 1951 refugee treaty did not incorporate special provisions for children. Children had to meet the same requirements as adults to qualify as refugees. In 1988, for the first time, the United Nations High Commissioner for Refugees created specific guidelines for dealing with child refugees. The guidelines emphasized the passive dependence of children and their need for special protection. A year later, a new international treaty addressed children's issues generally and made some specific references to refugee youth. However, this treaty (the Convention on the Rights of the Child) took a very different approach from the guidelines. It emphasized that children are independent agents with distinct preferences and rights. Thus, international law initially ignored children; when it began to address their needs, it first treated them as passive and dependent, but later treated them as more autonomous agents with rights.

These same transitions characterize the development of much international law in the twentieth century (Boyle *et al.* 2006). The most recent characterization of children as active agents under international law coincides with the rise of a similar perspective toward children within the social sciences.

The relatively recent creation of refugees as a formal legal category explains why social scientists only lately became interested in these individuals. Although sociologists have been studying migrants for a century, attention to refugees is much more recent. For scholars conducting research in this new area, an important question is whether voluntary migrants and refugees should be theorized separately (Hein 1993). The problem is that the legal distinction between refugees and other migrants is not necessarily socially meaningful. It is a laudable goal to develop social scientific theories that explain differences between groups of migrants, such as between migrants who are forced from their homes with little warning and migrants who are able to weigh their options and carefully plan their moves in advance. To do this, however, scholars cannot rely on the arbitrary legal definitions, but rather will have to identify independently socially meaningful distinctions between these groups.

## The refugee experience for children and youth

Young people who are forced to flee their homes face as much, or even more, hardship as older people. They may lose one or both parents, or other significant relatives, in the conflict or the flight. They are likely to have to assume greater household responsibility, such as finding food or caring for their younger siblings if their parents are killed or disabled. They often lose extended support networks in the general displacement of communities. Their education may be delayed or aborted because of the crises occurring around them. Because their lives suffer from upheaval during the most important socialization period of their lives, refugee children often suffer from mental health problems. There is a growing literature on the consequences of the refugee experience for young people. I will discuss a few illustrative studies here.

One focus of these studies is the mental health of refugees. Rousseau *et al.* (1998) found that refugees use dreams of the future as a tool to deal with the harshness of life in refugee camps. This can be very effective as a coping strategy, but it can also become an unhealthy obsession. Cindy Horst (2006) studied this phenomenon among Somali in the Dadaab refugee camp in Kenya. She found several factors that pulled individuals into these resettlement dreams, which Somalis call *buufis*. Poor living conditions in the camp and news of continuing conflicts in Somalia (undercutting chances of return) tended to promote *buufis*.

Although Horst did not discuss age variation specifically, young people appeared to be particularly affected by these resettlement dreams. She explained how, in Somali culture, young women and especially men are expected to travel as a way to gain education and life experience. Her analysis also suggested that younger individuals suffered more than adults because they did not have the life experience to imagine other alternatives to resettlement. For example, an older man told Horst that he was prompted to abandon *buufis* after witnessing the experience of his young nephew. His nephew had dreamed of moving to the United States, had put his life on hold in Kenya, and had made elaborate plans for what he would do after resettlement. When the US immigration agency failed to designate him a 'refugee', he was despondent and began to engage in bizarre behaviours. The young man had placed all his future aspirations on resettlement, while the older man was better able to distance himself from that future when he saw his nephew suffering. Once in the refugee camps, trauma and unsettledness can lead to mental illness; youth seem particularly susceptible.

Many of the outcomes of the refugee experience for young people are gendered. Young men may be viewed as potential combatants, which places them in mortal danger. Actual combatants may see them as a potential threat and kill them before they can be recruited into military service. Luling (2006) tells of young Somali men who were killed by members of their own clan because they had not learned and were unable to articulate their family connection in a moment of confrontation. For example, in a United Nations 'safe zone' in Srebrenica in the former Yugoslavia, Serbs slaughtered Bosnian boys over 12 along with all the adult Bosnian males (an estimated 8,000 individuals were killed) in 1995. Women and younger children were safely bussed out of the zone before the massacre began. Young male refugees are also at risk of being forcibly 'recruited' to participate in the hostilities. Here, an example is Somalia, where very young boys are actively participating in the country's civil war.

Girls and young women also face serious problems, but of a different nature. In times of turmoil, culture is often etched on the bodies of women and girls (Yuval-Davis 1997).

In other words, females bear the burden of showing that their society is civilized during war. Girls may be under enormous pressure to act and dress in particular ways. For example, after the civil war, Somali women in the refugee camps began to wear more conservative clothing than was typical prior to the war (Abdi 2007). Most wear a *jiilbab*, a long dress, covered with a *chador*, a long veil that covers the hair and neck and flows down to the waist. Rape has been widespread in the Dadaab refugee camp, and the hope is that the conservative clothing will make them generally less conspicuous to would-be rapists. Somali women and girls have also taken to wearing pants under the *jiilbab* as an additional physical barrier to rapists. The clothing signifies the community's civility and the individual woman's chastity, and it also provides (minor) impediments to would-be rapists. Children and youth, who may believe these clothing requirements are timeless rather than transitory, sometimes lead the enforcement of dress codes, harassing or stoning women who are not veiled (Hammami 1990).

The clothing is not a mere inconvenience; it is part of a package of disadvantage for females that particularly affects young girls. In Dadaab, girls may engage in prostitution or be vulnerable to sexual exploitation, sometimes by international aid workers, because of their extreme poverty (Abdi 2007). Female circumcision, which was widely practised in Somalia, is decreasing in most parts of the world, but appears to be stable or even be increasing in the Dadaab refugee camp (ibid.). Boys and girls are segregated and are being indoctrinated in the formal education system to believe that such segregation is normal (ibid.). Furthermore, as limited resources are restricting access to education, girls are disproportionately affected. Some parents are reluctant to send girls, particular as they reach the early teenage years, to coeducational schools. Middle East-based Islamic charities exacerbate these educational differences by providing scholarships mainly to boys (ibid.).

## Refugee children and youth after resettlement

While children often suffer disproportionately in the initial refugee experience, their flexibility and readiness to learn new skills can serve them well in the resettlement process. For example, they tend to pick up new languages and adapt to new social cues much more quickly and competently than their elders. This is one reason why recent migrant acculturation literature has focused specifically on 1.5 and second generation migrants, that is migrants who moved to a new country at a young age or who were born in a new country to immigrant parents.

Scholars once viewed acculturation as an either-or process. Migrants either became westernized or they did not. Today, theories of acculturation are more appreciative of the nuances of this process. First, cultures are diffuse and segmented. Scholars today believe that it is important to identify which particular variations of the host culture migrants adopt rather than view acculturation as an all or nothing process. Further, scholars today note that migrants may selectively retain some of their 'home' culture while still embracing portions of the host culture. For those young refugees who are fortunate enough to escape from the camps and resettle in Europe or the United States, successful resettlement depends on a number of factors. The factors that influence outcomes for young people are: (1) the experiences of the first generation; (2) the relationship between children and their parents, and their co-ethnic network; (3) barriers, such as discrimination, bifurcated labour markets, and inner-city subcultures which block upward mobility; and (4) family and community resources for combating those barriers

(Portes and Rumbaut 2001). In this section, I will consider how each of these relates to refugee children and youth.

In terms of refugees, two experiences of the first generation set these individuals apart from other migrants. First, formal refugees are legal migrants. They are legally entitled to live in the receiving country. This sets refugees apart from undocumented migrants. Although both types of individuals tend to be poor, refugees do not need to evade authorities and are somewhat less vulnerable to exploitation as a result. The second experience that is unique to refugees is that they are usually entitled to some financial support from the government. In the United States, the financial burden to support refugees is increasingly falling on their sponsors (often extended family), but the government continues to provide small amounts of aid in the form of subsidized English language classes, subsidized housing expenses, food stamps, etc. This support is minimal, but is important in comparison to the aid received by other migrant groups – that is, generally none at all. Both of these factors tend to provide the children of first generation refugees with some financial security.

In terms of the relationship between children and parents, refugees may be no different from other migrants. The first generation tends to have a more difficult time with the receiving society language than the 1.5 and second generations. This is good for the children because it facilitates their incorporation in the new country. However, there are also some potential drawbacks. The primary concern, which Portes and Rumbaut (2001) call 'dissonant acculturation' is that the child's knowledge of a new language and culture will so outstrip his or her parents' knowledge that the traditional family dynamic will be turned upside down. In other words, instead of the child relying on the parents to provide guidance, the parents become dependent on the child to navigate the new system. This can result in children shouldering too much responsibility early and making rash decisions with long-term negative consequences. The ideal situation, according to Portes and Rumbaut is for children and parents to learn the receiving society language at the same pace, with the parents providing guidance about which elements of the new culture the family will embrace. Portes and Rumbaut call this 'selective acculturation'. Wealthy, highly-educated immigrant families are the most likely to experience this type of acculturation. Generally, refugees are not wealthy or highly educated.

Role reversal in the family creates one obstacle to successful acculturation. Contextual factors provide other obstacles. These include racial, ethnic, or religious discrimination (see Waters 1999), blocked economic opportunities in the receiving country's labour market (see Bean and Stevens 2003), and, particularly in the United States, the adoption of a resistance-based counter-culture perspective toward the dominant ideas of the receiving country culture (see Waters 1999). Portes and Rumbaut (2001) propose that the best way to combat all of these barriers is with strong families and dense, supportive co-ethnic communities. Refugees often settle in the same community and provide support for one another (e.g., Fadiman 1997). For historical reasons, the connections between co-ethnics may vary and this also has an impact on the extent to which they can buffer children from the barriers to acculturation (Fuglerud and Engebrigtsen 2006). In terms of refugee resettlement communities, it is important to consider how the refugee experience itself may have weakened community ties (Boyle and Ali 2008). In any event, a strong community with a shared emphasis on education for the younger generation can pave the way through hardship and cultural misunderstandings to a successful outcome for young refugees in a new country.

## Conclusion and directions for future research

Much of the research relevant to young refugees touches on them only indirectly. Work on the refugee experience in general is not systematic in the selection of theories or uses no theories at all. This is unfortunate and impedes the systematic accumulation of knowledge in this area. One promising theoretical direction for this research would be to focus on the role youth play in cultural continuity and cultural change in the refugee context. This would complement and yet be theoretically distinct from the migrant resettlement literature. The resettlement literature is more theoretically developed and shows a greater appreciation of the importance of children for understanding accultura-tion. Especially as it relates to refugees, this work would benefit from greater attention to the role law plays is defining deserving or undeserving migrants and the consequences of these categorizations for acculturation.

## References

Abdi, C. M. (2007) 'Convergence of civil war and the religious right: reimagining Somali women', *Signs*, 33: 183–207.

Bean, F. D. and Stevens, G. (2003) *America's Newcomers and the Dynamics of Diversity*, New York: Russell Sage Foundation.

Boyle, E. H. and Ali, A. (2008) 'Culture, structure, and the refugee experience in Somali immigrant family transformations', *International Migration*. In press.

Boyle, E. H., Smith, T. and Guenther, K. (2006) 'The rise of the child as an individual in global society', in S. A. Venkatesh and R. Kassimir (eds) *Youth, Globalization and Law*, Stanford, CA: Stanford University Press.

Fadiman, A. (1997) *The Spirit Catches You and You Fall Down: A Hmong Child, Her American Doctors, and the Collision of Two Cultures*, New York: Farrar, Straus, and Giroux.

Fuglerud, O. and Engebrigtsen, A. (2006) 'Culture, networks and social capital: Tamil and Somali immigrants in Norway', *Ethnic and Racial Studies*, 29: 1118–34.

Hammami, R. (1990) 'Women, the *hijab*, and the *intifada*', *Middle East Report*, 164–5(May–August): 24–8, 71, 78.

Hein, J. (1993) 'Refugees, immigrants, and the state', *Annual Review of Sociology*, 19: 43–59.

Horst, C. (2006) '*Buufis* amongst Somalis in Dadaab: the transnational and historical logics behind resettlement dreams', *Journal of Refugee Studies*, 19: 143–57.

Luling, V. (2006) 'Genealogy as theory, genealogy as tool: aspects of Somali "clanship"', *Social Identities*, 12: 471–85.

Portes, A. and Rumbaut, R. G. (2001) *Legacies: The Story of the Immigrant Second Generation*, Berkeley, CA: University of California Press, and New York: Russell Sage Foundation.

Rousseau, C., Said, T., Gagne, M. and Bibeau, G. (1998) 'Between myth and madness: the premigration dream of leaving among young Somali refugees', *Culture, Medicine and Psychiatry*, 22: 385–411.

United Nations High Commission for Refugees (2007) *Global Trends: Refugees, Asylum-seekers, Retur-nees, Internally Displaced and Stateless Persons*, UNHCR, Division of Operational Services, Field Information and Coordination Support Section, June.

Waters, M. (1999) *Black Identities: West Indian Immigrant Dreams and American Realities*, Cambridge, MA: Harvard University Press.

Yuval-Davis, M. (1997) *Gender and Nation*, London: Sage.

# Part III

# Education

*Andy Furlong*

## Educational contexts and transitions

Patterns of educational involvement shape transitions in a variety of ways. Education may represent the starting point of a trajectory leading towards employment, but it also represents a resource that should provide young people with the skills to navigate future lives. The dynamic nature of change in contemporary society requires an ongoing debate over the organization of education, ensuring that the service delivered equips young people for the road ahead within a context of social justice. With education being delivered in different ways by national governments, international comparisons may be able to help researchers identify best practice and assess the extent to which local systems are meeting the needs of young people making transitions in increasingly complex contexts. The content of education, and particularly variation in the curricula offered to different socio-economic groups, also merits scrutiny, especially when we know that educational tracks form the bedrock of processes of social reproduction.

Issues relating to the forms of education suited to the needs of young people in late modernity are addressed by Wyn in Chapter 12. Arguing that the foundation for many educational systems that were laid in the 1950s still shape modern school contexts, she argues for a radical re-think of education, with priority being placed on involving young people as full participants in the learning process. Education is not simply about teaching skills and imparting subject-based knowledge; educating for modernity has to be about equipping young people with the skills to navigate careers that are increasingly characterized by change and precariousness. It should be about breaking down barriers between formal and informal learning, preparing young people for lifelong learning and helping them to invest in the identities that underpin successful transitions. While education in the Fordist era revolved around developing the hard skills that would help smooth the route to employment, in late modernity subjective competencies are the key to career success and young people who fail to become efficient navigators risk future marginalization.

Obviously some educational systems are more forward-looking than others, some countries organize education in ways that help smooth entry to employment, while others have much looser connections. In exploring the extent to which variation in transitional processes are shaped by institutional arrangements, in Chapter 13, Raffe highlights the difficulties in using international comparisons to identify transferable 'best practice'. Suggesting that it is possible to identify the 'key ingredients' that help shape successful transitions, he argues that both highly stratified systems and more open systems both make distinct contributions: the former promote smoother transitions to employment, while the latter may facilitate greater flexibility for young people.

Focusing on young people's subjective orientations to education, in Chapter 14, Biggart explores changing responses, highlighting processes of individualization and showing how subjectivities have become increasingly complex and multi-faceted. Biggart also shows the importance of 'identity work' and suggests that the class-based rejection of education that once characterized working-class positions has been replaced by new accommodations and ambivalences.

The increased engagement in secondary education and appreciation of the importance of credentials in modern labour markets have provided an incentive for young people to participate in higher education. Once the preserve of the privileged, higher education has become open to the masses, although less advantaged social groups still face barriers to access in all advanced societies. While inequalities of access are clearly visible and form the basis of discussions of the role of higher education in processes of social reproduction, in Chapter 15, Furlong and Cartmel highlight various forms of horizontal stratification that are somewhat more obscure, but which play a central role in the maintenance of inequalities, suggesting that even when they gain access to higher education, those from less well-off families have distinct (and poorer) higher educational experiences.

One of the forms of horizontal stratification discussed by Furlong and Cartmel relate to divisions between academic and vocational courses: divisions that are discussed more fully by Bills and Stone. Questioning whether vocationalism runs counter to the needs of young people in modern society, in Chapter 16, Bills reminds us that vocationalism has always been controversial. For some, the allocation of young people to vocational tracks in school may help reproduce inequalities by blocking opportunities for advanced study. At the same time, it may help smooth access to skilled employment for young people who lack the ability or aspiration for a university education. Once seen as a 'dumping ground' for low achievers, Stone argues, in Chapter 17, that, in the USA, the stigma attached to vocationalism has declined. Indeed, he shows that vocational education participation can be linked to improved educational outcomes both in terms of attainment in core skills as well as in the development of soft skills.

Together, the chapters in this section ask us to consider ways in which educational systems can be reformed in ways that provide young people with the skills that will help them navigate the complexity of late modernity. They also remind us of the need to reflect on the principles of social justice that should underpin educational systems and highlight entrenched inequalities.

# 12

# Educating for late modernity

*Johanna Wyn*

## Introduction

In this chapter, I argue that social change has far-reaching implications for education and learning, focusing on two central elements: (1) what young people need to learn in order to thrive in late modernity, and the meanings and uses of education that they are shaping; and (2) the emergence of new mass education systems designed to meet the needs of emerging economies. Young people's response to their changing world has involved new approaches to learning and diverse uses of both formal and informal education and learning. They expect to navigate their way in a context in which institutional pathways and structures are not able to provide certainty or predictability. This context of weakened institutional processes poses significant challenges for the design of a new generation of educational systems by governments. This is especially the case because many of the basic assumptions and structures on which the previous mass education sector (secondary education) is based have become increasingly less relevant in a post-industrial era.

In most Western countries, education systems underwent a significant transformation in the early 1950s, with the institutionalization of mass secondary education designed to serve the needs of industrially based economies. While different countries established distinctive secondary education systems, the options open to young people and the expectations of them were relatively similar within educational 'streams': technically based education or leaving school to go directly into the workforce prepared young people to work in 'manual' occupations and academically focused education, and engagement in further education at a university prepared young people for 'professional' or 'white collar' occupations. Educational policy was informed by the principle of structuring learning around: age-based groupings, normative expectations of young people at each age level, a deficit notion of 'student' and the strict separation of school and learning from the community, families and workplaces. The way young people were seen was based on an approach that focused on institutional control and normative behavioural expectations, supported by the rise of expert knowledge and the emerging discipline of developmental psychology.

The nature and meaning of education and learning are fundamentally implicated in the social changes that have occurred in Western countries over the past three decades.

The pace of change has meant that new skills need to be learned frequently and new circumstances regularly adapted to. Digital technologies have enhanced our capacity to access information and have created the expectation that individuals will learn how to use successive waves of new applications and forms of new technologies in personal life and in work settings. At the same time, the widespread emergence of flexible and precarious employment has meant that individuals need to be able to regularly learn new skills and take up new options in order to survive. This requirement for perpetual learning has meant that all stages of life require education and educating and all areas of life are learning opportunities. The idea of a 'totally pedagogised society' (Bernstein 2001), is taken for granted by young people as they actively seek to learn from their experiences, regardless of the setting (Stokes and Wyn 2007). For young people, formal education is only one site of learning and only one, sometimes marginal, part in a repertoire of learning approaches and sites. This means that in one sense young people themselves have begun to transform the contemporary meaning and uses of formal education and its relation to informal learning.

At the same time, governments have a significant stake in shaping education systems to ensure national competitiveness in a context where knowledge is a crucial resource as well as a commodity and an industry. Indeed, the Organisation for Economic Cooperation and Development (OECD) refers to contemporary 'globalising knowledge economies' that are connected locally and globally (OECD 2007a: 11). OECD reports, which inform the direction that educational policies in many Western countries take, promote the significance of higher education as the new mass education sector that will ensure economic development for nations, promote social cohesion and deliver prosperity to individuals (OECD 2007b). The completion of secondary education and participation in further or higher education have thus become normative for young people in late modernity. This development has put pressure on governments to transform education systems so that they are effective in meeting the needs of 'knowledge economies' (OECD 2007c). The completion of secondary education is normative and it is expected that young people will participate in post-compulsory education: tertiary education is the new mass education sector.

Responding to the changing nature of social, economic and political life in the post-industrial world, educational policies are focused on the production of young people who have the appropriate skills and dispositions to serve post-industrial economies. In late modernity, national investment in the education and training of young people is seen as a key to developing human and social capital as a basis for sustaining economic growth and competitiveness as well as for ensuring social inclusion and active citizenship. The transformation of education systems is based on the assumption that knowledge-based economies require workers with high levels of post-secondary and increasingly tertiary education who will return regularly to formal education throughout their working lives in order to stay competitive within labour markets that continuously require new sets of skills. Social groups that do not use education effectively will be marginalized from participation in economic activity (OECD 2007b).

Increasing rates of participation in secondary education (OECD 2007b), combined with high levels of immigration mean increased social diversity in school populations that include significant numbers of young adults. Yet, despite widespread recognition of the extent of social change, many elements of contemporary secondary school education, including ideas about young people and learning, date back to the 1950s. In general, secondary education has been more expanded than transformed, retaining older models and assumptions about the nature of learners and the form that education should take, and the new mass sector (tertiary education) has been grafted onto secondary education. In countries such as Australia, New Zealand and the UK, where traditionally school leaving was the major option for after compulsory schooling at the age of 15, the expansion of post-compulsory education has mainly involved an increase in participation by older students, leaving the educational frameworks and assumptions that have been inherited from an industrial era intact.

The challenge of educating young people in the period of late modernity and of constructing new education systems that meet their needs is thrown into clearer focus when we look at the nature of social change and how this has impacted on young people's lives. The following section describes key conceptual approaches that have contributed to an understanding of the impact of social change on both young people and education systems. In the final section, I turn to the issue of educating young people to live well in late modernity.

## Conceptual approaches

Many researchers draw on the work of Beck and Lau (2005), Beck and Beck-Gernsheim (2002) and Bauman (2001) to provide a conceptual framework for considering the characteristics of late modernity and the impact of social change on society. These theorists argue that late modernity is characterized by the fragmentation of traditions and a weakening of social institutions, creating a situation where people's identity has become a task rather than a given: 'Needing to *become* what one *is* is the hallmark of modern living' and the sources of collective identity that were characteristic of industrial societies have begun to lose their relevance (Beck and Beck-Gernsheim 2002: xv). Individuals have come to bear increasing responsibility for negotiating an unpredictable world. Despite the fact that social structures and processes that create inequality, marginalization and risk continue to have an impact on people's lives, these processes appear to be less visible to individuals. These ideas about the nature of late modernity and in particular the process of individualization, risk society and the disintegration of traditional institutions have influenced many youth researchers (e.g. Leccardi and Ruspini 2006; Furlong and Cartmel 2007; Henderson *et al.* 2007 and White and Wyn 2008). There is a convergence of opinion that the social, political and economic processes of late modernity have meant:

- Greater complexity of pathways through youth. Changes in the nature of work have meant that young people must make their own routes through education and work in new economies (Ball *et al.* 2000) and negotiate new sets of risks in the form of 'personal' choices (Furlong and Cartmel 2007). The individualization of the risks of changing skill requirements and the emergence of flexible and precarious labour markets mean that young people feel the need to hold their options open and to make decisions that enable them to balance being in the present with an orientation to the future. In many countries, the majority of young people are both workers and students, establishing a pattern in secondary school that they will continue throughout life (Stokes and Wyn 2007). The links between education and employment are also increasingly complex and unpredictable (Wyn 2006).
- Adulthood is achieved incrementally and earlier than for previous generations. The relevance of age as a marker of transition to adulthood is therefore reduced and new patterns of adult life are forged relatively early, breaking down clear

distinctions between youth and adulthood (Dwyer *et al.* 2005), as noted by youth researchers in many countries. For example, in Europe, Leccardi and Ruspini (2006) see a 'new' youth; in the United States, Arnett (2004) has identified 'emerging' adulthood and in the UK Henderson *et al.* (2007) explore the 'invention' of adulthood by young people. Paradoxically, in all Western countries, youth researchers note the increased length of time that young people spend in education, and the trend towards life-long education.

Other conceptual approaches have also been influential in understanding the relationship between young people and education in late modernity. These approaches draw on the work of Bourdieu (1976), Giddens (1991) and Foucault (1988) to provide a perspective on the identity-making that is a necessary element in young people's negotiation of risk societies. Various authors, especially those researching school-aged youth, have drawn on Giddens's concept of 'autobiographical thinking' which identifies the capacity to narrate and create one's self-history as a central aspect of identity-making, and reflexivity is seen as a central characteristic of contemporary identities (Giddens 1991: 54). Bourdieu's concepts of cultural and sub-cultural capitals have been especially influential in providing a framework for understanding the interaction between material structures (including class, race and gender) and individual subjectivities in the production and reproduction of social divisions through schooling. Researchers also draw on Foucault (1988) to understand the relationship between social conditions and the formation of dominant subjectivities and the ways in which social processes and institutions frame, reward and control the possibilities for being and becoming. These conceptual approaches have influenced significant research on young people and their relationship to schools and other institutions (e.g. Ball 2003; Davies 2004; Kelly 2006; McLeod and Yates 2006). This work provides evidence that:

- In late modernity, as some 'ways of being' have become more effective and better rewarded than others, new subjectivities have become dominant. Successful 'transition' into adulthood depends to some extent on being able to engage reflexively and continuously on the processes of constructing themselves as choice-makers and also to demonstrate that one takes individual responsibility, is resourceful and and 'reflexive, enterprising subject', regardless of age (Kelly 2006; McLeod and Yates 2006). Young people are required to hold a strong future orientation and to be able to plan the process of becoming an adult. These subjectivities are an essential resource base for the successful negotiation of education and labour markets in new economies, as well as other aspects of life.
- New forms of inequalities based on class and gender are emerging. There is evidence that the imperative to make and re-make oneself, to construct one's own biography and to 'be your own person' have had a stronger impact on some groups of girls than on boys (McLeod and Yates 2006). In particular, young women from high socio-economic backgrounds appear to be the most responsive to the need to perform required identities (as reflected in academic and labour market success). By contrast, young men from low socio-economic backgrounds are the least likely to be seen to need to be open to change with new times and continue to rely on 'ways of being' that served men from their communities well under different economic conditions and are the most likely to be unemployed (McLeod and Yates 2006; White and Wyn 2008).

The research evidence reveals that young people may in many respects be ahead of institutional change in gaining the skills and knowledge they need to be successful from diverse sources. Educational institutions are no different from other institutions in late modernity in that they have suffered a lessening of legitimacy and a tendency towards fragmentation and divergence. Formal education systems cannot make strong claims for legitimacy because learning itself has become de-institutionalized and individuals have become their own experts. Neither can they offer guarantees about the nature of the return on the investment of money and time that young people (and their families) are required to make in education, although some groups are able to use education more effectively than others. Young people understand that gaining educational credentials will not guarantee them a job and that they must actively construct education and employment biographies that make them attractive in precarious and changing labour markets. At the same time, the individualization of responsibility for creating effective pathways through education and work has heightened the relevance of subjectivities and the task of actively constructing one's biography. Identity work has become a significant new dimension of learning in late modernity.

## What and how young people need to learn

Addressing the question of what young people need to learn and what kinds of formal educational processes and curricula will prepare young people to live well in late modernity requires the acknowledgement that institutionalized, predicable connections between formal education and post-educational outcomes are increasingly non-existent and have become less relevant to many young people. While it is still the case that higher levels of education are almost universally associated with better pay and job security (OECD 2007b), the ways in which well-educated individuals secure 'good jobs' are diverse and the links between education and employment are complex (Dwyer *et al.* 2005). Even where young people graduate from a professional degree (e.g. teaching or commerce) research shows that they often do not expect to take up employment in their field of training or that they intend to work in that field for a short period of time only, seeking options to re-train in order to enter different fields of work (ibid.). The requirement (and often desire) to be self-navigators, and the extent of mobility mean that young people need to understand the nature of the social, economic and political world in which they are living, their relationships with others, locally and globally. Being good navigators requires a more conscious approach to personal development so that all young people have the capacity to see how their personal biography (past) has developed and how it may be constructed (in the present) to maximize their options (for the future).

While there has always been some degree of responsibility on individuals to make school–work connections and to determine what they should learn in order to live well, the scale of the shift towards dependence on individual resources in late modernity has made this a defining feature of young people's transitions. Meeting this requirement of educating for late modernity means that increasingly, responsibility for learning shifts from the educator to the educated. How young people learn in formal education settings may more closely approximate the way they learn outside of formal institutions, developing the capacities to understand what is relevant, how to access information, how to learn and how to develop knowledge.

Changes in the way in which young people live their lives mean that many elements of education systems that are currently taken for granted are becoming outmoded. There are many examples, including age-based learning, the idea of a mainstream, valuing young people for their future contributions only and the separation of learning institutions from communities. Exploring one of these examples in more detail, it is possible to see how the reliance on age as an organizing principle of formal learning reinforces a normative approach to learning and disconnects that learning from the context and circumstances of individuals and communities (and their diverse needs). This is especially the case with the senior years of secondary school, closing off options for young people and creating artificial barriers to learning.

The 'problem' of early school leaving is a case in point. In Australia, up to one quarter of young people leave school 'early' and do not complete their secondary education by the age of 18 (Wyn 2006). The age-based system of education means that it is very difficult for these young people to find their way back into formal education because very few schools offer a 'second chance' once the normative, education – age nexus is broken. The organizational reliance on age appears increasingly outmoded in an era of life-long learning. Even though schools contain increasing proportions of young adults, the assumptions are that they are being prepared to be decision-makers in their futures. Opportunities for participation in decision-making by young people in formal education (secondary or tertiary) remain limited, reflecting a view that young people are recipients of education not participants in learning. While this understanding of the role of young people may have served an industrial economy, it does not make a good fit with the demands of living in late modernity.

Educational systems have been slow to respond to the changes in young people's learning needs and some of the trends in contemporary educational approaches have further isolated education from broader social trends through an increased inward focus (e.g. standardized testing, ranking of school performance). Rather than developing a focus on the relationship between schools and other educational institutions to their communities and to the diverse needs of those who participate in these institutions, initiatives such as the 'school improvement' movement actively disavow the relationship between schools and their social and economic context and focus on universal notions of 'quality of teaching' based on normative expectations of a (disembodied) learner and a narrow notion of (academic) outcomes. New patterns of inequality of outcomes based on class, gender and geographic location are formed as some groups are more able than others to draw on cultural and economic resources to secure success.

In as much as educational policies have recognized the need for education to respond to social change, this has tended to rest on traditional assumptions about the preparation of young people to serve the economy. This has created a disjuncture between educational policies that continue to frame education within an industrial model (instrumental and vocationalist) and the requirements that young people themselves have for the capacity to be good navigators through new economies, to live well and to engage with complexity and diversity.

## Conclusion

Overwhelmingly, perspectives from youth research emphasize the impact of social change on how young people experience and manage their lives in late modernity. Young people need to be able to negotiate their way through both the uncertainty that is associated with personal transition and with wider social change. In general, the ideas that govern education have underestimated the impact of social change on young people's lives and their needs, focusing largely on the needs of new and emerging economies.

However, educational institutions are not immune to the effects of de-traditionalization processes that have characterized late modernity. Formal education is paradoxically becoming both more central and more marginal in young people's lives. Young people value formal learning because it offers the possibility of future success and security, and because educational credentials are increasingly a necessity for employment. However, learning in non-formal settings (for example, paid work in workplaces, in leisure pursuits, engaging in cultural activities and in voluntary work) is also valued by young people because, unlike formal education, it equips them to engage with immediate issues and rehearses the exercise of choice and decision-making. The fragmentation of social institutions (including families) also places greater emphasis on the conscious maintenance of personal relationships as a source of security. This means that personal and social development has achieved a new significance as an element of the skills and capacities that schools aim to support young people to learn.

As individuals bear the risks and responsibilities of wider social processes, they require increasingly sophisticated personal repertoires in order to manage. For young people, this means managing the balance between the future orientation of becoming and the necessity to have space to be in the present. Educational policies, from the OECD through to local educational jurisdictions, acknowledge the impact of social change and the need for a transformation of formal learning systems, but tend to focus exclusively on education as a tool for economic development. Educating for late modernity requires high levels of competence in literacies and numeracy, but it is selling young people short to focus on the preparation of labour market skills to ensure international competitiveness at the expense of the development of capacities that will enable all young people, regardless of gender or class background, to be successful navigators of uncertainty.

# References

Arnett, J. (2004) *Emerging Adulthood: The Winding Road from the Late Teens through the Twenties*, New York: Oxford University Press.

Ball, S. (2003) *Class Strategies in the Educational Market: The Middle Classes and Social Advantage*, London: RoutledgeFalmer.

Ball, S., Maguire, M. and Macrae, S. (2000) *Choice, Pathways and Transitions Post-16: New Youth, New Economies in the Global City*, London: Routledge/Falmer.

Bauman, Z. (2001) *The Individualized Society*, Cambridge: Polity.

Beck, U. and Beck-Gernsheim, E. (2002) *Individualization*, London: Sage.

Beck, U. and Lau, C. (2005) 'Second modernity as a research agenda: theoretical and empirical explorations in the "meta-change" of modern society', *The British Journal of Sociology*, 56: 525–57.

Bernstein, B. (2001) 'From pedagogies to knowledge', in A. Marais, I. Neves, B. Davies and H. Daniels (eds) *Towards a Sociology of Pedagogy: The Contribution of Basil Bernstein to Research*, New York: Peter Lang.

Bourdieu, P. (1976) 'The school as a conservative force: scholastic and cultural inequalties', in R. Dale, G. Esland, and M. MacDonald (eds) *Schooling and Capitalism: A Reader*, London: Routledge and Kegan Paul.

Davies, B. (2004) 'Identity, abjection and otherness: creating the self, creating differences', *International Journal in Equity and Innovation in Early Childhood Education*, 2: 58–80.

Dwyer, P., Smith, G., Tyler, D. and Wyn, J. (2005) *Immigrants in Time: Life-Patterns 2004*, Research Report 27, Melbourne: Youth Research Centre.

Foucault, M. (1988) 'Technologies of the self', in L. H. Martin, H. Gutman, and P. Hutton (eds) *Technologies of the Self: A Seminar with Michel Foucault* (eds) London: Tavistock Publications.

Furlong, A. and Cartmel, F. (2007) *Young People and Social Change: New Perspectives*, 2nd edn, Maidenhead: Open University Press.

Giddens, A. (1991) *Modernity and Self Identity: Self and Identity in the Late Modern Age*, Cambridge: Polity.

Henderson, S., Holland, J., McGrellis, S., Sharpe, S., Thomson, R. with Grigoriou, T. (2007) *Inventing Adulthoods, A Biographical Approach to Youth Transitions*, London: Sage.

Kelly, P. (2006) 'The entrepreneurial self and "youth at-risk": exploring the horizons of identity in the twenty-first century', *Journal of Youth Studies*, 9: 17–32.

Leccardi, C. and Ruspini, E. (eds) (2006) *New Youth? Young People, Generations and Family Life*, Aldershot: Ashgate.

McLeod, J. and Yates, L. (2006) *Making Modern Lives*, Albany, NY: State University of New York Press.

OECD (2007a) *Higher Education and Regions: Globally Competitive, Locally Engaged*, Paris: OECD.

—— (2007b) *Education at a Glance*, Paris: OECD.

—— (2007c) *No More Failures: 10 Steps to Equity in Education*. Paris: OECD.

Stokes, H. and Wyn, J. (2007) 'Young people's identities and making careers: young people's perspectives on work and learning', *International Journal of Lifelong Education*, 26: 495–511.

White, R. and Wyn, J. (2008) *Youth and Society: Exploring the Social Dynamics of Youth Experience*, 2nd edn, Melbourne: Oxford University Press.

Wyn, J. (2006) 'Youth transitions to work and further education in Australia', in P. Cartwright, J. Chapman and E. McGilp (eds) *Lifelong Learning, Participation and Equity*, Dordrecht: Springer.

# 13

# Explaining cross-national differences in education-to-work transitions

*David Raffe*

## Introduction

Indicators of 'successful' transitions between education and work, such as youth employment rates, vary widely across countries. So do other processes and outcomes of transition such as the duration of transitions, the speed with which new entrants converge towards adult labour-market patterns, the association between education and employment outcomes and social, gender and ethnic inequalities. These variations are not all due to compositional factors such as the different educational distributions of young people in each country. Nor can they all be attributed to the macroeconomic context, such as different national employment rates. At least some of the variation in countries' transition processes and outcomes reflects what researchers have variously called 'institutional arrangements' (Kerckhoff 1995), 'institutional effects' (Shavit and Müller 1998), 'transition systems' (Rosenbaum *et al.* 1990), 'coordination regimes' (Hillmert 2002) and 'institutional filters' (Blossfeld *et al.*, 2005). Here I use the term 'transition system' to describe 'the relatively enduring features of a country's institutional and structural arrangements which shape transition processes and outcomes' (Smyth *et al.* 2001: 19). In this chapter, I describe some of the main ideas and achievements of research on transition systems, drawing especially on analyses of longitudinal transition surveys.

## Examples of transition-system research

The different terms for transition system express broadly similar ideas, including the tendency for education-to-work transitions to vary across countries, the importance of educational, labour market and other institutions in explaining this variation and the path-dependence of national development. Nevertheless the variety of terminology reflects the range of disciplinary and theoretical traditions on which research into transition systems has drawn. Below I describe some of these research traditions and give examples of the studies they have influenced.

## The sociology of social stratification and social reproduction

Educational attainment and the first job entered after leaving education are important influences on future life chances, and they help to reproduce inequalities from one generation to the next. Moreover, their importance appears to vary across countries. As a result, sociologists studying the process of social stratification have examined the transition from education to work as a crucial stage in this process. One of the main studies in this tradition was led by Shavit and Müller (1998). Shavit's earlier work included a comparison (with Blossfeld) of educational inequalities in 13 countries; Müller had led a comparative study of social mobility in industrial nations with Erikson and Goldthorpe. Their transition research included 14 national case studies of the relationship of educational attainment to first occupation and early unemployment, and a comparison of the 14 countries which showed that this relationship was systematically related to four characteristics of education systems: standardization; stratification; the occupational specificity of vocational education; and the relative size of the tertiary sector. Another stratification researcher who turned his attention to education-to-work transitions was Kerckhoff (1995; 2000). Kerckhoff showed how the 'status attainment' approach, characterized by path models of individual progress and sometimes criticized for its individualistic orientation, could take account of macro- and meso-level influences by relating transition processes to features of the institutional context. For example, countries differed in the extent to which young people could increase their qualifications after entering the labour market (high in Britain, limited in France and Germany with the USA in between) and in rates of early work-life mobility.

## Life course perspectives

In showing how transition systems shaped sequences as well as outcomes of transition, Kerckhoff's work also exemplified a second strand of research, the sociology of the life course. This shared many of the concerns of stratification research but saw education-to-work transitions as aspects of a phase in the life cycle. Life-course researchers drew attention to the increasing duration, complexity and variability of transition sequences and the declining importance of 'normal biographies'. Moreover, education-to-work transitions interacted with other transitions to adulthood, including family, housing and lifestyle transitions. A classic study in the life-course tradition followed a cohort of young people in two English and two German towns through the final years of education and the first years in the labour market, using qualitative and quantitative research methods (Evans and Heinz 1994). Only recently have researchers acquired the comparative data and the conceptual frameworks with which to apply life-course perspectives to comparisons of larger numbers of countries (Blossfeld et al. 2005; Brzinsky-Fay 2007).

## Labour-market analysis

A third strand of research is the comparative analysis of labour markets by institutional economists and sociologists. Maurice et al. (1986) compared French and German workplaces and distinguished two types of space: qualification space (Germany) and organizational space (France), in which entry to employment and the relationship between qualifications and work were governed by different 'logics'. Their 'societal analysis' approach drew attention to the need to compare social institutions or processes – including education-to-work transitions – in their societal contexts. A closely related influence was the work on labour-market segmentation by writers such as Marsden (1986). National labour markets varied in the extent to which they were organized on occupational, internal or competitive lines. This, together with the level and mode of state regulation, affected the ways in which young people (and different categories of young people) were included or excluded from national labour markets. These ideas were explored in an early collection of comparative studies by economists and other social scientists edited by Ryan *et al.* (1991).

## Network analysis

A further influential strand is network theory, which has been used to explain job-finding processes and information flows about jobs and workers. Network analysis has tended to focus on micro-level relationships between individuals, but Rosenbaum *et al.* (1990) showed that it could be applied to macro-level differences between countries by distinguishing personal and institutional networks. The institutional networks connecting education and employment differed between countries, generating different transition patterns. The German apprenticeship system and Japanese school–employer linkages were contrasting examples of institutional networks which supported smooth transitions between education and the labour market; such institutional networks were present to a lesser extent in British training schemes but tended to be absent in the United States.

## Theories of globalization and social change

Some transition researchers (including Shavit and Müller 1998, described above) have used their analysis of institutional effects to test predictions of cross-national convergence based on theories of modernization, industrialism or globalization. The GLOBALIFE project used a collaborative methodology similar to Shavit and Müller's with participants representing 14 countries (Blossfeld *et al.* 2005). It examined how countries' 'institutional filters' – their education systems, employment systems, welfare regimes and family systems – mediated the impact of globalization and the uncertainty associated with it on transitions to adulthood, for example, on the timing of labour-market entry, the formation of stable relationships or becoming a parent. The project endorsed a transformationalist view in which the role of nation-states was changed but not removed by globalization.

## Policy analysis

As youth unemployment grew in the 1970s and 1980s, there was increased policy interest in reforming education and training to facilitate smoother transitions and to enhance national competitiveness in the new global economy. Cross-national comparisons were used to identify the most effective institutions and practices, especially in vocational education and training and in provision for early school leavers. Apprenticeships received particular attention. Young people experienced smoother transitions to work in countries with large apprenticeship systems, such as Germany, than in many other countries. However, attempts to replicate German-style apprenticeships in other countries proved largely unsuccessful. And some countries without apprenticeship systems, such as Japan, also achieved very successful transitions. International comparisons could not, it appeared, be used to identify transferable best practice. Such a conclusion would not have surprised the 'societal analysis' school, which stressed the need to see institutions such as apprenticeship in their national context, or theorists such as Rosenbaum *et al.* who presented the German apprenticeship system and Japanese school–employer linkages as alternative examples of effective institutional networks. A more sophisticated approach to comparative policy analysis emerged, exemplified by the OECD's Thematic Review of 'The Transition from Initial Education to Working Life', which used comparisons to identify the more fundamental 'key ingredients of successful transition systems' rather than specific institutions or policies to transfer. Based on case studies of 14 countries, it identified six key ingredients: a healthy economy; well-organized pathways that connect initial education with work and further study; widespread opportunities for workplace experience to be combined with education; tightly knit safety nets for those at risk; good information and guidance; and effective institutions and processes (OECD 2000).

## Dimensions, dichotomies and typologies

Despite its origins in diverse research traditions, transition-system research is to some extent unified by a common conceptual framework (Hannan *et al.* 1996; Raffe 2007). One element of this framework consists of the dimensions, dichotomies and typologies used to classify and categorize transition systems; another consists of the transition processes and outcomes which these systems shape. I discuss these elements below.

Researchers studying the effects of transition systems follow either an inductive or a deductive approach. The inductive approach compares transition patterns in different countries, and then looks for country-specific explanations for the differences that it finds. An example is the CHEERS project (*Careers after Higher Education: a European Survey*), which surveyed higher education leavers in 12 countries in the late 1990s (Teichler 2007). The deductive approach starts with a theoretical model of institutional differences and their effects on transitions, and then compares actual transition patterns to test the predictions of this model. Examples include the study by Shavit and Müller and the GLOBALIFE project, both described above, and Allmendinger's (1989) study which introduced the concepts of the stratification and standardization of education systems. The deductive approach has typically specified 'dimensions' of transition systems (such as stratification and standardization) whose effects on processes and outcomes of transitions are tested empirically. These dimensions include:

- characteristics of education and training systems, such as:
  - stratification;
  - standardization;
  - the size of the higher education sector;
- the scale of vocational education and training (VET);
  - the principal mode of VET (school-based or apprenticeship);
  - the occupational specificity of VET;
- characteristics of labour markets, such as:
  - the relative importance of occupational, internal and competitive labour markets;
  - the extent and nature of labour-market regulation;
- the nature and strength of institutional linkages connecting education and the labour market;
- dimensions reflecting other societal institutions, such as the family system and social welfare system.

This is not a complete list, but it still includes more dimensions than there are countries in many comparative studies. This makes it hard to test the relative importance of different dimensions through comparative analysis: 'degrees of freedom' are quickly exhausted. Researchers have responded to this problem by conducting more detailed comparisons which examine the processes underpinning each dimension, or by looking for connections between dimensions and developing simpler typologies.

Several dimensions are correlated. For example, occupational labour markets tend to be associated with specific vocational training and often with apprenticeship; education systems with large and vocationally specific vocational training sectors tend to be stratified; and the size of the higher education sector is often used as an (inverse) indicator of stratification. Hannan *et al.* (1996) reviewed the transition–system literature for the OECD's Thematic Review, and identified three dimensions as particularly important: standardization; stratification (or differentiation); and linkages with the labour market. Countries tended to cluster along the diagonal of the matrix based on these dimensions; much of the variation in transition systems could be understood as a single over-arching dimension or continuum, represented by this diagonal.

Other researchers reached similar conclusions. Reviewing the field in 2000, Kerckhoff (2000) described two types of transition systems. Type 1 was highly stratified and standardized, with large vocational sectors providing occupationally specific training. There were strong links between education and the labour market, and occupational labour markets dominated. Type 2 societies had more open education and training systems with weaker links between education and occupation. Germany was the paradigm example of the first type and the United States of the second. Many European countries, including France and the UK, were intermediate between these two types, suggesting that the typology could be better understood as a continuum or over-arching dimension along which transition systems could be placed, rather than a simple dichotomy.

The contrast between Type 1 and Type 2 summarized many of the empirical research findings before 2000. Young people in Type 1 systems specialized progressively through their educational careers. Transitions were smoother, more structured and faster, in the sense that the labour-market situations and behaviours of new entrants converged more quickly with those of experienced workers. Education and occupational outcomes were more tightly matched – horizontally and vertically – and skills were more important than experience in gaining access to employment. Vocational qualifications had value, especially for gaining access to skilled rather than unskilled manual jobs. Type 2 systems, by contrast, were more open, with more opportunities to change direction; transitions were less determined by social or educational origins, vocational qualifications were less important in the labour market and employment experience was more important. Some researchers argued that they engendered a greater sense of agency and enterprise.

However, much of this research was based on a small number of countries, in particular Canada, France, Germany, Japan, the UK and the USA. As more countries were included in comparative analyses, more complex typologies proved necessary. These needed to take account of dimensions such as the degree of labour-market flexibility or regulation, or the role of family systems, which were not adequately reflected in the single continuum described above. The CATEWE project (Comparative Analysis of Transitions from Education to Work in Europe) analysed national school–leaver survey data from five countries and European Labour Force Survey (ELFS) data for 15 European Union countries (Smyth *et al.* 2001; Müller and Gangl 2003). It found two main types of transition system in northern Europe, based respectively on occupational and internal labour markets, which were broadly similar to Kerckhoff's Types 1 and 2; but it also identified a third, southern European type characterized by inflexible labour markets and strong family support for young people's transitions. Other researchers found further distinctive types in central and eastern Europe (Kogan and Unt 2005) and in the countries of the former Soviet Union (Roberts 2006).

But even more detailed typologies were unable to capture all the variation in countries' transition systems. Countries varied widely even within the types identified by the CATEWE project. Moreover, typologies tended not to be robust; different studies generated different typologies depending on their methods and criteria. The initial report of the OECD Thematic Review, based on five countries, proposed a dichotomy similar to Kerckhoff's Types 1 and 2; the final report, based on 14 countries, rejected typologies in favour of a dimensions approach. Typologies are still used in the academic literature, but more cautiously; they have some explanatory value, and they can be useful for documenting difference and change, but their main value is heuristic. As ideal types, they help us understand the inner 'logics' of different transition systems.

## Transition patterns

National transition patterns are typically the dependent variables of comparative research on transition systems. That is, researchers have used the dimensions and typologies described above to explain aspects of transition such as:

- aggregate labour-market outcomes such as the (un)employment rate or occupational distribution;
- the association between education and labour-market outcomes, including the labour-market returns to educational level, the relative returns to general and vocational education, and the 'match' between occupation and field of study;
- gender, social and ethnic inequalities;
- flows between education, work and other statuses;
- the speed with which new entrants' patterns of employment and mobility converge with those of adults;
- subjective outcomes, including the perceived relevance of education to employment and the development of individual agency and self-efficacy.

These *national* transition patterns are in turn based on models of *individual* transitions of varying degrees of complexity. Many comparative studies have been based on a linear transition model which, at its simplest, involves a single step from initial education to first job, sometimes separated by a period of unemployment. There are practical reasons for this simple approach. Data sources typically include measures of initial education and first job, but even if they cover transition sequences in detail, as in the national school-leaver surveys used by the CATEWE project, they use nationally distinctive categories, concepts and time scales to describe them, making direct comparisons difficult.

The one-step transition model used by transition researchers raises two problems. First, it is difficult to define this single step in terms that are comparable and 'neutral' with respect to transition systems. When does a young person complete 'initial education'? When they cease studying full-time or when they achieve their highest qualification, perhaps through part-time study or workplace training? Does it include breaks in education? Similarly, what is a young person's 'first job'? Is it the first job ever entered, or the first job entered after leaving initial education? Is an apprenticeship a job? Do short-term, part-time or casual jobs count? And so on. These are not neutral questions: the answers may influence the conclusions of comparative transition studies. For example, the measured outcomes of apprenticeship-based transition systems may depend on whether apprenticeships are classified as jobs or as education. No single transition event such as first job can be defined neutrally with respect to transition systems because its significance will depend on the transition sequence of which it is part, which is in turn shaped by national institutions. And this is the second problem with the one-step transition model: it distorts reality, because it ignores the character of the education-to-work transition as a prolonged process, involving complex and variable sequences of transitions within and between education and the labour market, which may include transitions in both directions between education and work as well as dual status which combines the two and intermediate statuses between them.

The ideal study would compare transition sequences rather than single transition steps, but this is not easy, especially for large numbers of countries. The area-based Anglo-German study (Evans and Heinz 1994) used a comparative case-study approach, which described transition sequences within each country using country-specific terms and in sufficient qualitative detail to demonstrate the shaping role of national institutions. Scherer (2001) pioneered a quantitative approach which applied optimal matching techniques to household panel data for two countries. Brzinsky-Fay (2007) extended this approach to ten countries: monthly data on five statuses during the first five years in the labour market were used to identify 'labour market entry sequences' which varied across countries.

## Ways forward

The future of transition-system research may lie in developments at the micro, meso and macro levels of analysis. At the micro level it is likely to reflect the growing influence of the sociology of the life course and of policy interests in lifelong learning. The recent quantitative work comparing transition sequences, briefly described above, represents an important line of development. This approach could be extended to study transition sequences within the education system – between levels and types of education and training – as well as within the labour market. Hitherto the comparative analysis of educational pathways has been largely separate from the comparative analysis of transitions within the labour market. It could also be extended to explore the connections between education-to-work transitions and other transitions to adulthood, including family, household and lifestyle transitions. Further research directions may be driven by current policy interests in agency, career self-management and active citizenship, for example, to explore whether more open transition systems promote these qualities.

The meso level represents a gap to be filled. A body of research concerned with the effects of institutions has paid remarkably little attention to the ways in which institutions such as schools and companies actually function as organizations. Despite the theoretical interest in linkages between education and employment and in the practices of employers in different labour markets, there have been few cross-national studies of employer behaviour in relation to education-to-work transitions. Organizations which mediate between education and the labour market vary widely between transition systems, but have been neglected in comparative research. For example, there is little comparative evidence on the impact of different models of providing career education and guidance, despite growing policy interest in the issue.

The macro level presents the greatest challenge. The research field still lacks concepts of transition systems which reflect their diversity and have currency beyond the handful of well-researched North American and Western European societies. It also needs to conceptualize and explain changes in transition systems themselves, such as the changes observed in the former communist countries of central and eastern Europe and in other countries including Ireland and Mexico. Changes in transition systems pose several challenges for the research. They pose a methodological and conceptual challenge, of how to measure such changes and how to distinguish between changes in observed patterns of transition and changes in the institutional arrangements which shape these patterns. Second, they challenge the notion of transition systems as sources of national path-dependence, since transition systems themselves appear to change in response to wider social forces. Third, they challenge researchers to explain how and why transition systems change, and especially to determine the relative influence of policy decisions or other factors internal to a country, compared with cross-national 'global' influences. And finally, they challenge transition-system researchers to move beyond a comparative methodology which treats societies as independent, autonomous units of analysis, towards approaches which focus on their mutual influences and interrelationships. The future of transition-system research may depend on how it rises to these challenges.

## References

Allmendinger, J. (1989) 'Educational systems and labour market outcomes', *European Sociological Review*, 5: 231–50.

Blossfeld, H-P., Klijzing, E., Mills, M. and Kurz, K. (eds) (2005) *Globalization, Uncertainty and Youth in Society*, London: Routledge.

Brzinsky-Fay, C. (2007) 'Lost in transition? Labour market entry sequences of school leavers in Europe', *European Sociological Review*, 4: 409–22.

Evans, K. and Heinz, W. R. (eds) (1994) *Becoming Adults in England and Germany*, London: Anglo-German Foundation.

Hannan, D., Raffe, D. and Smyth, E. (1996) 'Cross-national research on school to work transitions: an analytic framework', paper to OECD, Paris.

Hillmert, S. (2002) 'Labour market integration and institutions: an Anglo-German comparison', *Work Employment and Society*, 16: 675–701.

Kerckhoff, A. (1995) 'Institutional arrangements and stratification processes in industrial societies', *Annual Review of Sociology*, 21: 323–47.

—— (2000) 'Transition from school to work in comparative perspective', in M. Hallinan (ed.) *Handbook of the Sociology of Education*, New York: Kluwer.

Kogan, I. and Unt, M. (2005) 'Transition from school to work in transition economies', *European Societies*, 7: 219–53.

Marsden, D. (1986) *The End of Economic Man?* Brighton: Wheatsheaf.

Maurice, M., Sellier, F. and Silvestre, J-J. (1986) *The Social Foundations of Industrial Power: A Comparison of France and Germany*, Cambridge, MA: MIT Press.

Müller, W. and Gangl, M. (eds) (2003) *Transitions from Education to Work in Europe: The Integration of Youth into EU Labour Markets*, Oxford: Oxford University Press.

Organisation for Economic Co-operation and Development (OECD) (2000) *From Initial Education to Working Life: Making Transitions Work*, Paris: OECD.

Raffe, D. (2007) 'The concept of transition system', paper presented at European Research Network on Transitions in Youth, Ghent, September.

Roberts, K. (2006) 'The career pathways of young adults in the former USSR', *Journal of Education and Work*, 19: 415–32.

Rosenbaum, J., Kariya, T., Setterstein, R. and Maier, T. (1990) 'Market and network theories of the transition from high school to work', *Annual Review of Sociology*, 16: 263–99.

Ryan, P., Garonna, P. and Edwards, R. (eds) (1991) *The Problem of Youth*, London: Macmillan.

Scherer, S. (2001) 'Early career patterns: a comparison of Great Britain and West Germany', *European Sociological Review*, 17: 119–42.

Shavit, Y. and Müller, W. (eds) (1998) *From School to Work*, Oxford: Clarendon Press, pp. 1–48.

Smyth, E., Gangl, M., Raffe, D., Hannan, D. and McCoy, S. (2001) *A Comparative Analysis of Transitions from Education to Work in Europe (CATEWE): Final Report*, Dublin: ESRI. Online. Available: www.mzes.uni-mannheim.de/projekte/catewe/publ/publ_e.html (accessed 27 July 2007).

Teichler, U. (2007) 'Does higher education matter? Lessons from a comparative graduate survey', *European Journal of Education*, 42: 11–34.

# 14

# Young people's subjective orientations to education

*Andy Biggart*

## Introduction

One of the central concerns of the sociology of education since its inception has been to document the nature of educational opportunities, inequalities and patterns of social reproduction. However, it was not until the 1970s with the theoretical development of interpretive approaches that young people's subjective orientations to education first became a major concern of research. Since then, the study of pupil cultures or young people's perspectives towards education has been a developing field, whereby not only have theoretical perspectives developed in terms of sophistication, but they have helped to document the changing nature of young people's cultural responses to the major shifts that have occurred in educational and occupational contexts over the past few decades.

## Early beginnings in the study of educational subjectivities

Early work on subjective orientations to education can be traced back to Werthman (1963) in the United States, who rather than coming from an educational perspective was working within the discipline of the sociology of deviance. His study of urban gangs in America challenged the traditional sociological view of the time that delinquent working-class pupils faced a problem of a monolith of middle-class norms and values against which they fared badly. Instead, he argued that gang members' responses within the classroom were predicated on the perceived fairness of individual teachers in response to individual grades. In this respect, behaviour or delinquency in school was perceived as both variable between teachers and one that appeared predicated on a perceived sense of social injustice.

In the UK, early interest in educational subjectivities stemmed from the influential work of Hargreaves (1967) and Lacey (1970) and their social systems approach. They argued that the emergence of different pupil subjectivities within the school could be understood by differentiation and polarization theory. Hargreaves, for example, follow-ing the re-organization of schooling along comprehensive lines, highlighted how streaming of ability within the school (differentiation) influenced teachers' perceptions and interactions with pupils, which in turn led to the emergence of two polarized pupil subcultures that he labelled 'academic' and 'delinquescent' Those within the academic subculture were seen as orientated to the values of the school and the teachers while the 'delinquescent' held polar opposite values that were negatively orientated.

Prior to this, there had been limited research into the study of young people's subjective responses to education, but the emergence of new interpretative approaches within the sociology of education led to a bourgeoning field of empirical study into pupil cultures located within the confines of the school. This was most evident during the 1970s when a number of influential studies highlighted patterns of cultural resistance particularly among working-class youth. One strand of this work focused on the institutional frameworks of the school and was primarily descriptive, with its focus on micro level processes within and outwith the classroom. This further developed the early work of Hargreaves and the way in which the organization of schooling, through allocating pupils to different bands or streams, led to the development of pro- and anti-school cultures. The other strand of work took this a step further, and while it also adopted an ethnographic approach, tried to connect the micro processes observed among young people to a broader macro framework. This line of work is mostly commonly associated with Paul Willis and his classic study, *Learning to Labour: How Working Class Kids Get Working Class Jobs*, which remains an important reference text to this day, but also Corrigan's study of working-class males in the North-east of England (Willis 1977; Corrigan 1979).

Willis's study differed in many respects from the earlier studies into young people's subjective responses to education. Although working with a Marxist tradition, he took a critical stance against other more deterministic theories, such as the work of Bowles and Gintis (1976), and argued that structural forces are mediated through the cultural sphere. In doing so, he placed a strong emphasis on young people's agency and shared how a group of working-class young people (the 'lads') were not failed by the school, teachers or social system, but actively sought to fail themselves. Willis explained the oppositional cultural resistance that characterized the lads' response to schooling as a collective response, one that sees through and penetrates, if only partially, the conditions of the working class under capitalism. As their chances of upward mobility within the system are negligible, they may as well reject educational conformity as it offered few or no rewards, and instead they may as well have a 'laff' and display their open hostility to the school and teachers. Willis argued the counter school culture they adopted tended to mirror that of the shop-floor culture with its strong emphasis on masculinity, but one that was also an aspect of wider working-class culture more generally, something that served to prepare them for the world of dead-end work.

While Willis's work was widely acclaimed, it has been subject to detailed criticism, in particular in relation to its romantic portrayal of the 'lads', its uncritical stance in relation to macho culture, and for downplaying working-class students who do not adopt strong forms of resistance to the dominant ideology of the school. Brown (1987), coming from a Weberian perspective, in a later ethnography, identified greater plurality of young people's subjective orientations to the school. In particular, he highlighted a further group of pupils the 'ordinary' kids, working-class young people who held an alienated but instrumental attitude toward the school. He was particularly critical of Willis's portrayal of the 'lads' as the normal working-class response to school and argued his analysis was flawed, as it failed to explain why large numbers of working-class kids did not reject school.

115

## Bringing in gender and 'race'

The subjectivities portrayed in many of these earlier ethnographic accounts often tended to be framed in terms of relative simple binaries or oppositions, in terms of pro- or anti-school cultures: the 'academics' and 'delinquescent' (Hargreaves 1967) 'lads' and 'ear 'oles' (Willis 1977) or in the US context 'jocks' and 'burn-outs' (Eckert 1989). Most of these early accounts of educational subjectivities were concerned with essentially white male working-class responses to the school. Feminists and those studying 'race' began to challenge such simple binary accounts of educational subjectivities, arguing subjective responses are cross-cut by social class, 'race' and gender, and highlighted how subjective cultural responses were much more complex than had typically been portrayed.

Fuller (1980), for example, showed how a group of West Indian girls adopted an ambivalent sub-cultural position to schooling that was both pro- and anti-school at the same time. She described how a group of West Indian girls adopted a similar anti-school perspective to their male black peers, or at least mimicked this position to avoid ridicule, while at the same time they held high-level aspirations and confidence in their own academic achievement. MacLeod's (1987) work in the United States drew heavily on the work of the French sociologist Bourdieu and his concept of habitus, in his study of two groups of working-class males, one predominantly white ('Hallway Hangers') the other black ('Brothers'). He argued the connection between objective structures and young people's subjective attitudes was a tenuous one. While both the groups in his study were seen to occupy similar class positions and lived within the same neighbourhood, the Hallway Hangers, on the one hand, rejected the American dream with its 'promise' of equality of opportunity – in a similar way to Willis's lads – while the Brothers, unaware of the structural constraints of 'race' and class, accepted the achievement ideology. Despite their structural location, they maintained high aspirations and ultimately blamed themselves for their subsequent failures.

## Changing educational and occupational contexts

Since these early studies into young people's subjective orientations to education, we have witnessed a period of significant social change. The relationship between education and employment has shifted dramatically, and educational credentials have become increasingly important in the contemporary context. Alongside this we have witnessed an unprecedented rise in educational participation within the upper secondary school linked together with a process of qualification inflation. With a collapse of the manufacturing sector and the youth labour market today there are few opportunities for those who leave school at an early age with minimal qualifications.

Policies have become increasingly driven by an economic prerogative to compete in a global labour market and create a knowledge-based society and educational provision has attempted to cater for all rather than an academic elite. This has led to an increasing vocational orientation to make the offer more attractive to those with lower levels of attainment and to try and entice all young people to remain in some form of education or training.

With the decline in manual employment and changing labour market experiences among working-class families, young people today tend to develop different responses towards education and the labour market to those held by members of earlier generations. As contexts have changed, young people have adapted the cultural responses of the previous generation to forms which are more compatible with labour demand in a post–Fordist economy. In this context, changes in the labour market and qualification inflation have had an important impact on the orientations of working-class youth towards education and the job market, whereby the responses which could once be described as collectivist have become more individualized.

In the 1990s, young people's subjective orientations began to be characterized by a growing individualization (Beck 1992) and it is now clearly possible to identify a broader range of cultural responses than those that were previously described by earlier studies. The social composition of the upper secondary school has changed and while middle-class 'cultural capital' (Bourdieu 1973; Ball *et al.* 2000) still provides educational advantages, schools now make greater effort to provide for pupils outwith the traditional academic mainstream.

As educational, labour market and social contexts have changed, so too have theoretical perspectives. The recent study of young people's subjectivities has been influenced by the emergence of post-structural perspectives within educational sociology, often drawing on Foucault and his concept of 'discursive power'. These perspectives have challenged a one step decoding of culture from social class location and have highlighted how subjectivities are complex and multi-faceted. They represent a move away from, and rejection of, grand theorizing, objectivism and essentialist thinking to more locally context specific analyses. However, they have often been criticized, among other things, for their relativism and a lack of applicability to the real world.

These post-structuralist perspectives, influenced by feminist writing have rejected earlier biologically based sex-role theories to explain gender differences in education and instead focus upon deconstructing sex/gender identities and reflect a more individualized or at least psychosocial approach where 'identity' as a concept has taken centre stage in theorizing. Walkerdine *et al.* (2001) have applied this approach to the contemporary study of the interaction between young women's subjectivities and their social class location. Other notable studies within this tradition include Mac an Ghail's study of masculinities and sexualities and Sewell's work on black masculinities (Mac an Ghail 1997; Sewell 2000). However, post-structuralist concerns within education are not only concerned with subjectivities according to the traditional sociological concerns of gender, 'race' and class but also with the intersections and interactions with other identity categories such as disability, Special Educational Needs (SEN) and Lesbian, Gay, Bisexual, Queer, Transgender and Intersex (Youdell 2006).

While earlier ethnographic studies had primarily focused on young people's subjectivities within the confines of the school and tended to ignore some of the wider contexts that may shape young people's educational perspectives, there has been increasing recognition of the way in which subjectivities may be shaped outside of the school context. The reassertion of the family as a site of influence on young people has gained greater prominence among contemporary accounts, but also out-of-school youth cultures and locality in the development and shaping of young people's educational subjectivities. Ball *et al.* (2000), perhaps influenced by post-structural perspectives, but also drawing heavily on cultural reproduction theory and the work of Bourdieu, highlight three key different arenas of action (Family, home and domesticity/Work, education and training/Leisure and social life) to help explain young people's subjective orientations to learning and the way in which they help shape their 'Learner Identities' and 'Imagined Futures'.

117

## Educational subjectivities and quantitative perspectives

The body of work discussed above has largely focused on ethnographic or biographical approaches which are particularly suited to the study of educational subjectivities, quantitative approaches have typically been concerned with identifying structural patterns in relation to educational inequality. Nevertheless, in the USA, young people's aspirations have long been seen as an important component of the influential Wisconsin model of status attainment. In contrast, in the UK, aspirations have tended to be overlooked as predictors of educational attainment and social mobility, although recent work in the UK has also demonstrated their importance. Using national birth cohort data, Schoon noted the significance of aspirations as a predictor of adult social status, and argued that teenage aspirations are 'a long-term protective factor moderating the impact of early socio-economic adversity on consequent attainments' (2006: 123). Furthermore, comparing birth cohorts over time, she argues that young people appear to have adjusted their aspirations upwards, reflecting changing labour market structures, and that positive future orientations appear to moderate the impact of early social risk associated with lower socio-economic background.

While Schoon's analysis of the UK context points to some protective aspects of positive future orientations, Schneider and Stevenson (1999) survey in the USA, where the massification of post-compulsory educational participation is well established, points to a more problematic interpretation of rising aspirations, what they call the 'ambition paradox'. Their analysis highlights a dramatic rise in aspirations in the 1990s compared to the past two decades, but also shows how, for many young people, the educational decisions and routes they take are misaligned with their ambitions. This highlights the greater complexity and uncertainty that characterizes the contemporary context. And while young people of all social backgrounds may have accepted that they need more educational resources, some lack sufficient direction and chose educational pathways with very low chances of realizing their aspirational goals.

Goldthorpe (1996), also coming from a quantitative perspective, offers an alternative explanation from the dominant cultural reproduction theories of educational inequality. He is critical of their inability to explain the large increase in educational expansion that has occurred over the past few decades. Using rational action theory, he argues that in terms of both continuity and change, patterns of attainment can be explained through the relative assessment of the costs and benefits of education. Breen and Goldthorpe (1997), developing this rational choice perspective further, argue that educational inequality can be understood through the concept of 'relative risk aversion' whereby all social classes are seen as being equally concerned with avoiding downward social mobility.

While the sort of weak rational choice theory they advocate provides a highly plausible explanation that can both account for contemporary social change and continuity in educational inequalities, Hatcher (1998) has confronted their model with a wealth of qualitative evidence. In doing so, he acknowledges that, among the middle classes, choices taken do generally appear uniformly rational and strategic, but argues that rational action theory has more difficulties in explaining the more diverse subjectivities among the working class.

Biggart and Furlong (1996), for example, in their study of young people's decisions to remain in the upper secondary school in Scotland, identified three distinct main orientations to post-compulsory educational participation: the 'hi-flyers'; the 'plodders'; and the 'drifters'. The 'hi-flyers' represented the traditional academic mainstream, predominantly middle class, who saw participation in the upper secondary school as a natural progression. The 'plodders' were middle attainers who did not take academic success for granted and tended to have an instrumental attitude to remaining at school in so far as they recognized the need to improve their credentials in a competitive modern labour market. While both of these groups clearly appeared to be acting in a rational and strategic way that fits with rational action theory, the 'drifters', who were mostly working class, had not made the same sort of cost–benefit analysis to remaining at school. With low levels of attainment and little prospect of significantly improving their educational credentials by remaining at school, aside from a vague awareness of the limited and uncertain opportunities open to them, they had given little thought about the consequences of post-compulsory educational participation.

## Conclusion

The situation in the UK in the early 1970s was much more clear-cut and highly structured when compared to the contemporary context. The young people in Willis' and Corrigans' studies could reject education as they saw it had little relevance for their future working careers. With the collapse of many traditional working-class forms of employment and the increasing proportion of jobs requiring higher levels of qualification, few young people today display such overt hostility, but instead adopt more passive forms of resistance.

With these changes in educational subjectivities we have witnessed a significant expansion in educational participation from all social classes as young people increasingly pursue higher levels of education, albeit for many in an instrumental fashion. And while the changes in labour market structures that have occurred in the recent past, with an expanded service and professional class, have increased the scope for individual agency and helped secure social mobility for many, whether this remains so is less clear.

With an expanding middle class and a degree of convergence of outlook among young people from all social backgrounds, comes a heightened risk of downward social mobility among the middle classes. As the majority of young people increasingly make a greater investment in education, their expectations about what this can deliver in terms of their future careers has been raised and we witness heightened aspirations among most young people today. However, there is little evidence to suggest that the knowledge society will be able to meet the demands of the heightened aspirations for all; as competition increases, a strong sense of agency may no longer be sufficient to secure upward social mobility. As a result, many may flounder and ultimately have to downgrade and revise their aspirations. While there will undoubtedly be both elements of upward and downward mobility for some, the middle classes who are able to draw upon their greater resources and social capital to strategically navigate their way to their desired outcomes, will tend to remain ahead in the race. As the room for agency diminishes, structural constraints, while never absent, may once again come more sharply into view.

## References

Ball, S., Maguire, M. and Macrae, S. (2000) *Choice Pathways and Transitions Post-16: New Youth, New Economies in the Global City*, London: RoutledgeFalmer.
Beck, U. (1992) *The Risk Society: Towards a New Modernity*. London: Sage.

Biggart, A. and Furlong, A. (1996) 'Educating "discouraged" workers: cultural diversity in the upper secondary school', *British Journal of Sociology of Education*, 17: 253–66.

Bourdieu, P. (1973) 'Cultural reproduction and social reproduction', in R. Brown (ed.) *Knowledge, Education, and Social Change: Papers in the Sociology of Education*, London: Tavistock.

Bowles, S. and Gintis, H. (1976) *Schooling in Capitalist America*, New York: Basic Books.

Breen, R. and Goldthorpe, J. (1997) 'Explaining educational differentials: towards a formal rational action theory', *Rationality and Society*, 9: 275–306.

Brown, P. (1987) *Schooling Ordinary Kids: Inequality, Unemployment and the New Vocationalism*, London: Tavistock.

Corrigan, P. (1979) *Schooling the Smash Street Kids*, Basingstoke: Macmillan.

Eckert, P. (1989) *Jocks and Burnouts: Social Categories and Identity in the High School*, New York: Teachers College Press.

Fuller, M. (1980) 'Black girls in a London comprehensive school', in R. Deem (ed.) Schooling for Women's Work, London: Routledge and Kegan Paul.

Goldthorpe, J. (1996) 'Class analysis and the reorientation of class theory: the case of persisting differentials in educational attainment', *British Journal of Sociology*, 47: 481–505.

Hargreaves, D. H. (1967) *Social Relations in a Secondary School*, London: Routledge and Kegan Paul.

Hatcher, R. (1998) 'Class differentiation in education: rational choices?', *British Journal of Sociology of Education*, 19: 5–24.

Lacey, C. (1970) *Hightown Grammar: The School as a Social System*, Manchester: The University Press.

Mac an Ghail, M. (1997) *The Making of Men: Masculinities, Sexualities and Schooling*, Buckingham: Open University Press.

MacLeod, J. (1987) *Ain't No Making It: Aspirations and Attainment in a Low-income Neighbourhood*, Boulder, CO: Westview Press.

Schneider, B. and Stevenson, D. (1999) *The Ambitious Generation: America's Teenagers Motivated but directionless*, New Haven, CT: Yale University Press.

Schoon, I. (2006) *Risk and Resilience: Adaptations in Changing Times*. Cambridge: Cambridge University Press.

Sewell, T. (2000) *Black Masculinities and Schooling: How Black Boys Survive Modern Schooling*. Stoke on Trent: Trentham Books.

Walkerdine, V., Lucey, H. and Melody, J. (2001) *Growing up Girl: Psychosocial Explorations of Gender and Class*, Basingstoke: Palgrave.

Werthman, C. (1963) 'Delinquents in school: a test for the legitimacy of authority', *Berkeley Journal of Sociology*, 8: 39–60.

Willis, P. (1977) *Learning to Labour: How Working Class Kids Get Working Class Jobs*, Aldershot: Ashgate.

Youdell, D. (2006) *Impossible Bodies, Impossible Selves: Exclusions and Student Subjectivities*, Dordrecht: Springer.

# 15

# Mass higher education

*Andy Furlong and Fred Cartmel*

## Introduction

In many western countries, higher education has recently become part of the normal, taken-for-granted, experiences of the middle classes and, despite persistent inequalities in access, the expansion of higher education has resulted in the increased participation of groups who once were largely excluded. Changes in the labour market have resulted in a serious decline in the number of quality jobs available to early school-leavers and, as a result, there is pressure on young people to remain in education so as to secure the most advantageous economic returns. With many governments committed to increasing participation in higher education, inequalities in access have become politically sensitive, especially as young people from working-class families and members of some minority groups remain seriously under-represented. Yet inequalities in access tell only a partial story: higher education is stratified in a variety of ways, all of which ensure that traditionally advantaged groups derive the greatest benefit.

In this chapter, we examine some of the key forms of stratification in the student experience and look at the distinctive forms of engagement linked to various divisions. We argue that, in different ways, the fragmentation of experience effectively ensure that those from less well-off families have distinct, and in many ways poorer, higher educational experiences, even when they manage to secure access to prestigious courses in elite institutions. Indeed, we can identify a range of mechanisms that help ensure that wider access does not result in a more open class structure or pose a threat to the reproduction of class advantage.

## Inequality in the age of mass participation

In the UK, as in most other advanced societies, there has been a sustained increase in higher educational participation over the past few decades. Higher education has been transformed from an elite to a mass experience. Yet while the numbers of young people entering higher education have increased among all social groups, in the UK, expansion has been achieved with very little impact on the overall social distribution of entrants. Indeed, commentating on trends in the social class composition of the higher educational sector, the Office for National Statistics state quite bluntly that 'the gap in participation rates between those from manual and non-manual classes has *increased* over the last 40 or so years' (Summerfield and Gill 2005: 36, our emphasis). In other words, the middle classes have managed to retain – and even increase – their advantages despite the shift from an elite to a mass system of higher education which has resulted in increased odds of attendance for all social classes.

The persistence and growth of class-based inequalities in access to higher education during a period in which the supply of places has increased can be partly explained by the underlying growth in income inequality in a number of advanced societies. In the USA, it has been argued that increasing income inequality has led to a 'greater dispersion of educational outcomes ... primarily because those at the bottom of the educational distribution fall further from the mean' (Haveman and Wilson 2007: 32). In other words, growing economic inequality has helped to polarize outcomes in secondary education which has knock-on effects on access to university.

At the very heart of the issue of fair access is the problem of school attainment and the educational advantages enjoyed by the middle classes, especially those with the ability to afford private education. For under-represented groups, the main barrier to accessing higher education stems from having inferior qualifications. Therefore the first and most significant step to social justice in higher education is about improving the quality of primary and secondary education, especially for those groups who are under-performing. But schools do not operate in a vacuum; patterns of parental encouragement and cultural capital represent a *habitus* (Bourdieu 1977) that has an important bearing on school experiences and performance. In the UK and many other countries, schooling is a stratified process. The existence of geographic catchment areas mean that many schools are dominated by members of particular social classes and aspirations in working-class schools can be restricted, while the use of academic and vocational streams also serve to reinforce socio-economic divisions (Ball 1981). With educational credentials used as currency to purchase access to higher education, admissions policies can maintain a veneer of fairness based on the perceived link between merit and performance. The failure by some groups to make significant in-roads to higher education can then be blamed on a lack of individual effort, ability or aspirations.

The policies of universities also play a role in the maintenance of inequalities and there is evidence suggesting that admissions officers have difficulty seeing beyond credentials or appreciating the sorts of hurdles faced by less advantaged applicants. In particular, a lack of understanding of working-class culture and a poor ability to 'read' the motives and commitment of non-traditional students may underpin some unjust decisions about admissions, especially when interviews play a part in the selection process. Poor levels of engagement with an interviewer and a lack of confidence to develop an argument can be interpreted as reflecting a lack of ability, as can an ignorance of 'high-brow' culture. More fundamentally, admissions officers may fail to appreciate that a potential student from a working-class family who attended a state school and who presents with relatively low grade credentials may be the intellectual equal of a middle-class student with strong credentials who has benefited from a private education. Indeed, while institutions may look sympathetically at the grades achieved by a working-class applicant, there is often a genuine (and misplaced) concern that such students are less able and may struggle to cope with their courses.

## Forms of horizontal stratification

While inequalities in access to higher education are clearly visible in all advanced societies, patterns of horizontal stratification, whereby inequalities are compounded by the
segmented nature of higher education, tend to be more obscure but are equally important. There are a multitude of divisions that result in the horizontal stratification of the
student experience, including the division between 'old' and 'new' universities, between
prestigious and less prestigious courses, between students living at home and those who
have moved to study and between those who enjoy student-focused lifestyles and those
who must combine study with extensive engagement in employment-related activities.
These divisions are significant in a number of ways: employers may favour degrees from
certain institutions, some specialisms open the doors to particularly rewarding careers
while others tend to provide routes into lower paid sectors of the economy. Moreover,
contexts can be significant, providing access to informal networks, an introduction to
middle-class lifestyles and assumptive worlds and providing different opportunities for the
enhancement of social capital. Importantly, the various forms of stratification that fragment
the student experience relate directly to labour market experiences and the reproduction
of class-based inequalities.

The most obvious dimension of horizontal stratification relates to institution hierarchies
and to the ways in which students from different social classes are allocated to institutions
that reflect their own socio-economic positions. Institutions of higher education organize
themselves in ways that help establish and maintain reputations, form exclusive 'clubs' to
signal their position and status and engage in exclusionary tactics in attempts to secure political and financial advantage. Thus, in the UK, the Russell Group of the 20 major research-
led universities regard themselves as occupying the apex of the hierarchy in terms of
status. Below the Russell Group in terms of status (and in terms of age), the 1994 group
is comprised of 19 of the smaller and more recently established research-led institutions.
A differentiation also tends to be made between the pre-1992 universities and the post-
1992 universities (mainly consisting of the former polytechnics). At the bottom of the
status hierarchy, are the colleges of further and higher education that award some degrees
as well as some sub-degree qualifications. In most advanced countries, despite professing
a commitment to the principles of social justice, institutions maintain their position in the
hierarchy through exclusionary practices. The marketing strategies they employ, for
example, clearly exploit their knowledge of class-based differences in taste and provide
signals about the social class positions and aspirations of existing and potential students.

By providing clear signals about their position in status hierarchies, universities are able
to target their preferred demographic, with those considered to be elite institutions targeting the most affluent market segments. While the older universities stress conservatism
and high culture, the new universities frequently seek to portray a 'down-to-earth' and
accessible image. As a consequence, there is a clear correspondence between the social
class of students and the institutions they attend. Students from the upper middle classes
are highly over-represented in a small cluster of Russell Group universities, such as
Oxford, Cambridge, St Andrews, Bristol and Durham (Sutton Trust 2000). In a less
privileged position, those from working class families are highly concentrated in the
former polytechnics and the college sector. To put this in context, Oxford, Cambridge,
St Andrews and Bristol all draw more than 85 per cent of students from the middle
classes. In sharp contrast, Wolverhampton, Bolton, Ulster and Bradford all draw more
than 45 per cent of their students from working-class families.

These forms of stratification are not simply brought about by the actions of admissions officers: the students themselves are actively involved in the choices that help reproduce advantage and disadvantage (Reay *et al.* 2005). Preferences are shaped by students' assessments of the quality of social life associated with different institutions (*Times Higher* 2007), by beliefs about teaching styles, approachability of staff and by impressions of the backgrounds of fellow students. In this respect, lecturers in the new universities may be regarded as being more friendly and approachable and as willing to spend time helping students with problems, while staff and students in older institutions can be seen by working-class students as culturally remote (Forsyth and Furlong 2003).

Feelings of cultural alienation between working-class students and those from under-represented minorities impact on patterns of peer interaction within an institution. From the perspective of working-class students, differences in accent can be crucial markers of social status that mark out potential friendship networks. Even basic cross-class conversations can be difficult and marked by misunderstandings with some young people saying that they were afraid to open their mouths in case they stood out as being different (ibid.).

Another important dimension of horizontal stratification relates to the distribution between subject areas and is manifest most strongly in the binary division between vocational and non-vocational subjects. With a few high prestige exceptions in areas such as law and medicine, vocational subjects were once uncommon within the university sector and tended to be located in colleges and polytechnics where they were studied at sub-degree level. Indeed, a substantial part of the growth of higher education has resulted from the establishment of degree entry in a range of areas that once either required diplomas or simply sought evidence of a good general education. Working-class students have always been more likely to study vocational subjects and subjects that have clear career links rather than general academic subjects, especially where these subjects are unfamiliar or perceived as being 'posh'.

In the UK, figures from the central clearing house for university entry (UCAS) show very clear differences in patterns of application to various subject areas that are linked to the social class of parents or aspiring students. With relatively few applications from working-class families, the middle classes dominate applications in all subject areas. However, in high prestige subjects, applicants are overwhelmingly drawn from the middle classes. In medicine and dentistry, for example, more than seven in ten applicants were from the managerial and professional classes compared to just one in ten from the routine and semi-routine classes. With subjects like nursing and physiotherapy requiring lower entry qualifications and being offered mainly in the new universities, working-class students can regard this area as more accessible (and perhaps more class-appropriate). As such, subjects allied to medicine (which includes nursing) attracts the largest number of working-class students: in 2006, 26 per cent of students applying for subjects in this cluster came from the routine and semi-routine classes.

Horizontal stratification between subjects that predominantly attract particular genders and minority ethnic groups is also significant. In the UK, in 2004/05, for example, four subject areas accounted for just over half the female students: subjects allied to medicine, education, business and administrative studies and social studies. Males tended not to cluster quite so tightly within a restricted range of subject areas, although 45 per cent of male students studied business and administrative studies, engineering and technology, computer science and social studies (Self and Zealey 2007). Indeed, despite a predominance of female over male undergraduates, females are over-represented in less prestigious subject areas (such as subjects allied to medicine). Similar patterns of stratification by subject apply to minority ethnic groups, partly, but not entirely, as a result of their concentration in new universities. Subjects like pharmacy and business, for example, have attracted relatively large numbers of minority ethnic applicants (National Statistics 2008).

While stratification by subject partly reflects the entry qualifications held by different groups, student choices also reinforce inequalities. Students from less advantaged families can be reluctant to choose courses that lack clear links to the occupational world, even when they had a strong interest in a non-vocational subject. Expressing a sentiment shared by several working-class students, in a recent Scottish study, young people sometimes spoke of the risk involved in doing 'degrees for positions that don't exist'; others stressed that they wanted to do a degree that was 'almost like an apprenticeship' because it removed worry and made the investment safer (Forsyth and Furlong 2003). Skeggs (1997) has also noted that working-class girls place a priority on practical skills (often involving care) while rejecting more academic subjects as 'useless'.

Patterns of residence also result in a form of horizontal stratification for students from less advantaged families as well as for mature students. In the UK, a recent report by MORI (UNITE/MORI, 2005) showed that when it came to choice of institution, the ability to live at home was twice as important for working-class than for middle-class students, even though three in five felt that students who live at home did not get the full benefit of the student experience. Similarly, in a recent report by Education Research Services (2007), it was argued that home-based students had a poor educational experience overall, being less likely to participate in optional parts of their course, such as work placements, reporting feelings of isolation from their fellow students due to limited opportunities for socialization and even being less likely to secure graduate employment. Patterns of social integration within an institution are also strongly affected by residential segregation and reinforced by the tendency of working-class students to continue to live with their parents, often commuting relatively long distances, and to prefer the company of friends in their local communities. As a result, even when working-class students enter prestigious courses, they may maintain a degree of social separation from their more advantaged peers.

Another powerful mechanism through which the experiences of middle-class and working-class students are stratified relates to patterns of engagement in paid work. While changes in student support have increased the pressure on students from all social classes to combine study with employment, the pressures on students from less affluent families is particularly acute. With the lives of some students being more employment focused than study focused, cross-class socialization becomes even more difficult and being a student comes to mean different things for different socio-economic groups with working-class students being more likely to be employed during term-time and likely to work longer hours. (Callender and Wilkinson 2003; Little 2006).

## Conclusion

The experiences of students in higher education have become increasingly diverse and fragmented. Whereas it was once common to think of the main divisions as represented by full and part-time students or between mature and younger students, the lines of differentiation have become ever more complex. In some respects, a process of differentiation can be welcomed as a move away from a 'one size fits all' model to one that

125

offers the possibility of becoming aligned with the non-linear and reflexive biographies that are the hallmark of late modernity. Yet crucially, the new complexity is perhaps more about class-based processes of stratification than about fresh opportunities.

The separation between old and new universities (and the more subtle distinctions that mark status within each of these broad categories), result in a class-based set of experiences that ultimately represent clear channels between unequal family origins and unequal labour market positions. Within institutions (especially the older ones) there are also clear divisions between prestigious and less prestigious courses and restricted patterns of interaction between students. There is little evidence that working-class students are becoming absorbed into the assumptive worlds of the established middle classes or developing the sorts of networks that will smooth access to traditional graduate careers.

The reproduction of inequalities through higher education is shaped not just by external structures (although financial and admissions policies play a central role) but by the choices made by students themselves as they seek experiences that work within their own comfort zones. Many of the choices and priorities that underpin processes of differentiation are conditioned by class so it is not surprising that the actions of students help reproduce inequalities. The dimension of these processes that tends to be overlooked relates to the active role taken by universities in developing marketing strategies that exploit class-based preferences and insecurities. Essentially, in the case of the established universities, these strategies run directly counter to their professed aim of widening access.

## References

Ball, S. J. (1981) *Beachside Comprehensive: A Case Study of Secondary Schooling*, Cambridge: Cambridge University Press.

Bourdieu, P. (1977) 'Cultural reproduction and social reproduction', in J. Karabel and A. H. Halsey (eds) *Power and Ideology in Education, Society and Culture*, London, Sage.

Callender, C. and Wilkinson, D. (2003) 2002/03 *Student Income and Expenditure Survey: Students' Income, Expenditure and Debt in 2002/03 and Changes since 1998/99*, Sheffield: Department of Education and Skills.

Education Research Services (2007) Education Research Services Bulletin, Winter. www.e-r-s.org.uk/ers_newsletter_01.html

Forsyth, A. and Furlong, A. (2003) *Losing out? Socioeconomic Disadvantage and Experience in Further and Higher education*, Bristol: Policy Press.

Haveman, R. and Wilson, K. (2007) 'Access, matriculation and graduation', in P. Dickert-Conlin and R. Rubenstein (eds) *Economic Inequality and Higher Education*, New York: Russell Sage Foundation.

Little, B. (2006) 'The student experience and the impact of social capital', in I. McNay (ed.) *Beyond Mass Higher Education: Building on Experience*, Maidenhead: The Society for Research into Higher Education and Open University Press.

National Statistics (2008) National Statistics Online, www.statistics.gov.uk/cci/nugget.asp?id=268 (accessed 26 February 2008).

Reay, D., David, M. E. and Ball, S. (2005) *Degrees of Choice: Class, Race, Gender and Higher Education*, Stoke on Trent: Trentham Books.

Self, A. and Zealey, L. (eds) (2007) *Social Trends No. 37*, London: Office for National Statistics.

Skeggs, B. (1997) *Formations of Class and Gender: Becoming Respectable*, London: Sage.

Summerfield, C. and Gill, B. (eds) (2005) *Social Trends, No. 35*. London: Office for National Statistics.

Sutton Trust (2000) 'Entry to leading universities', London: The Sutton Trust.

*Times Higher* (2007) 'Social life high on wish list', 7 December, p. 6.

UNITE/MORI (2005) *The Student Experience Report 2005*, London: Higher Education Policy Unit.

# 16

# Vocationalism

*David B. Bills*

## Vocationalism defined

Vocationalism refers to the subordination or accommodation of the educational system to the supposed needs of the economic system. In particular, vocationalism depicts a vision of schooling in which the chief function and responsibility of education are to meet the expressed needs of employers for useful skills. Most observers see vocationalism as a historical process, in which the liberal, moral, or civic purposes of schooling are steadily displaced by economic purposes. Analysts of vocationalism are often sharply divided on whether or not this accommodation is a good thing, and much of the literature on vocationalism is quite normative. Hayward (2007: 3), for instance, sees vocationalism negatively, defining it as 'the over-promotion of the work-related learning aims of secondary and tertiary education at the expense of the civic, aesthetic and moral purposes of education'. Others have defined vocationalism more positively as being of great benefit not only to employers, but to students, job-seekers, workers, and society more broadly.

There is no single entity that can be identified as vocationalism. As Ryan (2003: 159) observed, 'Vocationalism involves heterogeneous practices and multiple objectives.' Most importantly, vocationalism is not reducible to vocational education. While a narrowly vocational education comprises a particular aspect of vocationalism, the concept of vocationalism is broader, encompassing a range of practices and policies intended to maximize the occupational value of schooling. Among its staunchest supporters, vocationalism offers young people preparation for vocations – work that is meaningful and purposeful – rather than simply for jobs.

In one sense, vocationalism is a social movement. That is, there is an active and politically organized vocationalist community with its own professional associations, specialized journals, engaged core of advocates, and bureaucratic apparatus. Vocationalism is also an ideology, or at the very least an educational ideal, with its own system of beliefs, folk heroes, and guiding vision of what education should be.

The extent to which vocationalism has penetrated an educational system will vary across societies and historical periods. In principle, if not in practice, a society may organize its educational system around liberal or general studies with no explicit or even implicit connections to economic production. At the other extreme, virtually all curriculum, credentials, and pedagogy might be directed toward workforce preparation. What characterizes strongly vocationalized educational systems is that schooling is in the end more responsive to the economy than it is an innovative or independent force for the dissemination of other sorts of values and priorities.

Vocationalism can refer to educational preparation both for entry-level occupations of middling skill and income levels and for professional or high-skill positions. My focus here will be on vocationalism in secondary and tertiary schooling. I will not consider elementary education, although elements of vocationalism have penetrated curriculum and pedagogy even at that level. I will also ignore job training, a practice that is explicitly designed to enhance job skills, and which thus lacks the inherent tension between the competing civic or moral and economic purposes of schooling that characterizes other levels of the educational system.

Vocationalism typically brings with it the increasing involvement of the business community in the everyday operation of the educational system. This can take different forms, ranging from active partnerships between school and business through lobbying and otherwise influencing educational and labor force policy through the simple provision of money, equipment, or other resources. While business has rarely been indifferent to the output of the educational system, its direct involvement in schooling is almost certainly greater now than it has ever been. The relationships between business and education can be either consensual or conflictual, but the two institutions are in either case increasingly interconnected.

## A brief history of vocationalism

While the relationship between formal schooling and occupational entry is now so firmly established in contemporary industrial and postindustrial societies as to appear virtually innate, this relationship is actually a relatively recent development. Prior to industrialization and the expansion of mass education, young people acquired their job skills primarily through either their families or more formalized apprenticeships. In both the United States and much of Europe, the rapid expansion of both secondary and tertiary schooling beginning around the turn of the twentieth century (earlier in the United States, and a bit later in some other countries) was accompanied by the vocationalization of the educational system. Ryan (2003) characterizes the twentieth century as 'the century of vocationalism'.

The history of vocationalism has been a contentious one, marked by strikingly different visions of exactly how school should prepare young people for work (Kliebard 1999). The humanistic visions of figures such as John Dewey in the United States and Georg Kerschensteiner in Germany, calling for high academic standards and contextualized learning, have co-existed uneasily with more instrumental conceptions of schooling focusing on often narrowly defined but 'useful' job skills and knowledge. Likewise, the classical American debate over the proper direction for African-American education between the 'practical' vision of Booker T. Washington and the more occupationally ambitious vision of W. E. B. DuBois sets out in stark terms the contested nature of vocationalism. The history of vocationalism is simultaneously one of being highly valued and highly stigmatized.

The historical processes by which vocationalism has come about have differed across societies. In the United States, various forms of work-based education (although less commonly full-fledged apprenticeships in the European sense) eventually gave way in the 1880s to a form of vocational high schools known as manual training schools (Kliebard 1999). Late nineteenth-century vocationalism in the United States was often fueled by conflicts over unionization (Jacoby 2007). Early vocational education had powerful institutional backers. The National Association of Manufacturers (NAM), the American Federation of Labor (AFL), and the National Society for the Promotion of Industrial Education (NSPIE) all supported vocationalism, if often for quite different purposes. The rapid ascendancy of vocationalism over the ensuing decades was further encouraged by the elevation of Taylorism and Scientific Management as dominant business philosophies. Kliebard (1999) believes that the American educational system was essentially vocationalized by the end of World War II.

The fulcrum of American vocationalism shifted yet again in the 1950s and 1960s away from high schools and toward community colleges. Community colleges have always had multiple and contradictory purposes (Dougherty 1994). Their designers have as often focused on the role of community colleges in preparing students to transfer to four-year institutions as to prepare them for the workforce. Still, vocationalism has always been crucial to the community college mission. More recently, vocationalism has begun to shift toward a wide variety of private vendors and providers of 'educational services'.

The history of American vocationalism at the postsecondary levels of schooling, and particularly at the graduate level, is considerably different than its often stigmatized counterpart at the secondary levels. The ascendancy of professionalization in the nineteenth-century United States did much to vocationalize the university curriculum (Larsen 1977; Collins 1979; Abbott 1988). A series of broad structural changes including the emergence of mass education, the decline of liberal arts education (which had been the province of an elite class), and the increased role of science, rationality, and efficiency in virtually all sectors of the newly industrialized society together resulted in a historic shift to school-based occupational preparation and the dominance of the occupational major. These processes brought with them too the beginnings of educational credentialism in the United States.

Other nations have taken very different routes toward vocationalism, although the final result in industrial and postindustrial societies is virtually always an educational system that is to a great degree subservient to the demands of the workplace. Germany's 'Dual System', in which employers, employees, educational institutions, and the state collaborate on what has proven to be a highly durable system of skill formation, often serves as a model for an effective and efficient form of vocationalism. Evoking the concept of Beruf, which refers to the subjective meaning and honor attached to one's chosen work, the Dual System makes explicit the linkages between occupational preparation and quite specific forms of work. Nonetheless, the German model is now coming under increasing stress as it is faced with rapidly changing skill needs, structural transformations of the German economy toward services, and the mounting costs of maintaining an expensive apparatus of training.

The British history of vocationalism is different yet from that of either the United States or Germany. England did not develop mass schooling nearly as early as did the United States. Unlike the USA, apprenticeships in England grew out of a guild tradition and were heavily regulated by craft unions. As a consequence, England had much more of a tradition of skills being acquired at work. Over the past generation, this situation has

School-to-work policies differ across industrialized societies, but the increased demand of employers for skills is characteristic of all industrial and postindustrial societies. These ever more stringent skill demands are felt with particular force by young workers. Lacking the ability to observe these skills directly in job applicants, employers typically turn instead to an evaluation of the educational credentials of new workers. Many educational credentialists argue that this heightened demand for skills, certificates, and diplomas is less a rational response to technological and workplace change and more the acceleration of a process in which employers arbitrarily and unnecessarily increase their hiring criteria beyond any real change in the skills actually required to perform productively on the job. Extreme forms of educational credentialism seem to support extreme forms of vocationalism.

## Vocational education

While vocational education – coursework and curricula that are specifically designed to meet the needs of occupational preparation – is only one aspect of vocationalism, it is an extremely important one. Supporters of vocational education see it as the best long-term hope for young people for whom higher education is neither likely nor desired. Detractors of vocational education, in particular at the secondary level, counter with charges of blocked opportunities and class, gender, and racial privilege.

Somewhat paradoxically, in the United States the acceleration of vocationalism over the past generation has been accompanied by a sharp decline in traditional vocational education at the secondary level. Academic course taking has increased in American high schools since the mid-1980s while vocational education has declined. This is in part a response to more stringent high school graduation requirements set in motion by the report, *A Nation At Risk* (Gardner 1983) and similar reports of educational crisis and in part because of a more demanding job market. Also, the high costs of vocational education came under increasing scrutiny in the 1980s as the economy slowed, leading eventually to reduced government support.

The decline in vocational enrollments was not, however, a consequence of the growth in academic enrollments. Rather, many American students simply increased the number of credit hours they took in high school. The major shift was away from enrollments in general education and toward enrollments in college preparatory curriculum. In this sense, the declines in enrollments in postsecondary vocational education signal an even greater trend toward the vocationalism of the high school curriculum. The non-vocationally oriented general education fell by the wayside, while academic enrollments, by this point primarily a preparation for a vocationalized postsecondary tier, took on increased long-term vocational significance. The preparation of people for postsecondary education and the sorting and selection processes associated with this have become the centerpiece of contemporary vocationalism in that the ultimate aim is to channel people into jobs. In addition, in many cases such traditional subjects as math and science are now being packaged as practical and useful.

## The new vocationalism

Many critics (e.g., Grubb and Lazerson 2004) see American vocationalism as too narrowly focused on specific utilitarian and practical skills and capacities, and argue that the

acquisition of many of these skills will only prepare people for occupational obsolescence as the demands of the economy continue to shift. In part as a response to this criticism, an emerging and disparate body of thought collectively known as the New Vocationalism has emerged. Advocates of the New Vocationalism intend it to provide a more inclusive and general workforce preparation than existing models of vocationalism. Supporters of initiatives such as career academies, youth apprenticeships, tech–prep programs, co–op programs, work–based learning (WBL), and cognitive apprenticeships define vocationalism broadly to encompass generic and especially academic skills. Increasingly, scholars and practitioners of the New Vocationalism concern themselves not only with the curricular dimensions of vocationalism, but with its institutional setting in the workplace as well. Proposals to more closely align vocational education and academic education are in a sense a 'softer' vocationalism.

Scholars from different theoretical and normative perspectives understand the concept of the New Vocationalism quite differently. For some, the New Vocationalism is an exhortatory term, a call to action to meet the needs of a global economy. To others the term is more pejorative, signifying a dire warning of business encroachment on the democratic values and mission of education. While even its harshest critics acknowledge that the New Vocationalism is more than a simple repackaging of traditional vocationalism (Grubb and Lazerson 2004), there is no doubt that the New Vocationalism is subject to many of the same contradictions that have plagued vocationalism from its inception. The contradictions include the tensions between vocationalism and academic excellence, equity and equal opportunity, and social inclusion.

## Vocationalism and social stratification

One of the chief concerns of many critics of vocationalism is the potential of a vocationalized curriculum to reproduce or even exacerbate patterns of educational and socioeconomic inequality. Analysts have been especially concerned with the disproportionate placement of girls and women, racial and ethnic minorities, and economically marginalized groups in lower status vocational tracks. At its worst, vocationalism, and school tracking more generally, are held to provide a dumping ground for non–elite students.

The empirical evidence provides a mixed picture. Ainsworth and Roscigno (2005) maintain that the effects of high school vocational education are seriously reproductive. They report that participation in high school vocational education increases the likelihood of dropping out of high school and lowers the likelihood of subsequent college attendance. They find these disadvantages have especially detrimental effects for women, minorities, and lower SES students, even controlling for prior achievement and educational expectations. For researchers like Ainsworth and Roscigno and others who have reached similar conclusions, vocationalism is a story of blocked opportunities and foregone alternatives.

Others report less dismaying findings. Meer (2007), for instance, detected a comparative advantage for students who elect to participate in vocational education. In other words, some students are best served by following a technical track, while others are best served on an academic route. In general, proponents of vocationalism maintain that it can provide a ladder out of otherwise constrained life chances. Even such a perceptive critic as Ryan (2003) maintains that vocationalism raises the educational attainments (and thus socioeconomic attainments) of those of lower ability, motivation, and prior achievements.

The jury would still seem to be out on the stratifying effects of vocational education more narrowly and vocationalism more broadly. There remains a great deal of empirical and theoretical disagreement and uncertainty about such crucial issues as proper conceptualization and measurement, the lack of adequate statistical controls, the impact of sample or program selection effects, sample restrictions, and so on. We need a great deal more research on the role of vocationalism in social stratification.

## Research agenda

The focus of probably most research on vocationalism has been primarily on the individual-level effects of participation in vocational education. This research, conducted mainly by economists, has focused usefully but perhaps too narrowly on the question of whether or not vocational education is a good investment as a means of enhancing one's income and employment stability. There is also a substantial body of program evaluation of vocational education, again carried out primarily by economists. In some ways, these two strands of research are asking the same questions: to what extent does vocational education pay off in terms of employment and income prospects? What is the ratio of costs and benefits in vocational programs?

These are important questions and merit continued attention. There is still, however, much that we do not know about vocationalism, let alone about vocational education. Some of the more urgent questions are: How do systems of vocationalism differ across societies? What broader social structural and historical factors account for these differences? How has vocationalism changed over time? Questions like these are not only being raised by but are at the heart of the comparative and historical literature on welfare states, as well as by adherents to the 'varieties of capitalism' perspective.

What systemic implications does vocationalism (not only vocational education) have for social stratification more broadly? Do elite parents monopolize access to vocationalized schooling for their children as part of their 'strategies of reproduction'? Or does vocationalism provide an avenue to upward mobility for non-elite students that had not been previously afforded to them in general education curricula?

What does the trend toward vocationalism do to the shape and composition of the high school curriculum? How does it influence the postsecondary curriculum? Grubb and Lazerson (2004) have criticized the trend toward vocationalism as leading to the 'degradation of secondary education' while Labaree believes that vocationalism 'has reshaped education into a commodity for the purposes of status attainment and has elevated the pursuit of credentials over the acquisition of knowledge' (1997: 39). But advocates of the New Vocationalism say the curriculum has been strengthened and enriched through its Deweyan union of academic and vocational values. Empirical research is needed to settle these issues.

Finally, to a great degree, the concept of skills provides the foundation for all conceptualizations of vocationalism, but despite the centrality of skills we still fail to fully understand the role they play in postindustrial labor markets and occupational preparation. Much human capital theory to the contrary, skill is not the same thing as education, and in fact the relationship between the two can vary over time. Further, sometimes it is best to think of skills as characteristics of individuals, and other times to think of skills as characteristics of work tasks, jobs, or even of groups of workers.

# References

Abbott, A. (1988) *The System of Professions: An Essay on the Division of Expert Labor*, Chicago: University of Chicago Press.

Ainsworth, J. W. and Roscigno, V. J. (2005) 'Stratification, school–work linkages and vocational education', *Social Forces*, 84: 259–86.

Collins, R. (1979) *The Credential Society: An Historical Sociology of Education and Stratification*, New York: Academic Press.

Dougherty, K. J. (1994) *The Contradictory College: The Conflicting Origins, Impacts, and Futures of the Community College*, Albany, NY: State University of New York Press.

Gardner, D. P. (1983) *A Nation at Risk: The Imperative for Educational Reform: An Open letter to the American people. A Report to the Nation and the Secretary of Education,* Washington, DC: U. S. Department of Education.

Grubb, W. N. and Lazerson, M. (2004) *The Education Gospel: The Economic Power of Schooling*, Cambridge, MA: Harvard University Press.

Hayward, G. (2007) 'Forward: a century of vocationalism', *Oxford Review of Education*, 30: 3–12.

Jacoby, D. (2007) 'Plumbing the origins of American vocationalism', *Labor History*, 37: 235–72.

Kliebard, H. (1999) *Schooled to Work: Vocationalism and the American Curriculum, 1876–1946*, New York: Teachers College Press.

Labaree, D. F. (1997) 'Public goods, private goods: the American struggle over educational goals', *American Educational Research Journal*, 34: 39–81.

Larsen, M. S. (1977) *The Rise of Professionalism: A Sociological Analysis*, Berkeley, CA: University of California Press.

Meer, J. (2007) 'Evidence on the returns to secondary vocational education', *Economics of Education Review*, 26: 559–73.

Ryan, P. (2003) 'Evaluating vocationalism', *European Journal of Education*, 38: 147–62.

# Keeping kids on track to a successful adulthood

## The role of VET in improving high school outcomes

*James R. Stone III*

## Introduction

Low student achievement and dropout are twin problems tied to the public perception of the poor quality of US schools and the declining availability of skilled workers. In the 1980s and 1990s, the perceived decline in quality of America's schools was fueled by reports such as *A Nation at Risk* (Gardner 1983). In the more than two decades since, much education reform has been undertaken with the goal of improving US competitiveness in the global economy. In the early stages of these reform efforts, low-achieving students were assumed to be bound for work and often assigned to vocational education programs (now called Career and Technical Education; CTE). More recently, federally supported reform efforts have assumed that all students should be prepared to exit high school ready for college.

This chapter addresses how CTE has responded to the pressures of reform and the demands of the marketplace and outlines key pathways to postsecondary education and training that are intended to keep all students, but particularly the at-risk, on track for academic and economic success. I begin with a synopsis of the current policy context regarding access to education and career preparation and the tracking of students within what are sometimes exclusively academic or workforce-oriented tracks. This is followed by a brief discussion of the major themes driving educational reform in CTE, particularly a mandated focus on academic rigor. I then discuss three key concepts – engagement, achievement, and transition to postsecondary education and employment – in which CTE makes a difference to students' academic and employment outcomes at both the secondary and postsecondary levels.

Next, I address the fusion of CTE with the full span of the educational system and the demands of the labor market. The present policy context and educational system are structured with the expectation that all students will seek four-year degrees, regardless of the demand for such degrees in the labor market. By contrast, CTE provides students with desirable alternatives. Later sections address the variety and impact of postsecondary CTE programs and alternative government programs for postsecondary training and workplace preparation. These are followed by a description of how CTE prepares

low-ability youth for high-skill, high-quality jobs through classroom- and work-based learning and other strategies intended to increase transitions from education to work. The chapter concludes with a re-consideration of CTE as a first-chance system for academic and economic success.

## College and/or career: postsecondary education and CTE

At the heart of the debate over the role of CTE in US education is what Lewis (2000) has described as education's basic dilemma: maximizing each student's potential while simultaneously selecting and socializing all students for their future occupational roles and places in society. However, some argue that students who lack the ability or ambition to seek a university education should be taught a practical skill in high school so that they may be immediately employable upon graduation. Such students are usually placed in high school CTE. To others, this tracking practice conflicts with the ideals of a democratic society in which all students should be given the opportunity for higher education (Oakes *et al.* 1992). Nationally we have been reluctant to explicitly assign young people to inflexible educational tracks that prepare some for college and others for employment.

### Tracking

In every public school, student ability levels are often distributed in different learning groups, either within or across classrooms. At the high school level, these ability groups are known as *tracks* or *concentrations*. The highest academic track (about 32 percent of US high school students) leads students toward college. *General track* students (43 percent of the high school population) take varied general courses and may or may not achieve high enough grades and test scores in core subjects to attend university. Finally, *vocational track* students (the remaining 25 percent) are not expected to go to university (Levesque 2003). These students take courses preparing them for the labor market and are expected to enter the workforce after graduating. The vocational track traditionally was stigmatized as a dumping ground for low-achieving students, along with students with specific learning needs or behavioral problems who were deemed unfit for the general or academic tracks.

The stigma of CTE has diminished, however, as the academic and technical rigor of vocational content has increased. More academic content has been integrated into traditional CTE classes and curricula have been aligned more closely with industry standards. To reflect this shift, CTE reformers of the 1990s changed the nomenclature from *vocational education* to *career and technical education* (CTE).

### CTE and the labor market

The labor market's demand for highly skilled workers has also increased expectations for new graduates. The National Association of Secondary School Principals (2004) noted that the new global economy demands higher literacy, numeracy, and technical skills, and most high school students leave school with some form of education or training beyond high school (but not necessarily a four-year degree); and the ability to learn new skills and adapt to changing requirements. Such skills require not only mastery of core academic skills but also workplace literacy (Barton 2006). Effective CTE programs develop workplace literacy, often called 'soft skills' or 'employability skills', by combining

the best of classroom instruction with quality work-based learning. Examples of these are described later in this chapter.

## Seondary education reform: three key focuses

The national conversation about education and employment is largely driven by the belief that a solid academic education is the best solution for all youth in terms of future employment and earnings (ACT 2006). In addressing the question of how to improve students' educational and employment outcomes, I focus on three key areas in which CTE has been shown to make a difference: school engagement, student achievement, and successful transition to postsecondary education and employment.

### School engagement

One measure of school engagement is successful completion of high school within the expected period (by Grade 12 or age 18). In the United States, there has been a growing recognition that school completion is a problem for many youth. Current estimates of the magnitude of the problem place the high school completion rate between 66 percent and 88 percent with a consensus emerging toward the lower end of the range (Heckman and LaFontaine 2007). CTE has been shown to increase the holding power of school (Plank *et al.* 2005; Castellano *et al.* 2007)) especially for low-ability youth (Plank 2002).

### Student achievement

Criticism of the public school system has prompted a series of reforms, most emphasizing academic achievement. Common to these is the need to increase the rigor of the high school experience. The default measure of *rigor* is requiring students to take more academic coursework (e.g., mathematics, sciences, and foreign languages). However, the data do not suggest that requiring such coursework has improved performance. Measured maths ability for 17-year-old high school students, for example, remained at essentially the same level between 1990 and 2004, while science scores have declined. Overall scores for 2004 were not significantly different from those in 1973 (National Assessment of Educational Progress 2005). One unfortunate and perhaps unintended consequence of increasing the number of required academic courses is the reduction of instructional time for other kinds of coursework such as art, music, or CTE, which might engage students and provide workforce skills. One measure of this is the increased rate at which youth are leaving high school before graduation.

### Student transition

Other measures of the academic problem are college remediation rates. NCES (2004) documented that at least 30 percent of high school graduates require some remediation in reading, writing, or mathematics when they enrol in postsecondary education. Some studies place that figure at over 40 percent (Rosenbaum 2002). While many high school students plan to earn a college degree, their realities can be distressingly far from their aspirations. Rosenbaum noted that fewer than 42 percent of high school graduates obtain college degrees within 10 years of starting college; further, for students with poor grades, only 14 percent eventually earn a degree. For the other 86 percent, college aspirations may be harmful if they prevent students from preparing appropriate back-up plans, such as seeking out education and training for work.

Levesque *et al.* (2000) reported that initial college-going rates varied among curriculum tracks: 93 percent of college preparatory students enrolled in college within two years of high school graduation, as did 69 percent of general track students and 55 percent of CTE students. Many other CTE students enrol in college in their twenties, and within eight years of high school graduation, more than 80 percent of CTE students enrolled in some form of postsecondary education (40 percent earned a college degree). Vocational course-taking appears to increase the chance that a student will complete an associate's degree or a certificate rather than a baccalaureate (Silverberg *et al.* 2004) which may be appropriate given the vocational and technical nature of many community college programs.

## CTE participation and student outcomes

If CTE adds value to the high school experience of youth, especially in retaining lower ability youth, a sound policy approach would be to increase such course or program offerings. The data, however, suggest just the opposite. The National Assessment of Vocational Education (Silverberg *et al.* 2004) concluded that CTE participation has been fairly steady during the 1990s (about 25 percent of all graduates). The current wave of high school reform, with its emphasis on increasing graduation requirements, has reduced the curriculum space for many electives. Recent reports produced by the US Department of Education show a significant drop in CTE enrolment between 2000 and 2004 (National Center for Education Statistics 2007) as traditional academic coursework has increased. This decline comes at a time when groups such as the National Governor's Association have recognized the importance of keeping learning relevant as a means to engage students and specifically identify CTE as a part of that strategy (Meeder 2008).

Recent research shows promising outcomes for CTE students. They appear to have reversed a trend in mathematics course-taking patterns: they take more – and more difficult – mathematics (Stone and Aliaga 2007). In a longitudinal study of three US schools by Castellano *et al.* (2004), students in poor communities participating in CTE showed better growth in achievement for both reading and mathematics than those not participating. CTE students also exhibited better 'soft skills' compared to non-CTE students (Castellano *et al.* 2003). College attendance and completion rates and credential acquisition of CTE participants have also improved compared to others (Silverberg *et al.*, 2004).

## Making the connection between education and work: postsecondary CTE

The field's leading organization, the Association for Career and Technical Education (ACTE) has recommended that all students receive some kind of postsecondary education and training for the workforce. This would require the creation of a seamlessly integrated primary-to-16 educational system that includes workforce development, economic development, welfare reform, and adult education programs and that forms a 'coherent system focused on educational advancement, wage progression, and a higher standard of living for all, including diverse populations' (ACTE 2007: 1). Such a fusion of primary-to-16 education with the demands of the modern marketplace stands in marked contrast to the nation's current preoccupation with four-year college degrees.

One explanation for the nation's 'college for all' emphasis is that a college degree has become a proxy for employability or work readiness (Stone and Alfeld 2006). Believing that the high school diploma no longer signifies meaningful achievement, and lacking a national system of industry credentials, employers rely on college degrees. Recent national data indicate that there have been increases in college enrolment and completion since the early 1970s, the ramifications of which are still unclear. As noted earlier, Rosenbaum (2002) found that only a minority of US high school graduates complete college. Other studies put the success rate much lower, with less than 20 percent of all students completing a four-year degree within six years (National Center for Public Policy and Higher Education 2004). Regardless, such degrees are coming at increased costs to students and their families. The Public Interest Research Group (Swarthout 2006) found that more than two-thirds of college graduates leave with debt and between 23 percent and 55 percent of new graduates leave with debt described as unmanageable.

Recent projections from the US Department of Labor suggest a bifurcation of the labor market with roughly equal growth in professional and service jobs representing opposite ends of both education requirements and earnings. When specific occupations projected to add the most jobs in the next decade are examined, the list is comprised of health, service, sales, and office support positions. Hecker (2005) found that of the top 30 occupations of the future, only eight require formal post-high school education; the rest require no more than on-the-job training. Examining these and other data, Barton (2008) has challenged conventional wisdom about the ability of the US labor market to absorb the number of college graduates we are producing.

## The varieties and impact of postsecondary CTE

Within the postsecondary education system, postsecondary CTE is considered pre-baccalaureate education or training and takes varied forms. Numerous 16–24-year-olds avail themselves of courses and programs at their local community colleges – many without enrolling in formal programs. Postsecondary CTE includes offerings from two-year colleges (i.e., community and technical colleges), area vocational centers, proprietary schools, and adult learning centers as well as professional associations or labor unions and government agencies.

Community and technical colleges offer several types of credentials for students in a career pathway and adults engaged in continued education or transitioning between jobs. Four kinds of credentials are offered: (1) an Associate of Arts (A.A.), which is assumed to be a university transfer degree; (2) an Associate of Science (A.S.) degree, a blend of transfer and occupational credits; and (3) the associate of Applied Arts (A.A.S.), which is heavily vocational in content. In addition to these three, students often opt for a fourth variant; credentials requiring 6–18 months to complete (e.g., certificates in welding, carpentry). Bailey *et al.* (2004) found that 29 percent of all students enrolled in post-secondary education in 2000 were students in a vocational sub-baccalaureate program: 64.5 percent of these earned an A.A., whereas 33.3 percent earned a certificate. Grubb (1996) found that there were significant labor market payoffs for occupational course participation in community colleges, including increased earnings, dependent on degree, years of study, and field (related or unrelated).

139

## The varieties and impact of government programs

Outside of the postsecondary education system, at the national level, the US Department of Labor provides some support for low-achieving youth. The Job Corps is a no-cost education and vocational training program administered since 1964 focusing on out-of-school, low-income youth aged 16–24. More than 70 percent of enrolees are minorities. Job Corps participants learn a trade and are supported in earning a high school equivalency diploma or general equivalency diploma. Job Corps also provides career counselling and transition support to its students for up to 12 months after they graduate from the program. A study by Mathematica Policy Research, Inc. (MPR 2002) found that Job Corps participants improved their literacy skills, earned more after completing, received less welfare, and had fewer criminal arrests.

Other programs target youth with disabilities. Notable is the Job Accommodations Network, a technical assistance service provided to employers to attract, hire, and retain young workers with disabilities. Aside from data on the number of businesses seeking information, no studies examine the impact of this program.

Grubb (1996) found that the vast array of government-sponsored job training programs do not increase earnings substantially. He suggested that one explanation for the minimal effect of these programs on earnings is that they target and enrol individuals with substantial barriers to employment (e.g., low skill levels, drug and alcohol abuse problems, and physical disabilities) that are apparent to employers but not otherwise described by the data.

## The emerging workplace and CTE

Labor market trends indicate that many opportunities are available to non-college qualified youth if they possess the kinds of skills and training provided by secondary CTE programs and postsecondary CTE degree and certificate programs. Stone and Alfeld (2006) defined the basic skills for success in the modern workplace as reliability, positive attitude, willingness to work hard, ninth-grade or higher mathematics abilities, ninth-grade or higher reading abilities, the ability to solve semi-structured problems at levels much higher than today's high school graduates, the ability to work in groups, the ability to make effective oral and written presentations, and the ability to use personal computers to carry out simple tasks. Other reports (Mathematica Policy Research Inc. 2002; Barton 2005) concluded that employers place a higher premium on hiring individuals who show good work habits, confidence, and leadership skills – the so-called 'soft skills'. Many of these skills can be developed through classroom- and work-based CTE experiences.

### CTE strategies for successful transitions from education to work

Quality CTE programs include three kinds of activities: classroom instruction, work-based learning, and related student organizations. Each represents an opportunity: (1) to engage youth, make learning more interesting, and keep them in school; (2) to improve the academic and technical skills of youth; and (3) to motivate them to continue education and training beyond high school. Stern et al. (1995) reported on characteristics associated with quality school-to-work programs, which included classroom-based experiences, work-based learning experiences, and strategies for ensuring successful transition to continued education beyond high school.

### Classroom-based learning

Since the late 1980s, the CTE classroom has been used to improve student learning in academic subjects by contextualizing that learning in a practical context, giving concrete meaning to theories and abstract information (Stern *et al.* 1995). This effort is important for two reasons. First, the students who populate CTE classrooms often bring with them characteristics associated with lower academic ability. Second, the federal CTE legislation mandates academic rigor. Recently, the National Research Center for Career and Technical Education (NRCCTE) completed a large-scale experimental study of a pedagogic model of curriculum integration (Stone *et al.* 2005; 2006). In this study, students in the experimental classes significantly increased their scores on mathematics tests compared to students in traditional CTE classes, thus demonstrating the viability of building academic skills along with technical skills.

### Work-based learning

Work-based learning takes many forms. The one most associated with high school CTE is the *co-op*, also called an internship. Less intensive forms of work-based learning, like job-shadowing, involve additional students. Evidence of the impact or effect of participation in any of these or other forms of work-based learning is modest and mixed (e.g., Stern *et al.* 1995). Swail and Kampits (2004) documented an unusual effect of high school work-based learning or community service on college achievement. Students who participated had higher grade point averages than those who did not. Working outside of school can enhance youth development in ways that traditional classroom learning cannot (Stone and Mortimer 1998).

### Other strategies

Increasingly, the emphasis of the public education system is to move students toward postsecondary education. A number of strategies have been employed to increase the college-going rate of CTE students, most notably Tech Prep (Bragg *et al.* 2002). Silverberg *et al.* (2004) suggested that, while CTE students attend college at a lower rate than other students, over time, that difference declines. Despite the lack of supporting evidence, strategies such as dual enrolment and dual credit options are increasingly being implemented as a strategy to effect this transition. The current federal CTE legislation has wrapped this approach in law through what it defines as programs of study, which are intended to link secondary CTE programs with postsecondary programs leading to degrees or skills certificates.

## Conclusion

The current US political climate is such that all young people are expected to move through high school and into postsecondary education. The problem of preparing all students for success in the workplace thus becomes the domain of higher education. The reality of US higher education, however, does not match the rhetoric of many of the workplace assumptions behind the current 'college for all' philosophy. The United States does not have a well-developed second-chance system for either the high school dropout (or pushout) or the college dropout, and individual states vary in the quality and availability of programs to support such students. This argues for a public education system and related government policies that will improve the availability and quality of high school CTE – a first-chance system for academic and economic success. High-quality secondary and postsecondary CTE programs can improve the school-to-adult transition of youth by harnessing students' natural interests as tools to engage them in learning, using those interests to improve academic skills, and connecting student employment to in-school programs.

## References

Association for Career and Technical Education (2006) *Ready for College and Ready for Work: Same or different?* Iowa City, IA: ACTE.

—— (2007) *Expanding Opportunities: Postsecondary Career and Technical Education and Preparing Tomorrow's Workforce*, Position paper, Alexandria, VA:

Bailey, T., Leinbach, T., Scott, M., Alfonso, M., Kienzl, G. and Kennedy, B. (2004) *The Characteristics of Occupational Students in Postsecondary Education* (CCRC Brief), New York: Columbia University, Teachers College.

Barton, P. (2005) *One-third of a Nation: Rising Dropout Rates and Declining Opportunities*, Princeton, NJ: Educational Testing Services.

—— (2006) *High School Reform and Work: Facing Labor Market Realities*, Princeton, NJ: Educational Testing Service.

—— (2008) *How Many College Graduates Does the U.S. Labor Force Really Need?* Stanford, CA: The Carnegie Foundation for the Advancement of Teaching.

Bragg, D. D., Loeb, J. W., Gong, Y., Deng, C.-P., Yoo, J.-S. and Hill, J. L. (2002) *Transition from High School to College and Work for Tech Prep Participants in Eight Selected Consortia*, St. Paul, MN: National Research Center for Career and Technical Education (NRCCTE).

Castellano, M., Stone, J. R. III, Stringfield, S., Farley-Ripple, E. N., Overman, L. and Hussain, R. (2007) *Career-based Comprehensive School Reform: Serving Disadvantaged Youth in Minority Communities*, St. Paul, MN: The National Research Center for Career and Technical Education.

Castellano, M., Stone, J. R., III, Stringfield, S., Farley, E. N. and Wayman, J. C. (2004) *The Effect of CTE-Enhanced Whole-School Reform on Student Course Taking and Performance in English and Science*, St. Paul, MN: NRCCTE.

Castellano, M., Stringfield, S., Stone, J. R., III, and Wayman, J. C. (2003) *Early Measures of Student Progress in Schools with CTE-Enhanced Whole-School Reform: Math Course Taking Patterns and Student Progress to Graduation*, St. Paul, MN: NRCCTE.

Gardner, D. P. (1983) *A Nation at Risk: The Imperative for Educational Reform: An Open Letter to the American People. A Report to the Nation and the Secretary of Education*, Washington, DC: U.S. Department of Education.

Grubb, N. (1996) *The Returns to Education and Training in the Sub-Baccalaureate Labor Market: Evidence from the Survey of Income and Program Participation, 1984–1990*, Saint Paul, MN: NRCCTE (MDS-765).

Hecker, D. E. (2005) *Occupational Employment Projections to 2014*, Washington, DC: U.S. Department of Labor, Bureau of Labor Market Statistics.

Heckman, J. J. and LaFontaine, P. A. (2007) *The American High School Graduation Rate: Trends and levels*, Discussion Paper No. 3216, Bonn: Forschungsinstitut zur Zunkunft der Arbeit [Institute for the Study of Labor].

Levesque, K. A. (2003) *Trends in High School Vocational/Technical Course-Taking, 1982–1998*, Washington, DC: National Center for Education Statistics.

Levesque, K. A., Lauren, D., Teitelbaum, P., Alt, M., Librera, S. and Nelson, D. (2000) *Vocational Education in the United States: Toward the Year 2000*, Washington, DC: U.S. Department of Education, National Center for Education Statistics.

Lewis, M. V. (2000) 'Vocational education and the dilemma of education', *Journal of Vocational Education Research*, 25: 575–84.

Mathematica Policy Research, Inc. (2002) *Job Corps: An Education and Training Program for Disadvantaged Youth that Works*, Princeton, NJ: Mathematica Policy Research, Inc.

Meeder, H. (2008) *The Perkins Act of 2006: Connecting Career and Technical Education with the College and Career Readiness Agenda*, Washington, DC: Achieve, Inc.

National Assessment of Educational Progress (2005) *The Nation's Report Card Mathematics 2005*, Washington, DC: National Center for Education Statistics.

National Association of Secondary School Principals (2004) *Breaking Ranks II: Strategies for Leading High School Reform,* Reston, VA: National Association of Secondary School Principals.

National Center for Education Statistics (2004) *The Condition of Education 2004. Indicator 18: Remediation and Degree Completion*, Washington, DC: National Center for Education Statistics.

——(2007) *Findings from the Condition of Education 2007: High School Course Taking*, Washington, DC: National Center for Education Statistics.

National Center for Public Policy and Higher Education (2004) *Measuring Up,* San Jose, CA: National Center for Public Policy and Higher Education.

Oakes, J., Gamaron, A. and Page, R. N. (1992) 'Curriculum differentiation: opportunities, outcomes, and meanings', in P. W. Jackson (ed.) *Handbook of Research on Curriculum*, New York: Macmillan.

Plank, S. (2002) 'A question of balance: CTE, academic courses, high school persistence, and student achievement', *Journal of Vocational Education Research*, 26: 279–327.

Plank, S., DeLuca, S. and Estachion, A. (2005) *Dropping out of High School and the Place of Career and Technical Education: A Survival Analysis of Surviving High School*, St. Paul, MN: The National Research Center for Career and Technical Education.

Rosenbaum, J. E. (2002) *Beyond Empty Promises: Policies to Improve Transitions into College and Jobs* (ED-99-CO-0160), Washington, DC: U.S. Department of Education, Office of Vocational and Adult Education.

Silverberg, M., Warner, E., Fong, M. and Goodwin, D. (2004) *National Assessment of Vocational Education: Final report to Congress*, Washington, DC: U.S. Department of Education.

Stern, D., Finkelstein, N., Stone, J. R., III, Latting, J. and Dornsife, C. (1995) *School to Work: Research on Programs in the United States*, Washington, DC: Taylor and Francis.

Stone, J. R., III and Alfeld, C. (2006) 'The neglected majority-revisited', *Journal of Career and Technical Education*, 21: 61–74.

Stone, J. R., III, Alfeld, C., Pearson, D., Lewis, M. V. and Jensen, S. (2005) *Building Academic Skills in Context: Testing the Value of Enhanced Math Learning in Career and Technical Education*, St Paul, MN: NRCCTE.

Stone, J. R., III and Aliaga, O. A. (2007) 'Participation in career and technical education and school-to-work in American high schools', in D. Neumark (ed.) *Improving School-to-Work Transitions*, New York: Russell Sage Foundation.

Stone, J. R., III and Mortimer, J. T. (1998) 'The effect of adolescent employment on vocational development: public and educational policy implications', *Journal of Vocational Behavior*, 53: 184–214.

Swail, W. S. and Kampits, E. (2004) *Work-Based Learning and Higher Education: A Research Perspective*, Washington, DC: Educational Policy Institute, Inc.

Swarthout, L. (2006) *Paying Back, Not Giving Back: Student Debt's Negative Impact on Public Service Career Opportunities*, Boston: The U.S. Public Interest Research Group.

# Part IV

# Employment and unemployment

*Andy Furlong*

## Employment and unemployment in late modernity

Young people's experiences of employment have changed quite significantly in recent decades, although in some important respects similarities remain. Working lives tend to begin later with educational participation occupying young people for longer periods of time, although many young will combine study with part-time employment. Early working lives are frequently fragmented with young people engaged in a variety of jobs before developing more settled employment careers and, if they are fortunate, settling into longer-term careers. Some will encounter frequent periods of worklessness, although in many countries levels of unemployment are currently somewhat lower than they were in the 1980s and 1990s. At the same time, there are concerns about the precarious nature of many of the jobs secured by young people and it has been argued that non-standard, insecure, forms of work increasingly define modern employment contexts.

In describing young people's changing experiences of work, in Chapter 18, Mortimer argues that the 'single career' model is a thing of the past. Young people today tend to move jobs more frequently and often face the need to secure new qualifications and training. Career paths become much less predictable and young people are faced with the need to actively manage their own careers without the benefit of clear markers (especially in those countries that lack developed guidance systems). In these situations, some clearly struggle to move from 'survival jobs' to more secure sectors of the labour market while those who are more advantaged continue to make relatively smooth transitions. Despite strong initial ambitions, expectations change over time, falling into line with available opportunities and reflecting previous experience. Indeed, employment experiences remain highly stratified with factors such as social class, gender, 'race', ethnicity, neighbourhood and educational pathways having an important bearing on experiences.

While unemployment among young people has fallen in recent years, there are still concerns about its long-term impact, especially in the case of prolonged periods of worklessness. In highlighting debates about effective unemployment policy, in Chapter 19, Julkunen draws attention to the maintenance of long-standing divisions relating to social class and gender. She also highlights processes of change both in contexts of economic support as well as in the growing importance of new forms of marginality which suggest that the old dichotomy between employment and unemployment is somewhat dated due, in part, to the growth of insecure and marginal forms of working.

In Chapter 20, MacDonald is wary about the tendency of some academics to overstate the growth of precarious forms of employment without making clear differentiations about the extent to which different groups of workers have become vulnerable to insecurity. Here he makes an important distinction between *employment* insecurity and the increased precariousness of the *transitional* process. While the growth of employment insecurity as a general trend is often exaggerated, it is younger and less educated workers (especially those who live in depressed regions) who tend to experience insecure forms of working during the transitional process with a sizeable minority going on to experience fragmented careers. While there has been a tendency for policy-makers to argue that most forms of work experience will enhance employability, MacDonald argues that insecure and precarious jobs rarely represent stepping stones to stable employment but frequently lead to the long-term entrapment in marginal work forms with young people being churned between a series of poor jobs, interspersed with periods of worklessness.

Globally, young people encounter a range of different labour market contexts and face work situations that have changed in very different ways. Although timings, institutional frameworks and economic contexts differ, there are strong continuities in the long-term direction of change in advanced societies. In Japan, for example, levels of unemployment remained relatively low and transitions were characterized by stability during a period in which rates of unemployment in the West increased rapidly. Yet during the 1990s transitions became less stable, unemployment rose and there was a significant increase in the numbers of young people encountering precarious forms of employment and withdrawing from job-search activity. As Inui notes in Chapter 21, in Japan, even though concepts differ, there is evidence of a significant growth in the numbers of young people trapped in peripheral positions with few opportunities to develop skills. Moreover, as in the West, there has been a tendency to regard changes in the work situation of youth as reflecting poor motivation on the part of young people rather than acknowledging changing structures of opportunity.

While the advanced societies move towards a new modernity in which employment opportunities become less stable and individual life management becomes more significant, political change and rapid industrialization in China have led to a very different set of changes for young people. Whereas urban residents were once allocated jobs in state-run work units (and rural residents largely confined to agricultural employment), young people in China are increasingly finding jobs through their own initiative and, as Liu shows in Chapter 22, migration from the country to the town presents new opportunities as well as new forms of stratification. Migrant workers are often discriminated against, paid inferior wages and blamed for social problems. Other forms of stratification relate to gender, education and class as middle-class youth draw on family connections to secure advantaged forms of employment.

Processes of individualization and the need to actively manage careers mean that many young people seek increased control over their work situations. Self-employment can be seen as representing an attempt to break free of the sorts of constraints inherent in dependent employment relationships. From an econometric perspective, in Chapter 23, Blanchflower and Oswald examine some of the barriers that stand between young people and self-employment. Noting that the self-employed tend to be more satisfied with their lives and jobs, they argue that potential entrepreneurs tend to be held back by a lack of capital and show that those who inherit money before the age of 23 or who have parents who run their own businesses are more likely to become self-employed.

While processes of change are complex and far-reaching, the contributors to this part provide a fairly comprehensive flavour of key labour market trends affecting young people. It is argued that although situations have changed, key inequalities remain deeply entrenched and it is suggested that new concepts are needed to capture the fragmented careers experienced by many young people.

# 18

# Changing experiences of work

*Jeylan T. Mortimer*

## Introduction: the social context

Change in the experience of work in youth and young adulthood is inextricably tied to broad historical shifts in the transition to adulthood, the occupational structure, and the economy. During the past several decades, the process of becoming adult has become more prolonged, largely due to the extension of higher education. Moreover, no longer can it be said that there is a single, well-recognized and institutionalized 'pathway' to adulthood. In comparison to prior generations of young people, today's youth acquire the traditional role markers of adulthood, including finishing school, leaving their parental home, obtaining a full-time job, marrying, and becoming a parent, in a more variable and individualized sequence (Shanahan 2000).

The decline of well-paying, blue-collar employment, linked to the contraction of the manufacturing industry in the United States, makes it no longer feasible for young people to expect to obtain a middle-class life style with only a high school education (Schneider and Stevenson 1999). Today's youth and their parents understand that good, high paying jobs necessitate education beyond high school, and most adolescents aspire to obtain four-year college degrees.[1] A long-standing tradition of research in the United States, the 'status attainment' school, documents that educational attainment is the primary mediator of the link between socioeconomic origins and occupational destinations (Sewell and Hauser 1975). Youth whose parents have higher occupational prestige, education, and income encourage their children to obtain more education; their children, in turn, have higher educational aspirations, which promote higher educational and occupational attainments. Currently in the United States, young people's educational and occupational goals are quite ambitious; currently approximately 70 percent of high school graduates enter colleges or other institutions of higher education.

## Trends in the experience of employment through the school-to-work transition

Heinz (2003) documents shifts in employment during the past several decades in Europe and America that have dramatically altered the experience of work. Recent cohorts of young people entering the labor force encounter opportunities and constraints that reflect the effects of globalization, technological innovation, and rapid occupational change. The classic tripartite division of the life course into segments denoting education or preparation for employment, the work career, and retirement no longer holds. As a result of rapidly shifting technologies and occupational structures, workers can no longer expect to choose a single line of work, and follow a recognizable 'career path' within the same field during a lifetime of employment. Instead, workers are increasingly likely to experience multiple job and occupational changes, with need for 're-tooling', additional certification, degrees, or continuing education, so as to remain viable in highly competitive employment markets. Instead of following preordained, scripted career paths, the individual must construct his or her own trajectory.

Employers have responded to heightened competition by reducing personnel costs through downsizing and overseas outsourcing, and lessening their commitments to employees through non-standard employment contracts. Young workers increasingly find jobs through 'temp' agencies, rather than being employed directly by a firm. While temporary work is highly variable, it is likely to be part-time and involve frequent changes of employer and organizational venue, requiring considerable adaptation and flexibility. In this rapidly changing occupational and technological environment, youth's transition from 'survival jobs' to more stable full-time 'career jobs' becomes ever more challenging. Success will come for those who have access to, and can mobilize, diverse resources – intellectual, psychological, and all the various elements of capital, including social and cultural capital as well as human capital – to obtain their occupational objectives.

Unfortunately, most young people in the USA lack formal preparation for such sophisticated maneuvering through the labor market before they embark on their quest for 'career-like' employment. They receive little vocational guidance, since high school counsellors are mainly concerned with scheduling classes, making sure that students have completed the courses required for high school graduation, and gaining admittance to colleges. Nor are most students offered vocationally-relevant courses or programs or encouraged to assess their occupational goals and plan their employment futures. In fact, many parents are suspicious of any such vocational guidance or activities, fearing that they might divert their adolescent children from higher education. As a result, high school students typically give little serious thought to their future occupations, though most are able to respond when asked directly about occupational choices. Such responses feature the most prestigious and remunerative professional and managerial occupations. According to Schneider and Stevenson (1999), American young people are 'ambitious but directionless', having little sense of what is needed in the way of educational experiences or credentials that are needed for entry into particular lines of work.

Moreover, unlike other post-industrial modern societies, in North America there are few institutional bridges that effectively link education and work. Unlike the apprenticeship system of Germany, Denmark, and Austria, and the connections between high schools and employers in Japan, American youth have to rely on their own social contacts and experiences to help them to orient themselves to the labor market. The qualifications that most students receive (such as high school diplomas and BA degrees) are general credentials; in other modern societies they are more likely to be occupationally-specific (Kerckhoff 2003). As a result, neither employers nor novice job seekers have a good sense of what kinds of work an individual would be capable of doing. The absence of educational supports and school-to-work bridges contributes to long periods of 'floundering' – moving between jobs that are often little different from jobs held during high school, before settling into full-time work with 'career' potential.

In this context, youth who are able to obtain the highly coveted four-year college degrees enter the labor force in the most advantageous position. College placement services provide institutional supports that are lacking for the vast majority of labor force entrants who lack a four-year college degree: high school dropouts, high school graduates, and those who obtain 'some college'. Though the meaning of the B.A./B.S degree to employers is much debated; that is, whether it signifies achievements that will increase worker productivity, or alternatively, whether it indicates persistence and the capacity to learn; holders of four-year degrees (like those who obtain even more advanced professional and graduate degrees), clearly have the advantage.

Then how do young people prepare themselves for 'career-like' work in this increasingly challenging context? We find that they do this largely through their part-time work experiences while still in school. Whereas finishing school and beginning full-time work in fairly rapid succession once characterized the 'transition from school to work', this transition has now become a process typically lasting several years as young people combine roles as student and worker. Employment during high school has become a near-universal experience in the United States (Mortimer 2003); and patterns of investment in school and work developed in the adolescent years tend to persist as young people leave high school and enter colleges, technical institutes, or vocational schools (Staff and Mortimer 2007). So instead of finishing school and then beginning full-time work, young people today are more likely to simultaneously occupy the roles of student and worker (part-time or full-time) for long periods of time. Because their work during this long transitional phase needs to accommodate their responsibilities as students, their jobs are often characterized as 'survival' or 'stop-gap' jobs – part-time, transient, having low pay, without benefits, and predominantly in the service sector, rather than 'career jobs' – full-time, higher-paying, including health and retirement benefits, and diversified with respect to industry and occupational type.

We find evidence for two emergent 'tracks' in the transition from school to work in adolescence and young adulthood. Students upon entry to high school, who feel less confident about succeeding in the educational system, invest heavily in work during their high school years, working long hours on their jobs. These highly invested teenage workers, who pursue high intensity work (averaging more than 20 hours per week) during most months while they are attending school (in one study, 22 out of 24 months of observation), move more quickly after leaving high school than other students into 'career-like' work – jobs they identify as their careers (Mortimer et al. 2008). Though they may obtain some higher education at community colleges or vocational technical institutes, they are unlikely to obtain four-year college degrees. Clearly, during high school, they pursue a strategy to enhance their human capital through work experience, not through formal education.

Students who have greater educational promise upon entry to high school – those who have higher grades, higher educational aspirations, and who think of themselves as having stronger academic aptitude – are also employed during high school, but they limit

151

their hours of work so as to effectively accommodate their academic pursuits, extra-curricular activities, and time with friends and family. The steady, high duration-low intensity (less than 20 hours per week, on average) workers are more likely than youth who pursue other high school work patterns to achieve four-year college degrees. They learn to balance school and working while still in high school, and carry these time management skills into the college years. Though 'low promise' youth are less likely to pursue this pattern of working and studying during high school, when they do take this pathway, their chances of completing college greatly increase (Staff and Mortimer 2007).

In both cases, working and schooling, pursued in combination, continue over a long period of time. Both 'steady' and 'most invested' workers make the transition from school to work through several years of participation in both spheres. The process of entry into work take somewhat different form for students pursuing these divergent school and employment 'tracks', and results in positions that have a differential career potential, as indicated by income and advancement opportunities. Still, both move toward legitimate and highly valued objectives – higher educational attainment and career establishment. Of greater concern are students who are locked out of early employment opportunities (Newman 1999), or those who work only sporadically, with spurts of high-intensity employment that do not allow for the pursuit of the multi-faceted adolescent 'well-rounded' lifestyle, the accumulation of human capital through work that fosters early entry to 'career-like' employment, nor the development of time management skills that facilitate higher education.

## Objective and subjective occupational experiences

In examining the changing experience of work it is important to make an analytical distinction between objective and subjective experiences, although these experiences may be blurred empirically. Objective work characteristics refer to the structure of employment; ideally, they are measured by external observers (persons other than the worker). For example, the process of 'floundering' can be measured by how long it takes, after finishing school, for young people to locate stable, full-time employment. Wage rates, employment benefits, and task requirements can similarly be gauged. Objective features are of interest to government agencies concerned with matching workers and jobs and tracking the quality of employment through time. For example, the US Department of Labor's *Dictionary of Occupational Titles*, and more recently, O'NET classification[2] enable assessment of the cognitive demands posed by job tasks. Other objective features of work include its industrial and organizational location, whether there are career ladders which provide opportunity for mobility through a firm, the features of standard and non-standard employment relations referred to earlier, etc.

Subjective features of work experience, in contrast, refer to the worker's multifaceted reactions to their jobs. Most widely studied are job satisfaction and the worker's commitment to the job, occupation, and employer. They also include anxieties and feelings of insecurity, on the one hand, or feelings of confidence, ambition, and optimism as workers contemplate their occupational futures.

Whereas objective and subjective experiences tend to be related, that is, workers may be expected to respond positively to jobs with positive features ('good jobs', according to Kalleberg *et al.* 2000), it cannot be presumed that workers' subjective responses to the same work situation will be identical. Certain features of work are sometimes considered so important and compelling that all workers will respond similarly to them. For example, according to Kohn and Schooler (1983), workers respond similarly, and positively, to the degree of self-direction in their jobs irrespective of their demographic or other personal characteristics. According to another plausible point of view (Mortimer and Lorence 1995), workers' expectations and values influence their responses to their jobs. For example, one who seeks opportunities for work with people will not likely be satisfied or committed to employment that offers few such experiences even if the work is highly self-directed. Similarly, an ambitious youth who aims for a professional or managerial occupation with high prestige and economic compensation may be quite disappointed if only able to obtain a lower-level white-collar job, say, as a clerk in a bank. A supervisor in a fast-food restaurant coming from an impoverished background in a poor neighborhood might consider that job a 'career job'; to another, the same position constitutes a 'survival job' at best. Given the evidence that adolescents are becoming more ambitious, it is likely that they will be more dissatisfied with the jobs that are available to them as they enter the full-time adult labor force.

Whereas youth may attach very different meaning to jobs with the very same objective characteristics, the situation is complicated by the tendency for workers to change their orientations in response to the work experiences that are available to them. In fact, as they make the transition from school to work, young people's judgments about the 'importance' of various extrinsic (e.g. income, security, advancement opportunity, etc.) and intrinsic rewards (e.g. interesting work, responsibility, creativity, working with people and providing service to others) decline as they encounter the challenges of the labor market (Johnson 2001b).

There is substantial evidence that young people's judgments about work change over time in such a way that they become more congruent with the actual work that they experience. For example, youth who have a lot of autonomy in their jobs tend to increase their valuation of intrinsic rewards over time (Mortimer and Lorence 1979; Johnson 2001a); those who make a lot of money become more extrinsic, and less people-oriented, in their orientations. These tendencies help individuals to avoid psychologically dissonant states (wanting features of work that are unavailable) and to enhance their job satisfaction, thus perhaps mitigating the impacts of higher ambition.

Orientations toward work are more malleable and responsive to experiences in the workplace in the early phases of the career, when attitudes have not yet crystallized. Early experiences in the workforce that are positive and engaging – affirming the young worker's mastery of occupational tasks, the capacity to sustain employment and to be productive – would likely instil a positive work ethic, crystallize occupational values, and enhance commitment to work and career. Such salutary socialization processes would heighten expectations of success and foster ambition. Early success in the workplace can thus pave the way to subsequent achievement, as young workers accumulate the work experiences and contacts that facilitate continued occupational achievement and success despite economic cycles and organizational upheavals (mergers, downsizing, outsourcing, etc.). Though the 'single career' imperative may no longer be in force, and the need to flexibly move from job to job, and even from one occupation to another, may be increasingly prevalent, those who have accumulated the most human and social capital, including a sense of efficacy, confidence, and positive work values, will surely be in the more desirable, competitive position. Alternatively, sporadic work doing routine, dull tasks, interspersed with bouts of unemployment, or other failure experiences, would likely have quite different impacts – reducing confidence, commitment to work, and aspirations, or even withdrawal, insofar as possible, from this sphere and consequent dependency.

The rapidly changing occupational environment has the potential to erode both the objective and the subjective experiences of work; and much of the commentary on recent workforce transformations emphasizes the growing challenges in both spheres. As skilled manufacturing, white-collar and even service jobs are outsourced overseas, highly skilled professional and managerial employment and a pool of low-skilled service jobs remain. With job protections diminishing, workers are likely to face objective occupational downgrading after involuntary termination from prior jobs, and suffer in terms of their subjective experience of work – with declining job satisfaction and work commitment, along with increasing stress.

## Subgroup variation

Portrayals of the changing social context and experience of work during the transition to adulthood present a broad picture that varies considerably across subgroups in the US. For example, though the transition to adulthood has become more variable and unpredictable, some youth move smoothly through this formative period of the life course, experiencing what might be considered a standard or traditional pattern, finishing school and obtaining full-time work without undue difficulty. Others become caught up in an extended period of floundering in part-time non-standard 'youth jobs', with seemingly little direction or capacity to effectively maneuver through the myriad obstacles and pass the gatekeepers to secure 'career-like' employment.

As the transition to adulthood more generally (Mortimer *et al.* 2008), early work experiences differ considerably depending on family social class background and the socioeconomic features of the neighborhood. Affluent families can marshal their considerable economic and social resources in a manner that promotes the educational and occupational attainments of their offspring, including the use of private schools and tutors, the provision of growth-inducing summer travel and camps, and the capacity to draw on their considerable cultural and social capital to guide their children through college entrance and career entry processes (Furstenberg 2006). Aronson (2008) shows that children of lower social class background face hurdles at every step necessary for higher educational attainment, including gaining college admission, obtaining financial aid, achieving requisite grade point averages to stay in school, etc.

Newman (1999) has carefully documented, through her study of Harlem youth, that teenagers in impoverished, high crime neighborhoods have scarce job opportunities from which to choose (see also Wilson 1987). The more fortunate ones, able to land part-time jobs in fast food restaurants or in the retail or service sector despite the heavy competition, gain exposure to working role models who may steer them away from criminal activity and welfare dependency. Still, it is the unusual youth who is able to withstand the derision of peers, who may have access to far greater amounts of cash through illegal activities, and stick it out long enough to develop more conventional work and achievement orientations. Young people in depressed rural areas also face a very limited employment market, and must often make wrenching decisions about whether to stay or leave their home towns to obtain greater economic opportunity.

In addition to variation by social class background and urban/rural residence, the early experiences of work are likely to vary by other ascriptive divides, such as gender, race and ethnicity, and immigration status. Whereas women in the USA now surpass men in educational attainment, they still are underrepresented in many male-dominated fields, including science, mathematics, engineering and various technical fields; command lower incomes; bear the brunt of work-family conflict, especially when they enter parenthood (Ammons and Kelly 2008); and are much more likely than men to be subject to sexual harassment in the workplace (McLaughlin *et al.* 2008). African Americans continue to experience a higher risk of involuntary job dismissal than whites, even when numerous indicators of human capital and labor force position are controlled (Wilson 2005). In accord with the increasing ethnic diversity of American society, researchers are beginning to address the difficulties of immigrant children in achieving their educational and occupational ambitions (Feliciano and Rumbaut 2005), as well as the benefits and costs of work in ethnic enclaves. The latter can offer protections for young immigrant and minority workers against the injustice and discrimination encountered in the general workforce, while at the same time often limiting opportunity.

## Directions for future research

Continued study of the changing work experiences young people encounter as they make the transition from school to work is necessary given the critical character of this stage in the occupational career. Due to the rapid change in the occupational and social context and in youth adaptations, it is important to continuously monitor the changing experiences of work, and youth's reactions to them, during the transition to adulthood. We need research on the strategies youth use in adapting to changing labor force and occupational environments, especially those that prove successful in the more disadvantaged segments of the population. Given the importance of work for adult economic sustenance and lifestyle, the capacity of young people to establish themselves in this sphere can have major implications for their capacities to become economically independent of their families of origin (Schoeni and Ross 2005; Swartz 2008); the well-being of their families of procreation (Ammons and Kelly 2008), and even their capacities to form families; and for their personal well-being and mental health. Future investigations should address these important dynamics of spillover from work to other domains of young people's lives.

## Notes

1 In the USA, bachelor's degrees are typically structured as four-year programs, although many students take five or six years to complete their degrees.
2 Details of the O'NET classification can be found at www.online.onecenter.org.

## References

Ammons, S. K. and Kelly, E. L. (2008) 'Social class and the experience of work-family conflict during the transition to adulthood', *New Directions in Child and Adolescent Development*, 119: 71–84.
Aronson. P. (2008) 'Breaking barriers or locked out? Class-based perceptions and experiences of post-secondary education', *New Directions in Child and Adolescent Development*, 119: 41–54.
Feliciano, C. and Rumbaut, R. G. (2005) 'Gendered paths: educational and occupational expectations and outcomes among adult children of immigrants', *Ethnic and Racial Studies*, 28: 1087–118.

Furstenberg, F. F. (2006) 'Diverging development: the not so invisible hand of social class in the United States', paper presented at the biennial meetings of the Society for Research on Adolescence, San Francisco. Available at www.transad.pop.upenn.edu

Heinz, W. R. (2003) 'From work trajectories to negotiated careers: the contingent work life course', in J. T. Mortimer and M. J. Shanahan (eds) *Handbook of the Life Course*, New York: Kluwer/Plenum, pp. 185–204.

Johnson, M. K. (2001a) 'Change in job values during the transition to adulthood', *Work and Occupations*, 28: 315–45.

—— (2001b) 'Job values in the young adult transition: stability and change with age', *Social Psychology Quarterly*, 64: 297–317.

Kalleberg, A., Reskin, B. F. and Hudson, K. (2000) 'Bad jobs in America: standard and nonstandard employment relations and job quality in the United States', *American Sociological Review*, 65: 256–78.

Kerckhoff, A. C. (2003) 'From student to worker', in J. T. Mortimer and M. Shanahan (eds) *Handbook of the Life Course*, New York: Kluwer Academic/Plenum.

Kohn, M. L. and Schooler, C. (1983) *Work and Personality: An Inquiry into the Impact of Social Stratification*, Norwood, NJ: Ablex.

McLaughlin, H., Uggen, C. and Blackstone, A. (2008) 'Social class and workplace harassment during the transition to adulthood', *New Directions in Child and Adolescent Development*, 119: 85–98.

Mortimer, J. T. (2003) *Working and Growing Up in America*, Cambridge, MA: Harvard University Press.

Mortimer, J. T. and Lorence, J. (1979) 'Work experience and occupational value socialization: a longitudinal study', *American Journal of Sociology*, 84: 1361–85.

—— (1995) 'Social psychology of work', in K. Cook, G. A. Fine and J. S. House (eds) *Sociological Perspectives on Social Psychology*, Needham Heights, MA: Allyn and Bacon.

Mortimer, J. T., Vuolo, M. C., Staff, J., Wakefield, S. and Xie, W. (2008) 'Tracing the timing of "career" acquisition in a contemporary youth cohort', *Work and Occupations*, 35: 44–84.

Newman, K. S. (1999) *No Shame in My Game: The Working Poor in the Inner City*, New York: Knopf and Russell Sage Foundation.

Schneider, B. and Stevenson, D. (1999) *The Ambitious Generation*, New Haven, CT: Yale University Press.

Schoeni, R. F. and Ross, K. E. (2005) 'Material assistance from families during the transition to adulthood', in R. A. Settersten, F. F. Furstenberg, and R. G. Rumbaut (eds) *On the Frontier of Adulthood*, Chicago: University of Chicago Press.

Sewell, W. H. and Hauser, R. M. (1975) *Education, Occupation, and Earnings: Achievement in the Early Career*, Orlando, FL: Academic Press.

Staff, J. and Mortimer, J. T. (2007) 'Educational and work strategies from adolescence to early adulthood: consequences for educational attainment', *Social Forces*, 85: 1169–94.

Shanahan, M. J. (2000) 'Pathways to adulthood in changing societies: variability and mechanisms in life course perspective', *Annual Review of Sociology*, 26: 667–92.

Swartz, T. S. (2008) 'Family capital and the invisible transfer of privilege: intergenerational support and social class in early adulthood', *New Directions in Child and Adolescent Development*, 119: 11–24.

Wilson, G. (2005) 'Race and job dismissal: African American/White differences in their sources during the early work career', *American Behavioral Scientist*, 48: 1182–99.

Wilson, W. J. (1987) *The Truly Disadvantaged: The Inner City, the Underclass, and Public Policy*, Chicago: University of Chicago Press.

# 19

# Youth unemployment and marginalization

*Illse Julkunen*

## Introduction

The year is 1989 and Matti, 21, is unemployed. The unemployment rate is 4 per cent. The national situation is characterized by rapid economic growth, income equality and almost non-existent poverty. Matti is not yet established in the labour market and is not entitled to earnings-related unemployment benefits. For this he would have needed six months' previous work experience. He contacts the welfare office which asks him to contact the employment office. The welfare office also requires him to investigate if he has a right to a basic flatrate allowance. His employment benefits are suspended for one month. During that time Matti receives social assistance as a basic right. With the employment situation being relatively good, the employment office soon finds Matti a job.

The year is 2004 and Mikko, 20, is unemployed. The unemployment rate is 10 per cent and has fallen since the dramatic increase that occurred in the 1990s when it reached 17 per cent. Mikko has no work experience and is not entitled to earnings-related unemployment allowance as he lacks the required 10 months' work experience. As a newcomer he is not entitled to a basic allowance and is suspended for five months. He turns to the welfare office which asks him to contact the employment office. During that time he receives social assistance. The employment office designs a work activation plan and after three months he is offered a job training placement. He refuses to take the placement because of long distances to travel and is sent back to the welfare office which cuts his social assistance by 20 per cent. After refusing another offer the social assistance is reduced by another 20 per cent.

These case studies, drawn from Finland, highlight the changing situations for young unemployed people in Europe. They say something about the changed conditions in the European labour market and illustrate the difficulties faced by young people trying to get a foothold in the labour market. Despite relatively strong economic performance and an increase in productivity, employment situations have not improved. Radical policy changes have also occurred which have changed the circumstances of the young and unemployed. In this context it is important to learn more about how unemployment is understood and looked upon. How is unemployment related to marginalization and can we find new discourses, new concepts, which help us make sense of youth unemployment? These are broad questions which cannot be fully covered here. The aim, however, is to discuss how unemployment among youth relates to the discourses of late modern society and to highlight the challenges for policy.

Contextual factors are crucial in understanding the ways in which unemployment is shaped. Policy strategies construct citizenship, inclusion and participation. In particular, activation policies contribute to the shaping of the context in which youth unemployment exists. New forms of governance are being developed. Youth unemployment relates to the transformation of policies, governance and broader societal processes and also to the development of new theoretical perspectives. However, this is not to suggest that everything is being transformed. On the contrary, a large body of research suggests powerful continuities.

## The (un)employment situation

Youth (un)employment varies considerably across European countries. There are marked cross-national differences not only in terms of youth unemployment, but also in terms of the quality of the jobs in which young people are employed. National institutional differences regarding employment protection legislation and the vocational specificity of the education system also affect cross-national differences in labour market entry patterns.

The logic of social integration seems to follow the contours of the different welfare policy models in Europe. Unemployment policies, gender policy and forms of youth representation can be studied using a model of youth transition regimes which focus on education, training and labour market entrance. Such models see regimes as combinations of culture and institutional structures in which variations include the universalistic (e.g. the Scandinavian countries), liberal (e.g. Great Britain), employment-centred (e.g. Germany), sub-protective (e.g. the Mediterranean countries) and other complex models characteristic of post-communist societies. Thus, the educational and social lives of young people in different European societies are constructed around quite different welfare regimes leading to varied forms of individualization (cf. Walther *et al.* 2006).

In all advanced societies, there is a core of young adults who are employed in relatively stable positions, along with a sizable minority of low paid workers whose working lives can be described as discontinuous and fragmented. Educational expansion has increased the number of skilled young people available in the labour market, but, at the same time, has resulted in an oversupply of trained people (Shavit and Blossfield 1993). Moreover, a significant number of young people are engaged in sheltered forms of employment or in job preparation programmes, reflecting poor demand rather than deficits in supply. Marginalization is also reflected in high unemployment rates, particularly among immigrant and youth groups who experience difficulties in becoming established in the labour market and making transitions to adulthood. These difficulties have become more severe over time and have been accompanied by an increased polarization in youth society (Ohlsson 2006). This increased vulnerability has been highlighted in several studies (Solga 2002; Kogan 2004) and offers explanations ranging from displacement theory to human capital deficits, as well as drawing attention to selection effects that reflect the negative perceptions of employers.

Unemployment among young people does not necessarily lead to marginalization and social exclusion, in fact, the labour market experiences of young people are relatively unrelated to development later in life. Long-term effects will be dependent upon how they cope with unemployment, the duration of the unemployment period, their mental health status and educational qualifications (Hammer 2007). In the long run, long-term unemployment has a negative impact on young people's economic position. Studies also show the impact of long-term unemployment on the reproduction of class and gender relations with several studies (Halleröd and Westberg 2006; Fenton *et al.* 2006; Furlong *et al.* 2006; Shildrick and MacDonald 2007) highlighting the impact of early labour market experiences on future adult lives. Indeed, (un)employment patterns among younger people emphasize the continuing significance of long-standing social divisions relating to socio-economic advantage and gender-related disadvantage.

## Continuity and change

Unemployment as a social phenomenon has many facets. Talking about the unemployed tends to conjure up images of a certain group of disadvantaged people. Yet unemployment is defined in a range of ways and applies to different groups of people. In conceptualizing unemployment, the relational aspect as well as the process needs to be highlighted. Unemployment is an institutional construct and can be seen as representing what a given society regards as normal and acceptable at a given point in time (Halvorsen 1999). This process always includes interests, resources and power. Although the construct of unemployment appears to have relatively stable features, new elements can help redefine it. Numerous studies have, for example, shown how young people, differentiated by social class, gender, ethnicity, locality and education, follow different paths as they leave school and enter the labour market (cf. Furlong and Cartmel 2007). At the same time there is a tendency to broaden the definition to include young people not in training, education or work. Young people can fall off the administrative landscape and may not be registered as unemployed while not commencing further education. There has been a growing awareness of this hidden unemployment, particularly among the younger age groups, though there has been no definitive statistical evidence of this phenomenon.

Much recent research on youth unemployment has focused on transition processes. In these studies the main aim is to analyse how the process has changed over time. These studies document important aspects of social change. However, continuities and similarities may well be underestimated. This has much to do with a lack of good longitudinal studies. Goodwin and O'Connor (2007), completing a study started by Norbert Elias in the 1960s by re-interviewing respondents in 2002, have shown that young people's experiences of school-to-work transitions in the 1960s displayed many similarities to transitional experience today. That is, the transition process was characterized by complexity, uncertainty and risk.

Both continuity and change are also apparent in how unemployment is perceived. Changes can be seen in the ways in which unemployment was initially seen as a temporary problem, but subsequently as a global and structural problem. Policies have progressed from first being framed by moral issues, later seen as political issues and eventually seen as labour market policy and welfare issues. Nonetheless, there seems to be a thread of continuity running through these changes in that the individual aspects remain in the foreground, while structural causes remain hidden. Moreover, the moral aspect of work and the perceived need to control the unemployed are also ongoing (cf. Bakke 1969).

## Research discourses – governance and increased reflexivity

In discussing youth unemployment, two related discourses are particularly relevant. First, the governance of youth unemployment and policy issues, and, second, the biographical turn and the increasing reflexivity of individual and social life.

### The governance of youth unemployment – the policy issue

Rising unemployment rates have placed increasing pressure on welfare structures and since the 1990s unemployment has tended to be regarded as a structural phenomenon, rather than being caused by a temporary slump in demand due to economic downturns. External explanations for the situation have included the challenges of globalization and a knowledge-driven economy, while among the internal explanations inflexible labour markets and generous European welfare states have also been blamed. Since the 1990s there has also been a shift from passive to active labour market policies. A central idea behind this shift is that self-sufficiency in relation to welfare benefits is a precondition for individual welfare and for the welfare of the state; that welfare dependency in the longer term promotes poverty, inequality and long-term unemployment; that unemployment benefits have a disincentive effect on job search and re-employment as generous income replacement rates increase the level of minimum wages, which in turn decreases an individual's financial incentive for re-employment and, finally, that the effects of policies which aim to increase the efficiency of the labour market have generally been minor and inconsistent (cf. Malmberg-Heimonen 2005).

A central concern relates to the inconsistencies in contemporary labour market policy research. Some studies have found favourable employment effects in the use of financial sanctions to enforce participation in labour market programmes or job search activities, whereas other studies have not found any beneficial effects. Studies have also suggested that re-employment increases among persons with higher earnings-related unemployment benefits once benefit exhaustion approaches, but other studies have not found any such effects. Some studies have also indicated that earnings-related unemployment benefits are sufficient to prevent the adverse outcomes of unemployment, whereas minimum level benefits (such as flat-rate benefits and social assistance) seem to lack this preventative effect. Indeed, Van Oorshot (2002) claims that the fact that inequality among the long-term unemployed increasing indicates that contemporary labour market policies might not work for the more vulnerable groups of unemployed.

Recent policies addressing unemployment in general, and the integration of disadvantaged youth in particular, have stressed a need to mobilize individuals to engage more in their own processes of social inclusion and labour market integration. This approach has been addressed by individualizing activation policies and services.

However, many young unemployed people are not entitled to unemployment benefits because they lack work experience. Consequently, they are dependent on support from their family and/or social assistance (Hammer and Julkunen 2005; Hammer 2007).

Here Jones (1995; 2005) has focused on young people's experience of longer periods of dependency upon parents which have delayed access to the identities and activities which were previously regarded as signifying adult status, such as leaving the parental home.

## *Transitions, biographies and increasing reflexivity*

For young people, core changes in transitions also have an impact on patterns of (un) employment. Flexibilization and globalization have contributed to a decoupling of education and employment. Transitions to work have been prolonged, diversified, unstable and uncertain. In the course of this de-standardization, other transitions have also become fragmented, such as those associated with family formation, partnerships, lifestyles, housing and citizenship (Beck 2000; Pohl and Walther 2007). For young people, at the core of crisis is the disconnection between life trajectories, social roles and ties to the range of institutions able to give a stable shape to identity. One can enter the labour market, leave shortly afterward, and then re-enter it without being able to identify any progression towards adult roles. Similarly, vocational studies can be concluded without opening up access to a career or providing the means to live with a partner or create one's own family (Leccardi 2006).

Faced with these ambivalent states, a person's ability to devise cognitive strategies that can provide feelings of control over life becomes a key resource. Indeed, whereas many learners still pass through the educational system without encountering too many frustrations, others can feel out of step with the system in relation to both aspirations and identity formation (Bynner 2006). Late-modernity requires people not only to think as they go through life, but also to think about life. In the past, people could find security in believing in political and policy processes, today they are expected to rise above the situations, rise above contexts, and think about the world from a distance. This distanced reflection makes it possible to talk about a condition of choosing expertise or choosing social relations.

The processes of individualization prepare the individual for the challenge of actively participating in social contexts. Quite possibly life today is more demanding than it ever was, and represents a period of time in which many things can go wrong. One of the biggest problems of disengaged and frustrated learners is that their life course is marked by an accumulation of failures, not only in one area or at one point in time, but successively and in many different life arenas. By the time they leave education and have failed to find a job, their self-esteem has been bruised and they have lost trust in institutional help.

New motivational programmes, so–called engagement mentoring, have been devised as a response to these changes and tend to focus on socially excluded young people. They are closely connected with the professions of guidance and youth work from which mentoring has now evolved as a discrete practice. Essential in this development is the acknowledgement of individuals as organic, complex, dynamic entities in which all parts must be understood in relation to each other, in a holistic manner. Here a more accurate understanding of young people's dispositions (or habitus) may offer a great deal to policy and practice. It helps account for individual agency, including the pragmatically rational aspects of career and lifestyle decisions (Colley 2003). Availability of meaningful options also allows for biographical progress. This means, for instance, embedding activation in the personal counselling process where negative incentives may prevail.

# Researching youth unemployment – which glasses should we put on?

## *The structure and agency dimension*

Although much unemployment research has highlighted the heterogeneity of the phenomenon, the unemployed as a group are often depicted one-dimensionally, in fixed socio-economic classifications, without taking individual activity into account (Julkunen 2002). Moreover, the focus of unemployment research is sometimes considered narrow in that economic transitions are over-emphasized. Studies are also said to marginalize young people's own accounts of growing up and their active role in the process. In this context, dry, quantitative, empiricist and policy-driven mappings of youth unemployment and transitions have often taken precedence over more ethnographic and theoretically driven studies of youth cultural identities (Shildrick and MacDonald 2007). Shildrick and MacDonald claim that the tendency to adopt a structural perspective on youth unemployment can be counterproductive, primarily because it fails to prioritize the actual views, experiences and perspectives of young people. Williams and Popay (1999) have also argued that there seems to be a primary dichotomy between research paradigms in which structural and policy analyses are prioritized and perspectives that focus on the individual welfare subjects.

Several social scientists have addressed this dichotomy between structure and agency in an attempt to construct grand theory (Mills 1959; Merton 1972; Giddens 1979). As early as the 1930s, Talcott Parsons developed a voluntaristic theory of social action which was opposed to the view that reduced studies of social phenomena to interactions between individuals. Parsons' modernization theory has been useful in elucidating concepts such as social stratification and institutional relationship. The modernization theory has also had an effect on how young people's reactions to social circumstances are studied and interpreted (Lähteenmaa 2000). However, where Parsons's interest was primarily in systems and in how systems survive, others have focused primarily on human actions and the influence of social institutions. Giddens's structuration theory (1984) provides a theoretical framework that sees the individual as a reflexive agent who is both enabled and constrained by social structures and processes.

Young people both react to and act upon societal structures. The conditions encountered by individuals are themselves crucial to the successful mastering of specific tasks and societal contexts and also have an important impact on the way individuals come to understand their own life contexts. Actualization of the individual situations involves coming to terms with the range of possibilities and constraints that are encountered in social life. Young people learn from each other, they interact with each other and they develop new activities that help them overcome various obstacles and resolve some of the contradictions which arise from societal conditions.

Systems models show how structural and institutional patterns shape social relations. They also highlight the role of cultural and material factors in such relations, but are unable to help us understand young people's intentions and actions. People form and test their values and actions based on personal as well as on collective experiences, relations and notions. Culture and ethnicity are neither independent nor static entities, but change over both time and space. This means that both relational and agency perspectives have to be introduced to better understand those mechanisms facilitating and restricting the actions of young people.

162

## *Old and new concepts*

A number of concepts are used in describing the positions of young unemployed people such as social exclusion, marginalization, deviation, deprivation, segregation, and more recently bounded agency. In terms of theory it is important to differentiate between unemployment, poverty, deprivation, marginalization and social exclusion. There is no consensus on the definition of social exclusion which is a multidimensional concept. The core definition is often linked to poverty and unemployment (Berghman 1997). The term incorporates various social disadvantages including poverty, but goes beyond describing financial resources. According to classic unemployment research, unemployment either contains, or is a part of a process, whereby various social exclusion risks are accumulated (Jahoda *et al.* 1972). In the Scandinavian tradition, there has been a tendency to define long-term unemployment as a key form of social exclusion, although this has been criticized (Helne 2002). The relationship is based on the understanding of work as a basic human right having a positive impact on other spheres in human life.

Social exclusion has also been described as the process of becoming detached from the moral order or from prevailing norms in society (Room 1995) and, in so doing, it comes close to the concept of marginalization. Room suggests that social exclusion should be used to highlight the dynamic linkages between material situations, on the one hand, and attitudes and values on the other which may reinforce a situation of disadvantage. In line with this is Paugam's (1996) claim that extreme forms of marginalization occur when prolonged unemployment is coupled with a disintegration of the social networks that bind the individual to the community. Ohlsson (2006) discusses Kronauer's work where exclusion is referred to six dimensions of social exclusion: exclusion from the labour market; economic exclusion; cultural exclusion; exclusion by isolation; spatial exclusion; and institutional exclusion.

The concept of marginalization has been used to characterize an intermediate position, somewhere between full integration and social exclusion. The concept describes the risk of social exclusion in different dimensions. Young unemployed people are in a marginalized position, but may or may not be excluded from the labour market. Many researchers find this concept to be particularly useful for young people because it signals an intermediate position. Theoretically, marginalization builds on the work of Robert E. Park (1928) on cultural conflicts and its effect on the individuals. When the individual is marginalized, a certain personality type is created, the marginal man (although Park had a rather mechanistic view of the marginalization process).

Bourdieu's theoretical perspective can also be drawn on to examine the processes that contribute to marginalization and the conditions of broader society that sustain and reproduce them. Social processes can contribute to the creation of tensions between seeking to belong and being assigned to the margins. Taking direction from Bourdieu's (1990) theory of social relations, Lynam and Cowley (2007) illustrate ways in which discourses of marginalization and marginalizing practices associated with them can be interrupted, and in so doing work towards redressing processes that create a context for inequalities.

The discussion of social exclusion has mainly been influenced by European sociology and has often been linked to the notion of accumulation of deprivation factors. Some authors have suggested that the term should be used to identify structures in society that have an effect on individual marginalization or integration, such as the demographic and legal system, labour market, welfare system or the family. This may be seen as static and cross-sectionally based with little or no dynamic processing. It has also been claimed that binary categories of exclusion and marginalization become less adequate as parameters for understanding changing patterns of exclusion. The dichotomous nature of the concept is at the root of the problem, while the structural perspective may prove a hindrance for an incorporating process. Here Kronauer (1997) proposes a solution in which a semi-structural explanatory is used which views the young as an underclass (in line with Marxian terminology) and regards the actual exclusion as a process. This enables us to view young unemployed people's economic and material exclusion as structurally determined, and their ways of moving in and out of the position as a process. Indeed, Ohlsson (2006) argues that social exclusion as well as social inclusion must be understood as a process that change over time. Emirbayer and Mische (1998) also emphasize that structural contexts of action are themselves temporal as well as relational fields, multiple and overlapping ways of ordering time towards which young people can assume simultaneous orientations.

Agency remains an important concept in youth research generally and in work on youth unemployment more specifically (Mörch 1997; Mörch and Andersen 2006), although the tension between structure and agency remains unsolved. Here Emirbayer and Mische (1998) offer an analysis in which they disaggregate agency into its several component elements, demonstrate the different ways in which the dimensions of agency intertwine with diverse forms of structure and point out the implications of a differentiated conception of agency for empirical research. Emirbayer and Mische argue that the agentic dimension of social action can only be captured within the flow of time. This means reconceptualizing agency as a temporally embedded process of social engagement, informed by the past, but also oriented towards the future and the present. These entail the three constitutive elements of agency: iteration (past patterns), projectivity (future trends) and practical evaluation (the present). Here Emirbayer and Mische draw on Mead (1932) who insists that self-reflective activity which engages with the meaningful structure of the past is essentially referred to the future. This conceptualization may well encompass an extended dialogue between ideas and evidence to explore the beliefs and actions associated with life-chances under differing structural and cultural conditions. Evans's (2007) study has contributed to the re-conceptualization of agency as a process in which past habits and routines are contextualized and future possibilities envisaged in the contingencies of the present moment. Evans uses the concept of 'bounded agency' as an alternative to 'structured individualization' as a way of understanding the experiences of people in changing social landscapes.

The theoretical and disciplinary diversity in the field of unemployment research, while potentially an advantage, can also be seen as a handicap, as Raffe (2007) has claimed when addressing the transition-system research. Youth unemployment research has encouraged a wide range of hypotheses and explanatory models, but it may also have inhibited the development of research approaches which could test alternative explanatory models. In this context, research into youth unemployment still has much to accomplish.

## References

Bakke, E. W. (1969) *Citizens Without Work: A Study of the Effects of Unemployment upon the Worker's Social Relations and Practices*, New York: Archon Books.

Beck, U. (2000) *The Brave New World of Work*, Cambridge: Polity Press.

Berghman, J. (1997) 'Social protection in the European Union', in A. Bosco and M. Hutsebaut (eds) *Social Protection in Europe: Facing up to Changes and Challenges*, Brussels: European Trade Union Institute.

Bourdieu, P. (1990) *The Logic of Practice*, Stanford, CA: Stanford University Press.

Bynner, J. (2006) 'Re-thinking the youth phase of the life course: the case of emerging adutlhood?' *Journal of Youth Studies*, 8: 367–84.

Colley, H. (2003) *Mentoring for Social Inclusion*, New Jersey: Falmer Press.

Emirbayer, M. and Mische, A. (1998) 'What is agency?', *American Journal of Sociology*, 103: 962–1023.

Evans, K. (2007) 'Concepts of bounded agency in education, work, and the personal lives of young adults', *International Journal of Psychology*, 42: 85–93.

Fenton, S. and Dermott, E. (2006) 'Fragmented careers?: Winners and losers in young adult labour markets', *Work, Employment and Society*, 20: 205–21.

Furlong, A. (2006) 'Not a very NEET solution: representing problematic labour market transitions among early school-leavers', *Work, Employment and Society*, 20: 553–69.

Furlong, A., Cartmel, F. and Biggart, A. (2007) 'Choice biographies and transitional linearity: re-conceptualising modern youth transitions', *Papers: Revista de sociologia*, 79: 225–39

Giddens, A. (1979) *Central Problems in Social Theory: Action, Structure and Contradiction in Social Analysis*, London: Macmillan Press.

—— (1984) *The Constitution of Society: Outline of the Theory of Structuration*, Cambridge: Polity Press.

Goodwin, J. and O'Connor, H. (2007) 'Continuity and change in the experiences of transition from school to work', *International Journal of Lifelong Education*, 26: 555–72.

Halleröd, B. and Westberg, A. (2006) 'Youth problem: what's the problem?', *Acta Sociologica*, 49: 83–102.

Halvorsen, K. (1999) *Arbetslöshet som socialt problem*, HiO-rapport no. 13, Oslo: Högskolan i Oslo.

Hammer, T. (2007) 'Labour market integration of unemployed youth from a life course perspective: the case of Norway', *International Journal of Social Welfare*, 16: 249–57.

Hammer, T. and Julkunen, I. (2005) 'Surviving unemployment – a question of money or families', in T. Hammer (ed.) *Youth Unemployment and Social Exclusion in Europe*, Bristol: Policy Press.

Helne, T. (2002) 'Syrjäytymisen yhteiskunta', *Tutkimuksia 123, Stakes*.

Jahoda, M., Lazarsfeld, P. and Zeisel, H. (1972) *The Sociography of an Unemployed Community*, London: Tavistock.

Jones, G. (1995) *Leaving Home*, Buckingham: Open University Press.

—— (2005) 'Social protection policies for young people: a cross-national comparison', in H. Bradley and J. van Hoof (eds) *Young People in Europe: Labour Markets and Citizenship*, Bristol: Policy Press.

Julkunen, I. (2002) 'Being young and unemployed: reactions and actions in Northern Europe', *SSKH Skrifter 14*, Helsinki University.

Kogan, I. (2004) 'Last hired, first fired? the unemployment dynamics of male immigrants in Germany', *European Sociological Review*, 20: 445–61.

Kronauer, M. (1997) 'Soziale Angrenzung und Unterclass: Über neue Formen der gesellschaftliche Spaltung', *Leviathian*, 25: 28–49.

Lähteenmaa, J. (2000) 'Myöhäismoderni nuorisokulttuuri: tulkintoja ryhmistä ja ryhmiin kuulumisten ulottuvuuksista', *Nuorisotutkimusseura julkaisuja 14*, Helsinki: Hakapaino Oy.

Leccardi, C. (2006) 'Facing uncertainty. temporality and biography in the new century', in C. Leccardi and E. Ruspini (eds) *A New Youth? Young People, Generation and Family Life*, Burlington: Ashgate.

Lynam, M. J. and Cowley, S. (2007) 'Understanding marginalization as a social determinant of health', *Critical Public Health*, 17: 137–49.

Malmberg-Heimonen, I. (2005) 'Public welfare policies and private responses: studies of European labour market policies in transition', *People and Work Research Reports,* 68, Helsinki: Finnish Institute of Occupational Health.

Mead, G. H. (1932) *The Philosophy of the Present*, Chicago: Open Court Publishing.

Merton, R. K. (1972) 'Insiders and outsiders: a chapter in the Sociology of Knowledge', *American Journal of Sociology*, 78: 9–47.

Mills, C. W. (1959) *The Sociological Imagination*, London: Oxford University Press.

165

Mörch, S. (1997) 'Youth and activity theory', in J. Bynner, L. Chisholm and A. Furlong (eds) *Youth, Citizenship and Social Change in a European Context*, Aldershot: Ashgate.

Mörch, S. and Andersen, H. (2006) 'Individualisation and the challenging youth life', in C. Leccardi and Ruspini (eds) *A New Youth? Young People, Generation and Family Life*. Burlington: Ashgate.

Ohlsson, L. B. (2006) 'Young at the margins of welfare: a study of immigrant youth and labour market establishment', in L. Harryson and M. O'Brien (eds) *Social Welfare Social Exclusion: A Life Course Frame*, Lund: Värpinge Ord & Text.

Park, R. E. (1928) 'Human migration and the Marginal Man', *American Journal of Sociology*, 33.

Paugam, S. (1996) 'A new social contract? Poverty and social exclusion: A sociological view', EUI Working Papers RSC, no. 96/36.

Pohl, A. and Walther, A. (2007) 'Activating the disadvantaged: variations in addressing youth transitions across Europe', *International Journal of Lifelong Learning*, 26: 533–53.

Raffe, D. (2007) 'The concept of transition system: a review of recent research', paper presented at the European Research Network on Transitions in Youth Annual Workshop, Ghent, Flanders, 5–8 September 2007.

Room, G. (ed.) (1995) *Beyond the Threshold: The Measurement and Analysis of Social Exclusion*, Bristol: The Policy Press.

Shavit, Y. and Blossfield, H-P. (1993) *Persistent Inequality: Changing Educational Attainment in Thirteen Countries*, Boulder, CO: Westview Press.

Shildrick, T. and MacDonald, R. (2007) 'Biographies of exclusion: poor work and poor transitions', *International Journal of Lifelong Education*, 26: 589–604.

Solga, H. (2002) 'Stigmatization by negative selection: explaining less-educated people's decreasing employment opportunities', *European Sociological Review*, 18: 159–78.

Van Oorshot, W. (2002) 'Miracle or nightmare? A critical review of Dutch activation policies and their outcomes', *Journal of Social Policy*, 3: 399–421.

Walther, A., Du Bois-Reymond, M. and Biggart, A. (2006) *Participation in Transition: Motivation of Young Adults in Europe for Learning and Working*, New York: Peter Lang.

Williams, F. and Popay, J. (1999) 'Balancing polarities: developing a new framework for welfare research', in F. Williams, J. Popay and A. Oakley (eds) *Welfare Research: A Critical Review*, London: UCL Press.

Wolbers, M. H. J. (2007) 'Patterns of labour market entry', *Acta Sociologica*, 50: 189–210.

# 20

# Precarious work

## Risk, choice and poverty traps

*Robert MacDonald*

The boundaries between work and non-work are becoming more fluid. Flexible, pluralized forms of underemployment are spreading..

(Beck 1992: 142)

## Introduction

The facts of how youth transitions in western, industrialized societies have been radically restructured over the latter third of the twentieth century – and the consequences of this for young people – are well known. The extenuation, fragmentation, and increasing individualization and complexity of pathways to adulthood is the stuff of many contemporary studies of young people's lives. Less well understood is the significance of precarious work for young people under these changed conditions.

In general terms, global economic changes have seen the declining importance of youth employment, with labour market entry suspended pending lengthier periods of postcompulsory education. In the vision of a new, high-tech, knowledge economy offered by politicians, policy-makers and social commentators, professional and higher skilled employment dominates and low/no skill jobs disappear. Extended engagement in higher level education provides the expanded institutional pathway to this new world of work.

In considering the topic of young adults and precarious work, therefore, we are able to focus on particular, youth-related questions about changing transitions as well as broader sociological ones about change (and continuity) in the sphere of work and employment in late modernity. Because of youth's status as harbinger of the future, the nature of the younger generation's engagement in 'new' forms of employment has relevance beyond the sphere of youth studies.

First, the chapter considers the prevailing wisdom that standard forms of regular employment in stable jobs (taken to be typical of post-war, Fordist society) are being replaced by flexible forms of precarious employment that are now, in turn, seen as emblematic of late modern capitalism. Influential writers like Beck (1992) speak of the *general* social proliferation of risk, overriding older social divisions and certainties; rising precarious employment affects all sorts of work and workers. This chapter examines evidence about the social distribution of precarious employment. Second, it asks whether insecure jobs provide stepping stones to more secure ones or traps which curtail bio-graphical and social mobility. Third, patterns of choice and constraint that lie behind precarious employment are discussed. Fourth, the chapter examines the experience of doing this sort of work, with reference to qualitative youth and community studies, before considering the questions thrown up by this discussion, in conclusion.

## The growth of precarious work?

Beck has argued that the shift from a 'system of standardized full employment to the system of flexible and pluralized underemployment' (1992: 140) is indicative of late modern capitalism. The current and coming conditions of the industrialized societies are ones in which standard, stable, lasting, Fordist employment declines and flexible, impermanent forms of work proliferate. 'Contingent', 'atypical', 'non-traditional', 'non-standard', and 'insecure' work are commonly used (near) synonyms for precarious employment. As we will see, however, there are important category differences here. Narrow definitions of 'precarious' employment tend to focus on its contractual status (temporary or permanent) and/ or on length of job tenure. Others, like Vosko (2006: 3), prefer wider definitions in which impermanence is only one element. Referring to Canadian research, he states: 'Precarious employment encompasses forms of work invol-ving limited social benefits and statutory entitlements, job insecurity, low wages, and high risks of ill-health.'

Countering the social theoretical orthodoxy, some question whether rates of pre-carious employment, as narrowly defined, really are rising ('non-standard' employment – such as part-time work and self-employment – have shown greater upwards trends than, for instance, temporary employment; Butler and Watt 2007). According to a stinging essay by Fevre (2007), the idea of a new age of employment insecurity is a myth. He criticizes social theorists (citing Beck but also Sennett, Castells and Giddens) who have popularized the widely held but false notion that employment is increasingly short-term and unstable. Reviewing labour force survey data from the USA, the UK and con-tinental Europe, he says, *inter alia*, that average job tenure has not declined, that workers' feelings of *in*security have and that there is some evidence that rates of long-term employment are growing. For instance, he reports that the proportion of UK non-permanent employees was *lower* in 2006 (5.8 per cent) than in 1997 (8 per cent) and a *downward* trend in 'contingent' employment in the USA between 1995 and 2001. He does find some statistical evidence for a *gradual* increase in temporary employment in *some* affluent countries but not in the USA and the UK, those more liberal, deregulated labour market regimes said by social theorists to characterize the age of insecurity. Turning his guns more directly toward the theorists he names, he says: 'it has not been employment that has become insecure and flexible but social theory' that claims to describe social developments 'without undertaking empirical research' (ibid.: 531).

Further, empirically based arguments *against* the employment insecurity thesis come from an International Labour Office study of industrialized countries (Auer and Cazes 2003). It concludes that *long-term* employment relationships remain the norm for most European workers with no obvious trend toward their erosion. The proportion of longer-term, stable jobs is lower in the USA but again there does not appear to be a downward trend in these. Segmented, core–periphery labour markets are evident in industrialized countries but the proportions of workers in each segment generally remains constant.

Even if there appears to be limited evidence of a *general* rise in precarious work, importantly for our discussion, it is among younger and less educated workers that most insecurity is found (Cam *et al.* 2003). Average job tenure for 15–24 year-olds has declined in several industrialized countries over the past decade (Auer and Cazes 2003). From research in South-west England, Fenton and Dermott found the same in their survey-based testing of the 'fragmented employment' thesis. They found relative stability and perma- nency in the labour market careers of the majority of their sample. They add, however, that there was 'a sizeable minority, mostly of low paid workers whose working lives [were] discontinuous and fragmented … employment fragmentation is concentrated among young adults with less education and in lower status, lower paid occupations' (2006: 205).

## Stepping stones or traps? And is precarious work new?

Reflecting on the evidence of young people's disproportionate involvement in precarious work, Auer and Cazes (2003: 35) wonder whether: 'young people have to "queue" in temporary jobs while waiting for a permanent job or whether they are "trapped" in insecure, secondary jobs with no bridge to stable employment'. While acknowledging the limits of their evidence, they suggest that, because 'youth' is inherently temporary, 'younger workers would only temporarily be "outsiders" of the labour market'. The implication is that even if labour market insecurity is an increasing phenomenon for younger workers it is a passing one. Individuals will, in time, move through these jobs to more permanent ones. Quintini *et al.s*' summary of youth transitions in OECD countries, sides with this 'stepping stones' thesis (2007: 7):

> Unsurprisingly, youth represent a high proportion of new hires and job changers [and job quits] … youth tend to change jobs more frequently at the beginning of their career in search for the best possible match between their skills and those required by employers … this is just part of the natural dynamics of settling into the world of work.

This interpretation of precariousness as part of the *natural* dynamics of transitions to the labour market clearly stands at odds with grander social theoretical narratives of work insecurity as the leitmotif of a new age of risk. Theories of late or post-modernity can be criticized for overstating social *dis*continuity. Pollock (2002) argues that the under- employment said to be typical of a new risk society was not uncommon for youth in the earlier twentieth century. It was the post-war, 20-year period of full, regular employ- ment that Pollock sees as anomalous in recent history; 'labour market conditions that existed before this time and since are quite similar' (ibid.: 174). Beynon *et al.* (1994: 160) make a similar point: some working practices now labelled as *post*-Fordist actually represent 'a return to the undesirable past practices' typical of *pre*-Fordism.

Importantly, Quintini *et al.* (2007: 20), in reviewing *contemporary* evidence, describe how:

> The youth labour market is characterised by much turnover … some young people, particularly those with low educational attainment, can find it very hard to escape from spells of unemployment/inactivity punctuated by spells of employment, often

on temporary contracts. Many others, however, progress fairly smoothly into jobs with good career prospects.

This dynamic viewpoint requires us to consider how an episode of employment fits into longer-term labour market careers. In this sense, precarious employment is just part of a wider experience of economic marginality and instability typified by movement between different states. The flux, uncertainty and precariousness of *transitions* – rather than solely of *employment* – become significant. For this reason, academic and policy focus on discrete episodes and rigid categories (such as those who are 'not in employment, education or training') misses the way that disadvantaged young people can 'churn' around these categories (MacDonald and Marsh 2005).

## Precarious work through choice?

Some theories of risk and insecurity celebrate the opportunities for individual choice that 'portfolio working' and 'employment entrepreneurship' bring, as part of the active advancement of working lives (Handy 1994). Empirical studies tend to adopt a less positive tone. For instance, research on the cleaning, catering and security industries concluded that the greatest negative impact of precarious work comes to those at the bottom of the labour market. Here 'employment risk is something which traps, whereas for those with tradable skills higher up the income scale, risk may open up more opportunities than it closes down' (Allen and Henry 1997: 194, cited in Butler and Watt 2007: 137).

Similarly, the balance between individual choice and constraining social circumstance is crucial in understanding the meaning of precarious work. That young adults may have *socially divided* experiences of early adulthood (including this sort of work) is crucial to the debate between Bynner (2005) and Arnett (2006) about the validity of the latter's concept of a *general* phase of 'emerging adulthood'. Can young people's more fluid, uncertain movement around different labour market situations be understood as an expression of the 'choice biographies' said to be emergent under late modernity? Do they opt for 'non-standard employment to help maintain leisure-focused life-styles and as part of a strategy to avoid long-term commitment' (Furlong and Cartmel 2007: 43)? The answer depends on *who* it is that is doing the precarious work. Middle-class students 'paying their way' through university may do lower quality jobs to finance study and leisure, knowing that this employment is neither enduring nor constitutive of their transitions. For less advantaged young adults, denied greater room for post-16 manoeuvre, precarious employment can be a more serious and lasting affair that comes to *define* their labour market transitions and outcomes.

For such young adults, precarious work also tends to carry negative characteristics beyond its insecurity (hence some researchers' wider definitions of it). Typically, these are also low paid, low skilled and with poor terms and conditions of employment (e.g. lack of training or holiday, maternity and sickness entitlements). In the lower reaches of the labour market, the push to greater employment 'flexibility' (e.g. in terms of pay, worker roles and worker numbers) can slide into casualization. Felstead and Jewson (1999: 3) comment that 'the surge of non-standard work' in the UK 'is associated with rock-bottom wages, coercive management, intensified labour processes, unsocial hours and high rates of job turnover'. This neatly encapsulates the forms of casualized, 'poor work' reported in some recent UK studies.

# The experience of precarious employment

## Poor transitions in Teesside

The Teesside studies of youth transition and social exclusion, in which the author has participated, have documented the nature of 'poor work' for 15–25 year-olds growing up in some of Britain's poorest neighbourhoods (e.g. Johnston *et al.* 2000; MacDonald and Marsh 2005). Qualitative studies revealed complexity and change in these working-class young adults' lives but also how they were united by common, ongoing experiences of poverty in which precarious 'poor work' was central and causative.

Post-school labour market transitions were typified by rapid movement around poor quality and often unfinished training and educational courses, unemployment and low-paid, low/no skill jobs. Long-standing class-cultural values and practices framed how people got jobs and what they thought of them. Informal, localized, word-of-mouth job-seeking strategies predominated. The effective labour market for these poorly quali-fied young people became the sorts of lower quality jobs already done by those they knew. Yet, young adults displayed remarkably strong and enduring commitment to employment, despite recurrent encounters with poor work.

Interviewees often could not say definitively whether a job had been formally per-manent or temporary (many worked without written contracts). Their haziness also extended to the reasons why jobs ceased. Typically, their *experience* of these jobs was that they were temporary and not ended of their own volition. Being 'laid off', 'cancelled', 'sacked' or 'made redundant' were phrases used interchangeably and probably often wrongly to describe the loss of their jobs. For most, the job was simply not there for them any longer and they were not sure why this was the case. There was an implicit, weary acceptance that most jobs would be like this.

The Teesside studies show that low level, poor work has not been eradicated by the supposed shift to a new, high skill, information economy. Caring, cleaning, security, labouring and serving jobs (in shops and bars) were common for these interviewees, as was unskilled employment in food processing and textile factories. A more representative, UK national survey also reminds us that: 'there are substantial numbers of jobs at the lower end of the labour market with limited skills requirements despite the professionalization of employment in recent years' (Green and Owen 2006: ix).

Crucially, the stuttering labour market careers of the Teesside young adults did not lead onwards and upwards away from poverty. A follow up study of some of the sample as they reached their late twenties (Webster *et al.* 2004) concluded that the forms of precarious, poor work encountered in the late teenage years were ones that lasted. Contrary to the 'stepping stones' thesis noted earlier, MacDonald and Marsh (2005: 111–12) argue that these forms of work were not indicative of 'a separate *youth* labour market but a secondary labour market marked by the poorest conditions of work and pervasive unemployment and underemployment, to which many working-class people are now confined, regardless of age'.

## The working poor: life at the bottom of the labour market

There are few empirical studies available to confirm the Teesside researchers' refutation of 'the stepping stones' thesis. This would require larger, contemporary, longitudinal studies of the progress of cohorts of young workers as they reached their twenties (and beyond) which were focused enough to include sizeable proportions of the most socially disadvantaged. *Some* supporting evidence can be found. Furlong and Cartmel's (2004: 27) examination of the labour market careers of disadvantaged young men in Scotland found a similar pattern of precarious employment shaping labour market marginality:

> Their main problem was not finding work, but keeping it. This employment insecurity tended not to reflect negative attitudes ... or necessarily a lack of skills; it was almost entirely a consequence of the 'flexible' nature of low skilled employment in modern Britain.

Ethnographic and qualitative investigations of poverty and social exclusion also point to the role of low-paid, insecure work in entrapping people in those conditions. Indeed, the conditions of poor work are critical to understanding the problem of poverty in the USA. For instance, Barbara Ehrenreich (2002) worked undercover in a range of low-paid jobs, reporting the sheer daily grind and inability to make one's way that faces 'the working poor' in America. Using a similar method, Polly Toynbee's account of life in low-pay Britain makes the following point:

> Low pay is also fair enough if these jobs can be labelled 'entry-level', just a first step on a ladder. But it is now clear that very few of those in low-paid jobs can ever move far ... few make it to the next step. They inhabit a cycle of no-pay/low-pay job insecurity. This indeed is the end of social progress.
>
> (2003: 5–6)

David Smith's (2005) ethnographic study of white, working-class residents of an outer London housing estate captures the impact of a polarized, post-industrial labour market, particularly for younger generations. His findings are strikingly similar to those of the Teesside researchers:

> Practically all of those interviewed had considerable experience of entry-level jobs in the formal economy after leaving school ... few of these ... resulted in stable, reasonably paid work, the typical trajectory being into work patterns increasingly characterised by short-term, low-paid jobs.
>
> (ibid.: 95)

Thus, 'transience' became a 'definitive feature' of working lives for 'the irregular and low-paid workforce' (ibid.: 96). This study also reveals the significance of informal, cash-in-hand employment for those at the margins of the labour market. Informal work shades into formal work and, because of the bonds of trust in the networks that distributed each type of work, taking up cash-in-hand jobs can be a more reliable conduit to formal employment than official, employment service job-search strategies. Smith does not romanticize these informal jobs. They were often poorly paid and irregular and sometimes hard and exploitative; like those in the formal economy.

Smith's work shows, contrary to the dominant political discourse in the UK, that inclusion in paid employment does not signal social inclusion. Indeed, Byrne argues that low-paid work punctuated by unemployment 'represents the most significant kind of excluded life in our sort of society' (1999: 74). Byrne's theoretical discussion resonates with the details of Smith's study (and those of the Teesside researchers): episodic unemployment, job insecurity and poor work have become common *working-class* experiences, rather than the preserve of an underclass stranded beneath them.

Returning to theories of risk and individualization in respect of complex youth transitions, Furlong and Cartmel (2007: 35) argue that: 'the seemingly individualized churn within the precarious sector of the labour market can perhaps be regarded as part of a new set of class-based experiences'. The evidence from national and international surveys of precarious work shows that it is less educated and younger workers that take the brunt of precarious employment. Evidence from qualitative, community-based studies (e.g. in Teesside and London) show how engagement in precarious, poor work *reflects* and *adds* to class-based disadvantaged. Some of the Teesside interviewees described, for instance, how recurrent poor work 'cooled out' already modest employment aspirations. Repeated employment that provided no training and limited quality work experience 'scarred' labour market careers and made individuals increasingly unattractive to prospective employers with better jobs to offer. The longer the record of intermittent, low-level employment the less likely an individual is to access stable and higher level jobs. In other words, recurrent poor work spells cumulative disadvantage and further socio-economic marginalization. As McKnight points out (2002: 98), over the past 25 years the number and proportion of low-paid jobs have *increased* in the UK but the relative earnings of low-paid workers have fallen. She describes a low-pay/no pay cycle in which the low paid are more likely (than others) to be unemployed in the future *and* to re-enter low-paid work. Thus, for those disadvantaged workers at the bottom of labour market in industrialized societies like the UK and the USA, 'the precarious nature of many low-paid jobs' means that getting 'a job may only represent a turn in the cycle of poverty' (ibid.: 98). This analysis, like the others cited in this section, offers little support for the idea that precarious work might offer stepping stones out of poverty for disadvantaged young adults.

## Conclusion

What can we conclude? Bold visions of epochal, societal change can overlook contemporary empirical evidence (that seem to temper the generalized claims of theorists such as Beck) *and* evidence of insecure employment from earlier decades. Precarious employment has historically not been uncommon amongst semi- and unskilled workers in the UK (Pollock 2002). A career may be a middle-class expectation. One of the reasons that around half of the unskilled manual workers in Townsend's classic study (1979) were in poverty was because of the impermanence of their jobs.

The disjuncture between commonly held assumptions of rising rates of precarious employment and labour force surveys that cast doubt on these is partly explained by the gap between wide and narrow definitions. Quantitative surveys need fixed categories – and usually adopt narrow definitions of precarious employment – against which to measure social trends. Wider definitions would obviously generate greater prevalence but draw in messier, additional considerations that are less easy to capture statistically. Given the concentration of precarious employment amongst younger and less educated workers, one might also wonder about the reach and representativeness of labour force surveys on this question. Certainly the participants in the Teesside studies would have found it difficult to answer unequivocally survey questions about the nature of their employment (e.g. 'temporary or permanent?'), if they had ever received – and felt inclined – to answer them.

Issues of method may also help explain why precarious work is writ large in qualitative studies of the poor but appears oddly marginal in general surveys. The former zoom in to those places and populations where precarious work would seem to have grown in qualitative and quantitative significance over recent decades and where insecurity is just one negative feature of burgeoning poor work. Precarious work has a geography as well as a social demography. Thus, the averages produced by national labour surveys mask the higher significance of precarious work amongst economically marginal workers and neighbourhoods. Additionally, qualitative studies analyse the definitions and meanings that come from participants, who may be less concerned with technical, narrow definitions of precarious work and, instead, report their encounters with 'poor work' that is experienced as insecure and low paid and low skilled and low quality. Understandably, then, qualitative approaches present precarious work as more quantitatively abundant than do labour force surveys.

Regardless of the arguments about the prevalence of precarious work that can be had between social theory and empirical labour force data, a small number of recent, qualitative studies have revealed the growing importance of precarious work for the lives of *some* working-class young adults. These studies question the majority academic and policy viewpoint that precarious employment provides necessary and normal stepping stones into and then upwards in the labour market. The Teesside researchers argue that such jobs entrap young adults in economic marginality in the long term. They, like Smith and others, suggest that this pattern of employment insecurity underlying economic marginality has also become indicative of many working-class adults' experiences of the labour market in communities that, until recently, were built on skilled, lasting, regular employment. Maybe this is what is really new and most significant about precarious work? For some young people – growing up in localities stripped of traditional, employment routes to 'respectable', working-class adulthood – precarious, poor work has now become constitutive of lasting economic marginality and emblematic of longer-term processes of downward social mobility. Forthcoming research will test this thesis further, examining the labour market experiences of Teesside interviewees, now aged in their thirties (Shildrick *et al.* 2009). Longitudinal, qualitative research on these issues is rare but is perhaps the method best suited to understanding if, how and why – for perhaps only a minority of young adults – precarious work represents a 'new' route to lasting poverty and long-term marginality.

## Acknowledgements

Thanks to Colin Webster and Tracy Shildrick for their comments on an earlier draft of this chapter.

## References

Allen, J. and Henry, N. (1997) 'Ulrich Beck's *Risk Society* at work', *Transactions of the Institute of British Geographers (New Series)*, 22: 180–96.
Arnett, J. (2006) 'Emerging adulthood in Britain: a response to Bynner', *Journal of Youth Studies*, 9: 111–23.
Auer, P. and Cazes, S. (2003) *Employment Stability in an Age of Flexibility*, Geneva: ILO.
Beck, U. (1992) *Risk Society*, London: Sage.

Beynon, H., Hudson, R. and Sadler, D. (1994) *A Place Called Teesside*, Edinburgh: Edinburgh University Press.

Butler, T. and Watt, P. (2007) *Understanding Social Inequality*, London: Sage.

Bynner, J. (2005) 'Rethinking the youth phase: the case for emerging adulthood?', *Journal of Youth Studies*, 8: 367–84.

Byrne, D. (1999) *Social Exclusion*, Milton Keynes: Open University Press.

Cam, S., Purcell, J. and Tailby, S. (2003) 'Contingent employment in the UK', in O. Bergstrom and D. Storrie (eds) *Contingent Employment in Europe and the United States*, Cheltenham: Edward Elgar.

Ehrenreich, B. (2002) *Nickel and Dimed: Undercover in Low Wage USA*, London: Granta.

Felstead, A. and Jewson, N. (1999) 'Flexible labour and non-standard employment', in *Global Trends in Flexible Labour*, Basingstoke: Macmillan.

Fenton, S. and Dermott, E. (2006) 'Fragmented careers', *Work, Employment and Society*, 20: 205–21.

Fevre, R. (2007) 'Employment insecurity and social theory: the power of nightmares', *Work, Employment and Society*, 21: 517–35.

Furlong, A. and Cartmel, F. (2004) *Vulnerable Young Men in Fragile Labour Markets*, York: Joseph Rowntree Foundation.

—— (2007) *Young People and Social Change*, Maidenhead: McGraw-Hill.

Green, A. and Owen, D. (2006) *The Geography of Poor Skills and Access to Work*, York: Joseph Rowntree Foundation.

Handy, C. (1994) *The Empty Raincoat*, London: Hutchinson.

Johnston, L., MacDonald, R., Mason, P., Ridley, L. and Webster, C. (2000) *Snakes & Ladders*, York: Joseph Rowntree Foundation.

MacDonald, R. and Marsh, J. (2005) *Disconnected Youth? Growing up in Britain's Poor Neighbourhoods*, Basingstoke: Palgrave.

McKnight, A. (2002) 'Low-paid work: drip-feeding the poor', in J. Hills, J. Le Grand and D. Piachaud (eds) *Understanding Social Exclusion*, Oxford: Oxford University Press.

Pollock, G. (2002) 'Ignoring the past: underemployment and risk in late modernity', in M. Cieslik and G. Pollock (eds) *Young People in Risk Society*, Aldershot: Ashgate.

Quintini, G., Martin, P. and Martin, S. (2007) *The Changing Nature of the School to Work Transition Process in OECD Countries*, Discussion paper no. 2582, Bonn: Institute for the Study of Labour.

Shildrick, T., MacDonald, R. and Webster, C. (2009, forthcoming) *Two steps Forward, Two Back? Understanding Recurrent Poverty*, York: Joseph Rowntree Foundation.

Smith, D. (2005) *On the Margins of Inclusion,* Bristol: Policy Press.

Townsend, P. (1979) *Poverty in the United Kingdom*, London: Penguin.

Toynbee, P. (2003) *Hard Work,* London: Bloomsbury.

Vosko, L. (2006) 'Precarious employment', in L. Vosko (ed.) *Precarious Employment*, Montreal: McGill-Queen's University Press.

Webster, C., Simpson, D., MacDonald, R., Abbas, A., Cieslik, M., Shildrick, T. and Simpson, M. (2004) *Poor Transitions*, Bristol: Policy Press/JRF.

# 21

# NEETs, freeters and flexibility

## Reflecting precarious situations in the new labour market

*Akio Inui*

## Changes in youth transition and precariousness

As the transition from school to work in industrialized countries has become longer and more complicated, young people's condition has become fluid and precarious. In some countries, youth unemployment has increased, as have the number of young people who work in casual jobs or who are categorized as 'inactive'. Furthermore, more young people are changing their working conditions on a frequent basis; moving between unemployment and temporary jobs or from being inactive to pursuing training and education. These increases have made it difficult to examine young people's condition using the traditional categories of employed and unemployed. Consequently, new categories, such as 'NEET' and 'freeter' have emerged.

In the UK, the term NEET (*N*ot in *E*ducation, *E*mployment or *T*raining) was introduced in the early 1990s. Changes in UK policy disqualified 16 and 17 year-olds from claiming unemployment-related benefits and therefore the statistical category of 'unemployment' for this age group was removed. While the changes promoted increased educational participation and those without work faced pressure to join youth training programmes, there remained a considerable number of young people who were not in education, employment, or training. NEET was introduced as a new category to describe vulnerability and as a target for policy interventions (Furlong 2006).

In Japan, the term freeter has been used to refer to young part-time, and temporary workers (excluding student workers). Originally a slang term combining the words 'freelance' and 'arbeiter', (Arbeit being the German term for work) it was used to indicate a 'side job' ('McJob' or 'fiddly job' in the British literature). Although students frequently held part-time temporary positions, until the end of the 1980s most young people in Japan made smooth and direct transitions from school or university to relatively stable forms of employment. In the 1990s, transitions became much less stable and the number of freeters increased rapidly. At the end of the 1990s, the Japanese government began estimating the number of freeters, and the results were surprising. One estimate showed that among 15–34 year-olds, the number increased from 1.01 million in 1992 to 2.09 million in 2002 (MHLW 2004). Another showed an increase from 1.83 million in 1990 to 4.18 million in 2001 (Cabinet Office 2003).

The discrepancy between the two estimates is a result of the adoption of different definitions of freeters. The lower estimate includes non-students working in part-time or temporary jobs, as well as those unemployed and seeking such jobs. The higher estimate includes almost all non-regular employment (including agency work), as well as all of those who are not working but who are seeking any type of employment. With the increase of non-standard forms of employment, increasingly unemployed people hoping for regular work are only able to gain employment as freeters.

In the early 2000s, the increase in the number of 'inactive' young people began to attract public attention and attempts were made to estimate the numbers defined as NEET. The Japanese NEET differs from the UK concept: in particular it excludes unemployed young people. As unemployment has increased and the average duration of unemployment lengthened, more unemployed young people have taken a break from job-seeking because of the physical and psychological stress brought about by unemployment. As a consequence, there has been a large increase in the number of young people not actively seeking jobs, but who want to work (Cabinet Office 2005). One fairly reliable estimate shows that the most rapidly increasing segment in the last decade is the 'potential unemployed' segment – those who are not currently seeking jobs but who want to work (ibid.).

## Flexibilization of employment and peripherization of the youth labour market

As Beck (2000) has suggested, people's working conditions in industrialized countries have changed dramatically in the past few decades; changes that have had a significant impact on young people. Flexibility is a key aspect of these changes. Flexibility takes a variety of forms: production flexibility, such as outsourcing various employment functions; wage system flexibility, such as reducing the statutory value of minimum wage and restricting fringe benefits to a smaller group of employees; employment flexibility, such as replacing regular workers with casual workers, contract workers, agency workers, and home workers; regulation flexibility (deregulation), such as prolonging the duration of probation and cutting down statutory severance pay. Almost any type of flexibility increases insecurity for working people and heightens wage inequality. The restructuring of employment contracts has also affected workers' conditions: in particular, the growth of the service sector is associated with greater reliance on casual and insecure employment.

Since the 1980s, both the average unemployment rate and the variety of non-regular work have increased. For example, the average incidence of part-time employment in OECD countries rose from 5.0 per cent in 1990 to 7.5 per cent in 2004 for males, and 19.7 per cent to 25.4 per cent for females (OECD 2005). Those who were most affected by flexibilization were young people: the average incidence of temporary employment among 15–24 year-olds (25.0 per cent in 2000) was more than three times higher than among 25–54 year-olds (OECD 2002).

Although the increase in insecurity among young people has been common across industrialized countries in the past few decades, differences exist between countries in the modes of the precariousness. In most European countries, for example, youth unemployment began to increase from the late 1970s and early 1980s. In other countries, such as Australia, the increase of casualization among young people kept pace with, or even exceeded, the increase in unemployment. According to Furlong and Kelly (2005), while the unemployment rates among young people in Australia and the UK are almost at the same level, Australian rates of casual and part-time employment are much higher than in the UK. In Australia, between 1988 and 2001, the rate of casual employment among young people rose from 39 per cent to 66 per cent among 15–19 year-olds and from 17 per cent to 33 per cent among 20–24 year-olds (Watson *et al.* 2003).

In Japan, the youth labour market began changing later than in most Western countries, but the pace was rapid. Japan enjoyed a bubble economy up until the end of the 1980s, but after its collapse, insecurity in the labour market increased rapidly. Between 1990 and 2000, the unemployment rate more than doubled and the incidence of non-regular employment rose from 20.2 per cent to 26.0 per cent. Young people suffered from these changes much more than adults and were more severely affected by the casualization of jobs than from unemployment. The number of unemployed 15–24 year-olds rose from 468,000 in 1992 to 659,000 in 2002, but the number of freeters within the same age group increased even more – from 714,000 to 1,312,000. The non-regular employment rate among 15-to 24 year-olds, which was 13.4 per cent for males and 12.9 per cent for females in 1992, reached 42.5 per cent and 51.1 per cent, respectively in 2002. However, compared to other industrialized countries, Japan's youth unemployment rate is relatively low. The highest rate in the past three decades (2003) was 10.1 per cent among 15–24 year-olds, far lower than the OECD average (OECD 2005).

As casual workers, freeters experience various forms of insecurity. The first is poor employment protection: most are employed on fixed-term contracts. Typical durations are less than a year, but can be as short as a few months. Many freeters work beyond the assigned term by renewing the contract, but renewals are never guaranteed and dismissal brings no compensation. The second form of insecurity is low wages. In terms of average hourly wage rates, in 2002, male part-time workers earned 39.1 per cent of that earned by their full-time equivalents while females earned 53.2 per cent: rates which are lower than in other industrialized countries (OECD 1999).

Furthermore, many freeters are paid less than the poverty level wage. The third form of insecurity is that freeters have little access to social security. Many have no entitlement for unemployment insurance since entitlement is restricted to those who have been employed more than 20 hours per week continuously for more than six months. The fourth form of insecurity is that freeters have fewer opportunities to further their skills. Though Japanese companies provide a considerable amount of in-house training for their employees, most of this is restricted to regular employees; freeters receive only induction training, or no training at all.

Although the traditional Japanese employment patterns centred around life-long regular employment, low-wage, casualized employment has been relatively common since the 1960s. Indeed, while life-long employment was the norm for males, casual and part-time jobs were filled by housewives and students. Although the wages for casual jobs were very low – often below the poverty line wage – this was not seen as a serious problem since housewives' incomes were regarded as subsidiary to their husbands' while students were subsidized by their parents. The statutory minimum wage level was set in accordance with these social conventions.

In the 1990s, casual jobs became more widespread and involved groups other than housewives and students. However, the government's labour market policies, informed by neo-liberalism, deregulated non-regular employment protection. Alongside neo-liberalism, another position underlined the government's decision to avoid implementing protective and supportive policies for young people: the popularity of discourse decrying 'lazy and indulged youth'. Supporters of this viewpoint claimed that freeters and NEETs should not receive public support because they freely chose this way of life. Indeed, the few supportive policies introduced in the early 2000s (such as the 'Youth Independence and Challenge Plan' (*Wakamono Jiritsu Chosen Plan*)), focused not on labour market security, but on young people's motivation.

## The characteristics of young people in precarious positions

As precarious conditions increased for young people, it became more common to question their motivation. Some commentators blamed young people, accusing them of being work-shy or lazy, parasitically relying on public benefits or parental support. Others argued that young people had lost sight of transitional signposts because the traditional transition pattern had disappeared. Still others argued that those suffering most were disadvantaged youth who could find only insecure jobs.

In many industrialized countries, young people without secure jobs have been regarded as work-shy. In the UK, when youth unemployment increased in the 1980s, attention turned to levels of commitment among young people and the government eventually disqualified 16 and 17 year-olds from unemployment benefits. With 'guarantees' of training places and an allowance for participants, it was claimed that anyone refusing the offer had proved themselves to be unwilling to work and should therefore not expect support from the public purse.

When the number of freeters dramatically increased in 1990, they were described in Japanese public discourse as 'spontaneous' and criticized for deliberately avoiding serious, regular employment, choosing instead to rely on their parents in order to pursue carefree lives. When the government announced its estimation of NEETs in the early 2000s, most of the media blamed the idleness of youth – but these accusations were rooted in a fundamental misunderstanding of freeters' and NEETs' situation. Three factors led to such a misunderstanding.

First, young people in precarious situations, such as freeters and NEETs, are a heterogeneous group. Furlong (2006) points out that in the UK, the NEET category encompasses young people in a variety of situations including: the long-term unemployed; fleetingly unemployed; looking after children or relatives in the home; temporarily sick or long-term disabled; putting their efforts into developing artistic or musical talents; or simply taking a short break from work or education. Though the majority are disadvantaged youth who lack the resources to exercise choice, the category also includes more privileged young people who are able to exercise a significant degree of choice in how they manage their lives.

The situation is similar in Japan. The freeter category includes various kinds of young people such as those who want regular employment but can find only casual employment; those who work part-time while developing artistic or musical talents; and those who are trying various jobs to determine a suitable occupation. Japan's NEET category also includes young people who want jobs but are taking a break from job-seeking; those who are ill or disabled; those who are looking after children or relatives in the home and those who have withdrawn from social life.

This heterogeneity among young people reflects the growing precariousness associated with processes of change in industrialized countries. The changing patterns of young people's transition are described as tripartite biographies: the choice biography of those who exercise a significant degree of choice due to their superior access to resources; the normal biography of those who follow linear routes with minimal stagnation or deviation; and the risk biography of those who get into difficulty and become trapped in insecure conditions due to their lack of resources (Walther *et al.* 2005). Although the second group tend to experience relatively stable transitions, the transitions of the first and last groups are characterized by precariousness. It is important to note, therefore, that precarious transitions can be experienced by both advantaged and disadvantaged youth.

Second, Japan in the 1980s and 1990s provided a unique context for the economic challenges its young people were facing. Though Japan experienced a few economic downturns in the 1980s, these slumps were less serious than those in Western countries and Japan enjoyed a buoyant economy. Freeters first emerged in the late 1980s, attracting attention for representing a new lifestyle. Though the economy provided plenty of opportunities for regular employment, many young people were choosing freeter lifestyles to avoid the constrained, conformist working culture of Japanese companies. At this time, public opinion regarded these young people favourably, viewing them as seekers of a new work–life balance. Even in the 1990s, when the bubble burst and the number of freeters increased rapidly, this image persisted – freeters were still viewed as freely choosing their situation. However, an official government study in the early 2000s showed that three out of four freeters wished to have regular employment but were only able to find freeter jobs (Cabinet Office 2003).

The third reason for the misunderstanding relates to neo-liberal ideology. While neo-liberal policies can be associated with a rise in inequality, they also strongly emphasize self-help and regard disadvantaged people as lacking self-motivation. There is also a tendency to promote the view that the unemployed and those in unstable positions pose a threat to the social order. Commenting on the UK inner city 'riots' of the 1980s, Jones and Wallace (1992) argued that 'the media-created spectre of unemployed, alienated young men threatened the social order', and suggested that this interpretation prompted the UK government to expand youth training as a tool for social control. Similarly, since the 1990s, the Japanese media have often focused on and sensationalized crimes committed by freeters or NEETs and public discourses began to incorporate a 'youth-phobia' (Nakanishi 2004).

Though freeters and NEETs include both advantaged and disadvantaged young people, the number of disadvantaged young people in precarious situations far exceeds the number of advantaged young people. According to a recent comparative study of Japan and the UK, similar trends were apparent in both countries (Inui *et al.* 2006). In Japan, in 2002, while 83 per cent of males and 53 per cent of females aged 15–34 who had higher education diplomas were in regular employment, only 47 per cent of males and 11 per cent of females with minimum academic qualifications (junior high school) were in the same position. The prevalence of freeters, unemployment, and NEET among those with lower academic backgrounds (junior high school and high school) is much higher than that for those with a higher educational background. In the UK in 2003, while 86 per cent of males and 81 per cent of females aged 20–24 who had completed higher education were in regular employment or full-time education/training, only 55 per cent of males and 16 per cent of females who had no academic qualifications were in the same position.

# Conclusion

The precarious condition of young people in contemporary societies is a result of some complex factors. Precariousness spreads due to the fact that transition patterns are changing from traditional and predictable routes to plural, individualized pathways. Such changes potentially provide young people with more choices for managing their lives; and the increasing flexibility of work potentially provides both young people and adults with working patterns that can be adjusted to suit their particular needs. Among the freeters, for example, a small number deliberately choose this route to establish a new work–life balance, even though most are able to exercise few real choices. With proper wages, the freeter lifestyle has plenty to recommend it. Additionally, transitions are a time for identity-formation, requiring a process of experimentation (Côté and Allahar 1994). Therefore, a degree of work flexibility can serve as a tool to provide young people with the space to develop.

However, precariousness can easily turn to insecurity if there are not enough resources for every young person, and it is insecurity – not healthy precariousness – that leads to difficulties among young people. Disadvantaged young people suffer most, and we need more discussion and supportive policies to enable young people to realize their full potential in late modern contexts.

# References

Beck, U. (2000) *The Brave New World of Work*, Cambridge: Polity Press.

Cabinet Office (2003) *White Paper on People's Life 2003*, Tokyo: Cabinet Office.

—— (2005) *Seishonen no Syuro ni kansuru Kenkyu-Chosa* [Research on Young People's Employment Conditions], Tokyo: Cabinet Office.

Côté, J. and Allahar, A. (1994) *Generation on Hold: Coming of Age in the Late Twentieth Century*, New York: New York University Press.

Furlong, A. (2006) 'Not a very NEET solution: representing problematic labour market transition among early school-leavers', *Work Employment and Society*, 20: 553–69.

Furlong, A. and Kelly, P. (2005) 'The Brazilianisation of youth transitions in Australia and the UK', *Australian Journal of Social Issues*, 40: 207–25.

Inui, A., Furlong, A., Sato, K., Sano, M., Hirastuka, M., Fukit, H. and Miyamoto, M. (2006) Huantei wo Ikiru Wakamono-tashi [Young People Living in Precarious Situations: Freeter, NEET and Unemployed in Japan and the UK], Tokyo: Ohostuki-shoten.

Jones, G. and Wallace, C. (1992) *Youth, Family and Citizenship*, Buckingham: Open University Press.

Ministry of Health, Labour and Welfare (2004) *White Paper on the Labour Economy 2004*. Tokyo: Ministry of Health, Labour and Welfare.

Nakanishi, S. (2004) *Wakamono-tachi ni Nani ga Okiteirunoka* [What Is Happening Among Young People?], Tokyo: Kadensha.

OECD (1999) *Employment Outlook 1999*, Paris: OECD.

—— (2002) *Employment Outlook 2002*, Paris: OECD.

—— (2005) *Employment Outlook 2005*, Paris: OECD.

Watson, L., Buchanan, J., Campbell, I. and Briggs, C. (2003) *Fragmented Futures*, Sydney: Federation Press.

Walther, A., Sauber, B. and Pohl, A. (2005) 'Informal networks in youth transitions in West Germany', *Journal of Youth Studies*, 8: 221–40.

# 22

# The stratification of youth employment in contemporary China

*Jieyu Liu*

## Introduction

This chapter offers an overview of the youth employment situation in contemporary China and discusses the opportunities and problems which young people face as the country moves further toward a market economy. The chapter starts by introducing the social and historical contexts in which youth employment is situated and then shows the stratified nature of youth employment through the examination of young migrant workers and urban graduates. In particular, this chapter focuses on how labour market pressures have manifested themselves depending on the gender, educational background and residency status of a young person.

## Social and historical contexts

China was a planned economy for three decades following the communist takeover in 1949. Labour was considered a national resource that was owned by the state and all able-bodied urban residents were allocated jobs in government-run work units. Because the work unit provided lifetime employment security ('the iron rice bowl') and welfare services such as health care and housing, those leaving school during this time had little choice but to accept a state-provided job (Bian 1994). The government also strictly controlled rural–urban migration, requiring every Chinese citizen to be registered at birth with the local authorities as either an urban or a rural householder. This divided the population in two: rural householders were prohibited from migrating to the cities and expected to provide food for urban residents (Davin 1999). The only way in which someone born in the countryside could jump the divide and migrate to a city was through university education.

Following the death of Chairman Mao in 1976, China began the gradual transition to a market economy. In the countryside, collective farming was displaced by a return to family farming and the restrictions on rural–urban migration were reduced allowing millions of surplus agricultural workers to migrate to the cities (Li 1997). In urban China, private and foreign-owned enterprises were encouraged, exposing state-run businesses to market pressures, contributing to the demise of the macro-government job assignment system. Since the 1990s, most urban young have found jobs through their own initiative (Hanser 2002).

## Stratified youth employment

China's economic reforms have improved living standards immensely. However, the reforms have affected young employed workers differently depending on: their gender, their educational level, and whether they were born in the countryside or not.

### Young migrant workers

Estimates of the number of people who were born in the Chinese countryside but who now work in the towns and cities range from 70 to 100 million (Tan 2000). These young migrants work away from home either periodically, or for a single period of between a few months and a few years (although the number of migrants who have remained permanently in cities has recently started to increase). A number of factors contribute to this migration (Davin 1999; Zhang 2001): first, agricultural reforms in the 1980s greatly improved the efficiency of farming, generating a surplus of nearly 200 million rural farm labourers; second, a rapidly growing urban economy and the establishment of foreign enterprises demanded large numbers of cheap labourers; third, the gradual relaxation of state migration policy made it possible for rural migrants to seek employment in urban labour markets aimed at migrant workers; finally, on an individual level, rural youth expressed a desire to 'see the world'.

Studies have shown two key forms of segregation in the young migrant worker labour market: first, gender, and, second, institutional discrimination. In terms of gender, the primary jobs for migrant males are in construction and manual labour, while female migrants tend to be employed in export processing factories or the provision of domestic services (Xu 2000). Approximately two-thirds of all migrant workers are men (Tan 2000). This is largely because marriage enforces differing social obligations on rural men and women. For a man, the arrival of a wife means that he can pursue migrant work while his spouse looks after the farmland, domestic chores and his parents/children (Davin 1999). For a woman, marriage enforces responsibilities that tie her to the countryside and make any prolonged absence from home prohibitively difficult (Fan 2003).

Although rural men are more likely to migrate, the women who do migrate are more likely to be young and single (Tan 2000). This is partly because in rural areas girls are forced to give up education earlier (at the age of 16) and so chose to work in a city during the years between school and marriage (constraints on family finances mean that only boys can be afforded further education[1]) (Fan 2003). Another factor is that employers now target young, single migrant women as they are considered efficient, easy to control and capable of handling delicate work (Xu 2000). The result of these demographic trends is that while men and young women leave the countryside for better paid jobs in the cities, older and married women are tied to the land, and this has led to the feminization of Chinese agriculture (Jacka 2006).

In terms of institutional segregation, scholars found that despite the significant labour market reforms, state governments still require migrants to hold both a residence permit and an employment permit and large cities place restrictions on the trades and occupations migrants may undertake (Davin 1999). At an interpersonal level, migrants must also deal with a form of discrimination that is comparable with western racism; they are considered outsiders and blamed for social problems such as crime and disorder (Zhang 2001). This overt and covert discrimination means that employers often hire rural migrants to work for less pay and under worse conditions than their urban counterparts. Although migrants often experience unpleasant working conditions (many studies have documented the long hours, lack of labour safety and sexual harassment of young females), young migrants also claim that the experience has not only fulfilled their primary objective of earning more money but also broadened their horizons (Jacka 2006). First-person accounts by young migrant women describe the process as an important rite of passage that has made them wiser, more mature, and altered their aspirations.

To redress the institutional discrimination experienced by migrants, the national government is currently looking at various proposals designed to improve the conditions of migrant workers, for instance, raising the educational level of rural youth by popularizing vocational education,[2] implementing laws to protect migrant workers, and incorporating migrant workers into the social security system that is currently the preserve of urbanites only (see Wang 2002; Guo 2007).

## Urban graduates

The state-driven job assignment system was grossly inefficient and commonly criticized for the way it created a mismatch between graduates supplied and skills demanded. The 'mutual choice' system that has operated effectively since the late 1990s allows graduates and employers to choose one another without the state's direct interference. The only influence that appears to remain is the state's desire to produce patriotic professionals. Hoffman's study of a university in northern China, for example, found that the campus career service attempted to instil feelings of patriotic professionalism in the graduates and to mould them into responsible citizens (Hoffman 2001). The effectiveness of these attempts is questionable, however, since recent studies have shown that graduates prefer to work for foreign-owned and private-owned companies while state-owned enterprises have difficulty recruiting educated workers (Zeng 2004).

Having internalized the wider discourse of efficiency and competition accompanying China's transition to a market economy, urban youth show a competitive stance and seem keen to develop and demonstrate their abilities. A survey study in Southern China found that personal development was the biggest concern when looking for a job (salary was the second) (Tan and Ling 2004). This is supported by Hanser's (2002) study of university graduates in Northern China that found educated urban youths had forged 'enterprising selves' treating work as a realm for self-development and Liu's (2007) interviews with young women in Eastern China that found women had a sense of career building different from that of their mothers who saw work simply as a means of financial support. Unlike their parents who enjoyed lifetime employment stability and developed loyalty toward their work unit, university graduates seem to now long for professional mobility and often switch jobs to enjoy new and broader experiences (Hoffman 2001; Liu 2007). However, school graduates without a university education are less ready to speak about fulfilling personal desires through work and their job-related considerations focus more on salary and on working conditions (Hanser 2002).

The state promotes formal methods of graduate recruitment, that is, newspaper advertisements, campus fairs and municipal talent markets. However, many studies have found that family and personal connections continue to play a very important role in finding work, regardless of educational attainment (Zhang 2005). By studying the role of connections in finding work among redundant workers, Liu argued (2007) that prior status was maintained and reproduced in finding work through pre-existing connections (which arose because of similar lifestyles and socio-economic backgrounds). The use of connections appears to reinforce social hierarchies and inequalities – powerful families help their children gain better employment opportunities allowing social connections to be passed on to the next generation. Despite the common use of connections, however, Hoffman did find that there was also a desire 'to find a position on one's own, prompted by a lack of useful connections and an urge to prove that individual hard work mattered' (Hoffman 2001: 57).

Gender has also played an important role in securing employment. As an unexpected consequence of the strict implementation of one-child policy in urban China, the vast majority of urban girls born in the only-child generation have demanded their parents' full attention and benefited from an unprecedented level of educational investment (Tsui and Rich 2002). However, on entering the labour market, young women, even those who are highly educated, still face gender discrimination. Employers often cite women's psychological barriers to enterprise and the extra cost of their reproductive duties. Many job advertisements even specify a criterion of 'men only'. Aware of, and expressing resentment for this discrimination, young educated women are often driven to work harder in order to compete with their male counterparts in the labour market and many newly married female professionals express a tension between work and family life (Liu 2007). By contrast, women with less education and fewer job skills are least likely to feel disadvantaged by their gender because the service industry is booming in China which absorbs a large proportion of women workers (Hanser 2002). However, such jobs increasingly require the deployment of 'feminine' charms and skills, and thus young and attractive women are predominant in these 'youth occupations' (Wang 2000).

Millions of older workers were made redundant as part of the state's economic restructuring during the 1990s and so government policy has been targeted at alleviating the hardship of this generation. Recently, however, youth unemployment has become a political issue and demanded the attention of Chinese policy-makers and scholars. A study of the 2000 census found that people under the age of 34 comprised 70 per cent of the unemployed population and a recent survey of youth employment found that urban school graduates (junior middle school, senior middle school and vocational school[3]) made up 80 per cent of unemployed youths (Duan 2004). The unemployment rate of university graduates has also gradually increased over the past four years, reflecting the fact that university education has expanded rapidly since 1999 when it aimed to be made available to all (Zeng 2004).

A number of factors have contributed to the rise of unemployment among the young. First, parts of the Chinese economy are already moving from manufacturing to tertiary-level services and these require more experienced, capable employees. Second, the fast pace of change means that employers want to employ appropriately skilled staff who do not require long graduate training programmes. Third, there are huge regional disparities in employment opportunities: the cities of eastern and coastal China, the area which is considered modern and developed, are overwhelmed with youths seeking employment while in western China, which is considered underdeveloped and backward, there are positions that cannot be filled. Finally, the free flow of rural–urban migration has allowed rural youth to move to the cities and this has created an oversupply (see China Youth Union *et al.* 2005; Zhang 2005).

Scholars in China have made various suggestions to improve the current situation: some call for the reformulation of vocational schools to offer students work placement opportunities and to channel students into occupations that are required by the labour market; some call on graduates to re-adjust their employment expectations; while others even hark back to the job assignment system and suggest that the government should intervene (see Duan 2004; Wang 2002; Zeng 2004). These strategies seem to over-simplify the situation and overlook the disparity and diversity among youth employment in a vast nation such as China.

## Conclusion

This chapter has outlined the current trends and conditions of youth employment in China, drawing attention to the effects of location, education and gender. Young migrant workers battle institutional segregation, while urban graduates face market-driven employment pressures and female graduates must deal with gender discrimination. While the existing studies have helped draw attention to some of the problems faced by the contemporary Chinese labour market, there is room for more research. Studies produced by scholars within China tend to be policy-oriented, and despite a preference for quantitative methods lack standardized statistical data, providing a general picture with little in-depth understanding of how young people adapt to the working world. Studies conducted by scholars based outside China pay special attention to migrant workers but seldom from the perspective of youth transition. Moreover, China is large and diverse, some parts of the country are rich in industry and commerce but overpopulated with young graduates, while other parts are underdeveloped and their growth is stunted by the loss of young people keen to migrate. It is likely that the solutions to these competing problems will be found at a regional level but to assist in this judgement more region-specific studies are required.

## Notes

1 While a one-child policy is enforced in urban China, in rural areas, the policy is not strictly implemented and most families have more than one child.
2 Educational attainment in rural China is still relatively low: in 2003, approximately 80 per cent of those holding a university degree were urban household residents (Zhang 2005).
3 In China, children go to primary school from the age of 7–13 and then go to junior middle school from 13–16. This nine-year education is legislatively compulsory. Thereafter students may go to a vocational school for three years in preparation for work or go to senior middle school for three years in preparation for a university entrance exam.

## References

Bian, Y. (1994) *Work and Inequality in Urban China*, Albany, NY: State University of New York.
China Youth Union, Research Institute of Labour and Social Security and International Labour Organization (2005) 'Chinese youth employment – a survey report', *Economy Studies*, 80:1–14 [in Chinese].
Davin, D. (1999) *Internal Migration in Contemporary China*, New York: St. Martin's Press.
Duan, D. (2004) 'Analysis of Chinese Youth Unemployment', *Frontiers*, 12: 193–4 [in Chinese].

Fan, C. C. (2003) 'Rural-urban migration and Gender division of labor in transitional China'. *International Journal of Urban and Regional* Research, 27(1): 24–47.

Guo, X. (2007) 'Vocational education and rural youth development', *Science and Education*, 7: 87–90 [in Chinese].

Hanser, A. (2002) 'The Chinese enterprising self: young, educated urbanites and the search for work', in P. Link, R. P. Madsen and P. G. Pickowicz (eds) *Popular China: Unofficial Culture in a Globalizing Society*, Lanham, MD: Rowman & Littlefield, pp. 189–206.

Hoffman, L. (2001) 'Guiding college graduates to work: social constructions of labor markets in Dalian', in N. Chen, C. D. Clark, S. Z. Gottschang and L. Jeffery (eds) *China Urban: Ethnographies of Contemporary Culture,* Durham, NC: Duke University Press, pp. 43–66.

Jacka, T. (2006) *Rural Women in Urban China: Gender, Migration, and Social* Change, Armonk, NY: M. E. Sharpe.

Li, J. (1997) 'Occupational mobility of rural youth', *Youth Studies*, 3: 1–10 [in Chinese].

Liu, J. (2007) *Gender and Work in Urban China: Women Workers of the Unlucky Generation*, London: Routledge.

Tan, S. (2000) 'The relationship between foreign enterprises, local governments, and women migrant workers in the Pearl River Delta', in L. A. West and Y. Zhao (eds) *Rural Labor Flows in China*, Berkeley, CA: Institute of East Asian Studies, University of California Press.

Tan, J. and Ling, C. (2004) 'Urban youth: life and occupational development', *China Youth Studies*, 5: 52–60 [in Chinese].

Tsui, M. and Rich, L. (2002) 'The only child and educational opportunity for girls in urban China', *Gender and Society*, 16(1): 74–92.

Wang, J. (2002) 'Youth employment in China's socio-economic transition', *Youth Studies*, 1: 3–6 [in Chinese].

Wang, Z. (2000) 'Gender, employment and women's resistance', in E. J. Perry and M. Selden (eds) *Chinese Society: Change, Conflict and Resistance*, London: Routledge, pp. 62–82.

Xu, F. (2000) *Women Migrant Workers in China's Economic Reform*, New York: St. Martin's Press.

Zeng, X. (2004) 'Job seeking of college graduates in employment environment under transition', *Economy Studies*, 6: 87–95 [in Chinese].

Zhang, H. (2005) 'Chinese youth employment: problems and solutions 2005–20', *Youth Studies*, 3: 15–22 [in Chinese].

Zhang, L. (2001) *Strangers in the City: Reconfigurations of Space, Power and Social Networks within China's Floating Population*, Stanford, CA: Stanford University Press.

# 23

# What makes a young entrepreneur?

*David G. Blanchflower and Andrew Oswald*

## Introduction

A rule of thumb is that youth unemployment rates tend to be approximately twice the adult rate. The most recent 2006 figures, for example, from the 2007 OECD Employment Outlook, reveal a EU15 unemployment rate in 2006 of 16.1 percent among those 15–24 years of age, compared to a rate of 7.0 percent among those 25–54 and 6.4 percent for 55–64 year-olds. The figures for the OECD as a whole were 12.5 percent; 5.4 percent and 4.4 percent respectively. Unemployment rates for 18–24 year olds in 2006 were especially high in Belgium (18.9 percent); Finland (18.8 percent); France (23.9 percent); Greece (24.5 percent); Italy (21.6 percent); Poland (29.8 percent); Slovak Republic (26.6 percent) and Sweden (21.3 percent). In the UK, for example, the proportion of total unemployment accounted for by those aged 18–24 has increased steadily over the past decade: in 1997 it was 23.9 percent of the unemployed compared with 30.8 percent in the latest available data at the time of writing for June–August 2007 (Office for National Statistics 2007). Therefore in countries with the most severe youth unemployment rates, such as France, a quarter of young people can be looking for work. It is widely accepted that this is not merely a short-run waste of human resources and a source of unhappiness among Europe's young people. It may have long-term scarring effects on the working adults of the next generation. For many years, Europe has had a large group of young people outside education and the workplace. The persistence of the problem seems to demonstrate that standard economic policies have been insufficient. Western governments are searching for new alternatives. One is the idea that policy should attempt to create more entrepreneurship among the young.

It is not obvious that even a large new supply of young entrepreneurs would solve the jobs crisis. Nevertheless, there are a number of 'potential' benefits often discussed by commentators.

- Entrepreneurship may promote innovation and thus create new jobs.
- There may be a direct effect on employment if new young entrepreneurs hire fellow youths from the dole queues.

■ New small firms may raise the degree of competition in the product market, bringing gains to consumers.

■ Young entrepreneurs may be particularly responsive to new economic opportunities and trends.

■ Greater self-employment among young people may go along with increased self-reliance and well-being.

■ Economists have little evidence, however, on whether these hypothetical benefits exist in practice.

The beginning of the twenty-first century may mark a particularly appropriate time for young entrepreneurs. Some commentators argue that new opportunities abound – due to technological change, the fragmentation of markets, and increased deregulation across Europe.

In this chapter we address questions of the following kind:

■ Do young people want to be entrepreneurial, but are somehow prevented?

■ Are those who manage to become self-employed actually better off, in terms of well-being (not just income) than those who do not?

■ How, in a general sense, do young people perceive work?

## Background patterns in the data

The most commonly studied class of entrepreneurs is those who are self-employed. Columns 1 and 2 of Table 23.1 provide background information on self-employment rates for those aged 25 and younger and those older than 25 years of age for a large number of countries. Here we define the self-employment rate across workers so it is the proportion of workers who are self-employed. Table 23.1 shows that the self-employment figures vary greatly from one country to another. Figures are given in the table for the period 2001–6 from a number of Eurobarometers. Some of the patterns in Table 23.1 are due to the differing importance of the agriculture sector, nation-by-nation. So self-employment is particularly high in countries such as Turkey, Greece, Italy and Cyprus. For example, self-employment accounts for those over 25 accounts for 46 percent of workers in Greece, compared to less than 9 percent in Denmark. It is apparent that the self-employment rate of older workers is universally higher than it is for younger workers.

There is evidence from columns 3 and 4 of Table 23.1 that many more people would like to run their own businesses. The data come from 2000–04 and are identical to questions reported in the 1997/8 *International Social Survey Programme* examined in Blanchflower *et al.* (2001). It gives answers to one of the survey questions in a series of *Flash Entrepreneurship Eurobarometers* (see Blanchflower and Shadforth 2007). Respondents are asked:

Q. Suppose you were working and could choose between different kinds of jobs. Which of the following would you choose: being an employee or being self-employed?

Remarkably high numbers of individuals express a preference for self-employment. In most countries, large numbers of respondents said they would prefer being self-employed.

This is especially apparent for the young. As reported in Table 3 of Blanchflower *et al.* (2001), in an equation estimating the probability that an individual would like to be self-employed, age enters negatively, controlling for a variety of characteristics. Table 23.1 appears to indicate – assuming questionnaire material can be viewed as reliable – that *there is large latent demand for a kind of entrepreneurial behaviour – self employment.* People find self-employment intrinsically attractive.

**Table 23.1** Self-employment rates among workers only, 2001–06 (%)

| | *2001–06 Self-employment rate* | | *2001–04 Prefer self-employment* | |
|---|---|---|---|---|
| | *Over age 25* | *< age 25* | *Over age 25* | *< age 25* |
| Austria | 14.8 | 8.6 | 37.5 | 41.7 |
| Belgium | 15.5 | 10.6 | 34.6 | 48.3 |
| Bulgaria | 11.1 | 7.4 | – | – |
| Croatia | 12.3 | 5.3 | – | – |
| Cyprus | 32.7 | 29.8 | 62.5 | 68.4 |
| Czech Republic | 17.4 | 9.7 | 31.9 | 49.0 |
| Denmark | 8.5 | 3.9 | 36.4 | 59.0 |
| Estonia | 10.1 | 4.8 | 36.5 | 71.4 |
| Finland | 13.5 | 12.4 | 28.2 | 27.0 |
| France | 11.7 | 7.9 | 41.9 | 53.1 |
| Germany | 11.7 | 6.2 | 42.1 | 50.1 |
| Greece | 38.3 | 30.9 | 50.0 | 62.2 |
| Hungary | 10.0 | 6.0 | 45.0 | 67.7 |
| Iceland | 17.1[a] | 4.4[a] | 63.7 | 63.4 |
| Ireland | 19.5 | 10.6 | 58.6 | 60.0 |
| Italy | 29.5 | 23.6 | 54.1 | 73.8 |
| Latvia | 9.6 | 4.9 | 39.0 | 63.4 |
| Lichtenstein | 15.6[a] | 5.7[a] | 52.3 | 57.9 |
| Lithuania | 7.8 | 3.4 | 54.0 | 69.0 |
| Luxembourg | 10.7 | 6.4 | 46.5 | 54.3 |
| Malta | 13.4 | 3.0 | 45.3 | 54.7 |
| Netherlands | 13.7 | 8.7 | 32.1 | 43.8 |
| Norway | 11.4 | 1.9[a] | 37.2 | 63.9 |
| Poland | 22.3 | 10.0 | 53.8 | 53.7 |
| Portugal | 21.1 | 13.0 | 65.6 | 77.7 |
| Romania | 18.9 | 15.3 | – | – |
| Slovakia | 12.4 | 6.2 | 33.1 | 39.7 |
| Slovenia | 12.8 | 6.9 | 33.3 | 42.2 |
| Spain | 18.2 | 12.0 | 60.9 | 67.2 |
| Sweden | 11.5 | 6.9 | 35.0 | 45.2 |
| Turkey | 46.3 | 30.9 | – | – |
| UK | 10.8 | 6.8 | 44.1 | 49.0 |
| USA | 9.9[b] | 2.7[b] | 63.5 | 58.8 |

Source: Columns 1 and 2: *Eurobarometers* 2001–06 (*n* = 110,878). Columns 3 and 4: Flash Entrepreneurship Eurobarometers 2000–04. 'Suppose you could choose between different kinds of jobs, which one would you prefer, being an employee or being self-employed?'(*n* = 33,913).

Notes:
a estimates obtained from Flash Entrepreneurship Eurobarometers.
b estimates obtained from 2000, 2002, 2004 and 2006 General Social.
   Surveys pooled (*n* =11494 for age>25 and *n*= 1410 for age ≤ 25.

Who, then, becomes self-employed? Table 23.2 provides information from regressions on self-employment (the dependent variable is a one/zero) for three countries using large micro-surveys at the level of the individual from the UK Labour Force Surveys of 2001–07 (LFS); the Canadian Labour Force Surveys of 2001–05 (CLFS) and the Merged Outgoing Rotation Group files of the Current Population Survey of 2001–07 for the United States (MORG). There are nearly three million observations in total and nearly half a million young people between the ages of 16 and 25 in the data files. The procedure used is dprobit in STATA which fits maximum-likelihood probit models and is an alternative to probit. Rather than reporting the coefficients, dprobit reports the marginal effect, that is the change in the probability for an infinitesimal change in each independent, continuous variable and, by default, reports the discrete change in the probability for dummy variables. Table 23.2 models how personal characteristics are related to the chance of running one's own business. The probability of being self-employed for those aged over 25, in all three countries, rises with age and is higher for men (Blanchflower, 2000; 2004; 2007). In the case of the USA and Canada, the probability for older workers rises with education but declines with education in the UK (Blanchflower and Shadforth 2007). In Canada, the whites have especially high rates, but in the UK rates are especially high among Asians from India, Pakistan and Bangladesh and among Chinese while in the USA, rates are high for whites. In the case of the young, aged 25 and under, the probability is higher for men in the USA and the UK but lower in Canada. One half of all of the young self-employed in Canada are in childcare, jobs which are primarily held by young females. Probabilities decline with schooling in both Canada and the UK for the young; the differences in the probabilities by different levels of schooling are less marked for the young in the USA than for older workers.

Another important determinant of being self-employed that has been identified in the literature is having a self-employed parent. The probability of self-employment in the USA is substantially higher among the children of business owners than among the children of non-business owners (see Dunn and Holtz-Eakin 2000). These studies generally find that an individual who had a self-employed parent is roughly two to three times more likely to be self-employed than someone who did not have a self-employed parent. Broussard et al. (2003) found that the self-employed in the USA have between .2 and .4 more children compared to the non-self-employed. The authors argue that having more children can increase the likelihood that an inside family member will be a good match at running the business. One might also think that the existence of family businesses, which are particularly prevalent in construction and retailing, is a further way to overcome the existence of capital constraints. Analogously, Hout and Rosen (2000) found that the offspring of self-employed fathers are more likely than others to become self-employed and argued that the historically low rates of self-employment among African-Americans and Latinos may contribute to their low contemporary rates.

More recently Fairlie and Robb (2007) have demonstrated using data from the 1992 Characteristics of Business Owners (CBO) Survey that more than half of all business owners had a self-employed family member prior to starting their business. Conditional on having a self-employed family member, less than 50 percent of small business owners worked in that family member's business suggesting that it is unlikely that intergenerational links in self-employment are largely due to the acquisition of general and specific business human capital and that instead similarities across family members in entrepreneurial preferences may explain part of the relationship. In contrast, estimates from regression models *conditioning* on business ownership indicated that having a self-employed family

191

**Table 23.2** Probability of being self-employed in the UK, Canada and the USA, 2001–07 (dprobits)

| | UK > 25 2001–2007 | UK < 25 2001–2007 | Canada > 24 2001–2005 | Canada < 24 2001–2005 | USA > 25 2001–2006 | USA < 25 2001–2006 |
|---|---|---|---|---|---|---|
| Age* | 0.0033 (102.62) | 0.0060 (36.83) | 0.1545 (58.49) | −0.0026 (1.88) | 0.0037 (129.11) | 0.0037 (22.86) |
| Male | 0.0984 (142.97) | 0.0350 (40.90) | 0.0777 (77.35) | −0.0084 (7.78) | 0.0607 (91.85) | 0.0153 (20.48) |
| Mixed | −0.0070 (1.36) | −0.0049 (1.39) | | | | |
| Asian | 0.0399 (19.44) | −0.0038 (2.08) | | | −0.0230 (13.58) | −0.0074 (3.76) |
| Black | −0.0530 (20.60) | −0.0157 (5.51) | | | −0.0658 (54.42) | −0.0082 (6.25) |
| Chinese | 0.0646 (10.37) | −0.0113 (2.02) | | | | |
| Other race | 0.0015 (0.43) | −0.0151 (4.52) | | | −0.0443 (34.93) | −0.0097 (8.72) |
| Native American | | | | | −0.0463 (14.83) | −0.0007 (0.21) |
| Hispanics | | | | | −0.0540 (18.56) | −0.0135 (5.88) |
| School 2 | −0.0195 (15.64) | 0.0141 (6.15) | −0.0424 (19.45) | 0.0105 (0.94) | 0.0772 (21.74) | 0.0000 (0.00) |
| School 3 | 0.0307 (30.13) | 0.0193 (13.56) | −0.0441 (22.09) | 0.0188 (1.70) | −0.0543 (24.54) | −0.0199 (2.73) |
| School 4 | −0.0064 (6.07) | 0.0160 (10.80) | −0.0327 (13.24) | 0.0018 (0.18) | −0.0279 (12.19) | −0.0214 (2.68) |
| School 5 | −0.0150 (13.03) | 0.0261 (12.71) | −0.0395 (19.12) | 0.0108 (1.03) | −0.0478 (19.74) | −0.0166 (2.01) |
| School 6 | 0.0076 (6.08) | 0.0529 (19.01) | −0.0301 (13.39) | 0.0561 (4.72) | −0.0368 (15.22) | −0.0133 (1.46) |
| School 7 | 0.0214 (5.11) | 0.0362 (5.79) | −0.0214 (7.55) | 0.1669 (8.07) | −0.0281 (12.24) | −0.0224 (2.25) |
| High school graduate | | | | | −0.0376 (16.56) | −0.0178 (1.71) |
| 12th grade No diploma | | | | | −0.0421 (11.64) | −0.0141 (1.58) |
| 11th grade | | | | | −0.0331 (10.93) | −0.0125 (1.28) |
| 10th grade | | | | | −0.0279 (8.84) | −0.0063 (0.58) |
| 9th grade | | | | | −0.0315 (9.13) | −0.0045 (0.41) |
| 7th/8th grade | | | | | −0.0139 (4.02) | 0.0005 (0.04) |

| | UK > 25 2001–2007 | UK < 25 2001–2007 | Canada > 24 2001–2005 | Canada < 24 2001–2005 | USA > 25 2001–2006 | USA < 25 2001–2006 |
|---|---|---|---|---|---|---|
| 5th/6th grade | | | | | −0.0541 (15.44) | −0.0155 (1.78) |
| 1–4th grade | | | | | −0.0660 (14.29) | −0.0158 (1.69) |
| <1st grade | | | | | −0.0628 (8.76) | −0.0081 (0.64) |
| Year dummies | 5 | 5 | 4 | 4 | 5 | 5 |
| Area dummies | 19 | 19 | 9 | 9 | 51 | 51 |
| Pseudo $R^2$ | 0.0531 | 0.0766 | 0.0595 | 0.0529 | 0.0540 | 0.0322 |
| N | 1,041,559 | 171,194 | 567,691 | 129,690 | 1,026,349 | 185,067 |

Sources: UK – Labour Force Surveys, March 2001–June 2007; USA – Merged Outgoing Rotation Group files of the Current Population Survey, 2001–2006 and Canada – Labour Force Surveys, 2001–2005.

Mean self-employment rates

UK $\leq$ 25 years 3.5%; USA < 25 years 2.6%; Canada $\leq$ 25 years 4.7%; UK > 25 years 14.1%; USA > 25 years 13.4%; Canada > 25 years 17.7%

Notes: In the case of Canada, the age variable is for 50–54 and 20–24, half of the $\leq$ 24 year-old self-employed are in childcare. For Canada, education categories are excluded = university graduate degree; school 2 = university bachelor's degree; school 3 = post-secondary certificate or diploma; school 4 = some post-secondary; school 5 = grade 11 to 13, graduate; school 6 = some secondary; school 7 = 0 to 8 years schooling.

For the USA, excluded category is PhD, school 2 = MBA; school 3 = MA; school 4 = BA; school 5 = associate degree academic; school 6 = associate degree vocational; school 7 = some college no degree.

For the UK, excluded category is Degree or equivalent; school 2 = Higher Education; school 3 = GCE A Level or equivalent; school 4 = GCSE grades A*–C or equivalent; school 5 = Other qualification; school 6 = No qualification; school 7 = Don't know.

T-statistics in parentheses.

member plays only a minor role in determining small business outcomes, whereas the business human capital acquired from prior work experience in a family member's business appears to be very important for business success. Estimates from the CBO also indicated that only 1.6 percent of all small businesses are inherited, suggesting that the role of business inheritances in determining intergenerational links in self-employment is limited at best.

Columns 1 and 2 of Table 23.3 report the results of estimating the probability of being self-employed as in Table 23.2 but now for Europe using three *Flash Entrepreneurship*

**Table 23.3** Probability of being self-employed and choosing self-employment, 2002–04

| | Self-employment | | Choosing self-employment | |
|---|---|---|---|---|
| | *Over age 25* | *< age 25* | *Over age 25* | *< age 25* |
| Mother self-empl. | 0.0343 (6.37) | 0.0209 (3.68) | 0.0344 (3.75) | 0.0365 (1.78) |
| Father self-empl. | 0.0711 (16.31) | 0.0244 (5.42) | 0.0889 (12.64) | 0.0613 (4.04) |
| Age | 0.0176 (19.44) | −0.0079 (5.48) | −0.0049 (3.88) | 0.0142 (1.89) |
| Male | 0.0037 (1.14) | 0.0029 (0.92) | −0.0017 (0.32) | −0.0087 (0.72) |
| $Age^2$ | −0.0001 (21.09) | 0.0003 (7.75) | 0.0000 (3.42) | −0.0005 (2.44) |
| Austria | −0.0054 (0.49) | −0.0210 (2.90) | −0.0970 (5.38) | −0.0645 (1.41) |
| Belgium | −0.0194 (1.97) | −0.0155 (1.75) | −0.1175 (7.16) | −0.0541 (1.30) |
| Cyprus | 0.0518 (2.83) | −0.0200 (3.17) | 0.1592 (5.41) | 0.1655 (2.93) |
| Czech Republic | 0.0637 (4.36) | −0.0043 (0.60) | −0.1182 (5.33) | −0.0050 (0.10) |
| Denmark | −0.0526 (5.30) | −0.0174 (2.91) | −0.1164 (6.48) | 0.0593 (1.21) |
| Ireland | 0.0529 (4.34) | −0.0237 (3.74) | 0.1259 (6.72) | 0.0730 (1.91) |
| Estonia | −0.0151 (0.86) | −0.0205 (3.44) | −0.0698 (2.39) | 0.2067 (3.33) |
| Finland | 0.0002 (0.02) | −0.0114 (1.63) | −0.2043 (11.26) | −0.2395 (5.56) |
| France | −0.0613 (7.10) | 0.0586 (3.98) | −0.0475 (3.06) | 0.0105 (0.28) |
| Germany | −0.0118 (1.26) | −0.0178 (2.42) | −0.0342 (2.20) | 0.0028 (0.07) |
| Greece | 0.1006 (8.40) | −0.0133 (1.73) | 0.0208 (1.23) | 0.0795 (2.15) |
| Hungary | 0.0265 (1.91) | −0.0190 (3.05) | 0.0155 (0.72) | 0.1713 (3.35) |
| Iceland | 0.0396 (3.31) | −0.0219 (3.12) | 0.1174 (6.02) | 0.0730 (1.82) |
| Italy | 0.0073 (0.75) | −0.0182 (2.43) | 0.0764 (4.88) | 0.1992 (5.47) |
| Latvia | −0.0568 (3.31) | 0.0081 (0.59) | −0.0463 (1.62) | 0.1295 (2.42) |
| Lithuania | 0.0017 (0.16) | −0.0136 (1.53) | 0.0406 (2.19) | 0.0745 (1.75) |
| Lichtenstein | −0.0384 (2.19) | −0.0076 (0.51) | 0.0989 (3.41) | 0.1827 (3.26) |
| Luxembourg | 0.1507 (11.27) | −0.0150 (1.52) | −0.0236 (1.31) | −0.0029 (0.07) |
| Malta | −0.0495 (2.94) | −0.0161 (1.43) | 0.0046 (0.16) | −0.0130 (0.21) |
| Netherlands | −0.0133 (1.38) | −0.0121 (0.95) | −0.1553 (9.68) | −0.0858 (1.95) |
| Norway | −0.0024 (0.23) | −0.0200 (1.70) | −0.1240 (6.83) | 0.0527 (1.10) |
| Poland | 0.0154 (1.12) | −0.0124 (1.50) | 0.0758 (3.40) | 0.0185 (0.43) |
| Portugal | 0.0032 (0.31) | 0.0010 (0.09) | 0.2047 (11.94) | 0.2669 (7.51) |
| Slovakia | 0.0534 (2.78) | −0.0156 (1.40) | −0.1149 (3.85) | −0.0903 (1.54) |
| Slovenia | −0.0568 (3.36) | −0.0079 (0.97) | −0.1188 (4.09) | −0.0664 (1.18) |
| Spain | −0.0087 (0.90) | −0.0151 (2.19) | 0.1364 (8.39) | 0.1408 (4.04) |
| Sweden | −0.0230 (2.15) | −0.0190 (2.36) | −0.1251 (6.95) | −0.0604 (1.29) |
| USA | 0.0274 (2.63) | 0.0085 (0.98) | 0.1834 (11.31) | 0.1084 (3.04) |
| ALS 16–19 | 0.0145 (1.25) | 0.0092 (1.07) | −0.0452 (2.54) | −0.0470 (1.54) |
| ALS 20+ | 0.0274 (2.48) | 0.0038 (0.67) | −0.0411 (2.37) | −0.0355 (1.42) |
| Still studying | 0.0502 (4.35) | −0.0092 (1.52) | −0.0174 (1.00) | −0.0395 (1.33) |
| Pseudo $R^2$ | 0.0755 | 0.1433 | 0.0456 | 0.0426 |
| N | 35451 | 7133 | 33312 | 6886 |

Source: Flash Entrepreneurship Eurobarometers, 2002–04. T-statistics in parentheses.

Notes: Equations also include two-year dummies. UK is excluded.

*Eurobarometers*, 2002–04. Three of the five years of data used in Table 23.1 include information on whether the respondent's parents were self-employed. having a mother or a father self-employed or both, raises the probability of an individual being self-employed for both younger and older workers. Columns 3 and 4 now model the probability that an individual when offered the choice of being an employee or self-employed chooses the latter. A father who is self-employed is especially important here.

Columns 1 and 2 of Table 23.4 are similar to the first two columns in that they once again estimate self-employment probabilities. The main difference now is the much larger sample size as data are drawn from a long time series of various Eurobarometers, covering the period 1973–2006. Column 1 is for those aged over 25 and column 2 for younger workers. In total there are nearly 400,000 observations on 30 countries, including the ten Accession countries from Eastern Europe plus Malta and Cyprus, along with candidate countries of Norway and Turkey. The probability of being self-employed rises with age and is higher for men. As was found for the UK, self-employment and education are negatively correlated.

The data come from the *Eurobarometer Surveys of 1973 to 2006*. Happiness is U-shaped in age (Blanchflower and Oswald 2007) and married people are happier than singles and the unemployed have low happiness levels. Both young and old are the most unhappy if they lived in Bulgaria and the most happy living in Denmark. It is noticeable that for the two sub-samples the category 'self-employed' is statistically significant entering with a positive sign, showing that the self-employed have higher levels of satisfaction than the excluded category of employees with similar characteristics. Once more, therefore, the direct advantages to entrepreneurship seem clear. For whatever exact psychological reasons, self-employed young men and women are unusually satisfied with their *lives*.

In addition, self-employed young men and women are unusually satisfied with their *jobs*. The attitudes of young workers to various characteristics of their jobs are explored in Table 23.5. Data are taken from *Eurobarometer #54.2: Impact of New Technologies, Employment and Social Affairs, and Disabilities, January–February 2001*. The sample is restricted to workers only. These data were previously examined in Blanchflower (2004). Responses are reported in relation to job satisfaction; earnings; the type of work and travel-to-work time. In each case the dependent variable is coded one through ten: the respondent was told that '1' meant *not at all satisfied* and '10' meant *totally satisfied*. For each of the four variables the self-employed are especially satisfied and this is true for both the younger and older age groups. The self-employed like their jobs, the type of work they do, their earnings and the short travel to work times. Young workers are especially dissatisfied with their jobs in Greece and Portugal and with their earnings in Sweden.

## Entrepreneurship and capital constraints

Economists have amassed considerable evidence that potential entrepreneurs are held back by lack of capital. Blanchflower and Oswald (1998), for example, found evidence that the receipt of an inheritance or gift seems to increase a typical individual's probability of being self-employed. This emerges from British data, the National Child Development Survey. NCDS traces from birth a cohort of children born in 1958. These individuals have been followed for the whole of their lives. Blanchflower and Oswald find a large association between self-employment and receiving money early on. The inheritance effect is found at age 23 and 33. It is especially large in the former and

**Table 23.4** Probability of being self-employed and life satisfaction, Europe, 1973–2006

| | Self-employment probability | | Life satisfaction | |
|---|---|---|---|---|
| | Over age 25 | < age 25 | Over age 25 | < age 25 |
| Age | 0.0051 (78.24) | 0.0041 (9.73) | −0.0385 (32.78) | 0.0487 (9.57 ) |
| Age$^2$ | | | 0.0004 (36.57) | −0.0017 (11.73) |
| Male | 0.0575 (40.04) | 0.0397 (18.15) | −0.1025 (17.96) | −0.0800 (7.87) |
| Time trend | | | 0.0013 (4.17) | 0.0057 (8.70) |
| Self-employed | | | 0.0332 (3.81) | 0.0833 (3.23) |
| Home | | | −0.0374 (4.52) | −0.1420 (6.23) |
| Student | | | 0.0117 (0.27) | 0.1769 (6.45 ) |
| Retired | | | −0.0966 (10.77) | −0.3910 (10.27) |
| Unemployed | | | −0.9911 (83.73) | −0.9022 (47.85 ) |
| ALS 16–19 | −0.0278 (15.39) | −0.0121 (4.04) | 0.2396 (37.84) | 0.1637 (9.85) |
| ALS 20+ | −0.0241 (12.43) | −0.0026 (0.70) | 0.4823 (64.78) | 0.3882 (18.17) |
| Still studying | −0.0427 (3.52) | −0.0232 (2.80) | 0.2153 (5.16) | 0.3004 (10.40) |
| Married | | | 0.3956 (47.45) | 0.2260 (14.53) |
| Living together | | | 0.1876 (13.60) | 0.1477 (7.94) |
| Divorced | | | −0.3494 (25.48) | −0.7441 (14.63) |
| Separated | | | −0.4896 (22.23) | −0.5760 (8.28) |
| Widowed | | | −0.1866 (15.50) | −0.3171 (5.53) |
| Austria | 0.0867 (15.38) | 0.0383 (4.32) | −0.3099 (16.97) | −0.1591 (4.32) |
| Belgium | 0.0965 (24.890 | 0.0435 (7.29) | −0.2589 (21.19) | −0.0546 (2.30) |
| Bulgaria | 0.0344 (2.73) | 0.0812 (2.72) | −3.0543 (90.78) | −2.1829 (28.47) |
| Croatia | 0.0630 (4.77) | 0.0472 (1.54) | −1.2832 (36.10) | −0.3371 (4.09) |
| Cyprus | 0.2917 (25.09) | 0.3976 (13.16) | −0.2958 (7.92) | 0.1003 (1.21) |
| Czech Republic | 0.1251 (11.72) | 0.1325 (4.36) | −0.9971 (30.81) | −0.4984 (5.89) |
| Denmark | −0.0094 (2.70) | −0.0428 (7.67) | 1.0734 (85.34) | 1.1841 (45.79 ) |
| Estonia | 0.0102 (0.87) | 0.0383 (1.23) | −1.5259 (45.16) | −0.8716 (11.20) |
| Finland | 0.0526 (8.91) | 0.0642 (6.25) | −0.2058 (11.27) | 0.0033 (0.10) |
| France | 0.0612 (16.46) | 0.0038 (0.71) | −1.0225 (83.55) | −0.7695 (32.70) |
| Germany | 0.0083 (2.55) | −0.0168 (3.44) | −0.6872 (63.04) | −0.6765 (30.49) |
| Greece | 0.3664 (81.14) | 0.2722 (32.44) | −1.6083 (121.29) | −1.1353 (44.57) |
| Hungary | 0.0149 (1.13) | 0.0562 (1.76) | −1.9181 (58.49) | −1.2570 (13.13) |
| Ireland | 0.1980 (47.28) | 0.0794 (13.83) | 0.0840 (6.65) | 0.0710 (3.17) |
| Italy | 0.2013 (50.33) | 0.1839 (25.07) | −1.1271 (92.03) | −0.8733 (37.41) |
| Latvia | 0.0083 (0.72) | 0.0391 (1.44) | −1.8559 (55.77) | −1.0335 (13.62) |
| Lithuania | −0.0195 (1.52) | 0.0111 (0.33) | −1.9429 (57.38) | −0.6400 (7.79) |
| Luxembourg | 0.0245 (4.92) | −0.0053 (0.72) | 0.3288 (20.11) | 0.2194 (6.90) |
| Malta | 0.0741 (3.64) | −0.0019 (0.05) | −0.3693 (7.53) | −0.1810 (1.43) |
| Netherlands | 0.0234 (6.16) | 0.0002 (0.03) | 0.4361 (35.99) | 0.5910 (23.74) |
| Norway | 0.0127 (1.67) | 0.0287 (1.92) | 0.4358 (15.34) | 0.6090 (11.32) |
| Poland | 0.2116 (15.64) | 0.1336 (3.99) | −1.3646 (38.71) | −0.4069 (5.42) |
| Portugal | 0.1678 (36.73) | 0.0643 (9.79) | −1.5238 (109.95) | −1.0356 (40.25) |
| Romania | 0.1453 (11.64) | 0.2339 (7.49) | −2.4206 (70.68) | −1.6739 (20.67) |
| Slovakia | 0.0504 (4.84) | 0.0828 (2.76) | −1.7167 (53.90) | −1.2235 (13.55) |
| Slovenia | 0.0686 (5.64) | 0.0728 (2.28) | −0.3816 (10.92) | −0.0322 (0.42) |
| Spain | 0.1568 (33.14) | 0.0739 (10.52) | −0.6530 (46.20) | −0.3713 (14.53) |
| Sweden | −0.0014 (0.26) | −0.0040 (0.42) | 0.3476 (19.15) | 0.3740 (10.08) |
| Turkey | 0.4504 (29.35) | 0.3924 (14.10) | −0.8374 (19.54) | −0.4114 (5.89) |
| Cut 1 | | | −4.2661 | −3.3319 |
| Cut 2 | | | −2.4728 | −1.5287 |
| Cut 3 | | | 0.3414 | 1.3615 |
| Year dummies | 31 | 31 | 0 | 0 |
| Pseudo R$^2$ | 0.0845 | 0.0910 | 0.0873 | 0.0675 |
| N | 328,402 | 66,875 | 620,765 | 162,786 |

Source: *Trend Eurobarometers* 1975–2002 and various subsequent Eurobarometers. Excluded categories ALS < 16; UK.

Notes: Columns 1 and 2 are dprobits and columns 3 and 4 ordered logits. T-statistics in parentheses.

**Table 23.5** Satisfaction with work in Europe, 2001

| | Job satisfaction | | Job earnings | |
|---|---|---|---|---|
| | Over age 25 | ≤ age 25 | Over age 25 | ≤ age 25 |
| Self-employed | 0.3381 (5.65) | 0.9326 (4.37) | .0936 (1.56) | .9988 (4.64) |
| Age | 0.0049 (2.23) | −0.0216 (0.94) | 0.0008 (0.39) | −0.0090 (0.39) |
| Male | −0.0030 (0.07) | 0.0223 (0.20) | 0.1566 (3.59) | 0.1195 (1.08) |
| ALS 16–19 | 0.1423 (2.23) | −0.2252 (1.31) | 0.2206 (3.49) | −0.0879 (0.51) |
| ALS 20+ | 0.4378 (6.59) | 0.0807 (0.40) | 0.4233 (6.41) | 0.1031 (0.51) |
| Austria | 0.2657 (2.63) | 0.2908 (1.22) | 0.5696 (5.63) | 0.4538 (1.88) |
| Belgium | 0.0505 (0.50) | 0.2010 (0.76) | 0.1851 (1.80) | 0.3986 (1.52) |
| Ireland | 0.0540 (0.51) | 0.0013 (0.01) | 0.2219 (2.10) | 0.1859 (0.85) |
| Finland | −0.1928 (1.85) | −0.2734 (0.93) | −0.0874 (0.82) | −0.3348 (1.15) |
| France | −0.4279 (4.41) | −0.0522 (0.21) | −0.3728 (3.91) | 0.1271 (0.52) |
| Germany | 0.1111 (1.29) | 0.2221 (1.08) | 0.1229 (1.45) | −0.3793 (1.86) |
| Greece | −1.2589 (11.01) | −0.5374 (1.77) | −0.7227 (6.45) | −0.1713 (0.55) |
| Italy | −0.6131 (6.08) | −0.5364 (1.88) | −0.2770 (2.77) | −0.4883 (1.70) |
| Luxembourg | −0.0141 (0.11) | 0.3692 (1.18) | 0.3061 (2.44) | 0.1212 (0.40) |
| Netherlands | −0.2612 (2.72) | −0.0225 (0.08) | 0.2054 (2.15) | 0.0989 (0.36) |
| Portugal | −0.9700 (9.00) | −0.6069 (2.70) | −0.7309 (6.88) | −0.4553 (2.01) |
| Spain | −0.5587 (5.11) | −0.1172 (0.46) | −0.5402 (5.01) | −0.1857 (0.75) |
| Sweden | −0.0258 (0.27) | −0.2606 (0.92) | −0.6628 (6.64) | −1.0626 (3.86) |
| Cut 1 | −3.7005 | −4.3162 | −2.9266 | −3.3303 |
| Cut 2 | −3.1889 | −3.7244 | −2.2087 | −2.6258 |
| Cut 3 | −2.4993 | −3.1617 | −1.6023 | −1.9927 |
| Cut 4 | −2.0651 | −2.7134 | −1.0909 | −1.5023 |
| Cut 5 | −1.3011 | −1.9741 | −0.3906 | −0.7293 |
| Cut 6 | −0.7643 | −1.4938 | 0.1578 | −0.1874 |
| Cut 7 | 0.0230 | −0.66823 | 0.8778 | 0.5305 |
| Cut 8 | 1.1394 | 0.27187 | 1.9204 | 1.4938 |
| Cut 9 | 1.9043 | 1.21324 | 2.7514 | 2.4168 |
| N | 6,721 | 1,058 | 6,710 | 1,055 |
| Pseudo R$^2$ | 0.0156 | 0.0111 | 0.0131 | 0.0150 |

Source: *Eurobarometer 54.2: Impact of New Technologies, Employment and Social Affairs, and Disabilities, January–February 2001.* Excluded category UK0.

Notes:
(a) On the whole, how satisfied are you with your current job or business? Please use the following scale from 1 to 10, where '1' means that you are not at all satisfied and '10' means that you are totally satisfied.
(b) And how satisfied are you with your current job or business in terms of earnings?
(c) And in terms of the type of work you do?
(d) And in terms of the time it takes to travel to work?
T-statistics in parentheses.

younger group. Blanchflower and Shadforth (2007) showed using a subsequent sweep of the NCDS that the inheritances, received before the age of 23 raised significantly the probability of being self-employed more than 20 years later, in 2004/5 at age 46 or 47.

Blanchflower, Levine and Zimmerman (2003) reported evidence from the 1993 and 1998 Survey of Small Business Finances from the United States. Although this tells us only about one country, the survey responses were intriguing. Interviewing a sample of minority-owned firms, the main explanation given by people to the survey team was that they had difficulty obtaining capital. Earlier work by Evans and Jovanovic (1989) and Holtz-Eakin, Joulfaian and Rosen (1994) drew similar conclusions using different methods on US data. Finally, Lindh and Ohlsson (1994) adopt the Blanchflower–Oswald procedure and provide complementary evidence for Sweden. Blanchflower and Shadforth (2007) showed that rising house prices, which freed up capital constraints explain half of the recent increase in self-employment in the UK. This is consistent with Black *et al.* (1996), for example, who found that a 10 percent rise in the value of unreleased net housing equity increases the number of new firm (VAT) registrations by some 5 percent. Cowling and Mitchell (1997) estimate that in the UK a 10 percent rise in housing wealth increased the proportion of the workforce in self-employment by 3 percent.

## Conclusion

This chapter documents some of the patterns in modern microeconomic data on young people's employment, attitudes and entrepreneurial behavior. Among other sources, the chapter uses the Eurobarometer Surveys; the Labour Force Surveys from Canada and the Current Population Survey in the United States.

The first conclusion is that self-employed individuals – a special but well-defined entrepreneurial group – report markedly greater well-being than equivalent employees. Their job satisfaction and life-satisfaction are all higher than workers of identical personal characteristics. While this finding does not tell us how to create more entrepreneurs in society, it does suggest that self-employment brings direct microeconomic benefits to people. It raises a puzzle, too. If self-employment does this, why are not more individuals running their own businesses?

The second conclusion is that individuals *say* they would like to be self-employed. There is, according to the survey data, a large pool of potentially entrepreneurial people. Across the West, many millions of employees would apparently prefer to be self-employed. Questionnaire evidence, asking individuals about hypothetical outcomes, always needs to be treated with caution. Nevertheless, these answers are suggestive of an underlying interest in self-employment among large numbers of OECD citizens who are currently employees.

Third, we showed that another important determinant of being self-employed is having a self-employed parent. This appears to help young people to set up in business themselves. It is unclear whether this is done by inheriting the business, or working in the family firm or actually setting up a new business entirely.

How the chapter's findings can be exploited by the designers of economic policy is more complicated to judge. Econometric and questionnaire research suggests that the main constraint on new entrepreneurs is a lack of start-up and liquid capital (as summarized in the penultimate section). This does not mean that government cash ought to be handed out to those who wish to start a business. However, it indicates that plans to foster more entrepreneurship (if this is socially desirable) should begin by considering economists' evidence on the importance of capital constraints.

## References

Black, J., De Meza, D. and Jeffreys, D. (1996) 'House prices, the supply of collateral, and the enterprise economy', *Economic Journal*, 106, January: 60–75.
Blanchflower, D. G. (2000) 'Self-employment in OECD countries', *Labour Economics*, 7, September: 471–505.

—— (2004) 'Self-employment: more may not be better,' *Swedish Economic Policy Review*, 11(2): 15–74

—— (2007) 'Entrepreneurship in the United States', IZA Working Paper.

Blanchflower, D. G., Levine, P. and Zimmerman, D. (2003) 'Discrimination in the small business credit market', *Review of Economics and Statistics*, 85(4): 930–43.

Blanchflower D. G. and Oswald, A. J. (1998) 'What makes an entrepreneur?', *Journal of Labor Economics*, 16(1): 26–60.

—— (2004) 'Wellbeing over time in Britain and the United States', *Journal of Public Economics*, 88(7–8): 1359–86.

—— (2007) 'Is wellbeing U-shaped over the life-cycle?', NBER WP#12935. Washington, DC: NBER.

Blanchflower, D. G., Oswald, A. J. and Stutzer, A. (2001) 'Latent entrepreneurship across nations', *European Economic Review*, 45(4–6): 680–91.

Blanchflower, D. G. and Shadforth, C. (2007) 'Entrepreneurship in the UK', *Foundations and Trends in Entrepreneurship*, 3(4): 257–364.

Broussard, N., Chami, R. and Hess, G. (2003) '(Why) do self-employed parents have more children?', Working Paper, September.

Cowling M, and Mitchell, P. (1997) 'The evolution of UK self-employment: a study of government policy and the role of the macroeconomy', *Manchester School of Economic and Social Studies*, 65(4): 427–42.

Dunn, T. A. and Holtz-Eakin, D. J. (2000) 'Financial capital, human capital, and the transition to self-employment: evidence from intergenerational links', *Journal of Labor Economics*, 18(2): 282–305.

Evans, D. and Jovanovic, B. (1989) 'An estimated model of entrepreneurial choice under liquidity constraints', *Journal of Political Economy*, 97: 808–27.

Fairlie, R. W. and Robb, A. (2007a) 'Families, human capital, and small business: evidence from the Characteristics of Business Owners Survey', forthcoming, *Industrial and Labor Relations Review*.

Holtz-Eakin, D., Joulfaian, D., and Rosen, H. S. (1994) 'Entrepreneurial decisions and liquidity constraints', *Journal of Political Economy*, 102: 53–75.

Hout, M. and Rosen, H. S. (2000) 'Self-employment, family background and race', *Journal of Human Resources*, 15(4): 670–92.

Lindh, T. and Ohlsson, H. (1996) 'Self-employment and windfall gains: evidence from the Swedish lottery', *Economic Journal*, 106(439): 1515–26.

Office for National Statistics (2007) *Labour Market Statistics*, First Release, October Table 9(1).

# Part V

## Dependency and family relations

*Andy Furlong*

## Dependence, independence and housing transitions

The protraction of transitions to employment, the emergence of new norms and priorities regarding relationships and changes in welfare support regimes have all had an impact on patterns of dependence and independence. In many countries, marriage has ceased to be the most significant marker of residential independence, with young people experiencing different forms of independent living and negotiating complex housing careers that may involve periods of living alone, with peers and cohabiting with partners. In countries that once provided relatively generous forms of welfare support, cutbacks have meant that young adults are increasingly reliant on resources from their families for protracted periods of time. Familial dependence can reinforce inequalities when those from poorer families are unable to access the types of support necessary to facilitate educational progress or the pursuit of aspirations. Transitions to independent living involve the negotiation of a set of risks that can be reduced through intergenerational resource transfers, although some groups face grave difficulties. Early childcare responsibilities may limit opportunities, for example, while some will encounter periods of homelessness that can lead to long-term marginalization. In the extreme, these new complexities that shape the transition from dependence to independence may lead to a process in which young people withdraw from social life and rely on the extended support of their families.

By providing a comprehensive overview of patterns of leaving home in developed countries and changes in the factors that impact on housing transitions, in Chapter 24, Mulder draws attention to geographical differences in patterns of leaving home. In particular, she focuses on the distinct patterns that exist in the USA and Northern Europe on the one hand, and Southern Europe on the other. In the former regions, it is common for young people to leave the parental home early to live alone, with friends or to cohabit with a partner, while in the latter regions leaving home is still strongly tied to marriage. Mulder explains these differences in relation to factors such as welfare provision as well as deeply entrenched cultural factors. She also examines the impact of family resources, family structures and employment opportunities on patterns of home leaving.

In Chapter 25, Heath focuses specifically on the new forms of living arrangement encountered by single young people. She argues that the significance of alternative household arrangements are frequently overlooked, regarded as 'buffer zones' between family of origin and family of destination rather than being recognized as important new arrangements. As Heath argues, being 'young, free and single' often represents the preference of young people in their twenties who identify advantages in having access to a domestic space free of restrictions associated with parents or partners. However, she recognizes that shared forms of living are frequently associated with privilege, with the working classes facing greater risks.

The reproduction of inequalities through patterns of intergenerational resource transfer is a theme developed by Swartz and O'Brien in Chapter 26. Here it is noted that, in the light of declining support from national governments, the protraction of transitions has been facilitated by increased resource transfer. In the USA, for example, the majority of young people receive family support while in their early twenties, with around four in ten still receiving help in their late twenties. Yet in the USA as well as in Europe, high income families make significantly greater resource transfers, contributing to the reproduction of inequalities. From the point of view of parents, financial support is most likely to be forthcoming when it is seen to be contributing to education, employment or family formation.

While the age of marriage and parenthood has been increasing, concerns are frequently expressed over rates of teenage pregnancy. Rates of teenage childbearing are particularly high in the USA, partly due to the ethnic diversity of the population and partly due to high overall levels of poverty. In addition, in Chapter 27, Furstenberg suggests that rates of teenage pregnancy are affected by policies towards teenage sex and contraception: countries that attempt to discourage teenage sexuality tend to have higher rates of teenage childbearing than those that are more accepting of teen sex and promote contraception. Furstenberg is able to dispel several myths about the experiences of young mothers. Comparing their education, employment and marital experiences with those of young women from similar socio-economic backgrounds, he argues that long-term effects of teenage childbearing are modest. Moreover, in the long term, many young mothers are resilient and gain the motivation to succeed.

In terms of domestic transitions, the most visible signs of vulnerability relate to homeless young people. Homelessness, as McCarthy and colleagues stress in Chapter 28, is a process rather than a stable state in which young people frequently move from one type of shelter to another; staying with friends, sleeping on the streets or living in hostels. Homelessness among young people has increased significantly in recent years, with homeless youth tending to experience early transitions to adulthood. Youth homelessness can be linked to poverty, family breakdown, conflict and abuse. Despite the increase in homelessness, McCarthy and colleagues suggest that research on routes out of homelessness is underdeveloped, although access to resources either through the family or through government agencies is important. Employment also plays a significant role, although job instability and poor human capital can make it difficult for homeless youth to progress in career terms.

It is clear that patterns of dependence and types of housing transition encountered have changed quite radically, resulting in new opportunities as well as new inequalities. Researchers have to come to terms with the increased complexity of housing careers, as well as studying linkages between housing and experiences in other areas of life, particularly in the field of employment.

# 24

# Leaving the parental home in young adulthood

*Clara H. Mulder*

## Introduction

In the past few decades, young adults living in Europe, North America and Australia leaving the parental home has attracted considerable research attention from sociologists, demographers and geographers. This is not surprising given the great importance of leaving the parental home in the lives of young people and their parents. First of all, leaving home is an important marker in the transition to adulthood. It usually coincides with taking up major adult roles: running one's own household, making one's own financial and consumption decisions, and more generally taking responsibility for one's own life without regular parental supervision. Second, leaving home marks the start of the independent household career. It is usually seen as a prerequisite for living with a partner, marriage and having children. Third, leaving home marks the young adult's entry into the housing market. From the moment of leaving home, the young adult exerts a demand for independent accommodation. Finally, leaving home is an important event in the parent–child relationship: in the long and gradual process from dependence of children on parents to a more equal relationship, leaving home is the clearest and best datable step.

Apart from a small minority who stay in the parental home until the parents die or move out, most young adults in Western societies leave home and the vast majority of them do so before the age of 35 (in most countries: before the age of 30).

For most research purposes it is convenient – and not too far from reality – to consider leaving the parental home as an event that takes place in the life courses of individuals and that can be dated at one point in time. It should be acknowledged, though, that this is not an uncontested view. Some scholars have argued that leaving home should be regarded as a fluid process rather than a single event (e.g. Cherlin *et al.* 1997); that there are situations between living in the parental home and residential independence ('semi-autonomy'; Goldscheider and Goldscheider 1999); or that the process of leaving home is only completed after the young adult has reached not only residential but also financial independence (Whittington and Peters 1996). Furthermore, some of those leaving home return one or more times before leaving definitely: mainly students, but also those experiencing financial or social problems (Goldscheider and Goldscheider 1999).

## Leaving home in social-scientific research: questions and how they are usually addressed

Because nearly everyone in western countries leaves home at some time, the main interest of research into leaving the parental home is in the timing of leaving. The following type of questions is typically addressed in this research: How has the timing of leaving home changed over time? How does it differ between countries? How can the variation between individuals in the timing of leaving be explained? The most suitable method of answering such questions is event history analysis, also denoted as hazard analysis. This method requires data that include a measurement of the timing of leaving home, as well as measurements of explanatory factors and the changes in these factors up to the moment of leaving. Such data are typically derived from surveys based on a questionnaire probing into the life histories of respondents retrospectively, or sometimes from panel surveys in which respondents have been interviewed repeatedly to keep track of their behavior. Event history analysis can take into account information not only pertaining to those who have already left home, but also to those still living in the parental home.

Some young people leave home for marriage, some leave home for work or for enrollment in higher education, others because they want to gain independence from their parents, still others leave to join the military, to flee from conflict in the parental home or for specific other reasons. The factors underlying these different ways of leaving home are arguably different. It is therefore questionable whether it is possible to explain the timing of leaving home as if leaving home is one event. This is why many scholars have studied different ways of leaving home as separate processes, operating independently of each other. Buck and Scott (1993) distinguished two processes: leaving home to live alone, and leaving home to live with a partner. They convinced many researchers that the distinction of these two separate processes is essential to understanding the timing of leaving home. Other researchers have gone further and have distinguished three separate routes of leaving home: to live with a partner; for education or work; and for independence (De Jong Gierveld *et al.* 1991). Another study distinguished leaving home at a short distance from long-distance home-leaving (Mulder and Clark 2000).

Apart from studies of the timing of leaving home in western countries, some research work specializes in returning to the parental home or in leaving exceptionally early or exceptionally late (e.g. Goldscheider and Goldscheider 1999). There is also more qualitative work, focusing on what young people think about leaving home, what they expect from it, what they regard as appropriate timing and what pressure they feel from parents and peers to leave home (Baanders 1996). A small number of studies have devoted attention to leaving home among immigrants in Western societies and the differences with native-born (De Valk 2006, for the Netherlands; Bernhardt *et al.* 2007, for Sweden). Very few studies focus on leaving home in developing rather than Western countries (Johnson and DaVanzo 1998).

## Trends in leaving home in Europe and North America

### *Long-term change*

As shown by Van Poppel *et al.* (2004), the history of leaving home in industrialized countries did not follow monotonic trends. Periods in which the age of leaving home declined have alternated with periods in which it rose. In pre-industrial England, leaving home was much less connected with marriage than it became in the twentieth century. In the eighteenth century a considerable proportion of children as young as 15–19 and even 10–14 lived away from their parents to be a servant or for other jobs, which is not to say they had left the parental home permanently (Wall 1978). Findings for England and Wales, reported in Van Poppel *et al.* (2004), suggest that the mean age of leaving home for those born in 1750–1819 was 28.0 for men and 25.5 for women, and declined steadily afterwards to 21.8 for men and 23.9 for women born in 1890–1930 (implying that there was a time and place where women left home later than men; the reverse of today's gender difference).

### Trends since World War II

In the USA, the percentage of young adults aged 18–24 living with their parents declined continuously from just over 60 in 1940 to just over 40 in 1960, in line with a decline in the age at marriage (the major route from the parental home at that period). Between 1960 and 1970, it remained almost stable. Between 1970 and 1995 it rose again to just over 50 percent. This rise was entirely due to a trend reversal in the age at marriage. At the same time, the percentage living with the parents among those *not* married kept declining, from over 80 percent in 1970 to under 60 in 1994 (Goldscheider and Goldscheider 1999). These trends are illustrative of the trends in most European and North American countries, which can be summarized as follows. In the early postwar decades, leaving home and marriage were closely connected. The age at leaving home declined in association with the age at marriage. From around the 1960s, the age at marriage began to increase again. In North America and Northwest Europe, this increase in the age at marriage was partly, but not totally, compensated for by a rise in unmarried cohabitation. In the end, postponement of union formation (the formation of co-residential partnerships) was seen in all European and North American countries, pushing up the age of leaving home. Around the same time or a few years later, however, a formerly rare phenomenon began to gain importance in North America and Northwest Europe: living alone or with roommates after leaving home. This trend pushed down the age of leaving home. Depending on which trend has been strongest, the age of leaving home has either kept declining for quite long and then risen only moderately, as in North American and Central and Western European countries, or risen much more strongly, as in Southern and Eastern Europe (Cherlin *et al.* 1997; Corijn and Klijzing 2001).

## Large-scale patterns of leaving home: a North versus south and East divide

Today there are distinct patterns of leaving home in Europe (Billari 2004; Corijn and Klijzing 2001) and between the USA and European countries (Mulder *et al.* 2002). The most obvious difference is found between Northern Europe and North America on the one hand, and Southern and Eastern Europe on the other. The Northern pattern is characterized by early home-leaving, frequently to live alone or with roommates, either for independence or for enrollment in education. If young people leave home for a partnership, this is often for unmarried cohabitation. The Nordic countries (Norway, Sweden, Finland and Denmark) are the most 'extreme' in this respect. The Northern pattern is not universal to all of Northern Europe: for example, a strong connection of leaving home for marriage is found in Flanders, the Dutch-speaking part of Belgium (Corijn and Klijzing 2001). The Southern pattern is characterized by late home-leaving and a strong connection of leaving home with marriage. Italy and Spain are typical examples of this pattern. A strong connection between leaving home and marriage is also found in many Eastern European countries.

Several explanations for the diversity in leaving-home patterns, and in the transition to adulthood in general, have been put forward (e.g. Billari 2004). One explanation stresses institutional factors connected with the welfare state. Welfare states differ in the extent to which conditions for leaving home are favorable. Goesta Esping-Andersen has proposed a division into four welfare regimes. The social-democratic welfare regime, found in the Nordic countries, is oriented to individuals, and provides strong state support which facilitates leaving home to live alone at an early age for many. The liberal-market regime, found in the USA and the UK, is also oriented to individuals but is less generous in state support. The conservative continental regime, found, for example, in France and Germany, is more oriented to the family, and is characterized by fairly strong support provided by the state and semi-public non-profit organizations. The Southern European or familistic regime, found, for example, in Italy and Spain, is strongly oriented to the family and expects the family to provide support rather than the state. Connected with the welfare regimes, but changing faster than these, are social and economic policies: fiscal, family, housing, or labor-market policies.

Another explanation stresses long-term, persistent cultural differences. Various proposals have been made to divide the Western world into larger regions characterized by specific family systems (Van Poppel *et al.* 2004), that are thought to have existed a long time, to persist up to the present day and to continue to determine young adults' behavior with respect to leaving home, partnership formation, marriage and parenthood. The best-known example of such a division is the Hajnal line (proposed by John Hajnal), an imaginary line through Europe, connecting Trieste and St Petersburg. The area west of this line used to be characterized by nuclear families, late age at marriage, early age at leaving home, and servanthood as an important stage in the life cycle. East of the line, early and universal marriage and extended families were the rule. Another line has been drawn horizontally by David Reher and separates Northwestern Europe and North America from Southern and Mediterranean Europe. The Northern countries are characterized by weak family ties, individual independence and early severance of parent–child ties. The Southern countries are characterized by strong family ties and life-long commitments between parents and children.

## Determinants of leaving home

### Developmental readiness and age norms

To leave the parental home, a young person should have reached a certain maturity. Girls are thought to reach maturity somewhat earlier than boys and this probably explains why women leave home a year or two earlier than men, not only to live with a partner (which follows from the fact that women tend to marry men who are a few years older) but also to live alone.

Whereas leaving home before age 18 is considered by many as early or too early, there are also rather strong norms on what is late or too late. Billari and Liefbroer (2007) did not find any influence of variation between individuals in perceived societal age norms on the timing of their own leaving in the context of one country – the Netherlands. However, it is likely that young adults conform to general age norms and that differences in norms between countries play a part in the persistence of differences in timing between these countries. Furthermore, young people are surrounded by peers and parents who may express opinions about the proper age of leaving. Billari and Liefbroer found that the timing of leaving home in the Netherlands, particularly leaving home to live with a partner, was associated with perceived opinions of parents.

## The family of origin: resources and family structure

The family of origin plays an important part in leaving home. The impact of parental resources (mainly income) is considerable, but differs with age and with the way of leaving. Parents mainly use their resources to prevent early marriage and to encourage leaving home to live alone among older children (Avery *et al.* 1992, for the USA). The influence of parental resources has been shown to differ between transferable resources, such as income and parental education, and non-transferable resources, such as a good atmosphere, a caring family climate, or space and privacy in the parental home. Whereas transferable resources tended to speed up leaving home for education or independence, non-transferable resources slowed down leaving home for independence in the Netherlands (De Jong Gierveld *et al.* 1991). Family structure also affects leaving home: having divorced parents, and particularly step-parents, enhances the likelihood of leaving home at a young age, particularly among girls. Having step-siblings and being the oldest child also speeds up leaving home, whereas being an only child slows it down (Aquilino 1991, for the USA).

## Individual resources: income and education

In order to set up one's own household, individual resources are crucial. Whether a young adult has some income of his or her own has a positive impact on the likelihood of leaving home at a given point in time (Mulder and Clark 2000, for the USA); stable employment also has a positive effect (Nilsson and Strandh 1999, for Sweden). The amount of personal income was found to have a positive impact on leaving home to 'pre-marital residential independence' and an even stronger impact on leaving to marriage in the USA (Avery *et al.* 1992), but such an effect is not found for all European countries (Billari 2004). Enrollment in education generally hampers leaving home (Corijn and Klijzing 2001), but its impact differs strongly between leaving home to live with a partner (invariably a delaying effect) and leaving home to live alone (sometimes a positive effect for tertiary education; see Nilsson and Strandh 1999, for Sweden).

## Opportunity structures: education, jobs, housing, economic conditions

The availability and location of educational institutions, jobs and housing determine whether a young adult has an incentive to leave home (for example, if there is no local university or if better jobs are available elsewhere) or is constrained to do so (for example, if the cost of housing is prohibitive). Many young adults in Sweden and the USA feel obliged to leave home to go to college or university, whereas Italian universities are spread much more around the country so that students can stay at home (Cook and Furstenberg 2002). In the USA, those living in smaller towns leave home considerably earlier than those in large cities, probably because of the greater availability of jobs in the cities (Mulder and Clark 2000; living at college was excluded from their definition of leaving home). The higher the local costs of housing, the less likely young adults are to leave home to live with a partner (ibid.) and the more likely young adults who live away from the parents do so with roommates rather than alone (Haurin *et al.* 1997). Economic conditions are also important. In times of economic downturns or economic uncertainty, young adults tend to postpone leaving home, both to live alone and to live with a partner (Keilman 1987).

### Traditions, values, religion

Traditions, values and religion mainly influence leaving home because they influence the importance attached to closeness to parents, the centrality of marriage and family obligations and responsibilities. In the USA, non-religious people leave home earlier than liberal Protestants, whereas Catholics and Jews leave home later (Goldscheider and Goldscheider 1999). In the Netherlands, young people from specific migrant categories (Turks and Moroccans) were found to prefer younger ages for women to marry than native Dutch, but older ages to leave home (De Valk 2006).

## Avenues for future research

Leaving the parental home is a fascinating topic in social-scientific research because of its centrality in the transition from youth to adulthood, its implications for household and family formation and for housing demand, its diverse manifestations in different periods and different areas of the western world, and its intricate connection with parental resources, parental family structure, individual resources, the geographical opportunity structure, and values. The literature on leaving home in Europe, North America and Australia is huge, but several relevant aspects have remained under-researched. Not many studies in English are available on leaving home in Eastern Europe, and the literature on Southern Europe is also limited. Little is known about leaving home among children who immigrated with their parents to industrialized countries and among second-generation immigrants. Research into the influence of opportunity structures is scarce, both for opportunities in the area where the parental family lives and for those in possible areas of destination. The same is true of research into the role of social networks: siblings, other family besides the parents, and friends. Studies of the destinations of moves out of the parental home are scarce in any case: in terms of the type of accommodation the young adults move into, the distance to the parents, the type of residential environment (urban, suburban or rural area), and the geographical area. There are not many studies on leaving home very late or on prolonged co-residence with parents in older adulthood. Not much is known about the consequences of the timing of leaving home or its destination for the further life courses of the young adults and their parents. Finally, leaving home has hardly been studied for developing countries, even though the scarce literature suggests the mechanisms underlying leaving home in developing countries are rather different from those in western countries. So, despite the existing rich literature, there is ample room for improvement.

## Acknowledgement

The research for this chapter was made possible by the Netherlands Organisation for Scientific Research (NWO), Innovational Research Incentives Scheme (VICI) grant no. 453-04-001. For further reading, a good starting point is the work of Frances Goldscheider. She – along with other authors in the reference list – has published much more work on leaving home than could be discussed in this chapter.

## References

Aquilino, W. S. (1991) 'Family structure and home leaving: a further specification of the relationship', *Journal of Marriage and the Family*, 53: 999–1010.

Avery, R., Goldscheider, F. and Speare Jr., A. (1992) 'Feathered nest/gilded cage: parental income and leaving home in the transition to adulthood', *Demography*, 29: 375–88.

Baanders, A. N. (1996) 'Considerations in the decision to leave the parental home: Anticipated consequences and normative expectations', *Family and Consumer Sciences Research Journal*, 24: 272–92.

Bernhardt, E., Goldscheider, C., Goldscheider, F. and Bjeren, G. (2007) *Immigration, Gender and Family Transitions to Adulthood in Sweden*, Lanham, MD: University Press of America, Inc.

Billari, F. C. (2004) 'Becoming an adult in Europe: a macro(/micro)-demographic perspective', *Demographic Research*, Special collection 3: 15–44.

Billari, F. C. and Liefbroer, A. C. (2007) 'Should I stay or should I go? The impact of age norms on leaving home', *Demography*, 44: 181–98.

Buck, N. and Scott, J. (1993) 'She's leaving home: But why? An analysis of young people leaving the parental home', *Journal of Marriage and the Family*, 55: 863–74.

Cherlin, A. J., Scabini, E. and Rossi, G. (1997) 'Still in the nest: delayed home leaving in Europe and the United States', *Journal of Family Issues*, 18: 572–5.

Cook, T. D. and Furstenberg Jr, F. F. (2002) 'Explaining aspects of the transition to adulthood in Italy, Sweden, Germany, and the United States: a cross-disciplinary, case synthesis approach', *Annals of the American Academy of Political and Social Science*, 580: 257–87.

Corijn, M. and Klijzing, E. (eds) (2001) *Transitions to Adulthood in Europe*, Dordrecht: Kluwer Academic Publishers.

De Jong Gierveld, J., Liefbroer, A. C. and Beekink, E. (1991) 'The effect of parental resources on patterns of leaving home among young adults in the Netherlands', *European Sociological Review*, 7: 55–71.

De Valk, H. (2006) *Pathways into Adulthood: A Comparative Study on Family Life Transitions among Migrant and Dutch Youth*, Groningen: ICS.

Goldscheider, F. and Goldscheider, C. (1999) *The Changing Transition to Adulthood: Leaving and Returning Home*, Thousand Oaks, CA: Sage.

Haurin, R. J., Haurin, D. R., Hendershott, P. H. and Bourassa, S. C. (1997) 'Home or alone: the costs of independent living for youth', *Social Science Research*, 26: 135–52.

Keilman, N. (1987) 'Recent trends in family and household composition in Europe', *European Journal of Population*, 3: 297–325.

Johnson, R. W. and DaVanzo, J. (1998) 'Economic and cultural influences on the decision to leave home in peninsular Malaysia', *Demography*, 35: 97–114.

Mulder, C. H. and Clark, W. A. V. (2000) 'Leaving home and leaving the state: evidence from the United States', *International Journal of Population Geography*, 6: 423–37.

Mulder, C. H., Clark, W. A. V. and Wagner, M. (2002) 'A comparative analysis of leaving home in the United States, the Netherlands and West Germany', *Demographic Research*, 7: 565–92.

Nilsson, K. and Strandh, M. (1999) 'Nest leaving in Sweden: the importance of early educational and labor market careers', *Journal of Marriage and the Family*, 61: 1068–79.

Van Poppel, F., Oris, M. and Lee, J. (eds) (2004) *The Road to Independence: Leaving Home in Western and Eastern Societies, 16th–20th Centuries*, Bern: Peter Lang.

Wall, R. (1978) 'The age at leaving home', *Journal of Family History*, 3: 181–202.

Whittington, L. and Peters, H. E. (1996) 'Economic incentives for financial and residential independence', *Demography*, 33: 82–97.

# 25

# Young, free and single?

## The rise of independent living

*Sue Heath*

## Background

A distinctive feature of the emergence in many Western nations of young adulthood as a new life stage has been the parallel rise of independent living. Patterns in leaving home were considered in the previous chapter. Here we consider alternative living arrangements experienced by single young people on leaving the parental home, focusing in particular on shared households, and highlighting the significance of social class to understanding these trends. Patterns of household formation in the UK and Australia form the primary focus, although some of the themes discussed here are applicable elsewhere, including Northern Europe and North America.

Until relatively recently, research on young people and household formation has focused mostly on leaving and returning to the parental home (e.g. Jones 1995; Goldscheider and Goldscheider 1999), with little focus on young people's living arrangements once having left. The tracking of young people's domestic transitions in terms of movement from the parental household towards their own families has also tended to prioritise couple households as markers of authentic 'adulthood'. Considered historically, there is some logic to this: in the early 1960s, for example, the median age of first marriage in the UK was at its lowest recorded age and served as a reasonable proxy for the age of first leaving home.

However, a broader historical perspective highlights that the relatively low median age of first marriage during the immediate post-war years is in fact anomalous, and the close link between home leaving and marriage during that period certainly no longer pertains. In the UK, for example, the number of first marriages registered in 2005 was less than half those registered in 1970, while the median age of first marriage rose from 23 for men and 21 for women in 1971 to 30.6 and 28.4 for men and women respectively in 2001 (Heath and Cleaver 2003; Office for National Statistics 2005). Similar trends have emerged across Europe, albeit varying significantly between north and south, as well as in the USA and Australia. In the USA, the median age of first marriage was 27.1 for men and 25.3 for women in 2003, compared with 23.2 and 20.8 in 1970 (Fields 2004), and in Australia 23.3 for men and 20.9 for women in 1974, rising to 29.6 for men and 27.6 for women in 2006 (Australian Bureau of Statistics 1997; 2007).

Much of the shift towards later marriage in these nations is attributable to the growth of cohabitation (known in Australia as *de facto* living arrangements), which for many has emerged as an alternative living arrangement prior to or instead of marriage. In 2003, for example, 75 per cent of Australians cohabited prior to marriage (Australian Bureau of Statistics 2006). Cohabitation has *not*, however, simply replaced marriage as the primary reason for first leaving home in the UK and Australia, and the proportion of young people first leaving home in order to create *any* form of couple household is declining. Instead, young adults now leave home for a variety of reasons, and experience a diverse range of living arrangements across their twenties, including living alone, in communal establishments such as hostels and student residences, and in shared households.

Despite the increased likelihood of moving in and out of different living arrangements as a young adult, alternative household forms are largely neglected in existing literature or only acquire significance in as much as they are deemed to constitute a 'buffer zone' between the family of origin and the family of destination. Moreover, attainment of a couple household tends still to be constructed as the apex of a hierarchy of domestic arrangements to which all young adults should aspire. The existence of alternative households is then viewed largely as evidence of 'delayed' adulthood, rather than a new transitional pathway in its own right among contemporary young adults (see, for example, Bynner 2005; Arnett 2006). Couple relationships are by no means unimportant to young people, and most continue to attach special status to couple households. Nonetheless, they also attach a variety of interpretations to the concepts of independence and adulthood, not necessarily regarding their attainment as contingent on living with a partner (Holdsworth and Morgan 2005).

## Alternative household forms

It is, then, increasingly common for young people to spend time during their twenties living in 'non-familial' households, including living alone or with peers in shared households. Although unlikely to be permanent arrangements, growing evidence suggests that many young people expect to live in such households, and that they are adept at negotiating intimate relationships within and across different domestic settings. Only a minority of young people live alone or in shared households at any given point in time, yet increasing numbers are likely to do so *at some point(s)* in their twenties, if not beyond. In Australia, 21 per cent of 20–24 year-olds lived in peer-shared households in 2000, accounting for 39 per cent of all young people living independently, compared with 17.5 per cent of those living independently in 1980 (Burke *et al.* 2002). Strikingly, the growth of shared living has been at the expense of living alone: in 1980, 16 per cent of 20–24 year-old Australians lived alone, accounting for 26 per cent of all those living independently, in comparison with 5.1 per cent living alone in 2000, equivalent to 9.3 per cent of all those living independently (ibid.).

In the UK, while reliable figures are readily available on rates of living alone (5 per cent of 16 to 24 year-olds and 12 per cent of 25–44 year-olds in 2001, compared with 2 per cent of both age groups in 1973), reliable information on shared living remains elusive. 'Multi-person households' (a category which extends beyond peer-shared households) were lived in by only 4 per cent of the population in 2004, but the incidence among younger age groups is unclear. Nonetheless, around half of all higher education students live in the private rented sector at any given point in time, mainly in shared households (Rugg *et al.* 2000). Between 1994 and 2000, approximately 30 per cent of each successive cohort of 18 year-olds progressed into higher education, suggesting that at least 15 per cent of 18–21 year-olds lived in shared households during this period alone (HEFCE 2005). This figure (which excludes non-students) is likely to be higher now given increased participation rates.

As the link with student housing suggests, shared housing is often associated with economic constraint, with house sharers including many young people on low incomes and in receipt of housing benefits. In the UK, this is related to restrictions on housing benefit payments to under-25 year-olds only to those living in shared accommodation. Nonetheless, an evaluation of this policy found that most claimants *expected* to share at this stage in their life (Kemp and Rugg 1998). Despite this established link between sharing and disadvantage, shared housing is nonetheless increasingly associated with more privileged young people, notably graduates and/or young professionals. Analysis of data from the 1996 sweep of the UK 1970 Birth Cohort Study found that sharers were, on several counts, the most advantaged group among the entire cohort when analysed by their living arrangements at age 26, and that young people from relatively advantaged backgrounds accounted for the majority of cohort members living in shared households. Over half of male sharers and nearly two-thirds of female sharers had degree-level qualifications, two-thirds of both sexes were employed in professional or managerial positions, and sharers were over twice as likely as any other group to have fathers in professional and managerial occupations (Bynner *et al.* 1997).

In exploring why young people sharing these same characteristics lived in peer-shared households, Heath and Cleaver (2003) concluded that, while financial concerns were not insignificant, many sharers regarded their living arrangements as appropriate to the needs and demands of their current lifestyles, and did not experience their living arrangements simply – if at all – as products of constraint. These findings were confirmed in Australian research on shared households (Natalier 2002; McNamara and Connell 2007). It may no longer be sufficient, then, to assume that shared housing can be viewed simply in terms of financial constraint. Instead, it appears that many sharers, especially the more affluent, view their housing decisions in terms of an ongoing assessment of the material and non-material costs of different housing options, their attitudes towards 'settling down' and the desirability of an independent lifestyle. Their decisions cannot be divorced from economic considerations, but these are not the sole determinants; rather, they are grounded within the priorities they attach to financial savings, their housing quality, their potential for geographical mobility, the trade-off between company and privacy, and the desirability and feasibility of living alone or with a partner. On this last point, Heath and Cleaver (2003) found that most sharers in their research identified distinct advantages to a living arrangement which allowed for sexual freedom in their own domestic space while providing space away from partners when desired. While few sharers wanted to live in group households indefinitely, most regarded shared living arrangements as *currently appropriate* for someone of their age, and the right choice for the moment.

## Risk, individualization and new living arrangements

Independent living arrangements have, then, become culturally acceptable household forms among contemporary young adults in many developed nations. Group living is particularly common in the UK and Australia, while living alone is the preferred option in northern Europe, especially Scandinavia. In the UK, these developments have coin-cided with the rise of extended periods of overseas travel, in the form of 'time out' from work or study. Nonetheless, many young adults continue to follow highly standardized transitions to adulthood, marked by relatively early labour market entry, early partnership formation and early parenthood, often first leaving home to live with a partner rather than to live alone or with peers. In contrast, it is largely middle-class young people, especially students and graduates, who are at the forefront of the developments sum-marized in this chapter. Their transitional experiences are markedly different to those of their parents *and* their less advantaged peers, with relatively few now expecting to follow automatic and linear pathways from parental dependency to (co)dependency on a partner, even though most (heterosexual) young people continue to aspire to such a trajectory in the longer term.

Heath and Cleaver (2003) highlight the importance of considering a broad range of factors in explaining these shifts among more privileged young adults. Economic con-straints linked to educational and labour market transformations in recent decades are of course important, alongside employer demands and the perceived need for geographical mobility. The housing opportunities afforded by entry into further and higher education are also significant, as routes which provide exposure to, and expanded opportunities for, independent living arrangements. In analysing young people's housing transitions in England in the late 1990s, for example, Ford *et al.* (2002) identify five ideal-type housing pathways, based on the degree of planning and control exercised by young people, the extent and nature of any constraints, and the degree of family support available to them. They highlight the privileged housing pathway associated with student status, regarding it as the pathway with fewest constraints associated with leaving the parental home by virtue of providing access to various forms of student accommodation, including niche shared housing provision in the private rented sector. Exposure to student shared housing in turn fuels demand and provides access to *graduate* shared housing opportunities, including access via friends and acquaintances to networks of shared households in many locations, and providing a ready-made social life.

In contrast, young people from working-class families face greater levels of risk in their housing careers than their middle-class peers as a consequence of their relative economic disadvantage and their restricted access to ring-fenced sectors of the housing market. Graduates still encounter risks, but of a different kind, such as student debt, which impacts upon their ability to move into the property market on an individual basis early on in their careers, thus stoking demand for yet more shared households in both the private rented and owner-occupied sectors. Nonetheless, it is clear that in the realm of domestic and housing transitions, as in other spheres, higher education expansion is exacerbating, rather than reducing, inequalities among younger generations. Risk is by no means equally distributed, and the much debated 'choice biography' remains the preserve of the educated, mainly middle-class elite.

## Future research

Young adults' domestic and housing transitions remain an under-researched theme in youth studies, in some ways rather surprisingly so, given the inextricable link between transitions in these areas and broader school-to-work transitions. Looking to future research, one could argue that as there are so many unresearched topics in this field, any new contributions are to be welcomed. Nonetheless, at least two strands of research would be particularly beneficial, one linked to a specific set of research questions, the other linked to a call for a conceptual reorientation of existing research on domestic transitions.

First, we need to know more about the strategies adopted by young people in relation to meeting their housing needs and desires. House prices and rents continue to rise, in parallel with rising student debt and a slowdown of young people's average earnings relative to other age groups. Young people's prospects for getting a foothold on the housing ladder remain, therefore, limited at best. Many young people are resorting to shared mortgages with friends in order to cushion the burden of an initial outlay, raising important questions concerning the implications of such arrangements for trust, independence and the negotiation of friendships in such contexts. There is also evidence to suggest that young people are increasingly financially dependent on parents and other family members to give them a helping hand in relation to their housing costs. Financial transfers of this kind have long-term implications for the shaping of intergenerational relationships and obligations, and raise questions concerning the reinforcement of inequalities in the housing sphere.

Second, if assumptions of linear progression towards marriage and parenthood are increasingly out of touch with the reality of the lives of many heterosexual young people, then they are completely inadequate for the task of explaining domestic transitions among non-heterosexuals. A modest literature points to possible differences in experiences of leaving home for gay and lesbian young people in comparison with their straight peers, highlighting issues such as the role of coming out to parents in precipitating early home leaving and homelessness, and the negative experiences of gay and lesbian students in university halls of residence. Nonetheless, very little research focuses on the broader impact of being gay, lesbian or bisexual on experiences and expectations of domestic and housing transitions across the twenties and beyond. Research which normalizes such experiences would contribute to greater inclusivity within youth research, and would also – of necessity – bring researchers into a useful engagement with some of the normative assumptions which underpin transitions research more generally.

To conclude, the expectations of older generations concerning leaving home and 'settling down' are being rewritten by younger generations. Structural factors have undoubtedly shaped this process, but have also ushered in a generational re-evaluation of different domestic arrangements and what it means to be independent. Not all young people are able to negotiate these dramatic shifts from a position of strength, and those with few genuine options may feel themselves forced into household forms which are not of their choosing. For others, however, being young, free and single may represent a genuine preference during their twenty-something years, if not beyond, amounting to a redefinition of the boundaries of youth and adulthood.

# References

Arnett, J. (2006) 'Emerging adulthood in Europe: a response to Bynner', *Journal of Youth Studies*, 9(1): 112–23.
Australian Bureau of Statistics (1997) 'Family formation: age at first marriage', *Australian Social Trends 1997*, available at: www.abs.gov.au/ausstats/abs@.nsf/2f762f95845417aeca25706c00834efa/a8d1bea8a2ff1b33ca2570ec001b0dc3!OpenDocument (accessed 5 November 2007).

—— (2006) 'Marriages, divorces and de facto relationships, Year Book Australia 2006', available at: www.abs.gov.au/ausstats/abs@.nsf/0/C0771D0225B882D2CA2570DE0006B864?opendocument (accessed 5 November 2007).

—— (2007) 'Marriages, Australia, 2006', available at: www.abs.gov.au/AUSSTATS/abs@.nsf/allpri marymainfeatures/7947008D6F6787CFCA25739900118817?opendocument (accessed 27 November 2007).

Burke, T., Pinkney, S. and Ewing, S. (2002) *Rent Assistance and Young People's Decision Making*, Melbourne: Australian Housing and Urban Research Institute.

Bynner, J. (2005) 'Rethinking the youth phase of the life-course: the case for emerging adulthood?', *Journal of Youth Studies*, 8(4): 367–84.

Bynner, J., Ferrie, E. and Shepherd, P. (1997) *Twenty-Somethings in the 1990s: Getting On, Getting By, Getting Nowhere*, Aldershot: Ashgate.

Fields, J. (2004) 'America's families and living arrangements, 2003: population characteristics', *Current Population Reports*, P20–553, Washington, DC: US Census Bureau.

Ford, J., Rugg, J. and Burrows, R. (2002) 'Conceptualising the contemporary role of housing in the transition to adult life in England', *Urban Studies*, 39(13): 2455–67.

Goldscheider, F. and Goldscheider, C. (1999) *The Changing Transition to Adulthood: Leaving and Returning Home*, Thousand Oaks, CA: Sage.

Heath, S. and Cleaver, E. (2003) *Young, Free and Single? Twenty Somethings and Household Change*, Basingstoke: Palgrave.

Higher Education Funding Council for England (2005) *Young Participation in Higher Education*, Bristol: HEFCE.

Holdsworth, C. and Morgan, D. (2005) *Transitions in Context: Leaving Home, Independence and Adulthood*, Buckingham: Open University Press.

Jones, G. (1995) *Leaving Home*, Buckingham: Open University Press.

Kemp, P. and Rugg, J. (1998) *The Single Room Rent: Its Impact on Young People*, York: Joseph Rowntree Foundation.

McNamara, S. and Connell, J. (2007) 'Homeward bound? Searching for home in Inner Sydney's share houses', *Australian Geographer*, 38(1): 71–91.

Natalier, K. (2002) '"I'm not his wife": doing gender in share households', unpublished PhD thesis, University of Queensland.

Office for National Statistics (2005) 'Marriage decreases', National Statistics, available at: www.statistics. gov.uk/cci/nugget.asp?id=322 (accessed 27 November 2007).

Rugg, J., Rhodes, D. and Jones, A. (2000) *The Nature and Impact of Student Demand on Housing Markets*, York: Joseph Rowntree Foundation.

# 26

# Intergenerational support during the transition to adulthood

*Teresa Toguchi Swartz and Kirsten Bengtson O'Brien*

## Introduction

In many advanced industrial societies today, the transition to adulthood takes longer and has become more variable than it once was. While some countries facilitate this transition through social policies and institutions, others leave young adults to find their own pathways. In the latter cases especially, parents have stepped in to provide help. This support enables young people to explore and experiment with education, jobs, relationships and lifestyles with fewer risks. At the same time, however, private family support can exacerbate the impact of family background on attainment and reproduce inequalities. This chapter reviews recent research on the topic including how parents and their adult children understand these intergenerational connections, and discusses the implications of intergenerational support during this life phase.

## Changes in young adulthood

Researchers, as well as social commentators, have recently taken notice of marked changes in the transition to adulthood in many advanced industrialized societies. Social scientists have noted a prolonged transition from adolescence to independent adulthood, a change in the ordering of markers of the transition, and multiplicity of pathways to becoming an adult (e.g. Settersten *et al.* 2005). What is more, this elongated and variable process of becoming adult is often characterized by exploration and experimentation regarding work, relationships, lifestyles, and worldviews, as well as opportunities for re-examining and revising earlier choices and paths (e.g. Arnett 2004). Taken together, these changes have contributed to a new subjective understanding and experience of this phase of life (Arnett 2004; Hartmann and Swartz 2007).

Transformations in young adulthood are largely connected to broader structural shifts in the economy, welfare state, and family. Young adults are spending more time in school to meet rising educational demands, experiencing more challenges in finding adequate work and establishing careers, and delaying marriage and parenthood. Further, welfare state curtailment in many countries results in fewer social supports that could address the developing needs of this emerging social group. Yet within these broader trends, the specificities of national educational systems, labor and housing markets, social policies, and cultures shape the timing, sequence, and meanings of becoming adult within each country and for subpopulations within them (Cook and Furstenberg 2002). Like water, ice, and steam, the same elements produce different forms depending on the environment to which they are exposed.

This chapter focuses on the role of parents in responding to and facilitating these changes in the process of becoming an adult in advanced industrialized countries. Indeed, the protracted transition to adulthood has been made possible by parents and other family members willing to support young people and provide them with substantial family resources to navigate this extended transition (e.g. Scabini *et al.* 2006). Researchers have begun to take notice of the importance of intergenerational support given by parents to offspring in young adulthood, particularly in absence of other support mechanisms. While in some ways young adults have more independence and autonomy from family than ever before (Rosenfeld 2007), in some contexts parents have become even more important for contemporary adolescents and young adults. This is accentuated by the decline in other significant adult involvement in young people's lives (Scabini *et al.* 2006).

In this chapter we draw on recent research to help better understand the ways in which the transition to adulthood is what Scabini and colleagues have called a 'joint enterprise' involving the efforts and resources of both parents and young adults. We restrict our focus to research based on families in Western Europe and North America. First, we examine the ways that parents continue to support their young adult children through the protracted transition, enabling the exploration and experimentation that many have argued characterize contemporary young adulthood. Next, we look at norms and cultural understandings of intergenerational support during this life phase, finding that parents view their assistance not as a way to prolong youthful dependence, but rather in one of two ways: either as 'scaffolding' their adult children toward greater independence and attainment or as providing a safety net to reduce the risks associated with the uncertainty of modern society. We also explore relational dimensions of intergenerational support during this life phase. Finally, we reflect on the implications of these findings for changing family relations and social inequality.

## Intergenerational instrumental supports during the transition to adulthood

Changes in social, economic and structural circumstances affect intergenerational family structures and relations. While different from rearing minor children, active parenting is thus extended as parents work to bridge their offspring from the dependence of youth to the independence of adulthood through providing real, and needed, assistance to their adult children. For instance, in an analysis of families in the United States, Schoeni and Ross (2005) found that nearly two-thirds of young adults in their early twenties, and 40 per cent of those in their late twenties received financial support from their parents. American parents now expend a substantial portion of the total cost of raising a child during young adulthood (ages of 18–34), providing an average of $38,340 for their young adult child (ibid.: 405). Reflecting, and perhaps reproducing, class inequality in the United States, adult children in the top quarter of income categories receive at least 70 per cent more in material aid than children in the bottom quarter. This intergenerational transfer of financial support is largely one way during the young adult years, with aid flowing primarily from parents to young adult children and peaking when offspring are in their late twenties and early thirties (Cooney and Uhlenberg 1992).

Research on families in Europe finds similar trends (e.g. Brannen 2006, Kohli 1999). Not only do contemporary European young adults need more material support than their parents did to navigate the prolonged transition to adulthood, their parents, on the whole, also have more resources to share than previous generations due to their upward mobility post the Second World War (Brannen *et al.* 2004).

Although, parents across Europe are providing substantial aid to their young adult children, countries diverge in the extent of state support for young people in attaining education, training, employment, and housing (e.g. Cook and Furstenberg 2002). For example, the more limited welfare states in countries such as Italy, combined with traditions of family assistance, have resulted in parents continuing to provide substantial assistance to their young adult children. On the other hand, young adults in Scandinavian countries with more developed welfare states and relatively favorable labor markets for young people depend less on parents to make the transition to adulthood. Swedish young adults, for instance, are less likely to rely on their parents as they experience educational, training, labor market, housing, and policy conditions that enable them to launch into full adult autonomy earlier than young people from other countries.

Similar to what is found in the USA, within-country variation occurs as young adults from higher income groups receive more aid from their parents than those from lower income groups. Studies based on families in France and Germany find that the largest intergenerational financial transfers are given by parents with the most assets, and in Britain, young adults from the middle class receive more material assistance from their families of origin than their working-class or low-income counterparts (Kohli 1999; Brannen *et al.* 2004). And even in Sweden where the transition to adulthood depends less heavily on continued parental support, a loan system for funding higher education advantages Swedish young adults from more affluent families (Cook and Furstenberg 2002).

While the transition to adulthood in Europe and North America may now be characterized by choice, exploration, and experimentation, it also requires material resources to cover living expenses and the costs of trying out different paths. To a greater or lesser extent (depending on cultural and institutional contexts), continued parental support helps to minimize the risks and finances the modern transition to adulthood (Brannen *et al.* 2004; Scabini *et al.* 2006). Further research should be conducted that examines if and how parental support during young adulthood affects actual outcomes and attainment of the younger generation. In countries that heavily rely upon parents' generosity to assist young adults through education and into work, inequality between parents will likely result in the reproduction of inequality for the next generation as well.

### Housing and co-residence

Some forms of parental support are largely invisible, such as direct monetary aid, university tuition payments, or covering rent. Other forms are much more evident. One visible type of parental aid is in-home housing support which can be particularly helpful in contexts with high housing costs. Not only are co-resident young adults able to maintain their standard of living, they are also positioned to acquire more education and take on less debt than those who live on their own, affecting their earning potential and wealth accumulation later on in life (e.g. White 1994).

Researchers have observed variations in co-residence and home leaving in different countries associated with different housing costs, labor markets, educational systems, state policies, and cultures regarding independence and family life. In southern Europe (and Ireland), young people experience a difficult labor market, limited state support, and a culture of family assistance, resulting in leaving the parental home later than northern Europeans. In northern Europe, and especially in the Scandinavian countries, promising labor markets, lower housing costs, educational systems, and state supports allow for earlier independence and home leaving (Cook and Furstenberg 2002; Iacovou 2002). Young people in the United States also leave relatively early and for education, particularly whites who are not from economically disadvantaged backgrounds. Yet significant variation in co-residence by race and ethnicity exists in the USA, with Black, Hispanic, and Asian young adults staying in the parental home longer than whites (e.g. Goldscheider and Goldscheider 1999). In most of these countries, women leave home earlier than men and men are more likely to return once they have left and to stay longer upon their return (Kerckhoff and Macrae 1992; Iacovou 2002).

In fact, it is fairly common for young people to return home after an initial departure (e.g. Kerckhoff and Macrae 1992). These findings illustrate the gradual and uncertain process of launching from the home, and suggest the parental role as 'safety net', absorbing some of the risks of this exploratory, experimental phase and allowing many more options. Those young people without parents to return to may be less likely to try out uncertain paths, or more likely to experience significant problems if jobs, schooling, or relationships do not work out as hoped.

Just as most intergenerational material support flows from the older to the younger generation, co-residence in advanced industrialized societies more often meets the needs of children than parents (Logan and Spitze 1996). For the most part, co-residence during young adulthood can be viewed as a way in which parents support their children through young adulthood, enabling them to experiment, explore, or simply maintain lifestyles and consumption patterns that they could not otherwise. Although the dependence or semi-dependence of young adults who live with their parents is quite visible, it would be a mistake to think they are stagnant and not progressing toward adult independence, or that those who do not live at home are fully independent. Rather, young adults can and do make important transitions while living at home, and many who live outside of the home also receive some assistance from their parents, albeit in more invisible forms.

### Services and childcare

Parents also provide hidden help through practical assistance such as home upkeep and childcare. In the United States, parents from high and low income families supply similar amounts of help in terms of time – approximately 3,866 hours, or roughly two years of full-time labor to their children during the young adult years (Schoeni and Ross, 2005: 415). The transition to parenthood often garners parental help. Grandparents provide a great deal of care to grandchildren as their adult children work, especially in countries that lack strong state-supported childcare and have high maternal employment. In Britain and the United States, grandparents play a major role as regular or intermittent childcare providers (Brannen et al. 2004; Casper 1996). However, this pattern of intergenerational informal childcare is not present everywhere, and corresponds with welfare state supports as well as family practices. In the Nordic countries such as Denmark and Sweden, the majority of children attend formal services, and in Italy formal and informal childcare is less necessary as most young mothers remain out of the paid labor force (Brannen *et al.* 2004; Cook and Furstenberg 2002).

As we have seen, family continues to be an important institution for instrumental support in the transition to adulthood, providing young adults with opportunities for exploration and attainment. Yet we have also seen that all families are not equally positioned to provide similar levels of material aid, which likely contributes to the reproduction of inequality. Welfare state policies in the forms of funding and access to education, housing policies, and school to work or other employment programs can moderate the effect of family circumstances and the contingencies of the contemporary transition to adulthood.

The type and quality of parent–adult child relationships also likely influence intergenerational support. What is more, cultural expectations of intergenerational support impact on parental assistance during this life phase. After all, once children reach the age of majority, parents are not legally obligated to continue to support or house their grown offspring. At this point in the life course, support and even the relationship itself become volitional. In the next section, we discuss norms and expectations of intergenerational support, and the relevance of relationship quality.

## Cultural understandings and relational dimensions of intergenerational support

The transition to adulthood is not only a time of change for the maturing teen, but it is new terrain for many parents as well. While parenting may have once been considered an 18-year commitment, today it often extends beyond the adolescent years with the provision of instrumental as well as emotional support. In negotiating the types and degree of support parents are willing to provide in young adulthood, parents often implicitly convey cultural values and expectations, and these cultural understandings of intergenerational support are shaped by expectations of life course stages, as well as historical moment.

Today, parents of young adults see their children facing far different challenges than they themselves faced entering adulthood. Parents who became adults during the postwar period experienced strong economic growth and welfare state support that facilitated young people's educational and work attainment as well as the acquisition of housing. This meant that they did not need to turn to parents for support to achieve a smooth and relatively early transition to adult independence. Brannen and colleagues argue that the unprecedented upward mobility experienced by this post-war generation facilitated a 'freedom from' family of origin, and a focus on individual achievement and family of procreation (2004: 170). These more independent, internally focused nuclear families often include a cultural emphasis on children's development and close child–parent relations. Rossi and Rossi (1990) assert that parents internalize helping patterns toward their children that do not vanish at maturation.

Research suggests that parents more readily support young adult children when they view needs as legitimate and aimed at scaffolding toward independence. Parents are more likely to view financial support as legitimate when it aims to facilitate education, employment, family formation and other aspects of their offspring's independence (e.g. Goldscheider *et al.* 2001), and parent–child relations are closer when support is provided for these reasons (Aquilino 1997; White 1994). Providing this type of support reduces feelings of ambivalence for parents as they are simultaneously able to provide family support *and* encourage independence. Thus, rather than aiming to promote prolonged dependence, parental assistance seeks to facilitate autonomy and achievement.

Young adults are also keenly aware of the cultural expectations of independence as well as the economic and educational achievements expected of them. Young adults have come to expect, and even take for granted, continued parental help through the contemporary transition to adulthood, viewing it as an expected responsibility of parenting (Goldscheider *et al.* 2001; Brannen *et al.* 2004). Yet, young adults may feel ambivalent about receiving support from their parents when it challenges their newly emerging identities or status as adults. For example, this can be seen in the case of co-residence. Although living at home may provide many benefits for young adults such as enabling further education, allowing career exploration, maintaining a lifestyle or consumption level that would be impossible on the income of a student or entry level employee, and allowing for savings, these benefits also come with costs. Some studies find that young adults who reside with their parents report lower levels of trust, respect and fairness in their parental relationships and higher levels of conflict and issues of control, yet at the same time enjoy closer relations and share more activities with their parents than nonco-resident counterparts (e.g. Aquilino 1997). Thus, higher levels of involvement in one another's lives appear to foster both opportunities for closeness and conflict (Luescher and Pillemer 1998; Cook and Furstenberg 2002). The issues of control and conflict also may be highlighting the 'growing pains' of young adults exerting the very independence their parents are attempting to instill in them. So while enjoying the benefits of coresidence, young adults may also desire the greater freedom and status that accompanies independent living. Importantly, cultural contexts that view parent–adult child co-residence as normative foster less tension and ambivalence. We can see evidence for this in the case of Italy (Scabini *et al.* 2006) and for some immigrant communities in the United States.

Some argue that contemporary society is marked by an emphasis on self-realization, individuation, choice, and self-fulfillment (Giddens 1991). Changing structural conditions such as the uncertainty of the labor market with its accompanying requirement of flexibility, contribute to young people emphasizing 'freedom to' fashion oneself and one's life and developing identities based on expression, lifestyle, consumption, and autonomy (Brannen *et al.* 2004). Parents, too, have come to appreciate this understanding of life and adulthood for their children, even if they themselves have not been able to live it out (Scabini *et al.* 2006). Through experience, they have learned that lifetime employment, or even relationships, are no longer reliable, nor perhaps even desirable, and have come to value flexibility, choice, and personal fulfillment. Thus, along with providing resources that enable exploration and choice during young adulthood, they have also supplied emotional support and encouragement to their young adult children to do so.

## Relationship quality and intergenerational support

Although some sense of mutual family obligation remains, particularly in the parent–child stem family, today ongoing interaction and intergenerational support largely rely on choice and volition. After all, very few young people in the countries of focus depend on family land or other inheritance for livelihood. Nor do parents expect that they will exclusively depend on their children for ongoing care as they age. Because of this, the centrality of family ties for survival may have diminished. Ironically, at a time when young adults need their parents' help to navigate the changing transition to adulthood, intergenerational support may more heavily depend upon positive relations and affection.

Fortunately for many young people, it appears that on the whole parent–adult child relations are strong. Perhaps due to declines in the number of children per family or due to cultural shifts in childrearing ideologies/practices and lifestyle preferences of parents, both parents and young adults report close, high quality relations, with little 'generation gap'. While earlier research on adolescent and young adult–parent relationships focused on strain and conflict, contemporary research finds high levels of solidarity, affection, positive communication, and consensus (see Bengtson *et al.* 2002; Scabini *et al.* 2006). Perhaps reflecting or causing the high levels of instrumental assistance provided by parents to adult children at this life stage, affectional ties peak in the twenties (Rossi and Rossi 1990). Scabini *et al.* argue that in modern European societies, the relationship between parents and offspring during early adulthood is now less focused on separating from parents, but on restructuring relations to simultaneously allow for young adult autonomy and the continued parental support needed under new external objective circumstances (2006: 23). Italy offers a case in point. Italian young people carve out enough autonomy from parents for an active social, sexual, and consumption lifestyle, while still enjoying the housing support of their parents that facilitate achieving movement toward adulthood (Cook and Furstenberg 2002; Scabini *et al.* 2006). This restructured relationship enables the transition to adulthood to become a 'joint enterprise' shared by parents and offspring, when families of origin promote the autonomy and exploration of their young adult children, yet also provide them with guidance and instrumental and emotional supports that enable exploration of work and relationships without serious risks (Scabini *et al.* 2006). What is more, research finds that the quality of ties to parents and feelings of family solidarity and cohesion during the transition to adulthood has long-term significance for attainment, well-being and self-esteem (Bengtson *et al.* 2002).

## Conclusion

Changes in the transition to adulthood have meant changes for families. Parents have responded to shifting needs and desires of young adult children by providing them with continued support that enhances opportunities. Thus, families are adapting to collective problems that stem from broader structural shifts in the private sphere. Families with strong emotional attachments and more resources available may be better positioned to facilitate a smoother transition into adulthood for their children and help to minimize the risks of exploration. Yet support provided by the state in the form of affordable housing, funding for education, and structured school to work programs may moderate the effect of family circumstances. In those countries with limited welfare states, the private and hidden nature of interfamily support may not only reproduce existing inequalities, but they may also legitimate and reinforce ideologies of independence and individualism, while discouraging systemic solutions to shared societal problems.

While receiving support from one's family may imply a lack of independence, exchanges between family members are common throughout the life course. Emotional and instrumental support can be important at times of crisis, change or aging. Indeed, the transition to adulthood may be a critical time in restructuring relationships between parents and children with important implications for the quality of those relationships over the increased number of years parents and children can expect to share as adults, especially significant given changes in longevity. Further, patterns of intergenerational support established during this transition may affect intergenerational giving and care later in the life course, including when parents may have greater need for help.

# References

Aquilino, W.S. (1997) 'From adolescent to young adult: a prospective study of parent-child relations during the transition to adulthood', *Journal of Marriage and the Family*, 59: 670–86.

Arnett, J. (2004) *Emerging Adulthood: The Winding Road from the Late Teens through the Twenties*, Oxford: Oxford University Press.

Bengtson, V., Biblarz, T. and Roberts, R. (2002) *How Families Still Matter: A Longitudinal Study of Two Generations*, Cambridge: Cambridge University Press.

Brannen, J. (2006) 'Cultures of intergenerational transmission in four-generation families', *The Sociological Review*, 54: 133–54.

Brannen, J., Moss, P. and Mooney, A. (2004) *Working and Caring over the Twentieth Century: Change and Continuity in Four-generation Families*, Basingstoke: Palgrave Macmillan.

Casper, L. (1996) 'Who's minding our preschoolers?', in *Current Population Report*, Washington, DC: Government Printing Office.

Cook, T. D. and Furstenberg, F. F. (2002) 'Explaining aspects of the transition to adulthood in Italy, Sweden, Germany, and the United States: a cross-disciplinary, case synthesis approach', *Annals of the American Academy of Political and Social Science*, 580: 257–87.

Cooney, T. and Uhlenberg, P. (1992) 'Support from parents over the life course: the adult child's perspective', *Social Forces*, 71: 63–84.

Giddens, A. (1991) *Modernity and Self-identity: Self and Society in the Late Modern Age*, Cambridge: Polity Press.

Goldscheider, F. and Goldscheider, C. (1999) *The Changing Transition to Adulthood: Leaving and Returning Home*, Thousand Oaks, CA: Sage Publishers.

Goldscheider, F. K., Thornton, A. and Yang, L. (2001) 'Helping out the kids: expectations about parental support in young adulthood', *Journal of Marriage and the Family*, 63: 727–40.

Hartmann, D. and Swartz, T. (2007) 'The new adulthood? The transition to adulthood from the perspective of transitioning young adults', in R. Macmillan (ed.) *Constructing Adulthood: Agency and Subjectivity in the Life Course. Advances in Life Course Research*, vol. 10: New York: Elsevier, pp. 255–89.

Iacovou, M. (2002) 'Regional differences in the transition to adulthood', *The Annals of the American Academy of Political and Social Science*, 580: 40–69.

Kerckhoff, A. C. and Macrae, J. (1992) 'Leaving the parental home in Great Britain: a comparative perspective', *The Sociological Quarterly*, 33: 281–301.

Kohli, M. (1999) 'Private and public transfers between generations: linking the family and the state', *European Societies*, 1: 81–104.

Logan, J. and Spitze, G. (1996) *Family Ties: Enduring Relations between Parents and their Grown Children*, Philadelphia, PA: Temple University Press.

Luescher, K. and Pillemer, K. (1998) 'Intergenerational ambivalence: a new approach to the study of parent–child relations in later life', *Journal of Marriage and the Family*, 60: 413–25.

Rosenfeld, M. (2007) *The Age of Independence*, Cambridge, MA: Harvard University Press.

Rossi, A. and Rossi, P. (1990) *Of Human Bonding: Parent–Child Relations across the Life Course* New York: Aldine de Gruyter.

Scabini, E., Marta, E. and Lanz, M. (2006) *The Transition to Adulthood and Family Relations: An Inter-generational Perspective*, Hove: Psychology Press.

Schoeni, R. and Ross, K. (2005) 'Material assistance from families during the transition to adulthood', in R. Settersten, Jr., F. Furstenburg Jr. and R. Rumbaut (eds) *On the Frontier of Adulthood: Theory, Research, and Public Policy*, Chicago: University of Chicago Press.

Settersten, R. A., Jr., Furstenburg, F. Jr. and Rumbaut, R. (eds) (2005) *On the Frontier of Adulthood: Theory, Research, and Public Policy*, Chicago: University of Chicago Press.

White, L. (1994) 'Coresidence and leaving home: young adults and their parents', *Annual Review of Sociology*, 20: 81–102.

# 27

# Early childbearing in the new era of delayed adulthood

*Frank Furstenberg Jr*

## Introduction

Teenage childbearing has never been prevalent in most nations, even when fertility in the Western world was much higher than it is today. However, for reasons still incompletely understood, early family formation was more frequent in many parts of Eastern Europe and some Anglo-speaking countries. In these nations, early marriage was a distinct pattern, and it was not uncommon for teenagers to wed following a premarital pregnancy.

Although early marriage has all but disappeared in most industrialized countries, early childbearing continues to occur in high levels in many Eastern European and Anglo-speaking countries. The United States, in particular, has long been an outlier in this trend among high-income nations. Its rate of teenage childbearing is more than four times that of many European nations and more than twice that of Canada and Australia (Singh and Darroch 2000).

Despite these consistent distinctions, the rate of fertility among women aged 15–19 dropped rapidly during the past several decades, albeit more slowly in some countries than others, as the demographic transitions associated with adulthood have been delayed in virtually all industrialized nations. This chapter explores some of the reasons for the anomalous pattern in the United States, examines the consequences of early childbearing for teen mothers and their children, and discusses the efficacy of alternative policy approaches to lower early childbearing and lessen its adverse effects.

## The causes of early childbearing

Demographers have proposed a number of different explanations to account for different rates of early childbearing across countries. One important reason for the variation can be traced to the composition of national populations. It has long been the case that early childbearing is higher among African-Americans, Caribbean immigrants, and Native Indian populations whose kinship systems follow what Therborn (2004) refers to as the

Creole pattern of weak marital bonds and a pronounced matrilineal bias. The disparity between the United States and Europe noted above diminishes but does not completely disappear when comparisons are restricted only to non–Hispanic whites. Thus, the diverse population of the United States can explain part, but not all the differences in early childbearing.

Research has also shown that early childbearing occurs more frequently among the economically disadvantaged (Geronimus 2003). There is a modest correlation between levels of inequality and economic disadvantage and rates of early childbearing, presumably because the poor are less informed about contraceptive options and may also be less motivated to manage the timing of their first birth. In addition, less advantaged youth are more likely to begin to have sexual relations at earlier ages, use contraception less faithfully, and less often resort to abortion when pregnancy occurs (Hofferth and Hayes 1987). Of course, the poor are also less inclined to wed in the event of pregnancy, although marriage itself has generally become a less attractive option for young adults when pregnancy occurs. Generally speaking, higher poverty in a nation is associated with higher rates of early and unplanned births.

There are strong cultural, religious, and policy differences in how nations manage the sexual transition. Elsewhere I have proposed a theoretical approach to understanding when and why early childbearing will become a 'social problem' in the developing world (Furstenberg 1998). This approach builds on the premise that a nation's cultural beliefs and public policies toward regulating sexual activity are at the heart of the issue.

When premarital sexual behaviour is viewed as a religious and cultural anathema, there must be social mechanisms that control contact between young women and men, instil strong norms against sexual relations before marriage, and promote early marriage in the event that these norms are breached. Nations that attempt to discourage sexuality as a primary means of preventing early childbearing will generally be less effective in promoting contraceptive use (and perhaps abortion as well).

Most European nations have shifted away from strict control of sexuality and toward regarding sexual behaviour in the mid and late teens as normative, if not developmentally appropriate (Carpenter 2005; Schalet 2006). Accordingly, they have adopted pragmatic and public health approaches to avoiding the potentially adverse effects of sexual risk-taking. By contrast, the United States and, to a lesser extent other Anglo-speaking countries, continue to discourage premarital sex.

The lengthening period of early adulthood, now spanning from the late teens to the early thirties, when young people conclude their schooling, depart from the natal home, enter the labour force, and form a family, has made early childbearing (with or without marriage) more anomalous (Settersten et al. 2005). Clearly, however, the longer period that it takes youth to 'settle down' has also created a larger space in the life course when individuals are at risk of unplanned parenthood.

The United States, and to a lesser extent in Britain and New Zealand, continue to vigorously emphasize what I have called preventive approaches to postponing the onset of sexual intercourse rather than pragmatic strategies to avoid pregnancy and parenthood among sexually active youth. I have speculated that these policies help to explain why these Anglo-speaking countries have more early childbearing (Furstenberg 2007).

In sum, several reasons may explain the higher rates of teenage childbearing in Eastern Europe and Anglo countries: demographic differences, long-standing patterns of early family formation, different levels of commitment to avoiding premarital sex, and differential use of strategies for preventing unprotected sex. Depending on the country, these

227

different factors may play a more or less important role in accounting for the nation's prevalence of early childbearing.

## The consequences of early childbearing

The first studies of the consequences of early childbearing suggested that teen mothers were destined to lead a life of disadvantage (Campbell 1968). It was generally believed that these young mothers were likely to drop out of school, marry poorly or not at all, have more children than they wanted, and hence be in a poor economic position to support their children. Indeed, a huge amount of research, practice, and policy developed on the premise that reducing early childbearing was an effective strategy for breaking the cycle of disadvantage among the poor and disadvantaged minorities (Hayes 1987; Brown and Eisenberg 1995).

In recent years, research has begun to call that proposition into question. There are two related reasons why the initial studies may have exaggerated the impact of early childbearing on young mothers' life chances. First, the studies did not take adequate account of *pre-existing* demographic, social, and psychological differences between the women who had sex, became pregnant, and brought their pregnancies to term and those who postponed sex, used contraception effectively, or in the event of a pregnancy, obtained an abortion. It turns out that when investigators began to pay more attention to 'social selection' – the nonrandom nature of who is susceptible to early childbearing – the impact of early childbearing on the future educational, economic, marital, and childbearing outcomes is not nearly as large as most researchers had initially claimed.

As the statistical techniques for ruling out selection bias in data analysis have become more sophisticated, researchers have increasingly cast doubt on the importance of early childbearing as a determinant of women's prospects. While a lively debate continues over the precise magnitude of the effect of early childbearing on later life events, most researchers believe that the long-term impact on such things as earnings, marriage and divorce, and family size is only modest at most. (For a discussion of this debate, see Maynard 1997; Hoffman 1998; Geronimus 2003.)

A second and related reason for questioning the significance of early childbearing arises from studies of teenage parents and their offspring who have been followed for long periods of time. In my own study of a group of teenage mothers in Baltimore who were interviewed periodically from the mid-1960s when they first became pregnant to the mid-1990s when they had entered midlife, I discovered that the vast majority of teen mothers greatly improved their circumstances over the long term. Women who dropped out of school often returned later and managed to graduate from high school and some even entered college. Those who quickly had another child after their first birth did not invariably go on to have additional children after the second birth. Indeed, more than one-half of the women in the Baltimore study sought sterilization in their mid- or late twenties after a first, second, or third birth. Many of those who initially sought public assistance left the welfare rolls to return to work when their first child entered school. In fact, the vast majority of the women over time managed to become economically independent even if only one quarter of the sample made it into the middle class (Furstenberg 2007).

Moreover, their children, particularly their first-born daughters, were doing relatively well in their late twenties. Little more than one-third of the daughters had become parents in their teens while a substantial minority remained childless even in their late twenties when they were last interviewed. Most exceeded their parents' educational levels and found reasonable jobs by their adult years. By contrast, their sons were doing less well. A much higher proportion of their first-born sons were having severe difficulties in establishing social and economic independence in part because many had been caught up in the criminal justice system. Overall, the next generation did not look very different from the children of mothers who postponed childbearing but who had identical social and economic backgrounds.

Psychologically, I discovered that the teen mothers were far more resilient in adapting to early childbearing than many observers might have predicted. When asked to evaluate at the thirty-year follow-up how they had done in life, most reported they had accomplished more than they had expected, particularly given their shaky start. Compared with later childbearers in a national study, the women in Baltimore rated different aspects of their lives as favourably, if not more favourably, by mid-life. In part, they may have had lower expectations before and shortly after their first birth occurred. Hence as their lives unfolded, many were inclined to feel optimistic about what they had accomplished by their mid-forties. Indeed, the majority had traversed two public stereotypes, moving as they did from the highly negative image of 'a teenage mother' to the far more favourable image of 'a mid-life matriarch'.

It would be inaccurate to claim that early childbearing had no adverse effects on the population of women I studied in Baltimore. My study and a good deal of the recent research suggest small and persistent effects, which are likely attributable to life difficulties created, or at least aggravated, by early childbearing. An overwhelming number of the women in the Baltimore study experienced physical or mental health problems. Fewer than one-third of the women had formed stable and rewarding partnerships with men, and many had children or family members who were experiencing problems and disabilities associated with chronic economic hardship. Moreover, nearly one in ten had died. This figure is about twice as high as might be expected in the overall population of US women. However, the same level of problems was also evident among poor minority women more generally, regardless of the timing of their first birth (ibid.).

I conclude from the Baltimore study and related research on the life course of teenage parents that social scientists are inclined to underestimate the capacities of individuals to adapt to atypical events such as early childbearing. Their resiliency can be explained in various ways. First, many received considerable support from extended kin in ways that made it possible to return to school or enter the labour force.

Second, events after the birth of their child sometimes offset the difficulties created by having a child early in life. Many young mothers, faced with the responsibilities of rearing a child, resolved to get their lives together. Thus, the birth itself may have galvanized their motivation to succeed.

Third, many of the women found their way into remedial programmes and frequently took advantage of unforeseen opportunities. Experiences in later life were often put to good use. Women who went back to school or into the labour force revised their ambitions and found they could succeed even though they had started a family at an inopportune time.

There may be a tendency among social scientists, not to mention members of the mass media, to overstate the importance of early life events on the later course of life, particularly in the absence of longitudinal data. Seen from the perspective of later life, early childbearing is perhaps not as momentous as it seems at the time. Indeed, the first

229

assessments by the teen mothers of their well-being during the five years after delivery – when the young mothers were new parents – provided a much more negative picture of their lives than the information collected at later points in the study. By their late twenties and early thirties, most of the Baltimore women looked a great deal more mature and settled. While their lives were far from ideal, many, even most, had gained some measure of security, identity, and stability.

We know relatively little from this study about the specific processes that explain the course of development during the early adult years. A serious gap exists between what we know about the social and demographic trajectories of young lives and how young adults acquire a sense of self, social competencies and the ability to relate to others, and the skill of self-regulation and management required to perform social roles such as worker, parent, or partner.

## Early childbearing in the context of prolonged adulthood

Although I have suggested that early childbearing does not have the predictive power that has been widely assumed, and by implication its prevention might not be as potent a strategy for breaking the cycle of poverty as often claimed, it would be wrong to dismiss efforts to reduce unintended pregnancies and unwanted births. There are sound reasons for reducing unintended births, if only to allow couples to plan better for the care and support of their children. This is especially true as the timing of other adult transitions (such as work, education, and marriage) becomes more extended and the preparation for economic independence more prolonged. Although women can and do scramble the sequence of family-building, education, and employment, it is generally ill-advised to invest in children before one acquires the needed social capital (both psychological and material).

Children, it might be argued, will reap less from parental education and income when it is acquired after their birth or even after early childhood. The direct influence of parents on their children may well diminish after the preschool years. If that is the case, children should do better when their parents complete their education and gain experience in the labour market before, rather than after, they are born. (Of course, as we observed in the Baltimore study, economically disadvantaged women often do not accrue a great deal of human capital merely by delaying parenthood.)

In general, then, there are good reasons for discouraging early childbearing. It is typically unintended, and even when it is not, it is often ill-advised given the economic and social circumstances of the parents.

This brings us back to public policies to reduce teenage childbearing in contemporary societies. In the introduction of this chapter, I noted that societies have adopted very different strategies for curbing early childbearing with seemingly different effects.

I alluded to two approaches. The first I refer to as an upstream approach. This approach attempts to curb sexual activity during the teen years as a way of reducing early childbearing. This strategy is most popular in the United States, although it has found varying levels of support in other nations as well. A downstream approach, on the other hand, assumes that a high proportion of teenagers will engage in sex and takes measures to reduce the likelihood of pregnancy by promoting contraceptive use with the possibility of abortion in the event of conception. Most European nations have energetically promoted sex education and contraceptive use through the schools, mass media, and outreach by reproductive health agencies (Jones 1986).

Although some studies have attempted to examine the efficacy of these different strategies, there has been no definitive cross-national comparison on their effectiveness (Imamura *et al.* 2007). Plausibly, one could argue that the answer to the question of which approach works better is found in the rates of pregnancy and parenthood. However, a more convincing answer requires a careful analysis of sexual risk-taking among demographically and psychologically similar youth in societies that have established particular public policies.

It is also entirely possible that public policies *per se* are less important in determining rates of childbearing than the political and cultural differences that give rise to the policies. If that were true, trying to isolate public policies that work to reduce early childbearing would be an exercise in futility. Nevertheless, research is begging for more comparative research that addresses these questions.

## References

Brown, S. S. and Eisenberg, L. (eds) (1995) *The Best Intentions: Unintended Pregnancy and the Well-Being of Children and Families*, Washington, DC: National Academy Press.

Campbell, A. (1968) 'The role of family planning in the reduction of poverty', *Journal of Marriage and the Family*, 30: 236–45.

Carpenter, L. M. (2005) *Virginity Lost: An Intimate Portrait of First Sexual Experiences*, New York: New York University Press.

Furstenberg, F. F. (1998) 'When will teenage childbearing become a problem? The implications of western experience for developing countries', *Studies in Family Planning*, 29: 246–53.

—— (2007) *Destinies of the Disadvantaged: The Politics of Teen Childbearing*, New York: Russell Sage Foundation.

Geronimus, A. T. (2003) 'Damned if you do: culture, identity, privilege, and teenage childbearing in the United States', *Social Science and Medicine*, 57: 881–93.

—— (2004) 'Teenage childbearing as cultural prism', *British Medical Bulletin*, 69: 155–66

Hayes, C. D. (1987) *Risking the Future: Adolescent Sexuality, Pregnancy, and Childbearing*, vol. 1, Washington, DC: National Academy Press.

Hofferth, S. L. and Hayes, C. D. (1987) *Risking the Future: Adolescent Sexuality, Pregnancy and Childbearing*, Washington, DC: National Academy Press.

Hoffman, S. D. (1998) 'Teen childbearing isn't so bad after all … or is it? A review of the new literature on the consequences of teen childbearing', *Family Planning Perspectives*, 30: 236–43.

Imamura, M. *et al.* (2007) 'Factors associated with teenage pregnancy in the European Union countries: a systematic review', *The European Journal of Public Health*, 17: 630–6.

Jones, E. F. (1986) *Teenage Pregnancy in Industrialized Countries*, New Haven, CT: Yale University Press.

Maynard, R. A. (ed.) (1997) *Kids Having Kids: Economic Costs and Social Consequences of Teen Pregnancy*, Washington, DC: Urban Institute Press.

Schalet, A. T. (2006) *Raging Hormones, Regulated Love*, Chicago: University of Chicago Press.

Settersten, R. A., Jr., Furstenberg, F. F. and Rumbaut, R. G. (2005) *On the Frontier of Adulthood: Theory, Research, and Public Policy*, Chicago: University of Chicago Press.

Singh, S. and Darroch, J. E. (2000) 'Adolescent pregnancy and childbearing: levels and trends in developed countries', *Family Planning Perspectives*, 32: 14–23.

Therborn, G. (2004) *Between Sex and Power: Family in the World, 1900–2000*, Abingdon: Routledge.

# 28

# Homeless youth and the transition to adulthood

*Bill McCarthy, Monica Williams and John Hagan*

## Introduction

In the 1990s, UNICEF estimated that more than 80 million children and youth lived 'unaccompanied' in the world, mostly in 'developing' nations, but with large numbers of the homeless also living on the streets in the 'developed' world (Van der Ploeg and Scholte 1997). Precise counts of the size of the homeless youth population are impossible to obtain, in part because the population changes from day to day as some young people end their current period of homelessness while others begin theirs. Population counts are also influenced by other factors including inconsistent definitions of homelessness and youth, the political goals of governments and other data collectors, the expense under-taken to gather data, and the willingness of youth to count themselves as homeless. As a result, there is considerable variation in assessments of the homeless population. For example, estimates of the size of the homeless youth population in the United States in the late 1980s and early 1990s range from 100,000 to 750,000 (ibid.). These issues not-withstanding, it is widely acknowledged that the number of homeless youth throughout the world has increased dramatically in the past 40 years.

Although researchers have used a variety of definitions when studying homeless youth, most approaches agree that the absence of stable shelter and separation from family or guardians are key components of homelessness. Some definitions include specifications of the amount of time without shelter, the security of the available accommodation (e.g., sleeping in parks versus hostels) or the immediate reason for the homeless experience (e.g., whether youth left home voluntarily or were 'thrown out' by their family). Other approaches emphasize the extent to which individuals identify themselves as homeless. Some perspectives distinguish between homeless and street youth, reserving the latter term for youth who spend large amounts of time participating in street culture, regardless of whether or not they are homeless. However youth homelessness is defined, most researchers agree that it is a changing state in which young people move between living at home, being homeless and residing in some type of institutional setting such as foster care, juvenile detention, or jail. In addition, while on the streets, most youth move from one type of accommodation to another (e.g., back and forth between sleeping in a shelter or with friends). This instability leads some researchers to describe homelessness as a process – rather than a state of being (Wingert *et al.* 2005) – and to conceptualize its various elements as parts of a 'life cycle' of homelessness (Auerswald and Eyre 2002).

While homeless youth cycle through settings and accommodations, they also negotiate the transition from adolescence to adulthood. However, variation in the definitions of youth complicates our understanding of this transition. The term youth typically refers to the period between childhood and adulthood, but neither of these stages is clearly bound by specific ages. As a result, some researchers use a legal definition to demarcate youth, while others adopt the client age limits set by service organizations, or draw on definitions derived from research or theory.

In this chapter, we briefly review some key problems in making sense of the transition to adulthood. We then narrow our focus to homeless youth and review research that examines how these adolescents become homeless and the factors that help them exit the street. The transition into and out of homelessness is inextricably combined with the transition into adulthood. By definition, homeless youth are already involved in one of the common markers of adulthood – independent living – and in many cases, are involved in several others. Yet, only a few studies provide any analysis of the transition to adulthood among homeless youth, and this research mostly concerns Canada, the United States and Europe.

## The markers of adulthood

Research on the transition from adolescence to adulthood typically assumes that societies define distinct indicators that signify the end of adolescence and the start of adult life. Common demographic markers include independent living, completing education, finding full-time work, and forming a family (Mouw 2005). However, in the past 30 years, many of these transitions have become delayed, and for some youth are realized only in their late twenties or early thirties – a time of life that extends far beyond common conceptualizations of adolescence. The sequencing of the key transitions has also changed: fewer youth now follow traditional patterns in which the completion of one's education is followed by full-time work, marriage and childbirth (ibid.). Indeed, some scholars argue that the period between the late teens and mid-twenties has replaced adolescence as the 'most turbulent' for young people (Fussell and Furstenburg 2005).

A second problem with a focus on conventional signifiers of adulthood is that it often ignores the interpretive dimension or subjectivity of these markers. A growing body of research demonstrates that young adults vary in their interpretations of which events under which conditions signify adulthood (Brannen *et al.* 2002; Macmillan 2007); moreover, for many young people, adulthood is indicated by a combination of psychological achievements, such as being more independent, responsible and sensitive to others. As a result, some scholars suggest that a 'package' of social roles and personal qualities, rather than specific transitions, signifies entry into adulthood (Macmillan 2007).

The notion of a package highlights the diverse identities, or 'subjectivities' that influence adolescents' interpretations of adulthood. As they adopt, modify, and replace the multiple identities that adolescence and adulthood involve, youth reinterpret their status. For example, many adolescents make several of the transitions commonly associated with adulthood (e.g., finish their education, obtain full-time work and establish an independent household) and change many of their identities to reflect their new adult self, only to move back home, stop working and subsequently change how they view themselves.

The mutability of identities highlights a third complication in the transition to adulthood: agency. Adolescent's experiences and interpretations of the move to adulthood may be highly dependent on their self-image. Although all youth are influenced by social structures and forces, they are not equally determined by them. Those who have a strong self-image and possess a high degree of self-efficacy are more likely to believe that they can make decisions to change the direction of their life course. Yet, self-image adjusts as adolescents reflect upon their experiences and interactions with others. This shifting sense of empowerment may affect the timing, type and interpretations of the transitions they experience.

These and other factors trouble our attempts to understand the transition to adulthood. They remind us that although societies provide some normative indicators that distinguish adolescence from adulthood, many markers are ambiguous. They also highlight the non-linearity of the move to adulthood and the importance of adolescents' interpretations and agency in this process. This ambiguity and non-linearity are particularly pronounced for the homeless. Most of these youth have experienced some of the key changes associated with adulthood – independent living, ending one's education, full-time employment – but the timing of these experiences, their impermanence and the minimal commitments many homeless youth make to them challenge their usefulness as indicators of the transition to adulthood.

## Transition into homelessness

Much of the early research on homeless youth focused on runaways. Depending on the time of the research, the orientation of the researcher and the group studied, runaway behavior was variously attributed to economic conditions and a desire for excitement (e.g., during the Great Depression), as well as various psychological conditions (e.g., in the 1940s and 1970s narcissism, sexual precociousness and incorrigibility were commonly discussed). Most studies also considered the family backgrounds of these youth; however, it was not until the 1970s that researchers began to investigate more thoroughly the role of the family.

Since then, studies have repeatedly documented the disproportionate levels of physical, sexual and emotional abuse among homeless youth relative to other adolescents (e.g., Hagan and McCarthy 1997; Whitbeck and Hoyt 1999). Other family factors that increase the likelihood of adolescent homelessness include poverty, living with a single parent, parental instability (e.g., living with a succession of substitute parents/guardians), parental substance use, family conflicts due to an adolescent's sexual orientation (Cochran et al. 2002), and having been removed from one's family by a child protection agency. The 'risk amplification model' indicates that for many youth, it is the accumulation of these risk factors or their increased intensity that eventually results in their leaving home (Whitbeck and Hoyt 1999). Compared to other adolescents, however, youth who become homeless also report more personal troubles before they leave home, including problems with teachers and school work; more extensive contact with youth involved in crime; and higher levels of substance use, criminal involvement and contact with the police (Hagan and McCarthy 1997). Thus, while many homeless youth arrive on the street attempting to flee a dysfunctional family life, others have been cast out (e.g., 'throwaways') by dysfunctional parents or guardians or left home because of conflicts arising from personal troubles. In some cases, the decision to leave is also facilitated by the lure of the street – freedom from parental and school responsibilities, access to drugs and alcohol, and networks of street youth who support being homeless.

Although the majority of homeless youth are on the street in part because of their dysfunctional families, many see leaving home as their choice. They view themselves as 'survivors' taking control of their lives. Moreover, only a minority of youth stop all contact with their families. Phone calls, emails, and visits with family members are common. For many youth, contact with families is part of a cycle of moving back and forth between home and the street. These attempts at reconciliation may originate with the youth, with parents or other family members, or in some cases as a result of inter-ventions by representatives of charitable, social service or other state agencies (e.g., the police).

Research from the United States and Canada consistently finds that once they arrive on the street, most homeless youth spend much of their day searching for food, shelter and money; hanging out in public spaces with other homeless youth; and traveling from one social service agency to another to acquire various resources (Hagan and McCarthy 1997; Whitbeck and Hoyt 1999). In addition, homeless youth report more extensive involvement in a variety of types of crime compared to other youth; they are more fre-quently the victims of thefts and physical and sexual assaults; and they have more extensive contact with the police and other agents of the state. There is considerable city to city, and country to country variation in the social services available to homeless youth, and research suggests that the absence of social services contributes to several of the negative outcomes associated with homelessness (e.g., sleeping in dangerous places, panhandling, substance use and other crimes).

## Homelessness and the transition to adulthood

The transition from adolescence to adulthood is complicated for groups of 'vulnerable' youth such as the homeless (Osgood et al. 2005) who may not follow 'typical' patterns of life changes. These youth must overcome an array of structural, cultural, social and psy-chological barriers in their transition to adulthood. Key obstacles include the lack of support from families and others (i.e., limited positive social capital); educational deficits, limited employment experience and the habits that work encourages (i.e., limited con-ventional human capital); embeddedness in networks of individuals engaged in high–risk and often illegal activities (i.e., heightened access to criminal social and human capital); involvement in substance use, crime and other dangerous activities; psychological and emotional difficulties that may have originated in childhood but which have been exa-cerbated by being homeless (e.g., from biological handicaps to familial neglect and abuse); and the conditions of homelessness itself (e.g., the costs involved in the search for shelter, food, money, and social support).

Most research on homeless youth documents these difficulties while also commenting on the remarkable resiliency of many of these adolescents. Unfortunately, little systematic research examines which factors and conditions help youth successfully transition from homelessness to a more normative path to adulthood. In their interviews with 602 run-away and homeless adolescents in several Midwestern US cities, Whitbeck and Hoyt (1999) asked respondents about their future plans. They found that the majority of youth anticipated full-time work, completing their education and locating permanent, secure shelter. Some of these youth described concrete, achievable plans, but the plans of many were unrealistic or ill-defined. Whitbeck and Hoyt note that the viability of future plans decreased with the length of time a youth had been homeless and with the extent of his/ her involvement in street survival activities (e.g., panhandling, survival sex, theft), contact with other homeless youth, and physical or sexual victimization since leaving home.

In a study from Glasgow, Scotland, Fitzpatrick (2000) re-interviewed 25 homeless youth one year after her initial contacts with them. She reports that young people who stayed close to their family homes, remained in contact with family members and made use of local social services were most likely to transition successfully from homelessness during the period under study. The majority of these youth had established stable housing and they were able to find and keep a job. In contrast, youth who fared more poorly had traveled to urban areas far from the places in which they were raised, had less secure forms of shelter (e.g., more frequently slept on the streets) and had made extensive use of hostels that provided services to both youth and adults.

Wingert et al. (2005) also emphasize the importance of connections with others. In their research on 12 homeless adolescents in a mid-sized Canadian city, they argue that connection with an adult willing to invest in the youth was one of two factors that precipitated the transition from homelessness. Many of the adults that youth described were social service or care workers who helped them secure social assistance, housing, and employment. Other adults – in some cases extended family and friends – played similar roles (also see Whitbeck and Hoyt 1999). Studies consistently report that access to resources through family and government agencies plays a key role in successful transitions into adulthood (Osgood et al. 2005) and it is no surprise that this support helped youth access the resources they needed to exit the street.

The second factor that Wingert and colleagues highlight is an unexpected event such as the death of a friend, an arrest, or getting pregnant. Although these 'chance events' may encourage youth to leave the street, it is hard to establish their causal significance because we cannot assess whether a change would have occurred without the event. As Shanahan and Porfeli (2007) note in their research on chance events in the life course, the apparent randomness of these events also obscures the active choices people make that increase or minimize the likelihood of particular events: the decisions made by young people make some events all but impossible, while increasing the odds of others.

Other research suggests that finding stable employment may be important in helping homeless youth leave the street. The great majority of homeless youth (about 80%) have worked in the legal economy, a participation rate equivalent to the rate for most young people (about 80 percent of adolescents living in the United States participate in paid employment at some point in their high school years; see Hagan and McCarthy 1997). The jobs of the homeless and more securely housed youth – especially those from less well-off families – are also similar. Fast food restaurants, stores and other service jobs, as well as seasonal employment are the most common.

However, employment among the homeless differs from that for other youth in many important ways. There is more volatility in the employment of homeless youth; studies find that although most youth have worked since leaving home, only a minority were employed when they were interviewed (e.g., see Hagan and McCarthy 1997; Whitbeck and Hoyt 1999; Robinson and Baron 2007). Several factors contribute to this instability. Compared to other youth, homeless youth have higher rates of seasonal employment, work interruptions due in part to their greater mobility, incarceration and work termi- nations. As well, most homeless youth have not completed high school. Their limited human capital means that they are often the first workers to be let go when a business experiences a down-turn. Baron (2001) reports that most of the 400 homeless youth he interviewed in Vancouver felt that they lacked the appropriate skills and credentials to obtain employment (also see Hagan and McCarthy 1997).

Another distinctive characteristic of the work experiences of homeless youth includes the allocation of the money they earn. Most youth use their employment income to supplement allowances, money and subsidies they receive from parents and others (e.g., for shelter, food, clothing, technology); the great majority of homeless youth do not receive these types of financial supplements. As a result, homeless youth use a greater share of their employment income to purchase goods and services that families provide to other adolescents.

The majority of homeless youth also augment employment income with monies earned from quasi-legal and illegal activities. Gaetz and O'Grady (2002) note that most of the 360 homeless youth they interviewed in Toronto, Canada adopted a flexible set of economic strategies that combined part-time, seasonal or short-term jobs with social assistance, loans or gifts from friends, panhandling, cleaning car windows, and illegal activities (e.g., theft, drug selling, and prostitution). This pattern is not unique to homeless adolescents. Research on the urban poor, for example, documents how some members of the inner-city underclass participate in legal and illegal activities to generate the money they need to pay rent and purchase necessities and luxuries. Moreover, in their research on over 390 homeless Canadian youth in Toronto, McCarthy and Hagan (1991) find that although homeless youth report higher rates of offending than other youth, the proportion of youth involved in these activities increases substantially once youth become homeless.

Many homeless youth also lack the varied supports that other youth have to help them persist with work during difficult times and to reinforce the various returns that employment provides. As well, the networks of homeless youth are disproportionately populated by unemployed people who often sabotage attempts to find and keep a job (e.g., by encouraging youth to 'party' rather than report for work).

Although earning an income is the key reason homeless youth search for employment, work has other benefits. In the study described above, Gaetz and O'Grady (2002) report that homeless youth who had paid employment were more advantaged than were other homeless youth in terms of health, education, and housing situation. In research on over 475 homeless youth from Toronto and Vancouver, Canada, Hagan and McCarthy (1997) find that employment is negatively related to involvement in an array of street (e.g., hanging out on the street and panhandling) and illegal activities (e.g., drug use, theft, drug selling and selling sex). Hagan and McCarthy argue that work may actively decrease offending by increasing young people's involvement in the daily obligations of employment, by intensifying their investment in acquiring work skills, contacts and resources (i.e., increasing their human and social capital) and by heightening their awareness of the negative aspects of street life, including the deleterious consequences of hanging out with other homeless youth. Importantly, Hagan and McCarthy note that it is not employment *per se* that encourages these changes. Employment is not likely to instantaneously transform the lives of youth; instead, the positive effects of employment likely accrue over time as youth increase investments in their work and increase their human and social capital. Robinson and Baron (2007) underscore the importance of human and social capital in their research on the employment training program experiences of 32 homeless youth in Vancouver. They find that even though programs lacked the resources to educate homeless youth, they were instrumental in helping them acquire useful workplace skills and connections with people that increased these young people's work opportunities.

## Conclusion

Understanding social development involves more than applying markers and categories to life stages. This is especially true when studying complicated transitions such as the move from adolescence to adulthood, and when investigating this change in vulnerable populations such as homeless youth. Homeless youth experience traditional markers of adulthood earlier than most adolescents. Yet, for these youth, changes such as leaving family, ending education, participating in full-time work or cohabiting with a romantic partner are not clearly indicators of a triumphant transition to adulthood. Many of these youth lack many of the resources – from personal attributes and characteristics, to human and social capital – that increase the likelihood of success. Similar to other young people, homeless youth move back and forth between adolescent and adult activities and experiences. Moreover, their self-images straddle both statuses and although they often claim to be adults, they also see themselves as adolescents in particular settings, contexts and relationships.

Research suggests that providing stable housing, job training programs, and employment, as well as access to supportive adults increases the likelihood that homeless youth will leave the street and return to a more conventional developmental pathway. Although these resources will help end homelessness for individual youth, they do not address some of the fundamental, structural causes of homelessness. Solutions must also address the increasing instability of family life, the loss of employment opportunities, the shortage of affordable housing, and the diminishing interest in using taxes to provide assistance to those in need.

## References

Auerswald, C. L. and Eyre, S. L. (2002) 'Youth homelessness in San Francisco: a life cycle approach', *Social Science 512*.

Baron, S. W. (2001) 'Street youth, labour market experiences and crime', *Canadian Review of Sociology and Anthropology*, 38: 189–216.

Brannen, J., Lewis, S., Nilsen, A. and Smithson, J. (eds) (2002) *Young Europeans, Work and Family: Futures in Transition*. London: Routledge.

Cochran, B. N., Stewart, A. J., Ginzler, J. A. and Cauce, A. M. (2002) 'Challenges faced by homeless sexual minorities: comparison of gay, lesbian, bisexual, and transgender homeless adolescents with their heterosexual counterparts', *American Journal of Public Health*, 92: 773–7.

Fitzpatrick, S. (2000) *Young Homeless People*. London: Macmillan Press.

Fussell, E. and Furstenberg Jr., F. F. (2005) 'The transition to adulthood during the twentieth century', in R. A. Settersten Jr,. F. F. Furstenberg Jr. and R. Rumbaut (eds) *On the Frontier of Adulthood: Theory, Research and Public Policy*, Chicago: University of Chicago Press, pp. 29–75.

Gaetz, S. and O'Grady, B. (2002) 'Making money: exploring the economy of young homeless workers', *Work, Employment and Society*, 16: 433–56.

Hagan, J. and McCarthy, B. (1997) *Mean Streets: Youth Crime and Homelessness*. New York: Cambridge University Press.

Macmillan, R. (2007) 'Constructing adulthood: agency and subjectivity in the transition to adulthood', in R. Macmillan (ed.) *Constructing Adulthood: Agency and Subjectivity in Adolescence and Adulthood, Advances in Life Course Research*, 11: 3–29. New York: JAI/Elsevier.

McCarthy, B. and Hagan, J. (1991) 'Homelessness: a criminogenic situation?' *British Journal of Criminology*, 31: 393–410.

Mouw, T. (2005) 'Sequences of early adult transitions: a look at variability and consequences', in R. A. Settersten Jr., F. F. Furstenberg Jr. and R. Rumbaut (eds) *On the Frontier of Adulthood: Theory, Research and Public Policy*, Chicago: University of Chicago Press, pp. 256–91.

Osgood, D. W., Foster, E. M., Flanagan, C. and Ruth, G. R. (eds) (2005) *On Your Own Without a Net: The Transition to Adulthood for Vulnerable Populations*. Chicago: University of Chicago Press.

Robinson, J. and Baron, S. W. (2007) 'Employment training for street youth: a viable option?', *Canadian Journal of Urban Research*, 16: 33–57.

Shanahan, M. J. and Porfeli, E. J. (2007) 'Chance events in the life course', in R. Macmillan (ed.) *Constructing Adulthood: Agency and Subjectivity in Adolescence and Adulthood, Advances in Life Course Research*, 11: 97–119. New York: JAI/Elsevier.

Van der Ploeg, J. and Scholte, E. (1997) *Homeless Youth*. London: Sage.

Whitbeck, L. B. and Hoyt, D. R. (1999) *Nowhere to Grow: Homeless and Runaway Adolescents and Their Families*. New York: Aldine de Gruyter.

Wingert, S., Higgitt, N. and Ristock, J. (2005) 'Voices from the margins: understanding street youth in Winnipeg', *Canadian Journal of Urban Research*, 14: 54–80.

# Part VI

# Youth, culture and lifestyles

*Andy Furlong*

## Young people, culture and lifestyles

The ways in which young people spend their free time, their cultural tastes, the styles they develop and the visible differences between them and the previous generation frequently make media headlines. Such headlines are rarely positive; young people's activities are frequently portrayed as distasteful, dangerous or threatening and as signalling a decline in moral standards. 'Evidence' relating to the activities of young people is used to press for legislative change in a range of policy areas, to increase surveillance of youth and to justify the imposition of new restrictions on their activities.

In many senses, youth studies emerged as a sub-field within the social sciences as a result of concerns about the activities and patterns of consumption among young people in post-war Europe and America. Visible, and sometimes spectacular, differences in dress, tastes and consumption were seen as marking a generational change and as challenging the established order. Compared to pre-war generations, post-war youth had considerable disposable incomes and greater amounts of free time which facilitated creative styles and self expression. Understandably, social scientists were fascinated by these expressions of social change, by the manifestations of generational conflict and by visible differences in style and taste that could be mapped onto social class-based experiences. The UK-based CCCS, which was at the forefront of academic attempts to understand the changing experiences of young people in the 1960s and 1970s, linked youth cultures to processes of class-based resistance within changing industrial landscapes.

While culture and lifestyles are frequently portrayed as highly structured by factors like social class, gender, 'race' and geography, as in other areas of the social sciences there have been strong disagreements between those who portray cultural expressions as somewhat superficial manifestations of underlying socio-economic differences or regard youth as manipulated by the consumer industries and those who like to think of young people as creative actors engaged in a process of cultural change which ultimately shapes social and political relations. As in the social sciences more generally, post-modern perspectives have become increasingly influential, resulting in an increased tendency to advance explanations which rest on individual agency and a readiness to overlook the significance of structures. These tensions come across clearly in the chapters in this section. At one level, we are introduced to authors who highlight the liquidity of modern lives, the porous boundaries between styles and cultural expressions and those who continue to insist that young people's experiences in the contexts of leisure and consumption are highly segmented.

The chapters presented here describe and interpret the leisure activities of young people in contemporary societies, look at the ways in which leisure has changed and at the significant continuities in the ways they spend their time. New technologies affect forms of communication, patterns of belonging and empower some young people, while helping to exclude those without the means to participate. As consumers, young people are an important group with high levels of disposable income and, as Best points out in Chapter 31, the spaces occupied by youth are also those that attract the attention of the consumer industries. These interactions and their impact on young people's leisure are clearly illustrated in the changing urban nightscapes where manufactured 'cool' spaces are powerfully marketed and used to exclude those 'undesirable' individuals who have insufficient disposable incomes.

In contexts with strong links to youthful expression, chapters also focus on the role of popular music since the 1950s and the ways in which links between musical taste and sub-cultural membership has been theorized. The development of different youth styles are described, meanings explored and links to structural positions debated. The role of drugs and alcohol in the leisure lives of young people, a subject that frequently drives media-generated moral panics, are presented as activities that have long been central to the lives of young people; forms of entertainment that harm relatively few young people but which may enhance solidarity and belonging. Taken together, the chapters that make up this part not only provide a comprehensive overview of the changing leisure lifestyles of the young, but also help contextualize activities and remind us that if we scratch the surface there are some powerful continuities in the lives of young people in the post-war generations.

# 29

# Leisure activities, place and identity

*Joan Abbott-Chapman and Margaret Robertson*

## Leisure in the digital age

The widespread use by youth and young adults of global communication and information technology has led social scientists to re-conceptualize traditional categories of youth 'leisure', as contrasted with study and/or employment, in ways which now overlap and merge. Older generations' definitions of what constitutes 'leisure' must also be re-thought. For example, young people's 'spare' time may be perceived by parents as 'lost' or 'wasted' if it consists of 'hanging out' with friends apparently 'doing nothing' rather than 'constructive' or organized leisure activities. But their teenage children may use un-programmed 'time out' to relax and maintain social relationships or to withdraw and make sense and meaning of the barrage of sensations and information which daily bombard their lives, and to develop their own sense of independence and identity (Abbott-Chapman and Robertson 2001). Research shows youth find their own physical, psychological and digital spaces in which 'leisure' becomes a 'fluid' concept. The shifting kaleidoscope of leisure activities, fashion trends and 'must have' possessions in the digital age takes different forms for different age groups as youth and young adults move from family dependence to independence.

Most leisure activities, especially of younger teenagers, take place in and around the home and local neighbourhood and not, as is popularly imagined, in city centres. This suggests that, despite the process of individualization taking place in post-modern, globalized societies, most young people are still attached to home and family. While the boundaries of home and away, global and local are becoming increasingly blurred, international research suggests that young citizens of the global economy still retain their local cultural, even 'tribal' viewpoints and identities and that the 'local me' and the 'global me' (Zachary 2000) co-exist independently but inter-connectedly, through the cultural 'code switching' of which young people are becoming masters.

Individuals born between 1981 and 1995 and thereafter form the first generation born within the digital age. As 'digital natives' their lives are different from preceding generations. Personalized digital devices and associated tools of the Web 2.0 world of blogs, podcasts, vodcasts, YouTube, wikis and online games are for them integral components of self-expression (Richardson 2006). Social networking via digital media is independent of time and space and requires no mediation from adults (Robertson 2007). Leisure spaces for digital natives are connected 24/7 and (largely) independent of context and place. Intimate communications with friends and family merge with formal relationships of school, work and study, so that traditional lineal notions that separate play/leisure time and work, as 'free' time from 'non-free' time, have little relevance. These 'social geographies' represent the fluidity of space (Holloway and Valentine 2000). 'Loose Space' as the setting for impromptu activities differs from 'behaviourly controlled' leisure time associated with built spaces and organized activities such as sports (Frank and Stevens 2007: 3). This does not preclude involvement in sporting and cultural activities because young people are able to participate in both simultaneously – via mobile phones and text messaging.

## Participation in sport and cultural engagement

The majority of young people participate in some form of exercise or sport on a fairly regular basis, although this tends to diminish in the older age groups. Boys are more likely to participate in organized sports than girls. Childhood sports preferences may also find expression in young adults' participation in sport and outdoor physical activities (Perkins *et al.* 2004). Attendance at sporting events is popular, with highest attendance among young adults. The increase in sedentary leisure pursuits at home such as watching TV and videos, listening to radio, music CDs or tapes, and playing computer games has led to a decline in sports participation, with related health risks of obesity and muscular skeletal problems.

Today's youth have less interest in reading for pleasure than their parents' generation because of the smorgasbord of competing leisure activities. An Australian national survey showed only 8.5 per cent of youth surveyed read during their leisure time (ABS 2001). Girls spend more time reading than boys, although it is claimed that the publication of the Harry Potter books has engaged many boys in leisure reading for the first time. Only a minority of young people attend libraries, theatres, art galleries or museums in their leisure time. The most popular forms of 'cultural' entertainment are movies and pop concerts. Popular music-related activities (both listening to and making music) are especially significant for youth and are used to reinforce collective identities or to distinguish individual differences or values.

Dancing to loud techno music, often under flashing laser lighting, at raves, dance parties and night clubs is also popular among older teenagers and young adults. The 'vibes' induce a collective emotional state, which may be enhanced by the use of alcohol and so-called 'party drugs' such as ecstasy (Gourlay 2004), amphetamines or more recently the highly dangerous methamphetamine nicknamed 'ice'. Highly publicized cases of drug and alcohol abuse among sports 'stars' and 'celebs' do nothing to discourage drug and alcohol abuse among young people.

## Risk-taking and anti-social behaviour as 'leisure' activities

Potentially harmful and/or illegal risk-taking for 'under-age' youth, such as drug and alcohol abuse, cigarette smoking, unsafe sex, and gambling are prevalent teenage 'leisure' behaviours. Unsupervised internet access, especially by children and young teenagers, carries its own risks, through, for example exposure to predatory adults via chat rooms, or pornography websites (Mitchell *et al.* 2003). Research has suggested that gender differences in risk-taking have been diminishing in recent years with girls drinking alcohol, binge drinking and using illicit drugs to the same extent as boys, and to a much greater extent than their mothers' generation (Abbott-Chapman *et al.* 2008). A number of studies have highlighted the role which alcohol plays in Australian youth culture (White and Hayman 2006). Similar problems of drug and alcohol abuse as common features of 'modern society' are experienced in the USA, the UK and elsewhere. Excessive or 'binge' drinking among under-age drinkers is particularly concerning, leading not only to mental and physical health problems but to accidents, drunk driving, aggressive and anti-social behaviour, unwanted and unsafe sex and longer-term social and educational problems (Viner and Taylor 2007).

Leisure 'boredom' as well as the need for excitement and 'fun' have been blamed for a range of anti-social and illegal activities of an alienated minority, such as vandalism, graffiti, car theft and car joy riding (Mahoney and Stattin 2000). 'Swarming' is a recent phenomenon during which large numbers of youth unknown to the party givers, invited third and fourth hand by SMS text messages, gatecrash home parties in pursuit of alcohol, drugs, music and 'fun' (White 2006). Such gatherings may result in mob violence, including fighting police, if the crowd spills onto surrounding gardens and streets. Swarming should not be confused with the usually harmless and widely popular leisure activity of 'hanging out' with friends.

## Just 'hanging out' – enjoying unsupervised recreation

'Hanging out' in public spaces such as shopping malls and bus malls, to adult eyes apparently doing 'nothing', is a way of a group of friends 'chilling out' away from adult surveillance and of absenting themselves from stresses of modern living. Such groups are often mistakenly identified by adults as youth 'gangs' especially if they are distinguished by ethnicity and/or distinctive dress codes, and so become the target of public suspicion (White 1999). In fact, very few of these friendship groups ever become gangs, or engage in anti-social activity, and are usually loose-knit and transient. Shopping malls are popular venues providing the kinds of sheltered spaces where friends explore ideas and personal boundaries (Holloway and Valentine 2000). Brightly lit theme parks, brand name stores, video-gaming places, and markets are attractive places for 'hanging out' with friends and meeting other young people, by serendipity or arrangement. Researchers also note that localized culture characterizes games and greeting rituals.

Playing spontaneous games in the street is a rare sight in wealthy middle-class suburbs, perhaps because 'McMansions' typically have all the leisure stimulants within – gymnasium, swimming pool and sophisticated media equipment. In addition, free play of the past is now strictly controlled by parents who fear child abduction, and are themselves too over-committed to supervise. A British study 'showed that the radius within which children roam freely around their homes has shrunk by almost 90 per cent since the 1970s' (James 2007: 36). Once children cycled to school – they are now driven by parents or guardians. A decline in direct experience of nature is associated with increased popularity of park visits. Among those from low socio-economic urban backgrounds there are likely to be more outdoor and street leisure activities – most notably the culture of hip-hop born in the New York slums. Diversity is an important element in any discussion of global youth leisure patterns.

## Gender and class differences in leisure activity

Gender, class, cultural and religious differences differentiate leisure activities and places where activities are located. The types of leisure opportunities which may be enjoyed are related to disposable income and education, and social and educational differences have been linked with parental concern for adolescents' 'planned' leisure time (Zeijl *et al.* 2000). Students with strong religious commitment, of all faiths, are less likely than their peers to engage in risky leisure activities, despite significant declines in youth participation in organized religion (Abbott-Chapman and Denholm 2001). There are also gender differences in leisure preferences, which may be accentuated by religious and cultural differences. For example, girls prefer more indoor leisure pursuits in 'private' places and boys prefer more outdoor pursuits in 'public' places. Studies suggest that girls see 'unstructured' activities in places such as theme parks as dominated by groups of boys and unsafe. Girls are more likely to spend more time alone and in their bedrooms with their music, televisions and videos (James 2001).

Those who, for reasons of socio-economic or cultural disadvantage, are unable to access new electronic media are effectively excluded from current knowledge economies and the life-chances they offer. Social class and educational differences mark access to, and usage of, digital technology in leisure, and the amount of time available after formal commitments of work and study have been met. In the developing world millions of child workers living in poverty never experience leisure time and ironically are sometimes employed producing consumer and leisure goods for Western youth. In developed societies, Web based tools enable educated work and play to intersect in ways that are mutually supportive and enjoyable. The converse is true for the less well educated who experience pressure to take on second, often menial, jobs to pay for the 'leisure' trappings of the wealthy, including electronic gadgetry.

## Creating a 'private space' in which to relax and be myself

Young people's use of public and private spaces and the meanings they attach to them are important aspects of leisure (Tarrant *et al.* 2001). International research findings in the United Kingdom, Australia, Finland, Sweden, Hong Kong, and Singapore support the view that as adolescents develop independence and a sense of self, they need privacy and psychological 'space' away from the surveillance of parents and other adults (Robertson and Williams 2004). Teenagers' favourite places are often those in which to retreat from the things or people which 'bother them'. The home, spaces in the home such as own bedroom, and places in nature, in the countryside, public parks, or by the sea, have emerged as favourite places rather than entertainment and sporting venues in town centres. The reasons given for the choice of place make reference to privacy, peacefulness and relaxation. Leisure activities in the home or bedroom, include listening to music, watching TV, using the computer, and enjoying 'having my own things around me'. (Abbott-Chapman and Robertson 2001). Places in nature are favoured for 'hanging out' with friends, or 'thinking about things', and are also the site of a wide range of both structured and spontaneous sporting activities.

Paradoxically, growing numbers of young people combine the search for personal space and 'privacy' with social communication which involves degrees of self-exposure and self-advertisement, through internet communication. Popular websites are YouTube, a video-sharing website, where users can upload, view and share video clips, Facebook and Myspace, which are social networking interactive websites offering personal profiles, blogs, groups and photos, allowing people to exchange information with their friends. As of September 2007 Myspace had over 200 million accounts. Although there are privacy controls in place many young people do not bother to use them. These sites challenge the traditional meaning of 'public' and 'private' spaces and illustrate ways in which the global and the local can apparently co-exist independently but interconnectedly.

## 'Global me', 'local me' and the borders between

McDonald argues that a new social model of young people's leisure is replacing models associated with the industrial age. Digital natives focus on 'communication rather than function' (McDonald 1999: 3). The new model depicts young people's ability to link leisure, study and work activities in a seamless and productive mix of tasks and apparently successful outcomes. In formal education there is increasing recognition of these blurred boundaries. While games are associated traditionally with play, in the new leisure model games extend to formal spaces of study and provide the format for motivational learning (Robertson 2007).

This experiential continuum also has implications for future space usage. The 'always-on' imperative of Generation Y makes less obvious the need for private physical space in which to 'be alone' or with friends, noted in previous research. While privacy in a physical sense still remains important, the element of social separation from adults and authority figures may now be achieved in other ways by, for instance, mentally escaping into cyberspace with a quick SMS to a friend on the other side of the world or sitting in the seat alongside. The use of drugs and alcohol, and especially binge drinking, may also continue to provide socially less acceptable ways of getting 'out of it'. For today's youth are faced with the need to sustain and nurture their particular identity within a 'universalistic' globalizing world, through negotiating new personal geographies of time–space use. Compared with previous generations, when only the privileged few could venture beyond the boundaries of local communities for pleasure, teenagers can surf the planet through television and the Internet at any time and in any place, while still enjoying back-packing and international travel in 'real' time and space.

Research suggests this does not replace the need for close personal relationships with friends and family in the here and now. Multi-media transmissions, electronic communications and trans-national merchandising outlets for fashion, music and reading which dominate international youth culture enable 'webmasters' and transnational companies to mould behaviours, especially consumerist behaviours and values, in ways which may challenge values of parents, traditional cultures and communities, so that young people become depersonalized and dislocated. The escape from stress, the search for personal leisure 'space' in which to 'be myself' and the need to make meaning in an ever-changing world become youthful priorities. Thus the opportunity and freedom to 'play', to explore the physical, social and natural environment in real time, to 'anchor' identity and to seek pleasure and self-realization through interpersonal interaction with local peers, have become of increasing rather than of diminishing importance.

# References

Abbott-Chapman, J. and Denholm, C. (2001) 'Adolescents' risk activities, risk hierarchies and the influence of religiosity', *Journal of Youth Studies*, 4: 279–98.

Abbott-Chapman, J., Denholm, C. and Wyld, C. (2008) 'Gender differences in adolescent risk-taking: are they diminishing? An Australian inter-generational study', *Youth and Society*, in press.

Abbott-Chapman, J. and Robertson, M. E. (2001) 'Youth leisure and home: space, place and identity', *Leisure and Society*, 24: 484–506.

Australian Bureau of Statistics (2001) *Children's Participation in Cultural and Leisure Activities*, Canberra: Australian Bureau of Statistics, Catalogue No. 4901.

Frank, K. A. and Stevens, Q. (eds) (2007) *Loose Space*, London: Routledge.

Gourlay, M. (2004) 'A sub-cultural study of recreational ecstasy use', *Journal of Sociology*, 40: 59–73.

Holloway, S. L. and Valentine, G. (eds) (2000) *Children's Geographies: Playing, Living, Learning*, London: Routledge.

James, K. (2001) '"I just gotta have my own space!": The bedroom as a leisure site for adolescent girls', *Journal of Leisure Research*, 33: 71–90.

James, V. (2007) 'Lost in the concrete jungle', *Geographical*, November: 34–38.

Mahoney, J. and Stattin, H. (2000) 'Leisure activities and adolescent antisocial behavior: the role of structure and social context', *Journal of Adolescence*, 23: 113–27.

McDonald, K. (1999) *Struggles for Subjectivity*, Cambridge: Cambridge University Press.

Mitchell, K. J., Finkelhor, D. and Wolak, J. (2003) 'The exposure of youth to unwanted material on the internet: a national survey of risk, impact and prevention', *Youth and Society*, 34: 330–58.

Perkins, D. F., Jacobs, J. E., Barber, B. L. and Eccles, J. S. (2004) 'Childhood and adolescent sports participation as predictors of participation in sports and physical fitness activities during young adulthood', *Youth and Society*, 35: 495–520.

Richardson, W. (2006) *Blogs, Wikis, Podcasts*, Thousand Oaks, CA: Corwin Press.

Robertson, M. E. and Williams, M. (eds) (2004) *Young People, Leisure and Place: Cross-cultural perspectives*, New York: Nova Scientific.

Robertson, M. (2007) 'School governance and pedagogical reform – a matter of trust', *International Journal of Learning*, 13. Online at www.learning-journal.com (accessed 5/2/08).

Tarrant, T. M., North, A., Edridge, M., Kirk, L., Smith, E. and Turner, R. (2001) 'Social identity in adolescence', *Journal of Adolescence*, 24: 597–609.

Viner, R. M. and Taylor, B. (2007) 'Adult outcomes of binge drinking in adolescence: findings from a U.K. national birth cohort', *Journal of Epidemiology and Community Health*, 61: 902–7.

White, R. (ed.) (1999) *Australian Youth Subcultures: On the Margins and in the Mainstream*, Hobart: Australian Clearing House for Youth Studies.

—— (2006) 'Swarming and the social dynamics of group violence', *Trends and Issues in Crime and Criminal Justice*, No. 326. Canberra: ACT, Australian Institute of Criminology.

White, V. and Hayman, J. (2006) *Australian Secondary Students' Use of Alcohol in 2005*, Victoria, Australia: The Cancer Council.

Zachary, G. P. (2000) *The Global Me*, London: Nicholas Brealey Publishing.

Zeijl, E., Te Poel, Y., Du Bois-Reymond, M., Ravesloot, J. and Meulman, J. (2000) 'The role of parents and peers in the leisure activities of young adolescents', *Journal of Leisure Research*, 32: 281–301.

# 30

# Young adults and the night-time economy

*Robert G. Hollands*

## Introduction: understanding urban nightscapes

Economic and political restructuring over the past three decades has wrought many changes on the cities we live, work and play in. One part of this restructuring has been the development of a new urban brand which has reshaped many parts of city landscapes into corporate entertainment, nightlife and leisure hubs (Hannigan 1998; Gottdiener 2001), much of which is characterized by the ritual descent of young adults into city-centre bars, pubs and clubs especially during the weekend (Hollands 1995; Chatterton and Hollands 2001; Hobbs *et al.* 2003; Hatfield 2006). Visiting pubs, bars and clubs, has become an integral part of many young people's consumption lives today, with 80 per cent of the 15–24 year-old group visiting pubs and clubs in the UK (Mintel 2000: 15). This chapter analyses young adults' changing experiences of a 'night out' in the UK context (drawing primarily on three cities, Leeds, Bristol and Newcastle), and is concerned with the production, regulation and consumption of the 'night-time economy' (or 'urban nightscapes', see Chatterton and Hollands 2003).

To help unravel the relationship between youth and the night-time economy, this chapter draws upon two levels of analysis. First, such urban nightscapes can be understood through an integrated circuit of culture comprising processes of production, regulation and consumption. In this sense, while nightlife venues are clearly commercially manufactured by a range of multinational, national, regional and local operators, and regulated by various legislative frameworks and formal and informal surveillance mechanisms such as bouncers, CCTV, and pricing policies, there is also a lived consumer experience and the role young adults play in shaping such spaces. Second, urban nightscapes can be understood as a mixture of mainstream, residual and alternative nightlife spaces. Owned largely by international corporate players, mainstream nightlife is characterized by the well recognized commercially branded and themed premises found in all UK cities which cater to much of the hedonistic rituals one normally associates with a night out (ibid.). Residual, community spaces such as traditional pubs, ale houses and saloons, which were a significant feature of industrial cities, have been left to decline or have been eroded, due to the changing priorities of nightlife operators and consumer tastes. Finally, there are a range of independently run and alternative nightlife spaces which cater for more specific youth cultures, identities and tastes, some of which are self-organized, such as free parties, unofficial raves and squatted social centres (Chatterton 2002).

Clearly, such consumption spaces and their youth audiences are somewhat fluid and do at times overlap. However, the argument being made here is that, increasingly, urban nightlife has become dominated by mainstream production, through greater corporate control and concentration of ownership via processes of branding and theming (Klein 2000); mainstream regulation, through practices which increasingly aid capital accumulation and urban image-building (Harvey 1989); and mainstream consumption, through the adoption of new forms of segmented nightlife activity driven simultaneously by standardized, homogenous and commercialized provision and the impact of gentrification and the adoption of 'up-market' lifestyle identities amongst groups of young adults (Hollands 2002). Hence, although many city centres have achieved a 'cool' nightlife status and reputation, they have done so ironically by becoming more alike in terms of ownership, while also becoming more unequal and socially segmented consumption arenas, each with their own set of codes, dress styles, language and tastes (Chatterton and Hollands 2003). While young adults clearly do have an 'agency' role here, it is important to stress, borrowing rather liberally from Marx, that they 'make their own nightlife, but not under conditions of their own choosing'. Below we detail the domination of mainstream nightlife spaces over residual spaces, and some of the struggles by young people for alternative forms of nightlife provision.

## Mainstream, residual and alternative nighlife

Primary among the segmented spaces of the city at night is one that we have labelled the 'mainstream'. The mainstream proves difficult to define, partly because it often functions as 'the other', and partly because of its complex make-up (Thornton 1995). However, it is important to stress the enduring elements of the mainstream, In general terms, it includes the well-recognized weekend commercial provision of chain and theme pubs and traditional nightclubs which are characterized by smart attire, chart music, commercial circuit drinking, pleasure-seeking and hedonistic behaviour. Venues here range from large, somewhat tacky (what many refer to as 'cheesy') established nightclubs, theme and chain super-pubs, as well as more up-market and gentrified café and style bars, most of which are owned by multinational entities (around two-thirds of all nightlife premises in Leeds, Bristol and Newcastle are owned by international/national companies – see Chatterton and Hollands 2003).

Because the mainstream is such a large social space, it is inhabited differentially by a plethora of youth groups from across the middle-ground social spectrum including the young and aspiring working class, students, and a range of middle-class young professionals seeking more sanitized and gentrified styles (Hollands 2002). Differentiation is constructed around both labour market position and various taste communities based upon style, music, fashion and argot, and as fashion boundaries constantly shift, youth groupings within the mainstream compete for new positions and constantly seek out new spaces to re-differentiate themselves. In this regard, one of the main transformations within the mainstream is a clear attempt by commercial operators to introduce more gentrified environments (Chatterton and Hollands 2001), not least because they are seen as less trouble to regulate. For example, many of the new style bars have attempted to create an up-market feel with polished floors, minimalist or branded décor and a greater selection of designer drinks. Such new venues are perceived and experienced by young adults as more 'cosmopolitan'. As one of the female interviewees Sarah (aged 21) exclaimed in relation to them, 'there's just a better class of people' while another young women (Clare, aged 25) summed up the link between her identity and the style venues she frequented, with the simple comment: 'I'm a cocktail person.'

Gentrification, both in terms of displacing older users and upgrading the expectations of others, then, is a developing trend within mainstream nightlife and it is closely tied up with the middle classes as *driving* forward particular forms of downtown leisure and usurping older, established social spaces often linked to the industrial city. This perceived 'cosmopolitanization' has also been driven by the increased presence of young women within nightlife and the overlap between mainstream and gay cultures. One young woman, Rachel (19 years old), representing this shift with this comment: 'I'm a regular everywhere … I go to all the clubs so there really isn't anywhere that I wouldn't really not go.' While many night spaces remain heavily gendered and 'sexed' (Hollands 1995), the gentrification process has provided new opportunities for professional young women and gays to engage in the new seemingly diverse night-time economy (Chatterton and Hollands 2003).

The gentrifying mainstream has also attracted elements of the wealthier end of the student market and an increasingly older, more mature and upwardly mobile section of the local working-class population, who clearly view such places as sites to express their perceived mobility and status. Part of the explanation for the trend towards a more 'exclusive' mainstream can be found in theorizations about 'subcultural capital', within youth cultures (Thornton 1995). Understanding nightlife cultures as 'taste cultures' partly explains how hierarchies of style evolve and constantly change. Differences between youth groupings and cultures fuel a never-ending and tail-chasing game of 'cool-hunting' (Klein 2000).

However, while mainstream nightlife attempts to meet the style aspirations of white collar workers (including young professionals, graduates and service employees), ironically it also works to produce a rather predictable and serially-reproduced environment. Contrary to the postmodern consumer, many young professionals display conventional nightlife preferences rather than chasing the latest nightlife trends. In Wynne and O'Connor's (1998) study of middle-class city-centre livers in Manchester, they found that this affluent, mobile and largely childless group was not particularly exploratory in terms of cultural practices and represented a large 'open middle' of consumer taste. Much of this lack of experimentation reflects wider personal insecurities and a retreat to the familiar, in what is regarded by many as an increasingly complex and dangerous world. As one consumer we interviewed told us: 'I think I'm quite wary of going off the main track' (Charles, 22 years old). Self-exclusion from environments which consumers have little knowledge of is also a key element in the maintenance of segregated nightlife spaces. Such consumers are often unaware of other opportunities outside the growing mainstream. Hannigan (1998: 70) comments that to reduce the concerns of the middle classes over the safety of downtown areas, consumption experiences have become more sanitized and programmed. Increasingly, by regulating access, branding and rationalizing product sales and controlling movement through design of interiors, music and furniture, urban playscapes reflect the dystopic, standardized world of 'McDonaldization'.

Smith (1996), in his work on the gentrified city, suggests that upmarket developments represent a business and middle-class backlash against the urban working-class population. In light of this dominance of the mainstream, and more specifically the growth of up-market style bars, the fate of more 'residual' forms of urban night-life consumption has been one of rapid decline in many urban centres. These spaces are inhabited, or perceived to be occupied at least, predominantly by the young urban poor – the unemployed, welfare dependent and criminalized, which represent the other city of dirt, poverty, dereliction, violence and crime, in contrast to the stylish gentrifying mainstream (MacDonald and Marsh 2005). More connected to the city's industrial past, residual spaces are now surplus to requirements in the newly emerging post-industrial corporate landscape, replete with its themed fantasy world and expanding consumer power. Many groups, such as the young unemployed, homeless, poor and certain ethnic groups, are excluded, segregated, incorporated, policed and in some cases literally 'swept off the streets' (Chatterton and Hollands 2003), or are ostracized and labelled as members of the 'consuming underclass' as an interviewee, described them:

> Nasty, horrible creatures of society, who crawl out from under their stone on Thursday 'cos it's dole day. They put on the same frock every week 'cos they don't wanna buy a new one until they get too fat. Mainly seen wearing the PVC skirts and boob tubes, which are too tight, sort of sagging and not nice.
>
> (Mark, 22 years old)

Finally, a small number of young adults were less sanguine about the new outward stylization of much mainstream nightlife. Increasing corporate control of the style revolution means that for some young consumers, it is all style and no substance. The degree to which this stylization represents choice, or a 'real' step up the social mobility ladder, is highly debatable for some young people. As one interviewee stated (Colin, 25 years old): 'People want to belong to that elite crowd, but what people do not realize is that it is actually McDonald's with a marble bar.' A disenchantment with what is on offer in the labour market and mainstream nightlife has led many young people into forms of active resistance and the search for alternatives. While many alternative spaces are simply more bohemian versions of mainstream culture others openly identify themselves as actively oppositional against the mainstream (Chatterton 2002).

'Alternative' nightlife spaces, usually independently owned or managed, in the form of unique single-site music, club and bar venues, as well as less legal elements, such as one-off squats and/or house or free parties, form the basis of more localized night-life production-consumption clusters. Such places exist to meet the needs of particular youth identity groups, and styles here can be quite specific and related to certain genres of music, dance cultures, clothing styles and ethnicity (such as Goths, post-punk, grunge, indie, hip hop, garage, nu-metal, etc.) (Bennett 2000). Because they are less likely to be corporately owned, such places are typically found on the margins of city centres and consumption here is usually related to a conscious identity, style or lifestyle, and musical appreciation, rather than a passing consumer whim and it can sometimes combine arts, culture, performance and politics. Marginal spaces are often distinguished by an anti-aesthetic, setting them apart from the respectable, fashionable mainstream. Forms of regulation are also different. As one interviewee (Daryl, age 23) exclaimed about the free party scene:

> It's very, very different in the free parties. It's very anarchic, chaotic, messy, hazy. You don't have to worry about security ... This is all about de-regulation, you don't have to ask anybody for permission to do anything. There's a vibe there you won't get in a club.

The important point is that within such sites there is more of a blurring of the division between producers and consumers, through the exchange of music, shared ideas and values, business deals and networks of trust and reciprocity. At more underground sites such as illegal warehouse parties or squats, the line between production and consumption is literally indistinguishable (Chatterton 2002). At such sites the more fleeting and loose forms of tribal sociation, as suggested by writers like Bennett (2000) are identifiable. However, minority lifestyles do not negate the idea that social and spatial divisions, inequalities and hierarchies, continue to exist within urban nightlife. Urban youth nightlife cultures rather remain segmented around a dominant mainstream, with its various sub-divisions, and diminishing opportunities for alternative and residual experiences.

## Conclusion: youth, nighlife and the politics of 'going out'

While 'going out' is more likely to be experienced as 'fun' and as a non-serious form of leisure by young adults themselves, or viewed by society within the context of a 'social problem' discourse (related to binge drinking or violence), our analyses have demonstrated that the relationship between youth and nightlife has a more serious and political side to it. The structuring of nightlife infrastructure by corporate capital in terms of providing predictable forms of entertainment and producing particular leisure divisions, clearly influences and contours young people's experiences. On the other hand, nightlife experiences contain elements of agency and transgression. Young people then play an ambivalent role in nightlife both as avid consumers and as voracious cultural critics.

Engaging in nightlife activities continues to be both a popular leisure past-time for most young adults and forms an important marker of their identity (Hollands 1995; Chatterton and Hollands 2003). The popularity of predictable mainstream experiences remains and it is not that difficult to see why. A cursory glance might suggest that the growth of themed and branded nightlife venues seems to provide a greater variety of exciting places for young adults to consume. Yet our research reveals that underneath this glittering exterior is a growing concentration of ownership in the nightlife sector which results a lack of real consumer choice and diversity, which both blunts youth cultural creativity, and helps to create social and spatial segregation in cities.

Despite this, the night continues to be characterized by transgressive aspects, alternative spaces and resistant practices, even if this is a minority youth practice. Some of this dis-illusionment is symbolized through a 'brand backlash' (Klein 2000), exemplified through oppositional and alternative urban youth cultures such as the squatters movement, DIY culture and elements of the unofficial rave scene, as well as by more independent clusters of nightlife producers (McKay 1998; Corr 1999). Despite their fragility and limitations, these alternative cultures of the night function as important sources of creativity for young adults and provide opportunities for experimentation and transgression. They also represent the importance of the 'use' rather than the 'exchange' value of the city. The margins halt the drift towards passivity – the tendency for market forces and vested interests to encourage us to consume rather than create. As such, these alternative urban movements need to be encouraged and nurtured, involving young adults as active contributors to nightlife culture, rather than as passive consumers. Only then can nightlife cultures be built which counter-balance the seductiveness of corporate glam and the so-called entrepreneurial city, and instead serve the creative interests of young people rather than just the profits of the corporate nightlife machine.

# References

Bennett, A. (2000) *Popular Music and Youth Culture: Music, Identity and Place*, Basingstoke: Macmillan.

Chatterton, P. (2002) '"Squatting is still legal, necessary and free": a brief intervention in the corporate city', *Antipode*, 34: 1–7.

Chatterton, P. and Hollands, R. (2001) *Changing Our Toon: Youth, Nightlife and Urban Change in Newcastle*, Newcastle: Newcastle University Press.

—— (2003) *Urban Nightscapes: Youth Cultures, Pleasure Spaces and Corporate Power*, London: Routledge.

Corr, A. (1999) *No Trespassing: Squatting, Rent Strikes, and Land Struggles Worldwide*, San Francisco. South End Press.

Gottdiener, M. (2001) *The Theming of America: American Dreams, Media Fantasies and Themed Environments*, 2nd edn, Boulder, CO: Westview Press.

Hannigan, J. (1998) *Fantasy City: Pleasure and Profit in the Postmodern Metropolis*, London: Routledge.

Hatfield, P. (2006) *Bar Wars: Contesting the Night in Contemporary British Cities*, Oxford: Oxford University Press.

Harvey, D. (1989) 'From managerialism to entrepreneurialism: the transformation of urban governance in late capitalism', *Geografiska Annaler*, 71B: 3–17.

Hobbs, D., Hadfield,P., Lister, S. and Winlow, S. (2003) *Bouncers: Violence and Governance in the Night Time Economy*, Oxford: Oxford University Press.

Hollands, R. (1995) *Friday Night, Saturday Night: Youth Identification in the Post-industrial City*, Newcastle: Department of Sociology, University of Newcastle-upon-Tyne.

—— (2002) 'Division in the dark: youth cultures, transitions and segmented consumption spaces in the night-time economy', *Journal of Youth Studies*, 5: 153–73.

Klein, N. (2000) *No Logo*, London: Flamingo.

MacDonald, R. and Marsh, J. (2005) *Disconnected Youth*, London: Routledge.

Malbon, B. (1999) *Clubbing: Dancing, Ecstasy and Vitality*, London: Routledge.

McKay, G. (1998) *DIY Culture: Party and Protest in 90s Britain*, London: Verso.

Mintel (2000) 'Pre-family leisure trends', *Leisure Intelligence*, January.

Smith, N. (1996) *The New Urban Frontier: Gentrification and the Revanchist City*, London: Routledge.

Thornton, S. (1995) *Club Cultures: Music, Media and Subcultural Capital*, Cambridge: Polity Press.

Wynne, D. and O'Connor, J. (1998) 'Consumption and the postmodern city', *Urban Studies*, 35: 841–64.

31

# Young people and consumption

*Amy L. Best*

## Introduction

Contemporary youth and youth culture can hardly be understood without corresponding attention to the practices of consumption. For many youth, participating in the consumer realm is a defining feature of being young. The symbolic worlds of youth are enmeshed with the currents of a commodity culture such that youth speak a lingo that is steeped with the jargon of the market. Their references, jokes, and modes of address reflect their fluency in the language of the commodity market, its bewildering hold over them, and their ability to rework that language in ways that speak as much to their realities outside the market as to those inside it. Yet, the meaning of youth consumption has changed considerably as distinct patterns reflecting new configurations of time and space evolve. The explosion of the internet and our movement into a digital age as 'citizen consumers', the rise of conspicuous spending and a torrent of advertising, the emergence of segmented marketing as an alternative to mass marketing, the expansion of global markets, the proliferation of global and corporate mediascapes, the international consolidation of corporate power into mega-conglomerates, demands for external regulation by consumer advocacy groups in developed countries, and push back from the DIY (do-it-yourself), anti-globalization, and environmental movements all come to bear upon the distinct historical relationship between young people and consumption. Youths' consumer lives are further complicated by an ever-changing multi-ethnic and multicultural world marked by shifting borders and flow of movement, the ascendance of a racialized system through which meanings and symbols of cool are adjudicated in the commercial realm, a third wave of feminism with its easily commercialized symbols, and deepening social and economic inequalities.

The role of the consumer market in young people's lives has sparked much public and scholarly debate. Debates over the perils of excess consumption by young people, for example, has been the subject of much concern by educators, parents, policy-makers, and scholars, reflecting anxieties about the shifting place of young people in a rapidly changing cultural landscape. Youths' participation in the realm of consumption in the past century has generated much worry about their appropriate place in society, their sexuality, their unmediated access to adult forms of cultural knowledge, their self-esteem, and even their likelihood toward delinquency, though far less often calling into question their roles in supporting consumer capitalism itself. This concern, of course has taken various forms as the logic of rationalization and consumerism reorganize cultural fields thought to be impenetrable by market and commercial influence. A most recent version might perhaps be recognized in the global McDonaldization thesis (see Ritzer 2005) wherein a new form of cultural imperialism is thought to loom large, threatening local and indigenous culture as it forcefully advances a program of cultural standardization and homogenization as commercial forms of Western youth culture from MTV to *Beverly Hills 90210* are transmitted along global mediascapes, seeping into and colonizing the consciousness of entire generations as they embed themselves in the crevices of everyday life-worlds far removed from Hollywood and the cult of American celebrity.

From focused investigations of the formation and expansion of youth markets (Cook 2004), to how youth consume and are consumed (Steinberg and Kincheloe 1997), to the meanings young adults assign to their consumption as they struggle to participate in mainstream society (Best 2006) and alternately etch out in-group boundaries of sub-cultural scenes in opposition to the mainstream (Thornton 1995), youth scholars from different disciplines have sought to map the complex and contradictory coordinates connecting youth, commodities, consumption, and the market. Indeed, youth itself carries a symbolic value marketed to an ever-widening audience. An implicit assumption directing this rich and largely interdisciplinary body of scholarship is that to understand youth as a distinct stage in the life course and as a social, economic, and political category of identity and experience is to also investigate the emergence and expansion of a commodity culture. Most agree youth consumption is not simply an economic activity but deeply symbolic in its organization. While scholars have moved in various directions, I identify here three distinct narrative schema of youth and consumption: (1) the formation of youth markets and their expansion into a variety of social arenas; (2) youths' use of the market and its resources toward various ends; and (3) the meaning and consequence of youth consumption in late modernity and the rise of 'lifestyle choice' as the basis of identity and group membership. Each program has proceeded with varying attention to: (1) consumer capitalism's global expansion; and (2) how fields of consumption are consequential sites for the reproduction of social inequalities and social distinctions. In this sense the latter do not represent entirely distinct trajectories but have largely been taken up within and through the three narrative schema I identify.

## The formation and expansion of youth markets

Youth markets have grown considerably as marketers have aggressively pursued youth for more than a century, transforming their activities, identities, and social relations. Though a burgeoning market awareness of youth as consumers in the USA, for example, can be traced to the early 1870s, as the popularity of trading cards spread among an emerging middle class, most scholars agree juvenile markets exploded within the context of post-World War II America, a period of increasing economic prosperity and a dramatic expansion of the middle classes, and then later taking hold in the UK and the western portion of the European continent. Marketers were quick to capitalize on the changing economic and social reality of childhood and adolescence in North America and Western Europe, helping to catalyze swift changes in the leisure activities of young adults, the spaces they occupied, the activities in which they engaged, and the selves they imagined. As historian Grace Palladino (1996) has demonstrated, the category 'teen' itself was an invention of the American market, just as are more recent age-based categories; consider, for instance, the term 'tweens'. Feminist historians have shown how advertisers actively courted girls to establish brand loyalty, exploiting girls' concerns about popularity and appearance, drawing them into a world celebrating a conventional femininity centered on heterosexual romance, beauty, and the body. Over the second half of the twentieth century entire markets developed around the idea of distinct commodities for the teenage girl; make-up, clothes, music were promised to ensure a particular kind of teen experience for girls, one marked by success in school, in love and in life. By the end of the 1950s, girls' lives in large portions of the Western world played out within the trenches of a commodity culture.

Most youth historians agree that a confluence of forces conspired to cement young people's ties to a consumer market. In the US context, the growing freedom and independence of youth from family life that followed urban and industrial expansion, increasing school attendance and entrance into the labor force together played a role in shaping a band of youthful consumers.

Drawn into the folds of an ever-expanding culture of consumption shaped by the unrelenting drive for profit by consumer corporations, young folks today are immersed in a dizzying world of beepers and cell phones, cars, CDs, MP3 players, DVDs as they move across various cultural fields from school to home and in and out of a variety of leisure spaces (e.g., the arcade, internet coffee shops, the mall). As one example among many, today's American girl represents an estimated $9 billion cosmetic market. Of course, teens are not alone is this consumer world. As childhood scholars have demonstrated, the pre-adolescent is also assailed by a veritable windfall of messages intended to promote consumption of an endless array of consumer goods from bubble gum to Beanie Babies, McDonald's Happy Meals to Groovy Girls (Steinberg and Kincheloe 1997). Barbie, primarily marketed to younger girls and reigning as one of the most popular toys worldwide, has been the subject of much scholarly investigation. Tracing Barbie's cultural importance, feminist scholars have shown how Barbie operates under a veil of Imperial whiteness, promotes a narrow construction of the feminine body, and actively normalizes hyper-consumption (Chin 2001).

For decades, youth (teens especially) were thought to be big consumers of small ticket items: gum, hair accessories, lip gloss, CDs, comics, blue jeans, and so forth. This is hardly the case today as electronic, digital, and auto markets actively pursue youth. Young adults in North America and Western Europe have considerable disposable income relative to other generations before them. In the USA, the under-20 set are recognized by marketing insiders and scholars alike as the dominant marketing force surpassing their parents, the baby boomers, the original band of American youth consumers, in their ability to shape the direction of popular culture and consumer trends.

Naomi Klein (2002) points to categorical differences in how youth are targeted by marketers today in comparison to those of other generations, owing to categorical differences between the consumer world young people today occupy and a former social world where the commodity form was less ubiquitous. Young people today are becoming adults in the age of competitive advertising and accelerated meaning where the image matters more than the product, in a new branded world of hyper-marketing where segmented marketing has prevailed over mass marketing, endless corporate sponsorships and partnerships that are thought to have eroded the public sphere and civil

257

society and created a crisis of democracy. Indeed, one of the enduring features of the market that makes it so resilient is its adaptability as it relentlessly commodifies cultural forms, either folding them into already existing markets or carving out new ones.

Few spaces today occupied by youth exist beyond the sway of a consumer market. Even public schools, once thought to be beyond the reach of the market, have failed to avoid the pernicious influence of commodity relations as public resources for education recede and multinational corporations provide funding to schools, furnishing them with curricular materials, computers, electronic blackboards and other new media (consider Channel One), backboards, scoreboards and astro-turf most usually emblazoned with company logo. The high school prom is one example of a school scene among many that tie youth to cultural industries by harnessing their pleasure in consumption (Best 2000). Though it was an event that once played out in large part within the confines of a school's gym, it now involves 16-seater limousines, expensive dresses, luxury hotels, and rental accommodation for long weekends at the beach for many American students.

The success of advertising to youth, a number of scholars have argued, stems from its ability to align consumption with particular social meanings that resonate with young people. Many scholars have demonstrated how marketers have linked consumption with personal empowerment, freedom, and liberation. This is well illustrated in the phrase 'girl power', which originated with the London-based pop music group, Spice Girls, inspiring groups of girls to exercise their right to consume. While many have remarked that 'girl power' celebrates a form of feminist individualism more compatible with consumption than anything else, paradoxically young people have gained power through their participation in the commercial world (Harris 2004). Youth studies over the past 30 years have made visible the new areas of expertise and cultural authority youth have gained as consumers (McRobbie 1991). It is to these issues I now turn.

## Youths' uses of the market: resources of meaning and style

Markets play an ever-expanding role in the lives of youth, organizing their social spaces and social activities, as they forcefully attach themselves to signs that already register as repositories for youth culture and style, yet top-down approaches to understanding youth consumption have often overlooked the agentic possibilities in the consumer realm and the expressive promise of consumer choice seized by youth as they move in and around the market. Fueled by a moral protectionism that seems to rest on the enduring notion of youth as purity symbols, thought to be especially vulnerable to the polluting influence of a crass consumer culture, youth are often cast as passive consumers. It is perhaps not surprising, then, that such approaches have generated some critique for the over-determined relationship between the market and the formation of youth and youth culture they have assumed. Echoing the logic of the Frankfurt School which posited a determining capitalism whereby consumers were largely characterized as 'cultural dupes', fulfilling false needs as they blindly consumed, interiorizing wholesale the values and ideologies of the dominant culture through consumption, little room was left to theorize the various ways in which youths' consumer lives are differently negotiated (McRobbie 1991).

Hardly unidirectional, youths' consumer lives have proven to be anything but simple. The expansion of global markets, for instance, which has occurred at an accelerating pace in the past two decades has exercised tremendous influence over the formation of distinct youth cultures in settings where youth were rarely seen as a group apart from adults. As markets have opened, allowing for a seemingly infinite cross-flow of images, objects, money, bodies, and ideas along and over ever-shifting national borders and cultural-scapes, consumption has become a central means through which young people constitute themselves as having membership in distinct youth cultures and thus distinguish them-selves not only from other age-based groups but also from each other (Thornton 1995). For example, second generation American youth of the Indian diaspora combine tradi-tional forms of Bhangra dance with the sampling elements of American hip-hop to forge a distinct club culture and construct race and gender identities as they negotiate a highly commercial American youth culture, on the one hand, and the nostalgic constructions of an India frozen in time by the parent culture, (this despite rapid economic and social changes to India itself) on the other (Maira 2002).

Youth identity, youth experience, and youth culture are produced out of the resources offered by cultural industries but not determined by them. Youth use the objects offered by a consumer market toward their own ends: to construct identities, to express in-group solidarity, to define themselves apart from parents and others. Indeed, youths' struggles for freedom and independence often take shape within a consumer realm. Joan Jacobs Brumberg (1997) shows how the arrival of mass-produced clothing in the 1920s enabled girls to move out from under the yolk of maternal control since mothers no longer made their dresses, for example. This is because the meanings of cultural objects offered by the market are ascribed through production processes *and* consumption practices; in the words of Stuart Hall, meanings are 'encoded' in the production process but then 'decoded' as they are consumed, sometimes producing alternate readings than those intended.

The focus on the creative means by which youth used objects and forms available through the mass market to respond to a set of social and economic conditions that stunted mobility and constrained life trajectories is arguably the legacy of Birmingham's Centre for Contemporary Cultural Studies (CCCS) and its abiding interest in class and rituals of class resistance. Responding in large part to the Frankfurt School, CCCS scholars in the 1970s and 1980s sought to map the relationship between marginalized youths' structural location and the subcultural style through which oppositional youth cultures were formed (Hebdige 1979). Blending ethnography and semiotics to reveal the contested nature of youth engagement with the commodity form, much scholarly attention was given to young folks' use of resources provided by a consumer market to etch sub-cultural boundaries in particular. Dick Hebdige's (1979) seminal study of the Mods who used discarded market goods (e.g., clothes, record, clubs, hairstyles) as identity markers to craft an alternative youth culture against other youth cultures belonging to the mainstream serves as an important example. Investigation of the practices and spaces that constitute youth sub-cultural fields made visible the blurred boundaries that were once thought to distinguish production and consumption and our lives as producers and consumers. This point was well captured by Sarah Thornton (1995) as she demonstrated how youth develop types of sub-cultural capital to invoke distinct symbolic boundaries to distinguish the hip from the tragically un-hip mainstream within club culture. The consequence of such a shift was much greater attention to youth not simply as cultural consumers, but as cultural producers as scholars continued to map the increasingly complex relationship between youth and the consumer realm.

While much of the research on the formation of oppositional youth cultures has focused primarily on the rituals of resistance formed through consumption, a much smaller group of scholars have focused on the ways in which collective forms of *transformative* social action developed from youths' opposition to the consumer realm (Klein 2002). Musical and (maga)zine-based movements, most notable Riot Grrrls, have served as important conduits for girls to resist commodification, forge an alternative gender and sexual order and to articulate a feminist political agenda and a critical politics of consumption. Cultural jammers, young activists who protest the corporate control of everyday life, have been successful in disrupting the flow of information to the people, and provide another example.

Finally, youth studies that attempt to address questions relating to youth agency and the consumer market have also highlighted the importance of understanding the material contexts of consumption, arguing youths' investment in cultural forms are profoundly situational (Harris 2004). US feminist scholars showed us that while girls are consummate consumers of various media, spending countless hours watching television on the WB and UPN and music videos on MTV, listening to CDs of rappers Missy 'Misdemeanor' Elliot and Lil' Kim, reading magazines like *Cosmo Girl*, *Seventeen*, and the more recent *Teen Vogue* and *Teen People*, it is the social meanings they generate as they consume that are important to understand. British scholar Angela McRobbie (1991) demonstrated that teenyboppers (who are by default girls) consumed images of teen idols, courting them in the private space of their bedrooms. Their popular consumption of teen musical pop icons served as a way for young girls to work through romantic narratives in a setting with little risk of public condemnation, where the negotiation of feminine sexuality was a little less slippery since girls were unlikely to have much of an audience. Elizabeth Chin's (2001) investigation of poor, urban Black children's consumer lives and the public and private spaces wherein these lives unfold detailed how material context patterns relations of consumption where scarcity, unbridled fantasy, and desire bump up against each other, serving to both reveal and reproduce stark inequities that persistent racial segregation, de-industrialization, and urban renewal generate, serves as another example.

## Youth consumption in late modernity: the rise of lifestyle choice

A more recent direction among scholars has involved situating youths' consumer lives in the context of late modernity (Furlong and Cartmel 1997; McDonald 1999; Bennett 2003; Best, 2006). Youth consumption occurs within a changing social landscape, a post-traditional order where traditional moorings have been transformed by globalization, the acceleration of production and consumption in late capitalism, the hypermobility of communication systems and increasingly sophisticated media, where new forms of self-hood and social experiences have arisen, tied less to traditional organizations and institutions and increasingly to 'lifestyle choices' expressed through youths' consumption of cultural objects available in a commodity culture (Bennett 2003). In late modernity it is argued that status systems have become less fixed and tradition has receded as a guide for social action. In this context, identities can no longer be taken for granted, but are regarded as projects, things we must construct on our own (Slater, 1997; Bauman 2000). As Zygmunt Bauman has observed, 'needing to *become* what one *is* is a feature of modern living' (2000: 31). Linking these transformations of the self to a consumer culture, Don Slater writes,

> Modernity dismantles a stable social order which provides fixed values and identities ... the individual's boundaries, sources of meaning, social relations and needs

become blurred and uncertain. This is the context of consumer culture: it floods modernity with a torrent of values, meanings, selves and others, both filling in the cultural deficits of the modern world and constantly intensifying and exploiting them.

(1997: 99)

Youth live in a world increasingly structured by consumption where the social roles, norms, and institutions that had once anchored individual and collective identities (many social roles are less appealing than they once were) have given way to alternative forms of social existence arranged in terms of the 'individual as consumer', where competing ways of life lead to a proliferation of lifestyle choices (Slater 1997; Bauman 2000; Bennett 2003).

Advanced capitalism is seen here as having subverted the grand narratives that have traditionally directed the life course and this has direct relevance for young adults and their consumer lives. The certainty that one will marry, have children, buy a home, hold down a stable and permanent job belongs to a different era than the one in which today's youth are becoming adults. The erosion of this master narrative explains in part the turn to the consumer market as a field where meaning is created. Elsewhere, I have argued (Best 2006) that this can be seen through the relationship youth develop to cars, and the meanings they ascribe to them as vehicles of horizontal and vertical mobility, visibility, and freedom. Amid a rapidly changing world where traditional anchors of social existence have eroded, it is as consumers that young people claim and affirm membership in the larger community, helping to drive an ever-expanding consumer market. It is as consumers that they come to see themselves as individuals and it is also as consumers that they struggle to realize the cherished but elusive values of freedom and independence. Youth are increasingly drawn into the consumer market and into a culture of spending to forge their identities as individuals as much as to gain membership in specific groups. Their consumption of cultural forms and cultural experiences are much about being individuals, distinguishing oneself *from* the group as they are about keeping up *with* the group as so aptly captured in the edgy 'Drivers Wanted' advertising campaign launched by Volkswagen of America, 'On the road of life there are passengers and drivers'.

Yet, the endless possibility to reinvent identities, express group membership, tastes and aesthetic dispositions, and lifestyle choices through consumer practices is not without contradiction as what young adults desire slips away as they become entrenched in a culture of consumption. The basis of their individuality and group membership is increasingly dependent on what they consume and the means by which they find their place in the world inseparable from the market place. As a youth culture of spending intensifies in what a number of scholars regard as the new consumerism, marked by an upscaling of lifestyle norms, and the widening cleavage between the 'haves' and the 'have nots', many young adults, even before they are done with school, are locked into the cycle of work and spend (Schor 2000), the ground on which they move into the future increasingly shaky.

To study youth and consumerism, then, is to study material life and the maps of meaning upon which it relies. As youth continue to struggle to claim physical and rhetorical spaces against their relegation to the overflow of non-places (shopping malls come to mind) that pepper the contemporary modern landscape, to engage the market and its resources and to imagine lives outside it, attention must be paid to the complex and ever-changing webs of influence spun by a society increasingly structured around consumption if we are to understand youth at all, the lives they live, the selves they construct, and the meanings they generate.

# References

Bauman, Z. (2000) *Liquid Modernity*, New York: Polity.

Bennett, A. (2003) 'Subcultures or neo-tribes? Rethinking the relationship between youth, style and musical taste', in D. B. Clarke, M. Doel and K. L. Housiaux (eds) *The Consumption Reader*, London: Routledge.

Best, A. L. (2000) *Prom Night: Youth, Schools and Popular Culture*, New York: Routledge.

—— (2006) *Fast Cars, Cool Rides: The Accelerating World of Youth and Their Cars*, New York: NYU Press.

Brumberg, J. J. (1997) *The Body Project: An Intimate History of American Girls*, New York: Random House.

Chin, E. (2001) *Purchasing Power: Black Kids and American Consumer Culture*, Minneapolis: University of Minnesota Press.

Cook, D. (2004) *The Commodification of Childhood: The Children's Clothing Industry and the Rise of the Child Consumer*, Durham, NC: Duke University Press.

Furlong, A. and Cartmel, F. (1997) *Young People and Social Change: Individualization and Risk in Late Modernity*, Philadelphia, PA: Open University Press.

Harris, A. (2004) *Future Girl: Young Women in the Twenty-first Century*, New York: Routledge.

Hebdige, D. (1979) *Subculture: The Meaning of Style*, London: Routledge.

Klein, N. (2002) *No Logo*, New York: Picador.

Maira, S. M. (2002) *Desis in the House: Indian American Youth Culture in New York City*, Philadelphia, PA: Temple University Press.

McDonald, K. (1999) *Struggle for Subjectivity: Identity, Action and Youth Experience*, Cambridge: Cambridge University Press.

McRobbie, A. (1991) *Feminism and Youth Culture: From Jackie to Just Seventeen*, Boston: Unwin Hyman.

Palladino, G. (1996) *Teenagers: An American History*, New York: Basic Books.

Ritzer, G. (2005) *Enchanting a Disenchanting World: Revolutionizing the Means of Consumption*, 2nd edn. Thousand Oaks, CA: Pine Forge Press.

Schor, J. (2000) 'Towards a new politics of consumption', in J. B. Schor and D. B. Holt (eds) *The Consumer Society Reader*, New York: New York University Press.

Slater, D. (1997) *Consumer Culture and Modernity*, Oxford: Polity Press.

Steinberg, S. and Kincheloe, J. L. (eds) (1997) *Kinder-Culture: The Corporate Construction of Childhood*, Boulder, CO: Westview Press.

Thornton, S. (1995) *Club Cultures: Music, Media and Subcultural Capital*, Cambridge: Polity.

# 32

# Spectacular soundtracks

## Youth and music

*Andy Bennett*

## Introduction

This chapter considers the relationship between youth and music as this has been repre-sented and theorized since the 1950s. The first section of the chapter examines the socio-economic circumstances that gave rise to the mass production of popular music during the post-war era and its marketing as a 'youth' leisure form. The subsequent section considers the parent culture's response to popular music and its perceived impact on youth. This is followed by an examination of studies that interpret the significance of popular music for youth in terms of its cultural resonance with issues such as class strug-gle, economic inequality and racism. Attention then turns to a consideration of work which, influenced by postmodern theory and the cultural turn, has sought to position popular music's significance for youth not as a direct reflection of socio-economic experience but rather as a more fluid cultural resource through which young people are able to construct reflexive identities and lifestyle projects. The final section of the chapter considers the problem of defining the cultural relationship between 'youth' and music in the context of the early twenty-first century when the audiences for musics once termed 'youth musics' are increasingly multi-generational.

## Sign of the time: youth, music and social change

The cultural relationship between youth and popular music dates back to the mid-1950s. Following the Second World War, new mass production techniques and increasing affluence led to a consumer boom in the West. The teenager became a highly lucrative target for the new consumer industries who quickly established a range of fashion items, accessories, such as make-up and jewellery, and magazines primarily aimed at the youth market. In a parallel fashion, rock 'n' roll, a music derived from African-American rhythm and blues, rapidly gained popularity among youth due to its rawness and vitality while the visual image and vocal style of rock 'n' roll singers, from Elvis Presley onwards, proved an instant appeal for young audiences (Shumway 1992).

Since the 1950s, a succession of new genres has emerged, each giving rise to increasingly spectacular forms of youth cultural practice. During the mid-1960s, enhancements in recording studio technology created the experimental basis of psychedelic rock, the latter providing the backdrop for a new 'counter-cultural' youth movement that rejected the norms and values of the dominant parent culture (Bennett 2001). During the early 1970s, the counter-culture was supplanted by glam rock which challenged conventional notions of sexuality through the gender bending images of artists such as David Bowie (Hebdige 1979). Glam was followed by punk, a musical and stylistic commentary on both the pretentiousness of the hippie area and the rapid socio-economic decline of Britain and other western nations from the late 1970s onwards (Hebdige 1979). In the same era, reggae became 'a pan-Caribbean' music, reaching out through the work of artists such as Bob Marley to an African-diasporic youth dispersed around the globe (Gilroy 1993). During the 1980s, rap, originally an African-American street youth music, rapidly gained significance as a new global youth music combining politicized statements concerning racism and racial exclusion with new DJ and sampling techniques that allowed rap artists to drawn on existing musical texts combining them into new soundscapes (Rose 1994). The 1980s also saw the emergence of new electronic dance music forms such as house and techno. Initially part of an underground scene utilizing disused urban industrial buildings and rural greenfield sites, dance music quickly acquired a more mainstream status becoming an integral aspect of the urban night-time economy (Thornton 1995). Both rap and dance were heralded as more inclusive musical styles, appealing to multi-ethnic youth audiences and supplying a new aesthetic that owed little to the rock-dominated youth musics that had gone before. Nevertheless, guitar-based youth musics continued to thrive and in the early 1990s underwent a resurgence in the form of grunge, a punk-inspired style originating from the US city of Seattle and made globally popular through the work of groups such as Nirvana and Pearl Jam. Like punk, grunge became a soundtrack for socio-economically disaffected youth (Lovesey 2004). Guitar-based youth music also returned to popularity in the UK during this period with Britpop, a journalistic term that grouped together a loose affiliation of bands who cited British groups from the 1960s, such as the Beatles, the Kinks and the Small Faces as key influences. Although immensely popular, Britpop was criticized for its championing of a nostalgic representation of Britain as a 'white' nation – an image that glossed over contemporary Britain's multi-ethnic and multi-cultural composition (Cloonan 1997).

## Youth, music and moral panics

Since the emergence of rock 'n' roll, the response of the media and authorities to youth-based popular music styles has often been negative, resulting in various forms of censorship (Martin and Segrave 1993). Drawing on Becker's labelling theory, Cohen's (1987) instructive work on the media's coverage of clashes between mods and rockers in Southeast English coastal towns during the mid-1960s offers a model of deviance amplification beginning with the sensationalized media reporting of isolated, small-scale incidents of violence and dramatically escalating in response to aggressive policing strategies. Cohen's model was subsequently revisited and revised by Thornton (1995) in her work on the media's response to the British rave scene of the late 1980s. According to Thornton, in addition to creating a large-scale public moral panic, negative media reporting can serve to 'positively' reinforce a group's sense if itself as 'outsiders' and thus contribute to the process of constructing 'subcultural' identities. At the other end of the scale, a substantial amount of academic scholarship, often grounded in social-psychological perspectives, supports the more pathological interpretations of popular music's impact on youth pro- pagated by the media. A case in point is work by Epstein *et al.* (1990) that posits causative links between a preference among youth for musics such as heavy metal and rap and deviant/anti-social behaviour. In opposition to such work, sociologists have often sought to explain music's role in youth practices not as triggering deviant personalities but rather as creating spaces for the 'normalization' of extant forms of youth deviance, for example, the use of recreational drugs (Malbon 1999).

## Music and the rituals of youth

The theorization of youth and music was initially grounded in the work of the Birmingham Centre for Contemporary Cultural Studies (CCCS). The CCCS research focused pre- dominantly on youth style rather than music. Drawing on the ideas of Gramsci, the CCCS argued that particular post-war, style-based youth cultures could be interpreted as an expression of resistance to the hegemonic order of the dominant society (Hall and Jefferson 1976). Although the CCCS are typically associated with the study of white, male working-class youth cultures, notably teddy boys, skinheads and mods, their work also extends to the study of middle-class hippie youth, African-Caribbean youth and female, teenybopper culture (McRobbie and Garber 1976). Such a class-centred approach to the interpretation of youth style was, in turn, adopted by post-CCCS work on youth which centred more closely on music. For example, Willis's study of biker and hippie cultures argues that there is a strong homological resonance between the respec- tive class backgrounds and musical preferences of these youth cultural groups – the bikers preferring short, musically straightforward rock and roll songs, while the hippies' interest was in more musically complex, album-orientated progressive rock. Willis defines homology as 'the continuous play between the group and a particular item which pro- duces specific styles, meanings, contents and forms of consciousness' (1978: 191). A fur- ther CCCS-inspired reading of the cultural relationship between youth and music is seen in a study by Brake (1985) that endeavoured to illustrate that the essentially British-based analysis of the CCCS and post-CCCS work could be applied to other national contexts, notably the USA and Canada. The international-comparative aspect of Brake's work also provides a formative insight into the role played by local factors in the specific char- acteristics of youth cultures. In an early acknowledgement of the emerging hip hop culture, Brake suggests that the latter's centrally defining components – rap, graffiti and breakdance – became key resources through which working-class, inner-city, African- American youth were able to challenge their dispossessed, disenfranchised position in US society and begin to negotiate a new cultural space for themselves.

In the early 1990s, Weinstein (1991) took the class-based analysis of musical / stylistic preferences into new territory with her ground-breaking study of heavy metal, a genre that up until this time had been scarcely acknowledged in academic work despite its 25- year history. Revising the concept of subculture, to encompass the audience–performer interaction in the concert setting, Weinstein identified significant interactions between heavy metal performers and their audiences, the metal concert becoming the site for forms of subcultural ritual centred around male-bonding and camaraderie threaded through by a succession of subcultral anthems performed by the band. According to

265

Weinstein, for the predominantly white, male, blue-collar metal audience, their ritualistic practice in the context of the heavy metal concert both corresponds with and confirms their mundane, everyday practice characterized by skilled and unskilled manual work, male-dominated leisure patterns and patriarchal discourses underpinning working-class society.

## Postmodern musics, post-subcultural styles

During the 1980s, the emergence of rap and various new dance music styles dramatically altered the existing popular music soundscape, introducing new sounds that were not created using conventional rock and pop instruments but rather with record decks, samplers and various other pieces of digital electronic equipment. Such approaches to music making also facilitated the manipulation of existing recorded sounds in a way never before possible. The role of the DJ shifted dramatically. As Back (1996) observed, rap and dance music DJs became bricoleurs, taking existing fragments of sound and recombining them into new works. Acknowledging such sonic underpinnings, a number of observers claimed that it was representative of a new postmodern era characterized by an increasingly random ordering of images, sounds and styles from previous eras of music, fashion, and so on. In relation to the last point, Redhead (1990) suggested that within the dance music scene, the previous stylistic allegiances of youth culture could be seen to break down and were being replaced by a new, more individualistic 'post-subcultural' approach to stylistic appropriation. Such observations were to give rise to a new era, collectively referred to as post-subcultural studies, in the academic study of contemporary youth culture and its stylistic affiliations with music. Muggleton (2000) takes Redhead's concept of post-subcultural youth and combines it with elements of Weberian sociology and postmodern theory to construct a new youth cultural figure that he refers to as the 'post-subculturalist'. According to Muggleton, the musical and stylistic affiliations of the post-subculturalist cannot be mapped in relation to markers such as class, gender and ethnicity but rather reflect a new individualist sensibility in which image and taste form part of a reflexively derived lifestyle project. Significantly, however, for Muggleton, the stylistic and taste preferences of the post-subculturist are not the product of a radical postmodern effect. Rather, postmodernism has supplied the post-subculturalist with a creative licence to use his/her acquired knowledge and expertise of post-war youth cultural history and convention in a way that tastefully combines a pastiche of different youth cultural traits. In this sense, Muggleton's post-subculturalist can be seen to deploy a form of subcultural capital not dissimilar to that attributed to the 'serious' clubber in Thorton's (1995) work on dance music.

Relating the cultural fragmentation of youth style more squarely to developments in the musical soundscape of youth, Bennett (1999) argues that the eclecticism of contemporary dance music has played its own part in the breakdown of formerly more defined youth cultural affiliations and replaced these with a new individualized musical aesthetic. Drawing on the neo-tribal theory of Mafessoli (1996), Bennett argues that, in accordance with Mafessoli's definition of the neo-tribe as a more fluid and inherently fragile expression of social collectivity, so the dance music crowd is inherently temporal. For Bennett, the temporal bonds of the dance crowd resonate with the fragmented and ever shifting nature of dance music itself; moreover, the range of different dance music events – often featured in the same club setting – generate their own neo-tribal dynamic as individuals move between different crowds over the course of an evening or weekend. In a further Mafessolian-influenced study of dance music, Malbon (1999) similarly applied neo-tribal theory as means of positioning the dance music crowd as something removed from the more rigid subcultural affiliations identified among post-war youth throughout the 1960s and 1970s. For Malbon, however, rather than remaining fluid and shifting, the neo-tribal affiliations between clubbers slowly produce discourses of collectiveness which harden to produce their own conventions of inclusion and exclusion. Such discourses, however, are based more on taste, knowledge and commitment to the dance music scene rather than relating directly to issues of class, gender and ethnicity.

## Youth, music and ageing

As baby-boomers reflect back on the 40 years that have passed since the 'Summer of Love', a new series of debates are beginning in the study of youth and music. Many of those musics once described as youth musics now attract multi-generational audiences, as evidenced in the cliché that veteran rock groups such as the Who and the Rolling Stones now attract an audience ranging between the ages of 7 and 70. As such, the definition of youth and the continuing dominance of youth as an object of study in popular music studies is a contentious issue (Hesmondhalgh 2005). Other theorists suggest that youth now expresses a way of feeling rather than a way of being, something which is again placed in a context of popular music tastes which are no longer as staunchly dictated by age as they once were (Osgerby 2008). Focusing on the internal dynamics of multi-generational music scenes, some writers have suggested that age continues to play a major role with older 'scenesters' moving into background roles such as production and promotion (Andes 1998). Other observers go further than this, arguing that age becomes a palpable block to involvement in the scene, as ageing fans withdraw their interest and involvement altogether, except for occasionally listening to their old record collection or tuning into classic gold radio formats (Weinstein 2000).

Taking a different position, other work on multi-generational music scenes has examined the relationships underpinning such scenes. For example, in his study of the straight-edge scene, characterized by its collective eschewing of hedonistic behaviours – drugs, alcohol and sexual promiscuity – associated with a number of other music scenes, Haenfler (2006) suggests that older members of this scene assume a paternal role, overseeing the development of the scene and attempt to ensure that its original ethos is adhered to by younger members. Similarly, Bennett (forthcoming) considers the long-term impact of intense investment in a music scene on the lives of ageing fans. Applying Chaney's concept of lifestyle, Bennett argues that for many ageing fans, their continuing involvement in music cannot be attributed purely to nostalgia. Rather, suggests Bennett, the musical tastes and attendant identities acquired by ageing fans in their youth often continue to inform their lives in the present, impacting variously on issues such as image, health and well-being, career path, family life and political values.

## References

Andes, L. (1998) 'Growing up Punk: meaning and commitment careers in a contemporary youth subculture', in J. S. Epstein (ed.) *Youth Culture: Identity in a Postmodern World*, Oxford: Blackwell.

Back, L. (1996) *New Ethnicities and Urban Culture: Racisms and Multiculture in Young Lives*, London: UCL Press.

Bennett, A. (1999) 'Subcultures or neo-tribes?: Rethinking the relationship between youth, style and musical taste', *Sociology*, 33: 599–617.

—— (2001) *Cultures of Popular Music*, Buckingham: Open University Press.

—— (forthcoming) *Growing Old Disgracefully? Popular Music Fandom and Aging*, Hannover, NH: Wesleyan University Press.

Brake, M. (1985) *Comparative Youth Culture: The Sociology of Youth Cultures and Youth Subcultures in America, Britain and Canada*, London: Routledge and Kegan Paul.

Cohen, S. (1987) *Folk Devils and Moral Panics: The Creation of the Mods and Rockers*, 3rd edn, Oxford: Basil Blackwell.

Cloonan, M. (1997) 'State of the nation: "Englishness", pop and politics in the mid-1990s', *Popular Music and Society*, 12: 47–70.

Epstein, J. S., Pratto, D. J. and Skipper Jr., J. K. (1990) 'Teenagers, behavioral problems, and preferences for heavy metal and rap music: a case study of a southern middle school', *Deviant Behavior*, 11: 381–94.

Gilroy, P. (1993) *The Black Atlantic: Modernity and Double Consciousness*, London: Verso.

Haenfler, R. (2006) *Straight Edge: Hardcore Punk, Clean Living Youth, and Social Change*, Piscataway, NJ: Rutgers University Press.

Hall, S. and Jefferson, T. (eds) (1976) *Resistance Through Rituals: Youth Subcultures in Post-war Britain*, London: Hutchinson.

Hebdige, D. (1979) *Subculture: The Meaning of Style*, London: Routledge.

Hesmondhalgh, D. (2005) 'Subcultures, scenes or tribes? None of the above', *Journal of Youth Studies*, 8: 21–40.

Lovesey, O. (2004) 'Anti-Orpheus: narrating the dream brother', *Popular Music*, 23: 331–48.

Malbon, B. (1999) *Clubbing: Dancing, Ecstasy and Vitality*, London: Routledge.

Mafessoli, M. (1996) *The Time of Tribes: The Decline of Individualism in Mass Society*, London: Sage.

Martin, L. and Segrave, K. (1993) *Anti-Rock: The Opposition to Rock 'n' Roll*, New York: Da Capo.

McRobbie, A. and Garber, J. (1976) 'Girls and subcultures: an exploration', in S. Hall and T. Jefferson (eds) *Resistance Through Rituals: Youth Subcultures in Post-war Britain*, London: Hutchinson.

Muggleton, D. (2000) *Inside Subculture: The Postmodern Meaning of Style*, Oxford: Berg.

Osgerby, B. (2008) 'Understanding the "Jackpot Market": media, marketing and the rise of the American teenager', in P. Jamieson and D. Romer (eds) *The Changing Portrayal of Adolescents in the Media and Why It Matters*, New York: Oxford University Press.

Redhead, S. (1990) *The End-of-the-Century Party: Youth and Pop towards 2000*, Manchester: Manchester University Press.

Rose, T. (1994) *Black Noise: Rap Music and Black Culture in Contemporary America*, London: Wesleyan University Press.

Shumway, D. (1992) 'Rock and roll as a cultural practice', in A. DeCurtis (ed.) *Present Tense: Rock and Roll and Culture*, Durham, NC: Duke University Press.

Thornton, S. (1995) *Club Cultures: Music, Media and Subcultural Capital*, Cambridge: Polity Press.

Weinstein, D. (1991) *Heavy Metal: A Cultural Sociology*, New York: Lexington Books.

Willis, P. (1978) *Profane Culture*, London: Routledge and Kegan Paul.

# 33

# Youth people, drugs and alcohol consumption

*Shane Blackman*

## Introduction

This chapter will initially focus on the demonization of young people, and then outline the facts about youth consumption of drugs and alcohol. The aim will be to assess two different positions that have shaped the debate on youth and intoxication by looking, first, at functionalist theory and the concept of *risk*, and, second, the interpretative approach and the idea of normalization. The analysis shows contradictions and political alignments where theorists, practitioners, journalists, policy-makers, popular icons and politicians engage in hegemonic and counter-hegemonic claims focusing on the morality of intoxication and its consequences (Blackman 2004).

## Intoxication and the demonization of youth

The demonization of youth through representations of intoxication calls forth the fear of respectable society. In *Hooligan*, Pearson (1983) describes the historical legacy from the 1880s of how young people's actions, style and culture have been reported sensationally as deviant and socially menacing both by the tabloid newspapers and in policy docu-ments. The contemporary tabloid media also present voyeuristic images of ordinary young people, for example, Leah Betts and Rachel Whitear (both of whom died in drug-related incidents), or icons of youth such as Robbie Williams and Kate Moss, to show moral degradation. The theoretical basis to Pearson's argument derives from Stan Cohen's (1972) study *Folk Devils and Moral Panics*. For Cohen, government statements and media attention can combine so that moral panic successfully captures demonized youth and each successive folk devil is publicly paraded. In the 1960s, the mod youth culture was presented by the *Sunday Mirror* (31 May 1964) in terms of 'EXPOSING THE DRUG MENACE' warning of teenagers who are in the grip of 'pep-pills'. The *Daily Mirror*'s (17 January 1997) headline was 'ECSTASY SHOCK ISSUE' announcing that 'a million young people take E every weekend. It can make you a dead person.' In the 1980s, the Conservative governments defined the youth question as a problem of 'yob culture' and 'lager louts'. For the recent Labour governments, the solution was 'marching drunken louts off to cash machines to pay instant fines' which would cure the anti-social behaviour of young people. Engineer and colleagues (2003: 25) maintain that excess alcohol consumption among young people is now the norm and wider culture not only appears to support this lack of constraint; it promotes the aristocracy as role models, for example, in the *Daily Star* headline (14 December 2007) WILL'S & HARRY'S 15K BOOZE BENDER, where the two royals are described as 'ravers'. BBC News (14 September 2006) reported: 'Crackdown Urged on Youth Drinking'. The *Daily Mail* reported (21 February 2008) 'BOOZE BRITAIN': 'hard evidence links alcohol and youth crime'. It would appear that the demonization of young people in relation to intoxication occurs on a cyclical basis where youth over time are presented in a public gallery as different *folk devils* but institutionally conform to one social type, that of the 'deviant other'. In the twenty-first century, popular magazines have used this 'othering' as the point of departure to concentrate on youth difference and to celebrate youthful intoxication. Magazines such as *Loaded*, *Nuts*, *Maxim* and *FHM* describe young people as *lads* and *ladettes* in pursuit of the new intense pleasures of excess, confirming the negative label of demon but also promoting an ambiguous youthful assertiveness.

## Drug consumption facts

A significant feature of youth culture is argot, a subculture's secret code of style, drugs, language and music. This means that measurement of prevalence or occasional usage is primarily based upon estimates. Newcombe (2007: 31) suggests that approximately ten million 12–59 year-olds of UK population have used drugs. The British Crime Survey (BCS) in 1998 reported that young people aged 16–24 reported the highest level of drug misuse; some 49 per cent indicated they had used a drug in the last year. Drugscope in 2007 using the figures from the BCS for 2005/6 estimated drug use among 16–59 year-olds in terms of 'ever used' as 11,075.000 and those who have used drugs in the last year as 3,329,000 (Table 33.1).

The data presented show a decrease of cannabis, ecstasy, amphetamine, LSD and magic mushrooms and an increase in cocaine use among young people. On a similar basis, the United Nations (2008) (unodc.org) reports that use of cannabis in the United Kingdom has declined. Drugscope (2007: 37) states that according to Home Office research, the government estimates that there are 320,000 problem users. With a relatively small number of problematic drug users, this evidence questions the explanatory power of the *gateway theory* of drug use. Mack and Joy (2001: 62–8) maintain that the psychological gateway metaphor has been a powerful influence in American drug policy, similarly Blackman (2007: 52) identifies the acceptance of the hypothesis within the Social Exclusion Unit and the Connexions Service and importantly within the British tabloid media. However, it would appear that statistics on young people and drug use suggest that prevalence has declined; yet substance consumption remains relatively high or stable.

## Alcohol consumption facts

BBC News (14 September 2006) reported that British 15 year-olds are among Europe's heaviest users of alcohol. The Institute of Alcohol Studies (2008: ias.org.) states 'UK teenagers came at or near the top of the international league for binge drinking, drunkenness and experience of alcohol problems.' However, Plant and Plant (2006: 31) are

**Table 33.1** Proportion of 16–24 year-olds in England and Wales reporting to having used drugs in the last year (%)

| Drug | 1998 | 2006–07 |
|---|---|---|
| Cocaine | 3.1 | 6.0↑ |
| Crack | 0.3 | 0.4 |
| Ecstasy | 5.1 | 4.8 |
| LSD | 3.2 | 0.7↓ |
| Magic mushrooms | 3.9 | 1.7↓ |
| Heroin | 0.3 | 0.2 |
| Methadone | 0.6 | 0.1 |
| Amphetamines | 9.9 | 3.5↓ |
| Tranquillizers | 1.5 | 0.6↓ |
| Anabolic steroids | 0.5 | 0.2 |
| Cannabis | 28.2 | 20.9↓ |
| Ketamine* | n/a | 0.8 |
| Amyl nitrate** | 5.1 | 4.2 |
| Glues** | 1.3 | 0.6↓ |
| **Class A** | **8.6** | **8.0** |
| **Any drug** | **31.8** | **24.1↓** |

Source: British Crime Survey.

Notes:
↑↓ Statistically significant change 1998 to 2006/07
* Only included in BCS since 2006/07
** Not an illegal drug.

cautious about the evidence put forward focused on intoxication because of the problems of underreporting or of exaggeration. Measham (2006) and Chatterton and Hollands (2003) maintain that as a result of the rebranding of alcohol, new forms of socially acceptable binge drinking have emerged over the past ten years. At the same time this new culture of intoxication has attracted considerable political and media attention as being a social problem, especially the moral focus on increased binge drinking by young women, for example the *Daily Express* (15 December 2004) headline '"LADETTE" teenage girls try to ape hard-drinking'. Representations of intoxication are not new from Hogarth's *Gin Lane* (1750–51) to the British New Wave of films of the late 1950s and early 1960s, including *Room at the Top* and *Saturday Night, Sunday Morning*. These accounts portrayed young people's lives in harsh urban settings, where hard drinking was an integral part of life. Plant and Plant (2006: 29) using data from the British Beer and Pub Association show that alcohol consumption was high in the late Victorian period but from then till today use of alcohol seems to have moved through periods of high then lower use. Overall, they suggest that currently in Britain we are moving into a period of high consumption.

## Different sociological approaches: from the problem of order to identity

In sociology, two approaches to understanding youth and intoxication have been in contestation for nearly a hundred years. The *functionalist* and *interpretative* paradigms can be traced back to the founding figures of sociology, Emile Durkheim and Max Weber. In the twentieth century, the dominance in sociology of Talcott Parsons and Robert Merton's structural-functionalism defined youth issues as part of the problem of order. In Britain and America, the construction of deviancy theory exploited the popularity of psychoanalysis (Blackman 2004). In Britain, the work of both Cyril Burt and John Bowlby was important, particularly Bowlby (1953) who advanced a Freudian theory of youth deviance called the 'affectionless personality', based on the idea of maternal deprivation theory, more generally understood as the 'inadequate socialization' thesis. The consumption of intoxicants by young people was understood as dysfunctional for society and therefore seen as a threat to order or equilibrium. In Britain, Bowlby's theory of 'inadequate socialization' became fused with A. K. Cohen's (1955) theory of youth subculture to become the orthodox explanation of young people's use of intoxicants, as the theory enabled the separation between 'deviants' who used drugs and 'normal' people who did not.

The major challenge to the hegemony of the 'youth as trouble' model came from Phil Cohen (1972: 30) who created an epistemological break in the study of drugs and youth when he argued for a separation between youth subcultural practices and delinquency. Blackman (2004: 111) argues that this distinction became the subsequent basis of contemporary drug normalization theory because drugs were explained and understood 'as a recreational part of a subculture's signifying practices', first through the work of the Centre for Contemporary Cultural Studies, then more recently through postmodern and post-subcultural approaches. This marks the beginning of an approach in sociology where young people's culture and practices were seen as part of their subjectivity at the level of agency: youth intoxication came to be understood as sign of resistance and a signifier of identity rather than as a social problem.

### Risk and normalization

In contemporary sociology, we can identify two theoretical areas in relation to youth intoxication. First, the functionalist paradigm with a social policy focus, which centres on risk, control and regulation through prohibition linked to problems of health, crime and deviance. Second, the interpretative paradigm focused on normalization, which examines the social and cultural practices of youth intoxication from the position of ordinary and everyday life (South 1999).

A significant impact on the social pattern and cultural practices of young people's consumption of intoxicants has been due to recent changes in socio-economic policies, which created new levels of choice and market freedoms. Thus, in sociology, the emergence of the new concepts of risk and normalization has a symbiotic relationship to this social issue. The new cultures of intoxication have been brought to fruition and supported by market-oriented political policies where the growth and diversity in alcohol, ecstasy and cannabis products are related to re-commodification and the increased relaxed attitude towards usage and the powerful position intoxication holds as part of the commercial cultural support system, which is highly profitable and legitimate.

Recently, it has become fashionable to speak of youth intoxication within the discourse of 'risk taking'. The control of drugs and alcohol has increasingly come under what Rhodes (1997: 227) calls the 'dominant scientific construction of risk', which is preoccupied with an atomistic understanding of collective actions. Risk theory draws on popular explanations such as the gateway metaphor and the notion of peer pressure to advance the prohibition argument of drug desistance. The concept of risk carries its own legitimacy because it suggests that young people are in need of expert systems of adjustment and rehabilitation. The psychological basis to these approaches is criticized by Coggans and McKeller (1994) who see them as deficit theories, which rely on functionalist argument. The gateway idea presents a spurious association between soft and hard drugs, focusing on the psychological predisposition with little evidence of any causal effect. In prohibition policy the gateway effect is used to counter relaxation policies. Within drug control debates risk has become the new concept to advance positivistic solutions to the problems of youth intoxication. The new prevention science based on psychology and criminology presents risk theory as offering solutions to the problems of intoxication, but for France (2008) such new theories are atheoretical (Farrington 2002). What links the developmental psychology approach to risk and the postmodern understanding of risk is the principle of individualism.

In sociological theory, risk has emerged as a concept derived from postmodern approaches, in particular the work of Ulrich Beck, who sees social change creating increased uncertainty, described as the *risk society*. The idea of risk has entered the sociological mainstream as a tool articulating the conditions of postmodernity characterized by increased levels of personal, social and cultural insecurity. The attraction of postmodern theory is that it suggests an individual acts with purpose and in response to perceived social changes, thus it commendably stresses the creativity of the individual agent. However, Beck's postmodernist conceptualization of risk is primarily an individualization thesis, which identifies society as being in a process of transformation where individuals will be set free of constraining forms. A key weakness of the theory according to Furlong and Cartmel (2007: 12) is a 'tendency to exaggerate changes and to understate many significant sources of continuity'. Risk is neither open to all people to the same extent, nor with the same consequential outcome: risk is an ideological construction of the deviant other. What the theories of risk fail to grasp is that youth intoxication is a collective action. For the majority of young people, their leisure-based intoxication is derived from solidarity (Jackson 2004). The inability or reluctance to conceive of young people's actions on a collective basis results in a partial account of the social actions of youth intoxication.

A different and emergent position to understand youth intoxication has been that of 'normalization'. The conceptual origins of the term are related to the ethnographic work of Howard Becker, David Matza and Erving Goffman who advanced labelling theory through the symbolic interactionist tradition. These theorists were concerned with the notion of the 'everyday', focusing on how individuals negotiate and understand their daily activities. Parker and colleagues (1998) put forward the contemporary theory of drug normalization. The importance of the theory is to suggest that drug consumption has become more conventional and integrated into the lives of certain young people. Shiner and Newburn (1999) are critical of the normalization idea and its theoretical origins, which they see as lacking objectivity. They use the notion of desistance and assert that 'normative drug education', as defined by drug prevention, can correct inaccurate exaggerations about the widespread acceptability of drug and alcohol use by young people. In contrast, Blackman (2007: 57) argues 'Drug normalisation theory was created as a corrective to the stigmatised understanding of young people who consume drugs on a recreational non-problematic basis who are neither deviant nor criminal.' This debate recognizes that the theory remains controversial and is contested but its consequences have been important because it has enabled research to focus on the complexities of young people's lives and their use of intoxicants.

273

## Conclusion

This chapter has shown that different and competing academic and policy control discourses and corporate media interests surround the issue of young people's intoxication. At the centre of the debate is an opposition between power, politics and science. The British government (2008: wiredforhealth.gov) argues that normative drug education can be effective and reduce young people's use of intoxicants, but the organization 'Transform' maintains that prohibition is malfunctioning and causing increased personal, social, economic and cultural problems. The dominant policy of prohibition asserts its legitimacy through its claims to 'scientific facts', and at the same time the tabloid media's sensational and stereotypical reporting supports it. The alternative position of normalization is a corrective to the media demonization of young people and the academic paradigm of 'youth as trouble'. It does not seek to find fault or to blame young people for their use of intoxicants; it searches for understanding. Drugscope (2007: 7) states, 'The vast majority of people who use drugs come to no physical or psychological harm.' While most young people see drinking as a positive experience, increased and sustained 'binge drinking' is more likely to result in long-term health and personal problems. In the debate about intoxication and youth, it is clear that solutions to this issue will not be decided by objectivity or morality alone because intoxication is a matter of power and capital.

## References

Blackman, S. J. (2004) *Chilling Out: The Cultural Politics of Substance Consumption, Youth and Drug Policy*, Maidenhead: McGraw-Hill.
—— (2007) 'See Emily Play: youth culture, recreational drug use and normalization', in M. Simpson, T. Shildrick and R. MacDonald (eds) *Drugs in Britain*, Basingstoke: Palgrave-Macmillan.
Bowlby, J. (1953) *Childcare and the Growth of Love*, London: Penguin.
Chatterton, P. and Hollands, R. (2003) *Urban Nightscapes: Youth Cultures, Pleasure Spaces and Corporate Power*, London: Routledge.
Coggans, N. and McKeller, S. (1994) 'Drug use amongst peers: peer pressure or peer preference', *Drugs: Education, Prevention and Policy*, 1: 15–26.
Cohen, A. (1955) *Delinquent Boys: The Subculture of the Gang*, London: Collier-Macmillan.
Cohen, P. (1972) 'Subcultural conflict and working class community', in *Working Papers in Cultural Studies*, CCCS, University of Birmingham, Spring: 5–51.
Cohen, S. (1972/1980) *Moral Panics and Folk Devils*, Oxford: Martin Robertson.
Drugscope (2007) *The Essential Guide to Drugs and Alcohol*, London: Drugscope.
Farrington, D. (2002) 'Developmental criminology and risk focused prevention', in M. Maguire, R. Morgan, and R. Reiner (eds) *The Oxford Handbook of Criminology*, Oxford: Oxford University Press, pp. 657–701.
France, A. (2008) 'Risk factor analysis and the youth question', *Journal of Youth Studies*, 11: 1–15.
Furlong, A. and Cartmel, F. (2007) *Young People and Social Change: New Perspectives*, Maidenhead: McGraw-Hill.
Jackson, P. (2004) *Inside Clubbing*, Oxford: Berg.
Mack, A. and Joy, J. (2001) *Marijuana as Medicine*, Washington, DC: National Academy Press.
Measham, F. (2006) 'The new policy mix: alcohol, harm minimisation, and determined drunkenness in contemporary society', *International Journal of Drug Policy*, 17: 258–68.
Newcombe, R. (2007) 'Trends in the prevalence of illicit drug use in Britain', in M. Simpson, T. Shildrick, and R. MacDonald (eds) *Drugs in Britain*, Basingstoke: Palgrave-Macmillan.

Parker, H., Measham, F. and Aldridge, J. (1998) *Illegal Leisure: The Normalisation of Adolescent Drug Use,* London: Routledge.

Pearson, G. (1983) *Hooligan,* London: Macmillan.

Plant, M. and Plant, M. (2006) *Binge Britain,* Oxford: Oxford University Press.

Rhodes, T. (1997) 'Risk theory in epidemic times', *Sociology of Health and Illness,* 19: 208–27.

Shiner, M. and Newburn, T. (1999) 'Taking tea with Noel: the place and meaning of drug use in everyday life', in N. South (ed.) *Drugs: Cultures, Controls and Everyday Life,* London: Sage.

South, N. (1999) 'Debating drugs and everyday life: normalization, prohibition and "otherness",' in N. South (ed.) *Drugs: Cultures, Controls and Everyday Life,* London: Sage.

# 34

# Spectacular youth?

## Young people's fashion and style

*Paul Hodkinson*

## Introduction

The ways young people use clothing and other forms of bodily decoration as a means of expressing themselves have been an important focus for researchers of youth culture. There is a degree of agreement among scholars that style offers a means for adolescents to explore and express identity within a transitory period of the life course in which the dependencies of childhood gradually are relinquished without yet having fully been replaced by adult routines and responsibilities. Yet the details of how and why style is used and how this should be theorized and understood are the subject of considerable debate. This chapter outlines key elements of such debates, beginning with the influential work of a well-known group of theorists from Birmingham, UK, and developing a number of points of discussion which continue to dominate contemporary research of the subject.

## Spectacular style cultures

The best-known body of research on youth and style was provided by the University of Birmingham's Centre for Contemporary Cultural Studies (CCCS) in the 1970s. Focusing on the 'spectacular' fashions associated with *subcultures* such as teds, mods, skinheads, bikers and punks, the CCCS writers interpreted youth style as an expression of collective identity and defiance. Against the context of the partial decline of traditional working-class communities and the rise of rock 'n' roll and youth consumerism, it was argued that the visual uniforms of style subcultures represented a temporary or 'magical' solution to the confused and subordinated position of working-class young people (Cohen 1972). In the first instance, the adoption of such styles was argued to offer individuals a strong, defiant source of belonging during a time of uncertainty and, in placing emphasis on this, the CCCS drew upon subcultural theories emanating from US sociology (e.g. Cohen 1955). Yet the explanation of the neo-Marxist CCCS writers signalled a more specific role of style with respect to youth and social class. The adoption of collective stylistic uniforms was deemed simultaneously to represent, first, an expression of youthful difference from the traditional working-class culture of their parents and, second, a new stylistic form of class defiance against dominant bourgeois values (Cohen 1972; Clarke *et al.* 1976).

Of importance to this notion of style as resistance is the CCCS's understanding of the relationship between subcultures and the world of media and commerce. Although clearly linked to an embrace of consumer goods, it was argued that, rather than being 'bought off the shelf' or imitated from mass media, subcultural styles had emerged through the creative assembly by young people of a range of disparate items into coherent ensembles. Everyday items of clothing and other goods were selected, appropriated and, through their combination, assigned new subcultural meanings. The scooter, for example, was transformed by mods from an 'ultra respectable means of transport' into 'a weapon and a symbol of solidarity' (Hebdige 1976: 93), while the humble, functional safety pin became a symbolically important piece of jewellery within punk style. Having been thus assembled, each style was understood to perform a slightly different form of class resistance. The skinhead style, with its emphasis on traditional masculinity, was regarded as an attempt to stylistically reclaim a working-class community in decline (Clarke *et al.* 1976). Meanwhile, mods, it was claimed, were engaged in a stylistic parody of bourgeois values through appropriating a range of ultra-smart garments and combining them with scooters, pills and a hedonistic, rebellious lifestyle (Hebdige 1976).

Yet, for all their emphasis on fashion as an active, resistant form of youth expression, the CCCS's account also underlines the increasing power and influence of large-scale commerce over youth cultural styles. Not only are there occasional references to a 'conventional' culture, whose stylistic choices presumably were assumed to be dictated by media, but it is also suggested that resistant subcultural styles eventually would be exploited by fashion and music industries, stripped of their subversive meanings and sold back to broader sections of the population as packaged products (Hebdige 1976; 1979). Stylistic resistance, according to this view, could only ever be temporary.

The CCCS have proved enormously important to academic discussions about youth and style and their approach has generated points of contention which continue to dominate contemporary research agendas. In the following, we'll examine some of these.

## Social background or individual choice?

According to the CCCS, the style of subcultures was not a matter of individual preference or coincidence, but a grassroots reaction to the situation of being young and working class in post-war Britain. Yet others question whether we should understand young people's styles as an expression of class or indeed other fixed elements of social context. Some suggest the Marxist leanings of the CCCS prompted them to assume subcultural styles were attributable to class without providing empirical evidence of their demographic make-up or of the processes through which the groups emerged and recruited members (Clarke 1981). A related problem is that, while John Clarke *et al.* recognized that 'the great majority of working class youth never enters a tight or coherent subculture' (1976: 16), they were unable fully to explain what it was that prompted a minority to become involved in subcultures, while most of those who shared their class background did not. The implication is that other, more individually-specific factors must have played a role and that to explain stylistic choices purely as a response to class is over-simplistic.

Yet even if the CCCS's understanding of the link between youth style and social class background was justified, many argue that, as a result of social change, people's identities, tastes and lifestyles have since become less directly connected with the social status into which they were born. According to this view, previously significant markers of one's place in the world, including class, religion and locality, have become less influential, while the expansion and diversification of media and leisure industries have encouraged individuals to develop personalized consumer identities (Bauman 2001). And if such changes are indeed taking place, then it is perhaps logical to suggest that adolescents – already renowned for occupying an unstable and transitory period of life – may experience disconnection from traditional social categories particularly acutely. Thus, Muggleton (2000), Bennett (1999) and others argue that we should understand contemporary youth style not as an automatic response to social position but as a complex set of choices made by each individual. Rather than being locked into particular forms of stylistic expression as a result of their background, then, young people continually piece together their own identities.

Yet few would argue that traditional social categories have become entirely irrelevant to youth cultural expressions. Studies have repeatedly demonstrated complex but clear connections between ethnicity and particular forms of cultural expression (Nayak 2003; Huq 2006). Gender too remains of the utmost significance to young people's uses of style, with either dominant expectations or reactions to them comprising a key element of both majority and minority styles (Holland 2004; Harris 2007). Some research also suggests that social class retains significance. Thornton illustrates that the denigration within rave culture of 'mainstream' clubbers through the stereotype of 'Sharon and Tracy dancing around their handbags' reflected elitist assumptions relating to both gender and class (1995). More recently, Shildrick shows that class and neighbourhood remained strong predictors of youth style within the poor estates she studied, in which a clearly identifiable 'tracker' style was virtually ubiquitous (Shildrick 2006).

## Group styles or individual difference?

Another criticism of the CCCS is that they over-simplified the groups they examined, focusing on exclusive ideal-type group styles rather than on individual diversity or movement between groups (Clarke 1981). Observation of the recent expansion in the range of commercial styles on offer to consumers has prompted severe doubts over whether contemporary youth styles coalesce into neat subcultural affiliations. Rather, it is suggested that each individual compiles their own ensemble from the range of disparate items on offer and, in so doing, may draw from and cross-cut various genres or types. It follows that, rather than being fixed, individual styles and the DIY identities to which they are linked will fluctuate and change as young people develop their identities (Polhemous 1997). According to Muggleton, even those whose appearance resembles that of an identifiable subculture are at pains to emphasize self-expression and individual difference rather than group commitment (2000). The notion of the subcultural group is deemed to imply a set of collective restrictions which young people reject in favour of a 'fragmented, heterogenous and individualistic stylistic identification' (ibid.: 158).

For some, this elective, individualistic use of fashion and style renders the notion of subculture less useful in understanding such matters than another term, 'neo-tribe'. Drawn from the social theory of Maffesoli (1996), neo-tribe refers to groupings which offer an emotional attachment but whose boundaries are porous and whose membership is transitory: 'it is less a question of belonging ... than of switching from one group to another' (ibid.: 76). For Bennett, this emphasis on partial, temporary attachment to loose stylistic amalgams makes neo-tribe particularly suited to the cultural consumption practices of contemporary youth (1999).

Others, meanwhile, have criticized the specific tendency for subcultural theory to focus disproportionate attention on unusually spectacular or deviant youngsters (Laughey 2006). Studies of female youth cultural activities played an important role in the development of studies of 'ordinary' youth. Criticizing the marginalization of female youth within the work of their CCCS colleagues, McRobbie and Garber emphasized the prevalence among 1970s teenage girls of comparatively non-deviant indoor activities such as reading teen magazines and experimenting with clothes, makeup and hair (1976). The study of everyday fashion among young women has since developed into a significant body or literature which, among other things, has addressed the negotiation of youth with media representations of femininity. Other studies of 'ordinary' youth style include Willis's examination of the creative consumption practices of 'common culture' (1990) and Laughey's research on young people's everyday uses of music (2006). In contrast to previous emphasis on youth culture as a means of collective differentiation from parents, Laughey suggests that parents and siblings form significant components of individually unique portfolios of influence.

Yet the extent of the rejection of collective youth practices in individualistic 'post-subcultural' theories is regarded as unhelpful by some. Hesmondhalgh acknowledges that 'the CCCS subculturalists may at times have over-estimated the boundedness and permanence of ... group identities' but rejects Bennett's implication that 'relations between taste and identity are pretty much ... dependent on the whims of individuals' (2007: 40; also see Blackman 2005). Meanwhile, recent group-oriented studies have continued to demonstrate the significance of collective style identities. While outlining many of the complexities of club culture, Thornton identifies a clear set of collective standards through which clubbers both emphasized their collective difference from those outside their scene and judged and classified one another (1995). An emphasis on collective values also pervades Hodkinson's study of goths, which also illustrates the visual distinctiveness and consistency of the goth style, the strength of many participants' commitment to the group and a degree of separation between the subculture's networks and those of other groups (2002). Both studies retain the use of subculture as descriptor for the groups in question, even though they are critical of some elements of the CCCS's use of the term.

## Creative resistance or media manipulation?

A further area of contention pervading studies of youth culture since the 1970s is the extent to which young people's use of style may be regarded as active, or even subversive. As we have seen, the CCCS studies tended to assert that subcultural styles were assembled in a creative and autonomous fashion and that they communicated a youthful form of class resistance. The notion of youth style as an active and subversive form of consumption which defies the marketing of mainstream media and commerce and/or challenges dominant values has since been developed by others. Willis (1990) argues that elements of subversive creativity comparable to those previously identified in subcultures could also be observed in the stylistic consumption practices of broad sections of 'ordinary' youth. Such consumption was deemed to involve extensive knowledge, selectivity and imagination, reflecting grassroots interactions among friendship groups as much as the influence of media. As with the CCCS studies, the culture industries are relegated here to provider of raw materials, with young people themselves afforded the role of stylistic creators.

Studies focused upon gender and sexuality, meanwhile, have discussed a number of examples of the apparent challenging of dominant assumptions through style. Gotlieb and Wald (1994), for example, emphasize the subversive aspects of Riot Grrl style, in which participants and performers parodied the sexualization of women and the aggressive assertion of male sexuality within the rock industry. Overtly sexual clothing was combined with the aggressive deployment of the body and even the appropriation and adornment on the body of derogatory terms such as 'slut'. Meanwhile, both Siegel (2006) and Brill (2007) explore the implications of the apparent gender ambiguity on display within goth style, in which both males and females adopt a dark, feminine blend of clothing, jewellery and make-up. However, while Siegel concludes that goth style represents a form of gender resistance, Brill suggests that, in spite of challenging some conventions, the goth scene retains many dominant assumptions about masculinity, femininity and heterosexuality.

A key criticism of the CCCS, which also is applicable to some more recent studies such as Siegel's, is that the notion of style as resistance was in most cases based, not on an analysis of the views of those young people involved but on the external interpretation of the content of youth styles by academic 'experts'. Such an approach entails an assumption either that the interpretation of the critic is shared by those involved or that the subjective understandings of participants are unimportant. Acknowledging that many subculturalists would not have recognized themselves in his interpretations of their activities, Hebdige (1979) apparently opts for the latter view and alongside it an implication that youth styles acquire an external subversive significance independent of the motivations of their creators. Many researchers view such bypassing of the experiences of young people as problematic and, as a consequence, recent studies of youth and style often have adopted participant-centred approaches, characterized by interviews and often a combination of participation and observation.

A further objection to proclamations about the resistant qualities of youth style is that they sometimes can underestimate the influence of media and commerce. The ongoing diversification of culture industries arguably makes it increasingly unlikely that new styles or subcultures could emerge purely on the basis of youth spontaneity. Through the employment of 'cool hunters', among other tactics, commercial organizations seek to latch onto, publicize and exploit new styles before they even have been fully conceived. Meanwhile, youth media regularly construct and publicize new styles as an effective means to increase circulation and sell advertising space (Thornton 1995; Osgerby 2004). Rather than consisting of active appropriations, then, some suggest that even the most marginal of youth styles revolve around a form of niche marketing; they are, for the most part, bought off the shelf. From this point of view, the attribution of resistance to young people's uses of style – whether within spectacular subcultures or more ordinary contexts – may be dangerously complacent, constituting an uncritical endorsement of consumerism as the solution to social and cultural problems.

## Conclusion

Starting with the studies of spectacular subcultures carried out by the CCCS, this chapter has explored key issues in the study of youth and style, including the relationship between style and social background, the extent to which style is collective or individualized and debates about whether youth style can be active or resistant. In spite of the disagreements relating to these and other themes, the notion of youthful style as a response to the particular transitional circumstances of adolescence is broadly accepted. Yet in recent years, the categories of youth and youth culture in many societies have themselves become a little more ambiguous, with greater numbers of people retaining 'youthful' styles and pursuits well beyond the traditional age categories associated with adolescence. Rather than being a short-lived 'phase', it seems that some of the stylistic and behavioural features once regarded as the preserve of 16–25 year-olds are in fact becoming prevalent across a broader age range (Bennett 2007). A key focal point for future scholarship, then, is to establish what exactly we mean by youth style and what it is that substantially differentiates the practices and motivations of late teens from those of older consumers engaging in apparently similar activities.

## References

Bauman, Z. (2001) *The Individualized Society*, London: Polity.

Bennett, A. (1999) 'Subcultures or neo-tribes? Rethinking the relationship between youth, style and musical taste', *Sociology*, 33: 599–617.

—— (2007) 'As young as you feel: youth as a discursive construct', in P. Hodkinson and W. Deicke (eds) *Youth Cultures: Scenes, Subcultures and Tribes*, New York: Routledge.

Blackman, S. (2005) 'Youth subcultural theory: a critical engagement with the concept, its origins and politics, from the Chicago School to post modernism', *Journal of Youth Studies*, 4: 1–21.

Brill, D. (2007) 'Gender, status and subcultural capital in the goth scene', in P. Hodkinson and W. Deicke (eds) *Youth Cultures: Scenes, Subcultures and Tribes*, New York: Routledge

Clarke, G. (1981) 'Defending ski-jumpers: a critique of theories of youth subcultures', in S. Frith and A. Goodwin (eds) (1990) *On Record: Rock, Pop and the Written Word*, London: Routledge.

Clarke, J., Hall, S., Jefferson, T. and Roberts, B. (1976) 'Subcultures, cultures and class: a theoretical overview', in S. Hall and T. Jefferson (eds) *Resistance Through Rituals: Youth Cultures in Post-war Britain*, London: Hutchinson.

Cohen, A. (1955) *Delinquent Boys: The Culture of the Gang*, London: Collier-Macmillan.

Cohen, P. (1972) 'Subcultural conflict and working class community', *Working Papers in Cultural Studies*, 2: 5–70.

Gotlieb, J. and Wald, G. (1994) 'Smells like teen spirit: Riot grrrls, revolution and women in independent rock', in A. Ross and T. Rose (eds) *Microphone Fiends: Youth Music and Youth Culture*, New York: Routledge.

Harris, A. (ed.) (2007) *Next Wave Cultures: Feminism, Subcultures, Activism*, London: Routledge.

Hebdige, D. (1976) 'The meaning of mod', in S. Hall and T. Jefferson (eds) *Resistance Through Rituals: Youth Subcultures in Post-war Britain*, London: Hutchinson.

—— (1979) *Subculture: The Meaning of Style*, London: Methuen.

Hesmondhalgh, D. (2007) 'Recent concepts in youth cultural studies: critical reflections from the sociology of music', in P. Hodkinson and W. Deicke (eds) *Youth Cultures: Scenes, Subcultures and Tribes*, New York: Routledge.

Hodkinson, P. (2002) *Goth: Identity, Style and Subculture*, Oxford: Berg.

Holland, S. (2004) *Alternative Femininities: Body Age and Identity*, Oxford: Berg.

Huq, R. (2006) *Beyond Subculture: Pop, Youth and Identity in a Postcolonial World*, London: Routledge.

Laughey, D. (2006) *Music and Youth Culture*, Edinburgh: Edinburgh University Press.

Maffesoli, M. (1996) *The Time of the Tribes: The Decline of Individualism in Mass Society*, London: Sage.

McRobbie, A. and Garber, J. (1977) 'Girls and subcultures: an exploration', in S. Hall and T. Jefferson (eds) *Resistance Through Rituals: Youth Subcultures in Post-war Britain*, London: Hutchinson.

Muggleton, D. (2000) *Inside Subculture: The Postmodern Meaning of Style*, Oxford: Berg.

Nayak, A. (2003) *Race, Place and Globalization: Youth Cultures in a Changing World*, Oxford: Berg.

Osgerby, B. (2004) *Youth Media*, London: Routledge.

Polhemous, T. (1997) 'In the supermarket of style', in S. Redhead (ed.) *The Club Cultures Reader*, Oxford: Blackwell.

Shildrick, T. (2006) 'Youth culture, subculture and the importance of neighbourhood', *Young*, 14: 61–74.

Siegel, C. (2006) *Goth's Dark Empire*, Indianapolis: Indiana University Press.

Thornton, S. (1995) *Club Cultures: Music, Media and Subcultural Capital*, Cambridge: Polity.

Willis, P. (1990) *Common Culture: Symbolic Work at Play in the Everyday Cultures of the Young*, Milton Keynes: Open University Press.

# 35

# The experience of youth in the digital age

*Philippa Collin and Jane Burns*

## Introduction

Born into a digital world, young people today are considered significant actors at the forefront of an increasingly complex social, economic and political world. Traditional transitions (for example, from study to work or unemployment, or from dependence on family to independent living or economic independence) and the strategies young people use to navigate these are distinct from previous generations (Furlong and Cartmel 2007). Wyn and Woodman (2006) argue that a 'social generation' approach to the study of youth compels us to explore both how young people negotiate new social contexts and structures and how they make meaning through this process. One significant difference between the experience of people born after 1980 and their parents (and grandparents) is the role of new media and information communication technologies (ICT) in everyday life. Education, work and interpersonal relationships are increasingly mediated by ICT and in most parts of the developed world it is hard to imagine a youth without mobile phones or the internet.

What do we mean by new media and ICT? In the *Handbook of New Media*, Lievrouw and Livingstone (2006) propose that new media is made possible through ICT that can best be understood as 'infrastructures':

> *Infrastructure*s with three key components: *artefacts* or *devices* used to communicate or convey information; the *activities* or *practices* in which people engage to communicate or share information; and the *social arrangements* or *organizational forms* that develop around those devices and practice.
>
> (ibid.: 2)

This suggests that in order to make sense of the impact of ICT, research must take into account how young people negotiate and shape social structures, processes and make meaning through technology. Literature on youth and ICT is diverse and emerges from a range of disciplines including sociology, media studies, psychology, education and political science. While some studies look broadly at ICT, others explore particular technologies, such as the internet or mobile phones, or, particular online practices, such as 'blogging', 'mashing', chat rooms and gaming. However, though rapid innovation in mobile and digital technology (including media players and digital television) impacts on the experience of youth, the largest body of literature explores the role of the World Wide Web (WWW). As such, this chapter draws mainly on literature on the internet, but takes into account the critical role of other ICT and media for contemporary experiences of youth.

This chapter will review key debates in the literature. Though we argue that there are some far-reaching implications that span geographical, cultural, economic and social boundaries, we also acknowledge that these effects are not felt equally and the impact of differential access and use of ICT among young people must be considered in future research. Low e-literacy skills, speed of internet connection and location of access can have a perceived and real effect on young people (Livingstone 2006; Boyd 2008). As social relations, such as friendships and employment, become increasingly linked to digital connectivity, there are concerns about the impact of the 'digital divide' on citizenship and well-being (Stokes *et al.* 2004). Research indicates that class and level of education are predictors of internet use and quality of internet access (Willis and Tranter 2006; Livingstone *et al.* 2007; Vromen 2007) and young people from minority or marginalized groups, such as Indigenous people, report significantly lower levels of access (ABS 2002). As such, there is a need to look at how structural factors such as gender, economic status and cultural background impact on access to and use of ICT.

The literature reveals a complex and diverse range of perspectives and approaches. In this chapter we suggest that the current spectrum of literature can be summarized (though not limited) by considering the impact of ICT on two dimensions of the experience of youth: identity, social relationships and well-being; and citizenship and political participation.

## Identity, social relationships and well-being

With the development of communication technologies, social life has increasingly occurred beyond the limitations of geography and place, and identity is increasingly produced through action and performance (Giddens 1991; Castells 1997). The implications of ICT for identity production, and subsequently, the formation of communities online are of significant interest to scholars, though diverse technologies have been viewed in distinct ways. For instance, research on gaming initially explored the positive effects on creativity and learning, but has shifted in recent times to focus on the perceived negative impacts, particularly anti-social behaviour (Buckingham 2006). Conversely, research on the internet has largely focused on how the web can facilitate creative expression and provide new opportunities for young people to explore and experiment with identity through email, chat rooms, blogging and the production – as well as consumption – of online content (eg. Coleman and Rowe 2005; Montgomery 2007). Studies have also explored the way that young people use the internet to explore, challenge and perform dominant discourses of, for example, gender (eg. Harris 2004) and sexuality (e.g. Hillier and Harrison 2007).

One of the key theoretical questions shaping the study of ICT and youth identity relates to the changing boundaries between public and private. Scholars argue that the internet is making young people's private lives increasingly public (Harris 2004;

Livingstone 2006). The focus is now on understanding how this occurs and what effects this might have. Harris has argued that authoring oneself online is manifest in 'confessional styles' that transform 'intimate details and experience into material for popular consumption' (2004: 128). In this way, she argues, the distinction between the private and public is blurred – perhaps inverted. As such, by 'living large' online (ibid.: 128) through membership of online communities and the authoring and publication of online content, young people construct and claim new, legitimate spaces in the public sphere.

Using ethnographic research to examine social networking sites such as Friendster (www.friendster.com) and MySpace (www.myspace.com), Danah Boyd has theorized that by chatting on each other's profiles, young people are holding previously private conversations in new public spaces (Boyd 2008). Moreover, she argues that the emergence of *networked publics* signals a new kind of public (social formation) and space (locality). These networked publics are distinguished from other kinds of publics by being: persistent (permanent); searchable (individuals and their personal information can easily be located); replicable (information, comments and multimedia can be copied and disseminated); and populated by 'invisible audiences' (ibid.: 9). Subsequently, both the degree of agency and the structures that young people must negotiate are changing as interactivity enabled through bulletin boards, instant messenger and online chat is surpassed by 'open systems' technology of social networking sites, public publishing and virtual gaming environments. There is a pressing need to understand the nature and outcomes of young people's interactions with sites such as Bebo (www.bebo.com), Facebook (www.facebook.com), ActNow (www.actnow.com.au) and SecondLife (www.secondlife.com).

ICT as a range of new settings, activities and relationships also has implications for the health and well-being of young people. Questions of youth health and well-being are dealt with in this volume by West and Eckersley in Part VIII. Here we review the literature on the relationship between ICT and youth well-being, in particular, research framed around factors known to enhance well-being – engagement and valued participation, connectedness and meaningful relationships and skills.

Given the rapid evolution of the internet, much of the 'knowledge' about its impact focuses on dangers to the individual epitomized by concerns that it acts as a catalyst for negative interactions such as bullying, suicide, sexual predation and anti-social behaviours such as internet addiction (Ha *et al.* 2007; Mitchell *et al.* 2007; Tam *et al.* 2007). However, young people also report feeling empowered online, able to access immediate feedback and more confident in accessing and talking about sensitive topics (Gould *et al.* 2002; Nicholas *et al.* 2004) such as depression (Burns *et al.* 2007; Leach *et al.* 2007), sexuality or sexually transmitted diseases (Suzuki and Calzo 2004) and physical activity and nutrition (Spittaels and De Bourdeaudhuij 2006). However, the tendency of such research is to focus on outcomes, in isolation from young people's everyday lives.

Increasing knowledge and understanding about health issues are important but perhaps the greatest contribution the internet can make to well-being will be to reduce the stigma associated with mental health difficulties, promote help seeking in the offline world and build community and promote meaningful participation (Berger *et al.* 2005; Leach *et al.* 2007; Santor *et al.* 2007). For example, research on the role of online support groups finds they can 'clearly provide essential social support for otherwise isolated adolescents'(Whitlock *et al.* 2006), offer the 'same assistance strategies as face-to-face' groups (Winzelberg 1997) and provide 'a supportive conversation or a referral to appropriate help resources' (Barak 2007). A study of an online self-harm discussion group reported it as 'having positive effects, with many respondents reducing the frequency and severity of their self-harming behaviour as a consequence of group membership' (Leung 2007).

Such innovative web-based initiatives demonstrate that ICT – rethought of as a *setting* in which 'devices, activities and social arrangements' are activated – can have a powerful impact on the well-being of young people. ReachOut! (www.reachout.com.au) is an Australian initiative that utilizes a website, podcasting, digital storytelling, community forums, an online gaming platform, SMS and social networking site campaigns to deliver information, reduce mental health stigma and promote help-seeking (Burns *et al.* 2007). Online profiling, conducted in 2006, of 1,432 ReachOut! visitors (aged 16–25) shows that 75 per cent said they would return to the site if going through 'tough times' and 80 per cent would refer it to a friend. When repeat visitors were asked if they had sought help after visiting Reach Out!, 38 per cent said they had spoken to a mental health professional (ibid.). Research that accounts for the complex interplay between individual behaviour, interpersonal relationships and the settings in which young people spend their time (school, streets, church groups) – including the internet – will provide a richer understanding of the impact of ICT on young people's well-being.

Increased understanding of the role of ICT in young people's everyday lives has prompted a rethinking of the assumptions that have underpinned much of the existing research on identity, social relationships, well-being and ICT. Binary concepts that have traditionally been used to examine online behaviours and relationships, such as public/ private, real/virtual and online/offline now seem insufficient. Research is increasingly using mixed methods to understand not only rates of internet access and sites of online engagement, but the meaning young people ascribe to online activities and relationships (e.g. Livingstone *et al.* 2007). Mixed methods research has found that the online and offline worlds of young people are 'mutually constituted', meaning that young people primarily connect online to their existing (offline) friends and networks (e.g. Valentine and Holloway 2002; Boase *et al.* 2006). Simultaneously the internet provides the impetus for new forms of relationships and the transformation of the sites and substance of existing relationships between young people, their families, peers and the state.

## Participation and citizenship

The internet is shaping the experience of citizenship for young people in new and dynamic ways. There are broadly two approaches to the study of the internet and political participation among young people.

The first looks at how technology is extending or deepening democracy as a legal and administrative mechanism, and for strengthening the legitimacy of normative political ideas and culture. The focus is often on the opportunities and effectiveness of 'e-democracy' in strengthening existing institutional arrangements, linking decision-makers and political elites to citizens and extending government to marginalized or 'hard-to-reach' groups, such as young people. These perspectives view the internet as a vehicle for public information and 'civic education' (Montgomery *et al.* 2004) and are hopeful that the internet will foster 'active citizenship' – community engagement in government or 'youth service to the community' – through such mechanisms as online volunteer matching (Delli Carpini 2000: 347). However, the top-down nature of e-governance tends to focus on communicating policy to young people, being government/decision-maker-focused and limiting the degree to which young people can contribute to agenda-setting or decision-making. For example, government sites generally simply present information to young people, rather than seeking dialogue with them. There is also concern that digital technologies may reinforce structural factors such as levels of education and class enabling those who are already engaged to participate more, whilst further marginalizing those who are not (Norris 2001). Scholars therefore warn that unless the structural barriers to participation offline are addressed (including attitudes towards young people as *becoming* citizens), online initiatives may be of little consequence (Livingstone *et al.* 2007). For example, few top-down mechanisms link policy-makers with youth civic engagement taking place through NGOs, youth-led sites or social movements (e.g. Vibewire Youth Services [www.vibewire.net], ActNow [www.actnow.com.au] and TakingItGlobal [www.takingitglobal.org]).

The second approach challenges both the way that political participation is conceptualized and the way that it is researched. The internet has transformed the political actions of both individuals and groups who, through wide, shallow networks, use the internet as both a space and a tool for political communication (Bennett 2003). New communication practices enabled by the internet such as forums, electronic mail and open publishing software have shaped new settings for action, such as alternative media outlets (e.g. www.indymedia.org) (ibid.). The transformative power of the internet for political participation and citizenship lies in the value it holds for resource-poor political agents, minority and marginalized groups, such as young people.

Survey-based research in the UK (Livingstone *et al.* 2005) and in Australia (Vromen 2007) has explored a broad range of participatory opportunities undertaken online by young people, such as boycotting and ethical purchasing, conversations on issues of concern, searching for and sharing community or political information, visiting civic websites and creating content of a political nature for online distribution. Nevertheless, one of the key challenges is to define 'participation', and there is a pressing need to critically examine 'what exactly must young people do online before society will judge them "politically active" or "engaged in civic participation?"' (Livingstone *et al.* 2005: 289–90).

Research indicates that the internet can reinforce existing social and political awareness among young people (Mesch and Coleman 2007), but there is less evidence that it is a significant alternative vehicle for political socialization (Livingstone *et al.* 2005). However, there are recognizable, new forms of individualized participation such as online petitioning, blogging and contacting decision-makers via SMS (Stanyer 2005). Similarly, new forms of deliberation and communitarian action to share information and bring together new networks for action utilize email, user-generated content and social networking sites (Montgomery 2007; Vromen 2007). As such, scholars contend that there also remain significant opportunities to use the interactivity of the internet to bring young people and decision-makers together in processes of agenda-setting and debate (Coleman and Rowe 2005). For example, in the United Kingdom, the Hansard Society's *HeadsUp* (www.headsup.org.uk) initiative brings together students and Members of Parliament (MPs) in online discussions on political issues. The debates are timed to coincide with related events and inquiries of parliament. MPs report back to participants following forum discussions, drawing attention to parallels between the parliamentary outcomes and the conclusions of the HeadsUp forums (Ferguson 2007).

However, there are doubts that simply creating a website, blog or MySpace page is enough to engage young people in these processes or institutions. Boyd argues that for technology to engage people in democracy individuals must be able to negotiate their

287

identity, relationships and community as part of the political process (Boyd 2005). UK research has found that the more sites are 'managed' and controlled, the less inclined young people are to engage with them (Coleman 2008). Instead, young people want to be taken seriously as producers and partners in processes of online deliberation and engagement (Coleman and Rowe 2005).

Such considerations of the relationships between the internet and participation reveal processes of what Coleman has defined as 'managed' and 'autonomous' citizenship (Coleman 2008). In other words, the internet is a setting in which youth participation can be managed by traditional political institutions and structures. However, the internet also enables new, autonomous forms of citizenship to be performed that reach beyond, and are transforming, traditional political processes. Future research will be needed to understand how young people are mobilized in relation to these new forms of citizenship, and the ways they navigate these new terrains to undertake participatory actions.

## Conclusion

Current research and practice suggest that ICT has fundamentally impacted on the experience of youth across the globe. From a theoretical perspective there is a critical engagement with binary frames of reference, such as private/public, real/virtual and positive/negative to describe the impact of ICT on the experience of youth. In the process of engaging critically with these notions, there is an increasing interest in understanding the relationship between new media, ICT and young people's everyday lived experience.

The rise of ICT in everyday life has also sparked a transformation in empirical approaches to research whereby the internet is now understood as a new, though not separate, setting in which research can explore identity production and relationships and online activities that supplement or reinforce, rather than replace, offline activities across a range of social, cultural and political domains. At the same time, the literature indicates that future research must consider both the new opportunities created by ICT, as well as the enduring (offline) structures that shape different dimensions of the experience of youth.

## References

Australian Bureau of Statistics (2002) *National Aboriginal and Torres Strait Islander Social Survey*, Cat. No. 4714.0, Canberra: Australian Bureau of Statistics.

Barak, A. (2007) 'Emotional support and suicide prevention through the Internet: a field project report', *Computers in Human Behaviour*, 23: 971–84.

Bennett, L. (2003) 'Communicating global activism: strengths and vulnerabilities of networked politics', *Information, Communication and Society*, 6: 143–68.

Berger, M., Wagner, T. H. and Baker, L. C. (2005) 'Internet use and stigmatized illness', *Social Science and Medicine*, 61: 1821–7.

Boase, J., Horrigan, J. B., Wellman, B. and Rainie, L. (2006) *The Strength of Internet Ties: The Internet and E-Mail Aid Users in Maintaining Their Social Networks and Provide Pathways to Help When People Face Big Decisions*, Washington, DC: Pew Internet and American Life Project, Washington, DC. Online. Available at: www.pewinternet.org/pdfs/PIP_Internet_ties.pdf (accessed 12 January 2006).

Boyd, D. (2005) 'Sociable technology and democracy', in J. Lebkowsky and M. Ratcliffe (eds) *Extreme Democracy*, Lulu.com. Online. Available at: www.lulu.com (accessed 1 September 2007).

—— (2008) 'Why youth ♥ social network sites: the role of networked publics in teenage social life', in D. Buckingham (ed.) *Identity Volume*, Cambridge, MA: M.I.T. Press, 119–42.

Buckingham, D. (2006) 'Children and new media', in L. A. Lievrouw and S. Livingstone (eds) *The Handbook of New Media*, London: Sage.

Burns, J., Morey, C., Lagelée, A., Mackenzie, A. and Nicholas, J. (2007) 'Reach out! Innovation in service delivery', *Medical Journal of Australia*, S31–S34: 187.

Castells, M. (1997) *The Information Age: Economy, Society and Culture*, vol. 2: *The Power of Identity*, Oxford: Blackwell Publishers.

Coleman, S. (2008) 'Doing it for themselves: management versus autonomy in youth E-citizenship', in W. L. Bennett (ed.) *Civic Life Online: Learning How Digital Media Can Engage Youth*, Cambridge, MA: MIT Press, 189–206.

Coleman, S. and Rowe, C. (2005) *Remixing Citizenship: Democracy and Young People's Use of the Internet*, London: Carnegie Young People's Initiative. Online. Available at: www.carnegieuktrust.org.uk/ files/Carnegie_v3LRES_0.pdf (accessed 2 February 2006).

Delli Carpini, M. X. (2000) 'Gen.Com: youth, civic engagement and the new Information environment', *Political Communication*, 17: 341–9.

Ferguson, R. (2007) 'Chattering classes: the moderation of deliberative forums in citizenship education', in B. D. Loader (ed.) *Young Citizens in the Digital Age: Political Engagement, Young People and New Media*, Abingdon: Routledge.

Furlong, A. and Cartmel, F. (2007) *Young People and Social Change: New Perspectives*, 2nd edn, Maidenhead: Open University Press.

Giddens, A. (1991) *Modernity and Self-identity: Self and Society in the Late Modern Age*, Cambridge: Polity Press.

Gould, M. S., Munfakh, J. L. Lubell, K., Kleinman, M. and Parker, S. (2002) 'Seeking help from the internet during adolescence', *Journal of American Academy of Child Adolescent Psychiatry*, 41: 1182–9.

Ha, J. H., Kim, S. Y. Bae, S. C., Bae, S., Kim, H., Sim, M. *et al.* (2007) 'Depression and internet addiction in adolescents', *Psychopathology*, 40: 424–30.

Harris, A. (2004) *Future Girl: Young Women in the Twenty-first Century*, New York: Routledge.

Hillier, L. and Harrison, L. (2007) 'Building realities less limited than their own: young people practising same-sex attraction on the internet', *Sexualities*, 10: 82–100.

Leach, L. S., Christensen, H., Griffiths, K. M., Jorm, A. F. and MacKinnon, A. J. (2007) 'Websites as a mode of delivering mental health information: perceptions from the Australian public', *Social Psychiatry and Psychiatric Epidemiology*, 42: 167–72.

Leung, L. (2007) 'Stressful life events, motives for Internet use, and social support among digital kids', *Cyberpsychology and Behaviour*, 10: 204–14.

Lievrouw, L. A. and Livingstone, S. (2006) *The Handbook of New Media*, 2nd edn, London: Sage.

Livingstone, S. (2006) 'Drawing conclusions from new media research: reflections and puzzles regarding children's experience of the internet', *The Information Society*, 22: 219–30.

Livingstone, S., Bober, M. and Helsper, E. J. (2005) 'Active participation or just more information? Young people's take-up of opportunities to act and interact on the internet', *Information, Communication and Society*, 8: 287–314.

Livingstone, S., Coudry, N. and Markham, T. (2007) 'Youthful steps towards civic participation: does the internet help?', in B. D. Loader (ed.) *Young Citizens in the Digital Age: Political Engagement, Young People and New Media*, Abingdon: Routledge.

Mesch, G. S. and Coleman, S. (2007) 'New media and new voters: young people, the internet and the 2005 UK election campaign', in B. D. Loader (ed.) *Young Citizens in the Digital Age: Political Engagement, Young People and New Media*, Abingdon: Routledge.

Mitchell, K. J., Ybarra, M. and Finkelhor, D. (2007) 'The relative importance of online victimization in understanding depression, delinquency, and substance use', *Child Maltreatment*, 12: 314–24.

Montgomery, K. C. (2007) *Generation Digital: Politics, Commerce and Childhood in the Age of the Internet*, Cambridge, MA: MIT Press.

Montgomery, K., Gottlieg-Robles, B. and Larson, G. O. (2004) *Youth as e-citizens: Engaging the Digital Generation*, Centre for Social Media, American University. Online. Available at: www.centerforsocialmedia. org/ecitizens/youthreport.pdf (accessed 12 February 2006).

Nicholas, J., Oliver, K., Lee, K. and O'Brien, M. (2004) 'Help-seeking behaviour on the Internet: an investigation among Australian adolescents', *Australian e-Journal for the Advancement of Mental Health*, 3: 1–8.

Norris, P. (2001) *Digital Divide: Civic Engagement, Information Poverty, and the Internet Worldwide*, Cambridge: Cambridge University Press.

Santor, D. A., Poulin, C., LeBlanc, J. C. and Kusumaker, V. (2007) 'Online health promotion, early identification of difficulties, and help seeking in young people', *Journal of American Academy of Child Adolescent Psychiatry*, 46: 50–9.

Spittaels, H. and De Bourdeaudhuij, I. (2006) 'Implementation of an online tailored physical activity intervention for adults in Belgium', *Health Promotion International*, 21: 311–18.

Stanyer, J. (2005) 'The British public and political attitude expression: the emergence of a self-expressive political culture?', *Contemporary Politics*, 11: 19–32.

Stokes, H., Wierenga, A. and Wyn, J. (2004) *Preparing for the Future and Living Now*, Melbourne: Youth Research Centre.

Suzuki, L.K. and Calzo, J.P. (2004) 'The search for peer advice in cyberspace: an examination of online teen bulletin boards about health and sexuality', *Applied Developmental Psychology*, 25: 685–98.

Tam, J., Tang, W. S. and Fernando, D. J. (2007) 'The internet and suicide: a double-edged tool', *European Journal of International Medicine*, 18: 453–5.

Valentine, G. and Holloway, S. (2002) 'Cyberkids? Exploring children's identities and social networks in on-line and off-line worlds', *Annals of the Association of American Geographers*, 92: 302–19.

Vromen, A. (2007) 'Australian young people's participatory practices and internet use', *Information, Communication and Society*, 10: 48–68.

Whitlock, J. L, Powers, J. L. and Eckenrode, J. (2006) 'The virtual cutting edge: the internet and adolescent self-injury', *Developmental Psychology*, 42: 1–11.

Willis, S. and Tranter, B. (2006) 'Beyond the "digital divide": Internet diffusion and inequality in Australia', *Journal of Sociology*, 42: 43–59.

Winzelberg, A. (1997) 'The analysis of an electronic support group for individuals with eating disorders', *Computers in Human Behavior*, 13: 393–407.

Wyn, J. and Woodman, D. (2006) 'Generation, youth and social change in Australia', *Journal of Youth Studies*, 9: 495–514.

# Part VII

# Civic engagement and disengagement

*Andy Furlong*

## Civic and political engagement and disengagement

At election times, when politicians seek to engage citizens from a broad spectrum of the electorate, there are often discussions about the lack of engagement of young people and their general apathy regarding the political process. In most countries, even when voting is compulsory and failure to cast a ballot incurs penalties, young citizens are less likely than their elders to bother voting. This is not a new situation, although there is evidence suggesting that young people's interest and involvement have declined in recent years. Concern about young people's lack of involvement has led to renewed efforts to promote their involvement and even led to discussions of the ways in which new technologies can be harnessed to help engage an IT-literate generation. Yet in terms of involvement in traditional political mechanisms and interest, Harris reminds us in Chapter 37 that political institutions are developed by adults to serve their own agenda: whatever adaptations are made, it is important to be clear that institutions were never designed to engage young people – some of whom, by virtue of their age, will not even have the right to participate.

This section explores changing patterns of civic engagement among young people and examines some of the experiences that promote or discourage participation. Factors such as educational participation may promote political involvement, while the fragmentation of employment opportunities for less qualified young people can lead to a weakening of traditional sources of political socialization based on workplace solidarity. While changes may 'pull' in different directions, in Chapter 36, Flanagan argues that the class divide in civic participation has increased. Flanagan also makes an important point regarding the significance of historical contexts: in some periods of time, political issues dominate national agendas to such an extent that young people are forced to consider their position and encouraged by their peers to take a stand (the Vietnam War being a good example).

In terms of employment experiences, trade unions once played a key role in the political socialization of young people, providing an introduction to working-class politics and to representing a forum through which they could make their voices heard. Yet the demise of traditional employment contracts, the weakening of job security and the tendency for young people to combine study with employment have all contributed to a decline in union membership that has been particularly marked among young people. In Chapter 38, Carle suggests that, on one level, fragmentation of experiences has tended to result in young people seeking individualized rather than collective solutions while, at another level, more comprehensive legislation underpinning worker rights (especially in the European Union) effectively weakens trade unions.

The chapters in this section are not just about involvement in the 'traditional' political process: young people may not be enthused by party politics, but they do display high levels of interest and involvement in single issue politics and are engaged in less conventional ways in demonstrations, civic disruption and direct action. Recent involvement in anti-Iraq War demonstrations provides a good example, as does their participation in animal rights and environmental movements. The involvement of young people in single-issue politics has been significant globally in terms of political change: Flanagan highlights the ways in which young people invigorated the ANC in South Africa, Harris discusses their role in the dismantling of the communist regimes in Eastern Europe, and in Chapter 39, Akram looks at participation in urban riots, while in Chapter 40, Daiute explores the impact of their involvement in armed conflicts.

In many respects, it is important to be aware of the experiences of young people involved in more extreme forms of political engagement, as there has been a tendency to view such forms of involvement as criminal or as indicative of a lack of civic values rather than as forms of political action initiated by those who feel other avenues of protest are closed to them. In this context, in discussing young people's involvement in urban riots, Akram argues that rioters are often politically rather than criminally motivated, frequently involving young people whose lives have been characterized by severe poverty. Similarly, while recognizing that young people who are involved in armed conflicts tend to lack free choice, Daiute argues that young people are often extremely knowledgeable politically and have a strong awareness of the needs of their communities.

Overall, the chapters in this section provide a very broad perspective on young people's civic and political engagement and provide us with a greater awareness of the transformative capacity of young people as politically involved agents who are often key players in processes of change.

# 36

# Young people's civic engagement and political development

*Constance Flanagan*

## Introduction

Scholarly interest in youth and politics has waxed and waned with the times. Voting in elections is a major dependent variable in political science. Since age determines eligibility and since lower numbers of youth tend to vote, they have often been ignored. The intersection of youth and politics attracts attention when concerns about the younger generation's political interest and commitments intensify. Trends pointing to declines in conventional forms of engagement in younger generations has spurred today's interest. In any era, 18–25 year-olds are less likely than their elders to vote, to belong to political parties, or to read newspapers. However, young people today are also less likely than earlier generations of youth to get engaged in these ways (Levine 2007).

As scholarly attention has increased, the definition of civic engagement has expanded. In this chapter, the terms civic and political are used interchangeably based on the equivalence of the terms in the political theorist, Michael Walzer's definition:

> A citizen is, most simply, a member of a political community, entitled to whatever prerogatives and encumbered with whatever responsibilities are attached to membership. The word comes to us from the Latin *civis;* the Greek equivalent is *polites*, member of the polis, from which comes our political.
>
> (1989: 211)

This is a useful way to conceptualize citizenship with a decidedly 'youth' lens. In the context of their experiences of membership in local groups, institutions, and organizations, youth practice citizenship. In such contexts they learn what it means to be a member of a group, to exercise rights, have a say in the group's affairs, and learn to be accountable to fellow members and to the mission of the organization (Flanagan 2004). By working toward a common goal, they also learn to be agents of social change.

## Why focus on youth?

Psychological and sociological theorists consider youth a politically definitive period. This is a time in life for deciding about the direction of one's future. In the process, an individual tends to take stock of him/herself and his/her society. Whereas childhood and early adolescence tend to be highly structured, the transition to adulthood is marked by the young person's greater self-determination and independence of thought. Consequently, the political views of younger generations are rarely carbon copies of their parents' views.

Erikson (1968) captured the developmental imperatives that youth face when he described the key psychosocial tasks of these years as exploring and consolidating an identity. This entails seeking purpose, deciding on beliefs and commitments, and linking to others (in organizations, religious traditions, or social causes) who share such commitments. Developing an ideology enables youth to organize and manage the vast array of choices the world presents. Political ideologies are forming in adolescence when personal values, world views, and political attributions appear to be highly concordant (Flanagan and Tucker 1999).

Identity theorists extol the benefits for youth of a moratorium on social roles and commitments (Arnett 2000). Compared to older adults, youth are 'free' to explore different perspectives on social issues and different possible selves. Politically, they should be more independent than their elders, undecided about party affiliation, and more open to joining alternative (e.g. Green) parties. However, freedom from role and other social constraints is not, in itself, enough to motivate exploration and consolidation of political identities. At least two other factors are important. First, one also needs exposure to heterogeneous points of view. The classic case for the impact of new reference groups on the evolving political views of young adults was documented in Newcomb's longitudinal studies of women attending Bennington College in the 1930s. Exposure to progressive faculty perspectives on public issues – which departed from their parents' conservative convictions – was related to a shift in the women's positions toward greater identification with the policies of the New Deal, a political shift that lasted into their retirement years (Alwin *et al.* 1991).

Second, the freedom of youth may be wasted politically, if there are no pressures (whether historical or contextual) that motivate youth to grapple with social issues and take a stand. In this regard, Jennings' (2002) longitudinal study of a 1965 high-school cohort points to the opportunity that the college context provided during the political heyday of the late 1960s. Compared to peers who did not attend college, those who did were more likely to grapple with diverse perspectives on issues which helped them to clarify where they stood. Differences between the groups persisted into mid-life with the college attendees remaining more consistent in their political beliefs.

Importantly, it is not the mere fact of being in college that produces civic benefits but rather the exposure to different perspectives and the pressure to come to grips with them that helps youth crystallize their own views. As social movement literature has documented, for civic engagement in one's youth to have lifelong effects, one has to actively wrestle with the issues rather than watch from the sidelines. Citizenship figures prominently in most college mission statements and, in recent years, courses with a community service component have been on the rise. At the same time, universities have enacted policies that restrict the range of backgrounds and perspectives their students will naturally encounter. For example, computer matching services to help new students find roommates who are similar to them are now common practice. To improve their ratings in outlets such as *U.S. News and World Report*, universities seek students with high standardized test scores and attract them by increasing the proportion of merit vs. need-based scholarships and providing small 'honors' colleges within the larger public university.

Nonetheless, being in college (or other institutional settings such as work, faith-based organizations, etc.) enhances the likelihood of recruitment into civic activity. Verba *et al.* (1995) show that variation in civic participation among American adults can be explained by three factors: the fact that citizens who have *resources* can be active; those who are *engaged* are motivated or want to be active; and those who are *recruited* often say yes when asked. College plays a role in at least two and perhaps all three of these. Youth with more resources are more likely to attend college; additional political contacts and resources accrue with education. A wide range of organizations, clubs, and associations also are a typical part of student life and participation in such groups has both social and civic pay-offs. Student members of organizations are likely to get recruited into some community volunteer work or political activity even if the primary purpose of their organization is social. Civic skills and dispositions may accrue as a consequence of their volunteer work. It is less clear that college attendance impacts the motivation for civic participation. However, college attendance does seem to sustain the civic engagement of the highly motivated by offering structured opportunities for staying engaged.

## Class divide in opportunities for civic participation

What are the opportunities for civic participation for youth who do not go on to four-year colleges? Although education and participation have long been stubbornly linked (Verba *et al.* 1995), the class divide in civic participation has been growing. According to a 2006 report from the National Conference on Citizenship, those with a college education are far more likely than those with high-school diplomas to participate in a wide range of civic activities. In part, this growing divide may be due to the changing conditions associated with the transition to adulthood and the institutional lacuna for working-class and poor youth (Settersten *et al.* 2005). In earlier generations, youth who did not go on to college could expect to find full-time jobs, some unionized, with a living wage. Work provided structure and social connections; many young adults started families and set down roots in communities. Thus, the non–college-bound had several institutions (work, union, family) that provided structured opportunities (resources and recruitment) for getting engaged. In contrast, today, there is an institutional lacuna for youth who do not go on to college. They are more likely to be 'on their own' to identify opportunities both for personal achievement and for civic engagement. And what may pass as exploration may, in fact, reflect floundering in the absence of guidance or mentoring. Trends in North America and Europe indicate that there are growing numbers of late adolescents and early adults who are not connected to society via training, school, or work.

Inequalities in opportunities for civic engagement exist well before the young adult years. In poor communities, schools offer fewer extracurricular and service learning activities and communities offer fewer organized activities. The ratio of children to adults is much higher in resource-stressed communities (Hart and Atkins 2002). As a result, there is a smaller pool of the adult volunteers on which community-based youth organizations depend. In addition, young people are less likely to learn ways that citizens can get the system to work for them since their communities have fewer ties to public officials, less political clout, and fewer vibrant civic associations where public actions can be organized.

Nonetheless, there is a growing body of applied research and practice documenting youth activist projects in marginalized communities (see summaries in Sherrod *et al.* 2005). These projects harness young people's frustrations and direct their anger toward social change, often targeting basic needs for textbooks and transportation or tolerance in schools and communities. Political skills are gained as youth gather information and critically analyze issues, including the political/power dynamics that underlie them and, ultimately learn how to speak out on behalf of their group. Through such venues, they interpret the meaning of citizenship and understand their role as agents of change.

An institutional setting is one context in which political views and identities take shape. Historical context is another. If youth is a politically definitive time in the life course, then the historical events of the period when one comes of age provide fodder for political growth. In fact, historical events that occur during one's youth have a greater formative influence than those same events occurring in one's adulthood. The intersection of historical era with developmental timing has been the focus of sociologists and political scientists in the tradition of generational theory. Proponents of this theory point out that, as increasing numbers of the younger generations replace the declining numbers of their elders in society, the political landscape is bound to change (Delli Carpini 1989). The amount of political stability vs. political change is determined in part by the degree to which the younger generation adopts the views of their elders or crafts a distinct generational perspective. Thus, focusing on ways that younger generations negotiate salient social issues provides a lens on the future political landscape. Drawing from Mannheim ([1928] 1952), generational theorists contend that younger generations have a 'fresh contact' with their society, i.e., they see (objectively) similar issues and events from a perspective distinct from adults.

Stewart and McDermott (2004) argue that different forms of political engagement (e.g., conventional vs. protest politics) and the amount of political continuity or change they portend are shaped by different generations' relative tendency to identify horizontally (with peers) or vertically (with the parents' generation). If the period of one's youth intersects with a historical time of social discontinuity, it increases within generation identification. For example, in South Africa, activists in the Black Consciousness and Young Lions generations united around the cause of fighting apartheid. In today's democratic South Africa, activists in the younger generation are more likely to participate through intergenerational venues such as religious, traditional, and indigenous organizations.

In contrast to the theme of social change which tends to dominate generational replacement theories, socialization theory concentrates on intergenerational continuity, arguing that adult agents pass on to the younger generation a set of principles that sustain the system. An affective attachment to the political principles that sustain the system was thought to develop via the young person's sense of political efficacy, i.e., their sense that when people like them spoke, political authorities paid attention (Easton and Dennis 1969). Less attention was given to politics as a contestation of power or to the development of political consciousness in marginalized groups. Socialization theory also is less compelling in contexts of rapid social change when there is considerable discontinuity between the principles that organized society during the parents' formative years and the principles that dominate as their children come of age. For example, in Central and Eastern Europe in the early 1990s, the rapid pace of change from command to market economies and from single party to multi-party rule meant that the habits and practices of the parents' generation were poor guides for the political realities that their children faced.

## Opportunities for civic practice

Participation in organizations in one's youth is a precursor to civic engagement in adulthood. However, opportunities for engagement vary by age and class. In their national, longitudinal study following a 1965 high-school cohort into mid-life, Jennings and Stoker (2004) point to precipitous declines in civic engagement after youth graduate from high school. As explanation, they contrast the highly structured opportunities and norms for engagement in the high school setting with the greater dependence on individual initiative to find and join organizations in early adulthood.

Engagement in extracurricular and community-based organizations in adolescence does predict civic engagement in adulthood (Verba *et al.* 1995) but all organizations are not equal in this regard. In their analysis of two national longitudinal US data sets, McFarland and Thomas (2006) report that involvement as a youth in voluntary associations that entail community service, public speaking, debate, and performance, and religious affiliations are the strongest predictors of political involvement in young adulthood. After controlling for multiple social background and selection factors, they conclude that 'youth organizations that demand time commitments and that concern service, political activity, and public performance have the most significant positive relation to long-term political participation' (ibid.: 416).

The mechanisms underlying the long-term civic impact of organizational involvement in one's youth are not well delineated but several come to mind. First is a selection effect: joiners in youth become joiners in adulthood. As research on voluntarism suggests, their personalities may differ: volunteers are more likely than non-volunteers to exhibit positive emotions and social skills including openness, agreeableness, and extraversion (Matsuba *et al.* 2007). Second, once in an organization, an individual is likely to get recruited into other organizations and civic activities (Verba *et al.* 1995). Thus, engagement as a youth sets one on a recruitment trajectory, i.e., involvement in one group increases the likelihood of recruitment into others.

Third, although social rewards are the reason most youth initially join organizations, over time they are likely to develop an affinity and identification with the organization and its mission, and feel a sense of coherence between their own values and views and those of others in the organization (Erikson 1968). The public or collective identity they are forging is a necessary foundation for sustained civic action insofar as such action benefits the community, not just the self. We are more likely to forego individual gain on behalf of the good of a group if we feel a sense of solidarity with the group.

Solidarity or identification with a group or organization is related to a fourth reason why organizational engagement in youth is related to civic engagement in adulthood. By working with a group to achieve a goal, particularly if they succeed, they may experience a sense of collective efficacy, i.e., a belief in the capacity of the group to achieve something together. Since political goals are typically achieved through collective action, this is an important constituent for sustaining their engagement.

## Forms of youth political activism

Youth may be less likely than their elders to engage in conventional politics. But they are more likely to act on their beliefs in unconventional ways through public demonstrations, acts of civil disobedience, or even more disruptive forms of political action. Social movements literature has regularly documented the inverse relationship between age and the choice of militant strategies that may pose personal risks. Often, this has resulted in public and media derision and dismissal both of the message and of the youth. However, youths' impatience and penchant for militant action have invigorated organizations and political movements. In the struggle against apartheid in South Africa, it was the militancy of youth that rejuvenated the African National Congress. Likewise, the willingness of the Student Nonviolent Coordinating Committee (SNCC) to get arrested for acts of civil disobedience against segregation revitalized more mainstream Civil Rights organizations in the United States.

Contemporary studies also document how mainstream community organizations (e.g., 4-H) are reinvigorated when youths' perspectives are taken seriously. Across communities in the United States, young people are assuming leadership roles in public policy consultation, community coalitions for youth development, and non-profit organizations. These models reflect a new focus on positive youth development which frames youth as assets rather than risks to their communities (see entries in Sherrod et al. 2005). They also necessitate a new partnering style between the youth and adults in the organization. It is also noteworthy that several contemporary models of job and life skills training incorporate civic engagement as an integral element of training. Programs such as Youth Build, Youth ChalleNGe, AmeriCorps, and Youth Corps combine education, job skills training, and volunteer service. Consequently, youth have first-hand experience of the contributions they can make and the ways their training can be put to use.

Perhaps the biggest increase in youth civic engagement has occurred as a consequence of the institutionalization of community service/service learning in secondary and post-secondary education. In the United States, the past two decades have seen an exponential increase in the number of service learning courses offered in high schools with some cities and states mandating a specified number of community service hours as a graduation requirement. Although program quality varies, the ideal is that students engage in meaningful (rather than functional) work that addresses real community needs in projects that are sustained over time, and that they connect their experiences back to classroom learning. Research indicates that, even when mandated, engaging in quality service results in a growth in students' civic skills, democratic dispositions, and sense of efficacy in addressing community issues. Criticisms of the trends in service learning as a form of civic engagement contend that direct service in the absence of discussions about the underlying cause of public problems and policy options to address those problems, may divert youth toward charity and away from political action.

Similar trends in community engagement have occurred in colleges and universities where creative experiments in public scholarship and service learning emphasize the reciprocity between learning in the classroom and the community. These models of education emphasize its civic purpose and imply that it is myopic to focus only on credentializing students for the job market: preparing youth for the responsibilities of adulthood also means enabling them to assume their roles as citizens. Indeed, as the job market becomes less predictable and the nature of jobs more episodic, the centrality of work to identity may be changing. Civic identity and the purpose and sense of community derived from it may take on added meaning in the life narratives of younger generations.

Increasingly political issues transcend the borders of states and many new forms of youth activism reflect this transnational reality. Both the causes (e.g., workers' rights in sweatshops) and the methods (networking with IT) are transnational in their reach. Activists focus on justice in labor, environmental, and procedural practices and underscore the lack of accountability of new multinational entities (the WTO, G8, or the World Bank) to the people affected by their policies. Organizations such as the World Social Forum provide alternative images of a world other than the one these multinational entities portend.

Organizational styles reflect a new politics as well. In contrast to the centralized, hierarchical structures of political parties or labor unions, horizontal, loose networks with flexible membership and dispersed leadership are more typical. The new youth politics take advantage of the democratic potential of new media to share information, increase diversity of opinion, and to mobilize political actions. To date, social networking, virtual worlds, and gaming have largely been used for social and consumer purposes but time will tell how creative youth may be in exploiting their political potential.

The protracted period of 'youth' and the global space of their lives should motivate renewed attention to the civic engagement theme, including a critical look at the received wisdom about the developmental processes, forms, and timing of political identity formation. First, younger generations may take longer than in the past to explore political issues before deciding where they stand. The lower voting rates of today's 18–25 year-olds may be less troubling if they catch up by age 30. Second, there may be life-long civic benefits to an extended moratorium on social roles *if* youth get engaged and wrestle with public problems during these years. Of course, this implies a policy shift toward more programs in local and national service. Engaging in such work at a time when individuals are constituting their identities should inculcate a civic ethic well into the retirement years.

Third, the changing structure of work and declines in union membership have resulted in a growing class divide in civic participation and an institutional lacuna for working-class youth. Models of job training that include civic service hold promise but more creativity is needed to insure all young people have equal opportunities for civic practice. Fourth, migration of people from the developing to the developed world raises questions about the meaning of citizenship and the protections of 'stateless' citizens.

Finally, theories of youth political development may have underestimated the value of responsibilities in the consolidation of political identities. The freedom from social roles has been extolled as a major reason why youth is a politically definitive period. But such freedom may be put to other exploratory ends (binge drinking comes to mind) in the absence of social pressures. Youth are unlikely to take a stand until the personal relevance of a political issue is clear and the relevance of many issues may only become clear with the assumption of adult roles and responsibilities.

# References

Alwin, D. F., Cohen, R. L. and Newcomb, T. M. (1991) *Political Attitudes over the Life Span: The Bennington Women after Fifty Years*, Madison, WI: University of Wisconsin Press.

Arnett, J. J. (2000) 'Emerging adulthood: a theory of development from the late teens through the twenties', *American Psychologist*, 55: 469–80.

Delli Carpini, M. (1989) 'Age and history: generations and sociopolitical change', in R. S. Sigel (ed.) *Political Learning in Adulthood*, Chicago: University of Chicago Press.

Easton, D. and Dennis, J. (1969) *Children in the Political System*, New York: McGraw-Hill.

Erikson, E. H. (1968) *Identity: Youth and Crisis*, New York: W.W. Norton.

Flanagan, C. A. (2004) 'Volunteerism, leadership, political socialization, and civic engagement', in R. M. Lerner and L. Steinberg (eds) *Handbook of Adolescent Psychology*. New York: Wiley.

Flanagan, C. A. and Tucker, C. J. (1999) 'Adolescents' explanations for political issues: concordance with their views of self and society', *Developmental Psychology*, 35: 1198–1209.

Hart, D. and Atkins, R. (2002) 'Civic competence in urban youth', *Applied Developmental Science*, 6: 227–36.

Jennings, M. K. (2002) 'Generation units and the student protest movement in the United States: an intra- and intergenerational analysis', *Political Psychology*, 23: 303–24.

Jennings, M. K. and Stoker, L. (2004) 'Social trust and civic engagement across time and generations', *Acta Politica*, 39: 342–79.

Levine, P. (2007) *The Future of Democracy: Developing the Next Generation of American Citizens*, Medford, MA: Tufts University Press.

McFarland, D. A. and Thomas, R. J. (2006) 'Bowling young: how youth voluntary associations influence adult political participation', *American Sociological Review*, 71: 401–25.

Mannheim, K. ([1928] 1952) 'The problem of generations', in P. Kecshevich (ed.) *Essays on the Sociology of Knowledge*, London: Routledge and Kegan Paul.

Matsuba, J. K., Hart, D. and Atkins, R. (2007) 'Psychological and social-structural influences on commitment to volunteering', *Journal of Research in Personality*, 41: 889–907.

Settersten, R. A., Furstenberg, F. F. and Rumbaut, R. G. (2005) *On the Frontier of Adulthood: Theory, Research, and Public Policy*, Chicago: University of Chicago Press.

Sherrod, L., Flanagan, C. A., Kassimir, R. and Syvertsen, A. B. (eds) (2005) *Youth Activism: An International Encyclopedia*, Westport, CT: Greenwood Publishing.

Stewart, A. J. and McDermott, C. (2004) 'Civic engagement, political identity, and generation in developmental context', *Research in Human Development*, 1: 189–203.

Verba, S., Scholzman, K. L. and Brady, H. E. (1995) *Voice and equality: Civic voluntarism in American Politics*, Cambridge, MA: Harvard University Press.

Walzer, M. (1989) 'Citizenship', in T. Ball, J. Farrand and R. Hanson (eds) *Political Innovation and Conceptual Change*, Cambridge: Cambridge University Press.

# 37

# Young people, politics and citizenship

*Anita Harris*

## Introduction

This chapter addresses young people's engagement with the state, their communities, and with social and political issues, and how they enact their rights and duties as citizens. Over time, what is meant by politics and citizenship has come to include an increasingly wide range of practices, but these fundamentally still relate to how young people participate in the polity, the public sphere and civil society, including voting habits, civic knowledge, involvement in party politics, activism, consumption and production of political media, creation of community, and relationship to rights. This chapter looks at a range of predominantly Western approaches to youth, politics and citizenship by discussing the evolution of key concepts in the field, considering the special status held by youth as political actors, and by exploring the current challenges to theories and practice of youth participation and citizenship brought about by recent socioeconomic change.

## Defining young people, politics and citizenship: the evolution of key concepts

Theoretical approaches to youth, politics and citizenship are determined by historical moment, discipline and location. From the 1950s to the 1970s, the political socialization of children and young people was an important theme in US political science and psychology as well as in other areas such as Latin American sociology, especially given the emergence of the youth-led social movements of the late 1960s. This research focused on the psychological development of political consciousness. Since this time, according to Holdsworth *et al.* (2007), three key concepts have emerged: first, the 1970s and 1980s saw the development of interest in youth *participation* in decision-making. This era marked the first wave of an international cross-disciplinary youth rights movement championing the inclusion of young people in political spaces and public conversations that affect them. This recognition of the participatory rights of young people was enshrined in the 1989 United Nations Convention on the Rights of the Child.

The following period was characterized by debate on youth *citizenship*, including not only rights, but also civic and political knowledge and responsibilities. From the 1990s onwards there has been an explosion of interest and concern regarding young people's participatory citizenship: their awareness of and engagement in politics and current affairs, from their commitment to voting to their attendance at protests. Research projects out of political science, sociology and education have frequently identified a 'civics deficit' and many nations have developed policies, programmes and school curricula to address this problem. There have also been supranational policy recommendations such as the European Commission's 2001 White Paper on youth. Third, into the 2000s, the language of *civic engagement* has emerged, especially in sociological literature. Debates about youth and politics have been strongly influenced by Putnam's (1999) work on social capital and civic engagement in the USA to address their commitment to civil society, including volunteering and other kinds of community involvement.

Taken together, these key themes of political socialization, participatory citizenship and civic engagement form the foundation of contemporary studies on youth, politics and citizenship. Next, this chapter examines the particular circumstances of youth that give them a special status in the field of politics and citizenship, and then explores how theories and practice of youth participation have been transformed in response to recent socio-economic change.

## Young people's status as political actors

Young people have a special status as political actors for a number of reasons. First, the category of 'youth' straddles the formal age divide between those who have full citizenship rights, in particular, political rights, and those who don't. Commonly around the world, young people must be over 18 to vote or stand for office. At the same time, there is a huge variance within and across countries in the legal age for many other rights to be activated, for example, entitlement to an adult wage, access to unemployment or carer's benefits, or occupation of public space after certain hours. Further, the period of youth has been constructed as a time of citizenship training, during which young people are taught about political participation rather than facilitated to engage in it. As White and Wyn (2007: 112) note, citizenship is linked to adult status, and policy that addresses youth citizenship tends to treat young people as passive recipients of civic education that will prepare them for their future adult role.

Second, political institutions are created by adults to serve an adult agenda and are not structured around young people's interests or designed to engage them. Research has long indicated that young people feel marginalized by formal politics. There is a significant gap between what young people perceive as 'politics' and the issues they identify as important to them: politics is associated with formal political institutions, especially parliamentary processes. Young people do not tend to define their own concerns and the activities they engage in around these as politics. However, young people's lack of interest in and engagement with formal politics and political institutions is not the same as a lack of interest in political issues or an inability to act politically. As Vromen (2003) among others has demonstrated, young people's political interest and participatory practice can be better captured with more open typologies of politics.

Third, young people have always been the subject of fascination in politics because of the long-standing idea of a generation gap in political outlook and commitment. Youth is commonly associated with activism and with liberal politics. Young people of an earlier generation were the drivers of the 1960s Western social movements and more recently, youth have been instrumental in dismantling both communist and post-communist regimes in Eastern European countries, for example, Ukraine's Orange Revolution in 2004, and have been a strong presence in international protests against the war in Iraq and in the anti-corporate globalization movement. There is some evidence that young people are less conservative than older people, especially in relation to party preferences and social issues (Furlong and Cartmel 2007). However, youth has also been linked with apathy. Many studies have demonstrated that young people are less likely than older people to be interested in formal politics, to vote, to affiliate with a political party or to exhibit high levels of political knowledge (ibid.). For example, a 1999 survey of 90,000 youth in 28 countries found widespread scepticism about traditional forms of political engagement and shallow understandings of democracy (Torney-Purta *et al.* 2001).

Young people's role in politics occupies a special place in the public imagination because they are positioned paradoxically as both highly active and apathetic. This framing of young people takes on particular forms in contemporary thinking about issues for youth politics and citizenship because of recent socio-economic change.

## Current challenges to theories and practice of youth policies and citizenship

The contemporary conditions of economic rationalism, globalization and individualization mount a challenge to theories and practices of youth politics and citizenship. The current generation of youth no longer experiences a linear pathway to traditional adult status: compared to earlier generations, young people today stay in education and the family home longer and change jobs frequently rather than pursue a career for life (see White and Wyn 2007). This generation highlights the arbitrariness of age-based rights and the outdated perception of youth as passive citizens-to-be, for in many respects they are living simultaneously youthful and adult lives. Their experiences also raise questions about the paradoxical assumptions about young people as either apathetic or at the vanguard of social change, for while it can be argued that socio-economic changes have diminished traditional forms of citizenship and have marginalized young people from conventional political participation, new modes of youth engagement have emerged and older ones have re-emerged. Contemporary research on youth politics and citizenship complicates binary thinking about young people and politics.

### *Economic rationalism*

One trend in contemporary research on youth and politics documents how new economic conditions make it harder for young people to enact their citizenship status. Many young people struggle to achieve their social rights, that is, enjoy the economic security on which citizenship is predicated, in the context of a dismantled welfare system and neoliberal economic policies that devolve responsibility for economic security from the state onto the individual. Unlike previous generations, young people today do not have straightforward access to social security and at the same time face reduced employment opportunities. The new economy has made citizenship elusive for young people because they cannot move easily into economic independence, on which autonomy depends, but must now balance prolonged periods of training with insecure work in a highly competitive labour market (Jones and Wallace, 1992). Those working in the tradition of Marshall (1950), the influential theorist of citizenship as a tripartite system of rights, argue that young people cannot activate their participatory rights in isolation from these social rights. The privatization of formerly public services and spaces such as youth employment services or leisure facilities has also reduced young people's access to both the state and the public sphere and thereby has limited their opportunities to participate.

Other research focuses on how new economic challenges, in particular, the collapse of the youth job market, force young people to prioritize economic security over political rights. A study of youth in 41 countries found that failure to register to vote is a consequence of what the researchers call 'lifestyle' rather than apathy: young people were interested in politics, but often failed to register to vote because they moved so frequently for work-related reasons (Lagos and Rose 1999). In these ways, economic rationalism constrains participation.

## Globalization

Another focus for contemporary work on youth citizenship is the impact of globalization. Globalization is seen to loosen young people's traditional citizenship ties, especially in relation to national identifications, as a result of increased migration, the internet, the ease and popularity of travel and the powerful reach of a global youth consumer culture. Globalization has also meant that political and economic decisions and social and cultural trends occur supra-nationally, which can undermine young people's belief in the efficacy of the nation-state. The nation means different things to different youth in this context. In much Australian research, young people's attachment to national community is shown to be fairly weak. For example, Ang et al. (2006: 33) found their cohort of young Australians wary of excessive patriotism and open to cultural differences.

However, cosmopolitanism is not universally or evenly embraced. For example, in their six-country study of young people's citizenship and European identity, Jamieson et al. (2005) found that most were more strongly attached to their city, nation and region than they were to Europe. For some other young people again, 'the foreigner' has become a target for fears about social and economic change. There are some indicators that right-wing nationalism and even extremist ideologies gained currency among a minority of marginalized youth through the 1990s.

## Individualization

Contemporary youth politics and citizenship studies also grapples with the ways that individualization has replaced collective identification. Personal and lifestyle issues have become more significant for young people than movement- or party-based politics. According to theorists of individualization, traditional forms of fixed community and associational life have been replaced by transitory and multiple affiliations which do not lend themselves to 'thick' citizenship (Bauman 2001). This trend is often linked to the widespread disenchantment among young people with formal party politics. However, as Jamieson et al. (2005) show, low trust in political systems does not generally indicate low interest in social and political issues. For example, a 2002 UK Electoral Commission report found that of all the cohorts researched, young people were the least likely to vote, but also the most likely to have had discussions about political issues with friends and family (Russell et al. 2002). In spite of their finding that young people are sceptical about traditional forms of political engagement, Torney-Purta *et al.* (2001) note their openness to other kinds of civic and political participation. Similarly, a large US study of civic engagement found 15–25 year-olds half as likely as the 55+ cohort to be involved in electoral activities, but had twice the level of involvement in community activities (Keeter *et al.* 2002).

Theorists such as Inglehart (1990) suggest that young people have become more focused on quality of life concerns as a result of a generational shift from 'materialist' to 'post-materialist values', which is evident in the rise in commitment to issues such as the environment, peace, HIV/AIDs and animal rights. Similarly, while collectivist, hierarchical social movement politics has ceased to be popular with young people, there is evidence of new, more individualized forms of activism. These include computer hacking, culture jamming, brand boycotts and recycling, as well as the creative activities of the decentralized anti-corporate globalization movement. Other youth researchers argue that individualization has led to new socialities and communities. Terms such as 'neo-tribes', 'lifestyles' and 'scenes' describe loose networks that young people create in their leisure activities such as clubbing or online social networking. It is argued that the diminution of public space for young people to use both socially and politically and the rise of consumer culture in its place have seen young people carve out new spaces such as clubs, raves, hip hop gigs and the internet as alternative public spheres, or as sites of new community (Harris 2004).

## Continuities and geopolitical differences

Economic rationalism, globalization and individualization have had a significant impact on theories and practices of young people's participation. However, it is important not to overestimate the shift to new modes of politics and citizenship. Youth-led voter registration drives were held throughout the 1990s, some especially focused on marginalized populations such as African-American youth. The USA and Canada have both seen recent strong increases in youth voter turnout, and in Australia (where voting is compulsory) there has been a significant rise in youth voter registration. Roker (2007) notes the strong commitment young people, especially young women, have to traditional forms of social action. Vromen (2003) demonstrates that even a small expansion in definitions of participatory politics significantly increases the number of youth activities that can be counted. This picture unsettles the assumption that there has been a wholesale generational move away from conventional politics.

The internet has been an important force in the resurgence of youth engagement in formal politics, as it is now a key site for young people to express their views about politics and create new public spaces for articulation and exchange of politically and socially engaged ideas and activities. Many young people are keen bloggers and youth are the primary users of social networking sites, which themselves house tens of thousands of political groups. Politicians recognize the value of online activity and many use social networking and video-sharing sites to engage youth (albeit to questionable effect).

It is also important to recognize geopolitical differences in the forces that delimit or enable engagement. For example, Kovacheva (2005: 25) notes that in areas such as South-western and Eastern Europe, it is the ongoing centralization of political and social life rather than individualization which inhibits young people's participation. The political history of specific national contexts also cuts across assumptions about the value of youth engagement, for example, young political activists in South Africa have suffered mar-ginalization as a result of their engagement (see Everatt 2001). Young people's take-up of politics and citizenship is dynamic and it is most useful to look at their participation across a shifting spectrum that is shaped by local circumstances, socio-economic factors and demographic variables as well as global forces.

## Acknowledgements

Thanks to Lesley Pruitt for research assistance.

## References

Ang, I., Brand, J., Noble, G. and Sternberg, J. (2006) *Connecting Diversity: Paradoxes of Multicultural Australia*, Artarmon: Special Broadcasting Service Corporation.

Bauman, Z. (2001) *The Individualised Society*, Cambridge: Polity.

Everatt, D. (2001) 'From urban warrior to market segment? Youth in South Africa 1990–2000', in H. Helve and C. Wallace (eds) *Youth, Citizenship and Empowerment*, Aldershot: Ashgate.

Furlong, A. and Cartmel, A. (2007) *Young People and Social Change, New Perspectives*, 2nd edn, Maidenhead: Open University Press.

Harris, A. (2004) *Future Girl: Young Women in the Twenty-First Century*, New York and London: Routledge.

Holdsworth, R. (2007) *Civic Engagement and Young People*, Melbourne: Australian Youth Research Centre.

Inglehart, R. (1990) *Culture Shift in Advanced Industrial Society*, Princeton, NJ: Princeton University Press.

Jamieson, L., Wallace, C., Condor, S., Boehnke, K., Ros, M., Grad, H., Machacek, L. and Bianchi, G. (2005) *Orientations of Young Men and Women to Citizenship and European Identity*, final report, the European Commission, February 2005. Online. Available at: www.sociology.ed.ac.uk/youth/final_report.pdf (accessed 26 November 2007).

Jones, G. and Wallace, C. (1992) *Youth, Family and Citizenship*, Buckingham: Open University Press.

Keeter, S., Zukin, C., Andolina, M. and Jenkins, K. (2002) *The Civic and Political Health of a Nation: A Generational Portrait*. CIRCLE and The Pew Charitable Trusts. Online. Available at: www.civicyouth.org/research/products/youth_index.htm (accessed 19 November 2007).

Kovacheva, S. (2005) 'Will youth rejuvenate the patterns of political participation?', in J. Forbrig (ed.) *Revisiting Youth Political Participation: Challenges for Research and Democratic Practice in Europe*, Strasbourg: Council of Europe.

Lagos, M. and Rose, R. (1999) *Young People in Politics: A Multicontinental Study*, Studies in Public Policy Number 316, Centre for the Study of Public Policy, Glasgow: University of Strathclyde.

Marshall, T. H. (1950) *Citizenship and Social Class*, Cambridge: Cambridge University Press.

Putnam, R. (1999) *Bowling Alone: The Collapse and Revival of American Community*, New York: Simon & Schuster.

Roker, D. (2007) 'Young women and social action in the UK', in A. Harris (ed.) *Next Wave Cultures: Feminism, Subcultures, Activism*, New York: Routledge.

Russell, A., Fieldhouse, E., Purdam, K. and Kalra, V. (2002) *Voter Engagement and Young People*, London: The Electoral Commission.

Torney-Purta, J., Lehmann, R., Oswald, H. and Schulz, W. (2001) *Citizenship and Education in Twenty-eight Countries: Civic Knowledge and Engagement at Age Fourteen*, Amsterdam: International Association for the Evaluation of Educational Achievement.

Vromen, A. (2003) 'People try to put us down … participatory citizenship of Generation X', *Australian Journal of Political Science*, 38(1): 79–99.

White, R. and Wyn, J. (2007) *Youth and Society: Exploring the Social Dynamics of Youth*, 2nd edn, Oxford: Oxford University Press.

# 38

# Youth and trade unionism

*Jan Carle*

## Introduction: some basic concepts

This chapter begins by introducing some basic concepts before moving on to discuss trends and changes in trade union membership. One of the central issues addressed relates to why trade unions have a problem in attracting youth in modern society with various explanations considered including those that focus on occupational and industrial change and those that highlight changing values in modern societies.

In discussing trade union membership, two major concepts are important: first, the idea of membership density, second, variation in forms of membership. Ideas of membership density underpin any discussion of union membership with a distinction often made between gross and net density. Gross density refers to 'the total union membership including unemployed, students and retired workers as a share either of all wage and salary earners in employment or of the civilian labour force, which includes the unemployed' (Lesch 2004: 12). Lesch acknowledges that gross density can be problematic in situations where the number of retired workers, students and others with a loose or flexible relation to the labour market (such as young people in particular) are increasing in a given society. Net density is a more restricted concept and which focuses on active wage and salary earners and excludes unemployed or non-active members.

When exploring patterns of membership among young people, it is important to recognize that forms of membership typical in different occupations will have an impact on young people's experiences. At an extreme, where a 'closed shop' agreement exists, young people (as non-members) can be prevented from accessing jobs. Within the closed shop model, companies and organizations can only recruit existing union members, either through direct recruitment mechanisms or through the union as an intermediary gate-keeper. Imposing less strict (and therefore more youth-friendly) conditions is the 'union shop' model within which companies may only employ non-union members by using special contracts that are controlled by the unions. The 'agency shop' model allows companies more scope to hire also non-union members, although trade unions are involved in the recruitment process. Finally, the 'open shop' model provides equal opportunities for non-union and union members. From the point of view of the unions, these different models have a direct impact on membership density while from the perspective of young workers the degree of openness may have a direct impact on opportunities.

## Youth and trade unions: – some basic facts about trends

In a nutshell, in most advanced societies for which there are available statistics, union density has decreased significantly. A similar trend seems to be apparent in less developed countries where statistics are less reliable, such as in parts of Africa, Asia and Latin America. While union density peaked in many countries in the 1960s, since then the decline has been relatively steady (Ebinghaus and Visser 1999; Eurofond 2004; Checci and Visser 2005). This pattern has been reported to be particularly notable among young people (Spilsbury *et al* 1987; Freeman and Diamond 2003; Bryson *et al*. 2005).

Despite common trends, density rates vary hugely between countries. At one end of the spectrum there are countries such as Sweden with very high net density rates (82.2 per cent), while at the other end, countries like the USA have extremely low density rates (13.3 per cent) (Lesch 2004). Lesch also shows that while some countries have had quite stable (or even increasing) overall density rate since the 1960s (e.g. Sweden, Finland, Belgium, Norway and Denmark), in many other countries the decrease has been steady (e.g. the USA, Austria, Japan and Australia).

What stands out from the figures is, first, that a decrease in net density of membership describes the trend in many countries and, second, that young people are at the cutting edge of the changes. While the unions still play an important role in the administration of unemployment insurance in some of the Nordic countries (and consequently the added incentive for membership has meant that density rates have remained relatively high), even in these countries, density levels among young people have declined with many young people failing to join unions or abandoning their membership

## Reasons for change

### The question of power

In many respects, the scope for involvement with trade unions can be regarded as central to the democratic process in western societies. Democracy is not limited to the opportunity to participate in free elections, but also involves the right to form and participate in other representative bodies such as those elected to speak on behalf of groups of workers and represent them to management and government. For international bodies like the United Nations and the European Union, the possibility for workers to participate in trade union activities is regarded as a social right and as central to the process of citizenship. Writers such as Marshall *et al*. (1997) and Lukes (2004) regarded citizenship as involving possibilities for individuals and groups to influence social and political agendas. Access to work and the ability to influence the labour process were also regarded as part of the rights of citizens, and, in this context, trade unions have traditionally played an important role. They provide the working population with a voice and access to a representative body that can influence work contexts and employment security as well as perusing a broader social agenda. Indeed, in many countries, trade unions have been able to establish a role that goes beyond protecting working conditions and plays a part in the broader political arena as well as influencing social and cultural life. In such circumstances, union membership connects people on a social and political level and helps them to influence future agendas.

In contemporary society, trade unions can be regarded as being part of a process of extended citizenship, although perhaps they are not well adjusted to the rapid social changes that have taken place. In contexts that have become globalized and individualized, young people become connected in new ways and seek different ways to influence society and attempt to take control over their living conditions. Aside from trade unions, young people may be involved directly in political parties, may be part of grassroots movements or may even connect through internet-based activities. In trying to explain the decrease in union involvement among young people, researchers have tended to focus on broader processes of social change and the transformation of citizenship. In today's world, access to power and influence over social and political agenda can be secured in a wide variety of ways and young people are at the forefront of change.

## Change in rights and legal system

According to Lesch (2004), one of the main factors explaining country-specific differences in union density rates within Europe relates to the extent to which the 'Ghent system' has been adopted as a model that defines the position and influence of unions within the broader social and political system. The 'Ghent system' was introduced in 1901 and still operates in the Nordic countries as well as in Belgium. Under this system, unions not only represent members in negotiations over wages and working conditions, but also offer a range of other economic benefits as well as enhancing job security.

In the past, the strength of unions derived from their exclusive rights to negotiate with employers and represent their members. Membership had clear and positive benefits. While there were 'free riders' who benefited from the activities of the union without being members, union members often had exclusive rights and benefits. For young workers, an introduction to the benefits of union membership was part of the process of workplace socialization with older workers selling the benefits of membership. Today the situation is different in a number of respects. At a basic level, many of the conditions that were fought for and upheld by unions, such as minimal salaries and state pensions, are now provided by the state and therefore the cost of being outside a union is not so great. Indeed, the trend towards more comprehensive legislation governing workers' rights (particularly within the European Union) effectively undermines the role of trade unions as representatives and in turn they have a reduced scope for negotiation. Here one might expect that young people will increasingly be introduced to employment in contexts where labour conditions are governed by legislation rather than by union-led negotiation. In such circumstances the incentives for union membership are reduced.

On an international level, the overall trend has been for governments to legislate against closed shop agreements and launch reforms that favour open shop conditions. Rather than supporting bilateral agreements between employers and trade unions, governments have tended to intervene directly to underpin conditions through legislation. However, in the Nordic countries, contracts between unions and employers are still favoured. At the same time, some of the changes introduced by governments (who are perhaps less in touch with the concerns of young people) have caused unrest among younger workers. In France and Spain, for example, reforms introduced by national governments have resulted directly in conflict as attempts were made to 'open up' the market for young people. In France, the unions strongly opposed measures to 'improve' employment opportunities for young people by reducing their job security, leading directly to strikes and civil unrest. With unions failing to fight strongly for the rights for the young, young people may be less likely to join trade unions in the future.

## Industrial change

For young people, one of the key trends over the last few decades has been a general decrease in the numbers entering the labour market, an increase in educational participation, a growth in the numbers working on temporary contracts, an increase in numbers working in the service and in the 'new' economy and a decrease in young people in 'traditional' industrial working situations. Many of these trends have been triggered by the decline of traditional large-scale manufacturing industry and the growth of smaller service, caring and trading activities. These industrial changes have a huge impact on the unions since their roots have traditionally been firmly embedded in large scale manufacturing industries.

In the new areas of the economy, union activity lacks visibility, which impacts directly on recruitment. When unions are active in the workplace, with representatives and members able to talk to young workers in the employment setting, rates of membership among young people tend to be higher (e.g. Spilsbury *et al.* 1987; Freeman and Diamond 2003). The importance of being part of a union 'family' in highly unionized workplaces is even projected strongly on the web-pages of some unions, overlooking the fact that many young workers will be employed in small-scale settings without a tradition of union membership.

Machin (2003) argues that it is important to be aware of the impact of structural changes in the labour market and the ways in which they impact on the experiences of young people. Here he argues that one should distinguish between the age of the workplace and the age of workers within it. Compared to long-established companies, young enterprises typically have lower rate of union members; but companies that are relatively new also tend to employ a younger workforce, especially in the 'new' sectors of the economy such as computing and financial services. As the 'new economy' grows, so union density declines, even though the unions themselves are aware of these issues and have attempted to recruit in non-traditional fields (e.g. Dribbusch 2005).

In many cases, though, structural change has led to a situation where young people are denied the possibility of union membership because they are denied the possibility of becoming established in the labour market and are not considered as 'active' wage or salary earners. Indeed, for many traditional unions, especially those operating in male-dominated manufacturing industries, young people are regarded as 'potential' members of the future rather than as a possible source of available recruits who should be targeted despite, and even because, they hold temporary contracts or have precarious working situations.

## Change in socialization

Linked to industrial change, research shows clearly that family experience and traditions have a powerful effect on patterns of union membership: there are strong links between parents' membership and young people's membership. However, the association between parental membership and the union affiliation of young people has weakened over the past 10 to 15 years. Some have even argued that parental experiences of employment (especially the inability of unions to protect members in the face of rapid change), have begun to have a negative impact on political socialization and recruitment (Freeman and Diamond 2003).

### Change in attitudes

Despite these changes, on the whole, young people's attitudes towards trade unions remains positive (e.g. Freeman and Diamond 2003) and many young people, including the unemployed, those in precarious situations as well as those yet to enter the labour market, say that they are prepared to join a trade union and to participate in the political system in general (Carle 2003). Even those working in new areas of the economy are not ideologically opposed to unions, they simply do not see the point in joining and recognize that unions often have weak positions in the new markets (Freeman and Diamond 2003; Machin 2003).

### The change in working collective to the individualized worker

In many respects, the work situations of young workers are so different from those experienced by an older (and highly unionized) generation that changes in membership patterns are inevitable. Here Lysgaard (1961) argues that the ideal preconditions for union activity, situations where unions are able to speak for the workforce, stem from a set of common understandings rooted in collective experience. In such circumstances, workers may share attitudes and values, work in close proximity, are able to talk about common interests and able to learn from each other. Such situations tend to exist in traditional manufacturing environments, but are not part of the common experiences of today's youth. For young people today, fragmented work and life situations result in the search for individualized rather than collectivized solutions.

Related to this, Hirschman (1970) predicts that an individualized solution to workplace problems would be to seek an exit rather than seek a voice. If loyalty is not valued, employers treat workers as disposable objects and workers have few expectations of employment continuity, then any disappointment with salary or working conditions is likely to promote job search activities. In these circumstances, the position of the union is marginalized.

## Conclusion

What we are observing today is a clash between the new working conditions that are becoming increasingly common among young people and the old, collectivized, conditions that framed the workplace experiences of the previous generations. In the new contexts, unions lack visibility and influence and are failing to capture the loyalty of young workers. For Lysgaard (1961) it is vital that unions find ways of communicating and engaging with the new workforce and establish themselves as representatives of the young. Lacking a socialization in the process of workplace representation and working-class politics, young people often remain ignorant of the role of unions and seek individualized solutions to what they regard as personal problems. The role of the contemporary trade union movement is to help young workers make common links and help them recognize that the problems they face are experienced by their peers and, ultimately, require common solutions.

## References

Bryson, A., Gomez, R., Gunderson, M. and Meltz, N. (2005) 'Youth–adult differences in the demand for unionization: are American, British and Canadian workers all that different', *Journal of Labour Research*, 26.

Carle, J. (2003) 'Welfare regimes and political activity among unemployed young people', in T. Hammer (ed.) *Youth Unemployment and Social Exclusion in Europe*, Bristol. Policy Press.

Checci, D. and Visser, J. (2005) 'Pattern persistence in European trade union density: a longitudinal study analysis 1950–96', *European Sociological Review*, 21: 1–21.

Dribbusch, H. (2005) 'Unions take new initiative to tackle membership decline', *Eironline*. 24/06/2005. DE0506206F. Available at: www.eurofound.europa.eu/eiro/2005/06/feature/de0506206f.htm.

Ebinghaus, B. and Visser, J. (1999) 'When institutions matter: union growth and decline in Western Europe, 1950–95', *European Sociological Review*, 15: 135–58.

Eurofond (2004) *Trade Union Membership, 1993–2003*, European Foundation for the Improvement of Living and Working Conditions. Available at: www.eurofound.europa.eu/eiro/2004/03/update/tn0403105u.htm.

Freeman, R. and Diamond, W. (2003) 'Young workers and trade unions', in H. Gospel and S. Wood (eds) *Representing Workers: Union Recognition and Membership in Britain*, London: Routledge.

Hirschman, A. (1970) *Exit Voice and Loyalty: Responses to Decline in Firms, Organisations and States*, Cambridge, MA: Harvard University Press.

Lesch, H. (2004) 'Trade union density in international comparison', *CESifo Forum 4/2004*, 4: 12–17.

Lukes, S. (2004) *Power: A Radical View*, 2nd edn, Basingstoke: Palgrave Macmillan.

Lysgaard, S. (1961) *Arbeirderkollektivet: en studie i de underordnedes socisologi*, Oslo: Oslo University Press.

Machin, S. (2003) 'Trade union decline, new workplaces and new workers', in H. Gospel and S. Wood (eds) *Representing Workers: Union Recognition and Membership in Britain*, London: Routledge.

Marshall, T. H, Moore, R and Bottomore, T. (1997) *Citizen and Social Class*, London: Pluto Press.

Spilsbury, M., Hoskins, M., Ashton, D. N. and Maguire, M. J. (1987) 'A note on the trade union membership of young adults', *British Journal of Industrial Relations*, 25: 0007–1080.

# 39

# 'Riots' or 'urban disorders'?

# The case for re-politicizing urban disorders

*Sadiya Akram*

## Introduction

There has been a long-standing concern with 'rioting' in all First World countries, some of which is presented as criminal behaviour by bored and inactive youth, while at other times the political basis of their behaviour has been acknowledged. It is the argument of this chapter that acts termed as 'riots' are important political events, and those involved in these acts, 'the rioters', are politically motivated actors who deserve to be acknowledged as such. The terms 'riot' and 'rioter' are value-laden and normatively charged notions, which have been heavily disputed in the literature (Benyon 1987; Farrar 2002; Gilroy 2002; Dikec 2006). The language used in this discussion is important and will be discussed in more detail below, but for the purpose of introducing the subject matter, I will continue to use the terms 'riot' and 'rioter'. The analysis will focus on young people or youth involvement in politics, as they are the key cohorts involved in rioting.

It will be argued that existing literature on rioting has struggled to deal with the complex issue of locating political motivations in acts which are dominated by discussions on racialized criminality, violence, irrationality and spontaneous behaviour. These themes all serve to de-politicize the act of rioting. The chapter will examine trends in the literature on rioting and comment on the general neglect of a discussion of the political motivations of the actors involved. The analysis will be located within the broader context of a discussion on decreasing levels of political participation among young people in politics today, or at least in more traditional and more formal modes of political participation. Starting with the UK, the chapter will begin with a review of existing literature in the field of riots, a body of literature which grew in response to the riots; thus, the analysis will largely be temporal. Next, we will examine the riots in France in 2005 and attempt to show the deeply political nature of these events, despite state and popular discourses, which argued otherwise. The chapter ends by exploring future research agendas in this field and makes a plea to reconcile the more criminological aspects of riots, which are acknowledged, with the need to interpret them politically. First, however, we move to a discussion of terminology.

## 'Riots' or 'urban disorders'?

'Discourses' shape meaning and frame concepts, which may in turn develop socially and materially circumscribed boundaries (Fairclough 2002). The *Oxford English Dictionary* defines the term 'riot' as 'violent disturbance of the peace by a crowd' (2005: 1519). The term 'violence' is central to the dictionary meaning of the term 'riot' and leaves little room for any other form of analysis. Farrar (2002) argues that the concept of riot is the 'organizing tool' for a discourse that is generated not only in the media, such as the tabloid, broadsheet, radio and television, but is also legitimized in most of the official reports that are sometimes produced after these events (see the Cantle Report into urban disorders in Northern towns in England in 2001 (Cantle n.d.) and the Scarman Report into the riots in Brixton, in 1981 (Scarman 1981)). Farrar (2002) suggests that the discourse of the riot contains all the key terms of the dominant discourse on these events: youth, gangs, war, fire, drugs, and riot and de-limits a proper discussion of all of the issues at stake in the debate. The key problem in the official reports and in the media stories is that serious analysis of the cause of these events is pre-empted either by setting them within the discursive framework of 'riot', and, even where this term is partially replaced by 'disturbance', by erasing any detailed account which includes the meanings attached to these events by the participants themselves.

Paul Gilroy prefers the term 'disorderly protest' to riot and argues that while we cannot ignore the criminal elements involved, these events are to be understood as 'rational', and 'purposive' (2002: 327). Gilroy argues that these events are not reducible to 'marginality' and 'deviance', terms which imply that they are nothing more than 'crude reactions to crisis, lacking cognitive, affective and normative dimensions' (ibid.: 324). Gilroy (2002) also emphasizes the similarities between the disorders and social movement theory as discussed in the works of Touraine (1977). Dikec prefers the term 'revolts' to describe the riots arguing that they should be understood as 'unarticulated justice movements against spatial injustices' (2007: 155). Like Dikec, Gilroy is also keen to emphasize the 'local factors', which shape the riots (Gilroy 2002). Benyon (1987) prefers the term 'urban protest', whilst Rex (1979) opts for 'defensive confrontation' in place of 'riot'. Clearly, then, there is an attempt in the literature to change the language and ultimately, the discourse of rioting in order to identify their more political overtones. I opt for the term 'urban disorders' in this chapter, and, in doing so, aim to acknowledge the political motivations of the actors involved but also to locate the acts within their urban and local settings.

## Young people and political participation: an overview

It is important to locate the discussion on urban disorders within the broader literature on young people and their political behaviour. Voter turnout at elections in Britain has been steadily decreasing for all age groups, and, notably, among young people of voting age (Park 1998; Pirie and Worcester 1998; Eden and Roker 2000; Marsh *et al.* 2006). Indeed, there has been much talk of a crisis of youth political participation in Britain (Marsh *et al.* 2006). Pirie and Worcester (1998) claim that the 'millennial generation' of young people who reached the age of 21 just before or just after the turn of the millennium are an 'apolitical generation' as they are less involved in politics than the equivalent generation were 30 years ago, less likely to vote in national or local elections than older people now or young people 30 years ago, and, have little knowledge of politics at local, national or European levels. Similarly, Park's (1998) survey data of social attitudes among British youth indicate that teenagers and young adults are less likely to be involved in conventional politics, be knowledgeable about politics, have an attachment to any political party, or view voting as a civic responsibility.

While declining levels of political participation among young people may be the case, there is also research which questions the view that young people are politically apathetic or inactive. Eden and Roker (2000) and Marsh *et al.* (2006) take a broader view of the ways in which young people engage in political and civic life and suggest that while young people may be turning away from formal, mainstream politics, this does not mean that they are necessarily politically apathetic – rather, young people are reasonably interested in politics and political issues, but cynical about politicians and formal mechanisms for political participation. Eden and Roker (2000) argue, furthermore, that debates about young people and politics habitually fail to consider areas where young people *are* active. Their research suggests that certain types of youth civic participation are in fact increasing, particularly peer education, youth councils, youth-run and managed projects and peer support groups.

While recognizing the problems with young people's participation in more formal modes of political behaviour, Marsh *et al.* (2006), in their research, aim to establish how young people understand and 'live' politics. As such, they treat age, class, gender and ethnicity as political 'lived experiences' and conclude that young people are alienated, rather than apathetic, and that their interests and concerns are rarely addressed within mainstream political institutions. The authors argue that it is important to understand politics as a 'lived experience' for young people rather than a set of 'arenas' into which they do or do not enter. Marsh and colleagues argue that much of the research on political participation operates with a rather narrow conception of 'the political', which is generally 'arena-based', thus identifying particular areas of political participation and effectively imposing external and legitimized ideas of political participation upon the respondents. The authors advocate listening to how young people themselves conceive of, and experience, politics, and in turn that this will facilitate understanding of the distinctive issues and experiences that have an impact on young people's political engagement.

The approach taken by Marsh and colleagues highlights the importance of understanding the meanings actors attribute to their actions and might usefully be applied in understanding urban disorders. The restriction of the political to certain sanctioned arenas is restrictive and ultimately fails to locate political motives where there may be plenty.

## A critique of existing literature on urban disorders: the UK perspective

Britain is characterized by a history of urban disorders. Urban disorders have taken place in Brixton (1980, 1985, 1995), Bristol (1980), Notting Hill (1958, 1976), Toxteth (1981) and Handsworth (1981, 1985). Riots have also taken place in Bradford, Burnley, Leeds and Oldham in 2001 and more recently in Lozells, Birmingham, in 2005.

Existing literature on the disorders in Britain is largely structuralist in its mode of explanation and operates outside of important developments in understanding the dialectical relationship between 'structure and agency' (Archer 1995), thus failing to conceptualize agency and discuss the nature of political motivations. The more structuralist

315

attempts at explaining events tend to focus on, and emphasize the role of the police, of external agitators (the British National Party (BNP), the National Front (NF) and social deprivation factors). While this literature is often critical of those involved in the disorders, it can be sympathetic but provides very limited discussion of the motivations of the actors involved (Waddington 1992; Keith 1993; Hasan 2000; Bagguley and Hussain 2003). The more sympathetic accounts of the disorders tend to emphasize the deliberate political motivations of actors, but fail to explain why spontaneous political actions occur (Keith 1993; Gilroy 2002).

Bagguley and Hussain (2003) provide a useful critical account of the literature on urban disorders in the UK, examining disorders from the 1950s through to the more recent events of 2001. The authors attempt to identify continuities and discontinuities between the different disorders and suggest that some of the conclusions drawn in the literature are dated, and the benefit of hindsight necessitates re-evaluation. The analysis is largely structural in nature, identifying broad socio-environmental factors leading to the disorders.

According to Bagguley and Hussain (2003), explanations of the 1980s urban disorders tend to focus on the role of the police and the 'militarization' of policing methods with respect to Black neighbourhoods (Gilroy 2002). In addition, 'race' and racial discrimination are seen as key explanatory factors, as the unemployment status and social deprivation of those involved are seen as expressions of the wider structural subordination of Black people in Britain (Benyon 1987). The authors are critical of these interpretations arguing that existing literature ignores the role of South Asians in the riots of the 1980s as well as the role of women, children and the elderly in some instances. People of Afro-Caribbean origin were in the minority of those arrested for offences during the 1981 riots, however, this is not to say that they were multi-racial insurrections (Keith 1993). Furthermore, the authors suggest that the disorders of 1981 and 1985 should be seen as part of the same 'wave of action' starting in the 1970s, in that they were often in response to neo-fascist mobilization. The authors cite the passing of the 1981 anti-immigrant Nationality Act as a key contributory factor at the time, as many neo-fascist marches (usually the NF) were banned in cities across the UK and many anti-fascist marches also took place.

Bagguley and Hussain (2003) argue that the urban disorders of 2001, in Bradford, Burnley, Leeds and Oldham, are significantly more complex than previous disorders in the UK, as while police antagonism was a feature of the disorders, there were elements of the 1950s-style 'race riots' with South Asians and Whites attacking each other's properties; there was also evidence of collaboration between Whites and South Asians confronting the police as a common adversary. Highlighting continuities with past disorders, there was considerable neo-fascist mobilization in the areas of the disorders (in particular the BNP and the NF). A key feature of most of the disorders in previous decades which, was also a relevant factor to the more recent events in 2001, was the entrenched and long-standing poverty which characterized the communities involved in the disorders. Bagguley and Hussain argue that more recent disorders represent new modes of 'racialization' (see Miles 1989). Old racializations saw Afro-Caribbeans as having problems while South Asians had too much culture. New racialization is rapidly pathologizing South Asians, building on traditional stereotypes on topics such as Islamaphobia in the post-September 11th climate.

Michael Keith's (1993) analysis of the literature on urban disorders also focuses on problematizing traditional modes of explanation used to explain the disorders. Keith considers the American disorders of the 1950s and those that occurred in the UK in the

1980s and suggests that broadly the literature can be split into two areas: (1) identifying causes of the disorders, the 'recipe style analysis'; and (2), the romanticization of disorders as political mobilization. After highlighting the limitations of both approaches, I would argue, Keith reaches an impasse as he fails to reconcile the notion of disorders as partially strategic action, with a notion of spontaneity, and thus at the end of the analysis leaves many questions unanswered.

Government inquiries into the disorders provide an opportunity to analyse official state responses and, in Keith's opinion, both the Scarman Report into the events in Brixton and the National Commission on Civil Disorders Inquiry into the American disorders of the 1950s (commonly known as the Kerner Commision) provide a good example of the crude 'recipe analysis of riots' (Keith 1993: 76). In this mode of explanation, an attempt is made to identify all the different causal elements involved in the disorders, 'attributing to each an implicit proportion of the "blame" for disorder' (ibid.: 76). The Kerner Commission identifies three levels of blame, first; white racism in society; second; frustration, powerlessness and the legitimation of violence; and finally, 'incitement' and 'police behaviour' (ibid.: 77). Keith suggests that in the recipe analysis of disorders there is a false equivalence drawn between cause and blame, which is a link that exists in popular opinions about disorders but also dominates in the behaviouralist social sciences.

Paul Gilroy highlights the complexity of theorizing urban disorders arguing that while 'it is important not to exaggerate the uniformity of the disorders, it is important to look into local factors which have shaped each eruption' (2002: 324). Gilroy attempts to reconcile the notions of the spontaneity of the disorders with locating political strategy in the actions of those involved, by suggesting that while spontaneity and violence may be a feature of the disorders, 'this does not render them irreconcilable with a strategic long-term war of position' (Gilroy 1981: 221). Bagguley and Hussain (2003) accuse Gilroy of having a 'romantic' view of the 1980s disorders; while Keith is more sympathetic, suggesting that Gilroy recognizes the tension between social protest and its disorganized forms (Keith 1993).

While Keith's critique of existing rioting literature is certainly helpful, Keith fails to take the debate forward in terms of offering his own interpretations of disorders. Keith is clear that he wants to avoid developing crude chains of causality or romanticizing disorders into strategic political struggles. However, Keith argues that we need 'a notion of spontaneity that does not devalue the rationality of individuals yet at the same time conveys a notion of the social context in which such actions are situated' (1993: 94). Clearly, Keith is able to identify the problem with existing problems in the literature, however, he fails to provide sufficiently detailed explanations of the motivations of actors involved in the urban disorders.

## Urban disorders in France in October 2005

On the 27th October 2005, three young men in Clichy-sous-Bois, a banlieue[1] to the north-east of Paris, took refuge in an electricity substation in order to escape from the police, who they thought were chasing them. Two of the men were electrocuted and died and one was seriously wounded. The French police authorities have officially rejected the claim that they were chasing the three men, although the surviving young man maintains that they were (Dikec 2006; Murray 2006). The incident in Clichy-sous-Bois was the trigger incident for further urban disorders, which started on 28th October in

Clichy-sous–Bois and quickly spread to other social housing neighbourhoods of 274 communes, lasting for two weeks. During this period more than 10,000 vehicles were set alight and more than 3,000 people were placed under police custody, of which one-third were indicted (Dikec 2006; Murray 2006).

2005 was a difficult year for France, as it experienced some of the worst urban disorders it had ever known. France, however, has a history of urban disorders dating back to the 1970s. The 1970s saw similar incidents occur in the banlieues, although compared to them, the urban disorders of 2005 were unprecedented in terms of their magnitude and geographical extent. The 1980s saw five large-scale urban disorders in the banlieues and the 1990s saw 48 large-scale urban disorders in addition to some 300 on a smaller scale, referred to as 'mini-riots' (Dikec 2006).

The residential behaviour and status of Frances' ethnic minority population are central to understanding the disorders in France. Nearly all of the urban disorders of 2005 and of previous decades have taken place in social housing neighbourhoods, nearly all of them in banlieues, and the majority of the individuals involved have been non-white and of North African and Black origin. It is important to explain the significance of the 'banlieue' as it is central to understanding the French disorders. 'Banlieue' literally means 'suburbs' but unlike its British and American counterparts, in the French context, the term refers to an administrative concept and geographically denotes the peripheral areas of cities in general (ibid.: 7). The banlieues mostly consist of high-rise social housing projects where a large proportion of the country's ethnic minority populations live. The banlieues have been disproportionately affected by very high unemployment following the economic crisis of the 1970s and the ensuing process of economic restructuring. Levels of unemployment in these areas are exacerbated by discriminatory employment practices within the French labour market as well as relatively poor educational outcomes for ethnic minorities (Dikec 2006; Murray 2006; Salanie 2006). Dikec argues that in France the banlieues no longer serve as a geographical reference or an administrative concept, but stands for 'alterity, insecurity and deprivation' (2007: 8).

Dikec (2006) uses the term 'revolt' to refer to the urban disorders in France arguing that 'revolts are, in this sense unarticulated justice movements against spatial injustices addressing at once material, categorical and political conditions that are spatially produced' (ibid.: 155). Furthermore Dikec argues that the spatial injustice is not only linked to economic difficulties that restrict people to the banlieues but also from the discursive articulation of banlieues particularly in media and state discourses.

## Conclusion and future research agendas

This chapter has attempted to examine urban disorders and make the case for locating political motivations in acts which are more often than not thought to be largely criminally motivated. The spontaneity and lack of articulated political strategy of the actors involved in the disorders coupled with the violence often involved in these acts serve to undermine analysis of real political motives or grievances. While criminality may be a part of urban disorders, it is important not to allow these discussions to overshadow a discussion of political motivations, especially given the structural discrimination experienced by many of the actors involved in the disorders.

Limitations of space have prevented a discussion of methodology in this chapter, although this is an important issue if we are to examine the meanings that those involved in the disorders attach to the events. Collecting data on the individuals involved in urban disorders is notoriously difficult. Accounts of the disorders often rely on secondary sources of information or information collected by the media, public knowledge or through arrest data (Keith 1993). Modern usage of cameras has added more accuracy to identifying actors involved in these events; however, access to detailed camera footage can prove to be difficult. Nevertheless, it is important to use those sources that are available in order to add a degree of authenticity to the accounts we provide of the events. Keith uses state arrest data collected by the Home Office (ibid.). Such a source may be useful but remains necessarily flawed as any search for 'faces in the crowd' may be tainted by discretionary and discriminatory arrest practices. Collecting the accounts of those involved in urban disorders and understanding the meaning that they attach to events may be the next stage to developing more accurate explanations of urban disorders: this, I would argue, is an important and necessary task.

## Note

1 The term 'banlieue' is explained in more detail below.

## References

Archer, M. (1995) *Realist Social Theory: The Morphogenetic Approach*, Cambridge: Cambridge University Press.

Bagguley, P. and Hussain, Y. (2003) 'The Bradford riot of 2001: a preliminary analysis', transcript of paper delivered to the Ninth Alternative Futures and Popular Protest Conference, Manchester Metropolitan University, 22–24 April.

Benyon, J. (1987) 'British urban unrest in the 1980s', in J. Benyon and J. Solomos (eds) *The Roots of Urban Unrest*, Oxford: Pergamon Press.

Cantle, T. (n.d.) *Community Cohesion: A Report of the Independent Review Team*, London: Home Office.

Dikec, M. (2006) 'Badlands of the Republic? Revolts, the French state and the question of the banlieues', *Environment and Planning D: Society and Space*, 24: 159–63.

—— (2007) *Badlands of the Republic: Space, Politics and Urban Policy*, Oxford: Blackwell Publishing

Eden, K. and Roker, D. (2000) *'You've Gotta Do Something ... ': A Longitudinal Study of Young People's Involvement in Social Action*, Youth Research 2000, University of Keele.

Fairclough, N. (2002) *Discourse and Social Change*, Malden, MA: Blackwell Publishers Inc.

Farrar, M. (2002) 'The Northern "race riots" of the summer of 2001 – were they riots, were they racial? A case-study of the events in Harehills, Leeds Parallel lives and polarization', British Sociological Association, 'Race' and Ethnicity Study Group Seminar, City University, London (online paper).

Gilroy, P. (1981) 'You can't fool the youths: race and class formation in the 1980's', *Race and Class*, 23: 112–20.

—— (2002) *There Ain't No Black in the Union Jack*, London: Routledge.

Hasan, R. (2000) 'Riots and urban unrest in Britain in the 1980s and 1990s: a critique of dominant explanations', in M. Lavalette and G. Mooney (eds) *Class Struggle and Social Welfare*, London: Routledge.

Keith, M. (1993) *Race, Riots and Policing: Lore and Disorder in a Multi-racist Society*, London: UCL Press.

Marsh, D., O'Toole, T. and Jones, S. (2006) *Young People and Politics in the UK: Apathy or Alienation?*, Basingstoke: Palgrave Macmillan.

Miles, R. (1989) *Racism*, London: Routledge.

Murray, G. (2006) 'France: the riots and the Republic', *Race and Class*, 47: 26–45.

Park, A. (1998) *Young People's Social Attitudes 1998: Full Report of Research Activities and Results*, Keele: ESRC.

Pirie, M. and Worcester, R. M. (1998) *The Millennial Generation*, London: MORI/Adam Smith Institute.

Rex, J. (1979) 'Black militancy and class conflict', in R. Miles and A. Phizacklea (eds) *Racism and Political Action in Britain*, London: Routledge and Kegan Paul.

Salanie, B. (2006) *The Riots in France: An Economist's View*. Available at: http://riotsfrance.ssrc.org (accessed 12 April 2008).

Scarman, Lord (1981) *The Brixton Disorders*, London: HMSO.

Touraine, A. (1977) *The Self-Production of Society*, Chicago: University of Chicago Press.

Waddington, C. (1992) *Contemporary Issues in Public Disorder*, London: Routledge.

# 40

# Young people and armed conflict

*Colette Daiute*

## Introduction

After an almost-exclusive focus on the individual either in terms of trauma or personal traits, researchers and practitioners have begun to broaden the analytic lens to youth in society, thereby shifting from primarily medical-biological approaches to socio-cultural analyses of the impact of armed conflict on young people and their environments. This chapter reviews the major approaches and offers a rationale for broadening inquiry to political-historical analyses of conflicts that ensnare young people.

At the beginning of the twenty-first century, armed conflict continues to define the lives of millions of youth worldwide. During this transitional decade, 2 million children have been killed, 6 million seriously injured, and approximately 10 million affected by displacement, loss of family, and other consequences of armed conflict (www.crin.org). Adolescents and young adults are involved directly, albeit mostly not of their own choice, having been kidnapped, given sustenance after losing their families, or recruited with promises of glory. War-related activities by children and youth include acting as soldiers, engaging in acts of violence to prove their toughness, and performing practical roles in the field, such as courier, cook, medic, and sex slave. Young people have also witnessed violence, been used as weapons (such as adolescent girls' being raped for purposes of intimidation or ethnic cleansing) and have been involved indirectly by experiencing the myriad consequences of armed conflict. Young lives develop in playgrounds and sports fields littered with land mines, neck braces, and other remnants of war, in communities lacking political-economic infrastructures for education, in families suffering from psychological or physical disabilities, yet youth engage with these and the more positive aspects of their environments, such as social support and cultural heritage, in normative ways.

These material and symbolic conditions last for many years after the official end of armed conflict, on average seven years in the physical environment and political institutions (Collier 2003), up to 17 years in psycho-social effects (Amone-P'Olak *et al.* 2006), and across generations who transmit war experiences via social relations manifested in dreams, world views, and personalities (Caruth 1996; Danieli 2007). Sensitivity to such distal effects has led to increased focus on the socio-cultural nature of youth in armed conflict.

# Historical and intellectual development of research on youth and armed conflict

Scholarly research on youth and armed conflict has been organized into three distinct analytic perspectives, characterized in medical-biological, socio-cultural, and practice terms.

## *Medical-biological emphases*

Most research on the nature and effects of armed conflict on youth is organized in terms of a medical model (Summerfield 1999). Whether based explicitly or implicitly on assumptions about physical and mental health, research with youth in war-affected areas has focused on those directly involved, including child soldiers, young witnesses to violence, refugees, and those who have lost parents in armed violence. From this perspective, researchers and clinicians have measured the psychological impact of war with assessments of depression, post-traumatic stress disorder, and abilities to engage in the basic functions of daily life (sleeping, hygiene practices, eating, socializing, doing chores, etc.) (Weiss and Marmar 1997). Instruments used in this research paradigm measure reactions to conflict events over time, such as with paper and pencil scales including items like 'I thought about it when I didn't mean to', 'I had a dream about it', and 'I tried to remove it from my memory' (Weiss and Marmar 1997: 408–9). Patterns of responses by young people are analyzed in relation to personal psychological orientations, specific war-related events, and other factors, yielding some consensus that exposure to violence results in trauma reactions.

Consistent with research on war-related trauma is research measuring individual differences in psychological orientations like cognitive emotion regulation (Amone-P'Olak *et al.* 2007). For example, research assessing the cognitive emotion regulation strategies of 294 formerly abducted adolescents in rehabilitation centers in Uganda revealed relationships between certain strategies, war experiences, and measures of psychopathology. This illustrative study identified relationships among psychological strategies of rumination, planning, putting into perspective, other blame, and denial with psycho-pathological symptoms (PTSD, internalizing, externalizing), and reported war experiences. In contrast, high incidences of planning and/or putting into perspective were associated with fewer symptoms and events.

In another approach to studying individual differences, researchers measure personal characteristics such as resilience in the face of war-related violence. Across areas of armed conflict from Palestine to Bosnia, researchers have identified a relatively large number of 'resilient' individuals who do not manifest psycho-pathological symptoms, as well as others who 'recover' fairly quickly (Bonanno 2004). Such findings add to other recent observations about the over-determination of traumatic stress disorders, yielding motivation for socio-cultural approaches to research on human development in the context of war.

## *Socio-cultural perspectives*

From the perspectives of disciplines such as anthropology, developmental psychology, and education, researchers' questions and methods focus increasingly on meaning-making, often via interviewing and ethnographic accounts of social practices and discourse. Interview studies offer information about practices that embody cultural beliefs about the causes and effects of armed conflict, such as greeting and cleansing rituals for returning child/youth soldiers in Angola and Mozambique (Honwana 2006). Research focusing on meaning-making has also contributed insights into how young people acquire skills and goals for their future development from their participation in combat and non-combat roles in the field, as revealed in a study citing a teenage girl who expressed interest in pursuing formal medical training after having served as a medic for an armed guerilla group in the Philippines (Sta. Maria 2006). Highlighting the importance of culture is also the recent turn to consider the release of stress-related chemicals in the brain that occurs as a function of what counts as upsetting in a particular culture (Wilson 2007).

Another line of research with educators, students, and parents across four societies that experienced genocide and ethnic cleansing reported the need to understand youth development in relation to societal institutions (Weinstein *et al.* 2007). By weaving together stories across positions in civil society, these researchers identified contradictions between policies like banning ethnic talk about Hutu–Tutsi differences in Rwanda to forge a new collective civic identity, denying individuals' valued histories and traditions allowed resentments to fester and grow (Weinstein *et al.* 2007). Ethnographic research in other areas of Africa suggests skepticism about assuming what youth value most, as indicated in studies where youth emphasized economic issues like employment more than inter-group reconciliation as a means of healing in South Africa (Higson-Smith 2006) and on maintaining local ownership of natural oil resources in the Niger Delta (Ukeje 2006).

Exploring the distributed nature of experience in situations of armed conflict, researchers in post-war Yugoslavia asked youth to share stories of conflict (Daiute and Turniski 2005). Theory guiding this research posited that young people learn to express their knowledge and motivations relevant to important life events like armed conflict in terms of social relationships in everyday life. This study found that youth expressed different knowledge about the war, different orientations to those of other ethnic groups, and different personal goals when they narrated conflicts among adults (the war generation), among peers (the post-war generation), and in a realistic community event in the future. An overwhelming result was that youth tended to report inter-group conflict among adults, whom they also criticized as lacking the resources and will to create a better life. Rather than questioning the authenticity of any single narrative representation, the interpretation of these results is that the meaning of war-related events occurs in relation to physical and social contexts and, thus, is not a singular truth about any individual or generation. When the research design allows, moreover, individuals on the threshold of adult responsibilities and agency not only narrate a range of perspectives but also critique those that are dysfunctional for future development, as we see in the following comment by a Croatian youth:

> I do know that in my family there was optimism and hope for a better future. The Serbs had a plan to become a huge and a powerful nation. Conflict was solved with Croatia's victory in the war. Today we have an independent country. These hopes came true. But life in Croatia is not even close to the one we expected it would be (bad privatization, corrupted politicians, low life standards, etc.).

Another study exploring the persistence and transformation of frozen (ideological) narratives that may perpetuate inter-group hatreds involved 137 young people aged 12 to

27 living across four countries of the former Yugoslavia in a social history project about conflict. Results reveal the trans-generational communication of local war history in a complex way. Youth in Serbia, for example, narrated conflicts with intense inter-personal sensitivity, a hyper-vigilant orientation that may result from awareness that their nation is internationally known as the major aggressor in the recent war, while youth in Bosnia narrated conflict more distantly, an orientation that may result from being perceived primarily as victims (Daiute in press). Consistent with these results on the interaction of societal and personal perceptions of conflict is research indicating that, in contexts of long-term wars, research on violence prevention beneficially involves institutional as well as individual units of analysis, as has been done in the Middle East where a university was designed as a means for integrating Arab and Jewish Israeli youth so their views could be developed and expressed in a meaningful context (Hertz-Lazarowitz 2006).

## Field-based perspectives

Humanitarians, mental health professionals, non-governmental organization leaders, educators, and others who work in the field during and after armed conflict have offered observations that increase knowledge about youth and armed conflict. Although theirs is not a research agenda, fieldworkers provide compelling evidence to question perspectives that emphasize damage like PTSD and to suggest the importance of practice-based research with young people as agents of change in war-affected areas (IASC 2007). Based on their many years of combined practice in emergency contexts from Palestine, to Bosnia, to Acheh, and Rwanda, fieldworkers have observed that young people, in particular, are resilient and knowledgeable about their own and their community's needs, goals, and potential resources for addressing the emergency situation. The IASC report offers invaluable observations, which can serve as hypotheses for ongoing research, as well as guidelines for practice and policy, such as 'humanitarian action should maximize the *participation* of the local affected populations … local people [should] retain or resume control over decisions that affect their lives' (ibid.: 10); humanitarian actors should 'do no harm' (ibid.: 10), should 'build on available resources and capacities' (ibid.: 10), ensuring that they are 'integrated into wider systems (e.g. existing community support mechanisms, formal/non-formal school systems, general health services)' (ibid.: 11).

Another major field-based project related to research on youth and armed conflict is the United Nations Convention on the Rights of the Child (1989). Article 38 focusing specifically on armed conflict expresses goals and tensions inherent in this international treaty: 'States Parties shall refrain from recruiting any person who has not attained the age of fifteen years into their armed forces.' Even though the major goal of the Convention on the Rights of the Child is to define children as worthy of rights rather than only as possessions of their parents or the State, the Treaty sometimes acquiesces to require to ratifying States Parties in return for ratification, such as when allowing 15 year-olds to be recruited to fight the country's wars, while 18 is the standard age of protection for all the other articles of the CRC. In attempts to protect children further in such situations, the CRC process includes monitoring by the UN Committee on the Rights of the Child, which commissions non-governmental organizations to offer evidence-based perspectives 'alternative' to those of official state. One such report in Colombia, for example, included interviews with young people revealing violations like the following: 'I was promised a job and that they were going to pay me one million [Colombian pesos] for each guerilla leader that I killed. I am expert in explosives and then I can work planning mines and other explosives' (Alternative Report, p. 79).

Such increasing emphasis on story-telling, interviewing about local rituals, and other verbal testimony suggests the importance of cultural meaning-making about armed conflict, not only among those directly involved but also among post-war generations who often suffer from a 'conspiracy of silence' and denial caused, in part, by the desires of adults with armed conflict experience wanting to protect young people from the horrors of war (Danieli 2007). This focus on the symbolic realm of war-related effects and treatments is a shift from approaches emphasizing individual psycho-biological reactions. The use of means such as drawing, dance, and drama that allow children 'to tell without talking' (Apfel and Simon 1996: 14) likewise emphasize the release of stress, painful emotions, and repressed reactions, rather than interpretive interactions of individuals and societies. Ideally, future research and practice can integrate insights from medical-biological, socio-cultural, and field-based research, in particular, by adding political-historical factors.

## Principal contributions, criticisms and future directions

Now that socio-cultural perspectives have offered a theoretical and methodological shift away from an emphasis on psycho-pathology, research designs can do more to define political and institutions factors, such as accounting for how power relations influence public discourse about armed conflict and the related actions, which define human development and make their way into all research data. Toward this end, researchers can expand units of analysis from the individual and cultural context to global systems, sensitive to socio-political processes and structures. This means studying youth reactions not only as stable representations of authentic capacities or cultural meanings but as occurring in relation to specific institutional contexts (school, family, field of conflict), audiences (local peer groups, national evaluators, international actors, etc.), and purposes (being a friend, a meaningful contributor to a social group, a person with a future as a responsible and respected adult, a subject). Such approaches would, for example, examine displacement as a consequence of war having a major impact on youth and young adults.

The genre of adolescents' war literature offers poignant evidence of the ongoing importance of research on youth and armed conflict, as well as the need for increasing political analyses of impacts. The heart-breaking stories by Ishmeal Beah, a boy soldier in Sierra Leone (2007), and Zlata Filipovic (1994), a girl who lost her best friends, family and her childhood in Sarajevo, are two recent testaments to the defining effects of armed conflict on youth and, thus, on human development. Both stories narrate the transition from mundane childhoods of playing, going to school, learning hip hop, pulling pranks on friends, and suffering small disagreements with parents to killing on behalf of the country, dodging bullets to get water from the sole source across town, saying '"Goodbye" forever to a father who can't bear to look you in the eye' (Beah 2007), consoling one's mother who has just run across a bridge strewn with body parts, and many more acts that do not characterize the safe, supported, and creative development each young person and society deserves.

While we value personal accounts for their revealing detail, we must ask several questions from them, as from the previous research. These stories focus our attention on the individual and lead some to ask, 'What are these exceptional qualities of youth who escape, rise above it all, resist, etc.?' With the goal of understanding the interdependence of individual and societal development, we can, instead, focus on the individual's experiences in relation to the broader political–historical systems that create rationales, actions, and stories of conflict and peace. We researchers must begin to ask questions such as, 'What are the institutional practices that play a role in the development of individual and societal conflict stories over time?'; 'How are personal stories by youth moments of integration between socio-political narratives and subjective moments in real time and place in human development?' These questions direct our research to exploring how individuals, cultures, and nations are entwined. We must, at least in part, try to understand how young people who use their innocence to decry war also adopt societal narratives, whether to justify conflict, decry conflict, or transform it into mutual understanding and development.

If we are all implicated, we must move beyond absolute notions of perpetrator and victim to theory, design, and methods that will help us understand the broader local and global systems in which events and our interpretations of them develop. When focusing on how youth understand and critique the situations around them rather than focusing on what is wrong with youth, political–historical research can offer new insights about human development rather than illness (Daiute 2006). It is, moreover, the job of research to account for these developments in ways that are systematic rather than sentimental or sensational.

War and its consequences can no longer be isolated to specific locations. The broad distribution of armed conflict across fighters, bystanders, victims, and instigators, across time and place suggests an urgent need for new approaches to research, as well as for advocacy for ending the violence. As Zlata herself wrote in her diary at age 11, 'I'm not writing to you about me any more. I'm writing about war, death, injuries, shells, sadness and sorrow' (Filipovic 2006).

## References

Alternative Report to the Report of the Government of Reporting-Monitoring Colombia on the Situation of the Rights of the Child. Available at: www.crin.org

Amone-P'Olak., K., Garnefski, N. and Kraaij, V. (2007) 'Adolescents caught between fires: cognitive emotion regulation in response to war experiences in Northern Uganda', *Journal of Adolescence*, 30: 655–69.

Apfel, R.J. and Simon, B. (1996) *Minefields in Their Hearts: The Mental Health of Children in War*, New Haven, CT: Yale University Press.

Beah, I. (2007) *A Long Way Gone: Memoirs of a Boy Soldier*, New York: Farrar, Straus, Giroux.

Bonanno, G. L. (2004) 'Loss, trauma, and human resilience', *American Psychologist*, 59: 20–8.

Caruth, C. (1996) *Unclaimed Experience: Trauma, Narrative, and History*, Baltimore, MD: Johns Hopkins Press.

Collier, P. (2003) *Breaking the Conflict Trap: Civil War and Development Policy*, Washington, DC: The International Bank for Reconstruction and Development/The World Bank.

Daiute, C. (2006) 'The problem of society in youth conflict', in C. Daiute, Z. Beykont, C. Higson-Smith, and L. Nucci (eds) *International Perspectives on Youth Conflict and Development*, New York: Oxford University Press.

—— (in press) 'Critical narrating by adolescents in troubled times', in K. McLean and M. Pasupathi (eds) *Narrative Development in Adolescence*, New York: Springer.

Daiute, C. and Turniski, M. (2005) 'Young people's stories of conflict in post-war Croatia', *Narrative Inquiry*, 15: 217–39.

Danieli, Y. (2007) 'Assessing trauma across cultures from a multi-generational perspective', in J. P. Wilson and C. S. Tang (eds) *Cross-cultural Assessment of Psychological Trauma and PTSD*, New York: Springer.

Filipovic, Z. (2006) *Zlata's Diary: A Child's Life in Wartime Sarajevo*, New York: Penguin.

Hertz-Lazarowitz, R. (2006) 'Acceptance and rejection as a source of youth conflict: the case of Haifa University in a divided society', in C. Daiute, Z. Beykont, C. Higson-Smith, and L. Nucci (eds). *International Perspectives on Youth Conflict and Development*, New York: Oxford University Press.

Higson-Smith, C. (2006) 'Youth violence in South Africa: the impact of political transition', in C. Daiute, Z. Beykont, C. Higson-Smith and L. Nucci (eds) *International Perspectives on Youth Conflict and Development*, New York: Oxford University Press.

Honwana, A. (2006) *Child Soldiers in Africa*, Philadelphia, PA: University of Pennsylvania Press.

Inter-Agency Standing Committee (IASC) (2007) *IASC Guidelines on Mental Health and Psychosocial Support in Emergency Settings*, Geneva: IASC.

Summerfield, D. (1999) 'A critique of seven assumptions behind psychological trauma programmes in war-affected areas', *Social Science and Medicine*, 48: 1449–62.

Ukeje, C. (2006) 'Youth movements and youth violence in Nigeria's oil delta region', in C. Daiute, Z. Beykont, C. Higson-Smith and L. Nucci (eds) *International Perspectives on Youth Conflict and Development*, New York: Oxford University Press.

United Nations Treaty Collection (2001) Declarations and Reservations. Available at: www.unhchr.ch/html/menu3/b/treaty15/_asp.htm, 9 October.

UNHCR (2006) *Refugees by Numbers, 2006 Edition*. Available at: www.unhcr.org.

Weinstein, H. M., Freedman, S. W. and Hughson, H. (2007) 'School voices: challenges facing education systems after identity-based conflicts', *Education, Citizenship, and Social Justice*, 2: 41–71.

Weiss, D. S. and Marmar, C. R. (1997) 'The impact of event scale – revised', in J. P. Wilson and C. Tang (eds) *Assessing Psychological Trauma and PTSD: A Practitioner's Handbook*, New York: Guilford Press.

Wilson, J. P. (2007) 'The lens of culture: theoretical and conceptual perspectives on the assessment of psychological trauma and PTSD', in J. P Wilson and C. S. Tang (eds) *Cross-cultural Assessment of Psychological Trauma and PTSD*, New York: Springer.

327

# Part VIII

## Physical and mental health

*Andy Furlong*

## The physical and mental health of modern youth

Until relatively recently, the health of young people has been a largely neglected field of study. From a life cycle perspective, young people were regarded as being in peak health, having outgrown the health-related risks of infancy and childhood and yet to arrive at the stage where degenerative conditions of adulthood impact significantly on health. While these assumptions still underpin health policy, concerns about health-related behaviours of young people and their implications for long-term well-being and mortality are frequently expressed. The mental health of young people has also become a key area of concern, underpinned by evidence of widespread depression and psychological distress. While it is clear that some of the anxieties about the health risks faced by today's youth are over-reactions, significant changes have taken place that have implications for health. There is also evidence that one of the most significant determinants of health in childhood and adulthood, social class, is less pronounced in youth as young people come into contact with a greater range of influences.

In most advanced societies, despite improved standards of living and nutrition, improvements in young people's health has been negligible. As West observes in Chapter 41, increases in average height suggest improvements in overall health, yet this is countered by levels of obesity that have led some to argue that overall levels of life expectancy among this generation may actually fall. Levels of disease and disability among young people have changed little, although injury and deaths through accidents have declined. In developing countries the situation is very different. The HIV/AIDS 'epidemic' has had a devastating impact on young people with around 12 million 15–24 year-olds affected. While illustrating the positive impact made by some programmes, in Chapter 42, Mugisha highlights the vulnerabilities of young people and difficulties in delivering effective programmes in developing countries.

While health concerns linked to the sexual behaviour of young people are not confined to the developing countries, in the West there are also anxieties about the link between social change and health-related behaviours. In particular, smoking, alcohol and recreational drugs are all forms of consumption that have led to moral panics about the behaviour of modern youth. In many countries smoking is beginning to decline (although less so among females), yet it is still an activity that is most likely to develop in youth and although many will give up, others will continue smoking as adults with long-term health consequences. The use of illegal recreational drugs is also an activity that tends to begin in the teenage years although, as West reminds us in Chapter 44, for most usage is transitory and sensible. On the other hand, alcohol remains the drug of choice for most young people with excessive use linked to long-term health risks as well as the more immediate dangers of injury through accidents or violence.

While social class remains an important predictor of health-related behaviours, West argues that agency also plays a significant role. Health-related behaviours may cross-cut class, but they are linked to group membership, undertaken in the context of lifestyles and linked strongly to identity. Indeed, West suggests that, for young people, health-related behaviours such as smoking and drinking are symbolic dimensions of identity which may be as important as fashion or music.

While certain activities have clear consequences for health, much of the contemporary interest in young people and health centres on mental health and subjective well-being. Evidence from a range of countries shows that many young people suffer from mental health problems which have become more prevalent since the Second World War. In Chapter 43, Eckersley argues that it is difficult to establish long-term trends in mental health, but, using evidence from a range of studies, shows that between one in five and three in ten young people will experience significant psychological problems on at least one occasion with as many as one in two encountering less severe problems. Para-doxically, the vast majority of young people say that they are happy with their lives and both Eckersley and West acknowledge that young people can report positive well-being while displaying symptoms of psychological malaise.

For Eckersley, the materialism and individualization of Western societies can clearly be linked to dissatisfaction, anxiety and depression in youth. Individualism, he suggests, may provide new opportunities for creative expression and help free people from the bonds of tradition, but may also be a source of anxiety and disorientation. In this context, he suggests that young people may turn to party drugs and alcohol as a way of creating a sense of belonging.

The chapters in this section look at the health and health-related behaviours of young people and try to identify the ways in which broader socio-economic changes have impacted on their physical and mental health. The authors highlight some of the moral panics that have tended to overstate the issues linked to the health and health-related behaviours of contemporary youth, while acknowledging that there is clear evidence of changes that adversely impact on the health of young people.

# 41

# Health in youth
## Changing times and changing influences

*Patrick West*

## Introduction

Twenty years ago, the health of young people barely featured on the social and health policy agendas of national and international institutions, (re)affirming a widespread but fallacious assumption that youth and health go hand in hand (Bennett 1985). The assumption was sustained both by the paucity of research specifically focused on young people's health, and by the use of wide age bands (e.g. 0–16, 16–64 years) in official statistics, the effect of which typically rendered 'youth' invisible. Twenty years on, the situation could hardly be more different. Youth and health are now firmly on the policy and research agendas of most governments in the developed world, reflecting the wide-spread view that young people's physical and mental health has deteriorated over time, and without urgent action will continue to deteriorate.

This dramatic change in the significance attributed to young people's health has all the ingredients of another moral panic about youth, raising questions as to whether the claim of deterioration is real or not. Yet it has also occurred during a period of rapid social change, raising equally important questions as to what constellation of factors in late modernity might explain it. On the face of it, it is perplexing since it is not consistent with a simple materialist explanation; the populations of most developed societies have become richer, not poorer, over this period of time. Of course, what happens at a population level is not necessarily reflected in the material circumstances of youth, the evidence for which might be better indicated by trends in pocket money, youth unemployment or student debt. However, it does direct attention to a range of other factors including changes in family structure and functioning, education and the labour market, all of which can profoundly shape the transition from childhood through youth to adulthood, and in turn impact on health. In late modernity, it also highlights the potential importance of newer, 'postmodern', influences associated with consumerism and the media, which shape youth identities, youth cultures and lifestyles, and which may equally impact on health.

Against this background, the aim in this chapter is to provide a profile of health in youth together with evidence on time trends, to identify the principal social correlates, and how changes in these might explain changes in young people's health. To do this, we must first define what we mean by two key concepts: health and youth.

## Definitions and dimensions of health

Health is an elusive concept, a major paradox being that, within the biomedical model used in modern medicine, it is defined not in terms of the capacity or potential for health but by ill-health, typically indicated by disease, illness and sickness. From this perspective, disease (e.g. cancer) is a pathological process involving deviation from a biological norm; illness (e.g. symptoms) is the subjective experience of ill-health, most obviously distinguished from disease by the fact that each can exist in the absence of the other; and sickness is a social role negotiated between doctor and patient in the light of prevalent social norms and expectancies as well as medical knowledge. It is clear that each of these, including the definition and identification of disease, involves some measure of subjective judgement, a problem which is multiplied when attempting to define health itself. Yet it is widely acknowledged that health is not simply the absence of disease or illness, not least because people themselves identify positive physical or mental states such as fitness, energy and well-being as components of health (Blaxter 2004).

In recognition of the limitations of the biomedical model, several attempts have been made to define health in more positive and holistic terms which usually follow the World Health Organization's definition of health as 'a state of complete physical, mental and social well-being, and not merely the absence of disease or infirmity'. While well intentioned, this holistic approach runs the risk of including all of social life and human happiness as health, and conflating the causes of health with health itself. A recent example of this is the development of the 'Child Health and Illness Profile' (CHIP) in the USA (Starfield *et al.* 2002). These researchers argue that the parameters of relevance to young people's health differ from those in adulthood both because of the developmental nature of childhood and adolescence and because they anticipate (ill-)health later in the life course. Accordingly, in addition to dimensions which focus on current 'disorders', 'satisfaction' (perceived well-being) and 'discomfort' (physical and emotional symptoms), CHIP includes three other domains involving 'risk' (e.g. smoking), 'resilience' (e.g. family involvement) and 'achievement' (e.g. academic attainment). Only the first three of these overlap in any way with the biomedical model, the others indicating either states or behaviours with long-term consequences for health or failure to achieve normatively prescribed goals. While this approach may be useful for planning integrated services for young people, it seems limited as a research tool since it conflates health with its causes, thereby rendering any relationship with a predictor such as family life as tautological. In particular, it fails to distinguish health from health behaviours such as smoking or physical activity. It is not, therefore, the approach adopted here, not least because the vast amount of research on young people's physical and mental health has been conducted within a biomedical model.

Consideration of a broader concept of health does, however, highlight its multidimensional nature. Following a distinction between health status (a relatively long-term property of an individual) and health state (a shorter term property), Blaxter (2004) identified four dimensions: disease/impairment and 'fitness' reflecting two different dimensions of health status; psychosocial malaise and illness (symptoms), health state. The first dimension most closely corresponds with the biomedical model and includes physical and mental disorders and conditions defined by reference to taxonomies such as the International Classification of Diseases (ICD). Within social epidemiology, it is typically defined by reference to questions about '(limiting) long-standing illness' and/or subjective assessments of general health, variants of which are widely used in international research. 'Fitness', which most closely corresponds to a holistic definition of health, includes a range of physiological measurements such as height, weight, respiratory function and blood pressure. In contemporary society, obesity (measured by body mass index) is a major indicator of health status with known consequences for cardiovascular disease and disorders such as diabetes. Of the two health state dimensions, psychosocial malaise represents mental (ill-)health at a subclinical level and should be distinguished from psychiatric disorder which is defined by reference to the ICD or similar taxonomy. Finally, as the term implies, symptoms refer to subjective reports of illness. These dimensions of health are useful not merely as a guide to assimilating the evidence about the health of young people, but also for distinguishing between the social causes of shorter-term (health state) and longer-term (health status) health problems.

## Defining youth – early and later youth

Defining youth, as evidenced by other chapters in this volume, is no easier task than defining health. However, it is possible to offer a definition which is derived from life-course epidemiology, and to some extent 'focal' theories of adolescence, and which has particular relevance for health. At its simplest, it involves the idea of a change in the balance of influences on individuals as they move from childhood through youth to adulthood (West 1997).

In respect of the child/youth transition, this involves a shift in influences away from the family and home background to that of the school, peer group and youth culture. Although entry into primary school begins the process of disengagement, in most developed societies it is the transition to secondary school that marks the first major change in status. In addition to new influences arising from secondary education, this period is associated with a marked increase in exposure to peer group and youth cultural influences. There is, however, no corresponding exit point to mark the transition from youth to adulthood. Instead, and in recognition of the wide diversity in contemporary transitions, it can be defined as the point at which most adult roles are achieved. This has the dual advantage of recognizing that entry into adulthood is differentiated by social structure, and that beyond secondary education there is another change in the balance of influences on health, notably associated with entry into the labour market. While considerably oversimplifying the extent of cross-cutting influences, the distinction between the stages of 'early youth', primarily associated with secondary education, and 'later youth', associated with the post-school period, is useful in highlighting different sets of influences on health. It also has the advantage of focusing attention on the impact of changing influences on an individual's health state as compared with persisting influences on health status arising in an earlier period.

The distinction between early and later youth is also relevant to a consideration of the evidence base on young people's health. Because researchers have found it much easier to conduct studies in school than after leaving, there is much more data on the health of young people relating to the earlier than later period. While studies vary in the precise age groups investigated, in general the former refers to young people aged less than 16, the latter to ages 16–24. A major source for the younger age group is the WHO 'Health Behaviours in Schoolchildren' (HBSC) surveys, the most recent of which refers to data collected in 2002 in 34 countries (Currie *et al.* 2004). I also draw extensively on our own work in the West of Scotland, which refers both to early and later youth (West 1997).

## A profile of health in youth

Reflecting the dimension of 'disease/impairment', a key indicator of health status in youth is available from surveys which enquire about long-standing illness or disability. In the UK, the evidence is consistent over time in revealing rates of about 20 per cent in early youth which increase slightly in later youth, thereafter increasing steadily through-out the life course (Rickards *et al.* 2004). About half of young people responding posi-tively to this question go on to identify their condition as 'limiting activities', and among the wide range of conditions and disorders reported, respiratory (mainly asthma), mus-culo-skeletal and mental health problems predominate. Of course, even within this category, the extent of limitations is extremely variable, those more severely affected fulfilling criteria for 'disability'. These criteria differ even across developed nations, in Scotland involving about 2 per cent of young people aged 16–19, and 4 per cent aged 20–29. In the same country, 5 per cent of school-children are recognized as having 'special needs' and among students entering higher education a similar percentage dis-close a 'disability', the largest category being unseen disabilities like diabetes, epilepsy and asthma (Riddell and Banks 2001). In general, the prevalence of 'disease/impairment' remains fairly constant throughout youth, primarily reflecting exposures of one kind or another in the foetal and perinatal period, and early childhood.

Another widely used indicator of health status is based on subjective reports of general health, with typical response options, 'excellent', 'good', 'fair' or 'poor'. Surprisingly perhaps, in view of the simplicity of the question, it is a known predictor of morbidity and mortality in adulthood. In relation to (early) youth, the HBSC survey found that among 11, 13 and 15 year-olds in the combined international sample, 14 per cent of males and 21 per cent of females reported their health as only 'fair' or 'poor'. However, these figures conceal the fact that poorer health increases with age, and more so for females, such that, at age 15, 27 per cent of females and 16 per cent of males are so categorized. This pattern is consistent across all countries though young people's self-reported health is poorest in Eastern Europe, followed by the UK and the USA, and best in Southern Europe. Comparable figures for later youth are difficult to obtain because different response options are often used, but there is evidence from the UK that rates of 'poorer' health increase sharply between ages 14–15 and 16–24 year-olds.

The second dimension of health status, 'fitness', is represented by a number of physical measures, the most common of which are height and weight. Although height is not usually thought of as a health measure, it has been conceptualized as an indicator of health potential, shorter stature being predictive of future morbidity and mortality. In all developed nations, the height of children and young people has increased over time, suggesting on the logic of health potential that populations should be getting healthier. In combination with weight, however, this is clearly not the case, the evidence showing that rates of obesity have risen in all age groups, and in all developed (and most devel-oping) countries, to the extent that it is now regarded as a global epidemic. Usually measured by body mass index (BMI), and based on international cut-offs, it is estimated that at least 10 per cent of children and adolescents worldwide are overweight (adult equivalent BMI > 25) or obese (> 30), and this is highest in the Americas (32 per cent) followed by Europe (20 per cent) (Reilly 2006). In youth, the prevalence of overweight and obesity is similar in both sexes. In addition to known correlates with cardiovascular and metabolic health, most research suggests the major consequence of obesity in youth is psychosocial.

The third dimension refers to mental health, which in the case of psychiatric disorder clearly overlaps with the 'disease/impairment' dimension. Nevertheless, a number of (mainly US) studies have found rates of any disorder, based on symptoms alone, of up to 50 per cent. In recognition of the fact that this is simply not compatible with the concept of 'disorder', more recent studies incorporate impairment criteria with the unsurprising consequence that the prevalence is reduced considerably. In a major UK study of the mental health of children and adolescents (MHCA), the rate of any 'mental disorder' based on 'strict' impairment criteria was 11 per cent among 11–15 year-olds (Meltzer *et al*. 2000). 'Emotional disorders' (combining anxiety and depressive disorders) were slightly more common in females (6 per cent) than males (5 per cent), 'conduct disorders' more common in males (9 per cent) than females (4 per cent). These gender differences appear to be universal. Evidence that the prevalence of 'emotional disorders' increases in later youth is suggested in a meta-analysis of 26 epidemiologic studies focusing on 'depressive disorder' (Costello *et al*. 2006) which found the overall rate among 13–18 year-olds (6 per cent females, 5 per cent males) to be similar to that for all 'emotional disorders' in the younger age group in the UK study. Comparison with young people aged 18+ is difficult because of differences in psychiatric classification, but a UK study showed increases in 'neurotic disorders' in both sexes between age 16–19 (7 per cent males, 19 per cent females) and 20–24 (12 per cent males, 21 per cent females) (Meltzer *et al*. 1995).

As is evident from the difference in prevalence rates based on symptoms and impairment, mental health is best understood as a continuum ranging from relatively minor psychological morbidity to incapacitating disorder. One of the major instruments used in epidemiological research is the General Health Questionnaire (GHQ) which, because it refers to changes in emotional symptoms (depression and anxiety) in the recent past, is intended as a measure of health state (Goldberg and Williams 1988). Using particular cut-off points to measure 'caseness' (potential clinical significance), enables the prevalence of 'psychological distress' to be assessed. The results of several studies are consistent in revealing high levels of distress among young people, which increase from early to later youth, and which are higher among females than males. For example, in the first of our cohort studies in the West of Scotland, 'psychological distress among females increased from 19% at age 15 to 42% at 18, thereafter declining slightly to 37% at age 21, the comparable figures for males being 11%, 33% and 31%' (West and Sweeting 1996). The evidence, therefore, highlights the fact that mental health problems, particularly of an emotional nature, characterize the lives of a significant minority of young people.

The final dimension of health refers to symptoms of both a physical and psychological nature. The prevalence of such symptoms is remarkably high. For example, in respect of physical symptoms, among 15 year-olds in another of our West of Scotland studies, around two-thirds reported headaches/migraine, stomach-ache/sickness and colds/flu in the past month, and a half reported aches/pains and skin problems (Sweeting and West 2003). Similar high proportions reported malaise symptoms such as feeling nervous, worried or anxious, irritability and difficulty getting to sleep. Corresponding with the gender differences in 'psychological distress', females were much more likely to experience malaise symptoms, headaches and stomach-ache, there being no difference for other physical symptoms. Though there is considerable variation cross-nationally, this high level appears to characterize early youth in many countries, the HBSC average among 15 year-olds being 44 per cent of females and 26 per cent of males reporting 2+ symptoms more than once per week within the previous 6 months (Currie et al. 2004). As with health data in general, much less information is available relating to later youth. However, in one study of 18 year-olds using the same reporting time-frame, rates of most (especially malaise) symptoms were lower than similar symptoms reported by 15 year-olds (West and Sweeting 1996). It seems likely that the experience of symptoms is a particular feature of early youth, reflecting a range of physical and psychological changes together with exposures (e.g. cross-infection) associated with the school.

## Time trends – is the health of young people deteriorating?

As indicated at the beginning of this chapter, it is widely believed that the health of young people has deteriorated over time. In relation to physical health, the evidence is perhaps more equivocal than often supposed. On the positive side, mortality in youth, particularly from accidents, has declined substantially in virtually all developed societies, and health status (as indicated by disease/disability) has not markedly altered. Indeed, the secular trend in height (taller with each successive generation) can be seen as an indicator of increasing health potential, anticipating increased life expectancy. However, the evidence in relation to the 'obesity epidemic' complicates this picture hugely, suggesting the possibility that for the first time in more than a century, life expectancy may fall. Less well understood, but of potentially greater significance in youth when symptoms may be most marked, is evidence of increasing rates of allergic disorders, notably asthma. This appears to be another global phenomenon though the prevalence of asthma is highest in developed countries, rates rising in developing countries with increasing westernization (Beasley et al. 2000). Explanations include the so-called 'hygiene hypothesis', which postulates that reduced exposure to infectious diseases in childhood reduces the body's immunity to allergens, and it is also possible that it may in part be attributable to increased medical surveillance and, hence, diagnosis.

While concern about declining physical health has been expressed in relation to the whole population, in youth, it has been most sharply focused on mental health. The agenda for research on this issue was set by Rutter and Smith (1995) in the mid-1990s, who argued that in contrast to 'improvements' in physical health, there was emerging evidence that the mental health of young people in most developed countries had deteriorated since the end of the Second World War. Drawing together information from an extensive range of sources, they argued that the cumulative evidence supported the hypothesis in respect of suicide, depressive disorders, crime and conduct disorders and substance use, but not eating disorders. The strongest evidence, they argued, was provided by suicide statistics, reflecting both the availability of time-series data within particular countries and its (apparently) more objective status than either diagnostic records or subjective reports.

Since the publication of their seminal work, evidence has accumulated which is generally consistent with the view that mental health problems in youth have increased over time. Much of this work comes from the UK. Here, the picture in relation to youth suicide is complicated by different trends in two adjacent countries. In Scotland, the suicide rate for males (aged 15–29) doubled between 1980/2 and 2000/2, but during the same period there was little change in England and Wales (De Leo and Evans 2004). However, rates of suicidal ideation and non-fatal self-harm appear to have increased in the UK as a whole (Young *et al.* 2007). With respect to trends in depression and conduct disorders, the best evidence comes from a comparison of 'emotional problems' and 'conduct problems', reported by parents of 15 year-olds in three national studies conducted in 1974, 1986 and 1999 (Collishaw *et al.* 2004). This revealed that rates of 'emotional problems' in both sexes remained much the same over the first period, but increased markedly between 1986 and 1999. 'Conduct problems', by contrast, exhibited a steady increase over the whole period. Rather similar results for emotional problems were found in a comparison of 'psychological distress' in our own two studies of 15 year-olds in 1987 and 1999, although in this case gender differences were observed, the prevalence among females almost doubling over this period (from 19 per cent to 33 per cent), males exhibiting no increase (West and Sweeting 2003).

While similar patterns have been documented in countries as diverse as the USA, Sweden and Finland, not all the evidence is consistent with the view that mental health in youth has deteriorated. With respect to psychiatric diagnosis, Costello *et al.* (2006) in their meta-analysis, reported no increase in the prevalence of 'depressive disorder' over a 30 year period. At the other end of the spectrum, and focusing on measures of well-being rather than morbidity, successive HBSC studies in Scotland found an increase in levels of 'happiness' and 'confidence' among 11–15 year-olds between 1994 and 2006 (Levin *et al.* 2007). That this more positive picture co-exists with the negative picture emerging from our own studies, and in the same country, suggests the dimensions of well-being and ill-being may not be opposite poles on the same continuum.

## Determinants of health in late modernity

Within social epidemiology, the major focus of international research has been on variations in health by socio-economic status (SES), widely referred to as 'health inequalities'. There is now a vast evidence base testifying to the association between lower SES and poorer health as measured both by mortality and morbidity. Explanations vary, but they include a range of material and psychosocial exposures, beginning in-utero (or even before) and accumulating across the life course. Interestingly, poorer health is not confined to the poorest groups, but exhibits a gradient across all social classes and income groups, a pattern consistent with a psychosocial explanation in which an individual's position in the social hierarchy is seen to be of key significance for health.

While health inequalities were once understood to characterize all stages of the life course, closer investigation has revealed a different pattern in youth, which this author characterized as 'relative equality'. Initially based on the observation that, excepting deaths from accidents and violence, mortality differentials present in childhood seemed to disappear in youth, only to reappear again in early adulthood, the pattern was also seen for another health indicator, (limiting) long-standing illness. While a re-emergence of health inequalities between youth and adulthood can be understood within a life-course framework (e.g. exposure to new hazards in adulthood), a change in SES patterning between childhood and youth which involves 'equalization' of gradients present in the earlier period, is more difficult to explain. In an extensive review of evidence relating to the 'equalization hypothesis', the distinction between health status and health state proved useful, the evidence being weaker for 'disease/disability' (particularly severe impairment) and stronger for certain mental health indicators and physical and malaise symptoms (West 1997).

In the most recent test of the hypothesis, involving a comparison of SES patterning between ages 11 and 15, we found reductions in gradients for physical and malaise symptoms in males and for some physical symptoms in females, the pattern for malaise involving a strengthening of a reverse SES gradient already present at 11 (West and Sweeting 2004). This reverse gradient is consistent with a related finding of a higher rate of 'psychological distress' among females from middle-class compared with working-class backgrounds (West and Sweeting 2003). Despite this evidence of changing SES patterns between childhood and early youth, an equally prominent pattern in respect of health status measures (long-standing illness and self-rated health) was one of little or no SES variation throughout. While a number of other studies have confirmed this pattern of 'relative equality' in early youth, both in the UK and elsewhere (e.g. Modin and Ostberg 2007), it is by no means a universal finding. For example, a recent US study found consistent SES gradients in global health status across childhood and early youth coupled with an emerging gradient in acute respiratory symptoms in the later period (Chen et al. 2006). Similar gradients in 'mental disorder' (particularly 'conduct disorder') were found in the MHCA study (Meltzer et al. 2000), suggesting a different SES relationship with severe mental health problems than more minor psychological morbidity such as 'psychological distress'.

While much of the evidence on the SES/health relationship suggests early youth is different from other life stages, evidence of (re)emerging health inequalities in adulthood also suggests that new exposures associated with entry into the labour market, and the achievement of other adult roles, impact on health. Such experiences are SES related, the most extensively researched being unemployment, a much more common experience among young people from lower SES backgrounds. The evidence is consistent in showing an association between unemployment and poor mental health (including suicide and self-harm), and that while this is partly attributable to selection (young people in poorer health becoming unemployed), there is also a deleterious effect of unemployment on health (Platt and Hawton 2002). Expectations of unemployment have also been associated with poorer mental health (West and Sweeting 1996).

However, it should not be assumed that other labour market positions are risk-free. Contrary to what might be expected, students in higher education have higher rates of long-standing illness and poorer physical and (particularly) mental health than young people of similar age in the general population (Stewart-Brown et al. 2000), and in our own study, higher rates of transitory self-harm (Young et al. 2007). They have been described as a 'neglected group', which is surprising given they now comprise up to half the post-school youth population in the UK. In combination, these different exposures may go some way to explaining why in contemporary society, the (re)emergence of health inequalities appears to be delayed. Nevertheless, unless the effects of SES on health are being transformed in late modernity, it seems likely that the combined effect of early environments and those in adulthood, together with the effects of health behaviours (notably diet and smoking) will continue to produce the familiar picture of health inequalities later on in adulthood.

The pattern of relative equality in health in early youth raises the interesting question as to what influences might be operating during this phase that cut across class to promote equalization. One such factor is the young person's family, which although usually conceptualized as a key mechanism of class reproduction, is an independent influence on health. Research in this area usually divides into that on family structure, including the effects of parental separation or divorce, and family functioning, including parenting strategies. There is now a considerable body of evidence attesting to the generally negative health consequences of growing up in a lone-parent or reconstituted family compared with both birth parents, much of which has focused on mental health. For example, in the MHCA, the prevalence of 'emotional' and 'conduct disorders' was twice as high among 11–15 year-olds of both sexes in lone-parent and reconstituted families compared with those with two parents (Meltzer *et al.* 2000). That such effects can persist into later youth (and beyond) is indicated in another UK study involving two birth cohorts. Controlling for a range of characteristics prior to family break–up (including parental social class), higher 'malaise' was found among adults (aged around 30) whose parents had earlier divorced (Sigle-Rushton *et al.* 2005). Similar results have long been demonstrated in research on family functioning, poorer health irrespective of family structure being associated with a range of problems including family conflict, strained communication with parents and 'poor' parenting.

A second factor, with greater potential to cut across class, is the (secondary) school, which in the UK typically involves a degree of social mixing, and exposes young people from different social backgrounds to similar influences and stressors. Developed from educational research, a number of studies have begun to investigate whether there are 'school effects' on health and health behaviours like smoking; that is, an effect of schools themselves over and above the characteristics (SES etc.) of students attending them. The evidence to date is inconclusive, and though some studies (Sellstrom and Bremberg 2006) have demonstrated school effects on health (including 'psychological distress'), the effect is consistently smaller than that for health behaviours. One explanation for this may be that there is simply not much variation between schools in the factors which directly impact on health, which is not to say that the school environment is unimportant. An interesting development of this theme has been undertaken by Swedish researchers who conceptualize the school like an adult work environment, distinguishing between (school) work in terms of demand and control dimensions (Modin and Ostberg 2007). Higher levels of psychosomatic complaints and lower 'psychological well-being' were associated with 'strained' working conditions (high demand/low control), involving a fifth of all students. This finding held after adjusting for a range of factors including ability and social class, suggesting that for a significant minority, school is a major source of stress.

Closely associated with the school is the influence of the school peer group. Compared with the volume of research on health behaviours, there has been little attention to the relationship between health and peer group structures and related cultures aside from studies attesting to the negative effects of victimization on mental health (Hawker and Boulton 2000). A notable exception is the work of Goodman (Goodman *et al.* 2001) in the USA which focused on the relative importance of family SES and peer group position for health, using a ladder to represent the respective social hierarchies. Goodman found only a low correlation between the SES position junior high students ascribed to their family and their own subjective position in school. Further, (lower) school position was more strongly associated with depression, overweight and obesity than (lower) subjective family SES and, in the case of depression, with a more objective measure of SES (father's education). Together with evidence that health in early youth is not strongly differentiated by SES, these findings suggest that the peer group is the more important influence on health at this stage in the life course.

The peer group is also arguably the key social arena in which individual and group identities are shaped by wider cultural influences, notably that of consumer culture, and specific influences associated with youth (sub)cultures. These broader influences, which include the media (TV, magazines, etc.), advertising, and the music and clothing industries, are powerful determinants of youth identities, which are equally strongly desired by young people. Constant pressure, or inability, to conform to such identities may have profound consequences for young people, including their health. Evidence in support of this is provided by Schor's (2004) investigation of the US consumer industry, one component of which found an association between consumerist attitudes and poorer mental health.

With respect to specific youth (sub)cultures, which often re-fashion identities in opposition to mainstream consumer culture, there is very little evidence directly related to health. Despite the well-documented association between youth scenes and illicit drugs, from which health consequences may be inferred, most research on youth cultures has paid little attention to health. An exception is one of our studies which demonstrated a strong association between self-harm and Goth identification, an association specific to this sub-culture (Young *et al.* 2006). Interestingly, in common with several other sub-cultures (e.g. dance, rave, clubbing), Goths were equally likely to come from working-class as middle-class backgrounds, suggesting that many influences associated with youth (sub)cultures cut across class. Played out in the school and peer group, many of these consumerist, sub-cultural and related lifestyle influences highlight the mechanisms by which equalization of health in youth may occur. Such influences, sometimes termed 'postmodern', appear to be most pronounced in early youth, but it is evident they extend well into the post-school period.

## Changing times, changing influences

It seems clear that influences specific to youth (the school, peer group and youth culture) are at least as important, if not more so, than those arising from SES, and that the balance between them changes over the youth–adult transition. The question arises as to whether the balance of influences is also changing over time in late modernity. This question is highly topical, and is central to explanations of why the mental health of young people seems to be deteriorating. Rutter and Smith (1995) outlined several candidate explanations, chief among which were changes in material circumstances, changes in family structure, in education and youth cultures.

In most developed societies, the increase in mental health problems in youth has occurred in parallel with increasing population affluence. While this is clearly not compatible with a simple materialist explanation, it might equally be a poor indicator of material circumstances in youth. However, using several different indicators, evidence is accumulating which suggests that material factors have only a small part to play. This was the conclusion drawn by Rutter and Smith, based on the finding that trends in suicide, depressive disorder and conduct disorder exhibited little or no correlation with (aggregate) youth unemployment rates. More recently, Collishaw *et al.* (2007) have demonstrated that changes in levels of family income in the UK (as indicated by proportions in 'relative poverty') accounted for less than 10 per cent of the increase in 'conduct problems' in 15 year-olds between 1974 and 1999. They also showed that changes in family structure had an equally small explanatory role, similar increases in 'conduct problems' occurring in young people in intact, reconstituted and lone-parent families. Additional support for the view that material factors are of minor significance, and of particular relevance to early youth, is evidence that young people's own disposable income (pocket money, etc.) has increased over time, and massively in excess of inflation rates.

With respect to alternative explanations, there is as yet not much systematic research to go on, and conclusions therefore remain tentative. One possibility refers to the education system, and specifically increased pressures associated with an expansion of testing and higher educational expectations generally. Some support for this is provided by the comparison between our two West of Scotland cohorts; between 1987 and 1999, while worries about unemployment decreased, those relating to school work increased in females, but not males (West and Sweeting 2003). Possibly related is an increase in the salience of the peer group, and related youth sub-cultures, as both a source of support and influence. The most obvious consequences for health reside in associated lifestyles and substance (ab)use, though, as the Goths example illustrates, there may be more direct effects on mental health. Perhaps the most significant change of all, however, refers to the expansion of consumer culture generally, with its emphasis on materialism and individualism and power to shape acceptable youth identities. In the West of Scotland comparison, increased worries about appearance and body size, along with educational worries, completely explained the increase in 'psychological distress' in females. More generally, there is increasing evidence that suggests consumerism is bad for health, and via psychosocial mechanisms, mental health in particular. While this may impact on people of all ages, it is most likely to affect youth. The irony is that as young people become more affluent, so they become more embedded in consumer culture, which in turn may be a major factor in their deteriorating mental health.

## Conclusion

It seems likely that the assumption of youthful healthfulness has always been more myth than reality. Yet, it is only relatively recently that young people's health has become a specific focus of research, in large part because of concerns, verging on panic, that all is not well. The picture that has emerged is one which reveals a significant minority to have a range of chronic conditions (notably asthma), compromised health potential (notably obesity) and mental health problems of varying degrees of severity. Furthermore, although both medical and lay criteria defining morbidity themselves change over time, most of the evidence suggests the changes are real and indicative of deteriorating health in youth. These trends appear to characterize most countries in the developed world. Overall, it is a pessimistic picture, which justifies the concerns of governments and other institutions in the international community. However, the identification of positive alongside negative trends in two Scottish studies reminds us of the complexity of the issue, and in particular highlights the need to further explore positive concepts of health. A major focus of the research agenda over the foreseeable future will involve closely monitoring trends in a range of dimensions of health, including biological measures of 'fitness'.

It will also be crucial to gain a much more comprehensive understanding of the social determinants of health in youth and how the hypothesized balance of influences actually works to impact on health over the child/youth/adult transition. With the exception of severe conditions, perhaps the most surprising finding to date is the overall lack of relationship between SES and health in early youth. Given that the deterioration in physical and mental health has occurred over a period of increasing population affluence, this suggests strongly that we need to look beyond material factors for explanations. While the evidence base is certainly undeveloped, there are enough indicative studies to suggest that a much fuller investigation of the roles of the family (particularly family functioning), school (particularly sources of stress), peer group (particularly social position) and youth sub-cultures is warranted. Each of these is an arena within which wider influences are played out. In late modernity, perhaps the most important of these is consumerism which has both direct effects on young people's health and indirect effects operating particularly through peer group processes. It will be the task of research on youth and health to chart these relationships more fully and investigate how changes in their structures and related cultures are linked to changes in youth identity, and ultimately changes in health.

## Acknowledgements

Many of the ideas and findings reported in this chapter are based on research conducted in the Medical Research Council's Social & Public Health Sciences Unit at Glasgow University. The author would like to thank research colleagues who have contributed to this, in particular Sally Macintyre, Helen Sweeting and Robert Young. Patrick West is supported financially by the Medical Research Council of Great Britain.

## References

Beasley, R., Crane, J., Lai, C. and Pearce, N. (2000) 'Prevalence and etiology of asthma', *Journal of Allergy and Clinical Immunology*, 105: S466–S472.

Bennett, D. (1985) 'Young people and their health needs: a global perspective', *Seminars in Adolescent Medicine*, 1: 1–14.

Blaxter, M. (2004) *Health*, Cambridge, Polity Press.

Chen, E., Martin, A. and Matthews, K. (2006) 'Socioeconomic status and health: do gradients differ within childhood and adolescence?', *Social Science and Medicine*, 62: 2161–70.

Collishaw, S., Goodman, R., Pickles, A. and Maughan, B. (2007) 'Modelling the contribution of changes in family life to time trends in adolescent conduct problems', *Social Science and Medicine*, 65: 2576–87.

Collishaw, S., Maughan, B., Goodman, R. and Pickles, A. (2004) 'Time trends in adolescent mental health', *Journal of Child Psychology and Psychiatry*, 45: 1350–62.

Costello, E., Erkanli, A. and Angold, A. (2006) 'Is there an epidemic of child or adolescent depression?', *Journal of Child Psychology and Psychiatry*, 47: 1263–71.

Currie, C., Roberts, C. and Morgan, A. (2004) *Young People's Health in Context: International Report from the HBSC 2001/02 Survey. WHO Policy Series: Health Policy for Children and Adolescents*, Copenhagen: WHO Regional Office for Europe.

De Leo, D. and Evans, R. (2004) *International Suicide Rates and Prevention Strategies*, Göttingen: Hogrete and Huber.

Goldberg, D. and Williams, P. (1988) *A User's Guide to the General Health Questionnaire*, Windsor: NFER-Nelson.

Goodman, E., Adler, N., Kawahi, I., Frazier, A., Huang, B. and Colditz, G. (2001) 'Adolescents' perceptions of social status: development and evaluation of a new indicator', *Pediatrics*, 108: E31.

Hawker, D. and Boulton, M. (2000) 'Twenty years' research on peer victimization and psychosocial maladjustment: a meta-analytic review of cross-sectional studies', *Journal of Child Psychology and Psychiatry*, 41: 441–55.

Levin, K., Todd, J., Currie, D. and Currie, C. (2007) *Mental well-being of young people in Scotland: 1994–2006*, Edinburgh: Child and Adolescent Health Research Unit.

Meltzer, H., Gatwood, R., Goodman, R. and Ford, T. (2000) *Mental Health of Children and Adolescents in Great Britain*, London: The Stationery Office.

Meltzer, H., Gill, B., Petticrew, M. and Hinds, K. (1995) *The Prevalence of Psychiatric Morbidity among Adults Living in Private Households*, London: HMSO.

Modin, B. and Ostberg, V. (2007) 'Psychosocial work environment and stress-related health complaints: an analysis of children's and adolescents' situation in school', in J. Fritzell and O. Lundberg (eds) *Health and Welfare Resources: Continuity and Change in Sweden*, Bristol, The Polity Press.

Platt, S. and Hawton, K. (2002) 'Suicidal behaviour and the labour market', in K. Hawton and K. Van Heeringen (eds) *The International Handbook of Suicide and Attempted Suicide*, 2nd edn. Chichester: John Wiley & Sons.

Reilly, J. (2006) 'Obesity in childhood and adolescence: evidence based clinical and public health perspectives', *Postgraduate Medicine*, 82: 429–37.

Rickards, L., Fox, K., Roberts, C., Fletcher, L. and Goddard, E. (2004) *Living in Britain: No 31. Results from the 2002 General Household Survey*, London: TSO.

Riddell, S. and Banks, P. (2001) *Disability in Scotland: A Baseline Study: A Report for the Disability Rights Commission, Strathclyde Centre for Disability Research*, Glasgow: The University of Glasgow.

Rutter, M. and Smith, D. (1995) *Psychosocial Disorders in Young People: Time Trends and their Causes*, Chichester: John Wiley & Sons.

Schor, J. (2004) *Born to Buy*, New York: Scribner.

Sellstrom, E. and Bremberg, S. (2006) 'Is there a "school effect" on pupil outcomes? A review of multilevel studies', *Journal of Epidemiology and Community Health*, 60: 149–55.

Sigle-Rushton, W., Hobcraft, J. and Kiernan, K. (2005) 'Parental divorce and subsequent disadvantage: a cross-cohort comparison', *Demography*, 42: 427–46.

Starfield, B., Riley, A., Witt, W. and Robertson, J. (2002) 'Social class gradients in health in adolescents', *Journal of Epidemiology and Community Health*, 56: 334–61.

Stewart-Brown, S., Evans, J., Patterson, J., Petersen, S., Doll, H., Balding, J. and Regis, D. (2000) 'The health of students in institutes of higher education: an important and neglected public health problem', *Journal of Public Health Medicine*, 22: 492–9.

Sweeting, H. and West, P. (2003) 'Sex differences in health at ages 11, 13 and 15', *Social Science and Medicine*, 56: 31–9.

West, P. (1997) 'Health inequalities in the early years: is there equalisation in youth?' *Social Science and Medicine*, 44: 833–58.

West, P. and Sweeting, H. (1996) 'Nae job, nae future: young people and health in the context of unemployment', *Health and Social Care in the Community*, 4: 50–62.

—— (2003) 'Fifteen, female and stressed: changing patterns of psychological distress over time', *Journal of Child Psychology and Psychiatry*, 44: 399–411.

—— (2004) 'Evidence on equalisation in health in youth from the West of Scotland', *Social Science and Medicine*, 59: 13–27.

Young, R., Sweeting, H. and West, P. (2006) 'Prevalence of deliberate self harm and attempted suicide within contemporary Goth youth subculture: longitudinal cohort study', *British Medical Journal*, 332: 1058–61.

Young, R., Van Beinum, M., Sweeting, H. and West, P. (2007) 'Young people who self harm', *British Journal of Psychiatry*, 191: 44–9.

# 42

# HIV and AIDS, STIs and sexual health among young people

*Frederick Mugisha*

## Introduction

This chapter provides an up-to-date overview of research relevant to Human Immuno-deficiency Virus (HIV) and Acquired Immune Deficiency Syndrome (AIDS), other Sexually Transmitted Infections (STIs) and sexual health among young people, reflecting on trends and considering future research agenda. The chapter addresses three dimensions: (1) research on trends in the prevalence of HIV and AIDS, STIs and sexual behaviour; (2) developments in research on interventions to address them; and (3) research on challenges of delivering these interventions. Since the advent of the AIDS epidemic, research has concentrated on the first two dimensions, that is, measuring the extent and reasons to which sub-populations are affected and developing technologies and approaches to address them. Less research focus has been on understanding effective mechanisms for and challenges of delivering them in public and non-public endeavours. Yet without enhancing the effectiveness of their delivery, young people will continue to miss out on proven interventions. The chapter was based on a review of published and unpublished literature in the public domain. It is written to reach a wider audience; those who are familiar and those who might be unfamiliar with the subject of HIV and AIDS, STIs and sexual health among young people. The chapter is structured thus: the extent of the problem is first addressed, then the next section addresses intervention programmes, followed by the challenges of service delivery, and finally future research outlook.

## Extent of the problem

Globally, almost 12 million people aged 15–24 were estimated to be living with HIV/AIDS in 2002. About three-quarters of these live in Sub-Saharan Africa. The young age structure of countries hardest hit by the pandemic implies that about half of all new infections are now occurring among this age group (e.g. Summers *et al.* 2002). Since the vast majority of HIV infections are sexually transmitted, the vulnerability of young

344

people is strongly influenced by their sexual behaviour. However, positive changes are being observed in the prevalence of HIV, other STIs and behaviour among young people.

First, HIV prevalence among females ages 15–24 is higher than among males in most developing regions. This is especially true in Africa, where prevalence rates among females are more than double those of males (Glynn *et al.* 2001). Higher infection rates among females also hold, though to a lesser extent, for South and South-eastern Asia. Women, particularly girls and young women, face a higher risk of infection with HIV for physiological, social, and cultural reasons. The risk of infection during unprotected sex is two to four times higher for women than for men (United Nations Population Fund 2003). This disparity is due to several reasons: the viral load is generally higher in semen than in vaginal secretions; in vaginal intercourse a larger surface area is exposed to sexual secretions for a woman than for a man; and the vagina and cervix of adolescent women are less mature, with a thinner cell structure that allows the virus to pass more easily (Berman and Hein 1999). In addition, women face a higher risk of infection with HIV because of differences in patterns of heterosexual relations. In Sub-Saharan Africa, for example, where most infections are transmitted by heterosexual relations, young women generally face higher risks because they tend to have sex with and marry older men, who are more likely to be infected than younger men. Some of these relationships are based on economic gain, that is, they involve the exchange of gifts or money for sex. There is now a great deal of research showing that the power differentials inherent in such relationships make it difficult for young women to negotiate the use of condoms (e.g. Luke 2003).

Second, STIs enhance the probability that HIV infection will be passed between sexual partners (Cohen 1998). Due to data scarcity on the prevalence of other STIs among young people, trends are difficult to discern. Existing evidence, however, gives an impression that a substantial minority of young people may contract STIs. For instance,

**Table 42.1** Direction of change in the probability of females marrying, having premarital sex, and having sex by age 18: a comparison of 20–24 year-olds and 40–44 year-olds, demographic and health surveys (1990–2003)

|  | Number of countries | Increase | No change | Decrease |
|---|---|---|---|---|
| Per cent marrying by age 18 |  |  |  |  |
| Africa | 27 | 0 | 3 | 24 |
| Asia | 5 | 1 | 3 | 1 |
| Latin America/Caribbean | 9 | 0 | 3 | 6 |
| TOTAL | 41 | 1 | 9 | 31 |
| Per cent having premarital sex by age 18 |  |  |  |  |
| Africa | 27 | 20 | 7 | 0 |
| Asia | 5 | 1 | 4 | 0 |
| Latin America/Caribbean | 9 | 3 | 5 | 1 |
| TOTAL | 41 | 24 | 16 | 1 |
| Per cent having sex by age 18 |  |  |  |  |
| Africa | 27 | 5 | 14 | 8 |
| Asia | 5 | 2 | 2 | 1 |
| Latin America/Caribbean | 9 | 2 | 3 | 4 |
| TOTAL | 41 | 9 | 19 | 13 |

Source: DHS data as reported in National Research Council and Institute of Medicine, 2005.

studies in eight countries of various populations ranging in age from 12–24 show that between 3–12 per cent of males and 1–14 per cent of females had ever experienced an STI (Brown 2001) (Table 42.1).

Third, behaviour related to early age at sexual initiation, early marriage, and risky sexual practices is also changing. We are observing an increase in premarital sex before age 18, a decrease in the percentage marrying before the age of 18, and no change in the percentage having sex before the age of 18 (see Table 42.1) among females over a period of 20 years (National Research Council and Institute of Medicine 2005). Delays in age at marriage imply that there is a greater likelihood that first sex will be experienced prior to marriage exposing young people more. Condom use among sexually active young women is still relatively low, but increases are noticeable in Africa and Latin America. Table 42.2 shows the percentage of young women currently using condoms in successive Demographic and Health Surveys about ten years apart. In Uganda (see Table 42.2), which is often cited for its success in promotion of behaviour change, virtually no women aged 15–24 were recorded as using condoms in 1988–89, whereas about 10 years later the proportions among never married, sexually active women exceed one in

**Table 42.2** Percentage of young women currently using condoms in successive demographic and health surveys about ten years apart

| Age group and country | Year of study | | All sexually active | | Never married and sexually active | |
|---|---|---|---|---|---|---|
| | 1st | 2nd | 1st | 2nd | 1st | 2nd |
| 15–19 year-olds | | | | | | |
| Ghana | 1988 | 1998–1999 | 0.4 | 12.1 | 0.4 | 8.6 |
| Kenya | 1989 | 1998 | 0.3 | 5.5 | 0.3 | 4.3 |
| Senegal | 1986 | 1997 | 0.0 | 3.2 | 0.0 | 2.5 |
| Togo | 1988 | 1998 | 1.8 | 14.4 | 1.8 | 13.6 |
| Uganda | 1998–1999 | 2000–2001 | 0.0 | 11.8 | 0.0 | 36.7 |
| Zimbabwe | 1988 | 1999 | 0.8 | 6.5 | 0.8 | 4.4 |
| Bolivia | 1989 | 1998 | 0.1 | 4.3 | 0.0 | 2.9 |
| Brazil | 1986 | 1996 | 1.1 | 12.0 | 0.0 | 7.9 |
| Colombia | 1990 | 2000 | 1.5 | 12.7 | 0.6 | 10.0 |
| Dominican Republic | 1986 | 1996 | 0.0 | 6.6 | 0.0 | 3.3 |
| Guatemala | 1987 | 1998 | 0.9 | 3.6 | 0.0 | 0.2 |
| Peru | 1986 | 1996 | 0.0 | 6.6 | 0.0 | 3.3 |
| 20–24 year-olds | | | | | | |
| Ghana | 1988 | 1998–1999 | 1.2 | 7.1 | 0.2 | 3.6 |
| Kenya | 1989 | 1998 | 1.2 | 2.2 | 0.1 | 0.8 |
| Senegal | 1986 | 1997 | 0.0 | 2.7 | 0.0 | 2.1 |
| Togo | 1988 | 1998 | 1.5 | 9.6 | 0.9 | 7.2 |
| Uganda | 1998–1999 | 2000–2001 | 0.0 | 4.5 | 0.0 | 34.9 |
| Zimbabwe | 1988 | 1999 | 1.8 | 3.8 | 0.4 | 1.7 |
| Bolivia | 1989 | 1998 | 0.4 | 5.1 | 0.0 | 1.4 |
| Brazil | 1986 | 1996 | 0.8 | 8.2 | 0.3 | 4.1 |
| Colombia | 1990 | 2000 | 2.0 | 14.2 | 0.5 | 7.7 |
| Dominican Republic | 1986 | 1996 | 0.0 | 2.0 | 0.0 | 0.1 |
| Guatemala | 1987 | 1998 | 1.5 | 1.8 | 0.0 | 0.1 |
| Peru | 1986 | 1996 | 0.0 | 6.1 | 0.0 | 2.0 |

Source: DHS data as reported in National Research Council and Institute of Medicine, 2005.

three. Although the magnitude of the change varies, increases over time appear in all countries surveyed. Trends in the number of sexual partners could not be discerned, however, existing evidence suggests that a substantial proportion of those aged 15–19 reported having had two or more sexual partners during the past year ranging from 20–39 per cent in 5 of the 17 countries, and 40–61 per cent in the remaining 12 countries (Singh and Bankole 2001).

## Intervention programmes

Numerous health-related programmes directed towards young people exist, which are either single-component or multi-component. The single component programmes include: sexual and reproductive health education in schools, mass media and social marketing programmes, youth-friendly health services, peer promotion programmes, STI/HIV counselling and testing, youth centres, programmes targeting parents, and workplace-based programmes. Multi-component programmes, which are relatively new, include multi-component community-based programmes and comprehensive youth development programmes. Each of the programmes is examined in detail.

### Sexual and reproductive health education in schools

In countries with high school enrolment, sexual and reproductive health education programmes in schools have the potential to reach a large number of young people. The potential is enhanced with the high and rising school enrolment rates in many developing countries with the advent of free primary and secondary education. However, the curricula, content, duration, and format of these interventions vary but overall the programmes attempt to impart information on one or more of the following areas: sexuality, HIV/AIDS transmission and prevention, family planning, condoms, sexually transmitted diseases, and decision-making and refusal skills. Many of the programmes have demonstrated impact on knowledge and attitudes. Only a few have demonstrated impact on delayed age at first sex and numbers of sexual partners (see, for example, Harvey *et al.* 2000).

### Mass media and social marketing programmes

The use of mass media has the potential to reach large numbers of young people. Less research has been undertaken on mass media-based sexual and reproductive health interventions directed specifically to young audiences. However, communications research indicates that the media can be an effective strategy for influencing adult behaviours (Rogers 1995).

### Youth-friendly health services

Youth-friendly service initiatives are geared towards making the use of existing reproductive health services more acceptable and less traumatizing to young people. To date, only a small number of youth-friendly service programmes in developing country settings have been rigorously evaluated. Among the three with reported evaluation results, one found solid evidence of positive impact on service utilization by young people, one nominal impact, and one no impact (Institute for Reproductive Health 2001).

## Peer promotion programmes

Peer promotion programmes take advantage of the fact that young people spend a large amount of time interacting with other young people similar to themselves in school, at work, or in the community. These programmes recruit and train a core group of young people to serve as role models and sources of information for their peers. Peer promotion strategies have been associated with positive behavioural outcomes in several studies in Peru, Nigeria, Ghana and Cameroon (see, for example, Speizer *et al.* 2001).

## STI/HIV counselling and testing

Evidence from the United States indicates that HIV counselling and testing can be effective in changing high-risk sexual behaviours and reducing new STIs among both adults and young people (Kamb *et al.* 1998). The evidence from developing countries is sparse. However, the findings from a randomized control trial of a programme for unmarried young adults in northern Thailand indicated a significant effect on the proportion of young people seeking HIV testing. The magnitude of the effect (8 per cent) was modest, and no increases in other risk-reduction behaviours (e.g., condom use) were observed (Jiraphongsa *et al.* 2002)

## Youth centres

Youth centres generally have recreational and educational components, as well as reproductive health counselling and clinical components. Most youth centres also include peer educators who refer young people to the centre for both recreational and health service visits. The evidence on the impact of youth centres on service utilization is limited. The only rigorous study currently available is an evaluation of the Association Togolaise pour le Bien-Etre Familiale youth centre in Lomé, Togo (Speizer *et al.* 2004) which found that, while awareness of the youth centre increased from 6 per cent in 1998 to 42 per cent in 2000 among young people in Lomé, actual use only rose moderately, from 3 per cent in 1998 to 8 per cent in 2000 and 10 per cent in 2001.

## Programmes targeting parents

Parents play a key role in shaping young people's behaviours, yet are uncomfortable counselling their children on matters related to sex and contraception. Sexual and reproductive health and HIV/AIDS education programmes for parents have been designed directed to young people. When parents participate in such programmes, parent–child communication about sexuality increases, however, no evidence to date demonstrates an effect on the likelihood of initiating sex during the teen years (see Miller *et al.* 1998).

## Workplace-based programmes

Implementing workplace-based programmes is one way of reaching out-of-school young people. Placing reproductive health activities in workplaces that attract large numbers of young people is a logical strategy in such places. In two of the four evaluations of workplace-based reproductive health programmes for young people impact on behaviours was measured, and in both reported significant impact – one of them in Thailand targeting visitors to brothels (Celentano *et al.* 1998).

### Multi-component community-based programmes

In recognition of the multiple risk and protective factors present in the environment, multiple-component community-based reproductive health programmes for young people are increasingly being tried. Four recent studies of multi-component interventions in Bangladesh, Kenya, Mexico, and Senegal included: a community sensitization programme for community leaders, parents, and out-of-school youth; youth-friendly clinic services; and a school-based reproductive health information programme (YouthNet and Family Health International 2003). Positive changes in behaviour were observed in some sites, but these changes tended to be small and mostly statistically insignificant. Knowledge and attitudes did change in many of the sites. Such multi-component programmes are more promising when designed with input from the local community.

### Comprehensive youth development programmes

Youth development programmes consist of the provision of a range of development activities in one programme that address a wide range of needs of young people. These projects go beyond simply providing sexual and reproductive health education. They also focus on life options, educational aspirations, employment considerations, and psychosocial development needs. They also promote a safe environment in which young people can develop and are often focused on vulnerable populations, those who have missed the opportunity to go to school or dropped out prematurely. The only youth development programme in a developing country for which evaluation data are currently available is the Better Life Options Project designed by the Centre for Development and Population Activities and initially implemented in India in 1987 (Levitt–Dayal and Motihar 2000). This programme included non-formal education (literacy, post-literacy, and linkages with formal education), family life education, vocational skills training, health education and services, public awareness creation, and advocacy. The evaluation study found that females (ages 15–26) who had participated in the programme had a higher age at marriage and fewer children; were more likely to have participated in formal schooling; were more likely to be employed and earning cash; had greater confidence and self-efficacy; and had higher rates of contraceptive use, antenatal care, hospital deliveries, and use of oral dehydration solutions compared to young women with no programme exposure. While these results are promising, it should be noted that the extent to which the programme evaluation effectively controlled for participation (i.e., selection) bias is questionable.

## Challenges of maximizing the impact of services

To maximize the impact of services in promoting sexual health in adolescents, more innovative means of offering advice and promoting sexual health will be needed. There are at least two challenges to this: promoting and exploring deployment and use of new technologies, such as DVDs or CD-Roms; and ensuring effective accountability in service delivery. These two challenges are addressed in tandem. First, the challenge regarding promoting and exploring deployment and use of technologies is that most providers such as health workers are conservative with regard to adolescent sexuality, even with training. Education curricula that include topics on sexuality of young people are rare and where they do exist, relevant sections are frequently skipped over by teachers who are unprepared (DeJong *et al.* 2005).

Second, the manner in which service delivery is organized poses a challenge of ensuring effective accountability and which ensures young people continue to be denied effective interventions. Service delivery involves three main players: service providers, policy-makers and the young people (see Figure 42.1). The three players form a service delivery chain. Young people – as patients in clinics, students in schools, clients at youth centres – are the clients of service providers. They have a relationship with the frontline providers, with school teachers and health workers who provide them with services. Young people have a similar relationship when they purchase items or services in the market, such as a piece of soap. In a competitive-market transaction, they get the 'service' because they can hold the provider accountable. That is, the consumer (young person) pays the provider directly; he/she can observe whether or not he has received the piece of soap; and if he is dissatisfied, he has power over the provider either by refusing the soap, or refusing repeat business or, in the case of fraud, with legal or social sanctions.

For the majority of social services – such as reproductive health services or education – there is no direct accountability of the provider to the client. Why not? For a variety of good reasons, society has decided that the service will be provided not through a market transaction but through the government or any other party taking responsibility. First, these services are replete with market failures – with externalities, as when an infected child spreads a disease to playmates or a farmer benefits from a neighbour's ability to read. So the private sector, left to its own devices, will not achieve the level of health and education that society desires. Second, basic health and basic education are considered fundamental human rights. The Universal Declaration of Human Rights asserts an individual's right to 'a standard of living adequate for the health and well-being of himself and of his family, including … medical care … [and a right to education that is] … free, at least in the elementary and fundamental stages'. No matter how daunting the problems of delivery may be, the public sector cannot walk away from health and education. The challenge is to see how the government – in collaboration with the private sector, communities, and outside partners – can meet this fundamental responsibility.

The accountability is through a 'long route' (see Figure 42.1) – young people or clients as citizens influence policy-makers through elections, and policy-makers influence service providers, and service providers provide services to the young people or clients. When the relationships along this long route break down, service delivery fail and failure is manifested in absentee health workers, absentee teachers, disincentive for creativity and innovativeness. As a consequence, the young people – mainly the poor – suffer

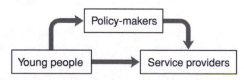

**Figure 42.1** Framework of service provision and accountability relationship.
Source: modified based on World Bank 2003.

ultimately with poor reproductive health outcomes. Emerging evidence suggests that this breakdown in accountability is one of the most important factors responsible for poor service delivery. In some cases, there is simply neglect due to lack of enforcement, in others, policy-makers and service providers collude to deny the young people services, yet in other cases policy-makers are not well facilitated to undertake their functions effectively. In the final analysis, even when there are effective interventions, the approach to service delivery and accountability means that the young people continue to be left out.

## Future research outlook

This chapter has reviewed research on trends, interventions, and challenges of service delivery in relation to HIV and AIDS, and sexuality among young people. Extensive work has been conducted on the trends that show improvements in the prevalence of the diseases as well as changes in sexuality-related behaviours. In addition, although not all interventions have consistently demonstrated positive impact, in part due to lack of rigorous evaluations, promising interventions addressed to young people exist. More research is required to provide more evidence on the effectiveness of a number of interventions preferably through randomized control trials. Research on mechanisms of ensuring effective and responsive service delivery, especially in respect of accountability is still lacking.

## References

Berman, S. and Hein, K. (1999) 'Adolescents and STDs', in P. Mardh, P. Sparling, K. Holmes, S. Lemon, W. Stamm, P. Piot and J. Wasserheit (eds) *Sexually Transmitted Diseases*, New York: McGraw-Hill, pp. 129–42.

Brown, P. H. (2001) 'Choosing to die: a growing epidemic among the young', *Bulletin of the World Health Organization*, 12: 1175–7.

Celentano, D. D., Nelson, K. E., Lyles, C. M., Beyrer, C., Eiumtrakul, S., Go, V. F. L. *et al.* (1998) 'Decreasing incidence of HIV and sexually transmitted diseases in young Thai men: evidence for success of the HIV/AIDS control and prevention program', *AIDS*, F29–F36.

Cohen, M. (1998) 'Sexually transmitted diseases enhance HIV transmission: no longer a hypothesis', *Lancet*, 3: 5–7.

DeJong, J., Jawad, R., Mortagy, I. and Shepard, B. (2005) 'The sexual and reproductive health of young people in the Arab countries and Iran', *Reproductive Health Matters*, 25: 49–59.

Glynn, J. R., Caraël, M., Auvert, B., Kahindo, M. J., Musonda, R., Kaona, F. and Buvé, A. (2001) 'Why do young women have a much higher prevalence of HIV than young men? A study in Kisumu, Kenya and Ndola, Zambia', *AIDS*, 4: S51–S60.

Harvey, B., Stuart, J. and Swan, T. (2000) 'Evaluation of a drama-in-education programme to increase AIDS awareness in South African high schools: a randomized community intervention trial', *International Journal of STD and AIDS*, 3: 105–11.

Institute for Reproductive Health (2001) *Reaching Adolescents at Family Planning Clinics: Applying the Reproductive Health Awareness Model (The Awareness Project Research Update)*, Washington, DC: Institute for Reproductive Health, Georgetown University Medical Center.

Jiraphongsa, C., Danmoensawat, W., Greenland, S., Frerichs, R., Siraprapasiri, T., Glik, D. C. and Detels, R. (2002) 'Acceptance of HIV testing and counseling among unmarried young adults in Northern Thailand', *AIDS Education and Prevention*, 2: 89–101.

Kamb, M. L., Fishbein, M., Douglas, J. M., Jr. and Rhodes, F. (1998) 'Efficacy of risk reduction counseling to prevent human immunodeficiency virus and sexually transmitted diseases: a randomized controlled trial', *Journal of American Medical Association*, 13: 1161–7.

Levitt-Dayal, M. and Motihar, R. (2000) *Adolescent Girls in India Choose a Better future: An Impact Assessment*, Washington, DC: The Center for Development and Population Activities.

Luke, N. (2003) 'Age and economic asymmetries in the sexual relationships of adolescent girls in sub-Saharan Africa', *Studies in Family Planning*, 2: 67–86.

Miller, K. E., Sabo, D., Farrell, M. P., Barnes, G. M. and Melnick, M. J. (1998) 'Athletic participation and sexual behavior in adolescents: the different worlds of boys and girls', *Journal of Health and Social Behavior*, 2: 108–23.

National Research Council and Institute of Medicine (2005) *Growing up Global: The Changing Transitions to Adulthood in Developing Countries: Panel on Transitions to Adulthood in Developing Countries*, ed. C. B. Lloyd, Committee on Population and Board on Children, Youth, and Families, Division of Behavioral and Social Sciences and Education. Washington, DC: The National Academies Press.

Rogers, E. M. (1995) *Diffusion of Innovations*. New York: Free Press.

Singh, S. and Bankole, A. (2001) 'Gender differences in the sexual and contraceptive behavior of young people: Sub-Saharan Africa and Latin America and the Caribbean', paper presented at International Union for the Scientific Study in Population Conference, Salvador, Brazil.

Speizer, I., Kouwonou, K., Mullen, S. and Vignikin, E. (2004) 'Evaluation of the ATBEF Youth Centre in Lome, Togo', *African Journal of Reproductive Health*, 3: 38–54.

Speizer, I. S., Tambashe, B. O. and Tegang, S. P. (2001) 'An evaluation of the "Entre Nois Jeunes" peer-educator program for adolescents in Cameroon', *Studies in Family Planning*, 4: 339–51.

Summers, T., Kates, J. and Murphy, G. (2002) *The Tip of the Iceberg: The Global Impact of HIV/AIDS on Youth*. Menlo Park, CA: The Henry J. Kaiser Family Foundation.

United Nations Population Fund (2003) *The Impact of HIV/AIDS: A Population and Development Perspective*, New York: United Nations Population Fund.

World Bank (2003) *Making Services Work for Poor People: World Development Report 2004*. Washington, DC: World Bank and Oxford University Press.

YouthNet and Family Health International (2003) *New Findings from Intervention Research: Youth Reproductive Health and HIV Prevention*, Arlington, VA: Family Health International.

# 43

# Progress, culture and young people's wellbeing

*Richard Eckersley*

## Introduction

The orthodox view of young people's health and wellbeing is of continuing improvement, in line with historical trends. In this chapter, I argue against this view because it over-estimates the importance of declining death rates and underestimates that of adverse trends in a range of non-fatal, chronic health problems, both physical and mental. These problems have their sources in quite fundamental features of modern societies, and optimizing wellbeing will mean making correspondingly fundamental social and cultural changes.

Young people reflect best the tenor and tempo of the times because they are growing up in them. Because of their stages of biological and social development, they are also most vulnerable to social risks. Many of the attitudes and behaviours – even the illnesses – that largely determine adult health have their origins in childhood, adolescence and early adulthood. So the health of young people shapes the future health of the whole population: their health is not only important in its own right, or for their sake, it is crucial to assessing the overall state and fate of societies.

I define health very broadly to include all aspects of wellbeing, not just clinical disease, disorder and disability. I use the terms 'health' and 'wellbeing' somewhat interchangeably and sometimes together to emphasize their many dimensions: illness and wellness, physical and psychological, objective and subjective. My focus, however, is on mental health and wellbeing; physical health is discussed elsewhere.

### Conceptual framework

Much of the evidence on which I draw comes from epidemiology. The analysis is informed by a psychosocial theory of health which states that the social determinants of health, and health inequalities, are not primarily, or fundamentally, material – resulting from differences in material exposures and experiences – but psychosocial – stemming from people's position in the social hierarchy and their perceptions of relative disadvantage (Eckersley 2006a). I have extended this theory beyond socio-economic inequality and disadvantage – the focus of epidemiology – and applied it to culture: that is, cultural factors can also influence people's perceptions and expectations, reducing social support and personal control, and causing stress, depression, anxiety, isolation, insecurity and hostility.

However, the way I think of culture – as a system of meanings and symbols that shape how people see the world and their place in it and give meaning to personal and collective experience – owes more to anthropology than to epidemiology, which understands 'culture' mainly in categorical terms of 'subcultures' or 'difference', especially ethnic and racial, and so, often, as one dimension of socio-economic status (ibid.). On the other hand, anthropologists are often sceptical of the notion that whole societies can be characterized by a few dominant themes, such as materialism and individualism. Instead, they focus on the details of population patterning and distribution, individual and group differences, and culture as local knowledge and daily life. So I also take from psychology and sociology, disciplines in which these cultural qualities are a major focus of research.

## Patterns and trends in young people's wellbeing

Consistent with a belief in human progress, the orthodox, or official, view of young people's health (and health generally) is that it is continuing to improve. For example, Lomborg, in a statistical assessment of the state of the world, concludes that humanity's lot has improved vastly in every significant measurable field and that it is likely to continue to do so: ' ... children born today – in both the industrialized world and developing countries – will live longer and be healthier, they will get more food, a better education, a higher standard of living, more leisure time and far more possibilities' (Lomborg 2001: 351–2).

At the national level, to take Australia as an example of the developed world, the official position, as articulated by the Australian Institute of Health and Welfare (AIHW 2004: 187), is that young people generally enjoy a level of health that is good and getting better. A corollary is that, with overall health improving, attention needs to be focused on those disadvantaged groups that lag behind (AIHW 2007: x).

Historically, the health of young people follows the overall trends in population health (Eckersley 2005). The toll of infectious diseases has fallen as a result of improved hygiene, nutrition and living and working conditions, and medical advances such as antibiotics and vaccines. The dramatic rise in life expectancy, which globally has more than doubled in the last 200 years, is one of humanity's greatest achievements. Mortality rates continue to decline, including among children and youth, and life expectancy to rise.

While mortality might have been a valid indicator of overall health historically, this is now questionable (especially in developed nations, but also increasingly in developing nations). Mortality and life expectancy do not reflect adequately the growing importance to health and wellbeing of non-fatal, chronic health problems. Nor is this shift in importance simply a result of the success in reducing mortality, or more (or better) diagnoses of chronic conditions. Modern medicine has contributed to the 'measurement problem' in keeping more people alive, but without, in many cases, preventing or curing disease and disability. However, there is increasing evidence that chronic problems are becoming more common for other reasons to do with changing lifestyles and social conditions. Just as we often wrongly equate quality of life with standard of living, we confuse how well people live with how long they live.

354

There are, therefore, growing 'scale anomalies' in generalizing about health trends from mortality rates. The figures for Australia illustrate this well. On the one hand, death now strikes only about 40 out of every 100,000 young people (0.04 per cent) each year, so falling mortality affects few people (AIHW 2007: 64). Moreover, the biggest cause of death among young Australians today is road accidents, and the drop in the road toll explains much of the decline in their mortality in recent decades. This has been a result of factors such as better roads, safer cars, seat belts and random breath tests, and says little about overall health and general living conditions.

On the other hand, large national studies have found that 27 per cent of Australians aged 18–24 experienced mental health problems in the previous year – the highest prevalence of all age groups – and that 14 per cent of children and adolescents (aged 4–17) were suffering mental health problems at the time of the survey (Eckersley 2005: 154–5; Eckersley, in press). Among Australians aged 15–24, mental disorders now account for 49 per cent of the burden of disease, measured as both death and disability (and 61 per cent of the non-fatal burden) (AIHW 2007: 20–1). This is by far the biggest contribution, well ahead of the next most important contributor, injuries, at 18 per cent.

Research in several developed countries suggests 20–30 per cent of young people are experiencing significant psychological distress at any one time, with less severe stress-related problems (including frequent headaches, stomach pains and sleeplessness) affecting as many as 50 per cent (Eckersley 2005: 147–69). Long-term trends in mental ill-health are very difficult to establish conclusively because of the lack of good, comparative data, and the issue remains contentious; not all studies show an increase. However, the evidence, both direct and indirect, taken together, produces a coherent and compelling, if still provisional, picture of declining psychological resilience and wellbeing. For example:

- A major US study has shown almost a half of Americans will experience a clinical mental disorder during their lives, and over a quarter will do so in any one year (Kessler *et al.* 2005a; Kessler *et al.* 2005b). The lifetime risk increases for successive generations: people aged 18–29 have an estimated lifetime risk four times that of those aged 60 and over.
- A UK study of health surveys carried out in 1974, 1986 and 1999 found a rise in some mental health problems among both boys and girls aged 15–16 (Collishaw *et al.* 2004). Overall, the prevalence of conduct problems increased from 7 per cent to 15 per cent, and that of emotional problems from 10 per cent to 17 per cent. The preliminary results from a more recent analysis of English health survey data from 1986 and 2006 also show that today's adolescents experience considerably higher rates of emotional problems, with the increases becoming more marked with increasing symptom severity (Collishaw *et al.* 2007).
- Swedish data suggest mental health has declined among children and youth, at least since the late 1980s (Hjern 2006; Stefansson 2006). The proportions of boys and girls who said they often or always felt unhappy rose markedly between 1988 and 2002. In 2001–2, 20–30 per cent of boys aged 11–15, and 30–40 per cent of girls, said they experienced every week one or more psychosomatic symptoms such as abdominal pains, headaches and disturbed sleep; the proportions have increased continuously since the mid-1980s.
- A large Australian survey of students from prep school to year 12 found that about 40 per cent of students could be described as displaying lower levels of social and emotional wellbeing (ASG 2007). From a fifth to a half of students said they: were

lonely, worried too much; were very nervous or stressed; had recently felt hopeless and depressed for a week and had stopped regular activities; lost their temper a lot; and had difficulty calming down when upset (indicating poor resilience).

Findings such as these not only challenge the picture presented by declining mortality, they run counter to other evidence that is used to support the orthodox view of young people's wellbeing: most say they are happy and satisfied with their lives. An Australian study found that over 80 per cent of young people aged 19–20 were satisfied with their lives – including lifestyle, work or study, relationships with parents and friends, accomplishments and self-perceptions. However, 50 per cent were experiencing one or more problems associated with depression, anxiety, anti-social behaviour (including illicit drug use) and alcohol use (Smart and Sanson 2005). The explanations for the apparent contradiction are complex, and include that evaluating one's happiness involves illusions, rationalization and mitigation, and that 'unhealthy' moods and behaviours do not necessarily equate to unhappiness and dissatisfaction (Eckersley in press).

## Explanations

An introductory commentary on a series of papers on adolescent health in the medical journal, *Lancet*, states the papers incorporate three fundamental principles: rapidly changing social contexts promulgate new and sometimes unexpected health threats; health and ill-health are understood best as a result of the complex interplay between biological, psychological and sociological factors; and the sociological factors have global reach in their effect on young people (Resnick and Bowes 2007). A wide range of such factors has been implicated in the patterns and trends in young people's health and wellbeing (Eckersley 2005):

- Changes in the worlds of family, work and education such as family conflict and breakdown, poverty and unemployment, job stresses and insecurity, and education pressures (the most commonly cited factors).
- Cultural changes, for example, excessive materialism and individualism (discussed later), and the emergence of a youth culture that isolates young people from adults and increases peer influence.
- Increasing media use and changing media content, linked to violence, consumerism, loss of community and social cohesion, vicarious life experiences, invidious social comparisons, and pessimism about global conditions and futures.
- The decline of religion, which 'packages' many sources of wellbeing, including social support, spiritual or existential meaning, a coherent belief system and a clear moral code (paradoxically, at a population or national level, research suggests religion is a health burden).
- Changes in diet, which have been implicated in many chronic health problems. For example, a large increase in the ratio of omega 6 to omega 3 fatty acids has been linked to cardiovascular disease and mood disorders.
- Comorbidity, especially between drug use and mental illness, but also between mental and physical problems such as the links between obesity and depression, and depression and heart disease.
- Environmental degradation, including widespread toxic chemical pollution, which affects neurological development and immune function.

Environmental changes loom large as a future risk to health, including mental health, especially global warming and its consequences. A major WHO report (Corvalan *et al.* 2005) warns that the dual trends of the growing exploitation of ecosystems and their generally declining condition are unsustainable. There is an increasing risk of 'non-linear changes' in ecosystems, including accelerating, abrupt and potentially irreversible changes, which could have 'a catastrophic effect on human health'.

There are several important points to note about these explanatory factors:

- They interact with other biological and social factors to produce individual, age and generational differences.
- The health effects are not usually independent, direct and immediate; rather the causal pathways are complex, effects being often interdependent, indirect, delayed, and spanning different levels or layers of causation.
- Trends in some factors provide indirect corroboration of evidence that psychosocial problems have risen among youth.
- Some of the factors that explain social patterns of health may not be implicated in the trends over time.

The last point is especially important in extending explanations beyond the usual social and economic focus. Studies typically show socio-economic gradients in mental health problems (that is, higher prevalence in lower-income and single-parent and blended families). However, the UK research (Collishaw *et al.* 2004; 2007) on time trends shows the rise in problems occurred across all family types and social classes, as does the Swedish research (Stefansson 2006) with socio-economic status. This suggests changes in these areas are not the main reasons for the trends.

## Materialism, individualism and cultural fraud

The more fundamental explanatory factors include the defining features of modern Western culture: materialism and individualism (Eckersley 2005: 77–104; 2006a). Research shows materialism (the pursuit of money and possessions) breeds, not happiness, but dissatisfaction, depression, anxiety, anger, isolation and alienation. People for whom 'extrinsic goals' such as fame, fortune and glamour are a priority in life tend to experience more anxiety and depression and lower overall wellbeing – and to be less trusting and caring in their relationships – than people oriented towards 'intrinsic goals' of close relationships, personal growth and self-understanding, and contributing to the community.

As materialism reaches increasingly beyond the acquisition of things to the enhancement of the person, the goal of marketing becomes not only to make people dissatisfied with what they have, but also with who they are. As it seeks ever more ways to colonize their consciousness, consumer culture both fosters and exploits the restless, insatiable expectation that there must be more to life. In short, the more materialistic people are, the poorer their quality of life.

Individualism (the relaxation of social ties and regulation and the belief that people are independent of each other) is supposed to be about freeing people to live the lives they want. Historically, it has been a progressive force, loosening the chains of religious dogma, class oppression and gender and ethnic discrimination, and so associated with the liberation of human potential. However, individualism is a two-edged sword. As sociologists have noted, the freedom people have is both exhilarating and disturbing: with new opportunities for personal experience and growth also comes the anxiety of social dislocation.

The costs of individualism relate to a loss of social support and personal control, both of which are important to resilience and wellbeing. These include: a heightened sense of risk, uncertainty and insecurity; a lack of clear frames of reference; a rise in personal expectations, coupled with a perception that the onus of success lies with the individual, despite the continuing importance of social disadvantage and privilege; a surfeit or excess of freedom and choice, which is experienced as a threat or tyranny; increased self-esteem, but of a narcissistic or contingent form that requires constant external validation and affirmation; and the confusion of autonomy with independence or separateness.

Mistaking autonomy for independence (or, to put it somewhat differently, redefining 'thinking *for* ourselves' as 'thinking *of* ourselves') encourages a perception by individuals that they are separate from others and the environment in which they live, and so from the very things that affect their lives. The more narrowly and separately the self is defined or construed, the greater the likelihood that the personal influences and social forces acting on people are experienced as external and alien. The creation of a 'separate self' could be a major dynamic in modern life, impacting on everything from citizenship and social trust, cohesion and engagement, to the intimacy of friendships and the quality of family life. It is no accident that the drugs most popular among youth today – such as alcohol and party drugs like ecstasy – are those that dissolve the boundaries of the self and induce a sense of belonging, a merging with others, so easing the pain of isolation.

In summary, the evidence suggests that individualism and materialism are powerfully and mutually reinforcing in their negative impacts. Broadly speaking, it would seem that they have produced a self that is socially and historically disconnected, discontented, insecure; pursuing constant gratification and external affirmation; prone to addiction, obsession and excess. Large numbers of people are medicating themselves to 'take the edge off the 21st century', to use one expression. We see these failings clearly in the lives of Hollywood-style celebrities, whose glamour, fame and wealth are so often a glittering veneer over deep insecurities, addictions and self-absorption.

Thus one of the most important and growing costs of our modern way of life is 'cultural fraud': the promotion of images and ideals of 'the good life' that serve the economy but do not meet psychological needs or reflect social realities. To the extent that these images and ideals hold sway over us, they encourage goals and aspirations that are in themselves unhealthy. To the extent that we resist them because they are contrary to our own ethical and social ideals (and to public health messages), they are a powerful source of dissonance that is also harmful to health and wellbeing.

## *Material progress and sustainable development*

Most, if not all, of the explanatory factors are associated with a particular form or model of national development, material progress, which focuses on economic growth and material welfare (Eckersley 2005; 2006b). Together with other evidence, the factors point to a state of 'overdevelopment', where social changes that were once beneficial to health have now become harmful. The various lines of evidence represent an intricate and complex web of cause and effect. They show that material progress does not simply and straight-forwardly make people richer, so giving them the freedom to live as they wish. Rather, it comes with an array of cultural and moral prerequisites and consequences that affects profoundly how people think of the world and themselves, and so what they do.

The costs to health and wellbeing can no longer be regarded as unfortunate side-effects of a model of progress whose major effects remain largely beneficial; they are a direct and fundamental consequence of how societies and cultures define and pursue progress. Consequently, material progress is coming under growing challenge from a new model, sustainable development, which does not accord economic growth over-riding priority. Instead, it seeks a better balance and integration of social, environmental and economic goals and objectives to produce a high, equitable and enduring quality of life.

## Conclusion

I have argued that, notwithstanding the complexities and uncertainties, the totality of the evidence suggests that fundamental social, cultural, economic and environmental changes are impacting adversely on young people's health and wellbeing, especially in Western societies. These changes make it harder for young people to feel accepted, loved and secure; to know who they are, where they belong, what they want from life, and what is expected of them: in short, to feel their lives have meaning.

There are several reasons why such a broad analysis of whether or not life is getting better or worse for young people is warranted:

- *Research*: The broad perspective is important as a framing or conceptual device. However elusive a definitive answer might be, the question generates questions that otherwise would not be asked. It encourages more transdisciplinary dialogue and synthesis, creating new perspectives and insights into many, more specific, issues about health.
- *Health*: Whether young people's health is located within a social world that is improving or deteriorating will determine what approaches we should take to health. If quality of life is improving for the majority, attention can legitimately be focused on the minority at risk; if not, then health promotion must include broader social reforms. The picture I have presented is, despite huge increases in health expenditure in rich countries, from an average 5 per cent of GDP in 1970 to 9 per cent in 2004 (OECD 2005), prevention and public health programmes receive only about 3 per cent of this expenditure. This trend is unsustainable and some reallocation of resources is essential.
- *Society*: We manage our societies with the aim of making progress, of increasing quality of life; we need to consider, and weigh, the patterns and trends in health and wellbeing in judging if this is the case. If young people's wellbeing is improving, then this challenges a major theme in contemporary social criticism; if it is declining, this substantially weakens the case for continuing on our present path of social development, a central tenet of which is that health is continuing to improve.

Historically, health professions, notably medicine, have been part of a broad, progressive movement that has increased life expectancy and quality of life. Today, they appear to be, at best, countering the growing harm to health of adverse social trends. At worst, they are becoming part of the problem because of an emphasis on a biomedical model that focuses on the treatment of individual cases of disease, at the expense of a social model of disease prevention and health promotion.

This emphasis limits the political significance of health. The politics of health is seen largely as the politics of healthcare services; it should be the politics of everything, the defining goal of government. The central purpose of our present social system is to create wealth; we need to make that purpose to create health. Making this change requires more than a change in policies. It means rethinking 'the defining idea' of how we make life better, redesigning the conceptual framework, or worldview, within which policy decisions are made.

## References

AIHW (2004) *Australia's health 2004*, Cat. No. AUS 44, Canberra: Australian Institute of Health and Welfare.

—— (2007) *Young Australians: Their Health and Wellbeing 2007*, Cat. No. PHE-87, Canberra: Australian Institute of Health and Welfare.

ASG (2007) 'The state of student social and emotional health', Melbourne, Australian Scholarships Group. Available at: www.asg.com.au/socialemotional (accessed 6 february 2008).

Collishaw, S., Maughan, B., Goodman, R. and Pickles, A. (2004) 'Time trends in adolescent mental health', *Journal of Child Psychology and Psychiatry*, 45: 1350–62.

Collishaw, S., Pickles, A., Natarajan, L. and Maughan, B. (2007) '20-year trends in depression and anxiety in England', poster paper presented at the International Society for Research in Child and Adolescent Psychiatry Conference, London, 21 June.

Corvalan, C., Hales, S., McMichael, A. *et al.* (2005) *Ecosystems and Human Wellbeing: Health Synthesis*, a report of Millennium Ecosystem Assessment. Geneva: World Health Organization.

Eckersley, R. (2005) *Well and Good: Morality, Meaning and Happiness*, Melbourne: Text Publishing.

—— (2006a) 'Is modern Western culture a health hazard?', *International Journal of Epidemiology*, 35: 252–8.

—— (2006b) 'Progress, sustainability and human wellbeing: is a new worldview emerging?', *International Journal of Innovation and Sustainable Development*, 1: 304–17.

—— (in press) 'The health and wellbeing of young Australians: patterns, trends, explanations, responses', in D. L. Bennett, S. J. Towns and E. L. Elliott (eds) *Challenges in Adolescent Health: An Australian Perspective*, Tel Aviv: Freund Publishing.

Hjern, A. (2006) 'Chapter 7: Children's and young people's health', *Scandinavian Journal of Public Health*, 34: 165–83.

Kessler, R. C., Berglund, P., Demler, O., Jin, R. and Walters, E. E. (2005a) 'Lifetime prevalence and age-of-onset distributions of DSM-IV disorders in the National Comorbidity Survey Replication', *Archives of General Psychiatry*, 62: 593–602.

Kessler, R. C., Chiu, W. T., Demler, O. and Walters, E. E. (2005b) 'Prevalence, severity, and comorbidity of DSM-IV disorders in the National Comorbidity Survey Replication', *Archives of General Psychiatry*, 62: 617–27.

Lomborg, B. (2001) *The Skeptical Environmentalist: Measuring the Real State of the World*, Cambridge: Cambridge University Press.

OECD (2005) *Health at a Glance: OECD Indicators 2005*, Paris: OECD.

Resnick, M. D. and Bowes, G. (2007) 'Us and them: worldwide health issues for adolescents', *Lancet*, 369: 1058–60.

Smart, D. and Sanson, A. (2005) 'What is life like for young Australians today, and how well are they faring?', *Family Matters*, 70: 46–53.

Stefansson, C-G. (2006) 'Chapter 5.5: Major public health problems – mental ill-health', *Scandinavian Journal of Public Health*, 34: 87–103.

# 44

# Health-related behaviours in context

*Patrick West*

## Introduction

Health behaviours, sometimes referred to as (health) risk behaviours, theoretically refer to any practices, habits or actions which, either in the short or long term, have an effect on health, either positively or negatively. In medicine generally, and life-course epidemiology specifically, they are often conceptualized as components of an individual's lifestyle, or even as lifestyles themselves. By virtue of human agency, or at least the potential for agency, they are distinguished from social structure (e.g. social class) which is typically understood as an external (material and/or cultural) constraint. In most studies, they are usually represented by four behaviours; diet, physical activity, smoking and alcohol consumption, and (increasingly) in the case of young people illicit drug use. Sexual behaviour is also referred to, but as the subject of another chapter, is not included here.

From a sociological perspective, these behaviours are not so easily reducible to lifestyle variables, nor are they necessarily dis-embedded from social structure. Each is imbued with social meaning, both in the way they are socially constructed through, for example, advertising and the media and in the way they are consumed, and displayed by individuals. For young people, they are especially strong signifiers of identity since they are so closely connected with the youth–adult transition, minimum ages for the legal purchase of tobacco and alcohol marking stages in the achievement of adult status in most developed countries. They are also remarkably precise signifiers of youth identities, group membership and subcultures, as indicated by the way particular young people engage in physical activity (and which activities), whether they smoke or drink (and which brands they consume) or use illicit drugs (and which drugs). The extent to which such health behaviours continue to be shaped by social structures such as social class, and the extent to which they are lifestyle choices, is an important indicator of where any society is positioned in late modernity.

This chapter begins with a brief overview of the social epidemiology of diet, physical activity, smoking, drinking and drug use among youth in developed societies, focusing on health consequences, prevalence issues, and age, gender and cross-national variations. A review of ethnic group and religious differences is beyond the scope of the chapter though they are clearly important (e.g. for diet and alcohol). Developing from this, against the background of the structure/agency debate (Furlong and Cartmel 2007), and representing the former by young people's social class of origin, the latter by various lifestyles, an assessment is made of the relative importance of each for health behaviours in contemporary society. The chapter concludes with a closer look at the social contexts within which young people's health behaviours are developed, and the social processes involved. It is within these particular contexts, notably the school and the peer group, that the meaning of health behaviours for identity, group membership and lifestyles can best be understood. Because most research has been undertaken on young people of school-age, the focus is primarily on 'early youth' though the implications extend beyond school.

## Health behaviours: a developmental approach

The development of health behaviours over the life course begins with a biological imperative (nutrition), which even in earliest infancy is shaped by social and cultural influences, notably in relation to maternal breast-feeding practices. Thereafter, the experience of childhood and youth is typically marked by a series of socially structured developmental stages; first involving physical activity (often normative within educational systems), and later on exposure to social contexts (often peer-related) involving substances (tobacco, alcohol and drugs) which also tend to be sequenced in terms of age-related norms and associated opportunities for access. While this oversimplifies the extent to which these substances are connected, research shows there is a connection (e.g. between smoking and drug use). The concept of sequence also directs attention both to the range of influences involved, and the way they typically change over the transition from childhood through youth to adulthood. At its simplest, it implies a weakening of structural influences over this period as agency increases, and suggests that young people's class of origin would be most important with respect to diet, and less so for substance use. Correspondingly, inasmuch as lifestyles represent chosen activities, we would expect a closer connection between lifestyles and substance use than diet.

## Diet

As indicated, young people's dietary habits are largely developed in childhood, food preferences for example tracking across the life-course, laying the foundation for current and future (ill-)health, the most prominent examples in contemporary western societies being overweight and obesity. From a dietary perspective, youth is a particularly important stage, the physiological changes associated with rapid growth in adolescence requiring a diet of high nutritional quality. However, evidence about the dietary habits, and nutritional intake, of young people generally belies this. For example, in the 'Health Behaviours in Schoolchildren' (HBSC) surveys, conducted in 2001/2 on over 160,000 young people in 35 countries (Currie *et al.* 2004), around a third of the total sample reported not having breakfast on school days (a widely used indicator of 'good' nutritional practice). Having breakfast decreased in all countries between ages 11 and 15, particularly among females, the largest gender difference occurring in the UK. This pattern is consistent with other evidence that young people are increasingly taking a 'grazing' approach to meals, consuming snacks with high sugar content rather than eating 'proper meals'.

The HBSC study also showed that on two other nutritional indicators (daily fruit and vegetable consumption), despite considerable cross-national variation, only around a third of the total sample consumed either on a daily basis. This too reduced with age, in this case more so among males. In one of our own studies in the West of Scotland, where diet is notoriously poor, two-thirds of 15 year-olds in 1999 were judged to have an 'unhealthy diet'. This almost certainly worsens in later youth, the British Scientific Advisory Committee on Nutrition (2007) highlighting the diet of 'young adults' (aged 19–24) as 'cause for considerable concern'. In an evaluation of successive national surveys on diet and nutrition, they noted that almost all (98 per cent) 19–24 year-olds consumed less than the recommended daily portions ($\geq$ 5) of fruit and vegetables, they had the highest salt and sugar intake of all age groups, and consumption of carbonated drinks had doubled over the previous two decades. In short, from a nutritional perspective, the diet of young people is just about as bad as it gets, and the evidence suggests it is getting worse.

## Physical activity

Physical activity refers to any activities involving energy expenditure, and as such extends beyond organized and recreational sports and exercise to encompass activities such as walking and cycling, and work–related activities both within the labour market and elsewhere (e.g. housework). The health benefits of physical activity are well documented for adults, most notably in relation to overweight and obesity, but also extending to cardiovascular and respiratory fitness, and mental health. For young people, the short-term health benefits are less obvious though there is evidence of modest effects on physical health and most, but not all, dimensions of mental health (Ströhle et al. 2007). Physical activity is notoriously difficult to measure both in defining levels with health-enhancing capacity, and assessing the extent to which these are achieved. Despite this, considerable efforts have been made to provide recommendations, the present international consensus for adults (18–65 years) being 30 minutes or more of moderately intense aerobic activity for 5 days a week (Haskell et al. 2007). For children and young people (< 18 years), the recommendation is for a minimum of 60 minutes of moderate activity every day.

Evidence about the extent to which young people achieve this is available in several school-based surveys. In the HBSC study, based on self-reported activity, only about a third of the total sample met the recommended level for 'moderate-to-vigorous' activity, though this varied between countries (highest in Ireland, lowest in France). It also decreased between ages 11 and 15, at each age males reporting higher levels, though the size of age and gender differences varied between countries. Interestingly, in another study of 9 and 15 year-olds in four European countries (Riddoch et al. 2004), which used objective measures (accelerometers), much higher levels of activity were recorded, almost all of the younger group and 82 per cent of males and 62 per cent of females aged 15 achieving recommended levels for moderate activity. Evidence relating to representative samples of young people in the post-school period is limited to self-report data. In the most recent Health Survey for England (Craig and Mitchell 2008), in the age group 16–24, 53 per cent of males and 33 per cent of females met the (adult) recommended levels. The lower level of physical activity among females is the most consistent finding of research in this area, the gender gap widening across the school years, and still further after school-leaving.

## Smoking

In contrast to diet and physical activity, smoking has long been regarded as the quintessential health behaviour of youth. While the later health consequences of smoking (e.g. cancers, obstructive lung disease) have been comprehensively documented, even early on in a smoking career, adverse effects on the respiratory system are evident. Smoking uptake mainly occurs in early youth, typically progressing through stages of anticipation, experimentation, occasional smoking to regular (daily) use of tobacco, the earlier the onset, the more likely young people will become regular smokers (Flay et al., 1983). In the HBSC total sample, among 11 year-olds, 15 per cent reported ever smoking, rising to 62 per cent at age 15, by which time 18 per cent were daily smokers. While there were some countries with particularly high (e.g. Greenland) and low (e.g. the USA) rates, in general there was remarkable consistency between nations. This is also true of the gender patterning of smoking which typically reverses from a male excess at 11 to a female excess by 15. Although for the majority of smokers, smoking develops in early youth, rates continue to rise in the post-school period right up to adulthood, by which time the gender pattern reverses again (West et al. 1999). There is evidence from a number of developed (but not developing) countries, as diverse as the USA and Sweden, that smoking is declining in youth, a pattern more pronounced among males than females.

## Alcohol

Drinking is a second health behaviour developed, or at least encountered, in youth. Reflecting different cultures of drinking, the HBSC study revealed considerable cross-national variation in frequency of drinking and drunkenness, Mediterranean youth reporting the lowest rates, countries in Western Europe, including the UK, the highest. In most countries, males reported more frequent drinking and generally more drunkenness than females though gender differences were much smaller in the UK. In one of our West of Scotland studies, among 15 year-olds in 1999, though more males (27 per cent) than females (22 per cent) reported regular (weekly) drinking, there was little gender difference in drunkenness, and similar proportions (13 per cent) exceeded the recommended level of alcohol units (14 for females, 21 for males) in the previous week. By the time this cohort reached 18 years of age, 80 per cent of males and 70 per cent of females were regular drinkers, 39 per cent and 27 per cent respectively exceeding these recommendations for a sensible level of alcohol consumption.

This level of drinking, and particularly the well-documented phenomenon of 'binge' drinking, have increased substantially over time and now appears to be widespread in many European countries and the USA. In the UK, binge drinking (twice the recommended daily amount on at least one day in the previous week) is most prevalent in both sexes (though higher for males) in the 16–24 age group (Self and Zealey 2007). In addition to alcohol-related accidents and violence, there is increasing concern that damage to vital organs, notably liver cirrhosis, is occurring at younger ages (e.g. BMA 2008).

# Drugs

Closely associated both with smoking and drinking is the use of illegal drugs, much of the medical literature being focused on the considerable health risks associated with 'hard drugs' like heroin and, more recently, the widely reported link between frequent cannabis use and psychotic symptoms (e.g. (Henquet *et al.* 2005)). Though undoubtedly serious, the cumulative evidence suggests that problematic drug use only affects a very small proportion of young people, the majority being 'recreational users', by far the most commonly used substance being cannabis. The international evidence shows that drug use generally, and cannabis use in particular, increased rapidly over the past two decades, though in some countries it may have plateaued, or even recently declined. Among 15 year-olds in the HBSC study, around 1 in 5 of the total sample reported ever having used cannabis, most within the previous year. Like drinking, this varied substantially between countries, the USA and Western Europe having higher rates than elsewhere, and in almost every country males had more experience than females. In our own West of Scotland study, among 15 year-olds in 1999, cannabis use in the past year was particularly high (31 per cent, males; 25 per cent females) though only about a half used it on a weekly basis. Among other drugs, amphetamine use (ever) was reported by about 10 per cent of both sexes, LSD by 9 per cent of males and 6 per cent of females, much lower proportions reporting substances like Ecstasy or cocaine.

Much less information exists on young people's drug use in the post-school period. An earlier study of ours, following a cohort from age 15–30, provides a rare longitudinal picture of drug use in later youth (Sweeting and West 2008). In this study, which started in 1987, rates of any drug use (ever) were comparatively low at age 15 (9 per cent), but rose sharply by 18 (32 per cent) and continued to rise to age 23 (58 per cent), thereafter only increasing marginally. Cannabis use increased most between ages 15 and 18 while the uptake of other drugs (principally amphetamines, LSD, amyl/butile nitrite, Ecstasy and cocaine) increased steadily with age. Of particular interest was the finding that for the majority of young people drug use was transitory, this being more likely among those with later initiation, and most evident among cannabis-only users. The results of this study are consistent with other research supporting the view that for most young people drug use is 'normalized', sensible and recreational (Parker *et al.* 2002). However, there is a smaller but significant group, who initiate earlier, who more closely fit the profile of problematic drug use, progressing from soft to hard drugs.

## Structural and lifestyle influences on health behaviours

Young people encounter multiple influences in the development of health behaviours. Some of these reflect wider influences emanating from global capitalism (e.g. the tobacco industry), national cultures (e.g. dietary habits), governments (e.g. smoking, drinking and drugs policies) and the media (e.g. teenage soaps and magazines) and related advertising. In any society, a key (perhaps the key) social structure within which such influences are assimilated and transmitted is that of social class, which in the case of young people refers to the class position of their family of origin. This may involve direct influences, of a health-enhancing (e.g. opportunities for physical activity) or health-inhibiting (e.g. family members' smoking) kind, together with indirect influences associated with (class-related) schooling, peer group activity and youth subcultures. Within these overlapping social and cultural contexts, young people develop various lifestyles which may reflect such wider influences, but are not simply determined by them since they contain the potential for agency. The extent to which youth lifestyles are structured by reference to social class, therefore, together with the way each is related to health behaviours, is one way of addressing the question of the relative importance of structure and agency in relation to those behaviours.

The evidence concerning the relationship of social class to health behaviours in youth shows there is no general pattern, but rather one characterized by variability. The strongest class patterning occurs in respect of diet. For example, in the Health Survey for England, among children (aged 5–15), the proportion meeting recommended levels of fruit and vegetable consumption (5+ portions per day) was directly related to parental socio-economic status. Similar results were found in our own West of Scotland studies of 15 year-olds, the proportion with an 'unhealthy diet' increasing with falling social class, a pattern continuing in the post-school period (age 18) when an additional deleterious effect of own unemployment was observed (Sweeting *et al.* 1994). With respect to physical activity, the evidence differs between earlier and later youth. The HBSC study, which used a measure of 'family affluence' to represent family socio-economic status, found a trend in almost all countries for activity levels to increase with family affluence, a pattern more marked in females than males. In the post-school period, however, when the effects of work-related activity kick in, the difference is less apparent, some studies finding little or no class differences.

For smoking, the picture differs again, depending both on young people's age and the amount of tobacco smoked. While in general, smoking is class-related in youth (as in adulthood), this is much more pronounced at younger ages (i.e. lower class youth start earlier) and evens out around the end of secondary school, particularly in relation to occasional rather than regular smoking (West *et al.* 2007). In respect of alcohol (often referred to as the 'middle-class' drug), the evidence shows little or no class differences in the frequency of drinking, amount consumed or drunkenness, though drinking contexts differ (e.g. higher class youth drinking with parents). Indeed, in one of a series of national studies of secondary school children in England, young people from more affluent backgrounds were more likely to have drunk alcohol in the previous week (Fuller 2005). Much less information exists about older youth, but in a systematic review of UK studies of drinking among university students (much more likely to come from higher class backgrounds), both males and (particularly) females were more likely to exceed recommended levels of 'sensible drinking' and engage in binge-drinking compared with their peers in the general population (Gill 2002). Even less information exists on the social class patterning of illicit drug use in youth, but excepting a small group of problem drug users the evidence suggests there is less of a relationship than often supposed. For example, in the English secondary school survey, young people from less affluent backgrounds were only slightly more likely to report using drugs in the previous year. Similar results were found in our West of Scotland studies, one of which extends well beyond school-leaving. In this cohort, there was little or no relationship between class of background and drug use (cannabis and 'hard drugs') at any point between ages 15 and 30, the only exception being a higher uptake of cannabis among higher class youth in the student years (Sweeting and West 2008).

The variability in social class patterning of health behaviours suggests both that the extent to which young people's lifestyles are class related, and the relative importance of each for the behaviours are also likely to vary. Beyond theorizing, there is very little empirical evidence to go on, one exception being a comparative study of young people (aged 15) in Helsinki and Glasgow (Karvonen *et al.* 2001). These investigators conceptualized lifestyles in terms of 'free-time' activity, using data relating to leisure pursuits to derive types of lifestyle. In each location, this resulted in the identification of four lifestyles labelled 'commercialized' (e.g. gigs/clubs), 'conventional' (e.g. hobbies), 'sports/ games' (e.g. physical activity) and 'street-oriented' leisure (e.g. 'hanging about on the street'). The findings revealed that 'commercialized' leisure was unrelated to class in both locations, a pattern extending in Glasgow to 'sports/games', but that 'conventional' leisure was more characteristic of higher class, and street-oriented activity of lower class youth in both locations. Importantly, while these lifestyles were strongly related to smoking, drinking and drug use, street-oriented and commercial lifestyles elevating rates, sports/games reducing them, social class was of little or no consequence for these health behaviours in both locations. In a related study (conducted only in Helsinki), which focused on young people's diet, social class proved to be much more important than lifestyle, though both commercial and street-oriented leisure were independently associated with the consumption of fast foods and sweets (Roos *et al.* 2004).

These findings demonstrate both the continued importance of class in structuring some lifestyles, notably distinguishing between conventional and street-oriented activities of higher and lower class youth, but that others, notably participation in commercialized leisure, cut across class. They also show that in respect of health behaviours, young people's diet is most strongly class-related (but not entirely so), and that though part of the explanation for class relationships with substance use (particularly smoking) emanates from associated lifestyles (particularly street-oriented activity), in major respects young people who smoke, drink and use drugs do so in the context of lifestyles irrespective of class.

## Everyday social contexts

These statistical relationships, though indicative of underlying processes, tell us little about the social contexts within which such lifestyles are actually played out, and even less about the meaning of these health behaviours for identity and group membership. Two of these contexts, which have particular significance for young people of school-age, are the school setting itself, and the peer group. A developing body of research attests not only to their importance for these behaviours, but also illuminates the role of agency in their development.

The school in most education systems has long incorporated health education, and more recently health promotion, as part of the official curriculum, a great deal of research dedicated to the evaluation of such programmes. A related stream of research, developing from studies of educational attainment, focuses on 'natural variation' between schools in pupils' health behaviours with a view to investigating 'school effects'; that is, an effect of schools themselves over and above the characteristics of individuals within them (e.g. their social class). Most of the work to date has been undertaken on smoking, the cumulative evidence strongly supporting an independent effect of the school. In one of our own West of Scotland studies, we investigated (secondary) 'school effects' in relation to a wider range of health behaviours at ages 13 and 15, specifically 'unhealthy diet', current smoking and drinking, and drug use ever (West *et al.* 2004). The findings revealed wide variation between schools in all health behaviours, but in respect of diet this was accounted for by differences in the social class composition of the schools, thereby confirming the primary importance of class of background for young people's dietary habits. In relation to each of the other behaviours, however, there was evidence of 'school effects', strongest with respect to smoking at age 13 and drinking at 15, less so for drug use. The findings also showed that these 'school effects' were largely explained by factors relating to school ethos, pupils in schools with a more inclusive ethos having lower rates of smoking, drinking and drug use.

While this evidence is compatible with the 'health-promoting school' concept, it is by no means the only possible explanation of 'school effects' on health behaviours. Since schools are a major (perhaps the major) context for peer group activity in youth, it is also possible that school differences reflect influences arising from the peer group rather than schools themselves. Indeed, given the long-established association in quantitative research between young people's smoking, drinking and drug use and that of their friends (e.g. for smoking, see West and Michell 1999), this appears entirely plausible. It is further suggested by a number of qualitative studies which identify the significance of health behaviours for individual identity and group membership and position in peer group hierarchies. For example, in one study of smoking (Michell 1997), two groups of smokers were identified, one reflecting a lowly social position (both males and females), the other reflecting the highest position in the social hierarchy (entirely females). These 'top girls' were attractive and very popular, their identities as smokers symbolizing their high (and highly valued) social status within the peer group. 'Top boys', by contrast were those with lifestyles strongly linked to sport. Bringing together the evidence from quantitative surveys and the insights of such qualitative studies is the focus of a major development in research on the peer group, which utilizes the methods of sociometry or 'social network' analysis (Luke and Harris 2007).

Social network analysis focuses on the connections between actors in a social system, in this case, the school peer group. Normally based on reciprocated friendships, the structure of the peer group can be represented by a map, or 'sociogram', showing the position of individuals within it (e.g. group member, dyad or 'isolate'), onto which any characteristic (e.g. smoking) can be added. Several other characteristics of individuals' social position (e.g. popularity) and the peer group as a whole (e.g. density) can also be measured. In an early sociometric study focusing on smoking, researchers found the highest rate among 'isolates', an unexpected finding which argued against simplistic notions of peer pressure. In a more recent study (Ennett et al. 2006), the same researchers uncovered a more complex set of relationships, which revealed smoking to be more common among those less embedded in the peer group generally, but in closer proximity to substance using groups (sometimes described as peripherals or 'hangers-on'). This also extended to two other health behaviours, alcohol and cannabis use, both additionally associated with high status (e.g. popularity) in the peer group.

The potential of sociometry is vastly extended by the very few studies with a longitudinal design, which enables investigation of the processes underlying change in peer group position. The key research question concerns the extent to which processes of selection (individuals are attracted to groups with similar characteristics, including health behaviours) compared with influence (individuals in groups adopt their characteristics) are involved. In general, and perhaps unsurprisingly, the evidence to date suggests that both processes are involved, individuals choosing their friends and groups, but also being influenced by them. For example, one of our own studies found that peripheral 'risk-takers' (smokers and cannabis users) tended to drift towards risk-taking groups over time and that this reflected the influence of popular and powerful individuals already in 'risk-taking' groups (Pearson and West 2003). In an important sense, as observed many times before, young people choose the influences they experience, and perhaps nowhere more so than in the context of their peer group. This observation goes right to the core of the structure/agency debate since it is within the context of young people's peer groups that choice and constraint are an everyday reality. The evidence from sociometric research suggests a stronger role for choice than commonly assumed, but it also raises the question of the way wider influences bear on the peer group itself, shaping the meaning of 'popularity' and in turn the experience of popular and unpopular students alike.

## Conclusion

Health behaviours in youth are important not just because of their consequences for health, but also because of the way they are integrally linked to young people's lives. Conceptualizing them as lifestyles in themselves misses this point. It is clear that, though there is some connection between them (notably smoking and drug use), each is distinguished by virtue of different associations with age, gender and particularly social class. Diet is much the most strongly class-related, reflecting early exposures in the family of origin. By contrast, smoking, drinking and drug use are more strongly linked with lifestyles developed in youth, which cut across class. This in itself is an important observation about their place as social indicators in late modernity. Inasmuch as this reflects the primacy of agency over structure, it also suggests that for most young people in contemporary society, health behaviours are largely chosen activities integrally linked to their lifestyles.

It is apparent too from the evidence about the way these health behaviours vary between schools and peer groups that, among school-aged youth, these are the most important contexts within which young people's lifestyles are played out. While schools themselves may impact on pupils' health behaviours, it is equally possible that this masks a more important effect of the peer group. Of particular importance are the sociometric studies which reveal connections (often highly gendered) between social positions in the peer group and smoking, drinking, drug use and sport. Although the focus of this research is on school-based networks, for many young people this extends beyond school boundaries (e.g. to commercial leisure settings or the street), in turn reinforcing peer group positions within school. Similar effects extend beyond school-leaving, though the relative balance between influence and selection is likely to change as the role of agency increases still further.

Sociometric studies also highlight the way health behaviours act as signifiers of individual and group identity. In this sense, they have similar symbolic significance to other well-documented indicators of youth style or subculture such as clothes or music preference, which are known correlates of substance use (e.g. for music, North and Hargreaves 2008). This focus on micro-contexts, however, should not blind us to the way wider influences define desirable youth identities and shape the processes by which these are evaluated within the peer group. In late modernity, such influences increasingly stem from advertising and the media, and appear to cut across class boundaries. However, because they define the attributes by which peer group position, popularity or rejection are achieved, they can be conceptualized as newer forms of social structure which circumscribe young people's agency. It is equally clear from the evidence presented in this chapter that while the peer group and associated lifestyles are the more important contexts for young people's health behaviours, wider influences associated with class and national cultures still matter.

## Acknowledgements

Many of the ideas and findings reported in this chapter are based on research conducted in the Medical Research Council's Social & Public Health Sciences Unit at Glasgow University. The author would like to thank research colleagues who have contributed to this, in particular Sally Macintyre, Helen Sweeting and Robert Young. Patrick West is supported financially by the Medical Research Council of Great Britain.

## References

BMA (2008) *Alcohol Misuse: Tackling the UK Epidemic*, London: British Medical Association.

Craig, R. and Mitchell, J. (2008) *Health Survey for England 2006: Latest Trends*, London: The Information Centre.

Currie, C., Roberts, C. and Morgan, A. (2004) *Young People's Health in Context: International Report from the HBSC 2001/02 Survey*, Copenhagen: WHO Regional Office for Europe.

Ennett, S. T., Bauman, K. E., Hussong, A., Faris, R., Foshee, V. A. and Cai, L. (2006) 'The peer context of adolescent substance use: findings from social network analysis', *Journal of Research on Adolescence*, 16: 159–86.

Flay, B. R., D'Avernas, J. R., Best, J. A., Kersell, N. W. and Ryan, K. B. (1983) 'Cigarette smoking: why young people do it and ways of preventing it', in P. J. McGrath, and P. Firestone (eds) *Pediatric and Adolescent Behavioural Medicine: Issues in Treatment*, New York: Springer.

Fuller, E. (2005) *Smoking, Drinking and Drug Use Among Young People in England in 2004*, Leeds: Health and Social Care Information Centre.

Furlong, A. and Cartmel, F. (2007) *Young People and Social Change: New Perspectives*, Maidenhead: Open University Press.

Gill, J. S. (2002) 'Reported levels of alcohol consumption and binge drinking within the UK under-graduate student population over the last 25 years', *Alcohol and Alcoholism*, 37: 109–20.

Haskell, W. H., Lee, I.-M., Pate, R. R., Powell, K., Blair, S., Franklin, B. A., *et al.* (2007) 'Physical activity and public health: updated recommendation for adults from the American College of Sports Medicine and the American Heart Association', *Circulation*, 116: 1081–93.

Henquet, C., Krabbendam, L., Spauwen, J., Kaplan, C., Lieb, R., Wittchen, H.-U. *et al.* (2005) 'Prospective cohort study of cannabis use, predisposition for psychosis, and psychotic symptoms in young people', *British Medical Journal*, 330: 11–14.

Karvonen, S., West, P., Sweeting, H., Rahkonen, O. and Young, R. (2001) 'Lifestyle, social class and health-related behaviour: a cross-cultural comparison of 15 year olds in Glasgow and Helsinki', *Journal of Youth Studies* 4: 393–414.

Luke, D. A. and Harris, J. K. (2007) 'Network analysis in public health: history, methods and applications', *Annual Revue of Public Health*, 28: 68–93.

Michell, L. (1997) 'Pressure groups: young people's accounts of peer pressure to smoke', *Social Sciences in Health*, 3: 3–17.

North, A. C. and Hargreaves, D. J. (2008) *The Social and Applied Psychology of Music*, Oxford: Oxford University Press.

Parker, H., Williams, L. and Aldridge, J. (2002) 'The normalisation of "sensible" recreational drug use: further evidence from the north-west England longitudinal study', *Sociology*, 36: 941–64.

Pearson, M. and West, P. (2003) 'Drifting smoke rings: social network analysis and Markov processes in a longitudinal study of friendship groups and risk taking', *Connections*, 25: 59–76.

Riddoch, C. J., Andersen, L. B., Wedderkopp, N., Harro, M., Klasson-Heggebo, L., Sardinha, L. B., et al. (2004) 'Physical activity levels and patterns of 9- and 15-yr-old European children', *Medicine and Science in Sports and Exercise*, 16: 86–92.

Roos, E. B., Karvonen, S. and Rahkonen, O. (2004) 'Lifestyles, social background and eating patterns of 15-year-old boys and girls in Finland', *Journal of Youth Studies*, 7: 331–49.

Scientific Advisory Committee on Nutrition (2007) *The Nutritional Wellbeing of the UK Population*, London: Scientific Advisory Committee on Nutrition.

Self, A. and Zealey, L. (2007) *Social Trends*, Basingstoke: Palgrave Macmillan.

Ströhlë, A., Höfler, M., Pfister, H., Müller, A.-G., Hoyer, J., Wittchen, H.-U. et al. (2007) 'Physical activity and prevalence and incidence of mental disorders in adolescents and young adults', *Psychological Medicine*, 37: 1657–66.

Sweeting, H., Anderson, A. and West, P. (1994) 'Socio-demographic correlates of dietary habits in mid to late adolescence', *European Journal of Clinical Nutrition*, 48: 736–48.

Sweeting, H. and West, P. (2008) 'Drug use over the youth-adult transition in a West of Scotland cohort: rates, pathways and socio-demographic correlates', *Addiction Research and Theory*.

West, P. and Michell, L. (1999) 'Smoking and peer influence', in A. J. Goreczny and M. Hersen (eds) *Handbook of Pediatric and Adolescent Health Psychology*, Boston: Allyn and Bacon.

West, P., Sweeting, H. and Ecob, R. (1999) 'Family and friends' influences on the uptake of regular smoking from mid adolescence to early adulthood', *Addiction*, 94: 1397–412.

West, P., Sweeting, H. and Leyland, A. (2004) 'School effects on pupils' health behaviours: evidence in support of the health promoting school', *Research Papers in Education*, 19: 261–92.

West, P., Sweeting, H. and Young, R. (2007) 'Smoking in Scottish youths: personal income, parental social class and the cost of smoking', *Tobacco Control*, 16: 329–35.

# Part IX

## Identities, values and beliefs

*Andy Furlong*

## Transforming identities values and beliefs

In youth studies, the focus on the construction and transformation of identities is a relatively new development. While psychological interest in individual development has been long-standing, in the past, the focus was on processes of adjustment to a relatively static social order and on cognitive disorders and adaptations. Contemporary interest in identity, especially sociological interest, can be linked to process of social change and the transformation of transitions that have resulted in fragmented experiences and protracted processes of exploration. The chapters in this section explore some of the complexities of identity formation in the late modern period, examine changing values, beliefs and aspirations as well as focusing closely on attitudes and values in the contexts of work, sexuality and religion.

In the Fordist era, with transitions being relatively linear and predictable, identities were often viewed as closely related to the structural predictors of transitional outcomes. In other words, factors such as social class and gender that shaped experiences were also integral to the process of identity formation. A young man from a working–class family moving into a manual occupation, for example, would probably have had a long-standing anticipation of such an outcome and his identity would have been shaped within the context of these expectations which would have been shared with family and friends. In the modern, post–Fordist, era, it is argued that the protraction and complexity of transitions result in greater uncertainty and more open possibilities to choose outcomes and shape transitional experiences. In turn, rather than being ascribed, identity formation becomes a project that must be actively managed and provides scope for individualized negotiation. As Côté makes clear in Chapter 45, contemporary perspectives on identity require us to take the role of agency more seriously and encourage us to consider the significance of greater fluidity of identities on transitional processes.

Young people's subjective interpretations of their own position and experiences offer valuable insights into the nature of late modern societies and offer fresh perspectives on the changes that have taken place. More broadly, Johnson and Monserud argue in Chapter 46 that young people's values and beliefs highlight patterns of generational change, offer clues about where societies are heading, and provide a basis for understanding motivation and behaviour. Evidence is provided to suggest that young people in contemporary societies have become less concerned with their communities and have become more materialistic.

One of the dimensions of young people's subjectivity that has been the focus of sustained academic analysis relate to occupational aspirations. In particular, in the USA, aspirations have long been used by quantitative researchers as key predictors of status attainment, while qualitative researchers have tried to understand the ways in which young people's aspirations are constrained by the desire to 'fit in' on a cultural level or maintain identities that are grounded in understandings of opportunity structures. While Jones and Schneider argue in Chapter 47 that young people's ambitions tend to reflect their knowledge of the occupational world, they also acknowledge that, irrespective of socio-economic background, high aspirations have become the norm with the vast majority of young people in the USA planning to attend college due to the strong links between higher education and future career opportunities.

This is a theme that is developed by Kelly in Chapter 48, who argues that the increased precariousness of labour market conditions requires new orientations to working life. The desire to construct a stable 'narrative of the self' in conditions of extreme uncertainty forces young people to cultivate an entrepreneurial self in which they constantly strive for self-improvement. Thus, the new work ethics which he describes highlight the adaptations that people are forced to make to get by in a world where opportunities are constrained.

While the work ethics of young people have long been of interest to researchers, until relatively recently young people's sexuality has either been overlooked or subject to simplistic interpretations. In Chapter 49, Holland focuses on the relationship between sexuality and gender, discusses the impact of hegemonic masculinity and institutionally reinforced 'heteronormativity', as well as looking at patterns of change and continuity and at resistance. Linked to themes developed by other authors in this section, she highlights the implications of economic change on sexualities and describes some of the implications of the multiple and flexible gender identities that have become common in the late modern era.

Youth is a time in which people reflect on the views of their parents and develop values and beliefs that are congruent with emerging adult identities. Among the core beliefs that may be questioned are those related to religiosity. In Chapter 50, Pearce and Denton suggest that, in general, religiosity will decrease in youth, but also remind us that many young people (especially those living in the USA) believe in God and practise their faith. While time trends show a decline in religiosity in youth in Europe and Australia, changes in the USA have been marginal. Moreover, while researchers frequently overlook religion, Pearce and Denton argue that religious teenagers tend to have more positive attitudes, higher self-esteem and lower levels of depression.

Youth-identity studies is an emerging field of interest; one which accommodates a range of empirical interests and which offers the potential form new theoretical insights. The chapters in this part help capture some of the possibilities for a new research agenda that puts a greater emphasis on young people's subjectivities while retaining an awareness of the impact of objective conditions.

# 45

# Youth-identity studies

## History, controversies and future directions

*James E. Côté*

## Historical and intellectual influences on the study of identity

Prior to the 1950s, the term 'identity' was found mainly in psychiatry and psychoanalysis. However, in the 1950s, based on the works of Erik Erikson, the concept became a 'reasonably value-neutral and interdisciplinary term' (e.g. Weigert *et al.* 1986: 29) with which to describe the effects of social change on social status, group allegiances, value acquisition, and the process by which people developed a sense of meaning and purpose in life. At the same time, theories of mass society emerged in the social sciences to account for the decline in traditional forms of community and a consequent rise in problems of identity (Stein *et al.* 1960).

Since the 1950s, concerns about problems in identity formation and identity construction have morphed into several approaches. In sociology, the term mass society has been replaced by the concepts like postmodernity and late modernity, although similar problematic societal conditions remain as likely sources of identity problems. In addition, a developmental psychology has emerged that 'normalizes' identity problems in inadequate maturation, rather than problematic societal conditions. It appears, however, that the societal conditions undermining problem-free identity formation and identity maintenance persist, to the point where the popular press now recognizes 'identity' as a key to the increased complexity of youth and young adulthood. (e.g., Frank 1997). At the same time, some developmental psychologists are completely re-evaluating the nature of the transition to adulthood with the proposition that there is now a new life stage – emerging adulthood – characterized by protracted identity exploration (Arnett 2000).

This chapter first reviews the major approaches and leading figures in the field of Identity Studies and then shows how this field is intersecting with Youth Studies, which will be referred to as 'Youth-Identity Studies'. From this foundation, the current controversies in the area are reviewed and the future prospects of the hybrid Youth-Identity Studies field are speculated upon.

# Major theories and theorists in identity studies

In the mid-1990s, Hall referred to the 'discursive explosion around the concept of identity' (1996: 1); more recently, Bauman (2001) has written about the 'thriving industry' of Identity Studies. Indeed, the concept of identity does not belong to any one discipline. Instead, it is used in a range of ways to describe or explain a variety of experiences and behaviors (Côté 2006). Accordingly, to give some order to its various uses, it is helpful to go to first principles of theory construction.

First, it is useful to separate psychological and sociological perspectives, the two dominant approaches (cultural studies will be treated as a sub-field of sociology). As one would expect, psychologists tend to take an individual focus, putting more emphasis on the mental traits, states, and dispositions of the person in predicting the subjective and behavioral properties of identity. In this sense, identity is the property of the person rather than of interaction or the group (cf. Côté and Levine 2002). And, as one would expect, sociologists tend to take a social focus, but it is important for non-sociologists to realize that the concern in many sociological analyses, especially those working at the micro level, is with interaction, not the group *per se*. This tradition dates back to the early symbolic interactionist and pragmatic approaches in sociology (e.g., Hewitt 2000). Accordingly, for sociologists of the social psychology tradition, identity tends to be viewed *not* as a property of the person so much as a property of interaction. In this way, identity is relational when it is viewed as embedded in interpersonal relationships. Sociologists who view identity as a property of the group tend to take macro approaches in the study of social identity arising from ethnicity, social class, and nationality.

Second, approaches can be classified in terms of their underlying epistemological assumptions. In this respect, theories in this field (as in others) differ in terms of what is believed to constitute identity (ontology), and how to study its manifestations (methodology). Epistemologically, theories in the social sciences differ in terms of two deep-seated divisions: whether social reality is to be understood (1) as fixed, obdurate, and independent of human consciousness (objectivism), or (2) as indeterminate and dependent on social constructions (subjectivism) (Côté and Levine 2002).

And, third, researchers hold fundamentally different assumptions regarding whether the existing social order is to be accepted as is (and therefore as inevitable), or whether it should be viewed critically as but one of many potentials contexts. The first, which can be called the status quo approach, asserts implicitly or explicitly that the existing order represents universal processes. In contrast, the critical researcher looks to 'transformative' influences on identity, based on the the argument that identity processes are contextual, and therefore no one form or content can be assumed to be an ideal. In accepting the inevitability of the status quo, the former approach assumes a certain benign functionality of social structures, while the later approach is not as sanguine about the benevolent nature of social structures, and specifies ways in which these structures create inadequate or sub-optimal identity formation (Côté 2006).

When these three binary heuristics are combined, eight approaches to the study of identity are identified, as shown in Table 45.1. Some of these approaches are more popular than are others. For example, the most popular psychological approaches in the field (the identity status paradigm and self-psychology; e.g., Marcia 1980; and Ashmore and Jussim 1991, respectively) take an individual focus, adopt objectivist epistemological assumptions, and have status quo orientations. Similarly, sociologists will readily recognize the symbolic interactionist (SI) approaches, although they may be more familiar

**Table 45.1** Fundamental assumptions in Identity Studies regarding epistemology and social order, by individual/social focus

| Epistemology | Individual focus | | Social focus | |
|---|---|---|---|---|
| | Status quo | Critical | Status quo | Critical |
| Objectivist | Identity status paradigm/ Self psychology | Critical/cultural psychologies | Structural Symbolic Interactionism | Late-modernism/ Critical social psychology |
| Subjectivist | Life history/ narrative approaches | Postmodernism (psychological variant) | Interpretative Symbolic Interactionism | Postmodernism (sociological variant) |

with the interpretive approach best known as the Chicago School rooted in the work of George Herbert Mead, than in the lesser-known structural approach of the Iowa School (e.g. Kuhn and McPartland 1954).

The differing epistemological assumptions of approaches to identity can be readily illustrated with reference to the two status quo SI approaches, where there is a fundamental fracture dating back to the 1950s stemming from differing interpretations of the seminal work of George Herbert Mead. Structural SI adopts an explicit quantitative methodology based on the assumption that the manifestations of identity are both observable and measurable (e.g. Stryker 1987). In contrast, the interpretative approach to SI, represented in the work of scholars like Goffman (1963) and Weigert et al. (1986), adopts an explicit qualitative approach (ethnographies) designed to capture the qualities of identities as they emerge through on-going international processes in day-to-day naturalistic settings. Structural SI investigates phenomena related to role playing, role salience and hierarchy, role conflict, and the like, while interpretive SI explores how people engage in role *making*, and other spontaneous forms of interaction associated with impression management and the presentation of self.

Finally, the difference between the views regarding the nature of social order – the status quo versus critical approaches – can be illustrated by contrasting the two status quo SI approaches with the two critical approaches that take a social focus. These critical approaches tend to be more macro-historical in orientation, providing a critical contrast of contemporary societal conditions in reference to past conditions, when the role-bases for identities were far different.

The late-modernist approach points to the ascriptive nature of identities in pre-modern societies, where social solidarity was greater but freedom of choice was constricted (Côté and Levine 2002; Furlong and Cartmel 2007). Accordingly, the focus is on the individualization process in late modernity, which emphasizes compulsory choice making in the absence of normative guidance, making the transition to adulthood more complex and uncertain. The work of Beck (e.g. 1992) exemplifies the European approach to late-modernity, while that of Wexler (e.g. 1992) represents a North American approach to 'critical social psychology', which problematizes identity processes in contemporary social contexts. The late-modernist approaches are objectivist to the extent that theorists view identities as relatively enduring attributes. For example, late-modernists view people as capable of agency, especially when they have a strong sense of self, and this agency helps them ride out the vicissitudes of late-modernity with a sense of continuous self-identity, or ego identity, intact (Côté and Levine 2002).

In contrast to the late-modernist approach, the sociological variant of the post-modernism is subjectivist in that it emphasizes the 'multiplicity, fluidity, and context-dependent operation' of identities, especially among the youth population (Rattansi and Phoenix 1997: 121). It is important for these postmodernists to see identity as 'de-centered' and 'de-essentialized' in contemporary contexts, because interactional processes are believed to be (now) inherently unstable. The key difference between the late-modernist and postmodernist approaches is with the view of agency and the potentials for individuals to direct their own development by anchoring their self- or ego-identity, as opposed to being buffeted about by contradictory 'postmodern' forces with no internal point of reference. This postmodern approach is exemplified in the work of theorists such as Bauman (2001) and Rattansi and Phoenix (1997) who see identity as: (1) located in the interactional realm as people engage in their day-to-day social engagements; (2) manifested in terms of its emergent and transitory properties; and (3) varying by the specific context in which the interaction takes place.

Finally, it is worth describing the remaining three approaches illustrated in Table 45.1, which all take an individual focus. First, those who take narrative and life-history approaches, as in the case of Chandler (2001) or McAdams (1993), believe that the study of identity formation requires a sensitivity to the emergent expressions of the various senses of identity that can only be captured using qualitative methods. Second, psychological variants of the postmodern approach, exemplified by Gergen's work (1991), examine the contexts in which certain societal conditions create a fragmentation of identity and an erosion of the sense of a unified core, resulting in the emergence of certain personality types (e.g. strategic manipulators, relational selves). And, finally, the individual-focused critical approaches adopt objectivist assumptions regarding the measurability and stability of identity processes, but do not assume that status quo conditions are necessarily benign in fostering optimal identity formation for a significant proportion of the population (e.g. Baumeister and Muraven 1996).

## The intersection of identity studies and youth studies: culture and identity

The area of Youth-Identity Studies is for the most part theoretically driven. Certainly, empirical work is important to this area, but most empirical studies launch from one of the theoretical positions identified above in ways that seek to validate the underlying theoretical principles without putting them to tests that could invalidate the theory, as is the practice in more empirically oriented sciences. This theory-based empiricism is undoubtedly due to the abstract and multidimensional nature of identity, which defies easy operationalization. Indeed, the reporting of these empirical studies is largely in discipline-based journals. More sociologically oriented studies of social identity and identity construction (youth subcultures and lifestyles, risk and social exclusion, and engagement and leisure) are published in outlets like the *Journal of Youth Studies* and *Young: Nordic Journal of Youth Research*. The former journal numbers its publications on identity in the dozens, while the latter does so in the hundreds. In contrast, more psychologically oriented studies of ego identity and identity formation (especially the correlates of identity status, and other Eriksonian-based concepts) are published in periodicals like the *Journal of Youth and Adolescence* and *Journal of Research on Adolescence*. Articles on identity during youth in psychologically oriented journals number in the thousands. In 2001, the journal *Identity: An International Journal of Theory and Research* was launched, with an aim of unifying the field by providing a common outlet, but it has published more psychologically oriented articles that reflect the orientations of its sponsoring society, the Society for Research on Identity Formation.

A synthesis of this vast empirical literature is beyond the space limitations of this chapter. Instead, a framework is offered that helps us understand social identity formation in broad historical terms. This framework helps adjudicate a major debate in the area of study, to be discussed next.

From a historical point of view, the protracted period of the life course currently designated as 'youth' appears only in modernist and late-modernist/post-modernist cultures (cf. Schlegel and Barry 1991). Table 45.2 shows the three periods of social change commonly used by sociologists to theorize what has happened over the past several centuries among Western societies, and societies influenced by the West. The distinction between pre-modern and early modern society corresponds to a widely accepted distinction between folk and urban society, a distinction that has been referred to in other terms such as agrarian versus industrial, folk versus urban, or *Gemeinschaft* versus *Gesellschaft* (Tönnies 1980). In most Western societies, this transformation was largely completed during the nineteenth century.

Table 45.2 helps us understand several debates in Youth-Identity Studies (cf. Côté 2006). Viewed in terms of historical changes in cultural dynamics, the social and cultural construction of youth becomes clearer. Table 45.2 also illustrates how the transition to adulthood has changed from one highly structured with social markers like marriage and family formation in pre-modernity, through a more prolonged one that is moderately structured with social markers in early modernity, to a prolonged and largely unstructured one in secular late-post-/modernity. Currently, then, youth and the formation of an adult identity can be a very prolonged and highly individualized process, making for a complex and uncertain period of the life course.

Further, the nature of the formation of social identities can be understood in terms of the structuring of the transition to adulthood in each historical period. In pre-modern societies where the transition is short and ritualized, social identities tend to be ascribed and identity formation is relatively linear from childhood to adulthood. In early modern societies, where the transition becomes extended, but still has certain social markers, the norm is increasingly that social identity is to be accomplished on the basis of the increasing choice. This choice is partly a necessary result of the decline in normative social markers in the transition to adulthood, but is limited by the structures of opportunity associated with class, gender, and race, which retain the certain ascriptive aspects of identity formation. Thus, more affluent males of the majority ethnic group will have more latitude in their identity formation. Finally, in late/post-modern societies, where

**Table 45.2** Culture, youth, and identity: structure of transitions to adulthood and parameters of social identity formation by socio-historical period

|  | Socio-historical period | | |
|---|---|---|---|
|  | Pre-modernity | Early modernity | Late/post-modernity |
| Transition to adulthood | Short and ritualized | Extended with social markers | Prolonged and individualized |
| Social identity formation | Ascribed | Accomplished | Managed |

the individualization process is more extensive because of the virtual disappearance of social markers for adulthood for young people in secular society, people are more likely to find themselves faced with the continual management of social identities, as they are formed and, thereafter, once they formed.

The requirement of social-identity management in secular late/post-modern societies has a number of implications that also shed light on debates in Youth Studies. For example, as opposed to being a birthright, or a sinecured social achievement, one's legitimacy in the public domain of the wider society can be continually called into question, in part because the logic of individualization carries with it the burden of personal responsibility (cf. Furlong and Cartmel 2007). In order to find a social location in the public domain in the first place, one often has to convince a community of strangers that one is worthy of their company, and this acceptance can be challenged at virtually any moment for many people, especially those in higher-status positions. Individual's now have to manage their lives by strategically finding their place or places, often repeatedly over their life course. Thus, in contrast to the past, it is common for people to move through a series of educational settings, jobs and careers, romantic relationships and marriages, and neighborhoods and urban settings, possibly gaining and losing acceptance a number of times.

Finally, it must be acknowledged that the individualization process and social identities continue to be circumscribed by class, gender, and race. Although the boundaries of these social statuses are more permeable and obscure than in early modernity, the access to certain social identities still depends on the specific circumstances found in the countries and culture in question, with some providing more opportunities than others (cf. Furlong and Cartmel's 2007 concept of the epistemological fallacy).

## Current controversies

The leading debate in Youth-Identity Studies is found between postmodernists and developmentalists. A recent special issue of *Identity: An International Journal of Theory and Research* (Côté 2005) dealt with these two inherently opposing approaches by using Rattansi and Phoenix's (1997/2005) work on the nature of youth-identity as an exemplar of the postmodern approach, particularly with its explicit critique of the prevailing developmental paradigm (i.e., the neo-Eriksonian, identity status paradigm).

Rattansi and Phoenix argue that developmental approaches to identity adopt modernist assumptions that decontextualize and ignore the subjectivities of young people's identities, as well as their contextual nature. They propose a framework based on six theoretical axioms to correct this bias:

- Identity is 'relational' in character, hinging on definition in relation to other identities, so is not 'centered' in the 'subject'.
- Identity relations are inherently unstable because of their oppositional nature, but social institutions function to normalize this opposition to disguise power relationships.
- People occupy multiple and contradictory positions and therefore have a range of social identities, with different identities having salience in different contexts. Accordingly, young people blend identity elements from their multiple positioning.

- Identities are always in process, and identity formation is never complete. Any apparent identity closures are 'provisional and conditional', as dictated by the various contexts in which the person must function.
- Unconscious conflict. The self is de-centered not only by context, but by unconscious mental processes.
- Fragmented context. Identity formation trajectories are uncertain and fragmented in ways that reflect dysfunctional institutional interrelations and contexts.

The assumptions underpinning Rattansi and Phoenix's axioms can be readily seen to correspond to those identified in Table 45.1 as associated with the critical, social, and subjectivist approach to identity.

Leading figures from the Eriksonian/Marcian tradition were invited to comment on this critique of the developmental paradigm in the special issue of *Identity* (e.g., Kroger *et al.*, in Côté 2005). Their responses include the assertion that many of the ideas underpinning these six axioms were actually proposed some time ago by 'modernist' identity theorists like Erikson. Moreover, Kroger argues that the social context does not have a unitary impact on young people, even if it is fragmented, and that this claim is based on the confusion between the structure of identity (which involves of continuity of functioning) and the content of identity (which includes social identities of race, class, gender, and so forth). Levine reminds us that personal agency is an important mediating factor in the impact of social conditions, and that any account of subjectivity needs to come to grips with the notion of agency and whatever 'core' aspects of human psychology might be responsible for it. And, Berzonsky (cited in Côté 2005) believes that postmodernists make 'category errors' in mistaking the manifestations of identity (social identity) for the underlying multidimensional basis of it (ego identity). Phoenix and Rattansi (cited in Côté 2005) respond to these and other rebuttals by noting the numerous points of agreement between postmodernists and developmentalists, although postmodernists want to move beyond the theoretical root of identity theory as represented by Erikson's 'grand theory'.

Those on apparently opposing sides of this debate actually agree on more matters than would appear to be the case at first blush. Why then, is there such rancour and antagonism in the literature between 'modernist' and 'postmodernist' positions (e.g. Hollinger 1994)? One way to approach this debate is to ask what would make both developmentalists and postmodernists happy in an integrated framework. It appears that many postmodernists would be happy with a framework that places a greater emphasis on youth subjectivity, where young people creatively engage contexts associated with personal and social identities, whereas many developmentalists would be happy if the importance of intrapsychic factors associated with agency were emphasized, such as ego identity processes coupled with the wilful assumption or forgoing of societal roles and commitments. If subjectivity is important, then agency must be as well.

If we are to follow the 'map' implicitly laid out in Table 45.1, and take the catholic view that each position is valid in terms of its claim to be methodologically rigorous in identifying its particular subject matter, a resolution of this debate is to recognize that each position is to be respected in its own terms. This catholic position further implies that it is incumbent on each youth-identity theorist to understand all of the perspectives represented in Table 45.1, because only then will each truly appreciate the multidimensional nature of identity and each other's approach to this multidimensionality.

## Future directions

When a broader, more catholic approach is taken to the disciplinary boundaries that divide youth–identity researchers, such as those depicted in Table 45.1, Youth–Identity Studies opens up in a way that invites theorists and researchers to both read each other's work and implement each other's methods to gain a better understanding of the new complexities of contemporary youth and young adulthood. The critiques of each other's position should most certainly be examined because they may help each position improve its grasp on identity and its structures and processes. However, when critiques form barriers to understanding as a result of intransigence, they become impediments to the field as a whole. Only by examining and overcoming prejudices and stereotypes that are the bulwark of disciplinary boundaries can the field mature.

For example, central to the postmodernist movement is the claim to have discovered the 'grand narrative' of modernity and to have successfully debunked it in various ways (i.e., claiming to have successfully uncovered the dangerous conditions created by the connections constructed among Enlightenment logics, science, notions of progress, and rationality). While this is an interesting and clever story to have weaved about the last five hundred years, many other equally interesting stories can be told about this period, particularly the story of the history of modern capitalism, which many people find to be a more plausible explanation for the social, economic, and technological changes that have challenged the human capacity for identity formation beyond parochial allegiances. This story about capitalism accepts the validity of historical materialism and some of the objectivist assumptions associated with it. This story also suggests that rejecting all objectivist assumptions is to accept a form of alienation from some basic realities of human existence and to leave us open to continued manipulation by Capital; indeed, to embrace a position entirely based on subjectivism is to condemn ourselves to perpetual self-doubt and infighting.

This type of disagreement over an imaginary grand narrative illustrates the stakes inherent in youth–identity studies: namely, to what extent is the period of youth in late/post-modernity to be conceptualized (1) as a period of growth and consolidation of strengths that *can* culminate in a coherent identity in spite of societal conditions that would alienate and fragment us, or (2) as simply the beginning of *inevitable* life-long identity confusion and crises, where we are all condemned to a de-centered existence with no sense of core self? Answers to this question take us to the heart of the human condition, and most certainly deserve our undivided attention.

## References

Arnett, J. J. (2000) 'Emerging adulthood: a theory of development from the late teens through the twenties', *American Psychologist*, 55: 469–80.

Ashmore, R. and Jussim, L. (eds) (1991) *Self and Identity: Fundamental Issues*, New York: W. Morrow.

Bauman, Z. (2001) *The Individualized Society*, Cambridge: Polity Press.

Baumeister, R. F. and Muraven, M. (1996) 'Identity as adaptation to social, cultural, and historical context', *Journal of Adolescence*, 19: 405–16

Beck, U. (1992) *Risk Society: Towards a New Modernity*, London: Sage.

Chandler, M. (2001) 'The time of our lives: self-continuity in Native and non-Native youth', in W. Reese (ed.) *Advances in Child Development and Behavior*, New York: Academic Press.

Côté, J. E. (ed.) (2005) 'The postmodern critique of developmental perspectives: Special issue', *Identity: An International Journal of Theory and Research*, 5: 95–225.

—— (2006) 'Identity studies: how close are we to developing a social science of identity? – an appraisal of the field', *Identity: An International Journal of Theory and Research*, 6: 3–25.

Côté, J. E. and Levine, C. (2002) *Identity Formation, Agency and Culture: A Social Psychological Synthesis*, Mahwah, NJ: Erlbaum.

Frank, T. (1997) *The Conquest of Cool: Business Culture, Counterculture, and the Rise of Hip Consumerism*, Chicago: The University of Chicago Press.

Furlong, A. and Cartmel, F. (2007) *Young People and Social Change*, 2nd edn, Maidenhead: Open University Press.

Gergen, K. J. (1991) *The Saturated Self: Dilemmas of Identity in Contemporary Life*, New York: Basic Books.

Goffman, E. (1963) *Stigma: Notes on the Management of Spoiled Identity*, Englewood Cliffs, NJ: Prentice-Hall.

Hall, S. (1996) 'Introduction: who needs identity?' in S. Hall and P. Du Gay (eds) *Questions of Cultural Identity*, London: Sage.

Hewitt, J. P. (2000) *Self and Society: A Symbolic Interactionist Social Psychology* 7th ed, Boston: Allyn and Bacon.

Hollinger, R. (1994) *Postmodernism and the Social Sciences*, Thousand Oaks, CA: Sage.

Kuhn, M. H. and McPartland, T. S. (1954) 'An empirical investigation of self-attitudes', *American Sociological Review*, 19: 68–76.

Marcia, J. E. (1980) 'Identity in adolescence', in J. Adelson (ed.) *Handbook of Adolescent Psychology*, New York: Wiley, pp. 159–87.

McAdams, D. P. (1993) *The Stories We Live by: Personal Myths and the Making of the Self*, New York: W. Morrow.

Rattansi, A. and Phoenix, A. (1997) 'Rethinking youth identities: modernist and postmodernist frameworks', in J. Bynner, L. Chisholm and A. Furlong (eds) *Youth, Citizenship and Social Change in a European Context*, Aldershot: Ashgate.

Schlegel, A. and Barry, H. (1991) *Adolescence: An Anthropological Inquiry*, New York: Free Press.

Stein, M. R., Vidich, A. J. and White, D. M. (1960) *Identity and Anxiety: Survival of the Person in Mass Society*, New York: The Free Press.

Stryker, S. (1987) 'Identity theory: developments and extensions', in K. Yardley and T. Honess (eds) *Self and Identity: Psychosocial Perspectives*, New York: Wiley.

Tönnies, F. (1980) 'Gemeinschaft und Gesellschaft', in L. A. Coser (ed.) *The Pleasures of Sociology*, New York: The New American Library, pp. 169–71.

Weigert, A. J., Teitge, J. S. and Teitge, D. W. (1986) *Society and Identity: Toward a Sociological Psychology*, Cambridge: Cambridge University Press.

Wexler, P. (1992) *Becoming Somebody: Toward a Social Psychology of School*, London: Falmer Press.

# 46

# Values and related beliefs

*Monica Kirkpatrick Johnson and Maria Monserud*

## Introduction

Adolescents' and young adults' values and related beliefs have been of great interest across the social sciences, despite ebbs and flows in the popularity of values as a concept in these disciplines. The growing capacity of adolescents to think abstractly and the centrality of identity development to adolescence and young adulthood make values fundamental to understanding these stages in the life course. Young people's values, or abstract evaluative beliefs that indicate good vs. bad or right vs. wrong, are most often assessed by asking research participants to rank or rate the importance of various behaviors (e.g., being honest, independent) or end states (e.g., wealth, inner peace) (Marini 2000; Hitlin and Piliavin 2004). Thus, they capture not only what young people think is right and wrong, but particularly in societies in which people have considerable freedom in shaping their futures, they also represent means and ends for constructing a life. Much scholarly attention has also focused on value-related goals, normative beliefs, and concerns of adolescents and young adults, which we include in this overview when they closely relate to its central themes.

Two key objectives underlie research on young people's values and related beliefs. First, they are used as a barometer for society and where it is headed. We ask whether the values of today's youth are different from ours or our parents and what that says for society's future. To use adolescents' values as a sign of what is to come as new genera- tions fill out the adult population requires an assumption that values be relatively stable throughout adulthood. Indeed, most research implicitly if not explicitly assumes that values are quite stable after crystallizing at some point in adolescence (Marini 2000; Hitlin and Piliavin 2004).

Given the volume of research making this assumption, surprisingly little research directly tests it. Some evidence of relative stability exists, yet scholars also acknowledge that values change somewhat with new roles and other experiences. The lack of empirical attention to this issue leaves room for claims of stability and malleability to coexist. Even if relatively stable, the transition to adulthood, with its many changes in roles, relation- ship networks, and institutional ties, may be a time of greater change in values than other periods of the life course. Despite heavy reliance on this assumption, the timing of 'crystallization' of values, if it does occur, is still unclear. As discussed at the end of this chapter, it may also be changing historically.

A second major objective of research on adolescents' and young adults' values and related beliefs is to understand behavior. Values are conceptualized as motivational beliefs and thought to work in conjunction with other factors in influencing behavior. Other things being equal, individuals behave in ways that are consistent with their values. A specific model of the value–behavior relationship is rarely offered, and specifying such a model is not usually a primary goal of adolescence research *per se*. When process is given any attention, values are usually thought to shape attitudes or other constructs that have more proximal effects on behavior.

There is perhaps more attention to how values are related to behavior in adolescence and early adulthood than at other life stages because decisions made during this period are believed to greatly affect the pathways individuals take with respect to education, work, and family. Secondary school and the years immediately following are a time of planning, and values guide thinking about the type of job one might want, whether and when to partner and have children, to leave or stay in the community in which one grew up, and a host of other related issues. The weight of these decisions, combined with the assumption that values are stable after adolescence, sustain much research on values for these age groups.

The remainder of this overview is organized into four parts. First, we consider research on historical trends in young people's values and related beliefs. Second, we examine work that is concerned with the major social sources of influence on values. Third, we summarize themes in value–behavior scholarship. And finally, we consider the limitations of scholarship in this area and suggest directions for future work.

## Historical change

Scholars in the USA have been particularly interested in an increasing emphasis among the young on what Easterlin and Crimmins (1991) refer to as 'private materialism' or values reflecting the pursuit of one's own well-being. The 1970s and 1980s saw young people attaching greater importance to being well-off financially, and increasingly interested in jobs with opportunities for advancement, high pay, status, and with substantial vacation (Easterlin and Crimmins 1991; Schulenberg *et al.* 1995; Watt 2004).

Concern for the welfare of the broader community declined during the same period. Studies show mixed evidence of whether or not the importance young people attach to contributing to society generally has diminished, but they consistently show young people expressing less concern about and becoming less committed to solving a variety of social problems including poverty, racial inequality, and protecting the environment (Easterlin and Crimmins 1991; Schulenberg *et al.* 1995; Astin *et al.* 2002; Watt 2004). Although there were signs that these trends might stall or reverse in the early 1990s, more recent analysis indicates that increasing materialism and declining concern for the welfare of the broader community continued through the 1990s (Astin *et al.* 2002; Watt 2004). Self-actualization values characteristic of the 1960s, such as the importance of finding purpose and meaning in life or developing a meaningful philosophy of life, similarly declined in the 1970s and 1980s, though leveled out in the 1990s (Astin *et al.* 2002; Easterlin and Crimmins 1991).

The general importance attached to having a good marriage and family life and viewing work as central in life remained reasonably stable over the last several decades.

Beginning in the 1960s, however, young people's beliefs have demonstrated increasing liberalization regarding gender roles and sexual freedom (Astin *et al.*, 2002). Studies document the increasing acceptability among youth of a variety of family paths, including non-married cohabitation and dual earner marriages, and a decline in the belief that lives are fuller and happier for those who marry (Schulenberg *et al.* 1995).

Bovasso, Jacobs and Rettig's study of change in moral judgments (1991), in which young people are asked to judge how right or wrong various acts are on a scale from 1 to 10, offers another approach. They conclude that severity of moral judgment was highest in the 1950s, with sexual and irreligious behavior judged less harshly by the 1960s, and selfishness and misrepresentation for financial gain judged less harshly by the 1980s. Feather (1980) also reviews a variety of studies in the 1960s and 1970s that make use of the Rokeach Value Survey, a popular instrument at the time. Rankings of traditional values including religion, patriotism, and leading a clean and moral life declined among young people during the period.

Cross-nationally, Inglehart and his colleagues argue values have changed in wealthy, postindustrial, nations along some similar, but also different lines than emphasized by US scholars. They suggest that traditional values, which emphasize religion, nationalism and obedience, are replaced by secular-rational values as nations develop economically. Survival values, which include materialism (on the rise in the USA), are replaced by self-expression values (e.g., Inglehart and Welzel 2005).

Two primary debates are evident with respect to historical change in values. First, whether changes evident among youth have also occurred among adults. Importantly, value change in society is often theorized to occur through cohort replacement (i.e. older cohorts are replaced in the population by younger ones who were socialized in a different historical milieu), but to the extent value change occurs after adolescence, life course change becomes a source of social change as well. Second, the primary sources of historical change in values are debated, both in the US and other industrialized nations. New media forms (e.g. internet) and the content of media messages are popular targets of investigation, as are changing gender roles and economic conditions (e.g. Astin *et al.* 2002; Watt 2004; Inglehart and Welzel 2005).

## Major sources of influence on values

Values are part of the cultural content internalized by members of society, and thus not only reflect a society's values at particular historical times, but also the subgroups to which individuals belong and the institutions to which they are exposed. Variation among adolescents' and young adults' values have been thus attributed to differences among their families and religious and racial/ethnic groups, as well as differences in lived realities tied to class and gender.

### *Family*

The family has long been considered the primary agent of children's socialization, including where they learn and internalize values. A large literature exists on the congruence between parents' values and beliefs and those of their adolescent offspring, though there is disagreement over the magnitude of intergenerational similarity. Greater congruence is evident in values related to major life concerns such as achievement, religion, and family, and between adolescents' values and their *perceptions* of their parents' values (Gecas and Seff 1990). Parenting styles that promote identification with parents (e.g., authoritative parenting) also foster value congruence (Gecas and Seff 1990; Pinquart and Silbereisen 2004).

Value congruence may result from familial socialization, but also exposure to similar socio-historical circumstances, and the relative contribution of each continues to be debated (Gecas and Seff 1990). Recent work on the intergenerational transmission of values also emphasizes that adolescents shape their parents' values. Pinquart and Silbereisen (2004) document bidirectional value transmission, with adolescents' values more likely to influence their parents' values in families with higher levels of authoritative parenting. They also found that intergenerational transmission of values requires that the values be relevant enough to provoke discussion between adolescents and their parents. Thus, it would seem adolescent-to-parent value transmission depends on value content and parenting styles, just as parent-to-adolescent transmission does.

## Religious and racial/ethnic groups

Families are, of course, located in cultural groups – religious and racial/ethnic – as well as socio-economic strata that shape values. In general, adolescents and young adults who are more religious are less materialistic, report more concern and responsibility for the well being of others, and attach more importance to finding purpose and meaning in their lives (Beutel and Marini 1995; Rahn and Transue 1998). Similarly, in assessing the importance of job features, more religious adolescents attach more importance to intrinsic, self-actualizing, features, as well as altruistic and social rewards, though they are also more concerned with job security than less religious adolescents are (Johnson 2002). These differences are thought to emerge because most religious traditions and doctrines tend to emphasize transcending material concerns, compassion, and helpfulness toward others in need. Not all faith communities extend this compassion toward outgroups (e.g. homosexuals), however, and studies also show religious fundamentalism associated with more conservative gender role beliefs (Moore and Vanneman 2003).

Although there has been some attention to racial/ethnic differences in values such as materialism (e.g. Rahn and Transue 1998) and materialistic, self-actualizing or social orientations toward work (e.g. Johnson 2002), most research on race/ethnicity centers around key values thought to differ cross-nationally, including individualism (orientation toward one's own welfare), familism (orientation toward the welfare of immediate and extended family), and collectivism (orientation toward one's larger community). Hispanic American and Asian American youth tend to hold stronger familistic and collectivistic values than non-Hispanic white youth, though not necessarily weaker individualistic values (Gaines *et al.* 1997). The varying role of values and beliefs in adolescents' lives is also a theme in recent research. For example, Asakawa and Csikszentmihalyi (2000) posit that the source of Asian Americans' academic success lies in cultural beliefs characteristic of Asian cultures that emphasize connectedness to others and interpersonal harmony. They argue these orientations facilitate the internalization of parental values regarding achievement.

## Socio-economic background

As is the case with race/ethnicity, studies concerned with the status of adolescents' and young adults' socio-economic backgrounds include values related to materialism, and young people's concern with material job features such as pay and security (Rahn and Transue 1998; Johnson 2002), though the value dimensions examined most often contrast self-direction and conformity to external authority. This distinction reflects a tradition of work in social stratification and values dating back to the 1960s. Kohn and his colleagues argue that a family's socio-economic position shapes adolescents' values via parents' values for their children (Kohn *et al.* 1986). Parents whose occupational positions allow for self-direction value it over conformity, and children both internalize their parents' values and experience greater opportunities for self-direction themselves, which also fosters a value for self-direction.

## Gender

Recently, whether gender differences exist in adolescents' and young adults' values and related beliefs has garnered increased attention. Studies generally support the idea that girls hold weaker materialistic values and stronger pro-social values that concern the wellbeing of others compared to boys (Beutel and Marini 1995; Rahn and Transue 1998; Astin *et al.* 2002). Girls also attach greater importance than boys to finding purpose and meaning in life (Beutel and Marini 1995). Girls are more committed to egalitarian gender roles and are more favorable toward dual-earner marriages and same-sex relationships, but are less accepting of casual sex (Astin *et al.* 2002; Schulenberg et al. 1995). With respect to what young people find important in choosing their work, gender gaps in materialism closed by the early 1990s (Marini *et al.* 1996). And while girls continue to place more importance on altruistic and social features of jobs, the extent of this difference narrows as young people move into adulthood (Johnson 2001). Consistent with their greater endorsement of self-actualizing values, girls also attach greater importance to self-actualizing job qualities (Marini *et al.* 1996). Although no study yet tracks the same values across the adolescent and young adult years, putting together the research on other-oriented general values during the teens and other-oriented job values during the transition to adulthood suggests two patterns: first, that gender differences grow during adolescence but narrow again as young people move into adulthood; and second, that such gender differences may be smaller or nonexistent among minorities (Beutel and Johnson 2004; Johnson 2002).

## Behavioral correlates

Values and related beliefs are implicated in some of the most important decisions adolescents make about risk behaviors, educational pursuits, career choices and family formation. Studies in this area rarely specify how values enter decision-making, however, or the circumstances under which they have greater or lesser influence. Moreover, it remains unresolved to what extent values truly motivate behavior or reflect rationalizations for what we do.

Studies indicate a correspondence, though not always a strong one, between values and behaviors from the same domain of life. For example, adolescents' other-oriented values predict participation in volunteer work during the years following (e.g. Oesterle *et al.* 2004) and stronger commitment to a set of conventional values, varyingly defined, is associated with lesser engagement in adolescent 'problem behaviors' including substance use, delinquency, and school dropout (e.g. Garnier and Stein 1998). The importance adolescents attach to different job qualities also predicts the extent to which they later work in jobs with those qualities (Johnson 2001).

Research on values relating to work and family indicates that values influence behaviors across life domains as well. For example, placing greater importance on extrinsic work rewards in one's future work as a high school senior is associated with earlier marriage and parenthood (Johnson 2005), possibly reflecting an awareness of how status attainment, family formation and supporting a family are linked, even if that understanding is underdeveloped. Clarkberg et al. (1995) find that young adults' union formation and their choices between marriage and cohabitation are influenced by values and attitudes relating to money, leisure, gender roles, and career, as well as toward marriage.

This area of values research is less well developed. In addition, we know little about how competing values across life domains play out across the life course. Specifically, when conflicts between valued end states arise (e.g. a happy family, a successful career, a healthy body), how do individuals resolve them? Or, do our flexible value systems allow for an after-the-fact resolution for wherever social forces lead us?

## Limitations and future directions

Research on adolescents' and young adults' values suffers from the limitations and concerns about the measurement and conceptualization of values more generally, and as indicated earlier, by the underspecified links between values and behavior (for general discussions, see Hitlin and Piliavin 2004 and Marini 2000). That these problems plague values research broadly does not give license to scholars of the early life course to ignore them. The extent to which values and related beliefs change over the life course is also an unresolved question deserving attention. Evidence that adolescents' values are transmitted to parents, and theories of historical change that emphasize shifts among all age groups (i.e. period effects rather than cohort effects), suggests some value change occurs in adulthood. Value change is also suggested by research that ties some aspects of adolescents' values to developmental processes. For example, Feather (1980) argues that because adolescents are particularly bothered by injustice and hypocrisy, and are working on developing autonomy, values of honesty, achieving true friendship, and having independence may take a prominent place in their value systems. It is perhaps stating the obvious, but a full understanding of adolescence and young adulthood cannot be built on studies of these age groups alone. Understanding value change across the life course is important to understanding values in adolescence.

Historical change in the structure of the life course in postindustrial societies like the USA also requires that we revisit our understanding of value development and change. The extent of value change across the life course may itself be historically variable. More years invested in educational qualifications, delayed family formation, and a lengthening period of dependence on natal families may correspondingly delay or lengthen identity development with implications for value development and change. Greater stability in values and other aspects of the self with age are usually considered to result from cognitive processes as well as environments that themselves become more stable with age. To the extent that many of the role transitions and experiences tied to becoming an adult occur later, stability of environment is delayed and values may exhibit greater malleability into older ages. Whether values truly crystallize or simply become increasingly stable with age, the process may take place later. This may be particularly true of values that young people have not had a chance to 'test drive' in earlier roles.

Trends toward individualization of the life course, in particular, may change the place of values in behavior. Individualization is often characterized as requiring more individual navigation of choices. Young people face a broadening set of choices with respect to school, work, and family. Should one cohabit with a romantic partner? Marry? Live independently? Individually navigated paths may allow for choices to reflect the personal preferences and priorities of youth, including chances to live consistent with personal values. At the same time, life paths may be increasingly dependent upon the resources youth bring with them, and growing economic inequality is likely to affect the options and navigational skills of young people as well as the ability of parents to guide and support their offspring as they make their way into adulthood. Mortimer and Larson write, 'For both rich and poor, the future puts greater responsibility onto their plates, requiring them to be volitional and agentic as they manage diverse components of fiscal, human, and social capital' (2002: 14). For some, a widening array of choices may mean greater behavioral expression of values. Others may be constrained in doing so.

Thus, social change pushes us to understand adolescents' and young adults' values along multiple fronts. Social change can alter cultural beliefs, including values internalized by the young, and so research on historical trends and their sources continues to be important. Social change has diversified the family contexts of socialization and introduced new socialization agents via television, gaming, and the internet. Social change can also alter institutions such as schools and labor markets and the skills young people need to develop if they are to be successful adults. Through their effects on the timetable and variability of the transition to adulthood, and not unrelatedly on identity development – its facets, its pace, its contexts, these changes likely have implications for value development and behavior that require future study.

## Acknowledgments

Work on this chapter was supported by a grant from the National Science Foundation (#0647333). We thank Ann Beutel and Steven Hitlin for helpful feedback on early drafts.

## References

Asakawa, K. and Csikszentmihalyi, M. (2000) 'Feeling of connectedness and internalization of values in Asian American adolescents', *Journal of Youth and Adolescence*, 29: 121–45.

Astin, A. W., Oseguera, L., Sax, L. J. and Korn, W. S. (2002) *The American Freshman: Thirty-Five Year Trends, 1966–2001*, Los Angeles: Higher Education Research Institute, UCLA.

Beutel, A. M. and Johnson, M. K. (2004) 'Gender and prosocial values during adolescence: a research note', *The Sociological Quarterly*, 45: 379–93.

Beutel, A. M. and Marini, M. M. (1995) 'Gender and values', *American Sociological Review*, 60: 436–48.

Bovasso, G., Jacobs, J. and Rettig, S. (1991) 'Changes in moral values over three decades, 1958–88', *Youth and Society*, 22: 468–81.

Clarkberg, M., Stolzenberg, R. M. and Waite, L. J. (1995) 'Attitudes, values, and entrance into cohabitational versus marital unions', *Social Forces*, 74: 609–32.

Easterlin, R. A. and Crimmins, E. M. (1991) 'Private materialism, personal self-fulfillment, family life, and public interest', *Public Opinion Quarterly*, 55: 499–533.

Feather, N. T. (1980) 'Values in adolescence', in J. Adelson (ed.) *Handbook of Adolescent Psychology*, New York: Wiley.

Gaines, S. O., Jr., Marelich, W. D., Bledsoe, K. L., Steers, W. N., Henderson, M. C., Granrose, C. S. et al. (1997) 'Links between race/ethnicity and cultural values as mediated by racial/ethnic identity and moderated by gender', *Journal of Personality and Social Psychology*, 72: 1460–76.

Garnier, H. E. and Stein, J. A. (1998) 'Values and the family: risk and protective factors for adolescent problem behaviors', *Youth and Society*, 30: 89–120.

Gecas, V. and Seff, M. A. (1990) 'Families and adolescents: a review of the 1980s', *Journal of Marriage and the Family*, 52: 941–58.

Hitlin, S. and Piliavin, J. A. (2004) 'Values: reviving a dormant concept', *Annual Review of Sociology*, 30: 359–93.

Inglehart, R. and Welzel, C. (2005) *Modernization, Cultural Change, and Democracy: The Human Development Sequence*, Cambridge: Cambridge University Press.

Johnson, M. K. (2001) 'Change in job values during the transition to adulthood', *Work and Occupations*, 28: 315–45.

—— (2002) 'Social origins, adolescent experiences, and work value trajectories during the transition to adulthood', *Social Forces*, 80: 1307–41.

—— (2005) 'Family roles and work values: processes of selection and change', *Journal of Marriage and Family*, 67: 352–69.

Kohn, M., Slomczynski, K. M. and Schoenbach, C. (1986) 'Social stratification and the transmission of values in the family: a cross-national assessment', *Sociological Forum*, 1: 73–102.

Marini, M. M. (2000) 'Social values and norms', in E. F. Borgatta and R. J. V. Montgomery (eds) *Encyclopedia of Sociology*, revised edn, New York: Macmillan.

Marini, M. M., Fan, P.-L., Finley, E. and Beutel, A. M. (1996) 'Gender and job values', *Sociology of Education*, 69: 49–65.

Moore, L. M. and Vanneman, R. (2003) 'Context matters: effects of the proportion of fundamentalists on gender attitudes', *Social Forces*, 82: 115–39.

Mortimer, J. T. and Larson, R. W. (2002) *The Changing Adolescent Experience: Societal Trends and the Transition to Adulthood*, Cambridge: Cambridge University Press.

Oesterle, S., Johnson, M. K. and Mortimer, J. T. (2004) 'Volunteerism during the transition to adulthood: a life course perspective', *Social Forces*, 82: 1123–49.

Pinquart, M. and Silbereisen, R. K. (2004) 'Transmission of values from adolescents to their parents: the role of value content and authoritative parenting', *Adolescence*, 39: 83–100.

Rahn, W. M. and Transue, J. E. (1998) 'Social trust and value change: the decline of social capital in American youth, 1976–95', *Political Psychology*, 19: 545–65.

Schulenberg, J., Bachman, J. G., Johnston, L. D. and O'Malley, P. (1995) 'American adolescents' views on family and work: historical trends from 1976–92', in P. Noack, M. Hofer and J. Youniss (eds) *Psychological Responses to Social Change*, New York: Walter de Gruyter.

Watt, T. T. (2004) 'Modern maturity: how the values and attitudes of adolescents have changed over the last twenty-five years', paper presented at the biennial meetings of the Society for Research on Adolescence, Baltimore, MD, March.

# 47

# The influence of aspirations on educational and occupational outcomes

*Nathan Jones and Barbara Schneider*

## Introduction

It is well established in the literature that one's economic and social position is linked to the social position of one's parents. Consequently children in families with limited economic and social resources are less likely to achieve their educational goals and occupational aspirations than their more advantaged peers.[1] Much of the research in this area has focused on differences in educational and career aspirations by race and ethnicity and socio-economic status to explain differences in educational attainment. However, researchers differ in how they specify the role of aspirations in their models with regard to the processes by which aspirations shape educational outcomes.

A primary challenge for this research has been in establishing a common conceptualization and measurement of aspirations. For example, do we measure what a student *hopes* to achieve or what they *expect* to achieve? Are we interested in an individual's educational plans or their occupational plans? Variation in how aspirations are defined has critical implications for how we think about the role of aspirations in predicting educational outcomes. It is possible that having high educational aspirations is a better predictor of achievement than having high occupational aspirations, or that expectations provide a more accurate measurement of someone's educational plans than a more abstract definition of aspirations would. Additionally, as the amount of schooling needed for more prestigious occupations has increased, researchers have had to adapt their definition of 'high' aspirations, further complicating the analysis of the relationship between aspirations and educational and career outcomes.

The term aspirations has been commonly associated with the early work of Sewell and Hauser (1972), who introduced the construct as an explanatory variable in their status attainment model. Models of status attainment prior to their work had focused on the structural processes by which individuals attain different economic and social positions in society, directing specific attention the antecedents of academic performance. Blau and Duncan (1967), for example, modeled the association between fathers' educational attainment and occupation status on their sons' educational attainment, first job, and subsequent occupation. They found that fathers' education and occupation each have an independent effect on their sons' careers, but these two factors interact as well; males in families whose fathers held higher levels of education and occupation were more likely to attain more prestigious jobs than males in less advantaged circumstances.

Sewell and Hauser (1975; 1980) expand on Blau and Duncan's work by using aspirations to explain the relationship between socio-economic background and educational and occupational outcomes.[2] In their 'Wisconsin Model', the authors measured educational aspirations by asking how much further beyond high school a student planned to go; a student was determined to have 'high' aspirations if they planned to attend four years of college or higher. Occupational aspirations were initially measured using occupational prestige scores developed through the North-Hatt Occupational Prestige Questionnaire.[3] Sewell and Hauser find that family background ascriptive characteristics are largely predictive of children's academic success. Children are socialized through their interactions with their significant others (i.e., their family members, peers, and teachers); through these relationships they develop aspirations that shape their educational outcomes. These aspirations, according to Sewell and Hauser, therefore are integral for predicting educational and occupational outcomes (Sewell et al. 1969; 1972).

The Wisconsin Model has played a foundational role in the way that sociological researchers have examined how family background characteristics influence educational attainment. Subsequent data collection has allowed Sewell and Hauser to refine their models and extend them to include experiences of the original survey participants, tracing their occupational success through various stages of adulthood. Surveys conducted from 1992–94, for example, provided updated data on occupations, health, wealth, marital status, child-rearing, and other measures of attainment in adulthood (Hauser et al. 1992; 1994). With longitudinal data that follows participants throughout their occupational careers, the role of aspirations remains prominent in explaining how plans made during childhood and adolescence have effects on educational attainment that follow individuals into adulthood.

However, despite its strength in explaining how family background and socio-economic status impact educational attainment status, the Wisconsin Model is limited to the extent to which it can explain variation by race/ethnicity or gender. This is due in large part to the fact that the foundational work in the areas was conducted primarily on samples of white males.[4] The status attainment model does not appear to hold up for African Americans, women, or students from low socio-economic backgrounds (Kerckhoff and Campbell 1977; Portes and Wilson 1976). Subsequent research on aspirations has since shifted to investigating more closely the relationship between aspirations and race and ethnicity, above and beyond any SES differences that emerge (Kao and Tienda 1998).

## The allocation model

Kerckhoff and Campbell argue (1977) that one potential reason that the socialization model does not work as well for blacks and other disadvantaged groups is that regardless of the cues they receive from their parents, teachers, and friends, their attainment is externally constrained. In Kerckhoff's (1976) model of allocation, individuals have little control over their occupational attainment; social structures place direct limits on the attainment of individuals according to their background. From this perspective, aspirations are conceived of as an index of one's knowledge of the 'real world' (ibid.). Rather than adjusting their aspirations based on feedback from others, students either lowered or raised their expectations as they became aware of the kinds of opportunities that are available to them. The role of significant others in the allocation model helped students to 'obtain an assessment of one's own relative position' (Kerckhoff 1976: 370). Kerckhoff's differentiation between aspirations (what one hopes to achieve) and expectations (what one expects to achieve), the latter of which he argues is a better predictor of attainment because it is based on an individual's assessment of their chances in the educational system. Findings from the allocation model show that the expectations of twelfth graders are much closer to their subsequent educational attainment than the expectations of ninth and tenth graders[5] (Kerckhoff and Campbell 1977; Portes and Wilson 1976), suggesting that students adjust their expectations as they gain insights into how the educational system operates.

## Blocked opportunities

For African American students, recognizing limitations to educational and economic success may produce skepticism about the value of education as a way of increasing occupational attainment (Fordham and Ogbu 1986; Ogbu 1991). The blocked-opportunities model posits that black students are likely to have lower aspirations because of their perceived value of education. The assessment of their chances at educational success is perceived as leading students to embrace an oppositional culture, thought of as the rejection of educational system and of the dominant culture in place. Ogbu theorizes that black students in the USA face the choice of fitting into this oppositional culture or of trying to 'act white'. Students close themselves off from positive academic outcomes, rejecting a culture that may not be prevalent across their peers and family members. As these students become more aware that they face blocked opportunities, they are more likely to adopt the oppositional culture.

A different trend is presented by McLeod (1987) in his analysis of working-class high school students over the course of a school year. Low-income black male students ('The Brothers') in his sample have higher aspirations than the low-income white male students ('The Hallway Hangers). This difference in aspirations is attributed in large part to the fact that the white students seem to have recognized that they are trapped in their current economic status while the black students hold onto their optimism that they will be successful. MacLeod argues that aspirations are 'leveled' as youth proceed through their daily lives and identify limits on their opportunities, suggesting that students may start with high aspirations, only to be discouraged by the realities of postsecondary entrance and the labor market. Schools play a large role in this leveling process, in part because they use 'meritocratic' criteria as a means of determining academic capabilities, which in turn legitimates students' low self-esteem (ibid.: 113).

## The attitude-achievement paradox

How else might we explain the gap between high aspirations and low educational outcomes for African American students that has been reported across multiple studies (Mickelson 1990; Hauser and Anderson 1991; Hochschild 1995; Ainsworth-Darnell and Downey 1998)?[6] Although this relationship has been referred to as the 'attitude-achievement paradox', Mickelson argues that the relationship between attitudes and achievement is not a paradox at all, but has resulted from an 'inadequate conceptualization and measurement of students' attitudes toward education' (1990: 45). This analysis makes a distinction between 'abstract' attitudes that reflect broadly-shared ideals about the value of education and 'concrete' attitudes that are based on life experience. When observing parents or other significant others, if job returns match educational credentials, students are likely to have a stronger view of the value of education. Drawing on this distinction, she argues that previous studies have relied on abstract attitudes toward education, which are likely to be similarly held by students from various racial/ethnic backgrounds. Her findings confirm this suggestion. Using survey items that more directly measured concrete beliefs about education (i.e. whether a student believes that their school effort and achievement will lead to a better job), Mickelson concludes that race and class are both associated with concrete attitudes toward education, which are in turn related to academic achievement.

With the two dimensions of attitudes in mind, other research has expanded on Mickelson's initial findings. For example, Kao and Tienda (1998) investigated patterns in concrete and abstract attitudes over time, hypothesizing that as students 'accumulate concrete scholastic experiences', their aspirations would become more concrete. This idea mirrors Kerckhoff and Campbell's (1977) distinction between aspirations and expectations, in which they found that as students progressed in their high school careers, their aspirations about what they hoped to achieve would fall in line with what they expected to achieve. Kao and Tienda find that black and Hispanic youth are less likely to have high aspirations throughout high school, suggesting that their aspirations are likely to shift from being more abstract to more concrete from early to later in their high school experiences.

Downey and Ainsworth-Darnell (2002), in contrast to Mickelson, question whether the attitude-achievement paradox is actually a paradox at all. That is, is it really true that black students say one thing (that education is important to them) but then demonstrate behaviors that contradict this belief? Using 10th grade data from the National Educational Longitudinal Survey 1988 (NELS: 88), a nationally representative sample of students, the authors have concluded that the correlation between attitudes and behavior is modest for all racial and ethnic subgroups, not just African Americans. Further, they find a consistently positive attitude-behavior association for blacks, which is even stronger than it is for whites in some situations, calling into question the assumption that African Americans are a population that looks substantially different than other racial and ethnic groups.

## Aligned ambitions

For the current generation of adolescents, high aspirations appear to be the norm. High educational ambitions can be found among nearly all US families irrespective of their financial and social resources (Wirt et al. 2005). Results from national surveys of parents and their adolescents show that over 90 percent of adolescents have the same high educational expectations for themselves as their parents have for them (Csikszentmihalyi and Schneider, 2000). It is important to consider across SES and race/ethnicity why students' aspirations do not match up with their achievement, as well as why some students make educational decisions in line with high aspirations while others do not. Schneider and Stevenson (1999) developed the concept of 'aligned ambitions' to explain the reason for this gap between aspirations and outcomes. They describe the value of having educational and occupational goals that are complementary as follows: 'Aligned ambitions reflect an adolescent's knowledge of the world of work and the educational pathways to different occupations. Such knowledge allows them to sustain higher levels of motivation and to make strategic choices about how to use their time and invest their efforts (ibid.: 79).

Thus, the gap between students with high ambitions who reach their occupational goals and those that do not can in part be explained by differences in information that students have at their disposal in order to follow through on their goals. One large category of students who do not have aligned ambitions are the 'drifting dreamers', students who may know what they want to do as a career but lack information about how much schooling it would take to achieve this goal as well as whether that job will be in high demand in the future. In contrast, students who are 'strategists' are more likely to develop a life plan toward an occupational goal, which orients students toward their future and provides them with a way to organize their time and to make educational choices. Interestingly, Schneider and Stevenson found no strong patterns of race, ethnicity, level of parent education, or gender on having aligned ambitions. The majority of students have misaligned ambitions, a finding that mirrors that of Downey and Ainsworth-Darnell (2002), and suggests that future research should focus less on differences in interest or motivation and instead on the critical role of information in children's ability to reach their occupational goals.

## Future directions

The importance of aligned ambitions will be particularly relevant given the changing occupational landscape. Approximately 90 percent of students now plan on attending college and the wage consequences of not completing college are high (Schneider and Stevenson 1999). Postsecondary education now appears to be a minimum requirement for most professional jobs, and the consequences of making the wrong educational choice appear to be greater than ever. At the same time, the nature of the labor force is changing, with a shift away from jobs in manufacturing to an increasing demand in science, technology, engineering and math (STEM) careers.

Consequently, with college becoming an increasingly popular post-high school choice, there is an increasing need for students to be strategic in the kinds of courses they take in order to differentiate themselves from others. Many of these courses appear to be those related to STEM. For example, not taking advanced courses in high school, such as physics and calculus, or not earning good grades in these subjects makes it harder to be admitted to a highly selective college and eventually graduate with an advanced degree (Schneider et al. 1998). Despite the potential benefit of these courses, research indicates that a substantial proportion of American students are not completing high school with levels of mathematical, scientific, and technical competencies necessary for success in higher education (Adelman 2006). Future research on aspirations should be particularly mindful of the ways in which the changes in occupational opportunities shape student decision-making.

## Notes

1 Black students have been found to earn lower grades, have higher rates of dropout, and have lower levels of educational attainment than their peers (Jencks and Phillips, 1998; Kerckhoff and Campbell, 1977; Portes and Wilson, 1976; Rothstein, 2004).

2 In addition to aspirations, they also included measures of academic performance and the social support adolescents perceive they are given from significant others (i.e. parents, peers, and teachers).

3 Today, revised measures of prestige and socio-economic status are used (Hauser and Featherman, 1977; Hauser and Warren, 1997; Nakao and Treas, 1994; Stevens and Chos, 1985; Stevens and Featherman, 1981). The most recent scores have relied on occupational prestige data collected in the 1989 National Opinion Research Center's General Social Survey (GSS). The Nakao–Treas prestige and SEI scores account for changes in the way occupations are viewed by the public (Nakao and Treas, 1994).

4 In later analyses that include women in the sample, the Wisconsin Model has worked less well (Sewell 1971).

5 Twelfth grade students are typically 17–18 years-old while ninth and tenth graders range from 14–16 years-old.

6 Hauser and Anderson (1991), for example, found that from 1976 to 1986, although the rate of college attendance dropped for blacks, this was not accompanied by a drop in aspirations.

# References

Adelman, C. (2006) *The Toolbox Revisited: Paths to Degree Completion from High School through College*, Washington, DC: U.S. Department of Education.

Ainsworth-Darnell, J. and Downey, D. (1998) 'Assessing the oppositional culture explanation for racial/ethnic differences in school performance', *American Sociological Review*, 63: 536–53.

Blau, P. M. and Duncan, O. D. (1967) *The American Occupational Structure*, New York: Wiley.

Csikszentmihalyi, M. and Schneider, B. (2000) *Becoming Adult: How Teenagers Prepare for the World of Work*, New York: Basic Books.

Downey, D. B. and Ainsworth-Darnell, J. W. (2002) 'The search for oppositional culture among Black students', *American Sociological Review*, 67: 156–64.

Fordham, S. and Ogbu, J. U. (1986) 'Black students' school success: coping with the burden of "acting White"', *The Urban Review*, 18: 176–206.

Hauser, R. M. and Anderson, D. K. (1991) 'Post-high school plans and aspirations of Black and White high school seniors: 1976–86', *Sociology of Education*, 64: 263–77.

Hauser, R. M., Carr, D., Hauser, T. S., Hayes, J., Krecker, M., Kuo, H. D. *et al.*, (1994) 'The Class of 1957 after 35 Years: Overview and Preliminary Findings (CDE 93–17)', *CDE Working Paper*, Madison, WI: Center for Demography and Ecology, University of Wisconsin-Madison.

Hauser, R. M. and Featherman, D. C. (1977) *The process of stratification: trends and analyses*, New York, Academic Press.

Hauser, R. M., Sewell, W. H., Logan, J. A., Hauser, T. S., Ryff, C., Caspi, A. and MacDonald, M. (1992) 'The Wisconsin Longitudinal Study: adults as parents and children at age 50', *IASSIST Quarterly*, 16(1/2): 23–38.

Hauser, R. M. and Warren, (1997) 'Socioeconomic indexes for occupations: A review, update and critique', in A.E. Raftery (ed.) *Sociological methodology* (pp. 177–298) Cambridge MA: Blackwell.

Hochschild, J. L. (1995) *Facing up to the American Dream*, Princeton, NJ: Princeton University Press.

Jencks, C. and Phillips, M. (eds) (1998) *The Black-white Test Score Gap*. Washington, DC: Brookings Institution.

Kao, G. and Tienda, M. (1998) 'Educational aspirations of minority youth', *American Journal of Education*, 106: 349–84.

Kerckhoff, A. (1975) 'Patterns of educational attainment in Great Britain', *American Journal of Sociology*, 80: 1428–37.

—— (1976) 'The status attainment process: socialization or allocation?', *Social Forces*, 55: 368–81.

Kerckhoff, A. C. and Campbell, R. T. (1977) 'Black-white differences in the educational attainment process', *Sociology of Education*, 50: 15–27.

McLeod, J. (1987) *Ain't No Makin' it: Aspirations and Attainment in a Low-income Neighborhood*, Boulder, CO: Westview Press.

Mickelson, R. A. (1990) 'The attitude-achievement paradox among black adolescents', *Sociology of Education*, 63: 44–61.

Nakao, K. and Treas, J. (1995) 'Updating prestige and socioeconomic scores', *Sociological Methodology*, 17: 3–72.

Ogbu, J. (1991) 'Minority coping responses and school experience', *Journal of Psychohistory*, 18: 433–56.

Portes, A. and Wilson, K. (1976) 'Black–white differences in educational attainment', *American Sociological Review*, 41: 414–31.

Rothstein, R. (2004) *Class and Schools: Using Social, Economic, and Educational Reform to Close the Black–white Achievement Gap*, Washington, DC: Economic Policy Institute.

Schneider, B. and Stevenson, D. (1999) *The Ambitious Generation: America's Teenagers, Motivated but Directionless*, New Haven, CT: Yale University Press

Schneider, B., Swanson, C. B. and Riegle-Crumb, C. (1998) 'Opportunities for learning: Course sequences and positional advantages', *Social Psychology of Education*, 2: 25–53.

Sewell, W. H., Haller, A. and Portes, A. (1969) 'The educational and early occupational attainment process', *American Sociological Review*, 34: 82–92.

Sewell, W. H. and Hauser, R. M. (1972) 'Causes and consequences of higher education: models of the status attainment process', *American Journal of Agricultural Economics*, 54: 851–61.

—— (1975) *Education, Occupation and Earnings: Achievement in the Early Career*, New York: Academic Press.

—— (1980) 'The Wisconsin longitudinal study of social and psychological factors in aspirations and achievement', in A. Kerckhoff (ed.) *Research in the Sociology of Education and Socialization*, Vol. 1: Greenwich, CT: JAI Press, pp. 59–100.

Stevens, G. and Chos, J. H. (1985) 'Socioeconomic indexes and the new 1980 Census Occupational Classification scheme', *Social Science Research*, 14: 142–68.

Stevens, G. and Featherman, D. C. (1981) 'A revised sociometric index of occupational status', *Social Science Research*, 10: 364–95.

Wirt, J., Rooney, P., Hussar, B., Choy, S., Provansnik, S. and Hampden-Thompson, R. (2005) 'Condition of education: 2005', U.S. Department of Education, NCES 2005–94. Retrieved August 13, 2006, www.epi.elps.vt.edu/Perspectives/2005094.pdf

# 48

# Generation Y, flexible capitalism and new work ethics

*Peter Kelly*

## Introduction

The starting point for the discussion in this chapter is the widespread, generalized claim that today's population of 16–24 year-olds – the most recent population to enter the labour markets of the industrialized liberal democracies – lacks a good, old-fashioned work ethic. In these discussions this generation, often referred to as Generation Y, is made knowable – at a very general level (the generalization of generations) – as a population that has a disposition to work that is characterized as being 'street smart', 'lifestyle centred', 'independently dependent', 'informal', 'tech savvy', 'stimulus junkies', 'sceptical', 'impatient' (Sheehan 2005, see also Berta 2001, Huntley 2006)

For management consultants Real World Training and Consulting (2002), Generation Y workers are 'not like us ... They don't have the same work ethic. They don't respect tradition.'

Now there is much that could be argued with in this sort of generalization. However, there is not the space here to develop a detailed critique of the concept of Generation Y. Instead, in the discussion that follows, I want to argue that rather than not having *a* work ethic Generation Y, if there is such a thing, is confronted by the new demands of the globalized, individualized and more precarious labour markets of the twenty-first century. These demands require new work ethics: new orientations to the conduct of a working life.

At the turn of the twentieth century, Max Weber published his provocative and highly influential work, *The Protestant Ethic and the Spirit of Capitalism* (Weber 2002). At a very general level, Weber's purpose was to explore the particular virtues that should be seen as attaching to work, and the particular influence that certain Protestant sects had on articulating these virtues. My purpose in making reference to the understandings of the spirit of capitalism that Weber explores is to lay the ground on which I am able to identify and analyse the new work ethics that provide the motive forces for the spirit of twenty-first-century, flexible capitalism.

I will suggest that the *essence* of the spirit of twenty-first-century, flexible capitalism is that the cultivation of the self is the enterprise to which all efforts should be directed in the pursuit of success, measured in terms of labour market participation. A Protestant ethic promised heavenly salvation and a good life now as the outcome of the pursuit of the individual's calling. I will argue that twenty-first-century, flexible capitalism is energized by a spirit that sees in the cultivation of the self an *ethically slanted maxim for the conduct of a life* (ibid.). This new ethic provokes a range of possibilities and limitations for the conduct of a life by the members of Generation Y: these can only be hinted at here and will be discussed, in closing, via the later work of Michel Foucault.

## Work in flexible, globalized 24/7, twenty-first-century capitalism

If I were to commence this discussion with a claim that at the start of the twenty-first century the nature and meaning of work has changed, I would likely provoke some argument – and some agreement. In many respects workers in the industrialized democracies are participants in a classic capitalist exchange relation in which they sell their labour (physical, mental, creative) in variously regulated labour markets. Those individuals and organizations that purchase labour then have some claims – often negotiated, contested, arbitrated – over what individuals are expected to do in terms of work processes and practices; when and where they are expected to do work; and the manner in which they should think, act and feel in relation to these paid work tasks and duties. Not much has changed then since the likes of Marx and Engels, and later, Weber were formulating frameworks for understanding capitalism and work. Yet, in many other ways, the meaning of work, the place of work in our lives, the times and spaces and places in which work occurs have been, and continue to be, transformed – particularly as a consequence of profound social, cultural, economic, political and technological changes over the last three decades.

These concerns have figured prominently in the sociology of so-called *new work orders* that has emerged in the last few decades. In the context of this discussion this literature highlights the emergence of widespread anxieties and uncertainties as individuals work away at constructing a coherent and continuing narrative of self, of identity, in an adult world of work that is increasingly precarious, uncertain, flexible (Bauman 2001; 2005; Beck 2000). As Zygmunt Bauman (2005: 27) argues, a 'steady, durable and continuous, logically coherent and tightly structured working career is … no longer a widely available option'. In new work regimes, the idea and the reality of a *job for life* disappears to be replaced by jobs that are 'fixed term, until further notice and part-time'(see also Kelly *et al.* 2007).

Richard Sennett's (1998; 2006) influential metaphor of *flexible capitalism* is particularly useful in exploring the issues I raise here. In *The Culture of the New Capitalism* (2006), Sennett identifies three key, unfolding, processes shaping the emergence of flexible capitalism. The changes Sennett describes are complex, contradictory and uneven. However, his analysis enables me to discuss changes in twenty-first-century work regimes that foreground the powerful demands for flexibility, both at the level of the organization, and at the level of the self.

The first of the processes that Sennett (ibid.: 37–47) identifies is the 'shift from managerial to share holder power' that has accompanied the freeing of vast amounts of capital to find optimal returns anywhere around the globe. Takeovers, mergers, acquisitions and buyouts have become the playthings of globalized, digitized capital. All enabled by the frenzied activity of wealth-holders seeking wealth creation; and facilitated by the demands for the interests of fluid, mobile, digitized capital to be accorded more currency/value than those of more territorially fixed players such as nation-states and flesh and blood workers (Beck 2000).

These globalized flows of often predatory capital, always on the lookout for bigger, better, faster returns on its risk activity, ushers in the second process energizing the flexibilization of capitalism. Sennett argues that 'empowered investors' demand short-term rather than long-term results. As Sennett indicates, there is little new in money chasing money. However, organizations have had to transform their organizational processes and structures to satisfy the fetishization of the short term by impatient capital: 'Enormous pressure was put on companies to look beautiful in the eyes of the passing voyeur; institutional beauty consisted in demonstrating signs of internal change and flexibility, appearing to be a dynamic company, even if the once-stable company had worked perfectly well' (2006: 40–1). In Sennett's understanding of flexible capitalism, this is a profound and continuing driver of change: the re-engineering of the organization – and I would add, of the self – that accompanies the myriad demands for flexibility and innovation signals a highly consequential break from the steel-hard shell of the Weberian bureaucracy.

The third driver of this post-bureaucratic, flexible capitalism is, for Sennett, the information, communication and transportation revolutions of the past three decades that have transformed the nature of all productive activities – service-based, manufacturing, agricultural and mining. As a consequence, twenty-first-century work looks different, is imagined and regulated in different ways. It can be undertaken by micro processor-governed machines and hardware that displace humans on a massive scale. It can be regulated within organizational architecture that, ideally, looks less like a pyramid, is flatter with less layers; and which constantly strives for real time rather than lag time in processes of command and control, but also of innovation and development. These forces are not just felt at the organizational level. They are highly consequential for the individual, who constantly encounters these *norms* of economic activity, and must make choices, fashion a self, practise his/her freedom in the spaces structured by these demands and expectations: How flexible are you? How enterprising are you prepared to be/become?

## New work ethics: the self as enterprise

In *The Protestant Ethic and the Spirit of Capitalism*, Weber's concern was with investigating the relationship between a Puritan/Calvinist view that hard work, done well, was its own reward, and a so-called spirit of capitalism. For Weber, the concept of the spirit of capitalism is an *ideal type* that is useful in trying to analyse the diverse, sometimes contradictory, motive forces of capitalist activities, and the behaviours and dispositions suited to these activities. Weber saw in the Protestant Ethic only one of the motive forces for the emergence of rationalized capitalism.

Weber provides an illustration of what he means by the spirit of capitalism via a 'document of that "spirit" which encapsulates the essence of the matter in almost classical purity' (2002: 8–9). What follows in *The Protestant Ethic* is an extended passage from the works of Benjamin Franklin (*Necessary Hints to Those that Would be Rich* (1736)), and *Advice to a Young Tradesman* (1748) – a passage that includes the following:

> Remember, that time is money. He that can earn ten shillings a day by his labour, and goes abroad, or sits idle, one half of that day, though he spends but sixpence during his diversion or idleness, ought not to reckon that the only expense; he has really spent, or rather thrown away, five shillings besides.

And:

> The most trifling actions that affect a man's credit are to be regarded. The sound of your hammer at five in the morning, or eight at night, heard by a creditor, makes him easy six months longer; but if he sees you at a billiard table, or hears your voice at a tavern, when you should be at your work, he sends for his money the next day; demands it, before he can receive it, in a lump.
>
> (Weber 2002: 9–11)

Weber makes no claims for the representativeness, even truthfulness of Franklin's incitements and advice. They are, as he stressed, illustrative of the concept that he has a mind to describe and explore. Indeed, for Weber, there is little doubt that what he calls 'this little sermon' is the 'characteristic voice' of the 'spirit of capitalism', although clearly it does not contain everything that may be understood by the term'. Moreover, the 'essence of this "philosophy of avarice" is the idea of the *duty* of the individual to work toward the increase of his wealth, which is assumed to be an end in itself'. This *spirit* has, for Franklin, 'the character of an *ethically* slanted maxim for the conduct of life [*Lebensfuhrung*]. *This is the specific sense in which we propose to use the concept of the "spirit of capitalism"'* (Weber 2002: 11, original emphasis)

A detailed critique of *The Protestant Ethic* is beyond the scope of this chapter. However, this methodological frame – in which Weber uses the homespun philosophy of Franklin to illustrate the ideal type of the spirit of capitalism – is generative for the work I want to do in identifying the spirit of twenty-first-century, flexible capitalism.

> 100 WAYS TO SUCCEED #5:
> TARGET #1: ME!
>
> Stand in front of the mirror ... Smiling. Saying ... 'Thank you'. Doing ... Jumping Jacks.
> Whatever. (See below.) ...
> Is there such a thing as 'powerlessness'?
> No! No! No!
> Take charge now!
> Task one: Work on ourselves.
> Relentlessly!
> 100 WAYS TO SUCCEED #17:
> WORK ON YOUR STORY!
>
> He/she who has the best story wins!
> In life!
> In business!
> Your career is ... a story.
> HE/SHE WHO HAS THE BEST STORY WINS!
> SO ... WORK ON YOUR STORY!
>
> MASTER THE ART OF STORYTELLING / STORYDOING / STORY PRESENTING!
>
> (Peters (2005) *100 ways to help you succeed/make money*,
> pp. 8–31, original emphases and punctuation)

What we see here are exhortations, incitements, advice for self-help, self-motivation, self-management and self-transformation that can be found in many other cultural spaces (physical and virtual) in globalized, twenty-first-century, flexible capitalism. They have a certain cultural significance, as ethically slanted maxims for the conduct of life, because they have significant resonance in a globalized information-scape: a large part of which is devoted to producing and providing advice on how to be successful and make money. In this sense, it is of less concern how many people read or take up Peters' suggestions. Although his renown and success would suggest that he has a substantial audience. Rather, the interest here is in the forms of knowledge of the self (rationalities) that frame these tips; and the techniques that are offered for working on the self, for transforming the self in the pursuit of success and wealth.

In this sense, I can argue that the essence of the spirit of twenty-first-century, flexible capitalism – expressed with passion and exuberance by Tom Peters – is that the cultivation of an entrepreneurial self is *the* calling to which individuals should devote themselves. That is, the self is the enterprise to which all efforts should be directed in the pursuit of wealth and success. Twenty-first-century, flexible capitalism is energized by a spirit that sees in the cultivation of the self – as an ongoing, never ending enterprise – an ethically slanted maxim for the conduct of a life. The cultivation, conduct and regulation of the self is a relentless project shaped by a variety of frameworks that promise to support, facilitate and energize this project. This spirit is analysable as an institutionally structured, individualized entrepreneurialism; a structured series of incitements to manage the lifecourse as an entrepreneurial DIY project (Beck 1992). Here, Continuous Quality Improvement migrates from organizational process to processes of self-formation!

## Looking forward in closing: Foucault and the critique of new work ethics

At the start of the twenty-first century, the ways in which large numbers of us in the industrialized democracies sell our time, skills and efforts in the world of paid work are damaging for our health and well-being and our relationships. These ways of working require us to commit more to the organizations we work for, and they subject us to an intensification of the expectations related to our performance. For more and more of us, work, and the salvation that it promises, are an increasingly precarious, stressful, unhealthy experience (Bauman 2005).

Quite possibly, if the generalized characterizations of Generation Y have any purchase, young people experience this uncertainty, precariousness and demands for flexibility in different ways as they enter the globalized labour markets of twenty-first-century, flexible capitalism for the first time. There is much research to be done on the nature and consequences of this developing experience. In closing I want to sketch a framework that can shape this analysis and critique.

In his later work on the care of the self and governmentality Michel Foucault (see, for example, 1986; 1991) was largely concerned with analysing the government and regulation of freedom; and the ways in which individuals in the liberal democracies are encouraged and compelled to develop a self that is capable of practising a well-regulated autonomy. In this sense, we are understood as individuals who practise our freedom in limited fields of possibility: fields that are shaped by relations of power and forms of knowledge about the ways in which the self should understand and govern itself.

We can, in this sense imagine labour markets as fields of possibility shaped by ethically slanted maxims for the conduct of a life. New work ethics provide frameworks for coming to know and understand how one should act, behave and think in relation to specific ends, and in a particular, limited, field of possibilities. These ethics are culturally and historically located; they are produced and circulated within generalized, and more specific, configurations of time and space – such as families, relationships, schools, offices, factories, communities. These frameworks function as truths in terms of the ways in which they are translatable through time and space; in the ways in which they have, and produce, significant resonances in particular times and spaces.

Foucault's analytical framework throws into relief questions about the ways in which we practise our freedom, and are governed as subjects who are free to choose, and who must carry the consequences of the choices we make (Rose 1999). To practise one's freedom is to develop certain behaviours and dispositions in fields where others seek to manage or encourage appropriate orientations to work and its place in the conduct of a life. The research challenge here is to explore some of the emerging, and longer-term, outcomes of processes of individualization that compel members of Generation Y (and all of us who want to work and conduct a life in the liberal democracies) to be involved – relentlessly – in the forms of self-improvement demanded by globalized, flexible capitalism.

100 WAYS TO SUCCEED #23:
DESIGN MEANS YOU!

Sure, 'design' means DHL spending Gazillion$$$$ on…YELLOW. IT'S THE NEW BROWN.
But that's not all.
I 'am' design!
It's near the Heart of the Matter in a BrandYou World.
(Hint: We live in a BrandYou World…like it or not.)
You = Desire to Survive = BrandYou = Branding Fanatic = LoveMark Fanatic = Design Fanatic.
Q.E.D.                    (Peters, 2005, *100 ways to help you succeed/make money*, pp. 41–2)

QED, indeed.

# References

Bauman, Z. (2001) *The Individualized Society*, Cambridge: Polity Press,
——(2005) *Work, Consumerism and the New Poor*, Maidenhead: Open University Press.
Beck, U. (1992) *The Risk Society*, Cambridge: Polity Press.
—— (2000) *The Brave New World of Work*, Cambridge: Polity Press.
Berta, D. (2001) 'Workforce said to enter a new age with changing values', *Nation's Restaurant News*, June 11.
Foucault, M. (1986) *The Care of the Self*, New York: Pantheon.
—— (1991) 'Governmentality', in G. Burchell, C. Gordon and P. Miller (eds) *The Foucault Effect: Studies in Governmental Rationality*, Hemel Hempstead: Harvester Wheatsheaf.
Huntley, R. (2006) *The World According to Y: Inside the New Adult Generation*, Sydney: Allen and Unwin.
Kelly, P., Colquhoun, D. and Allender, S. (2007) 'New work ethics? The corporate athlete's *back end index* and organisational performance', *Organization*, 14: 267–85.

Peters, T. (2005) *100 ways to help you succeed/make money*, www.changethis.com/14.100Ways (accessed 22 February 2007).

Real World Training and Consulting (2002) 'The generation gap', available at: www.rwtraining.com/Issue20.html (accessed 1 April 2005).

Rose, N (1999) *Powers of Freedom*, Cambridge University Press: Cambridge.

Sennett, R. (1998) *The Corrosion of Character: The Personal Consequences of Work in the New Capitalism*, New York: W. W. Norton & Co.

—— (2006) *The Culture of the New Capitalism*, New Haven, CT: Yale University Press.

Sheehan, P. (2005) *Generation Y*, Prahran: Hardie Grant Books.

Weber, M (2002) *The Protestant Ethic and the 'Spirit' of Capitalism: and Other Writings*, London: Penguin.

# 49

# Understanding the sexual lives of young people

*Janet Holland*

## Introduction

The explosion in studies of sexuality, and its journey to a more central position in the social sciences began with the AIDS crisis when it became clear how little was known about contemporary sexual behaviour and the implications this might have for the AIDS epidemic. Many studies took an epidemiological or quantitative approach to sexual practices, what, how often, with or without condoms? (Johnson *et al.* 1994). Initially gay men were the target, seen as a group at risk, but the emphasis changed from risky groups to risky practices as it became clear that heterosexuals were not immune. Similarly the sensitive nature of the enquiry and the search for meanings to understand behaviour led to increasing use of qualitative approaches. The large field of youth studies encompasses a range of perspectives, typically breaking young lives into segments – psychological development, family, education, work, although pioneers advocate a holistic approach – or regard them as problems. Their sexuality is often ignored or marginalized in these studies, perhaps entering through the focus on problems requiring control. They might be drug users, smoking and drinking too much and becoming sexually active too young or in ways regarded as inappropriate by adults. Teenage mothers are a typical concern from a policy and research perspective. In addition, building on a long history of school ethnography, a large number of studies have examined the behaviour of young people in relation to sexual values, beliefs and practices and the concomitant construction of masculinity and femininity in schools.

Those researching and writing about young people's sexual lives and sexuality stand somewhat apart from the mainstream of youth studies, which draws on social theory generally, and draw particularly on feminist and sexualities theorists (e.g. Foucault 1979; Connell 1995). They oppose essentialism as a way of understanding masculinity and femininity, and operate with a broadly social constructionist, or a deconstructive, post-modern or queer approach, although feminist materialism continues as important. Following on from feminist gender work and masculinity studies, many look at young men and women separately, but others grapple with both, just as they grapple with the relationship between sexuality and gender. This chapter draws largely on studies in Anglophone and European countries to examine how the sexual lives and sexualities of young people have been studied and understood, and pursues five intersecting themes that emerge as critical in the literature: the relationship between sexuality and gender; hegemonic masculinity and male power; institutional reinforcement of heteronormativity; change and continuity – changing masculinities and femininities; and resistance.

## Sexuality and gender

This relationship is at the core of normative heterosexuality (heteronormativity, Warner 1991; the heterosexual matrix, Butler 1993), and a crucial theme in feminist and sexuality studies in general and of young people in particular. Richardson (2001: 5491) has identified five approaches to the relationship between sexuality and gender: gender subsumes sexuality, sexuality subsumes gender, they are inherently co-dependent, there is complex interplay between them, and they can be analytically separated. Nayak and Kehily (2008), for example, favour a combination of the complex interplay (following Butler) and analytical separation. They oppose gender seen as a product or outcome of the sexed body, which collapses sex and gender. They highlight gender as a lived process by suggesting the concept of gender practices, a negotiation occurring within a set of social and historical forces enshrined in the law, religion, family, schooling, media, and work. This formulation is helpful in understanding the interplay between continuity and change in the sexual lives of young people reported and theorized in the literature. A further contribution to this understanding comes from a psychosocial approach, where unconscious anxieties and processes are seen as contributing to the tenacity of certain positions taken up within femininity and masculinity (Hollway 1989; Mac an Ghaill 1994; Frosh *et al.* 2002; Walkerdine *et al.* 2001). Combining these strands suggests that structural and material, social and discursive and individual psychological elements are relevant in understanding continuity and change in the construction of masculinities and femininities.

## Heterosexual power

Connell's concept of hegemonic masculinity, the normative heterosexual masculinity in any specific historical or social context, defined in distinction from subordinated masculinities and homosexuality, has played an important part in studies of sexuality. It can be seen as linked to male power, and power more generally, for example in Holland *et al.*'s (1998: 24/25) work on young people, where heterosexual power is seen as socially constructed through a set of interrelated, interacting, permeable 'layers'. This construction can vary over time and cultures and the layers are: *Language*, including beliefs, norms, values, identities, discourses; *Agency and action*, how people produce their relationships, accept or resist constructions of masculinity and femininity; *Structured institutionalized power relations*, how heterosexuality is constructed as hierarchical social relationships, and the barriers to change posed by the family, law, economy, state; and *Embodied practices*, sexual experiences and their meanings. They identify the heterosexuality that impinged on the young people in their study as male-dominated, although young men could lack power or negotiate egalitarian relationships, and young women could be empowered or exercise power over partners. The analysis clearly allows for variability and change through the different layers, but the defining characteristic of heterosexuality, embedded in the heteronormativity of social life, reported as experienced by the young women and men in the study was the place of hegemonic masculinity indicated by their title 'The male in the head'. This signals the asymmetry, institutionalization and regulatory power of heterosexual relations, and the silencing of female desire. A 16-year-old working-class young woman comments:

> The girl is not meant to want sex, even if she does, and she's not meant to say that she does, but I mean a boy, he's meant to be sort of more dominant, 'I want sex', you know, caveman type of thing.

A 21 year-old young man recognizes the pressures:

> I don't think it's anything innate that makes men and women very different ... I think you get roles thrust upon you and the women's movement has been very good in pointing out the roles, the stereotyped roles that women are forced into. But men are forced into stereotyped roles as well, and some of them are more subtle, because it looks as if they are getting what they want ... their power roles should be the ones they want most, but they are not always.

Writers examining young masculinities take up this point and stress the vulnerabilities associated with the acquisition of a heterosexual masculine sexual identity. Mac an Ghaill describes the elements involved as consisting of contradictory forms of compulsory heterosexuality, misogyny and homophobia, but marked by ambivalence and contingency, played out in different ways in different contexts. Connecting social and psychic processes, he describes young heterosexual males as involved in a double relationship, rejecting and traducing the 'other', women and gays (external) while expelling femininity and homosexuality from within themselves (internal). Some of the young men he talked to recognized these desires, William described himself and close friend wanking each other when really drunk, and subsequently having to move apart because they had got too close. He said

> I'm not a bender or anything. I don't give a fuck about the sex, I know some girls now. But I wish we were still mates. It's great to be close, you know what I mean, really close just to one person and just the two of you know.
>
> (Mac an Ghaill 1994: 99)

The male peer group plays a significant part in policing the boundaries of acceptable masculinity, making William's desires literally unspeakable. They create an unsupportive competitive environment, a gender police that makes individuals highly vulnerable, unable to express these types of emotions and desires, which if voiced would place them in danger of being labelled wimps, sissies, gay. Several researchers write of homosexual young men going along with and acting out homophobic practices under this peer group pressure.

Frosh *et al.* (2002) point out that some young men suffer from the narrowness of conventional masculinities: those who are bookish, not physically hard, are dependent and emotionally vulnerable. But in general the demands of hegemonic masculinity can render them vulnerable in three ways: they may simply fail to measure up to the cultural requirements of hegemonic masculinity; negotiating sexual encounters can engage their emotions and connect them to their need for affection, leaving them open to pain and rejection; sexual relationships with women can render them vulnerable, since particular women might resist conventional femininity, and so threaten conventional masculinity. Some of the young men in Frosh *et al.*'s study negotiated places for themselves that were non-hegemonic yet clearly 'masculine', for example, they were 'hard' but need not show it since they demonstrated dominance through academic work, muscular intellectualism, an alternative acceptable masculinity in appropriate context.

## Institutional reinforcement

A number of ethnographers working in schools have seen the school as reproducing hierarchical relations of gender, heterosexuality, class and race, a major institutional site of the production of the heterosexual matrix. This takes place in a context where informal cultures of the school are often saturated with sex and sexuality through innuendo, humour, commentary and acting out, but the official school and curriculum seeks to deny the sexual. Robinson (2005) explored the relationship between dominant constructions of masculinities and the sexual harassment of young women in Australian secondary schools from a postmodern perspective. Following earlier studies identifying sexual harassment as about male power over females, she indicates that it is also about male power in male groups. Sexual harassment is constituted within broader cultural values and power relationships around gender and sexuality and their intersections with other sites of difference, such as 'race,' ethnicity, sexuality and class. The boys in her study see their harassing behaviour as 'normal' and expected by their peer group. A number of studies delineate the prevalence of hegemonic heterosexuality in schools in various ways, and the surveillance and control that is exercised in the formal and informal school, where teachers too can be cultural accomplices in its construction (Steinberg *et al.* 1997; Youdell 2005). Taylor (2006) highlights the intersection of class and sexuality for young working-class lesbians in school in a society that normalizes middle–class experience, where they experience themselves as the wrong sexuality, the wrong class and having the wrong family.

In contrast to the focus on the part played by schools in *reproducing* hierarchical relations of gender, class, and race, recent work on sexuality has turned to investigate schools as *productive* of sexuality, and of gendered/sexualized identities, within a framework of normative heterosexuality. Drawing on a range of theoretical resources, from postmodern, to queer, to psychosocial, it includes research on gay and lesbian identities and an examination of masculinities. In opposition to the impetus of the school, which is seen to naturalize gendered and heterosexual hierarchy, this work denaturalizes gender and sexuality. It draws attention to discourses, processes and practices in school that produce gendered relations and normative heterosexuality, but emphasizes that they also provide spaces for resistance and reworking dominant norms.

Mary Jane Kehily's (2002) ethnography provides an example. Keen like many others to identify the young people as active autonomous agents, she identifies *student sexual cultures* as providing critical spaces for agency and autonomy in the otherwise controlling environment of the school. They are spaces for social learning and the negotiation and enactment of sex-gender identities, where young people draw on popular culture and other cultural resources to construct, perform, and police versions of masculinity and femininity, a more positive take on the peer group: 'From the perspective of young people themselves, their informal peer group cultures remain one of the few sites within school that is not shaped by the demands of teachers, parents, politicians and policy makers.'

From empirical findings, many of these researchers see the school as producing normative heterosexuality, more so in fact than the more variable society at large with the latter offering the possibility of more fluidity in sex-gender identities through public representations and individual practice. But in that process of production, schools provide spaces for change, resistance, and the generation of alternative discourses of masculinity and femininity.

## Change and continuity

Over the past 30 years dramatic changes *have* occurred in the lives of young people, often represented as a transformation in the possibilities for young women. The new girl order is contrasted with a crisis in masculinity. In the postmodern era the certainties of the past crumble and identities, masculinities, and femininities become multiple and more flexible, the time is ripe for self-invention. The crisis for young masculinities derives from just this disappearance of the traditional ways of doing boy into man, of traditional male work as the economy moved from production to service, and of the male breadwinner role in the family. Boys' underachievement at school is contrasted with increasing educational success of girls. The new girl order is one in which success at school and work and concomitant economic independence means that girls really can have it all, particularly in terms of consumption and lifestyle. They can also experiment with masculine behaviour, and in the process become problems once more, trouble and in trouble, 'ladettes' becoming publicly drunk and violent, engaging in casual sex with multiple partners. All of these patterns of behaviour are heavily inflected with class. Middle-class boys do achieve at school, black and white working-class boys are a problem; working-class girls are more likely to be ladettes, or described as such. They are also more likely to adopt a sexualized hyper-femininity.

There is a strong strand of feminist work that, despite the apparent and dramatic changes in many aspects of young women's lives, sees the reinscription and reinstatement of heterosexual normativity in operation through many social and cultural mechanisms, including the market and manipulations of consumption. They see the feminist language of freedom and emancipation being used to sell lifestyles, to evoke sexualized hyper-femininity and conformity to particular body images (Aapola *et al.* 2005; McRobbie 2006).

## Resistance

The interplay between continuity and change plays through many studies in this area, and some researchers seem to be desperately seeking 'resistance'. Some of the school studies illustrate this trend, but while resistance and alternative discourses are found, most conclude that any clear shift away from normative heterosexual identities and practices seem tenuous. Louise Allen (2003) found some resistant conceptions of the sexual self, a 17-year-old young woman inspired her title: 'I mean you have got our stereotypical, women want commitment and love, and guys just want a fling, but I think that girls are pretty much like that as well' (laugh). Allen's participants indicated both resistance and accommodation to the dominant discourse. Anna (17) calls on a discourse of female sexuality that legitimates desire within which she can resist being positioned as a slut: 'I was called a slut when I cheated on someone and I was called a slut … but a slut is supposed to be someone who sleeps around, I don't sleep around.'

Allen also found young men who expressed the desire for love and commitment, but for both young men and women, this alternative approach was a minority activity, often contingent on them being in a safe research space to express it.

Fiona Stewart (1999) similarly pursued alternative discourses, suggesting that developing a 'critical consciousness' might enable a young woman to break from the confines of conventional (disempowering) femininity. She found some adopting alternative challenging femininities, by taking a proactive approach and initiating sexual contact, by owning their sexual desire, and engaging in other forms of sexual practice than penetration, often indicating a transition from relative powerlessness in relationships to one of more control. Renold and Ringrose (2008) use a dazzling array of concepts in their hunt for ruptures, resistances and subversion in the regulation of normative heterosexuality amongst tween and teen young women. They found resistance among the girls in their study to the current pressure for a hyper-sexualized femininity, but that social class was implicated in how it played out. Middle-class girls could project this hyper-femininity onto working-class girls as the 'other'. Renold and Ringrose continue the search for the ruptures that will open a space for alternative feminine sexualities.

## Conclusion

Jeffrey Weeks has described UK history over the past half century as featuring amazing (if patchy) change in terms of sexual freedom, exemplified by the change from the illegality of homosexuality to citizenship partnerships, gay marriage sanctioned by the state. But he suggests that

> Whatever the moves towards formal equality, and whatever the local successes of both long-term economic and social shifts and ideological transformations, the traditional assumptions about the social meanings of masculinity and femininity remain deeply embedded in everyday practices and in the psychic and emotional relationships between men and women.
>
> (Weeks 2007: 142)

Studies do show change in the sexual lives, beliefs and practices of young people over time, accompanied by the continuity to which Weeks refers.

## References

Aapola, S., Gonick, M. and Harris, A. (2005) *Young Femininity: Girlhood, Power and Social Change*, Houndmills: Palgrave.

Allen, L. (2003) 'Girls want sex, boys want love: resisting dominant discourses of (hetero)sexuality', *Sexualities*, 6: 215–36.

411

Butler, J. (1993) *Bodies that Matter: On the Discursive Limits of 'Sex'*, London: Routledge.

Connell, R. W. (1995) *Masculinities*, Cambridge: Polity Press.

Foucault, M. (1979) *The History of Sexuality*, vol. I: *An Introduction*, London: Allen Lane.

Frosh, S., Phoenix, A. and Pattman, R. (2002) *Young Masculinities: Understanding Boys in Contemporary Society*, Houndmills: Palgrave.

Holland, J., Ramazanoglu, C., Sharpe, S. and Thomson, R. (1998/2004) *The Male in the Head: Young People, Heterosexuality and Power*, London: Tufnell Press.

Hollway, W. (1989) *Subjectivity and Method in Psychology*, London: Sage.

Johnson, A., Wadsworth, J., Wellings, K. and Field, J. (1994) *Sexual Attitudes and Lifestyles*, London: Blackwell.

Kehily, M. J. (2002) *Sexuality, Gender and Schooling: Shifting Agendas in Social Learning*, London: Routledge.

McRobbie, A. (2006) 'Four technologies of young womanhood', paper presented at the Centrum für Interdisziplinäre Frauen und Geschlechterforschung, Berlin.

Mac an Ghaill, M. (1994) *The Making of Men*, Buckingham: Open University Press.

Nayak, A. and Kehily, M. J. (2008) *Gender, Youth and Culture: Young Masculinities and Femininities*, Basingstoke: Palgrave.

Renold, E. and Ringrose, J. (2008) 'Regulation and rupture: mapping tween and teenage girls' resistance to the heterosexual matrix', submitted for publication.

Richardson, D. (2001) 'Sexuality and gender', in N. Smelser and P. Baltes (eds) *International Encyclopedia of the Social and Behavioural Sciences*, New York and Oxford: Elsevier.

Robinson, K. H. (2005) 'Reinforcing hegemonic masculinities through sexual harassment: issues of identity, power and popularity in secondary schools', *Gender and Education*, 17: 19–37.

Steinberg, D. L., Epstein, D. and Johnson, R. (1997) *Border Patrols: Policing the Boundaries of Heterosexuality*, London: Cassell.

Stewart, F. J. (1999) 'Femininities in flux? Young women, heterosexuality and (safe) sex', *Sexualities*, 2: 275–90.

Taylor, Y. (2006) 'Intersections of class and sexuality in the classroom', *Gender and Education*, 18: 447–52.

Walkerdine, V., Lucey, H. and Melody, J. (2001) *Growing up Girl: Psychosocial Explorations of Gender and Class*, Houndmills: Palgrave.

Warner, M. (1991) 'Introduction: fear of a queer planet', *Social Text*, 9: 3–17.

Weeks, J. (2007) *The World We Have Won: The Remaking of Erotic and Intimate Life*, London: Routledge.

Youdell, D. (2005) 'Sex–gender–sexuality: how sex, gender and sexuality constellations are constituted in secondary schools', *Gender and Education*, 17: 249–70.

# 50

# Religiosity in the lives of youth

*Lisa D. Pearce and Melinda Lundquist Denton*

## Introduction

After a significant period of marginalization, the social scientific study of religion, especially in the lives of youth, has experienced a resurgence. A renewed interest in the social importance of religion stems from the growing acknowledgement that religion persists and matters for global, local, and individual identity, social relationships, and well-being. For this chapter, we focus on religiosity in youth, or more specifically adolescence, which we define as the second decade of life (ages 10–20). Adolescence is a time in the life course for which the study of religion is particularly important for two reasons. First, the confluence of dramatic biological, psychological, social, and economic changes in adolescence suggests this is a prime time of life for religious or spiritual change and development. Further motivating the study of religiosity among youth is the question of whether religion might serve as a protective factor in the face of the challenges of adolescence. In this chapter, we review the current state of three primary streams of research on religiosity and youth:

- the extent to which young people are religious;
- factors that shape youth religiosity;
- the influence of religion in the lives of young people.

We discuss the theoretical backgrounds from which these bodies of research flow, summarize key findings, and suggest future areas of inquiry. We focus on multiple dimensions of religiosity, including expression of religious beliefs, practices, and salience. Space limitations prevent a full discussion of all the relevant literature with regard to religious lives of youth. Instead, we rely heavily on similar past reviews (e.g. Donahue and Benson 1995; Regnerus 2003) and add findings from the National Study of Youth and Religion (Smith and Denton 2005) and other recent, comprehensive studies of adolescent religiosity both inside and outside the United States.

## What are youth like religiously?

Although primarily descriptive in nature, the study of patterns of youth religiosity grows from a few theoretical assumptions. A common, yet debated, perspective on adolescence is the storm and stress model – that adolescence is a turbulent time due to vast hormonal change (Hall 1904). Although researchers now generally agree that adolescence is not inherently stressful, it is still viewed as a period of great change. The resulting stress is sometimes argued to increase rebellion against family religious values, and to dampen religious belief, practice, and salience. These ideas predict relatively low and decreasing levels of religiosity among youth.

More recent developmental theory on the shape and dynamics of religiosity in adolescence focuses on cognitive change, such as the move from concrete to abstract thinking, the expansion of autonomy, and the development of meaning-making capacities (Benson and King 2005). Sociological theories about religiosity in young people primarily emphasize decreases in parental authority and increases in peer influence (Regnerus *et al.* 2003). Combining these theories suggests that religiosity may increase or decrease in adolescence, in connection to the social contexts in which various developmental processes are taking place. Although adolescent experiences may, on average, lead to decreases in religiosity, there will also be interesting subgroups of young people who maintain or increase their personal religiosity, and this will be discussed in the next section of this chapter. We now discuss research on aggregate levels and change in religious beliefs, practices, and salience for youth.

When it comes to religious beliefs, data from the National Study of Youth and Religion show that 84 percent of American teenagers (ages 13–17) believe in God, 12 percent are unsure, and only 3 percent do not believe in God (Smith and Denton 2005). Between four and six out of ten American teenagers say they believe in angels, demons, divine miracles, and life after death (Smith and Denton 2005). In comparison, Francis and Kay (1995) find that among a representative sample of 13–15 year-olds attending school in England and Wales, 39 percent believe in God and 41 percent believe in life after death. Mason, Singleton, and Webber (2007) report that just over half of Australian youth born between 1981 and 1995 believe in God. Although levels of adolescent religious belief are lower in England, Wales, and Australia compared to the United States, this is expected given the unique religious contexts of those three countries. What has yet to be studied is to what extent changes in religious belief occur over time, within and across these and other countries' adolescent populations.

Just less than half of American youth publicly practice religious faith (Donahue and Benson 1995). Four out of ten teenagers report attending religious services weekly or more, praying daily or more, and being currently involved in a religious youth group. These numbers have remained relatively stable across youth of the same age between 1976 and 1996 (Johnston *et al.* 1999; Smith and Denton 2005). Regarding other organized religious activities, about half of American teenagers attend Sunday school monthly or more, have participated in at least one religious summer camp, and nearly three in ten have participated in a religious missions or service project (Smith and Denton 2005). Several studies have found a small but noticeable decline in religious service attendance between ages 13 and 18 (Regnerus *et al.* 2003), though drastic changes in religious practice during adolescence appear rare (Regnerus and Uecker 2006). Studies of youth religious involvement in England, Wales, and Australia show much lower religious participation and more steep declines in the adolescent years (Francis and Kay 1995; Mason *et al.* 2007).

Slightly more prevalent than religious practice among youth is personal religious salience and experience. About half of US youth report their religious faith to be at least very important, identify as very close to God, have made a commitment of their life to God, experience powerful worship, receive answers to prayer and guidance from God, and lack religious doubt (Johnston *et al.* 1999; Smith and Denton 2005). Alternatively, about half of American teenagers express weak or no subjective attachment to religion or religious experience. Benson *et al.* (2005) find that the percent of youth reporting that religion or spirituality is 'quite' or 'very' important remains stable from ages 12 to 18, suggesting that personal dimensions of religiosity are less likely to decline through adolescence than public religious involvement.

Most of what we know about youth religiosity comes from surveys which map the general patterns well. Studies of youth have begun to add more measures of religiosity, and a few large studies have been funded to focus on religion. One limitation of current survey research on youth religiosity is that most surveys of this nature are fielded in English-speaking countries. Research outside these settings, and in contexts of non-Western religions, will further advance our understandings of youth religiosity, its contexts, and its consequences. Also, by relying on large-scale, longitudinal surveys, research on religion and youth is constrained to the time scale of when waves of data collection are produced, usually spans of three to five years. Other research designs incorporating more frequent measurement, like online diaries or beeper time use studies, may allow for more precise timing of religious change or more continuous measurement of variance in youth religiosity.

Ethnographic research adds depth and nuance to our understanding of youth religiosity. For example, although survey results from the National Survey of Youth and Religion suggest that significant numbers of teenagers profess conventional religious beliefs and engage in regular religious practices, findings from 267 semi-structured interviews with a subsample of the survey respondents reveal a surprising lack of articulacy about religious beliefs and the significance of religious practice. For many of these youth, faith operates in the background, not as a central feature of their everyday lives (Smith and Denton 2005). In another study involving participant observation and in-depth interviews with teenagers, Lytch (2004) discovers factors that strengthen adolescents' connection and commitment to religious congregations. Also, ethnographic work by Clark (2003) examines the ways that youth embrace spirituality outside the boundaries of traditional religious faith. These studies are an important window on how adolescents enact their religious beliefs and practices.

## Which factors shape youth religiosity?

By far the most commonly cited source of religiosity among youth is parental religiosity (Regnerus *et al.* 2003; Mason *et al.* 2007). Theories of socialization hold that parents teach and set examples for their children in ways that reinforce their own religiosity. Matching prior research, Smith and Denton (2005) find that most American teenagers are highly similar to their parents in religious belief and affiliation and attend religious services with at least one parent.

As youth age, parental influence lessens (although rarely disappears), and peer influence heightens. Potvin and Lee (1982) develop and test a theory of religious development that integrates the individual development of autonomy with the influence of peer context.

They show that parental influence lays a foundation of belief and practice and then an adolescent begins to co-construct his/her religious identity with peers. Examining school peer context, Regnerus and Uecker (2006) find that schoolmates' religiosity is protective against religious decline and heightens the odds of a sharp jump in religious service attendance. When it comes to closest friendships, however, Smith and Denton (2005) find that only half of teenagers' closest friends share their religious beliefs, most are not involved in the same religious groups, and few discuss religion with friends. It is still debatable how strong a role peers play in religious development. Future research capitalizing on the theory and methods of social networks research could shed considerably more light on the role of peers in religious development.

Certain religious traditions motivate higher levels of religiosity from both youth and adults. Smith and Denton (2005) find youth who identify as Latter Day Saints at the high end of religiosity, followed by Conservative and Black Protestants, then Mainline Protestants and Catholics, with Jewish and unaffiliated teens at the lowest end on traditional measures of religiosity. They suggest that theories of institutional strictness and subcultural identity might explain these patterns. Aside from religious affiliation, characteristics of clergy and youth leaders and program quality are also likely to influence youth religiosity (Lytch 2004).

There are other social characteristics that are related to higher religiosity in adolescence and across the life course. Females report higher religious involvement and salience than males, African-American youth report higher participation and importance than other race and ethnic groups in the United States, youth from the American South are most religious, and youth from the West are least religious (Benson and King 2005; Regnerus et al. 2003). Interestingly, Mason et al. (2007) have documented a gender convergence among Australian youth, where females are no more religious than males on a wide range of indicators. Finally, more recently emergent in this literature are discussions of personality characteristics that might influence religiosity. It may be that youth who are less risk averse and more extroverted are drawn to religion and remain religiously involved (Regnerus and Smith 2005).

## What impact does religiosity have on the lives of youth?

Researchers consistently find positive relationships between adolescent religiosity and life outcomes (Smith and Denton 2005; Regnerus 2003). Regarding mental health, religious teenagers report higher self-esteem and more positive attitudes about life (Smith and Denton 2005). Smith and Denton (2005) also report that highly religious teenagers are less likely than religiously disengaged teenagers to feel sad, misunderstood, invisible, or to be unhappy with their physical appearance. Other research finds religiosity among adolescents to be inversely related to depression, suicide ideation, and suicide attempts (Donahue and Benson 1995). Wallace and Forman (1998) discover that religious youth are more likely to engage in activities that are beneficial to their physical health, such as exercise, eating properly, and getting enough rest.

Another area where religion appears to be related to the life outcomes of adolescents is in their family relationships and ties to other adults in their lives. Parent–child relationships are stronger among those who report religious commitment or involvement (Regnerus 2003). Smith and Denton (2005) also find that religiously devoted adolescents report being closer to and getting along better with parents and siblings. In addition, they find that religiously devoted youth have stronger connections to other adults, reporting higher numbers of supportive adults in their lives, more comfort interacting with adults, and greater levels of network closure with respect to their parents and other adults that they know and trust.

The educational experiences of youth are correlated with their religious participation. Some have argued that conservative religious backgrounds limit educational aspirations and achievement (Regnerus 2003). However, additional work by Beyerlein (2004) shows that this effect is limited to fundamentalist and Pentecostal groups. Other studies show that youth religious participation improves a variety of educational outcomes, especially for those who come from disadvantaged backgrounds (Regnerus 2003).

Adolescent religiosity has been found to be a protective factor against delinquency and risk behaviors (Smith and Faris 2002). Highly religious adolescents are less likely to report smoking regularly, drinking frequently, getting drunk, or using marijuana, and their parents are less likely to report them as being rebellious or having a bad temper (Smith and Denton 2005).

Adolescent religiosity is often inversely related to early initiation of sexual activity and frequency of sexual activity (Regnerus 2007). Smith and Denton (2005) find that highly religious youth are more likely to report that they believe sex should wait for marriage and less likely to approve of teenagers engaging in sex. These beliefs about postponing sexual involvement are also reflected in the lower rates of sexual activity (and fewer sexual partners when they are sexually active) found among highly religious youth.

Altogether, there is a relatively consistent link between adolescent religiosity and various life outcomes. These empirical studies are based on specific hypotheses grounded in a general understanding of religion as an institution that provides support, meaning, and social control across the life course. However, there has been little theoretical work on why religion might be so prosocial for adolescents. One important contribution in this area is the work of Smith (2003).

Smith (2003) proposes nine mechanisms through which religion may have a positive influence on youth, grouped into three categories. Smith first outlines Moral Orders as a group of mechanisms that may guide life choices and commitments. These might include moral directives taught by religion, spiritual experiences that reinforce and solidify moral commitments, and involvement in a religious community where role models provide examples of life practices for youth to emulate. The second group of mechanisms, Learned Competencies, represents how religion provides adolescents with skills and knowledge that improve their overall well-being. Within congregations, youth may learn community building and leadership or coping skills to navigate the situations and stresses they encounter in life. Further, religious involvement may expose adolescents to alternative forms of cultural capital – such as knowledge of music, world history, religions and cultures – that contributes to constructive outcomes in youth's lives. The third group of mechanisms, Social and Organizational Ties, represent how religious involvement contributes to the social capital of youth, and embeds them within dense social networks, often creating network closure. Through organized religion, adolescents come in contact with peers and adults who provide social and organizational ties from which they can benefit. Smith concludes that the presence of these three groups of mechanisms within religious congregations creates a context in which religion can 'positively and constructively influence outcomes in American youth's lives (ibid.: 27). This theoretical work is an important step toward generating larger theoretical frameworks in a field of study that tends to be more focused on documenting relationships between religiosity and outcomes than on explaining why these relationships exist. Of course, the ideas in Smith's framework depend on an assumption that religious communities are comprised of positive interactions and role models. This is not necessarily always the case, so future research should examine the extent to which congregation characteristics facilitate or pose barriers to adolescent well-being.

There now exist many studies that show positive connections between religiosity and adolescent well-being, and theory is beginning suggest richer explanations for these processes in youth. However, another weakness of this stream of research is how little attention is paid to the causal nature of the relationship between religiosity and well-being. We know little about what non-religious parent and family characteristics select youth into, and support continued religious involvement. To the extent these unobserved factors correlate with adolescent well-being, we risk overestimating the causal relationship between religiosity and well-being. Increased efforts to theorize and test causal models of influence using cutting edge statistical methods will shed more light on the causal nature of the relationships uncovered. Also important to this effort are more ethnographic, especially observational, studies of youth religiosity. Most studies in this tradition rely heavily on semi-structured interviews, which are an important window on the narratives and descriptions youth give of their religious lives, but no substitute for witnessing how religiosity unfolds and matters in adolescence.

## Conclusion

The study of religion in the lives of young people has come far, especially in recent decades. We now have rich information on patterns of youth religiosity, a good understanding of factors that shape adolescent religiosity, and a growing body of research outlining positive and protective relationships between religion and youth outcomes. However, there is still a need for continued research in this area – especially comparative research that can shed light on US or Western-based observations. We encourage better investigation of the factors that select families and youth into religious practice and identities and support their continuance in order to produce more confident estimates of so-called 'effects' of adolescent religiosity. We also promote a larger role for semi-structured interviewing and observational methods in this field. We are excited about the future of research on religion in adolescence and the contributions poised to emerge. Despite past generations' predictions of the waning importance of religion to social life, religion thrives and many young people receive religious socialization and develop their own personal religious identities. These identities have implications for other realms of life, so we must continue striving to better understand how youth are religious, the factors that shape their religiosity, and the influence their religiosity has on other aspects of life.

## References

Benson, P. and King, P. (2005) 'Adolescence', in H. R. Ebaugh (ed.) *Handbook of Religion and Social Institutions*, New York: Springer.
Benson, P., Scales, P., Sesma, A. and Roehlkepartain, E. (2005) 'Adolescent spirituality', in K. A. Moore and L. H. Lippman (eds) *What Do Children Need to Flourish?* New York: Springer.

Beyerlein, K. (2004) 'Specifying the impact of conservative Protestantism on educational attainment', *Journal for the Scientific Study of Religion*, 43: 505–18.

Clark, L. S. (2003) *From Angels to Aliens: Teenagers, the Media and the Supernatural*, New York: Oxford University Press.

Donahue, M. and Benson, P. (1995) 'Religion and the well-being of adolescents', *The Journal of Social Issues*, 51: 145–60.

Francis, L. J. and Kay, W. K. (1995) *Teenage Religion and Values*, Leominster, Herefordshire: Gracewing.

Hall, G. S. (1904) *Adolescence: Its Psychology and its Relations to Physiology, Anthropology, Sociology, Sex, Rime, Religion, and Education*, 2 vols, New York, Appleton.

Johnston, L. D., Bachman, J. G. and O'Malley, P. M. (1999) *Monitoring the Future: Questionnaire Responses from the Nation's High School Seniors*, Ann Arbor, MI: Institute for Social Research.

Lytch, C. (2004) *Choosing Church: What Makes a Difference for Teens*, Westminster: John Knox.

Mason, M., Singleton, A. and Webber, R. (2007) 'The spirituality of young Australians', *International Journal of Children's Spirituality*, 12: 149–63.

Potvin, R. and Lee, C-F. (1982) 'Adolescent religion: a developmental approach', *Sociological Analysis*, 43: 131–44.

Regnerus, M. (2003) 'Religion and positive adolescent outcomes: a review of research and theory', *Review of Religious Research*, 44: 394–413.

—— (2007) *Forbidden Fruit: Sex and Religion in the Lives of American Teenagers*, New York: Oxford University Press.

Regnerus, M. and Smith, C. (2005) 'Selection effects in studies of religious influence', *Review of Religious Research*, 47: 23–50.

Regnerus, M., Smith, C. and Fritsch, M. (2003) *Religion in the Lives of American Adolescents: ARreview of the Literature*, Research Report #3 of the National Study of Youth and Religion, Chapel Hill, NC, University of North Carolina.

Regnerus, M. and Uecker, J. (2006) 'Finding faith, losing faith: the prevalence and context of religious transformations during adolescence', *Review of Religious Research*, 47: 217–37.

Smith, C. (2003) 'Theorizing religious effects among American adolescents', *Journal for the Scientific Study of Religion*, 42: 17–30.

Smith, C. and Denton, M. L. (2005) *Soul Searching: The Religious and Spiritual Lives of American Teenagers*, New York: Oxford University Press.

Smith, C. and Faris, R. (2002) *Religion and American Adolescent Delinquency, Risk Behaviors and Constructive Social Activities*, Research Report #1 of the National Study of Youth and Religion, Chapel Hill, NC, University of North Carolina.

Wallace, J. M. and Forman, T. A. (1998) 'Religion's role in promoting health and reducing risk among American youth', *Health Education and Behavior*, 25: 721–41.

# Part X

# Crime and deviance

*Andy Furlong*

## Young people, crime and juvenile justice

Fears about young people, their involvement in illegal activities and the supposed threat that they pose for the moral order have long underpinned relations between generations. From the perspective of large sections of the adult population, young people must be tamed, civilized and taught respect for authority. They must learn that crime does not pay and that there is no bypassing legitimate employment as the route to prosperity. In most advanced societies these long-standing concerns about the socialization and civilization of youth have reached a stage where balanced debate has been superseded by a moral panic and where juvenile justice policies are being framed by a media–driven agenda in which young people are increasingly portrayed as a dangerous class whose actions threaten both property, and person, as well as the respect that once made for harmonious community relations.

Changes in patterns of criminality are often open to interpretation and may reflect the priorities of law enforcement officials and changes in legislation as much as underlying transformations in the behaviour of young people. Indeed, perceived increases in law-lessness among young people can lead to the introduction of new offences as politicians try to convince the concerned public that they are in control of the 'youth problem' and able to maintain order in the face of the threat from the younger generation.

In some respects, the fear of the younger generation stems from a poor understanding of the nature of changes in contemporary society and the way in which they impact on young people. The protraction of youth and the precarious nature of employment opportunities mean that it takes much longer to acquire the 'trappings' associated with adulthood and, hence, longer to 'grow out of crime'. Adulthood brings with it a whole set of responsibilities that have a protective effect: stable partners, jobs with regular wages, housing, domestic commitments and so on. As Schaeffer and Uggen note in Chapter 51, the withdrawal from criminal activities can be linked to a process of maturation and to increased self-control associated with the increase in responsibilities attached to various new roles. Offending behaviour, which increases during the early teenage years, peaks in the late teens and falls sharply from that point on.

In many countries, concerns about lawlessness among youth, which can be amplified by the media and which does not always relate to 'objective' increases in offending, have led to the introduction of new legislation and harsher sentencing policies. In relation to the USA, in Chapter 55, Harvey and Kupchik describe the ways in which school students are subject to intrusive surveillance techniques including random searches and the presence of armed guards on school premises. They also note lower tolerance levels relating to those guilty of minor transgressions and the increased tendency to transfer young people (especially those from poor backgrounds and youths of colour) to adult courts where they are treated more harshly.

A number of authors draw attention to the ways in which activities that were once regarded as trivial misdemeanours associated with youthful behaviour are increasingly being criminalized. In the UK, zero tolerance approaches have led to the introduction of a wide range of new policies which effectively criminalize activities that were once seen as little more than a minor nuisance. In Chapter 52, France describes policies introduced under the Blair government, such as Anti-Social Behaviour Orders (ASBOs), which effectively blur the distinction between criminal and civil law and can be issued by the police or local authorities to anyone 'causing alarm, distress or harassment'. Breach of the conditions of an ASBO can lead to a jail sentence.

One of the key problems with zero tolerance polices is that they draw minor offenders into the criminal justice system. Rather than providing young people with the space to grow out of crime, they result in a situation where harsher penalties are applied. In turn, it becomes difficult for young offenders to avoid being labelled as criminal, which can make it more difficult for them to obtain the employment that has been linked to desistence.

Concerns about youth crime tend to be underpinned by concerns about challenges to middle-class securities and by fears of opposing classes and immigrant groups. As White observes in Chapter 54, those targeted by the criminal justice system tend to be the least advantaged, but it is crime rather than its root causes – poverty, racism, etc. – which tends to be the main policy focus.

When opportunities to make a decent living through 'legitimate' activities become difficult, then, as White notes, criminal activities may provide opportunities that are 'more rewarding, secure and satisfying' than the low-paid and precarious, albeit 'legitimate' alternatives. In Chapter 53, Hagedorn focuses on youth gangs, which he argues are often central to culture and cohesion in poor neighbourhoods. Whereas gangs are often portrayed as abnormal, Hagedorn argues that many gangs have been in existence for several decades, and, with links to politics and music, can sometimes be regarded as 'agents of change'.

While the field of youth crime is a broad one, the chapters in this part encourage us to overlook the fears and prejudices that often characterize presentations in the media (and which underpin the policy agenda) and begin to link the activities of youth to new experiences and to constrained opportunities in late modernity. Rather than engaging in a war with the younger generation that only serves to alienate and disadvantage, a modern approach should perhaps be based on tolerance and empowerment.

# 51

# Juvenile delinquency and desistance

*Shelly Schaefer and Christopher Uggen*

## Introduction

According to the United States Office of Juvenile Justice Delinquency Prevention (OJJDP), juvenile courts handled approximately 1.6 million delinquency cases in 2002 (Snyder and Sickmund 2006). About 58 percent of these cases were formally processed and two-thirds of these formally processed cases were adjudicated delinquent. Adjudication is recognition by the juvenile court that there is sufficient evidence to determine that the juvenile committed a delinquent act. Of those adjudicated delinquent, four of every ten will return to court on a subsequent charge; of those age 14 and younger with at least one prior referral, about 75 percent will return to court (ibid.).

As the above statistics indicate, many youth who enter the juvenile justice system will continue offending during the adolescent years and, often, into young adulthood. This chapter reviews the literature and empirical evidence on juveniles' pathways *out of* crime and their desistance from criminal behavior. Because many researchers consider minor or low-level delinquency to be normative during adolescence, we concentrate our attention on juveniles who are more frequent or serious offenders (Moffitt 1994; Laub and Sampson 2001).

To explore the processes and mechanisms involved in desistance from juvenile delinquency, this chapter will proceed as follows. First, we review literature on trajectories of juvenile offending to establish the difference between general and more persistent offenders. Second, we briefly review maturational, developmental, and life-course theories of desistance, then highlight the evidence bearing on each theory. Third, we discuss criticisms and gaps in the current state of knowledge regarding juvenile desistance. Finally, we summarize the factors that are positively linked to successful routes out of crime.

## Juvenile offenders: persistent predators or adolescents misbehaving?

Terrie Moffitt (1993) offers an influential typology that distinguishes between two types of offenders, the adolescent-limited and the life-course persistent offender. The adolescent-limited group represents a large portion of the juvenile offender population. For Moffitt, adolescent-limited offenders are those for whom delinquency is confined to their adolescent years, is sporadic over time, and desists as they mature. In contrast, life-course persistent offenders are those who display anti-social or delinquent behavior at every life stage and continue criminal behavior into adulthood (ibid.). The life-course persistent group makes up a small percentage of the juvenile delinquent population, but commits a significant proportion of all serious juvenile offenses.

As discussed above, we here concentrate on desistance or routes out of juvenile offending for serious or life-course persistent offenders (ibid.). The life-course-persistent group is characterized by neurological difficulties, cognitive delays, school problems, and poor child and parent interactions. Early anti-social problems give way to a trajectory and accumulation of delinquent behaviors that continues, in some form, throughout the life course. This early presentation of delinquent behavior also slows progress toward developmental milestones such as educational success, forming positive peer relationships, and learning impulse control. Moffitt theorizes that this is because anti-social behaviors diminish the life-course-persistent offender's ability to maintain conventional behaviors and attain success by conventional means (ibid.).

Gottfredson and Hirschi's (1990) general theory of crime similarly points to a strong correlation between past criminal behavior and future criminality. They suggest that the persistence of criminal behavior over time, coupled with impulsivity or low self-control, increases the risk of a crime-prone lifestyle. Gottfredson and Hirschi suggest that individual criminal propensity stabilizes after early childhood, such that some individuals will commit crimes throughout life regardless of their environment, social bonds, or later social interventions. On this view, desistance from crime is largely a matter of simple aging.

Testing Gottfredson and Hirschi's theory, Nagin and Paternoster (1991) attribute the positive correlation between past criminality and future criminality to processes of 'state dependence'. On this view, the behavioral act of committing crime actually changes one's propensity for future crime, as it affects future life choices (ibid.). In short, the behaviors associated with crime and the consequences of an initial criminal act can increase the likelihood of a trajectory or pathway that includes future crime.

## Pathways to change: understanding routes out of crime

While these theories suggest some stability in offending, most juvenile delinquents will ultimately desist from crime. Nagin and Paternoster (1991) find that whether individuals desist from crime is not solely determined by age or low self-control, as Gottfredson and Hirschi contend, but also by processes of within-individual change. One way to examine such differences is to examine the rise and fall of offending trajectories, which can help identify pathways of desistance. The research typically adopts one of three general perspectives, emphasizing either maturation as a correlate of desistance, desistance as a developmental stage, or age-graded informal social controls.

### Maturation and age as a correlate of desistance

We earlier touched on the proposed relationship between maturation, as defined by age, and desistance. Glueck and Glueck (1950) emphasized maturation, or desistance with age, in their pioneering research on crime over the life course. The Gluecks followed 500 delinquent boys and 500 non-delinquent boys from 1940 through 1965 to analyze the development of criminal offending. Based on their analysis of these data, they developed a theory of maturation and desistance from criminal offending. Glueck and Glueck (1974) argue that once individuals reach a particular developmental stage where their physical, emotional, and intelligence levels are integrated and achieved, they attain the self-control necessary to determine that committing crime does not lead to satisfaction.

Building on Glueck and Glueck's (1950; 1974) theory of maturation, Gottfredson and Hirschi (1990) expanded the concept of self-control and age and its relationship to desistance. According to this view, some juveniles have a propensity to commit crime due to a lack of self-control that remains stable over time. They will commit less crime as they age, but their rates will remain higher throughout the life course than those who exhibit greater self-control. For Gottfredson and Hirschi, external factors such as family, school, peers, and employment do *not* directly influence an individual's propensity to commit crime. Instead, juveniles will inexorably discontinue crime as they age. To illustrate this relationship, Gottfredson and Hirschi plot age-crime curves based on the number of arrests by age. Such graphs show a dramatic spike in arrest rates for adolescents beginning around the age of 12 and peaking by age 17. A steep decline follows through age 28, at which point about 85 percent of the initial offenders will have desisted from crime as measured by arrest (Hirschi and Gottfredson 1983; Farrington 1986; Gottfredson and Hirschi 1990; Moffitt 1994).

More recently, researchers have revisited issues of maturation and desistance from a developmental social and psychological perspective. Chung *et al.* (2005) view psychosocial maturity as central to making a successful transition from adolescence to adulthood. Individuals who lack psychosocial maturity thus remain in a stage of delinquency for extended periods. The authors surmise that adolescents successfully transition to young adulthood by virtue of three psychosocial maturation skills: mastery and competence of knowledge and skills related to societal activities; interpersonal relationships and social functioning with others; and, the ability to self-define and self-govern by behaving responsibly and morally without external social controls.

Due to incarceration or displacement, Chung *et al.* posit that many adolescents in the juvenile justice system are delayed in psychosocial maturation, which makes it difficult for them to transition successfully into adulthood. Chung and colleagues therefore advise that psychosocial maturation, rather than age *per se*, should be taken into account when developing rehabilitation programs for juvenile offenders. Thus, if juveniles are placed in rehabilitative programs or interventions that exceed their level of psychosocial maturity, their offending will continue unabated. These authors advocate for juvenile justice reforms based on a developmental approach, focusing on psychosocial maturation that smooths the passage to adulthood.

### Desistance as a developmental stage

Theorists who view routes out of crime from a developmental perspective concentrate on the stages, progressions, growth, and evolution of pathways. Developing over time, these pathways are influenced by personality, cognitive transformations, and relationships and interactions with the social environment (Laub and Sampson 2001).

## Personality

As noted above, Moffitt's typology (1993; 1994) suggests that the ability to leave crime is dependent upon whether juveniles fall into the adolescent-limited or life-course persistent group. Adolescent-limited offenders dabble in delinquency during their adolescent years, primarily due to peer influence, but quickly desist from delinquent behavior in late adolescence. Life-course-persistent offenders, in contrast, continue offending into adulthood. Although they may reach some age-appropriate developmental milestones, such as employment and marriage, they find it difficult to completely 'leave their past selves behind' (Moffitt 1994: 45; Laub and Sampson 2001).

## Cognitive transformations

The concept of leaving past selves behind is closely linked to cognitive and phenomenological approaches to desistance. Rather than asking why people desist, such approaches instead ask how people in the same situation experience, interpret, and react differently (Maruna 2001). For Shadd Maruna (2001), desistance involves a cognitive transformation and a personal redemption script with three elements: (1) the development of a core belief that the true self is a good person; (2) an optimistic perception of personal control over one's destiny; and (3) finding a new purpose in life and becoming a productive member of society. From this perspective, a juvenile's route out of crime involves a cognitive transformation in support of behavioral changes, which, in turn, engender a law-abiding lifestyle.

Studies examining juvenile delinquency and desistance have generally focused on males, with the work of Giordano *et al.* (2002) representing an important exception. They conducted interviews at two periods with both male and female adolescent offenders, examining gender-based differences in desistance patterns. The first interviews occurred in Ohio detention facilities in 1982, with the follow-up interviews occurring 13 years later in 1995. Using life-history narratives, the authors identified cognitive shifts and individual role changes in the process of desistance. Giordano *et al.* (2002) found that women identified religion and children as motivating life changes, though many of the women had lost custody of their children during the time between the two interviews. Males, on the other hand, identified treatment and prison as well as family roles as catalysts for change.

## Symbolic interactionism

Cognitive approaches are closely related to social-psychological models of symbolic interactionism. Symbolic interactionist theories of crime and the life course are generalized from Mead's (1934) broader theory of the self and others. For example, Heimer and Matsueda (1994) attribute delinquency to delinquent views of the self formed in interaction with others, in addition to attitudes favoring delinquency, social approval for delinquency, delinquent peers, and a history of delinquent habits. To test their theory of symbolic interactionism, Heimer and Matsueda using three waves of data from the National Youth Survey. They find that juveniles who view themselves as rule-violators from the standpoint of their parents and friends – that is, they believe that their parents and friends perceive them to be rule-violators – are most likely to persist in delinquency.

To understand desistance and the transition away from crime, Matsueda and Heimer (1997) look to adult work and family roles. When juveniles take on new roles, their concept of self begins to shift. In most cases the commitment to family roles (as spouse or parent) and work roles (as co-worker, supervisor, or employee) lowers the likelihood of criminal behavior. In some cases, however, off-time events such as teenage pregnancy can solidify already marginalized identities, and foster criminal behavior. In general, however, Matsueda and Heimer explain the life course transition away from crime as a function of family and work roles and the changing conception of self that accompanies these new roles.

## Age-graded informal social control and desistance

Whereas symbolic interactionist models suggest that adult role behavior may encourage desistance or persistence in crime, informal social control theory focuses more exclusively on the controlling or crime-reductive effects of adult social bonds. Sampson and Laub (1993) argue that desistance from crime is tied to the informal social controls and social bonds formed over the life course. This perspective may appear similar to the developmental approaches to desistance reviewed earlier, with one key difference. Whereas developmental approaches emphasize how past behavior and life circumstances influence present and future behavior, informal social control theory concentrates on within-individual change over the life-course (Laub and Sampson 2001). On this view, the development of social bonds, in particular marital bonds, offer a potential turning point that engenders desistance from crime (Laub *et al.* 1998; Sampson and Laub 1993). Beyond the simple fact of marriage, the timing and quality of marital bonds also shape desistance patterns (Laub *et al.* 1998).

More recently, Laub and Sampson (2003) point to changes in everyday routines as the mechanism linking family bonds to desistance from crime. Being married and having a family results in less time with peers, possible relocation, and greater direct social control from a partner. Similarly, employment creates social capital by conferring meaning and identity, as the threat of losing employment significantly alters an individual's decision to continue offending (ibid.).

For young offenders, however, Staff and Uggen (2003) report a more complicated relationship between employment and desistance. They found that adolescents who hold jobs with greater autonomy, higher wages, higher status, and more hours per week actually commit more delinquency than adolescents who hold less attractive jobs. In contrast, jobs that provide conventional learning opportunities and support education are associated with reduced delinquency. There is thus some evidence that jobs must be age-appropriate, as employment that places adult-like responsibilities on juveniles can actually perpetuate delinquency (ibid.).

The effects of both employment and marriage on desistance appear to operate, in part, through their effects on peer relationships. For example, Mark Warr (2002) suggests that marriage reduces the time spent with delinquent peers, which in turn engenders desistance from crime. Warr develops a theory of desistance that unites theories of informal social control with elements of Sutherland's (1947) differential association theory, emphasizing that delinquency is learned from peers or from significant others in intimate groups. In simple terms, strong bonds and family attachments can prevent adolescents from associating with delinquent peers, which decreases the likelihood of delinquent conduct. Nevertheless, Warr (2002) cautions that once delinquent peer bonds are formed, the effects of parental bonds and attachments are greatly reduced.

## Identifying chronic offenders and successful interventions

This chapter has provided a brief overview of the literature on juvenile delinquency and desistance, emphasizing studies that focus on chronic or persistent juvenile offenders. How are these chronic juvenile offenders identified and what sorts of interventions are available to hasten their exit from criminal activity? In reviewing the literature on risk classification and intervention programs, Jones *et al.* (2001) caution that policy-makers and researchers should not assume that identification and intervention efforts can be easily transplanted across programs and populations. Depending on the sample, researchers, and methodology employed, our review suggests that several factors influence desistance: age, childhood characteristics, social and psychological maturation processes, personality, cognitive development, external influences, and social bonds in the form of marriage, some types of employment, and pro-social peers. Further progress in disentangling the routes out of crime for juvenile offenders will require close collaboration between researchers, policy-makers, and practitioners who work with young people on a daily basis.

## References

Chung, H. L., Little, M. and Steinberg, L. (2005) 'The transition to adulthood for adolescents in the juvenile justice system: a developmental perspective', in W. Osgood, E. Foster, C. Flanagan, and G. Ruth (eds) *On Your Own Without a Net*, Chicago: University of Chicago Press.

Farrington, D. (1986) 'Age and crime', in M. Tonry and N. Morris (eds) *Crime and Justice: An Annual Review of Research*, Chicago: University of Chicago Press.

Giordano, P. C., Cernkovich, S.A. and Rudolph, J.L. (2002) 'Gender, crime, and desistance: toward a theory of cognitive transformation', *American Journal of Sociology*, 107: 990–1064.

Glueck, S, and Glueck, E. (1950) *Unraveling Juvenile Delinquency*, New York: Commonwealth Fund.

—— (1974) *Of Delinquency and Crime*, Springfield, IL: Charles C. Thomas.

Gottfredson, M. and Hirschi, T. (1990) *A General Theory of Crime*, Palo Alto, CA: Stanford University Press.

Heimer, K. and Matsueda, R. (1994) 'Role-taking, role commitment, and delinquency: a theory of differential social control', *American Sociological Review*, 59: 365–90.

Hirschi, T. and Gottfredson, M. (1983) 'Age and the explanation of crime', *American Journal of Sociology*, 89: 552–84.

Jones, P., Harris, P., Fader, J. and Grubstein, L. (2001) 'Identifying chronic juvenile offenders', *Justice Quarterly*, 18: 479–508.

Laub, J., Nagin, D. S. and Sampson, R. J. (1998) 'Trajectories of change in criminal offending: good marriages and the desistance process', *American Sociological Review*, 63: 225–38.

Laub, J. and Sampson, R. (2001) 'Understanding desistance from crime', in M. Tonry (ed.) *Crime and Justice: A Review of Research*, Chicago: University of Chicago Press.

—— (2003) *Shared Beginnings, Divergent Lives: Delinquent Boys to Age 70*, Cambridge, MA: Harvard University Press.

Maruna, S. (2001) *Making Good: How Ex-Convicts Reform and Rebuild Their Lives*, Washington, DC: American Psychological Association.

Matsueda, R. and Heimer, K. (1997) 'A symbolic interactionist theory of role transitions, role-commitments, and delinquency', in T. Thornberry (ed.) *Developmental Theories of Crime and Delinquency*, New Brunswick, NJ: Transaction Publishers.

Mead, G. (1934) *Mind, Self, and Society*, Chicago: University of Chicago Press.

Moffitt, T. (1993) 'Adolescent-limited and life course-persistence antisocial behavior: a developmental taxonomy', *Psychological Review*, 100: 674–701.

—— (1994) 'Natural histories of delinquency', in E. Weitekamp and H. Kerner (eds) *Cross-National Longitudinal Research on Human Development and Criminal Behavior*, Dordrecht: Kluwer, Academic.

Nagin, D. and Paternoster, R. (1991) 'On the relationship of past to future participation in delinquency', *Criminology*, 29: 163–89.

Sampson, R. and Laub, J. (1993) *Crime in the Making: Pathways and Turning Points through Life*, Cambridge, MA: Harvard University Press.

Snyder, H. N. and Sickmund, M. (2006) *Juvenile Offenders and Victims: 2006 National Report*, Washington, DC: U.S. Department of Justice, Office of Justice Programs, Office of Juvenile Justice and Delinquency Prevention.

Staff, J. and Uggen, C. (2003) 'The fruits of good work: job quality and adolescent deviance', *Journal of Research in Crime and Delinquency*, 40: 263–90.

Sutherland, E. (1947) *Criminology*, 4th edn., Philadelphia, PA: Lippincott.

Warr, M. (2002) *Companions in Crime: The Social Aspects of Criminal Conduct*, Cambridge, MA: Cambridge University Press.

# 52

# Young people and anti-social behaviour

*Alan France*

## Introduction

The language of anti-social behaviour has strong relationships to developments in the United Kingdom although its theoretical and empirical roots are from the United States of America (Millie *et al.* 2005). Within other western and developed nations the concept of anti-social behaviour is not a common part of academic or political language. For example, we do not see it discussed in public or policy debates in any substantial manner in the European Union, Australia or even the USA. This being said, concerns about behaviour, which is now being seen in the UK context as anti-social, such as 'incivilities' and 'minor' forms of misbehaviour within community settings, has a long history in US criminology and has recently infiltrated policy developments in some European nations (Burney 2005). The policy concept of anti-social behaviour though, is fundamentally a British phenomenon and a concept used to explain and define certain types of behaviour as criminal or deviant. There is also much uncertainty about what it means and how it can be defined (and measured) and much discussion over how anti-social behaviour is constructed around 'common-sense' understandings. For example, the UK government has continually claimed that we all understand what it is, even though a definition is hard to find. It tends therefore to be assumed that there is a consensus over its meaning, while in reality no such agreement exists (Millie *et al.* 2005). It is also worth acknowledging that anti-social behaviour is not necessarily defined as just a 'youthful activity'. In fact, its history is linked more to criminological debates on neighbourhood decline in the USA. This tends to see youth criminal behaviour as only one of many indicators of social decline. But in the UK context, anti-social behaviour has, over the past ten years, been more synonymous with problematic youthful activity in local neighbourhoods. It has also been used by both the media and government as a way of focusing attention on young people's relationships, not only with their communities but also as a symbol of a decline in 'respect' and an indicator of their lack of interest in making a positive contribution to society (France 2007).

## The 'emergence' of anti-social behaviour

A major influence in shaping our understanding of anti-social behaviour and the role it plays in modern society has arisen from the work of American criminologists and sociologists of the 1970s and 1980s. They were concerned about community safety and were looking at ways to prevent crime in neighbourhoods. Its roots can be traced as far back as the Chicago School although recent debates tend to link it with the work of Wilson and Kelling in the 1980s on the 'broken windows thesis': 'if a window in a building is broken and *is left unrepaired*, all the rest of the windows will soon be broken. This is true in nice neighborhoods as in run down ones' (1982: 31, original emphasis).

According to Wilson and Kelling, symbols of decline, such as broken windows, excessive litter, graffiti, rough sleepers, public drinking and buildings in disrepair, are indications that 'no one cares' in such neighbourhoods. The lack of attention by local adults and community representatives to these problems symbolizes that it is a neighbourhood where community controls are weak and therefore creating an environment where criminal behaviour can flourish. Wilson and Kelling (1982) do not see this as an inevitable outcome but they do see the withdrawal of neighbourly contact as an invitation to a 'criminal invasion'. In this context the 'broken windows thesis' contends that disorder causes crime. Some criminologists writing on this thesis have argued that such incivilities can actually be seen as causal or a sequential development of criminal behaviour (Skogen 1990). Early forms of incivilities in neighbourhoods are understood as prerequisites for worse behaviour to come by delinquents. This suggests that such behaviour is linked to the lack of control functions such as monitoring delinquents' whereabouts, having clear rules set and regulation of behaviour in the community and the family. Criminal activity is seen as progressive and starts with incivilities and minor forms of criminal behaviour which then lead to further and more serious criminal activities. If this is not controlled early, criminality in neighbourhoods or individuals will increase. What such an approach fails to address is why such behaviours arise in the first place or an understanding of their context. For example, writers such as Sampson and Raudenbush (2001) contend that the 'broken windows thesis' fails to contextualize such behaviour arguing that crime and disorder needs to be understood by recognizing its relationship with poverty and disadvantage. They argue that disorder and crime share common roots (not one leading to the other) and the collective efficacy of a neighbourhood, or the levels of trust and participation in a neighbourhoods, are greatly affected by the structural position and levels of disadvantage.

Discussions on anti-social behaviour have also emerged in the work of criminal career researchers (Farrington 1996). Through longitudinal research, they have been exploring the relationships between early problem behaviour and future offending. In their analysis, early signs of anti-social behaviour in the activities of children and young people are seen as strong indicators of future offending and for the development of a criminal career (ibid.). Behaviour such as truancy, vandalism, or incivilities on the street are understood as risk factors that indicate a child or young person will be involved in future problem behaviour (Farrington 1996; Rutter *et al.* 1998). Much of this approach is influenced by social psychology seeing the behaviour of the anti-social child or young person as being linked either to a generic propensity to be involved in activities that are anti-social or arising from cognitive dysfunctioning where they cannot differentiate between right and wrong (Rutter *et al.* 1998).

While there is a growing literature that supports these claims, it does have its problems. In this context, anti-social behaviour is usually defined as the opposite of pro-social

431

behaviour, for example, being a nuisance, being in trouble or involved in activities that go against community or legal norms as opposed to being well behaved in school, not being involved in trouble and acting legally. It assumes behaviour as dichotomous (criminal or non-criminal) and that a consensus exists over what a pro-social life is. Such assumptions fail to acknowledge that conflicts and disagreements exist over norms and values and that the legal definition of what is criminal can be ambiguous (France 2008). Similar to the weakness of the 'broken windows thesis', it also focuses on anti-social behaviour as actions of individuals giving limited recognition to the social context of such behaviour. While there is a strong tradition within social psychology that emphasizes environmental factors in behaviour, those advocating criminal career methods tend to see it as a marginal factor (France 2008). Anti-social behaviour has to be seen in its social context, recognizing who is defining it, and why it is important at a particular moment in time as a significant influence on shaping how certain forms of behaviour are being constructed as problematic (Squires and Stephen 2005). Finally, it is important to acknowledge that the relationship between anti-social behaviour and future problem behaviour is not predictive or causal (France 2008). Evidence from longitudinal surveys propose a link between the two yet there are no guarantees that the outcome of identifying someone as being anti-social in their early years will lead to future offending behaviour. In fact, questions exist over how it is being measured and how identifying someone as a problem may lead to stigmatizing them and increasing the chances of them becoming a future offender (France 2008).

## 'Zero tolerance' and community safety

The emergence of anti-social behaviour or incivilities as a subject for policy to address has seen a wide range of interventions and programmes being constructed both in the USA and the UK. One of the first major policy interventions, influenced by the 'broken windows thesis', was that of 'zero tolerance'. This was initiated in New York in the US under the leadership of William J. Bratton, the New York Commissioner of Police. He claimed that the city had stopped caring for itself and that a new form of policing was required if crime was to be tackled. This included increasing the number of police officers on the beat, increasing the usage of police powers to enforce city ordinances to reduce incivilities such as graffiti, littering and public drinking, a greater use of stop and search powers and making sure that all minor offences were prosecuted. In a UK seminar in 1997, Bratton claimed that such an approach had been successful and that within three years homicide had dropped by 51 per cent, violent crime fell by 38 per cent and overall crime dropped by 37 per cent. 'Zero tolerance' was claimed as a successful way of tackling the wider crime problem (Burney 2005).

The New York experience had a significant influence on the UK where zero tolerance was seen as a way of tackling 'low levels' of youth crime. It had a significant impact on policies targeted at increasing community safety while also creating new forms of community policing (Crawford 2002). In the past seven years, New Labour have developed a range of policies for local councils and the police that aim to provide an environment of tackling anti-social behaviour and creating zero tolerance in communities. These include:

- Child curfews. In 2001, the government introduced powers for local authorities and the police to run and enforce child curfews for all children under the age of 15 in an identified community or neighbourhood.

- Dispersal orders. In 2003, the government gave powers to local police to disperse groups of two or more people where their presence or behaviour has resulted, or was likely to result, in a member of the public being harassed, intimidated, alarmed or distressed. No offence has to be committed, but refusing to comply will result in an offence. Between 2004 and 2006, over 1,000 areas were designated as such across England and Scotland.
- Fixed penalties for wide range of low-level crimes, i.e. fly posting/graffiti and litter were created in 2003. Also new powers to fine perpetrators of such crimes given to community wardens, private security guards and community safety officers, as well as the police.
- Powers to confiscate noisy stereos and TVs and for local authorities to close noisy pubs and clubs.
- Begging becomes a recordable offence.
- Ban on selling spray paint to under-16s and restrictions on selling replica guns and air rifles to young people.
- Media allowed to name and shame 'anti-social children'.

How effective these approaches are to tackling anti-social behaviour remains unknown.

## Anti-Social Behaviour Orders (ASBOs)

At the heart of New Labour's crime reduction plans for tackling anti-social behaviour have been Anti-Social Behaviour Orders (ASBOs). This new power was created under the 1998 Crime and Disorder Act and is seen as blurring the boundaries between civil and criminal law. The local authority or police can give the ASBO to anyone over the age of 10 who is thought to be causing alarm, distress and harassment. It is not issued through a criminal court but by a civil procedure. At present, it lasts for a minimum of two years but can be imposed for longer periods of time. Breaking the ASBO can lead to up to five years' imprisonment and the standard of proof required for giving a person an ASBO in the first place is less than in a criminal offence. This gives substantial powers to the police, housing offices and other local authority agencies. ASBOs are not concerned with causes of crime but with managing individual behaviour. They can also represent the interests and voices of the most powerful within community settings (Brown 2004), allowing community representatives to decide what happens to young people who are defined as a problem. Recent research suggests that over 4,000 ASBOs have been issued by local authorities and, of these, a third are breached and two-thirds result in jail sentences (Youth Justice Board 2005). This can increase the number of young people going to prison, although research shows that a number of those who breach their ASBOs are already at risk of being imprisoned (Home Office 2005). While such legislation provides a quick route into prison for some, it also creates the possibility for an increase in the number of young people who have low levels of anti-social behaviour being criminalized and pushed into the youth justice system (Muncie 2004).

## Early intervention and prevention

Tackling early onset of anti-social behaviour has also been a major policy initiative in the UK. Prevention has become a significant policy development where professionals are being required to identify those children and young people who are 'expressing' anti-social behaviour early in their personal and social development (France 2008). In the UK, this has seen new forms of social prevention practices being developed that target those identified as future problems early. For example, social programmes such as the On Track Early Intervention and Prevention Programme and the National Children's Fund both aimed to target families and individuals who were showing signs of anti-social behaviour and who might be future problems for the state (ibid.). Concerns over early signs of anti-social behaviour has also shaped the new support services for children, young people and families. In 2007, the Sure Start Programme became a central feature of everyday life for those families seen as being likely to rear anti-social, problem children. Targeting resources at early intervention and prevention has become a core strategy for national policy making. In the English youth justice and education system, similar developments have taken place. For example, assessment of levels of anti-social behaviour, such as truancy, nuisance activity, and mixing with other anti-social young people has been seen as indicators in identifying risky individuals, which then helps the state manage the youth problem of crime and disorder.

## Conclusion: anti-social behaviour and understandings of youth

There is little doubt that the emergence of anti-social behaviour as a core concern of policy-makers has increased the negative perceptions of young people as a problem. Media representations and national government's focus on youths 'causing trouble' on the streets and in their communities have been at the heart of how the young have been portrayed over the previous ten years (Muncie 2004). While it is hard to deny that there are problems in some communities and with certain families and their children, the majority of young people are fundamentally law-abiding and have little to do with anti-social behaviour. The evidence and theoretical base for this approach also remain problematic. Evidence of what being anti-social means and how it influences future behaviour remains contestable and it raises questions why, at a time when youth crime has been declining for over ten years, national government in the UK has given this so much attention. In fact, there remains significant worries that the UK is acting illegally by denying young people their rights through using civil legislation that leads to them either being denied the right to the use of public spaces and facilities or being criminalized when, and if, they break either dispersal or anti-social behaviour orders. In other words the 'new' crimes, as defined by the anti-social behaviour agenda, are increasing the ways that young people are being monitored and policed while also increasing their risks of being criminalized (France 2008). The danger here is that there are more pathways into criminality for young people The early intervention and prevention agenda also has problems in that it is built upon a static and dichotomous view that someone's behaviour in their early years will have a major impact in their youth. This does not recognize the dynamic nature of change that can and does take place in the child and youth stages of the life course or the contextual influences that can shape life trajectories (France and Homel 2006).

## References

Brown, A. P. (2004) 'Anti-social behaviour, crime control and social control', *Howard Journal*, 43: 203–11.

Burney, E. (2005) *Making People Behave: Anti-social Behaviour, Politics and Policy*, Cullompton, Devon: Willan Publishing.

Crawford, A. (2002) *Crime Prevention and Community Safety: Politics, Policies and Practices*, London: Longman.

Farrington, D. (1996) *Understanding and Preventing Youth Crime*, York: Joseph Rowntree Foundation.

France, A. (2007) *Understanding Youth in Late Modernity*, Maidenhead: Open University Press.

—— (2008) 'Risk analysis and the youth question', *Journal of Youth Studies*, 11: 1–15.

France, A. and Homel, R. (2006) 'Societal access routes and developmental pathways: putting social structure and young people's voice into the analysis of pathways into and out of crime', *Australian and New Zealand Journal of Criminology*, 39: 295–309.

Home Office (2005) *Defining and Measuring Anti-social Behaviour*, London: Home Office.

Millie, A., Jacobson, J., McDonald, E. and Hough, M. (2005) *Anti-social Behaviour Strategies: Finding a Balance*, Bristol: Policy Press.

Muncie, J. (2004) *Youth and Crime*, 4th edn, London: Sage.

Rutter, M., Giller, H. and Hagell, A. (1998) *Anti-Social Behaviour by Young People*, Cambridge: Cambridge University Press.

Sampson, R. and Raudenbush, S. (2001) *Disorder in Urban Neighbourhoods – Does It Lead to Crime?* Washington, DC: National Institute of Justice.

Skogen, W. (1990) *Disorder and Decline: Crime and Spiral of Decay in American Neighbourhoods*, New York: Free Press.

Squires, P. and Stephen, D. (2005) *Rougher Justice: Anti-social Behaviour and Young People*, Cullompton, Devon: Willan Publishing.

Wilson, J. Q. and Kelling, G. L. (1982) 'Broken windows: the police and neighborhood safety', *Atlantic Monthly*, 249: 29–38.

Youth Justice Board (2005) *Anti-Social Behaviour Report*, London: Youth Justice Board.

# 53

# Youth in a world of gangs

*John M. Hagedorn*

## Introduction

Gangs are a reality for youth in every corner of the globe. But while gang research has been largely concentrated in the United States and lately in Europe, the overwhelming majority of organized or semi-organized street youth hang out in the shanty towns, townships, barrios, and favelas of Africa, Latin America, and Asia. This vast number of gangs, street children, militias, crews, sets, cartels, child soldiers, and the like present a challenge to how we understand the problems of youth.

There are two different approaches to this challenge. The one favored by US and 'Euro-gang' criminologists applies a formal definition of a 'gang' to the youth they study. This deductive, mainly structural approach is largely concerned with adolescent criminal behavior and how to strengthen methods of social control by the state or civil society. In the past decade, a comparative focus has been in fashion, but restricted almost solely to studying youth groups in western countries.

Another approach casts a more global net. Rather than trying to fit a group of youth into a western-based definition, this inductive, more cultural perspective examines a variety of street-socialized youth groups as well as their identities of resistance. This approach includes in its vista western-style gangs, but also considers other types of youth groups as well as conventional and unconventional organizations that often recruit them. Thus 'gangs' are described on a continuum of youthful non-state actors with potential for social change as well as violence and threats to order (Hagedorn 2008).

## Western gang research

The formal sociological study of gangs had its origins in Chicago nearly a century ago. Conceptualized as by-products of urbanization, immigration, and industrialization, gangs formed spontaneously in the 'interstices' of Chicago's rapidly changing neighborhoods. Frederic Thrasher, the 'father' of gang research, defined a gang based on the process of how it emerged from an adolescent play-group.

The gang is an interstitial group originally formed spontaneously, and then integrated through conflict. It is characterized by the following types of behavior: meeting face to face, milling, movement through space as a unit, conflict, and planning. The result of this collective behavior is the development of tradition, unreflective internal structure, esprit de corps, solidarity, morale, group awareness, and attachment to a local territory.

(Thrasher 1927: 57)

Thrasher looked at how adolescent gangs were sometimes manipulated by politicians, and remarked how a few evolved into adult criminal gangs. But his research focused on the *adolescent* peer group, and transitions of gangs to conventional and unconventional adult organizations were minimized. Ironically, Thrasher's research took place during Prohibition in the 1920s, but the young adult crews of Al Capone and Bugsy Moran went almost unnoticed in his book, *The Gang*.

In keeping with the reform-oriented outlook of the 'Chicago School' of sociology, gangs were seen as fundamentally transitory, unsupervised peer groups, fated to disappear as youth matured into adulthood as their ethnic group assimilated. Race and ethnicity were downplayed, since crime rates, according to the research of Chicagoans Shaw and McKay (1943), were stable over time in a specific 'slum' even as one immigrant group replaced another. Thus, the Chicago sociologists pointed out, gangs and criminal behavior were not the psychological or cultural property of a particular ethnic group, but of specific urban spaces. Girls were almost completely ignored.

The sociological concern with group process was continued with William F. Whyte's (1943) study of corner groups in a Depression-era Italian neighborhood of Boston. Whyte's study described the organized nature of the 'slum', contradicting the Chicago School concept of 'social disorganization'. Whyte also examined the ties of corner groups to a variety of legitimate and illegitimate adult organizations. His 'corner boys' were in fact young adults not adolescents.

One set of 1950s and 1960s research began to examine American youth and their gangs with less attention to specific neighborhood context. The universal definitions proposed by this group, including Walter Miller (1958), Lewis Yablonsky (1966), and later Malcolm Klein (1995) conceptualize 'the gang' as a specific form, distinct from other youth groups. In a break with the Chicago School, these definitions included criminal behavior. Miller and Yablonsky took this orientation further by looking for stable cultural traits of gangs. For Yablonsky, the gang was a 'near-group' that was by nature violent. For Miller, gangs were the product of a lower-class, ethnically neutral culture with 'focal concerns' of 'trouble, smartness, excitement, fate, and autonomy'.

This inclusion of anti-social behavior and criminality as a defining characteristic of 'the gang' did not go unchallenged in the turbulent 1960s. Richard Cloward and Lloyd Ohlin (1960) related variation in 'neighborhood opportunity structures' to gang behavior and Jim Short and Fred Strodtbeck (1965) empirically upheld the Chicago tradition of defining gangs through their processes of development. Joan Moore's (1978) research was also in the group process tradition, but, importantly, Moore conceptualized East Los Angeles gangs in the context of the history of their barrios and structures of institutional racism. Moore also included girls and women in her study, and followed up her 1970s data by returning to East Los Angeles a generation later to track how the barrio and its gangs had changed (Moore 1991).

At the end of the 1960s, most US gangs were Latino and African American, and responses to gangs were becoming more punitive. By the late 1980s and 1990s, gang research was being conducted within a context of deindustrialization, following the paradigm of William Julius Wilson with a growing concern for how joblessness and mass incarceration affected the life chances of black and Latino youth. This turn was sparked by my own research on Milwaukee gangs and by Carl Taylor (1989) in Detroit, Diego Vigil in Los Angeles, and later several researchers in St. Louis.

Still most studies were of male gangs in a single-city. An older British tradition of youth subcultures paralleled American gang research. Some specialized research has been devoted to transnational organized crime, but this topic has been compartmentalized and has remained separate from the study of 'youth gangs'. By the century's end in several European countries, gangs or 'troublesome youth groups' began to attract the attention of researchers, including Malcolm Klein of the United States. Klein *et al.* (2001) initiated a 'Euro-gang' research agenda that confronted the 'paradox' that while European gangs were not like the media stereotype of US gangs, US gangs didn't fit those stereotypes either. Klein thus sought to debunk journalistic, sensationalist descriptions of gangs and foreground his long-standing hybrid group process/criminalized definition. The Euro-gang researchers adopted a consensus form of Klein's definition as the basis for investigating European 'gangs' (Decker *et al.* 2005).

> [Gangs are] any durable, street-oriented youth group whose involvement in illegal activity is part of their group identity.

This definition, Klein pointed out, excluded a host of criminal, nationalist, prison, and other groups that alienated youth might join in their transition from adolescence. Comparative studies of gangs in advanced western countries sought to apply this definition and devise programs and law enforcement tactics to best address what was seen as a growing 'gang problem'.

## A world of gangs

Klein *et al.*'s (2001) definition-based approach intentionally excludes the group experiences of millions of poor youth, particularly in Africa, Latin America, and Asia that do not rigidly conform to western definitions of 'the gang'. We have no reliable estimates of the numbers of these diverse street-oriented groups. Much of the research on this topic can be found as studies of 'street children', 'children in organized armed violence', or post-conflict youth groups, not gangs.

Today, urbanization, poverty, and ethnic conflict provide ideal conditions for the growth of 'gangs' and similar youth groups. According to the UN Population Fund (2005)

- Today's generation of young people is the largest in history. Nearly half of the world's population (almost 3 billion people) is under the age of 25.
- Over 500 million youth live on less than US $2 per day. Some 238 million, or 22.5 per cent of the world's youth live in extreme poverty, on less than US $1 per day.
- About 85 per cent of the world's youth live in developing countries. Asia alone is home to 70 per cent of the developing world's young people.
- The poorest, least developed countries tend to have the largest shares of young people as a proportion of their populations.

These are startling figures. For example, in Nigeria alone, 'youth' defined in the more extensive African manner, number more than 100 million. Youth make up 60 per cent of the population of El Salvador. Manuel Castells (2004) argues that conditions of economic polarization and social exclusion have created a devastated 'Fourth World' in cities around the globe, including the ghettoes of the United States. These dismal conditions, some African researchers argue, have created 'monsters' and all sorts of armed groups eager to recruit desperately poor young people to add to their ranks.

Starting more from literatures on armed conflict, a diverse set of researchers have begun to look at the situation of 'children in organized armed violence'. A comparative ten-nation study, *Neither War nor Peace* (Dowdney 2005), applied the child soldiers literature to youth in non-civil war conditions in Rio de Janiero, Cape Town, Port au Prince, Chicago and elsewhere. In the Third World, the decline of the state has meant the erosion of social benefits coupled with policies of repression, in Latin America called 'mano dura'. The legacies of civil war, ethnic and tribal inequalities, liberation struggles, displacement and forced immigration, drug trafficking, and the vast underground economy, have created conditions for the decades-long persistence of groups of armed young men and, infrequently, women. These armed groups play important roles for youth as they are growing up in ghettoes, favelas, barrios, shanty towns, and townships. Luke Dowdney (2003) was instrumental in both the study of drug factions in Rio de Janiero, and in persuading the United Nations to expand its focus on child soldiers to the conditions of youth in cities with no official state of war.

In cities as diverse as Rio de Janiero, Chicago, Los Angeles, Kingston, and Cape Town, specific gangs have persisted for more than 50 years. Like other 'institutions ' in the organizational literature, they adapt to new conditions and change in order to survive. In neighborhoods where these institutionalized gangs thrive, youth have an ever-present 'opportunity structure' for employment, security, and solidarity. While not all cities have developed institutionalized gangs, the seeds of such lasting forms are being sown even in European cities like London and Paris where large non-white, unassimilated ethnic groups reside. In countries where incarceration is a common solution to the gang problem, the prison becomes part of the cycle of institutionalization and a further training ground for young men in the organization and culture of the gang.

But institutionalized gangs are not the only kind of young adult organization eager to recruit youth. In Medillín, for example, the drug cartels, revolutionary guerrillas, and right-wing militia all compete for the allegiance of thousands of youth gang members. Interestingly, in Colombia, unlike most other countries, the armed groups are open to females as well as males. In most countries, armed groups are symbolic of traditional notions of masculinity or hyper-masculinity, and in some countries like South Africa, rape is not an uncommon gang-related behavior. Gang activity for females most everywhere is still mainly an adolescent phenomenon, and still typically overlooked (Chesney-Lind and Hagedorn 1999).

Post-conflict societies often are the site for the persistence of armed groups who provide illicit opportunities for youth. The demobilization of armed groups after a civil war creates chaos since formal labor markets are seldom able to provide sufficient jobs and schools are inadequate, if they exist at all. This leaves the door open to armed groups participating in the underground economy. For youth growing up in desperate conditions, such armed groups become a viable, immediate option.

A survey of post-conflict literatures, as well as historical US gang studies, also reveals substantial, if intermittent, political involvement of gangs and other armed groups. Western criminology has largely dismissed the potential of gangs to enter politics, but in fact there has been a long tradition of such behavior, traced back to the 'Gangs of New York' of Asbury's fame and the recent popular movie of the same name. Gangs, the underground economy, and politics have always gone together in American cities.

In the 1960s, powerful social movements drew gangs into nationalist politics in the USA, Brazil, South Africa, New Zealand, and other countries. A more recent relationship between politics and gangs has been demonstrated in Brotherton and Barrios's (2003) study of the Latin King and Queen Nation in 1990s New York. A demoralized rejection of politics for criminality also can be seen in the emergence of *maras* (gangs) in Guatemala, El Salvador, and Honduras as civil war wanes and in the underground activities of some Protestant militias in Northern Ireland after the Easter Accords.

Western gang research has consciously chosen to exclude this broader study of youth and their organizations in its definitional approach. A positivist methodology of fitting a youth group into a strict, criminalized definition has advantages for law enforcement but reifies youth groups into set forms that exclude or downplay youth's potential to become agents for social change.

## The power of identity

How can any review of youth be complete without considering culture, and above all today, the lure of hip hop and 'gangsta rap'? Hip hop is a world-wide youth culture, with raps resounding from Cape Town to Rio, to London, Cairo, Hong Kong, and back to its origins in the South Bronx. Those who study the culture of youth have largely been separate from the more structural, social control-oriented 'gang research'.

This is even more problematic, given the origins of hip hop in gang culture. Afrika Bambaataa, one of hip hop's South Bronx founders, was a warlord in one of the largest New York gangs of the 1960s, the Black Spades. Bambaataa left gang life, and with Kool Herc developed a music of the streets aimed to lure youth away from gangs and violence. In the late 1980s, hip hop was discovered by corporate America and its 'message'- turned on its head with the promotion of a violent, misogynist 'gangsta rap' celebrating the gang lifestyle and bringing mega-profits to media corporations.

Thus today on the streets, life imitates art imitating life: street gangsters mimic the gold-chained, women-adorned, chauffeured image of studio gangsters who are rapping their stereotyped rhymes of violence purporting to represent the streets. Cornel West (1993) has been among those who have looked carefully at the world of gangsta rap, and sharply criticized its values, but also contrasted it to a deeper, more historic understanding of hip hop culture.

Hip hop can be an expression of nihilism, but is also a response to it. Hip hop culture expresses an existential staring into the void, seeing the intractability of bleak conditions and the permanence of racism, yet refusing to yield. It is a culture of agency for youth, incorporating frustration and anger and providing a cultural outlet. As Grandmaster Flash rapped in the early days:

> Don't ... push ... me ... I'm ... close ... to ... the ... edge. I'm ... trying ... not ... to ... lose ... my ... head. It's like a jungle sometimes I wonder how I keep from going under.

Hip hop has become the predominant youth culture around the world as young people, following the lead of Afrika Bambaataa, look for cultural alternatives to a world of gangs. Hip hop is also a 'Black Atlantic' culture, to borrow from Paul Gilroy (1993). It is a global pastiche of black cultural responses to racial oppression. While the 'gangsta' persona is a marriage of nihilism and consumerism, the ongoing struggle within street culture refuses to die out. Many youth link their oppositional cultural identity to social movements for change and perform in neighborhood clubs, barbershops, and corner gatherings in US ghettoes and in youth spaces around the world.

This strand of cultural analysis has been almost totally lacking among gang researchers. Culture, for classic gang research, was experienced mainly as a 'lack', of the weakening bonds of traditional culture in a modern, industrializing world. Second-generation immigrant youth in the United States were the proto-typical gang members, experiencing a culture clash of Americanization with old world traditions. The forging of stronger social controls in the city was the preferred solution for social disorganization theorists from Robert Park to William Julius Wilson.

But immigration today differs from the industrial-era 1920s. The UN estimates the world today has more than 175 million immigrants, and even in the USA, the foreign-born population is approaching record levels. The world's workforce has been globalized, but the notion of simple assimilation to host countries is no longer a given. Thus many Turks in Germany, Maghreb Muslims in France, and Mexicans in the United States maintain close connections with their home countries and their cultural traditions whether or not they intend to return.

Gangs may become 'Americanized' through gangsta rap and assimilated to western societies, but also may take pride in an ethnic, 'resistance identity'. The banlieux uprisings in Paris of Muslim youth and their gangs were a prime example of this contradiction. The spread of American gangs, like Calle 18, Mara Salvatrucha, and the Latin Kings is a predicable consequence of US interventionist policies, deportations, and transnational immigration flows.

Manuel Castells (2004) is among those who analyze the nihilism of the ghetto and its gangs as a component of a larger cultural phenomenon. As the world spins of out control with flows of capital deciding the fate of nations, displacing millions, and diffusing a homogenizing global culture enforcing the conformity of consumption, many people rebel and retreat into local identities. These identities are often racialized and stress local territory or religion. As racial, tribal, ethnic, or religious minorities are marginalized, cultural reactions set in, what Castells calls 'the exclusion of the excluders by the excluded'.

While themes of cultural reproduction and resistance have been examined in the subculture literatures in Britain as well as the United States, most western gang research has turned away from a cultural orientation. The restriction of 'gang identity' to criminal behavior freezes youth in only one aspect of their lives. The struggle of youth to define their lives through their music, ethnicity, religion, or heritage is not seen as especially important for western gang research. For example, there are few studies of the struggles of female gang members to reconcile traditional gender roles with other realities of racism and oppression. Adolescent gang girls might be said to be 'fighting female' as Mary Devitt and I put in a study of Milwaukee female gangs. The girls we studied loved to fight their rivals, but were also fighting a restrictive gender role. One reason for the nearly universal falling off of gang membership by adult females, is that the identity of 'mother' competes with street identities in ways that 'father' does not.

# The future of gang research

It can be argued that one problem with western criminology is *myopia*, or 'the inability to see distant objects as clearly as near objects'. This is an all too human trait as well as a common disease in empirical research. In this era of globalization, myopia is especially vexing but eminently treatable. Among the social sciences, criminology has been slow to embed globalization in its research, and the study of gangs is still dominated by American concepts and US-trained social scientists. The Euro-gang research agenda can be seen as a small step toward a broader, transnational, comparative study of gangs, but not without its drawbacks.

It must be admitted that the definition-based approach to the study of gangs is useful in narrowing academic and public focus on gangs as a specific kind of problem within communities. In this approach, the multiple, conflicting identities of youth are downplayed in a search for 'the gang' and statistical comparisons of 'gang vs. non-gang' activity in order to zero in on a specific type of social problem. The alternative method that prioritizes identity focuses on race, religion, ethnicity, and gender and how these master identities influence street youth. It also examines how youth and their organizations can move from one identity to another and may become part of the solution, not just a part of the problem.

The definition-based approach of Euro-gang research has settled on an American-based criminalized conception of gangs. It is difficult to see how such an approach can be helpful in understanding the dizzying variety of youth groups around the world and the diverse outcomes of their lives. Looking to categorize a specific group as 'a true street gang' may fit western criminologists' theoretical concepts, but also excludes most of the forms of youth organization in the world from the attention of criminology.

It could be that western and especially American criminologists have something to learn from researchers looking at youth in post-conflict societies, at 'children in organized armed violence', street children, and at other forms of youth groups. The volatility of these groups, their members' multiple, conflicting identities, and their capacity to change challenges those who want to build walls around a specific kind of youth group, i.e. 'the gang'. It questions those who see 'the gang' as a qualitatively different entity from other kinds of youth groups. If the nature of youth is to change, might change also characterize their groups or 'gangs' in Lagos as well as Berlin or New York City?

This means that the array of institutionalized young adult groups that persist in so many cities around the world should also be a major focus of 'gang' research. Organizations of armed young men provide an opportunity structure for marginalized youth in thousands of cities around the globe. As we say in Chicago, 'the gang is always hiring'. In the no-exit ghettoes, favelas, townships, and barrios of the world, semi-permanent armed groups reproduce youth gangs who are not likely to go away soon, no matter what we do. More and more cities are beginning to see the institutionalization of gangs or the persistence of many types of armed groups. The realistic choices of many poor youth for survival, identity, and support now include joining the world of gangs.

This scenario may not be as bleak as it seems. Youth culture may have been channeled by 'corporate hip hip' into consumerism, misogyny, and violence, but it is also a culture of resistance. The gangs of 'gangsta rap' are only one identity of young people, and hip hop culture is a maze of contradictions and contested meanings. The 'gangsta' persona tells youth to keep 'your mind on their money and your money on your mind' but youth have more on their minds than money. Youth have always been the leading force in social movements and their resistance today, no matter how often misdirected, may signal a new era of hope. Unfortunately, it also is true that their message of rebellion may not be understood by an older generation deafened by the hard core beats of youth's music and unwilling to open ears, eyes, and minds to new ideas.

Social change today, as always, is bound up with the actions of youth. What may be crucial is whether the hundreds of millions of marginalized youth, and their gangs, will be included or excluded from emerging social movements.

## References

Brotherton, D. and Barrios, L. (2003) *Between Black and Gold: The Street Politics of the Almighty Latin King and Queen Nation*, New York: Columbia University Press.

Castells, M. (2004) *The Information Age: Economy, Society and Culture*, vol. II: *The Power of Identity*, 2nd edn, Malden, MA: Blackwell.

Chesney-Lind, M. and Hagedorn, J. M. (eds) (1999) *Female Gangs in America: Essays on Girls, Gangs, and Gender*, Chicago: Lakeview Press.

Cloward, R. and Ohlin, L. (1960) *Delinquency and Opportunity*, Glencoe, IL: Free Press.

Decker, S. H., Scott, H. and Weerman, F. M. (eds) (2005) *European Street Gangs and Troublesome Youth Groups*, New York: AltaMira.

Dowdney, L. (2003) *Children of the Drug Trade; A Case Study of Children in Organised Armed Violence in Rio de Janeiro*, Rio de Janeiro: 7Letras.

—— (ed.) (2005) *Neither War nor Peace: International Comparisons of Children and Youth in Organised Armed Violence*, Rio de Janeiro: 7Letras.

Gilroy, P. (1993) *The Black Atlantic: Modernity and Double Consciousness*, Cambridge, MA: Harvard University Press.

Hagedorn, J. M. (1998) *People and Folks: Gangs, Crime, and the Underclass in a Rustbelt City*, 2nd edn, Chicago: Lakeview Press.

—— (2008) *A World of Gangs: Armed Young Men and Gangsta Culture*. Minneapolis: University of Minnesota Press.

Hagedorn, J. M. and Devitt, M. L. (1999) 'Fighting female: the social construction of the female gang', in M. Chesney-Lind and J. M. Hagedorn (eds) *Female Gangs in America: Essays on Girls, Gangs, and Gender*, Chicago: Lakeview Press.

Klein, M. (1995) *The American Street Gang*, Oxford: Oxford University Press.

Klein, M., Kerner, H., Maxsen, C. and Weitekamp, E. G. M. (eds) (2001) *The Eurogang Paradox: Street Gangs and Youth Groups in the U.S. and Europe*, Dordrecht: Kluwer.

Miller, W. (1958) 'Lower class culture as a generating milieu of gang delinquency', *Journal of Social Issues*, 14: 5–19.

Moore, J. W. (1978) *Homeboys: Gangs, Drugs, and Prison in the Barrios of Los Angeles*, Philadelphia, PA: Temple University Press.

—— (1991) *Going Down to the Barrio: Homeboys and Homegirls in Change*. Philadelphia, PA: Temple University Press.

Shaw, C. R. and McKay, H. D. (1943) *Juvenile Delinquency and Urban Areas*, Chicago: University of Chicago Press.

Short, J. F. and Strodtbeck, F.L. (1965) *Group Process and Gang Delinquency*, Chicago: University of Chicago Press.

Taylor, C. (1989) *Dangerous Society*, East Lansing, MI: Michigan State University Press.

Thrasher, F. (1927) *The Gang: A Study of 1313 Gangs in Chicago*, Chicago: University of Chicago Press.

United Nations (2005) 'Report on the World Social Situation', Washington, DC: UN Department of Social and Economic Affairs.

West, C. (1993) *Race Matters*. New York: Vintage.

Whyte, W. F (1943) *Street Corner Society*, Chicago: University of Chicago Press.

Yablonsky, Y. (1966) *The Violent Gang*, New York: The Macmillan Company.

# 54

# Young people, crime and justice

*Rob White*

## Introduction

Most juvenile justice systems deal predominantly with offenders from working-class backgrounds (including indigenous and ethnic minority people), and thereby reflect the class biases in definitions of social harm and crime, as well as basing responses on these biases (White and Cunneen 2006).

In so doing, they reinforce the ideological role of law and order discourse in forging a conservative cross-class consensus about the nature of social problems. The reinforcement of this discourse also unwittingly enhances the legitimacy of coercive state intervention in the lives of working-class people, even if under the rationale of 'repairing harm' as in the case of restorative justice. At a social structural level, such processes confirm the role of 'crime' as the central problem (rather than poverty, unemployment, racism), neglecting or avoiding entirely the roles of class division and social inequality.

This chapter provides a brief survey of key issues pertaining to juvenile justice in advanced capitalist countries such as Australia, the United Kingdom, the USA and Canada. Differences between a social control agenda, and a social empowerment agenda, are explored through consideration of two broad interrelated tendencies within juvenile justice. The first tendency is for criminal justice authorities to rely upon risk assessment as the preferred mode of understanding and intervening in young people's lives. The focus on the individual as potential threat or problem is reinforced by policy frameworks that stress the responsibility of young people for their own actions.

The countervailing tendency, however, acknowledges the limitations of the risk model, and provides a more sophisticated consideration of the interplay between structural conditions and subjective choices when it comes to youthful offending. This approach to intervention demands an active role on the part of the offender. This can take the form of repairing the harm associated with offending. It can also manifest in rehabilitation strategies that emphasize offender competencies and potentials. Before considering these different types of intervention within juvenile justice, however, it is important to set youth offending into social context.

## Young people and the crime problem

Unemployment, poverty and declining opportunities directly affect the physical and psychological well-being of young people. This is significant insofar as such social problems are entrenched at a spatial level, and are increasingly concentrated in specific locations within our cities. This is sometimes referred to as a process of ghettoization. The social costs of marginality are inevitably translated into the economic costs of crime.

The social costs of marginality are also transformed into behaviour that is officially defined as 'anti-social' and 'dangerous'. All of this is bound to have an impact on the self-image of marginalized young people and their efforts at self-defence in a hostile environment. The pooling of social resources and the construction of identities that are valued by others (if only one's peers) find expression in a range of cultural forms, including various youth subcultures and 'gang' formations (Hagedorn 2007; Cunneen and White 2007).

It is the poor who constitute the 'perishing classes' of today, those most vulnerable to hunger, desperation, demoralization and want. And, in many different national contexts, it is the 'ethnic' poor, especially, who constitute the 'dangerous classes' of the early twenty-first century. It is they who are frequently portrayed in the mass media as 'the enemy', 'them', the Other (see, for example, Poynting et al. 2004). The visible face of crime in our cities is that of street crime. It is also that of the ethnic minority. It is those people in positions of disadvantage, those who have been politically and socially marginalized, who are the key targets for media vilification and state intervention.

The criminalization industries of the state and the media reflect concern about the growing reality of subsistence criminality driven by an expanding layer of poor and unemployed which has emerged from global political-economic restructuring. Thus, a key site of contemporary class struggles is that of 'law and order'. On the one hand, deprived individuals, families and communities will organize their own means and forms of subsistence and enjoyment. They will especially do so under circumstances in which they are excluded from desirable areas in which to live and are separated from opportunities to find paid work. Moreover, even if work is there to be had, illegality may be far more rewarding, secure and satisfying as a source of income than the insecurities and exploitations of precarious employment in the formal sectors of the economy.

On the other hand, the ideological representation of the poor and deprived as an irresponsible 'underclass' is built into the policy apparatus of the state in relation to both welfare and criminal justice. Unemployment and any resistance to enforced participation in poor workplace situations are reduced to 'bad attitudes' and 'bad families'. The response therefore is to impose varying forms of mutual obligation on the poor – below poverty line benefits and inadequate services in return for work search obligations and the imposition of training and employment programmes. For those who do not play the game, there is exclusion from state support. For those who ignore the game and make a living through alternative means, there is state coercion – in the form of increased policing, harsher sentencing and greater use of imprisonment.

The crux of state intervention is how best to manage the problem of disadvantaged groups (their presence and activities), rather than to eradicate disadvantage – for to eradicate it would require action to reverse the polarizations in wealth and income, to pit the state directly in opposition to dominant class interests. That starting point for analysis of juvenile justice, therefore, is acknowledgement that it is the most disadvantaged and vulnerable young people who receive the most attention from justice officials at all levels of the system, from police through to detention centre staff (Cunneen and White 2007), a trend that tells us as much about the operation of the juvenile justice system as it does about the young offender. Hence, crime and delinquency are socially patterned: certain categories of young people are criminalized more than others and this is entirely related to social circumstance.

## Risk and responsibility

The social composition of young offenders is basically the same regardless of jurisdiction. Responses to youth offending is, however, a different matter. Comparative analysis of juvenile justice systems and processes indicate a number of global commonalities, as well as important national and regional differences in the perception and treatment of young people (Muncie and Goldson 2006). General trends include a winding back of welfare provision and greater focus on deeds rather than needs, adulteration in some jurisdictions where young people are increasingly formally being treated as adults, and re-penalization of many aspects of juvenile justice – including use of youth curfews, mandatory sentencing, zero tolerance policing, and the like – as well as detention, greater attention given to concepts and practices of restorative justice, and at least some acknowledgement of the importance of the UN Convention on the Rights of the Children in deliberations about juvenile justice.

As Muncie (2005) emphasizes, global processes of neo-liberalism are translated into a multiplicity of social forms with great variation, depending upon specific local contexts. How international trends are played out at the national and regional level is contingent upon a range of factors, not the least of which is local history and local sensibilities.

Having said this, there are two interrelated policy emphases – each of which confirms a social control orientation within juvenile justice – that are worthy of close attention. These can be described as the emphasis on risk and risk aversion, and the emphasis on responsibilization. Prediction of risk has emerged as one of the most far-reaching changes in theory and practice in relation to juvenile justice in many different jurisdictions. Indeed, the concepts of risk (risk factors, risk assessment, risk prediction, risk management) permeate juvenile justice systems.

There are at least four different ways that the concept and measurement of risk are used in juvenile justice (Cunneen and White 2006: 102–3):

- in the context of risk and protective factors associated with offending behaviour;
- as an assessment tool for access to programmes for young people under supervision or serving a custodial sentence;
- as a classification tool for young people in custody to determine their security ratings;
- as a generic measure for activating legal intervention (for example, 'three-strikes' mandatory imprisonment).

When combined with government attempts to get tough on crime, especially when it relates to juvenile offenders, the emphasis on risk can open the door to highly punitive and highly intrusive measures.

The conceptual perspective that is often used to frame 'youth' and youthful 'deviance' is the 'risk factor' paradigm (Farrington 1994). This generally involves the charting of specific risk and protective factors that are seen to influence how individuals negotiate

446

particular transitions and pathways in their lives. Multi-factoral analysis of specific factors is statistically correlated with certain types of behaviour and certain types of people. The implication is that if certain factors are added up, there will be a predictable certainty that deviancy (or pathology) will result.

This kind of risk assessment is finding increasing favour in the juvenile justice field (MacDonald 2006; Muncie and Goldson 2006; Case 2007). It is not simply being used as a diagnostic tool (i.e., to pinpoint a person's specific needs and deficits), but also in a prognostic manner, to determine which young people are most likely to offend. Specific profiles of young people are constructed whereby all young people within a certain range of empirical indicators (e.g., age group, school record, type of family, previous criminal record) are dealt with according to the risk that they (presumably) pose now and into the future.

By their very nature, these kinds of risk assessment tools fail to capture the historical dynamics of societies. The tools reinterpret certain characteristics as representing the failings of individuals. This is because they are constructed on the basis of individualized data, rather than analysis of, for example, how state policy affects particular groups. The formation of specific kinds of groups and specific kinds of individuals, as the outcome of inequality, discrimination and the absence of opportunity, is basically lost in such analysis (Cunneen and White 2006). In its stead, it is the consequences of these processes that are central to who is or who is not deemed to be at risk.

For example, the combination of poverty, poor parenting, bad schooling and unemployment (as measured on pre-determined scales) might be said to equate to deviant behaviour (as defined in conventional criminal justice terms). Such calculations are then used to 'read back' into the life circumstances of certain individuals the probable trajectory that they will take. Interventions can then be organized even before the risk has actually been realized in practice. The paradoxical element of this process is that the 'at risk' come to be stigmatized, adding to their sense of difference and marginality (White and Wyn 2008). Moreover, the phenomenon of 'false positives' means that individuals may suffer the negative consequences of unwanted and unneeded intervention solely due to their membership of a 'high risk' group rather than due to their individual risk profile or actual behaviour (see Case 2007).

In other words, the justification for intervention is based upon employment of a social categorization that precludes us thinking about the young person in any way except as deviant (even if expressed as 'at risk' rather than 'criminal' as such). This is essentially a question of social control.

It is somewhat ironic that while risk is constructed in relation to the notion of determinism (one's social background, for example, determines the likelihood of engaging in juvenile crime), the other leading concept underpinning juvenile justice puts the emphasis on voluntarism (the element of free will in human behaviour).

The notion of responsibilization has several interrelated components. According to Muncie (2004), these include:

- communities should take primary responsibility for crime;
- prevention: individuals should be held responsible for their own actions;
- families, in particular, parents, have a responsibility to ensure that their children do not develop anti-social tendencies.

A fundamental premise of responsibilization is that responsibility for safety and well-being is no longer in the hands of the (welfare) state, but rather has been transferred back to communities, families, and individuals. It is yet another aspect of individuation, the notion that it is up to the individual to make a life for themselves, to negotiate their own pathways through the economic and social structure, and to accept that life is basically a do-it-yourself kind of project.

With regards to juvenile justice, there has been a significant shift in recent years away from a welfare or treatment perspective and towards a justice or retributive view of young offenders. Young offenders are seen to be responsible for their own actions, and so must suffer their just deserts for any transgressions they have committed. The burden of responsibility basically falls on the individual to atone for or change their behaviour (Muncie 2004). As seen below, however, juvenile justice nevertheless still allows for rehabilitation and restorative justice modes of intervention as well.

A hybrid system that combines punitive features with reparation philosophies makes sense to the extent that it reflects the profile of young offenders. The serious and per-sistent offender – typically those young people from marginalized, disadvantaged and oppressed communities – is liable to be punished up to and including the use of deten-tion. The low-risk offender, however, is made to make amends for their wrongdoing by repairing the harm and perhaps making an apology. Meanwhile, the potential offender is dealt with through deployment of risk assessment technologies and ongoing surveillance in order to prevent future deviation. Varying means of social control and intervention do not preclude the possibility of adopting policies that simultaneously offer social empowerment possibilities.

## Restorative justice and rehabilitation

Restorative justice refers to an emphasis on dealing with offenders by repairing harm, and in so doing involving victims and communities as well as offenders in the reparation process. Restorative justice thus emphasizes re-integrative and developmental principles and offers the hope that opportunities will be enhanced for victims, offenders and their immediate communities, with the direct participation of all concerned in this process.

Depending upon the specific way in which restorative justice has been institutionalized within a particular jurisdiction – for example, through juvenile conferences, victim–offender mediation, circle sentencing or offender restitution schemes – the focus will generally be on specific events and people (Cunneen and White 2007). That is, it is usually the case that the idea of social harm is conceptualized in immediate, direct, and individualistic terms. One consequence of this is that the emphasis on repairing harm tends to be restricted to the immediate violations and immediate victim concerns, thereby ignoring communal objectives and collective needs in framing reparation pro-cesses (White 2003). Thus, the emphasis remains that of changing the offender, albeit with their involvement, rather than transforming communities and/or changing the conditions under which offending takes place.

In some practical circumstances, restorative justice may be effective in providing offen-ders with greater developmental opportunities, and in ensuring greater victim and com-munity satisfaction and engagement in criminal justice matters. The practices of restorative justice do indeed contain the seeds for creatively and constructively responding to the injustices of life suffered by most offenders (see, for example, Bazemore and Walgrave 1999). At the least, restorative justice implicitly offers recognition that families and communities have an important role to play in trying to grapple with the causal reasons for personal offending. In some exceptional cases, restorative justice also offers young people themselves a pivotal role in the justice process as decision-makers, as well as participating as offenders or victims.

In many cases there is an emphasis on active agency. This refers to the idea that young people are to be held directly accountable in some way, and that they are meant to do things, for themselves, rather than simply being passive actors in the criminal justice system. Importantly, when they engage in doing something (e.g., painting a fence), this is generally constructed as being to the benefit of somebody else (e.g., a victim of graffiti). Restorative justice thus involves acts of giving, as well as acts of forgiving. The offending act may be condemned, and respect for the offender maintained (Braithwaite 1989), but young offenders are nonetheless expected to repair the harms they have caused.

This aspect of restorative justice – the notion of actively giving of oneself – also features in other approaches to juvenile offending. Desistance theories, for instance, include both psychological and sociological emphases, and are concerned with those processes (and outcomes) whereby young people desist or stop from offending. For example, Barry (2006) examines youth offending from the point of view of diverse forms of social, cultural, economic and symbolic capital. She argues that it is not just the accumulation of capital that preoccupies young people, but also its expenditure. In discussing why young people persist or desist in offending behaviour and activities, Barry (2006) argues that achieving social recognition is vital for young people to gain a sense of achievement and social belonging as they move through the childhood and teenage years.

The family of origin and one's local community provide the platform upon which capital accumulation grows and develops. But it is the expenditure of accumulated capital that brings the rewards of individual gratification and social stability. Examples of this include such things as buying your own clothes, engaging in volunteer work, and generally encouraging and helping others. Social recognition and self-esteem, generally, are built through expenditure of capital (doing something for oneself and for someone else). If this is so, then it also ought to be an important component in the development of juvenile justice intervention strategy.

Such thinking is also mirrored in the concepts underpinning the 'good lives' model of rehabilitation (Ward and Maruna 2007). This model argues that we need to go beyond a simple 'risks' framework for dealing with offenders. Rather, it is important to focus on promoting human goods (that is, providing the offender with the essential ingredients for a 'good' life). Again, the emphasis is on active engagement, and on those human characteristics (e.g., needs such as autonomy, relatedness, competence) that offenders share with the rest of the population. Rehabilitation is thus construed as being mainly about capacity building rather than personal deficits.

Rehabilitation is meant to involve the offender in a process of enhancement and empowerment, focused on the goal of achieving a good life. The point of such intervention is to achieve a result whereby the offender will be seen as a community asset rather than a liability or in need of stringent supervision.

The capacity or capability aspect of rehabilitation directly involves providing individuals with the internal and external conditions necessary to attain valued outcomes in ways that match their abilities, preferences and environments. Internal conditions refer to psychological characteristics such as skills, beliefs and attitudes, while external conditions refer to social resources, opportunities and supports.

(ibid.: 174)

Hence the goal of rehabilitation within this framework is to display the talents and skills of the offender in a useful and visible role, giving the person individual agency.

Both the 'social recognition' theory of Barry (2006) and the 'good lives' perspective of Ward and Maruna (2007) acknowledge the dynamic interplay of structure and agency — of how personal choices and personal values are made and experienced within the confines of certain external material constraints. For young people especially, social intervention based upon these approaches has to take seriously the narrative accounts of the juvenile offenders themselves. They also have to address those internal and external factors that impinge upon young people's sense of self and their place in the world.

By focusing on self-empowerment and self-determination through capacity development, models of intervention based upon the notion of positive strengths operate on the assumption that increases in the positives will naturally result in decreases in the negatives, for example, desistance from offending.

## Social justice and community building

Since there are strong connections between community circumstances that give rise to street crime (such as economic marginalization), and the community relations that sustain them (such as ethnic identification), community processes are also most likely to provide the best opportunities for their transformation. Community-based approaches have a number of dimensions, that include both direct service provision and efforts to build non-oppressive relationships at the local level. Some are directed at youth specifically; others are designed as whole-of-community strategies that benefit people across the local area in a variety of ways.

Community-based approaches also include those that involve large-scale, and often non-youth-specific measures. Urban renewal projects and community empowerment programmes, for example, are meant to increase work opportunities and civic participation among local residents. Low neighbourhood attachment, economic deprivation and adversity, and low community organization are implicated in the constitution of crime-prone areas, so any solution will have to address these kinds of issues.

Community reputation, especially if accompanied by stigma associated with gangs, crime and anti-social activities, has a dramatic impact on life within particular locales. Young people who live in stigmatized areas are more likely than others who do not live there to suffer the negative consequences, in the form of reduced job opportunities and difficulties in moving out of the neighbourhood. A 'bad' community reputation may occasionally translate into a gang mentality based upon defensiveness and re-assertion of worth in the face of a hostile 'outside' world. Changing the community's reputation through communal development is one way in which to address these issues.

Community crime prevention is about getting people involved, voluntarily and enthusiastically, in doing things that they want to do. An example of youth-oriented strategy is the employment of detached youth and community workers to provide supervised recreation and leisure activities and after-school programmes. These workers go to where the young people are, and they intervene in a low-key supportive fashion that is founded upon trust and mutual respect. Youth and community detached work is most strategically effective when merged with wider community development types of interventions and citizen participation.

The development of pride in one's local area can be important in changing negative attitudes and anti-social behaviours into more positive, liberating directions. This requires conscious efforts to positively portray local areas and suburbs; for community and state agencies to work together to enhance opportunities through the use of strategic initiatives that involve citizens (such as creation of local sports teams); building pride and aspirations by emphasizing each person's strengths, capabilities and skills and allowing them to take responsibility to make their neighbourhood something to be proud of; and concerted efforts at physical renewal through projects such as tree planting, mural painting, landscaping of parks and shopping complexes, and painting of homes by tenants, and by initiatives such as establishment of a local garden club.

In the end, what is to be done about juvenile crime cannot be divorced from the kinds of values and society we wish to have and promote, as well as questions of 'what works' in specific situations. Community crime prevention strategies, for example, are preferable to strict law enforcement approaches insofar as they open the door to more socially inclusive ways of dealing with the crime problem. There is an intrinsic connection between criminal justice and social justice. Hence the ongoing tensions between social control and social empowerment agendas within juvenile justice will not disappear unless and until there is significant societal change.

# References

Barry, M. (2006) *Youth Offending in Transition: The Search for Social Recognition*, London: Routledge.

Bazemore, G. and Walgrave, L. (1999) 'Restorative juvenile justice: in search of fundamentals and an outline for systemic reform', in G. Bazemore and L. Walgrave (eds.) *Restorative Juvenile Justice: Repairing the Harm of Youth Crime*, Monsey, NY: Criminal Justice Press.

Braithwaite, J. (1989) *Crime, Shame and Reintegration*, Cambridge: Cambridge University Press.

Case, S. (2007) 'Questioning the "evidence" of risk that underpins evidence-led youth justice interventions', *Youth Justice: An International Journal*, 7: 91–106.

Cunneen, C. and White, R. (2006) 'Australia: control, containment or empowerment?', in J. Muncie and B. Goldson (eds) *Comparative Youth Justice*. London: Sage.

—— (2007) *Juvenile Justice: Youth and Crime in Australia*. Melbourne: Oxford University Press.

Farrington, D. (1994) 'Early developmental prevention of juvenile delinquency', *Criminal Behaviour and Mental Health*, 4: 209–27.

Hagedorn, J. (ed.) (2007) *Gangs in the Global City: Alternatives to Traditional Criminology*. Urbana, IL: University of Illinois Press.

MacDonald, R. (2006) 'Social exclusion, youth transitions and criminal careers: five critical reflections on "risk"', *Australian and New Zealand Journal of Criminology*, 39: 371–83.

Muncie, J. (2004) 'Youth justice: responsibilisation and rights', in J. Roche, S. Tucker, R. Thomson and R. Flynn (eds) *Youth in Society: Contemporary Theory, Policy and Practice*. London: Sage, in association with The Open University.

—— (2005) 'The globalization of crime control – the case of youth and juvenile justice: Neo-liberalism, policy convergence and international conventions', *Theoretical Criminology*, 9: 35–64.

Muncie, J. and Goldson, B. (eds) (2006) *Comparative Youth Justice*, London: Sage.

Poynting, S., Noble, G., Tabar, P. and Collins, J. (2004) *Bin Laden in the Suburbs: Criminalising the Arab Other*, Sydney: Sydney Institute of Criminology.

Ward, T. and Maruna, S. (2007) *Rehabilitation: Beyond the Risk Paradigm*. London: Routledge.

White, R. (2003) 'Communities, conferences and restorative social justice', *Criminal Justice*, 3: 139–60.

White, R. and Cunneen, C. (2006) 'Social class, youth crime and justice', in B. Goldson and J. Muncie (eds) *Youth Crime and Justice*, London: Sage.

White, R. and Wyn, J. (2008) *Youth and Society: Exploring the Social Dynamics of Youth Experience*, 2nd edn, Melbourne: Oxford University Press.

# 55

# Youth and punishment

*Angela Harvey and Aaron Kupchik*

## Introduction

The aim of this chapter is to examine the role of punishment for juveniles who are arrested for crimes, with a specific focus on the United States. We discuss how a contemporary understanding of youth and punishment is shaped by prior research on the origin and continuing legacy of the juvenile court, contemporary policies that serve to question legal distinctions between childhood and adulthood, and the future of research for juvenile court practices and policies. Due to the enormous variations in how young people are punished across nations, we focus only on American juvenile justice, though it is important to note that some of the trends we discuss have also been observed in other Western European nations as well (Tonry and Doob 2004).

## The rise of the American juvenile court

The initial development of the juvenile court in the late nineteenth century was based on the modern idea that children were vulnerable, innocent, and dependent beings whom parents needed to protect (see Ariès 1967). Moreover, the juvenile court was founded on the idea that the state could act in the child's best interest by providing rehabilitative services to address the environmental factors presumed to have brought them to the court in the first place (Rothman 1980; Feld 1999). This *parens patriae* philosophy of the juvenile court led to the practice of removing children (mostly poor, immigrant children) from their homes and placing them in Houses of Refuge, in order to teach them middle-class morality.

It is clear from the literature that the social welfare rhetoric justifying the development of the juvenile court was not implemented to alter the circumstances of youth who made poor decisions, but rather as an institutionalized form of control over lower-class, minority youth (Platt 1977; Rothman 1980; Feld 1999). For example, the dominance of middle-class and elite women in this 'moral crusade' ensured that the guiding philosophy of rehabilitation would be based on middle-class values of the home, family life, and supervision. The effect of this was to expand governmental control under the guiding principles of social welfare by inventing new categories of youthful misbehavior, specifically, behaviors that were primarily exhibited by lower-class and immigrant families (Platt 1977). For example, as Feld (1999) explains, only two years after the establishment of the first juvenile court in Cook County, Illinois, in 1899, reformers broadened their definition of delinquency to include incorrigible acts, which would not be considered criminal if committed by an adult, but rather, included things such as truancy or sexual immorality.

## The contemporary juvenile court

### Rehabilitation versus punishment

The juvenile court's guiding principle that young people's immaturity necessitates a rehabilitative approach has been challenged repeatedly. In the hundred years following the development of the first juvenile court, politicians and the general public have repeatedly made calls for harsher punishments for delinquents. To some extent, this is a result of increasing rates of juvenile violence in the 1960s, and the subsequent attack on the rehabilitative ideal that followed (Allen 1981). More recently, the societal perception of delinquency has changed as a result of being confronted with media portrayals of rising violent youth crime, primarily of homicides and gang activity, yet these types of crimes are the least common antisocial behaviors of teenagers (Kunkel 1994). Additionally, the U.S. Supreme Court helped to marginalize the rehabilitative role of the juvenile court by finding, in *In Re Gault* (1967), that the juvenile court does not operate from a purely rehabilitative model, thus requiring formal due process rights for young people.

These calls for punishment and reductions in a rehabilitative approach seem to have had a substantial effect. As we discuss below, over the past three decades, juvenile courts have incarcerated increasing numbers of youth and have vastly increased the numbers of young people who are defined as beyond the capacity of the juvenile court, and transferred to adult, criminal courts (Feld 1999). However, these shifts are often not as complete as they may at first appear; even when juvenile courts across the country have adopted formal, legal policies from a political perspective of being 'tough on crime', most juvenile courts still include a rehabilitative rationale as the model of practice (Feld 1999; Kupchik 2006; Harvey 2007).

On the other hand, it is clear from the research that juvenile court practices do not reflect rehabilitative ideals for certain groups of juveniles, since outcomes for juveniles vary based on race, ethnicity, gender, and class (for a review, see Zatz 2000). For example, the literature suggests that court actors' perceptions of accountability and amenability to treatment result in more punitive outcomes for poor, youths of color (for a review, see Engen *et al.* 2002). Even attempts to limit court actors' ability to hand out unequal punishment, through sentencing policies that address the offense rather than the offender, have not resulted in equal treatment of youth. This is partly because court actors' perceptual differences of accountability arise early in the juvenile justice process (e.g., arrest, the decision to prosecute) and thus shape subsequent case outcomes (Bishop and Frazier 1996; Harvey 2007).

In addition to race, ethnicity, and class, research indicates that court actors make use of defendants' gender for case-processing decisions. However, there are differences in the

453

literature regarding how court actors treat females depending on the court decision examined. For example, research that focuses on entry-point decisions such as arrest, competency to stand trial, and transfer to criminal court find that girls are afforded less leniency and treated more harshly than boys (Gaarder and Belknap 2002; Harvey 2007). On the other hand, research that examines incarceration decisions have mixed results; some find that males are more likely to be incarcerated than females (Kupchik and Harvey 2007), while other scholars find support for equal treatment of males and females once legal factors such as the defendant's prior record and severity of offense are considered (Steffensmeier *et al.* 1993). Although the results are mixed in terms of *how* gender is used for case-processing decisions, it is clear that court actors use gender as an attribute of blameworthiness that results in gendered outcomes (see also Gaarder *et al.* 2004).

Thus, though the US juvenile justice system was based on a rehabilitative approach, this approach has been challenged repeatedly and applied in different ways based on the gender, race/ethnicity, and class statuses of young people. In the following section, we discuss in greater detail contemporary policies that illustrate these trends.

## Contemporary juvenile court policies

Throughout the past 30 years, the USA and other Western nations have observed increasing calls for harsh punishment for criminal offenders, generally (Garland 2001); public and political responses to juvenile offenders have followed suit. As a result, a number of policy clusters have been implemented in juvenile courts throughout the USA that question the distinction between juvenile and adult offenders on which the initial juvenile court was predicated, and call for increasing penalties for young offenders. In the following section, we discuss three types of policies that embody these trends: transfer to the criminal court, competency to stand trial, and an increasing connection between formal juvenile justice systems and public schools.

The first of these three policy types, transfer to the criminal court, is a direct rejection of the philosophy that guided the initial juvenile court: that young people are fundamentally different than adults and need different responses to their offenses (i.e., interventions, treatments, and punishments) than adults. Transfer policies have spread rapidly throughout the USA since the late 1970s. In a variety of ways, these laws mandate that certain young people below the age of 18 be removed from the juvenile court and prosecuted in criminal (adult) court instead. The ways that transfer works vary across states; some states' laws allow judges to decide who should be sent to criminal courts, others allow prosecutors to directly file cases in criminal rather than juvenile court, and other laws establish categories of offenses and offenders that are automatically excluded from juvenile court (e.g., 17 year-olds who are arrested for robbery). All available estimates suggest that the numbers of young people transferred to criminal court have expanded greatly over the past few decades as a result of these policy shifts (see Fagan and Zimring 2000).

These transfer policies are promoted as ways to provide appropriate responses to 'adult-like' juvenile offenders and to better protect the public. Unfortunately, the available evidence suggests that these transfer policies fail to achieve these goals. Though those transferred to criminal court are punished more severely than similar young people in the juvenile court (Fagan and Zimring 2000), several studies now find that re-arrest rates among those transferred are higher than those of similar young people who are prosecuted in juvenile court (see McGowan *et al.* 2007). Additionally, research suggests that these policies disproportionately transfer poor, youth of color to criminal courts (Bortner *et al.* 2000). Moreover, other evidence suggests that criminal court judges, prosecutors and defense attorneys who deal with those transferred often divert from normal criminal court process to incorporate practices usually found in juvenile court, as they informally attempt to undo much of what these transfer laws mandate (Kupchik 2006). The single clearest achievement of transfer laws is that they symbolize the public's demand for punishments for juvenile offenders and a dissatisfaction with a juvenile court perceived as failing to protect the public from young predators. Importantly, this declaration of adult-style punishment for young people comes at a time when a growing body of evidence is illustrating clear physiological distinctions between cognitive capacities of adolescents and adults (see Grisso and Schwartz 2000)

The second policy type that we discuss here, competency to stand trial (CST), is an important indicator of changes in punishing young people, but for different reasons. This policy shift represents a further departure from the ideals that gave rise to the initial juvenile court. A number of states have begun to evaluate whether adolescents are sufficiently mature and competent to be formally tried for their offenses. This is an ironic policy shift, given that the juvenile court was created over 100 years ago because its founders believed that there needed to be a court for dealing with offenders who were not competent, due to their youthfulness. By considering young people's competency to stand trial, juvenile courts are asserting greater formality in case processing by suggesting juveniles must be autonomous actors capable of defense strategizing, a direct contradiction to the court's founding *parens patriae* philosophy.

Since CST is a relatively new policy consideration (most states did not address juvenile CST until the late 1990s), it is unclear how competency cases are selected and how this process affects juveniles' ultimate case outcomes. It seems safe to assume that since CST determinations occur at the beginning of juveniles' cases, being subjected to this review is likely to influence court actors' future decision-points such as disposition (see Bishop and Frazier 1996). Indeed, in a recent study, Harvey (2007) finds that CST significantly influences case outcomes, as juveniles who receive the competency defense receive more lenient punishments than those not afforded this process. However, among young people subjected to CST processes, those who are found incompetent to stand trial receive harsher punishments than those found competent to stand trial. This may be because prosecutors use plea bargains to subvert the CST process for fear that these juveniles will have their charges dismissed because of incompetence and so, when juveniles refuse to accept the plea, prosecutors argue for harsher penalties. The effects of CST in juvenile courts clearly illustrate the court's difficulties managing the role of youthfulness or immaturity in shaping punishments, since CST can serve as both a beneficial and detrimental defense strategy for juveniles' case outcomes.

In addition to changes in how juvenile courts deal with offenders, we also consider one way in which the pool of cases that reach the court has broadened: through tighter links between schools and formal juvenile justice institutions. During the past few decades in the USA – during which juvenile courts have increased punishments and transfer laws have spread – schools have also altered their approaches to surveillance and punishing young people. It is now common to find armed and uniformed police officers, surveillance cameras, and random searches by drug-sniffing dogs in schools. When students misbehave, they are more likely than in years past to be suspended or expelled, as many schools have adopted 'zero-tolerance' policies that mandate suspension or expulsion regardless of the severity of the particular act (Kupchik and Monahan 2006).

One potential effect of these policies is for more youth to be referred by schools to juvenile courts. Student misbehaviors that in years past would be dealt with only within the school may now be matters for courts to oversee. This means that young people who behave in normal (though harmful) ways (e.g., participating in a schoolyard fist–fight) are more likely than before to be stigmatized by criminal courts and excluded from school, both of which may decrease their future life opportunities (see Davies and Tanner 2003).

As these three policy clusters illustrate, there have been important changes over the past several years in how young people are officially punished. Those who misbehave are now more likely to be officially arrested and sent to court, are at greater risk of harsher punishment or of transfer to adult criminal court, and if they go to juvenile court, they face a more formal, punishment-oriented institution. These shifts suggest that calls for punishing youthful offenders have been heeded, and that the theoretical separation of juveniles and adults that gave rise to the initial juvenile court has been challenged in several ways.

## Future research agenda

Despite a great deal of research on this topic in recent years, there is much more we need to know. As the number of juvenile court and school policies that call for greater punishment continues to grow, the research community needs to continue to understand the theoretical and practical causes and consequences of these policies. For example, since young people who are transferred to juvenile courts by prosecutors or categorically excluded from the juvenile court are considered adults from their initial court involvement, they are not represented in counts of transferred youth. As a result, we have only estimates (but no actual counts) of how many individuals under the age of 18 are prosecuted as if they were adults; this is an important issue that should be resolved.

What we do know from the empirical literature and policies discussed in this chapter is that juvenile courts across the USA need to formally examine how the discretionary powers available in this context can be managed more effectively. Even among federal mandates to address minority over-representation in the juvenile justice system, contemporary research clearly suggests there has not been enough attention given to these issues. There is also sufficient research demonstrating the negative effects of transferring young people to criminal courts for policy-makers to reexamine the effectiveness of transfer laws. It is evident that the juvenile court does a better job than the criminal court at achieving the ultimate goal of reducing recidivism (see McGowan *et al.* 2007). However, the system must work harder at achieving the necessary balance of maintaining a system that addresses youths' individual needs, but is fair to *all* juvenile offenders, while still holding youth accountable for their misdeeds.

## References

Allen, F. (1981) *The Decline of the Rehabilitative Ideal: Penal Policy and Social Purpose*, New Haven, CT: Yale University Press.

Ariès, P. (1967) *Centuries of Childhood: A Social History of Family Life*, New York: Vintage Books.

Bishop, D. M. and Frazier, C. E. (1996) 'Race effects in juvenile justice decision-making: findings of a statewide analysis', *The Journal of Criminal Law and Criminology*, 86: 392–415.

Bortner, M. A., Zatz, M. S. and Hawkins, D. F. (2000) 'Race and transfer: empirical research and social context', in J. Fagan and F.E. Zimring (eds) *The Changing Borders of Juvenile Justice: Transfer of Adolescents to the Criminal Court*, Chicago: The University of Chicago Press.

Davies, S. and Tanner, J. (2003) 'The long arm of the law: effects of labeling on employment', *Sociological Quarterly*, 44: 385–404.

Engen, R. L., Steen, S. and Bridges, G. S. (2002) 'Racial disparities in the punishment of youth: a theoretical and empirical assessment of the literature', *Social Problems*, 49: 194–220.

Fagan, J. A. and Zimring, F. E. (2000) *The Changing Borders of Juvenile Justice: Transfer of Adolescents to the Criminal Court*, Chicago: University of Chicago Press.

Feld, B. (1999) *Bad Kids: Race and the Transformation of Juvenile Court*, New York: Oxford University Press.

Gaarder, E. and Belknap, J. (2002) 'Tenuous borders: girls transferred to adult court', *Criminology*, 40: 481–517.

Gaarder, E., Rodriguez, N. and Zatz, M. S. (2004) 'Criars, liars, and manipulators: probation officers' views of girls', *Justice Quarterly*, 21: 547–78.

Garland, D. (2001) *The Culture of Control: Crime and Social Order in Contemporary Society*, Chicago: University of Chicago Press.

Grisso, T. and Schwartz, R. G. (2000) *Youth on Trial: A Developmental Perspective on Juvenile justice*, Chicago: University of Chicago Press.

Harvey, A. (2007) '(De)constructing youthfulness in juvenile court: an analysis of competency to stand trial', unpublished doctoral dissertation, Arizona State University, Tempe.

Kunkel, D. (1994) *The News Media's Picture of Children*, Oakland, CA: Children Now.

Kupchik, A. (2006) *Judging Juveniles: Prosecuting Adolescents in Adult and Juvenile Courts*, New York: NYU Press.

Kupchik, A. and Harvey, A. (2007) 'Court context and discrimination: exploring biases across juvenile and criminal courts', *Sociological Perspectives*, 50: 417–44.

Kupchik, A. and Monahan, T. (2006) 'The new American school: preparation for post-industrial discipline', *British Journal of Sociology of Education*, 27: 617–31.

McGowan, A., Hahn, R., Liberman, A., Crosby, A., Fullilove, M., Johnson, R., *et al.* (2007) 'Effects on violence of laws and policies facilitating the transfer of juveniles from the juvenile justice system to the adult justice system: a systematic review', *American Journal of Preventive Medicine*, 32: 7–28.

Platt, A. (1977) *The Child Savers: The Invention of Delinquency*, 2nd edn, Chicago: University of Chicago Press.

Rothman, D. J. (1980) *Conscience and Convenience: The Asylum and its Alternative in Progressive America*, Boston: Little, Brown.

Steffensmeier, D., Kramer, J. H. and Streifel, C. (1993) 'Gender and imprisonment decisions', *Criminology*, 31: 411–46.

Tonry, M. and Doob, A. N. (2004) *Youth Crime and Youth Justice: Comparative and Cross-national Perspectives*, Chicago: University of Chicago Press.

Zatz, M. (2000) 'The convergence of race, ethnicity, gender, and class on court decisionmaking: looking toward the 21st century', *Criminal Justice*, 3: 503–52.

# Author index

Aapola, S. 410
Abbott, A. 129
Abbott-Chapman, J. 243, 245, 246
Abdi, C. M. 92
Adelman, J. 396
Aldrdge, S. 59
Ali, A. 93
Ainsworth, J. W. 132
Ainsworth-Darnell, J. 394–96
Alfeld, C. 139
Aliaga, O. A. 138
Allahar, A. 181
Allen, F. 453
Allen, J. 170
Allen, L. 410
Allmendinger, J. 108
Alwin, D. F. 294
Ammons, S. K. 155
Amoner-P'Olak, K. 321–22
Andersen, S. 164
Anderson, D. K. 394
Andes, L. 267
Ang, I. 304
Anyon, J. 52
Apfel, R. L. 325
Apple, M. 51
Aqulino, W. S. 207, 222.
Archer, M. 315
Aries, P. 452
Aronson, P. 154
Arnett, J. J. 7–8, 39–42, 44, 100, 212, 217, 375
ASG. 355
Asakawa, K. 387
Ashmore, R. 376
Astin, A. 385–86, 388

Atkins, R. 295
Auer, P. 168–69
Auerswald, C. 233
Australian Bureau of Statistics. 211–12
Australian Institute of Health and Welfare. 354–55
Avery, R. 207

Baanders, A. N. 204
Back, L. 266
Bagguley, P. 316–17
Bailey, T. 139
Bakke, E. W. 160
Ball, S. 99–100, 117, 122
Baltes, P. B. 41
Bankole, A. 347
Banks, P. 334
Bankston, C. 77–78
Barak, A. 285
Baron, S. W. 236–37
Barrios, L. 440
Barry, H. 379
Barry, M. 449–50
Bazemore, G. 448
Bragg, D. D. 141
Barton, P. 136
Bassinin, C. 74–76
Bauman, Z. 2, 62, 99, 261, 278, 304, 376, 378, 400, 403
Baumeister, R. F. 378
Beah, I. 325
Bean, F. D. 93
Beasley, R. 236
Beck, U. 31, 63–64, 84, 117, 161, 167–68, 177, 377, 400, 403
Beck-Gernsheim, E. 99

Beckerman, Z. 34
Belnap, J. 454
Benson, P. 413–16
Berger, M. 285
Berghman, J. 163
Bengtson, V. 223
Bennett, D. 331
Bennett, A. 252–53, 260–61, 264, 266, 278–79, 281
Bennett, L. 287
Bernhardt, E. 204
Berman, S. 345
Bernstein, B. 53, 98
Berta, D. 399
Best, A. L. 256, 258, 260
Beutal, A. M. 387–88
Beyerlein, K. 417
Beynon, H. 169
Beynon, J. 313–14, 316
Bian, Y. 182
BIBB. 8
Biggart, A. 118
Billari, F. C. 205–7
Bishop, D. M. 453, 455
Blackman, S. 269, 272–73, 279
Blackshaw, T. 17
Blanchflower, D. G. 189–91, 195, 197–98
Black, J. 198
Blanden, J. 61
Blatterer, H. 28
Blaxter, M. 331
Blau, P. M. 392
Blossfeld, H-P. 6–7, 105–7, 158
Boase, J. 286
Bonanno, O. 322
Bortner, M, A. 455
Boulton, M. 339
Bourdeiu, P. 16, 34, 62, 74, 100, 117, 122, 163
Bourgois, P. 60
Bovasso, G. 386
Bowlby, J. 272
Bowle, S. 15, 115
Boyd, D. 284, 288
Boyle, E. H. 90, 93
Bradley, H. 34
Braithwaite, J. 449
Brake, M. 22, 265
Brannen, J. 27, 219–22, 233
Breen, R. 118
Bremberg, S. 339
Brill, D. 280
British Crime Survey. 270–71
Britton, L. 70
Brotherton, D. 440
Brown, A. P. 433
Brown, M. 66
Brown, P. 19, 115

Brown, P. H. 346
Brown, S. S. 228
Broussard, N. 191
Brumberg, J. J. 259
Brush, L. 61
Bryson, A. 308
Brzinsky-Fay, C. 106–11
Buck, N. 204
Buckingham, D. 284
Burke, T. 212
Burney, E. 430, 432
Butler, J. 407
Butler, T. 71, 168, 170
Bynner, J. 5, 7–8, 32, 44, 83, 161, 170, 212–13
Byrne, D. 172

Cairuth, C. 321
Caldas, S. 77–78
Callender, C. 125
Calzo, J. P. 285
Cam, S. 169
Campbell, A. 228
Campbell, R. T. 393–95
Cantle, T. 314
Carle, J. 311
Carpenter, L. M. 227
Cartmel, F. 18, 23–24, 35, 67, 69, 99, 158, 170, 172–73, 260, 273, 293, 303, 362, 377, 380
Case, S. 447
Casper, L. 220
Castellano, M. 137–38
Castells, M. 60–61, 284, 439, 441
Cazes, S. 168–69
Chandler, M. 378
Chatterton, P. 249–53, 271
Checci, D. 308
Chen, E. E. 338
Chen, X. 43
Cherlin, A. J. 203, 205
Chesney-Lind, M. 439
Chin, E. 257, 260
China Youth Union. 185
Chisholm, L. 5, 32
Chos, J. H. 397
Chung, H. L. 425
Clarkberg, M. 288
Clarke, G. 277
Clarke, J. 277
Clarke, L, S. 415
Clarke, W. A, V. 204, 207–8
Clay, A. 22
Cleaver, E. 211, 213–14
Cloonan, M. 264
Cloward, R. 437
Cochran, B. N. 234
Coggan, N. 273
Cohen, A. H. 272, 276

Cohen, M. 345
Cohen, P. 272, 276–77
Cohen, S. 264, 269
Coleman, J, S. 5, 74–76
Colley, H. 161
Collier, P. 321
Collins, R. 15, 129
Collishaw, S. 337, 340, 355, 357
Connell, J. 213
Connell, R. 60, 406
Cook, D. 256
Cook, T. D. 208, 219, 221–23
Cooney, T. 219
Corijn, M. 205–7
Corker, M. 82
Corr, A. 253
Corrigan, P. 115
Corvalan, C. 357
Costello, E. 335, 337
Côté, J. 44, 181, 376–77, 379–81
Cowley, S. 163
Cowling, M. 198
Craig, R. 363
Crawford, A. 432
Crimmins, E. M. 385
Crenshaw, K. 49
Csiksentmihayi, M. 34, 387, 395
Cunnen, C. 444–48
Currie, C. 336, 362
Curtis, P. 67, 71

Daiute, C. 323–24, 326
Danieli, Y. 321, 325
Darroch, J. E. 226
Davanzo, J. 204
Davies, B. 100
Davies, S. 456
Davin, D. 182–84
De Bourdeaudhuij, I. 285
De Jong Gierweld, J. 204, 207
De Leo, D. D. 337
De Valk, H. 204, 208
Decker, S. H. 438
Dejong, J. 350
Delli Carpini, M. X. 286, 296
Denholm, C. 246
Dennis, J. 296
Denton, M. L. 413–16, 477
Dermott, E. 159, 169
Devadson, R. 10
Devine, F. 19
Diamond, W. 308, 310–11.
Diepstraten, I. 35
Dikec, M. 313, 317–18
Donahue, M. 413, 416
Donnellan, M. 42
Doob, A. N. 452

Dougherty, K. J. 129
Douglass, C. B. 43
Dowdney, L. 439
Downey, D. B. 394–96
Dribbusch, H. 310
Drugscope. 270, 274
Duan, D. 185–86
Du Bois Reymond, M. 32, 34
Duncan, O. D. 392
Dunn, T. A. 191
Dwyer, P. 100–101

Easterlin, R. A. 385
Easton, D. 296
Ebinghaus, B. 308
EC. 33
Eckersley, R. 353–54, 356–58
Eckert, P. 116
Eden, K. 314–15
Education Research Services. 125
Egerton, M. 19
Ehrenreich, B. 172
Eisenberg, L. 228
Elias, N. 24–26
Emirbayer, M. 164
Engebrigsten, A. 93
Engen, R. L. 453
Ennett, S. T. 368
Epstein, J. S. 265
Erikson, E. H. 294, 297
Ester, P. 78
Eurofond. 308
Evans, D. 197
Evans, K. 7, 106, 111, 164
Evans, R. 337
Everatt, D. 306
Eyre, S. 233

Facio, A. 43
Fadiman, A. 93
Fagan, J. A. 454
Fairclough, N. 314
Fairlie, R. W. 191
Fan, C. C. 183
Faris, R. 417
Farrar, M. 313–14
Farrington, D. 273, 425, 431, 446
Feather, N. 386, 389
Feld, B. 452–53
Felstead, A. 170
Fenton, S. 159, 169
Ferguson, K. 75
Ferguson, R. 287
Ferve, R. 168
Field, F. 61
Fields, J. 214
Filipovic, Z. 326

Fine, M. 49
Finnegans, W. 61
Fitzgerald, M. 70–71
Fitzpartick, S. 236
Flanagan, C. A. 293–94
Flay, B. R. 364
Fordham, S. 394
Forman, T. A. 416
Forsyth, A. 124–25
Foucault, M. 100, 403, 406
France, A. 273, 430, 432, 434
Francis, L. J. 414
Frank, T. 375
Franks, K. A. 244
Franklin, B. 401
Frazier, C. E. 453, 455
Freeman, R. 308, 310–11
Frosh, S. 407–8
Fuglerud, O. 93
Fuller, E. 366
Fuller, M. 116
Furlong, A. 18, 23–24, 35, 67, 69, 99, 118, 124,
   159, 170, 172–73, 176, 178–79, 260, 273,
   283, 303, 362, 377
Furstenberg, F. F. 54, 208, 219, 221–23, 227–28,
   233
Fussell, E. 233

Gaarder, E. 454
Gaines, S. O. 387
Gannier, H. E. 388
Garland, D. 454
Gatez, S. 237
Gambalos, N. L. 43
Gamoron, A. 56
Gangl, M. 6, 109
Garber, J. 265, 279
Gardener, D. P. 131, 135
Gecas, V. 387
Geirgen, K. 378
Geronimus, A. T. 227–28
Giddens, A. 100, 162, 284
Giedd, J. N. 41
Gill, B. 122
Gill, J. S. 366
Gilroy, P. 264, 313–14, 316–17, 441
Gintis, H. 15, 115
Giordano, P. C. 426
Glueck, E. 424–25
Glueck, S. 424–25
Glynn, A. 69
Glynn, J. R. 345
Goffman, I. 377
Goffredson, M. 424–25
Goldberg, D. 335
Goldscheider, C. 203–4, 208, 211, 220–21
Goldscheider, F. 203–4, 208, 211, 220–21

Goldson, B. 446–47
Goldthorpe, J. H. 19
Goodman, E. 339
Goodwin, J. 23–24, 26, 159
Gotlieb, J. 280
Gottdiener, M. 249
Gou, X. 184
Gould, M. S. 285
Gourlay, M. 244
Green, A. 171
Grisso, T. 455
Grob, A. 40
Grubb, W, N. 131, 132, 133, 139, 140

Ha, J. 255
Haenfler, R. 267
Hagan, J. 234–37
Hageborn, J. M. 436, 439, 445
Hall, G. S. 434
Hall, S. 16, 265, 376
Halleröd, B. 159
Halvorsen, K. 159
Hammami, R.92
Hammer, T. 159–60
Handy, C. 170
Hanifan, L. 74
Hannan, D. 109
Hannigan, J. 249
Hanser, A. 183–85
Hargreaves, D. H. 114–16
Hargreaves, D. J. 369
Harris, A. 258, 260, 278, 284, 305
Harris, J. K. 368
Harrison, L. 284
Hatfield, P. 249
Hart, D. 295
Hartmann, D. 217
Harvey, A. 453–55
Harvey, D. 250, 347
Hasan, R. 316
Haskell, V. H. 363
Hatcher, R. 118
Haurin, R. J. 208
Hauser, R. 149, 392–94, 397
Haveman, R. 122
Hawker, D. 339
Hawton, K. 338
Hayes, C. D. 227–28
Haylett, C. 62
Hayman, J. 245
Hayward, G. 127
Heath, S. 53, 211, 213–14
Hebdige, D. 259, 264, 277, 280
Hecker, D. E. 189
Heckman, J. J. 137
HEFCE 213
Heimer, K. 426–27

Hein, J.90
Hein, K. 345
Heinz, W. R. 7–9, 37, 106, 111, 150
Helne, T. 163
Henderson, S. 99–100
Henquet, C. 363
Hertz-Lazarowitz, R. 324
Henry, N. 170
Hesmondhalgh, D. 267, 279–80
Hewitt, J. 376
Higson-Smith, C. 323
Hillier, L. 284
Hillmert, S. 105
Hirschman, A. 311
Hitlin, S. 384, 389
Hirchi, T. 424–25
Hjern, A. 355
Hobbs, D. 249
Hochschild, A. 60–61
Hochschild, W. 407
Hodkinson, P. 279
Hofferth, S. 227
Hoffman, L. 184–85
Hoffman, S. D. 228
Holdsworth, C. 212
Holdsworth, R. 301
Hollands, J. 407
Hollands, R. 249–53, 271, 278
Hollinger, R. 381
Holloway, S. L. 244–45, 286
Holloway, W. 407
Holtz-Eakin, D. 191, 197
Home Office. 433
Honwana, A. 313
Horst, C. 91
House of Commons Select Committee. 66–67
Hout, M. 191
Hoyt, D. R. 234–36
Huntley, R. 399
Huq, R. 278
Hussain, Y. 316–17

Iacovou, M. 220
Imamura, M. 231
Inglehart, R. 304, 386
Institute of Alcohol Studies. 270
Institue for Reproductive Health. 347
Inter Agency Standing Committee (IASC). 324
Inui, A 180

Jacka, T. 183–84
Jackson, P. 273
Jacobs, J. 386
Jahoda, M. 163
James, K. 246
James, V. 246
Jamieson, L. 304

Jefferson, T. 16, 265
Jenkins, R. 25
Jenks, C. 396
Jennings, M. K. 294, 297
Jewson, N. 170
Jiraphongsa, C. 348
Johnson, A. 406
Johnson, L. D. 414–15
Johnson, M. F. 387–89
Johnson, M. K. 153
Johnson, R. W. 204
Johnston, L. 170
Jones, E. F. 231
Jones, G. 160, 180, 211
Jones, P. 428
Jovanovic, B. 197
Joy, J. 270
Jugend. 35
Julkunen, I. 160, 162
Jussim, L. 376

Kay, W. K. 414
Kalleberg, A. 152
Kamb, M. L. 348
Kampits, E. 141
Kao, G. 395
Karoven, S. 367
Kehily, M. J. 407, 409
Keilman, N. 208
Keeter, S. 305
Keith, M. 67, 317, 319
Kelling, G. L. 431
Kelly, E. L. 155
Kelly, P. 100, 178, 400
Kemp, P. 213
Kerckhoff, A. 105–6, 109–10, 151, 220, 393–95
Kessler, R, C. 355
Kholi, M. 219
Kincheloe, J. L. 256–57
King, P. 414, 416
Kliebard, H. 128–29
Klein, M. 437–38
Klein, N. 250–51, 253, 257
Klijzing, E. 205–7
Kohn, M. L. 153
Kogan, I. 110, 158
Kovacheva, S. 305
Kronauer, M. 164
Krüger, H. 37
Kuhn, M. H.
Kuhn, T. 9
Kunkel, D. 453
Kupcaik, A. 453–55

Lacey, C. 114
LaFontaine, P. A. 137
Lagos, M. 304

Lähteenmaa, J. 162
Landolt, P. 76
Lareau, A. 53
Lash, S. 83
Larson, M. S. 129
Larson, R. W. 390
Lau, C. 98
Laub, J. 423, 425–27
Laughey, D. 279
Lazerson, M. 131–33
Leach, L. S. 285
Leccardi, C. 11, 161
Lee, C-F. 415
Lehmann, W. 8
Leisering, L. 11
Lesch, H.H. 307–8
Levesque, K. A. 136, 138
Levin, K. 237
Levine, P. 293, 376–77
Levitas, R. 82
Levitt-Dayal, M. 349
Lewis, M. V. 136
Lewis, P. 67
Li, G. 54
Li, J. 182
Lievrouw, L. A. 283
Lin, N. 74, 76
Lindh, T. 197
Ling, C. 184
Little, B. 125
Liu, J. 184–85
Livingstone, S. 283–87
Logan, J. 220
Lombourg, B. 354
Lòpez Blasco, A. 34
Lorence, J. 153
Lovesey, O. 264
Luescher, K. 222
Luke, D. A. 368
Luke, N. 345
Lukes, S. 308
Luling, V. 91
Lynam, M. J. 163
Lysgaard, S. 311
Lytch, C. 415–16

Mac an Ghail, M. 117, 407–8
McAdams, D. P. 378
McCarthy, B. 234–37
McCarthy, C. 49–51
McDermott, C. 296–97
McDonald, K. 247
McDonald, R. 22, 159, 162, 170–71, 252, 260, 447
McDowell, L. 17, 60
McFarlane, D, A. 297
McGowan, A. 454, 456

McKay, G. 253
McKay, H. D. 437
McKeller, S. 273
McKnight, A. 173
McNamara, S. 213
McLaughlin, H. 155
McLeod, J. 66, 100, 116, 394
McPartland, T. S. 377
McRae, J. 220
McRobbie, A. 258, 260, 265, 279, 410
Machin, S. 310–11
Mack, A. 270
Maffesoli, M. 278
Mahoney, J. 245
Maira, S. M. 259
Malbon, B. 254, 265, 267
Malmberg-Heimonen, I. 160
Mannheim, K. 22, 296
Marcia, J. E. 376
Marini, M. M. 384, 387–89
Marmar, C. R. 322
Marsden, D. 107
Marsh, D. 314–15
Marsh, J. 170–71, 252
Marshall, T. H. 4
Marshall, V. W. 4
Mason, M. 414–16
Martini, L. 264
Martsueda, R. 426–27
Maruna, S. 426, 449–50
Mason, D. 68, 71
Matsuba, J. K. 297
Maurice, M. 106
Maynard, R. A. 233
Mead, G. H. 164
Measham, F. 271
Meeder, H. 138
Meer, J. 132
Meltzer, H. 335, 338–39
Mennell, S. 24
Merton, R. K. 162
Mesch, G. S. 287
Mikleson, R. A. 394
Miles, R. 66, 316
Miller, K. E. 348
Miller, W. 437
Millie, A. 430
Mills, C. W. 162
Mische, A. 164
Mitchell, K. J. 245, 285
Mitchell, J. 363
Mitchell, L. 198
Mitchell, P. 198
Modin, B. 338–39
Moffitt, T. 423–24, 426
Monahan, T. 455
Montgomery, K. C. 284, 286

Moore, J. W. 437
Moore, L. M. 387
Mörch, S. 164
Morgan, D. 212
MORI. 125
Morrow, V. 74
Motihar, R. 349
Mortimer, M. L. 43
Mortimer, J. T. 4, 141, 151–54, 390
Mount, F. 62
Mouw, T. 233
MPR 140
Muggleton, D. 266, 278
Mulder, C. H. 204–5, 207–8
Muller, W. 6–7, 105–7, 109
Muncie, J. 433–34, 446–48
Muraven, M. 378
Murray, G. 317–18

Nagin, D. 424
Nakanishi, S. 180
Nakao, K. 397
Natalier, K. 213
National Assessments of Educational Progress. 137
National Association of Secondary School Principals. 136
National Centre for Public Policy and Higher Education. 139
National Centre for Education Statistics, 137
National Education Longitudinal Survey. 395
National Research Council and Institute of Medicine. 345–46
National Statistics. 125
Nayak, A. 278, 407
Nelson, L. J. 43
Newburn, T. 273
Newcombe, R. 270
Newman, K. S. 154
Neoman, K. 60
Nicole, K. 34
Nilsson, K. 207
North, A. C. 369

Oaks, J. 136
O'Connor, H. 23, 26, 159
O'Connor, J. 251
OECD. 98, 101, 108, 359
Oetberg, V. 338–39
Office of National Statistics. 211
Ogbu, J. 394
O'Grady, B. 237
Ohlin, L. 437
Ohlsson, H. 197
Ohlsson, L. B. 158, 163–64
Oliver, M. 82
Osgerby, B. 267, 280

Osgood, D. W. 235–36
Osterberg, V. 338–39
Oswald, A. J. 195

Palladino, G. 257
Park, A. 314–15
Park, M, J. 42
Park, R, E. 163
Parker, H. 273, 365
Parson, R. 16, 75
Passeron, J-D. 16
Paternoster, R. 424
Patterson, O. 68
Paugams, S. 163
Payne, M. 36
Pearson, H. 273
Pearson, M. 369
Perkins, D. F. 244
Peters, H. E. 203
Peters, T. 402, 404
Pheonix, A. 378, 380
Phillips, M. 396
Pikkerty, T. 49
Pilavin, J. A. 384, 389
Pilcher, J. 22
Pillemer, K. 222
Pirie, M. 314
Plank, S. 137
Plant, M. 270–71
Platt, A. 453
Platt, S. 338
Pohl, A. 161
Polhemous, T. 278
Pollock, G. 169, 173
Pontin, R. 415
Popay, J. 162
Porfeli, E. J. 236
Portes, A. 93, 393–94
Portes, T. 76
Poynting, S. 445
Putnam, R. 16, 75

Quintini, G. 169

Raffe, D. 5, 164
Raffo, C. 34
Rahn, W. M. 387–88
Rattansi, A. 378, 380
Raudenbush, S. 431
Real World Training and Consulting 399
Ream, R. 74, 76
Reay, D. 124
Redhead, S. 266
Regnerus, M. 413–17
Reich, R. 49–50
Reilly, J. 335
Reeves, M. 34

Renold, E. 411
Resnick, M. D. 356
Retting, G. 386
Rex, J. 314
Rhodes, T. 272
Rich, L. 85
Richardson, D. 407
Richardson, W. 244
Rickarts, L. 334
Riddell, S. 83, 85, 87, 334
Riddock, C. J. 363
Ringrose, J. 411
Riseborough, G. 15
Ritzer, G. 256
Robb, A. 191
Roberts, B, W. 42
Roberts, K. 7, 83, 110
Robertson, M. E. 243–44, 246–47
Robinson, J. 236–37
Robinson, K. H. 409
Rogers, E. M. 347
Roker, D. 305, 314–15
Room, G. 163
Roos, E. B. 367
Rosa, H. 36
Rose, N. 404
Rose, R. 304
Rose, T. 264
Rosen, H. S. 191
Rosenbaum, J. 105, 107
Rosenbaum, J. 137, 139
Rosenberger, N. 43
Rosenfeld, M. 218
Roscigno, V. J. 132
Ross, K. 218, 220
Ross, K. E. 155
Rossi, A. 221, 223
Rossi, P. 221, 223
Rothman, D. J. 452
Rousseau, C. 91
Rowe, C. 287–88
Rumbaut, R. G. 93, 155
Ruspini, E. 36, 98, 100
Russell, A. 304
Rutter, M. 336, 340, 431
Ryan, P. 107, 127–28, 132

Saez, E. 49
Salanie, B. 318
Salmela-Aro, K. 21
Sampson, R. 423, 425–27, 431
Sanson, A. 355
Santor, D. A. 285
Saunders, P. 19
Savage, M. 19
Scabini, E. 218–19, 222–23
Scarman, Lord, 314

Scherer, S. 111
Schneider, B. 118, 149–50, 395–96
Schor, J. 261, 340
Scott, J. 204
Scottish Executive. 82, 87
Schalet, A. T. 227
Schlegel, A. 379
Schoeni, R. F. 155, 218, 220
Scholte, E. 232
Schooler, C. 153
Schoon, I. 118
Schulemberg, J. E. 42, 385–86, 388
Schwartz, R. G. 455
Segrave, K. 264
Seff, M. A. 386
Self, A. 124, 364
Sellstrom, E. 339.
Sennett, 400–401
Setterson, R. 217, 227, 295
Sewell, T. 117
Sewell, W. H. 149, 392–93, 397
Shadforth, C. 189, 191, 197–98
Shakespeare, T. 82
Shanahan, M. J. 149, 236
Shannon, M. J. 4, 8–9
Shavit, Y. 7, 105–7, 158
Shaw, C. R. 437
Sheehan, P. 399
Sherrod, L. 296, 298
Shildrick, T. 159, 162, 174, 278
Shiner, M. 273
Short, J. F. 437
Shumway, D. 263
Siegel, C. 208
Sigle-Ruston, W. 339
Silbereisen, R. K. 387
Sickmund, M. 423
Silverberg, M. 138, 141
Simon, B. 325
Singh, S. 226, 347
Skeggs, B. 17, 62–63
Skogen, W. 431
Slater, D. 260–61
Smart, D. 355
Smith, C. 413–17
Smith, D. 172, 174, 336, 340
Smith, D. J. 68
Smith, N. 251
Smyth, E. 105, 109
Sneed, J. R. 41
Snyder, H. N. 423
Solga, H. 158
South, N. 272
Speizer, I. 348
Spilsbury, M. 308, 310
Spittaels, H. 285
Spitze, G. 220

Suires, P. 432
Staff, J. 151–52, 427
Stanyer, J. 287
Starfield, B. 332
Stattin, H. 245
Stauber, B. 8–9
Staudinger, U. M. 41
Steffensmeier, D. 454
Stefansson, C-G. 355, 357
Steinberg, D. L. 409
Steinberg, S. 256–57
Stein, J. A. 388
Stein, M. R. 375
Stephen, D. 432
Stern, D. 140
Stevens, G. 93, 397
Stevens, Q. 244
Stevenson, B. 118, 149–50, 395–96
Stewart, A. J. 296
Stewart, F. 411
Stewart-Brown, S. 378
Stoker, L. 297
Stokes, H. 98–99, 284
Stone, D. 81
Stone, J. R. III. 138–39, 141
Stradl, M. 207
Strodtbeck, F. L. 437
Ströhlë, A. 363
Stryker, S. 377
Summerfeild, C. 122
Summerfeild, D. 122
Summers, T. 344
Sutton Trust. 123
Suzuki, L. K. 285
Swail, W. S. 141
Swarthout, L. 139
Swartz, T. S. 155
Swartz, T. 217
Sweeting, H. 335–38, 341, 365–66

Tam, J. 285
Tan, J. 184
Tan, S. 183
Tanner, J. 456
Tanner, J. L. 7–8, 40, 42
Tarrant, T, M. 246
Taylor, B. 245
Taylor, C. 438
Taylor, Y. 409
Teichler, U. 108
Therborn, G. 226
Thomas, R. J. 297
Thorlindson, T. 78
Thornton, S. 250–51, 256, 259, 264, 266,
    279–80
Thrasher, F. 437
Tilly, C. 64

Tonnes, F. 379
Tonry, M. 68, 452
Torney-Purta, J. 303, 305
Touraine, A. 314
Townsend, P. 173
Toynbee, P. 172
Transue, J. E. 387–88
Tranter, B. 284
Treas, J. 397
Tsui, M. 185
Tucker, C. J. 294
Turnski, M. 323

Uecker, J. 414, 416
Uggen, C. 427
Uhlenberg, P. 219
UKEJE. 323
Unicef 36
UN Census 70
UNHCR 90, 327
United Nations Population Fund. 345, 438
Unt, M. 110
Urry, J. 83

Valentine, G. 244–45, 286
Van Der Ploeg, J. 239
Van Eijck, K. 17
Van Hoof, J. 34
Van Krieken, R. 25
Van Oorshot, W. 160
Van Poppel, F. 204–6
Vanneman, J. 387
Verba, S. 295, 297
Vinken, H. 78
Vinter, R. M. 245
Visser, J. 308
Voskon, L. 168
Vromen, A. 284, 287, 302, 305

Waddington, C. 316
Wald, G. 280
Walgrave, L. 448
Walker, S. 66
Walkerdine, V. 117, 407
Wall, R. 205
Wallace, C. 180, 303
Wallace, J, M. 416
Walther, A. 32, 158, 161, 180
Waltzer, M. 293
Wang, J.184, 186
Wang, Z.185
Ward, T. 449–50
Warner, M. 407
Warr, M. 427
Waters, M.93
Watson, L. 178
Watt, P. 71, 168, 170

Watt, T. T. 385–86
Weber, M. 399, 401–2
Webster, C. 68, 70, 171
Weeks, J. 411
Weigert, A. J. 377
Weinstein, D. 265, 267
Weinstein, H, M. 323
Weis, D. S. 322
Weis, L. 51, 55–56
Wellman, B. 78
Welzel, C. 386
Werthman, C. 114
West, C. 440
West, P. 333, 335–38, 341, 364–68
Westberg, A. 159
Wexler, P. 377
Whitbeck, L. B. 234–36
White, L. 220, 222
White, R. 99–100, 245, 302–3, 444–48
White, V. 245
Whitlock, J. L. 285
Whittington, L. 203
Whitty, G. 51
Whyte, W. F. 437
Wilkinson, D. 125
Williams, F. 162
Williams, L. M. 42
Williams, M. 246
Williams, P. 246
Willis, P. 15, 54, 83, 115–16, 265, 279
Willis, S. 284
Wilson, G. 155
Wilson, J. P. 323

Wilson, J. Q. 431
Wilson, K. 122, 393–94
Wilson, W. J. 154
Wingert, S. 233
Winzelberg, A. 285
Wirt, J. 395
Witzel, A. 9
Wolkowitz, C. 1
Woodman, D. 4, 23–24, 283
Worchester, R. M. 314
Wyn, J. 4, 23–24, 98, 100, 102, 283, 302–3, 447
Wynne, D. 251

Xu, F. 183

Yadlonsky, Y. 437
Yates, L. 100
Yates, S. 36
Youdall, D. 117, 409
Young, M. F. 51
Young, R. 337–38, 340
Youth Justice Board. 433
Yuval-Davis, M. 91

Zackary, G. P. 243
Zarrett, N. 42
Zatz, M. S. 453
Zealey, L. 124, 364
Zeijl, E. 245
Zeng, X. 184–86
Zhang, H. 185
Zhang, X. 184–86
Zimring, F. E. 454

# Subject index

A Nation at Risk 131, 135
ability groups 136
abortion 42, 227–28, 230
abuse 202, 234–35
accidents 245, 329–30, 336–37, 355, 364
acculturation 89, 92–94
activism 298–99, 301, 303, 305
admissions officers 122, 124
adolescence 2–4, 7, 22, 39–42, 76, 217, 233–35,
    238, 256, 281, 294, 297, 332–33, 353, 362,
    378, 384–86, 388–89, 393, 413–16, 418, 423,
    425–26, 438
adolescent-limited approaches 423–24, 426
adulthood 3–9, 11–12, 22–24, 26, 29, 32, 39,
    42–44, 56, 67, 69–70, 81, 83, 86–87, 99–100,
    106–7, 111, 135, 149, 154–55, 158, 167, 170,
    174, 202–3, 206, 208, 211–12, 214–15,
    217–19, 221–24, 227, 230, 232–36, 238,
    294–98, 329, 331–34, 337–38, 353, 362, 364,
    366, 375, 377, 379, 380, 384–85, 388–90,
    393, 421, 424–27, 452; arrested 44; delayed
    226; emerging 7–8, 11, 39–44, 100, 170;
    young 1–3, 12, 39–42, 49, 68, 76, 130, 149,
    151, 203, 211, 217–22, 297, 375, 382, 384,
    389, 423, 425
African-Americans 53, 55, 66, 68–69, 128, 155–56,
    191, 226, 263–65, 305, 393–95, 416, 437
African-Caribbean 66–71, 226, 265, 316, 345
agency; biographical 9–11 bounded; 163–64;
    personal/individual 10–12, 4–5, 7–8, 12, 31,
    34, 109–11, 161–64, 234, 241, 250, 253, 260,
    272, 285, 315, 323, 330, 361–62, 366–67, 369,
    373, 377–78, 381, 407, 409, 440, 449, 450
agency workers 177
agriculture 183, 189

alcohol 18, 55, 235, 242, 244–45, 247, 267,
    269–71, 273, 329, 330, 356, 358, 361–62,
    364, 366, 368; abuse 140, 244–45
aligned ambitions 395–96
allocation model 393–94
alternative household forms 202, 212
ambition paradox 118
amphetamines 244, 270–71, 365
anti-globalization 255
anti-school cultures 115–16
anti-social behaviour 67–68, 244–45, 270,
    284–85, 356, 424, 430–34, 437, 445, 447,
    450; Anti-Social behaviour Order (ASBO)
    422, 433–34
anxiety 330, 335, 354, 356–58
apartheid 296, 298
apprenticeship 10, 83, 107–9, 111, 125,
    128–30, 132, 150
armed conflict 292, 321–26, 439
arrested adulthood 44
aspirations 4, 7–8, 11, 18, 62, 68, 91, 116,
    118–19, 122–23, 137, 154, 161, 184, 201,
    251, 358, 373–74, 392–97, 451; educational
    96, 138, 149, 151, 349, 392–93, 417;
    occupational 10, 173–74, 392–93
autobiographical thinking 100

baby boomers 22–23, 257, 267
Bangladeshi 70–71, 191
banlieue 317–19
Barbie 257
Beattie Committee 87
Bebo 285
beliefs 28, 127, 164, 227, 294, 298, 323, 373–4,
    384–90, 395, 406–7, 411, 413–17, 449

bhangra 259
binge drinking 62, 245, 247, 253, 270–71, 274, 299, 364, 366
Biographical Action Orientation (BAO) 9–10
biography 1–12, 18, 33, 100–101, 118, 160–61, 168, 180; choice 170, 180, 214; individualized 20, 35; normal 37, 106, 180; reflexive 126; yo-yo 32, 35
bisexual 117, 215
Black youth 33, 66–67, 69–70, 116–17, 220, 260, 316, 318, 393–97, 410, 416, 438
bling 16, 58, 62
blogs 243, 247, 284, 287, 305
body work 61
Britpop 264
broken windows thesis 431–32
Brothers 116, 394

Cannabis 270–72, 365–66, 368
Career and Technical Education (CTE)135–42
Careers 3, 6, 17, 39–43, 64, 95, 108–9, 119, 123, 126, 130, 145–46, 151, 169–73, 214, 217, 380, 393, 395–96; fragmented 9, 146–47; housing 201–2, 214; portfolio 58, 63
Careers Service 87
casual sex 388, 410
casualized labour 47, 60–61, 170, 178
Catholics 208, 416
Centre for Contemporary Cultural Studies (CCCS) 15, 241, 259, 265, 272, 276–80
Chavs 16, 58, 62, 64
Chicago School 377, 431, 437
child soldiers 322, 436, 439
childhood 3, 11, 20, 22–23, 25–26, 32, 68, 76, 83, 230, 233, 235, 244, 256–57, 276, 294, 325, 329, 331–34, 336–38, 353, 362, 379, 393, 424, 428–29, 452
chronic conditions 341, 354
churn 146, 170, 173
citizenship 4, 98, 111, 158, 161, 284, 286–88, 293–96, 299, 301–6, 308–9, 358, 411
Civic engagement 287, 291–95, 297–99, 302, 305, 315, 450
closed shop 307, 309
clothes 49, 59, 61, 257, 259, 279, 369, 449
club culture 259, 279
cocaine 270–71, 365
cohabitation 205, 212, 386, 389
college 7–9, 17, 42–43, 52, 87, 123, 131–32, 135–42, 149–52, 154, 207–8, 228, 294–95, 298, 374, 393, 396–97; community 124, 129, 138–39, 151; graduates 6, 9, 137–39
competency to stand trial (CST) 454–55
comprehensive schools 15, 52, 114
condoms 345–47, 406
conduct disorders 335–40

consumer culture 258, 260–61, 304–5, 340–41, 357
consumption 4, 5, 20, 33, 36, 43, 55, 62, 203, 220, 222–23, 241–42, 249–53, 255–62, 269–73, 279, 284–85, 301, 329, 361, 363–64, 366–67, 410, 441
contraception 202, 227–28, 348
Convention on the Rights of the Child 90, 301, 324, 446
co-residence 219–20, 222
crime 16, 67–68, 70, 154, 180, 184, 234–35, 252, 270, 272, 336, 421–28, 431–34, 437–38, 444–47, 450–53
criminal justice system 66–67, 229, 422, 444–45, 447–49, 451
cultural capital 16–17, 34–35, 53, 60, 69, 71, 100, 117, 122, 150, 251, 259, 266, 417
curfews 432, 446
curriculum 33, 51–52, 95, 101, 128–29, 131–33, 136, 138, 141, 258, 302, 347, 350, 367, 409

dance music 264, 266–67
degrees 59, 86, 101, 123–25, 135–41, 149–53, 155, 186, 194, 213, 396
delinquency 67–68, 114, 256, 272, 388, 417, 423–28, 446, 453
democracy 258, 286–87, 303, 308
dependence 1, 12, 26, 35, 90, 101, 154, 160–61, 201–3, 218, 220, 222, 243, 276, 283, 297, 389, 424
depression 285, 322, 329–30, 335, 337, 339, 354, 356–57, 374, 416
deprivation 68, 70, 163, 272, 316, 318, 450
diet 338, 356, 361–69
disability 42, 47–48, 81–88, 91, 117, 140, 179, 229, 321, 329, 334, 336, 338, 353–55
disadvantaged groups 3, 8, 14, 34, 58, 63, 68–69, 71 84, 87, 155, 159–60, 170, 172–73, 179–81, 220, 227–28, 230, 254, 393, 417, 445, 448
discrimination 34, 66, 68, 71, 82, 92–93, 155, 183–86, 316, 318, 357, 447
disease 42, 63, 285, 329, 332–36, 338, 347, 350–56, 359, 364, 442
divorced parents 196, 207, 228, 339
domestic transitions 202, 211, 215
drifters 118–19
drop-outs 6, 228
drugs, 55, 70, 235, 242, 244–45, 247, 265, 267, 269–74, 314, 329–30, 340, 358, 361–62, 365–67; hard 273, 365–66
dual system 129
dysfunctional families 234–35
dyslexia 85–86

ear 'oles 54, 116
early school leavers 102, 107, 121
early youth 333–34, 336, 338–42, 362, 364

earnings 137, 139–40, 157, 160, 173, 195, 197, 215, 228

ecstasy 244, 269–72, 358, 365

educational attainment 43–44, 53, 87, 106, 116, 118–19, 122, 149, 152, 154–55, 169, 185–86, 332, 367, 392–94, 396

emerging adulthood 2, 7–8, 11, 39–44, 100, 170, 375

emotional difficulties 87, 235, 332, 335, 337, 339, 355; support 86, 221–23

employability 11–12, 136, 139, 146

employment 1–9, 11–12, 15, 17–18, 31, 36, 43, 58–61, 709–1, 83, 85–87, 95–96, 99, 101, 103, 105–7, 109–11, 116, 119, 123, 125, 130, 133, 135–37, 140, 142, 145–46, 149–54, 157–61, 167–74, 176–80, 182–86, 188, 201–2, 207, 219–22, 230, 234–38, 243, 280, 284, 291–92, 303–4, 307–11, 318, 323, 349, 421–22, 425–28, 439, 445, 447, 450; blue collar 33, 60, 149, 266; casual 178–79; fixed term 178, 400; flexible 3, 83; informal 172, low paid 12, 17, 47, 55, 60–61, 64, 158, 169–70, 172–74, 422; non-standard 6, 150, 152, 168, 170; part-time 18, 59, 83, 110–11, 125, 145, 150–51, 154, 168, 176–79, 237, 400; precarious 3, 60, 95, 98–99, 101, 145–46 167–74, 176–77, 179–81, 310–11, 374, 400, 403, 421–22, 443; self-10, 146, 168, 189, 190–98; temporary 168, 170, 173, 177;

entrepreneurial self 374, 403

entrepreneurs 146, 170, 188–89, 190–98

epistemological fallacy 18, 23–24, 380

equalization hypothesis 338

ethnic minorities 32, 34, 36, 48, 53, 66–67, 69–72, 76, 78, 92–93, 105, 110, 124–25, 132, 202, 252, 255, 264, 316, 323–24, 357, 361, 379, 386–87, 395, 416, 437–39, 441, 444–45, 450; ethnicity 2, 7, 32, 44, 47–49, 53–54, 56, 66–71, 76, 78, 82, 155, 159, 162, 220, 245, 266–67, 278, 315, 376, 392–93, 396, 409, 442, 453–54

Facebook 247, 285

family formation 6, 41, 44, 69, 161, 202, 208, 222, 226–27, 379, 388–89

fashion 16, 243, 247, 250, 252, 263, 266, 276–30

femininity 58, 60, 62, 64, 257, 279, 280, 406–11

fertility 18, 43, 226

fiddly jobs 176

flexibilization 161, 177, 401

flexible capitalism 399–404

folk devils 269–70

Fordism 47, 95, 117, 167–69, 373

foster care 232

four year degrees 135–36, 139

Frankfurt School 258–59

freeters 176–81

functionalism 14–15, 22, 269, 271–73

future orientation 100, 103, 118

gambling 244

gangs 114, 245, 314, 422, 436–43, 450

gangsta rap 440–42

gateway theory 270

gays 117, 215, 251, 406, 408–9, 411

generation gap 223, 302

generation X 22

generation Y 22, 247, 399–400, 403–4

gentrification 250–51

Ghent system 309

girl power 258

glam rock 264

globalization 7, 107, 150, 160–61, 255, 260, 303–5, 442

God 374, 414–15

goths 59, 252, 279, 340–41

governance 158, 160, 286

graduates 6, 8, 18, 86, 136–40, 149, 151, 184–86, 213–14, 251

grandparents 36, 220, 283

habitus 10, 25, 53, 62, 116, 122, 161

Hallway Hangers 116, 394

happiness 42, 195, 332, 337, 356–57

health behaviour 329–30, 332, 334, 338–39, 361–70; chronic 353–54, 356; education 347, 349, 367; inequality 337–38, 353; mental 42, 48, 85–86, 91, 155, 159, 229, 285–86, 322, 329–42, 353, 355, 357, 363, 416; physical 42, 245, 336, 353, 363, 416; reproductive 230, 347–49, 350–51; sexual 344, 347, 349

heavy metal music 265–66

hedonistic behaviour 249–50, 267, 277

heroin 271, 365

heteronormativity 374, 407–8

heterosexual 214–15, 257, 280, 345, 406–11

high flyers 118

high school diplomas 139, 151, 295

higher education 1, 18–19, 40, 48, 83, 85–87, 96, 98, 108–9, 121–25, 131, 136, 139, 141–42, 149–52, 154, 180, 204, 212–13, 214, 219, 334, 338, 341, 374, 396

hip hop 246, 252, 259, 265, 305, 325, 440–42

hippies 264–65

HIV/AIDS 25, 305, 329, 344–45, 347–48. 351

homelessness 201–2, 215, 232–38, 252

homophobia 408

hoodies 62

horizontal stratification 96, 123–25

hostels 85, 202, 212, 232, 236

households 5, 40, 48, 70, 91, 111, 182, 186, 202–3, 207–8, 211–15, 233

housing 20, 50, 71, 93, 106, 161, 172, 182, 198, 201–3, 206–8, 213–15, 218–21, 223, 236,

237–38, 318, 421, 433; shared 213–14; transition 201–2, 214–15

human capital 34, 77, 133, 150–52, 155, 158, 191, 194, 202, 230, 235–36, 382

identity 7–8, 39, 49–50, 52, 58–59, 62, 66–67, 83–84, 99–100, 117, 161, 230, 243, 247, 251–53, 256, 259, 271–72, 276, 279, 284, 286, 288, 294, 297–99, 304, 323, 330, 342, 361–62, 367, 369, 373, 375–82, 384, 389–90, 400, 408, 413, 416, 427, 438, 440–42; formation 8, 49, 161, 181, 373, 375–76, 378–79, 381–82

illegal activities 154, 235, 237, 245, 421, 434, 438

imagined futures 117

immigrants 50, 53, 68, 76, 92–93, 155, 158, 204, 208, 222, 226, 316, 422, 437, 441, 452–53

impairment 48, 82, 84–87, 332, 334–35, 338

income 44, 53, 58–60, 122, 128, 133, 140, 149, 152–53, 155, 157, 160, 170, 178, 189, 202, 207, 213, 219–20, 222, 226, 230, 237, 241–42, 246–47, 340–41, 357, 394, 445

independence 5, 12, 26, 41–42, 83, 179, 201, 203–7, 212, 215, 218, 220–23, 229, 243, 246, 257, 259, 261, 283, 294, 303, 358, 389, 410

individualism 3, 58, 63, 223, 258, 273, 330, 341, 354, 357–58, 387

individualization 2, 7, 18, 20, 63, 96, 99, 101, 117, 146, 158, 161, 164, 167, 173, 213, 243, 273, 303–5, 330, 377, 380, 390, 404

informal learning 95, 98

information communication technology (ICT) 283–86, 288

injury 321, 326, 329, 355

insecurity 69, 126, 146, 152, 168–70, 172–74, 177–81, 251, 318, 354, 356, 358, 445

internet 51, 78, 244, 247, 255, 257, 283–88, 304–5, 309, 386, 390

intersex 117

intoxication 269–74

Jews 208

Job Corps 140

job satisfaction 152–54, 195, 197–98

job tenure 168–69

joblessness 66, 68, 71, 438

juvenile courts 423, 452–56

knowledge economy 167

knowledge society 6, 31, 119

labelling theory 264, 273

labour markets 1, 3, 5–11, 16, 20, 33–35, 47, 58–61, 64, 68–69, 71, 83, 85–87, 92–93, 96, 98–101, 103, 105–11, 116, 9, 121, 123, 126, 145–47, 157–61, 163, 167–74, 176–79, 183, 185–86, 214, 250, 252, 304, 307, 310–11,

318, 331, 333, 338, 363, 374, 399–400, 403–4; segmentation 107

ladettes 58, 62–63, 270–71, 410

lads 15, 17, 27, 54, 58, 83, 115–16, 270

lager louts 270

late adolescence 39, 295, 426

later youth 333–36, 339, 363, 365–66

learner identities 117

learning difficulties 84–87

leisure 17, 62, 103, 117, 170, 242–47, 249, 251, 253, 256–57, 263, 266, 273, 278, 304–5, 354, 367, 369, 378, 389, 450

lesbians 117, 215, 409

life chances 3, 5–6, 8, 16, 19–20, 34, 64, 85–87, 106, 132, 164, 228, 246, 238

life course 1–8, 11–12, 32–33, 35–37, 83, 106, 111, 150, 154, 161, 203, 208, 221, 223, 111, 150, 154, 161, 203, 208, 221, 223, 227, 229, 234, 236, 256, 261, 276, 296, 332, 334, 337, 340, 361–62, 379–80, 384, 386, 389–90, 413, 416–17, 423–27, 434

life management 2, 31, 34, 146

lifelong learning 11, 34, 83, 95, 102, 111

lifestyle transitions 106, 111

lifestyles 5, 17, 32, 62, 67, 106, 111, 123, 152, 155, 161, 180–81, 185, 213, 217, 220, 222–23, 241–42, 250, 252–53, 256, 260–61, 263, 266–67, 277–78, 304–5, 330–31, 340–41, 354, 356, 361–62, 365–69, 378, 399, 410, 424, 426, 440

linear transitions 1–2, 4, 23, 41, 83, 110, 126, 180, 214–15, 303, 373, 379

Lisbon Summit 33

lone parents 68–69, 339, 341

long-term illness 81–82

LSD 270–71, 365

magic mushrooms 270–71

manufacturing industry 8, 58–59, 83, 116, 130, 149, 154, 185, 310–11, 396, 401

marginal man 163

marginalization 68–69, 71, 81, 86, 95, 99, 157–59, 163–64, 173, 201, 279, 306, 450

marriage 5–6, 11, 18, 23, 32–33, 37, 39–40, 43–44, 183, 185, 195–96, 201–7, 211–12, 215, 217, 266–68, 230, 233, 246, 348–49, 379–80, 385–86, 388–89 411, 417, 426–28, 441

Marxist 14–15, 115, 164, 250, 276–77, 400

masculinity 47, 60, 69, 115, 277, 280, 374, 406–11, 439

materialism 305, 330–31, 340–41, 354, 356–58, 374, 382, 385–88, 406

McDonaldization 251, 256

McJobs 176

media 17, 61–62, 70, 179–80, 229–30, 241–42, 244–47, 254, 258, 260, 264–65, 269–71, 274, 277–80, 283–84, 287–88, 298–99, 301, 314,

318–19, 331, 340, 347, 356, 361, 365, 369, 386, 407, 421–22, 430, 433–34, 438, 440, 445, 453

mental health 42, 85–86, 91, 155, 159, 229, 285–86, 322, 324, 329–42, 353, 355, 357, 363, 416

meritocratic 14, 17, 19, 63, 394

migrants 68, 92–94, 146, 182–84, 186, 208

minimum wage 130, 177–78

mobile phones 244, 283–84

mods and rockers 16, 59, 259, 264–65, 276–77

moral panic 16, 22, 242, 264, 269, 329–31, 421

morbidity 334–35, 337–38, 341

motivation 19, 34, 132, 146, 161, 179–80, 202, 229, 247, 280–81, 295, 313–18, 322–26, 403

music 16, 18, 137, 179, 242, 244–47, 250–53, 257–58, 260, 263–67, 270, 277, 279, 330, 340, 369, 417, 440–41; popular 242, 244, 263–64, 266–67

Muslims 67, 441

navigation 2, 4–5, 7–9, 11, 31–34, 36, 87, 93, 95–97, 101–3, 119, 218–19, 223, 283, 288, 390, 417

NEET 8, 36, 70, 87–88, 176–77, 179–80

neo-liberalism 12, 34, 48, 63, 72, 179–80, 446

new vocationalism 131–33

night-time economy 249, 251, 253, 264

non-linear transitions 23, 126, 234, 357

normalization thesis 269, 272–74

obesity 244, 329, 333–36, 339, 341, 356, 362–63

official knowledge 49, 51–52

open shop 307 309

opportunity structure 4–5, 7–8, 207–8, 374, 437, 439, 442

parental support 179, 219, 223

parenthood 5, 18, 39–40, 43–44, 155, 202, 206, 214–15, 217, 220, 227, 230–31, 389

peer groups 325, 369, 437

physical activity 285, 290, 332, 361–67

plodders 118–19

podcasts 243, 286

police 70–71, 234–35, 245, 252, 316–18, 408–9, 422, 432–34, 446, 455

political activism 298; awareness 287 consciousness 296, 301; engagement 291–92, 296, 303, 305, 315; issues 159, 185, 287, 291, 299, 301–2, 304, 315; parties 292, 294, 297, 301, 303–4, 315; rights 302, 304; socialization 287, 291, 300–302, 311

poor work 170–74, 445

portfolio careers 58, 63, 170, 279

post-adolescence 39

post-compulsory education 18, 98–99, 118

post Fordist 117, 169, 373

post-materialist values 305

postmodernism 82–83, 169, 241, 243, 266, 273, 279–80, 382

post-subculture 266, 272

poverty 68–69, 82, 87, 90, 92, 157, 160, 163, 167, 171–74, 178, 202, 227, 234, 246, 252, 292, 316, 340, 356, 385, 422, 431, 438, 444–45, 447

premarital sex 39–30, 43–44, 227, 345–46

prostitution 92, 237

Protestant 208, 416, 440; work ethic 399–402

psychedelic rock 264

psychiatric disorder 42, 333, 335

psychosocial disorder 332–33, 335, 357

punishment 252–56

punk 252, 264, 276–77

qualifications 15, 18, 60, 70, 83, 106, 109–10, 116–17, 122–25, 145, 151, 159, 180, 193, 213, 389

queer 117, 406, 409

race 44, 47–50, 53–56, 61, 66–68, 70–71, 76, 89, 100, 116–17, 119, 154, 192, 220, 241, 259, 316, 379–81, 387, 392–93, 395–96, 409, 416, 437, 442, 453–54; discrimination 34, 66, 68, 71, 92–93, 155, 316, 357

racism 184, 263–64, 317, 422, 437, 441, 444

rap 264–66, 440–42

rape 92, 439

rational action theory 19–20, 118–19

raves 244, 250, 253, 264, 278, 305, 340

recreational drugs 265, 329, 330

reflexivity 1–2, 8, 18, 100, 126, 160–63, 266

refugees 48, 54, 89–94

reggae 264

religion 37, 56, 89, 208, 246, 278, 356, 373–74, 386–87, 407, 413–18, 426, 441–42

resistance 15–16, 47, 54–55, 78, 93, 115, 119, 241, 252, 259, 265, 272, 277, 279–80, 374, 409–11, 436, 441–42, 445

resource transfers 201–2

respiratory health 333–34, 228, 363–64

restorative justice 444, 446, 448–49

retail trades 17, 60, 154, 191

riots 67, 180, 184, 260, 292, 313–18

risk behaviours 42, 361, 388, 417; biography 180; society 16, 58, 63, 69, 99, 169, 273; -taking 8, 42, 231, 244–45, 272, 368

rock 'n' roll 263–4, 276

runaways 234–35

rural areas 43–44, 68, 74, 84, 146, 154, 182–86, 208, 264

Russell Group 123

Scarman Report 314 317

school effects 339, 367–68

school-leavers 6–8, 15, 26, 60–61, 84–85, 87, 121, 130
self harm 62, 285–88, 340
self improvement 63, 374, 404
self-esteem 62, 161, 223, 256, 258, 374, 394, 416, 449
self-harm 62, 285–86, 337–38, 340
self-socialization 8–9, 11
service sector 17, 59, 61, 151, 154, 177
sexual exploitation 92; freedom 213, 386, 411
sexuality 202, 227, 256, 260, 264, 280, 284–85, 47–48, 350–51, 373–74, 406–11
sexually transmitted infections 42, 285, 344–48
shared housing 211–14
shopping malls 62, 245, 261
skills 6–7, 9, 11–12, 17–18, 28, 59, 61, 64, 75, 85, 92, 95, 98, 101, 103, 109, 125, 127–33, 136–37, 140–42, 146, 152, 169–72, 178, 184–85, 237, 284–85, 295–96, 298, 323, 347, 349, 390, 403, 417, 425, 449–51; basic 15; 140; core 96; social 8–9, 62, 297; soft 96, 136, 138, 140
skinheads 16, 265, 276–6
slums 246, 437
smoking 244, 329–30, 332, 338–39, 361–62, 364–69, 406, 417
social assistance 6, 8, 121, 157, 160, 236–37
social capital 6, 16, 34, 48, 53, 60, 72, 74–79, 85, 98, 119, 123, 153–54, 230, 235, 237–38, 302, 390, 427, 427
social class 7, 8, 14, 18–19, 32–34, 43, 47–49, 51–52, 54–56, 66, 70–72, 84–86, 116–19, 122–25, 145, 154, 159, 211, 241, 246, 276, 278, 329–30, 337, 339, 357, 361–62, 365–67, 369, 373, 376, 411
social divisions 18, 47, 67, 100, 159, 167
social exclusion 3, 8, 48, 67, 71, 82–83, 87, 159, 163–64, 171–72, 378, 439
social injustice 114
social justice 87, 95–96, 122–23, 450–51
social mobility 14, 19, 58–59, 61, 106, 118–19, 168, 174, 252
social movements 63, 127, 287, 294, 298, 301, 305, 314, 440–42
social reproduction 2, 95–96, 106, 114
social stratification 106, 132–33, 162, 388
social structure 6, 11, 54–55, 99, 162, 234, 283, 333, 361, 365, 369, 376, 393, 448
socialization 4, 8–9, 11, 14, 16, 25, 44, 54, 91, 125, 153, 272, 287, 291, 296, 301–2, 309–11, 386–87, 390, 393, 415, 418, 421
sports 17–18, 50, 244, 321, 363, 367, 451
status attainment 106, 118, 133, 149, 374, 389, 392–93
step-parents 207
stepping stone thesis 146, 168–69, 171, 173–74
straight-edge scene 267

street youth 232, 235, 264, 436, 442
structured individualization 7, 164, 403
students 8, 41, 43, 52–55, 59, 85–87, 99, 115, 122–27, 129, 131–33, 135–42, 150–52, 155, 170, 176–78, 186, 203, 208, 212–15, 246, 250, 258, 287, 294–95, 298, 307, 323–24, 338–39, 350, 355–56, 369, 393–97, 422, 455
style 59, 62, 64, 241, 250–52, 258–59, 264–66, 269–70, 276–81, 269
sub-cultures 340, 369
subjective orientations 96, 114–17
substance use 42, 234–35, 336, 362, 367, 369, 388
suicide 285, 336–38, 340, 416
surveillance 241, 245–46, 249, 336, 409, 422, 448, 455
survival jobs 145, 150, 153
symbolic interaction 273, 276–77, 426–27
symbolic violence 63

teachers 15, 23, 34, 70, 78, 114–15, 234, 350, 393, 397, 409–10
techno music 244, 264
teddy boys 16, 59, 265
teenage childbearing 202, 226–27, 230
teenage mothers 202, 226–27, 229–30
teenage pregnancy 202, 427
teenagers 59, 263
teenybopper 265
tertiary education 98–99, 127, 207
text messaging 244–45
theft 235–37, 245
tobacco 361–62, 364–66
trade unions 291–92, 307–12
training 5–12, 15, 18, 36, 69–71, 83, 85, 87, 98, 101, 107–11, 116–17, 128–30, 135–36, 138–40, 145, 157–59, 170–71, 173, 176, 178–80, 185, 219, 237, 273, 298, 299, 302, 304, 323, 349–50, 399, 439, 445
trajectory 35, 41, 85, 95, 150, 172, 214, 297, 424, 447
transfer policies 454
transgender 117
transitions 1–12, 18, 20, 22–24, 26, 29, 39–41, 44, 48, 58, 64, 66–72, 81, 83, 85–87, 90, 95–96, 99–101, 103, 105–12, 130, 135–37, 139–42, 145–46, 149–55, 158–59, 161–62, 164, 167, 169–71, 173, 176, 179–82, 184, 186, 201–3, 208, 211–12, 214–15, 217–24, 226–27, 323–26, 238, 281, 283, 295, 321, 325, 331, 333, 340–41, 361–62, 373, 377, 379, 384, 388–89, 390, 411, 425–27, 437–38, 447
truancy 68, 431, 434, 453

underemployment 167–69, 171
unemployment 9, 15, 18, 70, 83, 100, 106–7, 110, 130, 145–47, 153, 157–64, 169, 171–73,

176–80, 185, 188, 195–96, 237, 252, 283, 302, 207–8, 311, 316, 318, 331, 338, 340–41, 356, 366, 444–45, 447; benefits 157, 160, 179
UNICEF 36, 232
United Nations 90–91, 301, 308, 324, 345, 438–39, 441, 446
University 9, 19, 59, 74, 85, 96–97, 122, 124, 129, 136, 170, 176, 182, 184–86, 207, 215, 219, 324, 366
urban disorder 313–19
urban nightscapes 242, 249
urban protest 314

values 15–16, 19, 36–37, 76, 114–15, 132–33, 153, 162–63, 171, 208, 221, 244, 247, 253, 258, 260–61, 264, 267, 277, 279, 292, 294, 297, 305, 311, 373–74, 384–90, 406–7, 409, 414, 432, 440, 450–52
vandalism 245, 431
violence 62–63, 70–71, 245, 252–53, 264, 313–14, 317–18, 321–22, 324, 326, 330, 337, 356, 364, 436, 438–40, 442, 453
vocational education and training 6–7, 9–10, 106–8, 110, 127, 129, 131–33, 135–39, 141, 184
vocational guidance 150
vocational tracks 96, 132, 136

vocationalism 96, 127–33
volunteering 295, 297–98, 302, 388, 449
voting 291, 293, 299, 301–2, 305, 314–15

welfare, dependency 154, 160, 252; regimes 5–7, 12, 20, 36, 81, 83, 107–8, 133, 158, 160, 201, 206, 218–19, 221, 223, 303, 446–47
well-being 42, 74–77, 79, 155, 189, 198, 223, 230, 267, 284–86, 329–30, 332, 337, 339, 350, 385, 387, 403, 413, 417–18, 445
West Indians 116
wider access 121, 126
Wisconsin model 118, 393, 397
work ethics 153, 374, 399, 401, 403–4
work-based learning 132, 136–37, 140–41
working poor 171–72
work-life balance 180–81
World Health Organization 332

Yobs 16, 58, 62, 270
youth culture 15–16, 22, 47, 59, 79, 117, 245, 247, 250–51, 253, 255–56, 258–59, 261, 265–66, 269–70, 276, 279, 331, 333, 340, 356, 440–42
youth work 161
youth-Identity Studies 374–75, 377–82

# eBooks – at www.eBookstore.tandf.co.uk

## A library at your fingertips!

eBooks are electronic versions of printed books. You can store them on your PC/laptop or browse them online.

They have advantages for anyone needing rapid access to a wide variety of published, copyright information.

eBooks can help your research by enabling you to bookmark chapters, annotate text and use instant searches to find specific words or phrases. Several eBook files would fit on even a small laptop or PDA.

**NEW:** Save money by eSubscribing: cheap, online access to any eBook for as long as you need it.

## Annual subscription packages

We now offer special low-cost bulk subscriptions to packages of eBooks in certain subject areas. These are available to libraries or to individuals.

For more information please contact webmaster.ebooks@tandf.co.uk

We're continually developing the eBook concept, so keep up to date by visiting the website.

## www.eBookstore.tandf.co.uk